THE VOICES OF EDEN

A History of Hawaiian Language Studies

THE VOICES OF EDEN

EDEN

A History of Hawaiian Language Studies

Albert J. Schütz

University of Hawai'i Press
Honolulu

Library of Congress Cataloging-in-Publication Data
Schütz, Albert J., 1936–
The voices of Eden : a history of Hawaiian language studies /
Albert J. Schütz.
p.   cm.
Includes bibliographical references and index.
ISBN 0–8248–1637–4
1. Hawaiian language—History.   I. Title.
PL6441.S38   1994
499'.4—dc20   94–30968
                                              CIP

Plate 7.1, *The Alphabet,* is used with the permission of the
Mission Houses Museum Library.

Camera-ready copy was prepared by the author.

University of Hawai'i Press books are printed on acid-free paper
and meet the guidelines for permanence and durability of the
Council on Library Resources.

For Renée Heyum,
who has always been a help and an inspiration
for any student of Pacific languages
and cultures

CONTENTS

ACKNOWLEDGMENTS

For their financial aid that allowed me to research and write this book, it is a pleasure to thank the following organizations within the University of Hawai'i: the Research Relations Fund, the Dean's Research Support Fund, and the Social Science Research Institute.

For their help with my quest to learn more of 'Ōpūkaha'ia, who was not only the inspiration for the Congregational Mission to Hawai'i, but also the first in a long list of people who wrote about Hawaiian grammar, I should like to thank the following people and organizations: Samuel and Nancy Martin, who assisted with my pilgrimage to Cornwall, Connecticut, the place where 'Ōpūkaha'ia worked and died; the Cornwall Historical Society (Michael R. Gannett, President), Peter Marshall Hammond of the United Church of Christ (First Church of Christ, Second Congregational Church, Cornwall).

The following people helped me by answering questions about their particular language specialties: Katherine Klingebiel and Jean M. Toyama (French); John E. Crean, Jr. (German); Anatole Lyovin (Greek); Greg Lee Carter, Emily A. Hawkins, Noenoe Moan, Puakea Nogelmeier, No'eau Warner, and Laiana Wong (Hawaiian); Richard A. Benton and Kerry E. Stevens (Māori); Austin Dias (Spanish); Robert J. Ball and Miriam E. Sinclair (Latin).

For answering my questions about various aspects of Hawaiian history, I should like to thank Agnes Conrad, Edgar Knowlton, Robert J. Morris, and James D. Rumford.

The following people read part or all of the manuscript at various stages of its completion, and helped immeasurably by spotting errors and suggesting improvements in style: Wendy Arbeit, Elizabeth Bushnell, O. A. Bushnell, John P. Charlot, Noenoe Moan, Robert J. Morris, Kenneth L. Rehg, and James D. Rumford.

I should also like to thank my colleagues Michael L. Forman, George W. Grace, and Donald M. Topping for always being willing to discuss ideas and offer suggestions for improving various pieces of the manuscript.

For helping me face the challenge of producing computer-generated, camera-ready copy for the press, thanks are due Karen L. Ah Mai, Byron W. Bender, Robert W. Hsu, and Johnny On.

As with all my previous research, this project would not have been possible without the excellent collection and staff of both the Hawaiian and Pacific Collections at Hamilton Library, University of Hawai'i at Mānoa. In particular, I should like to thank Renée Heyum, Emeritus Pacific Curator; Lynette T. Furuhashi, Pacific Librarian; Nancy J. Morris, Charlot Curator; and Karen Peacock, Pacific Curator. Special thanks are due Chieko Tachihata, Hawaiian Curator, for the invaluable help she provided by reading several drafts of this bibliography, not only weeding out inconsistencies, but also suggesting many useful new entries.   Any errors that remain are, of course, my responsibility.

I am also grateful to Marilyn L. Reppun, Hawaiian Mission Children's Society Head Librarian, and Barbara E. Dunn, Hawaiian Historical Society Librarian, for the help and guidance they provided.

In addition to these special collections at the University of Hawai'i, I have also, over the past thirty years or so, worked in the following collections, all of which have added to my knowledge about the history of the study of Pacific languages: Alexander Turnbull Library, National Library of New Zealand, Wellington; Auckland Institute and Museum Library; Auckland Public Library; Bernice P. Bishop Museum Library, Honolulu; The British Library, London; Cambridge University Library (England); Cooke Library, Punahou School, Honolulu; Cornwall Free Library, Cornwall, Connecticut; Essex Institute Library, Salem, Massachusetts; Hawaiian Mission Children's Society Library, Honolulu; Hawaiian Historical Society Library, Honolulu; Hocken Library, University of Otago, Dunedin; Houghton Library, Harvard University, Cambridge, Massachusetts; Mitchell Library, State Library of New South Wales, Sydney; Peabody Museum Library, Salem, Massachusetts; School of Oriental and African Studies Library, University of London; Staatsbibliothek zu Berlin/Preußischer Kulturbesitz; Sterling Memorial Library, Yale University, New Haven; Tozzer Library, Harvard University, Cambridge, Massachusetts; Widner Library, Harvard University, Cambridge, Massachusetts; Yale Anthropological Library, New Haven; and Yale Divinity School Library, New Haven.

INTRODUCTION

Hawaiian history has been studied and described from many different points of view—cultural, archaeological, geographical, and botanical, among others. But very little has been written about Hawai'i's postcontact linguistic history: how outsiders first became aware of the Hawaiian language, how they and the Hawaiians were able to understand each other, and later, how they tried to record and analyze Hawaiian vocabulary and grammar.

Our first records of European contact with the Hawaiian language are in the journals from Captain James Cook's third voyage, in which he and some of his crew recorded their efforts to communicate with this latest (and for Cook, the last) branch of the Polynesian peoples encountered on their exploration of the Pacific. Luckily for those of us interested in language, we had our counterparts over two centuries ago: some people who wrote down just a few words of Hawaiian, and others who were curious enough to set about gathering much longer lists of words. These reports vary in quality as well as in scope, often reflecting the native languages, training, and attitudes of those who collected them. None of them resembles in the slightest the full-scale dictionaries produced later. But they are our only written records of the Hawaiian language at that time and, if examined closely enough, can yield clues as to what it was like then.

Just as these brief sketches contrast strongly with the latest Hawaiian dictionaries, so do some of the early statements about so-called primitive languages differ from our better understanding of language today. These differences reflect not only an increase in our knowledge about Hawaiian in particular during the last two centuries, but also some major changes in the way people view language in general.

The first change was one concerning attitude: observers have gradually realized that the word *primitive* is not properly applied to language. Whether a culture used stone or steel for its tools, its language was a complex instrument, capable of expressing anything that needed to be expressed. Usually, the "faults" noted by casual observers were matters of vocabulary, easily solved by creating new words through borrowing or expanding the meanings of old ones. But sometimes they were the result of inadequate observation. Indeed, only a few years after

Adelbert von Chamisso claimed that Hawaiian had only two pronouns, scholars realized that the language's pronoun system possessed several useful distinctions that English could express only through context.

The second change was the development of a procedure for describing and transcribing speech sounds—that is, phonetics. Although phonetics by itself is not an adequate foundation for a writing system, it is an essential tool for understanding the sounds of a language, which underlie the grammar as well. We will see, against the unfolding background of successive work on the language, how phonetic methodology changed (reversed itself, actually) in the years between Cook's first contact and the missionaries' standardization of the alphabet in 1826.

The third major change was one of theory: the gradual development of an idea eventually called the *phonemic principle*. From our position, which is concerned mainly with the relationship between Hawaiian sounds and an efficient writing system, this principle highlights the *function* of sounds—that is, to keep otherwise identical words separate. In practical terms, this means that variation of a sound, no matter how extreme it may seem from an outside point of view, is of no account unless it interferes with meaning. For example, for Hawaiian, it did not matter whether a speaker said (what sounded like) *lua* or *rua*, for the word still meant 'two', no matter which variant was used. As a matter of fact, this kind of variation and the missionaries' eventual solution to the problem was an implicit statement of the phonemic principle, which was not made explicit until years later. Here was the beginning of the realization that phonetics alone could not serve as the basis for an adequate writing system.

This capsule course in phonetics and the phonemic principle brings us to a related topic. A discussion of language does not have to be filled with jargon. However, there are certain fundamentals to understanding and explaining how a language works. For example, one cannot talk about sounds without knowing something of phonetics. Lay terms for language (such as *guttural, melodic, lilting, subtle and rhythmic, soft, filled with musical cadences*) will not suffice, because they are mostly impressionistic and nearly always meaningless.

Thus, although one cannot describe accurately what a consonant or vowel sounds like, one *can* describe how it is produced. The mechanics of producing a sound forms the basis of articulatory phonetics. In brief, a consonant is described in terms of its manner of production (for example, whether by temporary stoppage or friction, or by some other means), where it is made, whether or not the vocal cords are vibrating, and whether or not it is accompanied by some additional modification, such as a noticeable puff of air. Vowels, more elusive creatures, are described by noting which part of the tongue is relatively high or low, and whether the lips are rounded or spread.

As for grammar, we must assume that the reader understands certain basic terms, such as names for parts of speech and for the grammatical categories of classical languages. For those who have not had the advantage of learning phonetics, Latin grammar, or even English grammar from a very traditional point of view, a further explanation of these technical terms can be found in a reputable desk dictionary.

When linguists write about a language, they use certain conventions to make sure the reader understands the status of a cited form. Square brackets enclose phonetic symbols, slant lines enclose phonemic symbols—that is, the *distinctive* sounds of the language—and italics indicate written or printed forms. In other words, a symbol in square brackets refers to the *form* of a sound, a symbol in slant lines to its *function*, and italics to its *written form*. A gloss, which is just a rough translation of a form, is enclosed by single quotes. A grammatical explanation, on the other hand, appears in roman type, not set off by quotation marks, but sometimes by parentheses if necessary for clarity. The following examples illustrate these conventions for Hawaiian sounds and words.

Early writers wrote *b* for what was actually an unaspirated [p].

Hawaiian /w/ was sometimes interpreted by English speakers as [w], other times as [v]. It was written as both *w* and *v*, but finally *w* was chosen as the official way to represent the sound.

Hale 'house' was a word that was already familiar to the explorers who knew the Tahitian word *fare*.

Ua (aspect marker) was until fairly recently interpreted as a tense marker.

Phonetics, phonology, grammar, historical-comparative linguistics, sociolinguistics—some of the divisions of the general field of language study—are not exact sciences. I have tried to sketch some of the ways in which the discipline has changed over the period we are concerned with. Another, more elusive, variable is the human element. It consists of qualities difficult to measure, such as personality and intelligence. Still, whenever possible, I have tried to tell something about the people who figure in this history.

Here is a general *dramatis personae*, listed in order of appearance.

First, explorers, statesmen, naturalists, all visiting Hawai'i only briefly, and just occasionally curious enough to gather a few Hawaiian words or to make pronouncements about the nature of the language.

Longer-term visitors came later: beachcombers, traders, missionaries, and teachers, these with a practical (and sometimes theoretical) interest in the language.

Professional linguists came still later—during the second half of the twentieth century, in fact, for even then, the discipline was, if not still in its infancy, then not much advanced beyond its adolescence.

Finally, in the last two decades of this century, most of the interest in Hawaiian has been generated by a somewhat different kind of professional: the person who is interested mainly in the preservation of the language as a living, growing, changing entity.

THE VOICES OF EDEN

A History of Hawaiian Language Studies

CHAPTER ONE

Background

-0-0-0-0-0-

We had been approached several times by some canoes at a distance, but none of them would come near enough to converse with us or that we might see what sort of people they were until we anchored and furled our sails: Those who came first were armed and appeared inexpressibly surprized, though not intimidated: They shook their spears at us, rolled their eyes about and made a variety of wild uncouth gesticulations: But we had exchanged but few words with them before we found to our joy and surprize that with little variation their language was the same as that of our acquaintance at the southern islands (John Ledyard's Journal [1783]:66–67).

About a half mile up the Waimea River on Kaua'i, not very far inland from the remnants of the fabled Menehune Ditch, lies an unmarked and nearly unknown historic spot—the site of the *heiau* where, on 21 January 1778, Dr. William Anderson collected the word list that gave the outside world its first look at the Hawaiian language.[1]

On his short stroll up the Waimea, Anderson was accompanied by Captain James Cook and the artist John Webber. Each of these observers recorded his impressions in a different way, consistent with his profession. In his journal, Cook painted a picture of the *heiau* in words: an oracle tower about twenty feet high, four buildings, a chiefs' burial plot, and a four-foot stone wall surrounding the whole area. This verbal description was enhanced by Webber's sketches of different views of the ceremonial structure, backed by the gentle profile of low mountains in the background. Anderson, on the other hand, recorded the scene in a different way—not only through his eyes, but through his ears as well: from Hawaiian speakers he collected the names of the plants, animals, and artifacts seen on the way to the *heiau*, and those of many ceremonial items in the *heiau* itself.

Over two centuries later, it is only through archaeological records that we can find the site, for it has been completely transformed. All traces of the *heiau*, even the stones, are gone, now overlaid with structures of another culture, but ironically with a similar function—the buildings of the Honpa Hongwanji Mission of Hawai'i.

1

This, then, is where Europeans first attempted to describe the Hawaiian language, even if only a small part of it. Anderson's list of nearly 250 words and phrases made its public appearance in a phenomenal best-seller in late eighteenth-century England. Published in 1784, sold out in three days, and in its third edition by the next year, the official account of James Cook's third and last expedition—*A Voyage to the Pacific Ocean, Undertaken by the Command of His Majesty, for Making Discoveries in the Northern Hemisphere*—gave an eager and impatient English-reading public the final installment of one of the world's greatest adventure stories.

For many of these readers, one of the most exciting "discoveries" of the third voyage was the first European sighting of the Hawaiian Islands—so far from Tahiti and New Zealand in miles, but so near in customs, language, and appearance. The fact that the islands were also the scene of James Cook's violent death (a startling contradiction to the romantic image that many Europeans had of the Pacific) could not help but heighten Europe's fascination with Hawai'i.

Scholars, generally content with less sensational amusements, looked to the new volumes for a continuation of the richness of discovery offered in the accounts of the previous two voyages. For those armchair philologists interested in the novelty of *lingua incognita* (with again perhaps a touch of romanticism), Cook's *Voyage* was a small treasure trove.

And what was the first example of this new language presented to European readers? *Aloha*? *Haole*? No. Oddly enough, Cook's first citation of Hawaiian, clear to us now, reveals a natural but total misunderstanding on his part. When the Hawaiians boarded the ship for the first time, they were keen to possess the bits of iron they saw, pointing to them and saying (as Cook wrote it) *Hamaite*. He surmised that the word probably referred to "some instrument, in the making of which iron could be usefully employed." But this spontaneous exclamation was actually the phrase *He maita'i*! (*t*, not *k*, was used on Kaua'i then) 'It's good!' (Apparently the Hawaiians were familiar with iron from the nails and other small pieces of hardware on wood that had been washed ashore as jetsam from distant shipwrecks.)

Cook recorded a few other words in his narrative, some of which have even made their way into English dictionaries: *maro* (*malo*) 'loincloth', *taboo* (*kapu*) 'sacred, forbidden' (possibly the first borrowing from Polynesian into English; Cook learned the word in Tonga and used it in the report of his second voyage), and names for such common plants as *tee* (*kī*) and *taro* (*kalo*).

But other than the occasional Hawaiian word in Cook's journal, the bulk of the language sample was collected by Anderson, who was acting as unofficial naturalist for the expedition.

Anderson was one of the first of a series of intellectually gifted Europeans who approached the newly discovered Pacific islands with calipers, sketch pads, and butterfly nets to collect curiosities and put order into what they often conceived as a pristine but chaotic world. Later, missionary-linguists used such phrases as "rude" "barbaric," or "not yet brought into system" to describe their impressions of the language. As for Anderson's own opinion along these lines, we can only guess, for the Hawaiian section of his journal was lost sometime after its contents were used to augment the official account of the third voyage.

CONNECTIONS

With the advantage of historical hindsight, we can see that the European discovery of Hawai'i in the last half of the eighteenth century coincided with a number of ideas or events that affected the first reports about the Hawaiian language and culture. But first of all, Cook's encounter with Hawai'i was not just coincident with, but was a part of, one important development: the great voyages of discovery that put the finishing touches of clarity and detail on the hitherto indistinct map of the Pacific. As for those influences on the reports, they fall into three main groups—philosophy, language, and religion:

1. The idea of the Noble Savage: the most popular theme of eighteenth-century romantic naturalism.
2. The state of language study in the eighteenth century: how several scholars viewed English grammar, and the development of phonetics and phonology.
3. Evangelical revival movements in England and America.

The Noble Savage

The descriptions of Pacific islands, especially Tahiti, included in the accounts of Wallis, Bougainville, and Cook are closely bound to the intellectual interests of Europe in the latter half of the eighteenth century. At that time, the Age of Enlightenment was opening minds to new ideas, or at least encouraging a more critical look at old ones. One of the features of this movement (but with much more ancient origins) was a reverence for a return to nature, idealizing any beings who appeared to be free and untrammeled—even peasants and children. Other ideas that enter into the concept are that of a Golden Age, the biblical tradition of the Garden of Eden, an earthly paradise, and medieval legends of "an island of peace and plenty hidden afar in the western seas" (Fairchild 1928:6). The idea of the Noble Savage was, in a sense, a philosophers' construct that combined many of these features, and was reinforced by such fictional characters as Man Friday and the reports of explorers, beginning with Columbus and continuing through the next three centuries.

Such a philosophy seemed tailor-made for the Tahitians—or at least for European perceptions of the Tahitians. The discovery of groups of people unknown to Europe and living in what seemed a physical and social paradise proved what had until then been only a theoretical notion: that mankind in its pristine state, uncorrupted by the forces of "civilization" (as defined by Europe), was superior. In short, the Noble Savage had been found. As Alan Moorehead (1966:41) explained it,

> Europe in the seventeen-seventies seems to have been specially ripe for the notion of an earthly paradise. Rousseau had written his *Discours sur les arts et sciences* in 1749, and for twenty years the theory of the simple and unsophisticated man living in Arcady had intrigued philosophical imagination.[2] The discovery of Tahiti was the perfect dénouement, the apparent reality of the preconceived idea. The island was like one of those unseen stars which eventually come to light after the astronomers have proved that it must exist ... And now Cook brought back the proof that it really did exist, this golden island inhabited by happy, healthy, beautiful people, and who, best of all, knew nothing of the cramping sophistries of civilization.

Still working with the wisdom of hindsight, it is not hard to see the circularity in this so-called proof. Indeed, the reports were rather like self-fulfilling prophecies, for writers distorted facts to fit their preconceived notions. For this particular transgression, John Hawkesworth is often cited as a prime example. Engaged to take the rough edges off Cook's narration of his first voyage, Hawkesworth not only smoothed Cook's prose, but embellished it as well, leaning heavily toward Rousseau and the Noble Savage.

But observers often distorted their reports in a different way, one that seems at odds with the Noble Savage philosophy. Moorehead (1966:49, based on Smith 1960) described the difficulties that faced the painter or engraver who relayed the visual images of Polynesia from their home ground to Europe:

> To see these objects accurately, to divest himself of the European attitude, to refrain from the temptation to paint a pretty composition—this was the artist's problem if he was going to represent the Pacific without prejudice, and it is hardly surprising

that the weaker brethren fell along the way so that their breadfruit trees grew up into English oaks and their Tahitian girls were transformed into nymphs surrounded by classical waterfalls in a soft English light.

If we apply this model to language as well, we can see that many of the reports about the Hawaiian language suffered in similar ways. First, the writers had preconceived notions about what a "primitive" language should be like (in spite of the fact that the adjective is meaningless). These notions found expression in the terse characterizations of Hawaiian that appeared, mostly just after contact, but some surprisingly late. Some of the adjectives used to describe the language in general fit the model: *childlike, primitive, simple,* or *undeveloped.* This last attribute seems especially apt, for it would be the linguistic manifestation of "living in a state of nature." Here, it seems that the Savage was found to be not so much Noble as Simple. In the next chapter, such opinions about the language are examined in more detail.

As for the breadfruit-into-oaks approach, there are abundant examples. With respect to writing systems, the lack of a phonetic alphabet in the eighteenth century meant that most observers wrote Hawaiian words "as they heard them," usually the way they wrote words in their own language. Even more visible in the early descriptions is the tendency to analyze Hawaiian grammar according to the accepted classical grammatical models. Thus Hawaiian grammatical features were constantly being compared to those of European languages. Moreover, we will see that writers often faulted Hawaiian for an apparent lack of generic terms. This was also an implicit comparison, as was the perpetual surprise at the small number of consonants and vowels in the sound system.

It may be that Hawai'i suffered less from these distortions than did Tahiti. First, by no means did all of the European intelligentsia embrace the Noble Savage notion. From the very beginning there were detractors, whose voices, at first ignored, were heard more clearly as less romanticized reports made their way from the Pacific. And as a tragic and dramatic event, Cook's death could not help but lift the scrim of romanticism and cast a harsh light on what lay beyond. Nor was there a Hawkesworth to sift and embellish Cook's account of the third voyage. But the clarity was short-lived. True, the Hawaiian islands did not have to endure a misnomer like the "Friendly Islands," which Tonga had borne since Cook's first false impression there, but from our language-centered point of view, many of the reports about Hawaiian speech suffer from prejudice and an excess of romanticism.

This, in an oversimplified way, describes the philosophical background for many of the first observers of the Hawaiian language. But we
must know something of their linguistic backgrounds as well. In other
words, what were people thinking and writing about language in 1778
and the following years?

The Study of Language in the Eighteenth Century

Language certainly played a part in the Noble Savage theme, but in
the minds of the observers, the quality "primitive" was attached more to
the *use* of the language than to the language itself. "The notion that the
savage is a natural poet is perhaps the most widespread and enduring
aspect of the Noble Savage idea" (Fairchild 1928:444). As for Rousseau's writings on language, they are mostly ruminative, discussing such
highly speculative (and unprovable) topics as the origin of language,[3]
and affecting people's attitudes about language more than their ability to
describe it (see chapter 2). Three works of this period that had a much
greater, albeit indirect, influence on the descriptions of Hawaiian were
Thomas Dilworth's *New Guide to the English Tongue* (1740), Samuel
Johnson's *Dictionary of the English Language* (1755), and Noah Webster's *Grammatical Institute of the English Language* (1783). Of course,
one could turn to many other eighteenth-century essays about language,
but because these three books were so widely used in Europe and
America, they can serve as samples of how the writers whose works we
will examine later were trained to think about language.

"Tho. Dilworth, Schoolmaster" (as he was described on the
frontispiece of his textbook) was in a sense Schoolmaster to the entire
English-speaking world in the middle decades of the eighteenth century.
As a self-advertisement on the first page of his book proclaims, his work
was recommended "as the most useful Performance for the Instruction
of Youth [and] designed for the Use of SCHOOLS in *Great Britain,
Ireland*, and in the several *English* Colonies; and Plantations abroad."
Its success can be gauged by noting that the version I have at hand,
1788, is the fifty-second edition. By that date it had already been
printed in America for more than forty years, originally through the
efforts of Benjamin Franklin. From its remarkable printing history alone
we might infer that almost all students educated in Great Britain or
America at that time received their basic knowledge of English structure
from this book. Moreover, the content of the lessons was designed to
extol the moral virtues of Protestantism, preserve the existing relationship between masters and servants, and further the good works of King
George[4] and the British Parliament.

For those pursuing the study of English at a higher level, the major reference work available was Samuel Johnson's dictionary. In addition to its contribution to English lexicography (and the anecdotal value of some of its whimsical entries), Johnson's dictionary is important in the history of linguistics for its insightful comments on the relationship between English sounds and the letters that represent them. He wrote in the preface about the difficulties inherent in writing a previously unwritten language:

> As language was at its beginning merely oral, all words of necessary or common use were spoken before they were written; and while they were unfixed by any visible signs, must have been spoken with great diversity, as we now observe those who cannot read to catch sounds imperfectly, and utter them negligently ... The powers of the letters, when they were applied to a new language, must have been vague and unsettled, and therefore different hands would exhibit the same sound by different combinations.

Next, in his discussion of possible spelling reform, he commented succinctly on the nature of speech in general and of the sound-symbol relationship as well. Some spelling reformers had attempted, he wrote,

> to accommodate orthography better to the pronunciation, without considering that this is to measure by a shadow, to take that for a model or standard which is changing while they apply it. Others ... have endeavoured to proportion the number of letters to that of sounds, that every sound may have its own character, and every character a single sound. Such would be the orthography of a new language to be formed by a synod of grammarians upon principles of science.

Later, we will see that this seemingly logical criterion of *one sound per symbol, one symbol per sound* was not so easy to apply, for just what constituted a "sound" was often open to question.

Meanwhile, on the other side of the Atlantic, nationalism nourished by the American Revolution prompted an interest in the *American*, as opposed to the *English*, language. Benjamin Franklin, partly through promoting Dilworth's book, had already made his contribution to American education by introducing the study of grammar. Thomas Jefferson was another advocate for an American language, foreseeing a gradual separation of the speech of the new nation from that of its former colonial master. But the greatest influence on this movement was exerted by Noah Webster, whose spellers and grammar books replaced Dilworth's grammar and eventually were almost universally used in America. Webster's system of noting the various pronunciations of vowel letters influenced Samuel Ruggles's sketch of Hawaiian grammar (1819; see chapter 6), and his speller was used by the American missionaries who began in 1820 to teach English to the Hawaiians.

The point needs to be made that these three works did not deal with *general* linguistics, for that discipline was not developed until late in the next century. Instead, they concentrated on English, explaining the often idiosyncratic relationships between spelling and pronunciation, and analyzing the grammar mainly in the framework that had been used for Greek and Latin. This means that readers of these works did not learn the techniques for "reducing a language to writing" or for describing its grammatical structure.

However, the state of the study of English in the eighteenth century as related to Latin and Greek provides some interesting parallels with the beginning study of Hawaiian. English was considered a barbarous tongue until the last quarter of the sixteenth century, when scholars finally admitted it to the company of respectable languages. Once they realized its merits, they attempted to "regulate" it. Richard Foster Jones (1953:287–88) sketched the result of the effort:

> Latin, however, was not entirely content to be pushed aside. When the grammarians proceeded to regulate the vernacular, it was not unnatural that they should accept the former as a model, though the differences between the two languages were apparent, and though they refused to see in this difference evidence of the inferiority of their own tongue. Ben Jonson especially tried to introduce the whole Latin system of conjugations, declensions, and the like, and to force the native tongue to conform to it. Sooner or later a realization of the difference between the two languages and a desire for linguistic independence were sure to change the practice.

In chapter 12, we shall examine the extent to which the Latin model was applied (with varying degrees of success) to Hawaiian grammar.

Evangelical Revival Movements in England and America

Most of the discussion of language just referred to concerns words: even treatments of Latin grammar were word centered, focusing on the functional suffixes attached to (especially) nouns and verbs. The final item in our group of connected events also concerns the notion of *word*, but chiefly in its metaphorical sense: *In principio erat verbum* ... In the beginning was the Word ...

The discoveries of the several Polynesian societies in the Pacific coincided, at least partly, with such religious movements as the Evangelical Revival in Britain and the Great Awakening in America. If some people were convinced by the romanticized reports of the explorers that the Polynesians' societies were noble ones and their languages simple or "undeveloped," others were just as firmly convinced that the islanders were living in sin and their souls were sorely in need of saving. Hence, the Polynesians were not only drawing room curiosities but also grist for the missionary mill. As Newbury (1961:xxvii) wrote, "The coincidence of geographical discovery and evangelical revival was too striking to be anything less than a divine summons to convert the latest-known corner of the earth." Or, as he put it more succinctly, "The missionary followed the seaman."[5]

It is interesting that the very traits that led some European intellectuals to admire the Polynesians inspired a rather different group of people to try to change them. Ironically, the philosopher Denis Diderot warned against just such a probability: "... one day they (the Christians) will come, with crucifix in one hand and the dagger in the other to cut your throats or to force you to accept their customs and opinions; one day under their rule you will be almost as unhappy as they are" (from *Supplément au Voyage de Bougainville*, quoted in Moorehead 1966:43).

One of the principal missions to Polynesia was sponsored by the London Missionary Society (LMS), founded in 1795. It was not, however, the first; its Tahitian venture followed an unsuccessful attempt by Spanish Catholics by about twenty years. Volume 1 of the *Transactions of the Missionary Society* (1795–1802) tells some of the philosophy behind the movement. The historical introduction begins with a condemnation of Popery, suggesting how much more success the earliest missions would have had if they had only been Protestant. This is followed immediately by a reference to the early voyages (p. x):

> The voyages of discovery ... in the Southern Ocean brought to light vast countries, before unknown, and innumerable groups of fertile islands, which invite the visits of the humane, to soften, by civilization, the savage customs of their inhabitants, and to communicate to them the inestimable blessings of true religion.

Note the about-face from the naturalist point of view, which condemned the excesses of civilization. The writer went on to say that there turned out to be little "which would excite commercial attention,"[6] so that the inhabitants, "after having awakened the investigations of curiosity, were ready to be abandoned to their original ignorance and barbarism." The idea was driven home by a metaphor with an indirect reference to Bligh's voyage on the *Bounty*: "The bread fruit-tree was carried to the Leeward Islands, but the seeds of the tree of life were withheld from the islands of the south."

Bligh and the *Bounty* also make an unexpected appearance in the linguistic history of Polynesia, and the tie that binds all these topics together is the work of Thomas Haweis, the founding father of the LMS. Haweis was said to have been inspired to form a South Seas mission after reading Cook's *Voyages*. Apparently finding William Anderson's Tahitian word list less than useful,[7] Haweis set about collecting another vocabulary. His papers (Haweis 1795–1802) tell how this was accomplished:

> During my stay at Portsmouth the clergyman had very obliging-ly communicated to me the papers of the mutineers [i.e., from the *Bounty*] who had resided at Otahetie for two years, and during the time of their confinement under sentence of death had drawn up large Memoirs of their transactions and a vocabulary of the language.

Haweis transcribed a copy of this vocabulary for the missionaries, who studied it on their voyage to Tahiti.

Haweis was also an early link between the LMS and the Hawaiian mission, for his sermon on 15 November 1795 that led to the founding of the Society included a proposal for a mission to the Sandwich Islands as well. Another twenty-five years passed, however, before his hopes were fulfilled.

Church historians often trace the beginning of the American mission to Hawai'i back to 1809, the year the young Hawaiian 'Ōpūkaha'ia arrived in New England. But, as with so many aspects of Hawaiian history, the real beginning lies with Cook. As noted above, Haweis was motivated to found the LMS when he read the accounts of the three voyages, and Cook was the one who put the islands on Europeans' and Americans' maps, opening the way for more ships to call. *Voyages to Hawaii before 1860* (Judd and Lind 1974) shows that between the years 1786 and 1820, more than one hundred ships called at ports in the Hawaiian Islands.

One of these ships, the *Triumph*, under the command of Captain Caleb Britnall, carried the fourteen-year-old 'Ōpūkaha'ia from the Kona Coast to the coast of New England. 'Ōpūkaha'ia, whose connection with our theme is described more fully in chapter 6, eventually converted to Christianity and inspired the forming of the Congregational mission to Hawai'i.

But a seed cannot grow well in rocky soil. Extending this meta-phor, all the conditions were right in New England in the second decade of the nineteenth century for a mission not only to grow, but to flourish. "This was the Second Great Awakening, of the New Light Theology, of revivals at Yale and at Litchfield [Connecticut], of the formation of the

Board of Commissioners for Foreign Missions" (Reuman 1968:[8]). Then as now, evangelists commanded large audiences, and they entreated the local church members to support missions not only in the nearby Western Reserve of America, but in far-off Polynesia as well.

All these favorable conditions led to the official forming of the Hawaiian Mission on 15 October 1819 and, eventually, to a concerted effort to analyze the Hawaiian language that it might be more effectively used to convert the speakers to Christianity.

-0-0-0-0-0-

These, then, were the three movements of the latter part of the eighteenth century that affected the way Europeans and Americans reacted to newly discovered languages: developments in philosophy, language study, and religion, all resulting in a confluence of ideas, emanating from people of different backgrounds and different, sometimes conflicting, interests.

Chapter 2 expands on one of these themes: the philosophical construct of the Noble Savage, as reflected in a range of comments on the nature of the Hawaiian language.

NOTES

[1] Some of the following material appears in Schütz 1991b.

[2] Although Moorehead brought in Rousseau's name at the very beginning of his chapter on the Noble Savage, I am trying to keep some distance between the writer and the concept (following Spate 1988, based on Fairchild 1928). As Fairchild concluded (p. 139): "The fact is that the real Rousseau was much less sentimentally enthusiastic about savages than many of his contemporaries, did not in any sense invent the Noble Savage idea, and cannot be held wholly responsible for the forms assumed by that idea in English Romanticism."

[3] Rousseau's even better-known contemporary in Great Britain, Samuel Johnson, "dismissed speculations about the beginnings of man and of language as useless, idle prattle." In a slightly different context, he said, "Rousseau *knows* he is talking nonsense, and laughs at the world for staring at him" (Stam 1976:63–64).

[4] No doubt the author was assiduous in keeping such information up-to-date, but the succession of Georges in England would have made it unnecessary until 1830, long after Dilworth's death.

[5] This philosophy was stated somewhat less subtly by Denzil Carr (1951: 15): "Sailors and missionaries have many things in common, for they both go after the natives hammer and tongs."

[6] The London missionaries did not abandon commercialism altogether, however. To supplement the subscriptions that supported most of the work of the Society, Thomas Haweis, the founder, had hopes of bringing a cargo back from Tahiti. And his "Particular Directions given to the Missionaries at their Leisure Hours" include, among more scholarly activities, directives to wash the soil for minerals and to "find out where the natives get their pearls" (Haweis Autobiography, vol. 1).

[7] Others complained about this and other published word lists in the Cook material, but one wonders if they read the guide to pronunciation carefully enough. Anderson's Tahitian word list, which appears in the account of Cook's second voyage, is fairly accurate, considering the circumstances under which it was collected. For a more detailed account, see chapter 4.

CHAPTER TWO

The Noble Savage Speaks

-o-o-o-o-o-

In speaking, they pronounce through the nose and throat, and their language approacheth nearest to the High-Dutch or German, of any I know in Europe; but is much more graceful and significant (Jonathan Swift's Gulliver's Travels, A Voyage to the Country of the Houyhnhnms, *chapter 3).*

As the exploration of the South Pacific revealed an exotic world to the artists and scientists on Captain Cook's three expeditions, often they had no choice but to perceive the new in terms of the old. In chapter 1, a visual analogy was used to highlight the concept that the translation of images from one culture to another is not a simple matter. This theme is from Bernard Smith's thought-provoking study, *European Vision and the South Pacific* (1960), in which he noted that the eighteenth-century expeditions' artists had to interpret visual images according to the "pictorial conventions of the time." Not only was their perception filtered through their own culture, but often it was further altered—sometimes subtly, sometimes blatantly—by the imagination of the engraver or painter who prepared the final version for the public.

In the illustrations in Smith's work, the depiction of tropical flora provides dramatic evidence of the differences between the original drawing and the final product. For example, in some renderings of coconut trees, the engraver's versions look rather more like spiders on stilts, or a portent of John Wyndham's triffids.

But it was not only the pictorial records that suffered in the metamorphosis of primary records. In a similar but less obvious way, the linguistic data from Cook's third voyage also changed as they passed from manuscript to print, as we will see in chapter 4.

Perhaps, in observing a foreign culture, we can never see through a glass with perfect clarity. But the degree of resolution depends on how far we can place ourselves from our own culture and its particular prejudices. This difficulty is not diminished with respect to language; possibly we may be even less conscious of the linguistic prejudices than of the cultural ones.

13

BACKGROUND

In the middle and latter parts of the eighteenth century, observations about "exotic" languages suffered a special kind of distortion, one related to the theme introduced in chapter 1: the Noble Savage. At that time, some philosophers were intrigued by the question of language origin, a topic that has moved in and out of scientific favor many times (Stam 1976:1). The beginnings of the popularity of the topic in modern times can be traced to the early years of the eighteenth century and the works of Giambattista Vico. Vico's account is full of oppositions. For example, he wrote of three different kinds of languages—those of gods, of heroes, and of men—and of the tension and constant struggle between the *nobilitas* and the *vulgus* (*op. cit*, p. 16). In retrospect, it seems logical that the ideas of the origin of language and the Noble Savage should be combined into the concept of "primitive" language.

For a much later opinion on the relationship between so-called primitive languages and the origin of language in general, note the following comment from William Churchill (1912:10). (He was writing about the language of Easter Island, not Hawaiian, but the principle is the same.) To justify burdening the reader with a description of a language so far from the linguistic mainstream, he noted that the end product was

> far more comprehensive than a mere dictionary of the speech of a
> sociologically unimportant folk. Its purpose is to provide the
> orderly arrangement of the material whereby we enter upon the
> systematic study of the principles and the methods of the most
> elemental types of human speech. As the placing of the Sanscrit
> within the reach of investigators created the science of compara-
> tive philology, even so I indulge myself in the reverent aspiration
> that the presentation of these data for a widely extended speech of
> the isolating type will carry our students very close to one of the
> origins of human utterance of ideas, so close that philology may
> then be justified in calling upon psychology to explain the process
> whereby the primitive man has learned to differentiate his animal
> cry into thought-directed speech.

And herein lies the connection with European views of the Hawaiian language: some people may have been ready to apply the Rousseau model not only to the new societies found in the Pacific, but to their languages as well. Cook's volumes both stirred interest in such a topic and provided data, albeit limited, to be used to support or refute the notion. In addition to the individual vocabularies in the body of his narratives, in the appendix to his account of the third voyage is a comparative chart suggesting the extent of what was eventually called the Malayo-Polynesian (Austronesian) language family. The chart lists numerals from one to ten in about forty languages, including Hawaiian.

Cook's report provided the first raw material for theorizing. As more outsiders became better acquainted with Hawaiian, they began to give their impressions, commenting first on the "sound" of the language, and then on its vocabulary and its grammar.

The Sound and Sounds of Hawaiian

One of the first things that struck those who heard Hawaiian for the first time was the general Polynesian pattern of what is called phonotactics: every syllable ends with a vowel. Another feature, just as prominent, is that there are no consonant clusters. Finally, as an individual detail, there are no sibilants—that is, *s*-like sounds.[1] All these characteristics delight singers, outclassing even Italian. But apparently that advantage was not in the minds of most observers. The topic was usually mentioned when Hawaiians struggled with the very different sound patterns of English: a plethora of consonant clusters, syllable-final consonants, and sibilants. Missionary Hiram Bingham, who arrived in Hawai'i in 1820, later wrote of the Hawaiians' difficulties in pronouncing English, indirectly reflecting his opinion of the sound of Hawaiian (1847:155):

> Sibilants and compound consonants are exceedingly difficult, if not impracticable, to the unlettered Hawaiian. Had we made the Hawaiian people, as we found them, pass through the Israelitish ordeal of distinguishing and pronouncing correctly the words *Sibboleth* and *Shibboleth*, to save their lives, it is not probable that one in a thousand would have succeeded, even if each had been allowed a whole day, with patient instruction, in the trial to adjust and control the vocal organs right.

Several writers found such patterns—that is, the absence of sibilants and consonant clusters—lacking variety. For example, Lorrin Andrews (1838:396) wrote: "As might be expected, where the letters are so few, and their combination into words so regular, the language, to foreigners, is very monotonous. The guttural sounds are frequent, for many vowels come together which do not form diphthongs."[2]

William Ellis (1825 [1979]:336), on the other hand, found the language "smooth" and well adapted for poetry, apparently more so than the other Polynesian languages, because Hawaiian used *l*. (Is *l* a more poetic sound than *r*?) Still, he found the poetry "rude" and proposed a chicken-and-egg puzzle for the relationship between the language and the art form, wondering which came first: a fondness for poetry, or the "multiplicity of vowels"?

Along these lines of perceived simplicity is an often-repeated canard that many utterances in Hawaiian consisted entirely of vowels. Typical of such statements is that made by Richard Brinsley Hinds around 1840 (Kay 1968:109): "The words are frequently a curious string of vowels; many words consist entirely of them. Consonants are not much used." Almost every amateur who tried to characterize the language included a similar linguistic party piece. For example, Adelbert von Chamisso (Chapin 1973:102), writing in 1837, but who was unlikely to have heard the language since his visit to Hawai'i in 1816–1817, wrote:

> The wealth of vowels in Hawaiian is such that there are words with eight of them in a row: *hooiaioia* 'certified', and one can talk coherently for some time completely without resorting to a consonant: *Ua oia au, e ue ae oe ia Ii, e ao ae oe ia ia, e i ae oe ia ia, rua* ... etc. 'I am he', 'Greet Ii', 'Teach him', 'Say to him that ...'

Samuel H. Elbert (1969c:vii) rewrote each of the words or phrases in the modern orthography, showing that one consonant appeared repeatedly— the glottal stop, not yet recognized as a consonant in Chamisso's time.

M. A. Donne (1866:84–85) presented a variation on the theme, beginning with the effect that such a sound system had on the hearer:

> To our ears Hawaiian sounds feeble, indistinct, and unsatisfying; and no wonder, since it has only seventeen letters, and some of those left out are the ones we could least spare from our own language. The Hawaiians manage to do without *c, f, g, j, q, s, x, y,* and *z.* Their syllables are very short, generally having only two letters, and never more than three, and they always end with a vowel. Two consonants are never allowed to come together in any case, and there are many words formed of vowels only; indeed it is possible to make a whole sentence in Hawaiian without using a single consonant.

In 1862, Manley Hopkins contrasted the Hawaiians' behavior with his perception of the nature of their language (p. 246–47). "It appears strange, and contrary to analogy," he wrote, "that a people of bold and forcible character should express themselves in a language more fitted for the Sybarites." After a brief European language tour, in which Teutonic speech was characterized as "angular," that of the Latins called "vocal and emasculated derivations," and Greek as "born of masculine energy and elegant fancy," Hawaiian was given the following poetic simile:

> The Hawaiian language is so soft as rather to be compared to the warbling of birds than the speech of suffering mortals. It is usually said to contain but twelve letters, namely, seven consonants, and five vowels.

(Not every observer agreed with this characterization; George Mortimer [1791:51] described the language as "very thick and guttural"!) Hopkins continued:

> The language may, says Sir George Simpson,[3] be considered as pleasing and agreeable to the ear after a time, though at first it sounds childish, indistinct, and insipid. It lacks, of course, everything like force and expression; and the natives are by no means to be compared as orators with the aborigines of North America. The language is not capable of reaching the lofty strain of the Blackfeet, the Crees, or the Saulteaux, but flows on in a mellifluous feebleness, which, though it never offends the ear, always leaves us unsatisfied.

Statements of this type seem to reach their zenith (or nadir) in Erasmus Darwin Preston's comment (1900a:46): "In passing, we may say that the Hawaiian consonants are probably the softest and most effeminate of the Oceanic group."

In spite of its likeness to warbling birds for some hearers, Hawaiian had quite a different effect on others. Adelbert von Chamisso (Chapin 1973:103) wrote: "Our ear perceived neither prosody nor accent in the spoken language of Hawaii ..." Had this observation been accurate, such features would have made Hawaiian a very unusual language indeed.

On the other hand, Andrews (1854:19) emphasized the role that accent had to play (in his opinion), because of the low number of vowels and consonants:

> From the fewness of the letters and syllables in the language, it must necessarily be that many words of the same letters must have different significations; and so it is, but it is greatly remedied in Hawaiian as in other languages, by different tones, accents, or pronunciations, ... making in fact a different word to the ear, though not to the eye. The enunciation of some of these tones and accents are [*sic*] exceedingly difficult for an adult foreigner ever to obtain.

The Hawaiians' apparent inability to distinguish between what seemed to speakers of English to be two distinct sounds also caught the

attention of observers. On this topic, the well-known linguist Henry
Sweet wrote (1900:27):

> Civilized languages, which are spoken by populous communi-
> ties and over areas of some extent, and which involve copious
> vocabularies and the expression of complex and varied thought,
> must be precise in their articulation; and the habit of precise
> articulation becomes so ingrained in the speakers of these
> languages that ... they regard all deviations from their
> accustomed organic positions as impossibilities.
>
> Under different circumstances, different ideals may prevail.
> Many savage and half-civilized communities certainly seem to
> take sound-change much more lightly than we do. Trustworthy
> observers tell us, for instance, that in one of the Polynesian
> languages of the Pacific, Samoan, the consonant (k) existed only
> in the single word *puke*, "catch!"; that it was then substituted for
> (t) more and more in some of the Samoan islands, and then spread
> rapidly over the whole group. Whitmee remarks, speaking of
> Samoan, "many of the natives are exceedingly careless and incor-
> rect in the pronunciation of consonants, and even exchange or
> transpose them without confusion, and almost unnoticed by their
> hearers; as in *mānu* for *nāmu* 'a scent,' *lagoga* for *lagona* 'to
> understand,' *lavaau* for *valaau* 'to call'; but they are very
> particular about the pronunciation of the vowels."
>
> Strange as such a state of things may seem, much of it is
> evidently only an exaggeration of what happens in all languages.
> Among the island populations of the Pacific the tendencies to
> careless articulation which exist everywhere are allowed greater
> scope partly from the intellectual indolence of the speakers, partly
> from the want of external restraint. In small, scattered communi-
> ties which are constantly liable to be broken up into still smaller
> ones, the instability of external circumstances reflects itself in the
> language. Such languages are like the language of children: they
> are always starting afresh, and are in a constant ferment of experi-
> ment and phonetic licence checked only by the necessity of being
> intelligible to a small circle of hearers. The temperament and cir-
> cumstances of these people are both those of children, and their
> sound changes have a childish character. The instability of their
> surroundings gives their speech that tentative character which we
> observe in the articulation of infants.

Preston (1900a:46–47) classed Hawaiian sound changes (such as
those found in rapid speech) into two categories, *cacophony*, and the
indefinable term often used in nineteenth-century grammars, *euphony*.
After discussing the different ways some European languages "satisfy

the ear," Preston summarized his Weltanschauung-like findings, managing to insult each group in passing:

> The methods employed exemplify characteristic national traits. The Hawaiian accomplishes his purpose in any way that diminishes labor; he therefore cuts out rather than introduces. The energy of the Anglo-Saxon prompts him to interject something, and the Latins, true to their natural instinct, sacrifice symmetry of form to euphony of sound.

Just as speakers of Indo-European languages were struck by the alien sounds of Hawaiian and how different the patterns of its vowels and consonants were from those of their own languages, so were they apparently surprised by the way the Hawaiians' view of the world was reflected by its vocabulary.

Vocabulary

One of the popular misconceptions about "primitive" languages, unfortunately still held, is that somehow cultures can survive with a few hundred words, enhanced by gestures. For example, Philibert de Commerson, naturalist on Bougainville's expedition, thought that Tahitian had only about four or five hundred words (Rensch 1991:404). Hawaiian seems to have escaped that judgment, perhaps because it was considered another Polynesian dialect and, by the time of Cook's third voyage, enough was known about Tahitian to dispel the tiny-vocabulary myth. But it *was* thought that the syllable structure of Polynesian languages severely limited the number of words that could be formed. George Grey, well known for his work at the New Zealand corner of the Polynesian triangle, came up with figures to refute the idea (Grey and another, n.d.). First he listed forty Hawaiian syllables and then showed potential number combinations in two-, three-, and four-syllable words (table 2.1).

TABLE 2.1
POTENTIAL VOCABULARY SIZE

1-syllable words:	40
2-syllable words:	1,560
3-syllable words:	59,280
4-syllable words:	2,193,360
Total:	2,254,240

As impressive as this total is, Grey's figures are actually low, for several reasons. Working backward from his figures, we find that even if we use his definition of a syllable (a vowel alone, or a consonant plus a vowel), since he apparently did not count the glottal stop as a consonant, there should be forty-five syllables (8 [consonants] x 5 [vowels] = 40, + 5 more consisting of a vowel alone).

Moreover, the figure for two-syllable words uses the formula n ($n-1$), which is the standard way of counting different pairs. It ignores sequences of the same syllable (e.g., *lele* 'fly', *kaka* 'rinse'). Thus, the formula should be n^2, n^3, etc.

Finally, Grey's analysis of one short vowel per syllable is a simplistic and unrealistic way of describing the language, since it ignores long vowels, short diphthongs, and long diphthongs. If we use combinations that actually occur in the language (not all diphthongs occur both short and long), we find that twenty-five different vowels and diphthongs can serve as the center of a syllable (see Schütz 1981:25). In combination with the eight consonants, we arrive at a figure of 225— i.e., (8 x 25) + 25—potential one-syllable forms. Thus, Grey's figures can be revised as follows:

TABLE 2.2

POTENTIAL VOCABULARY SIZE (ADJUSTED)

1-syllable words:	225
2-syllable words:	50,625
3-syllable words:	11,390,625
4-syllable words:	2,562,890,625
Total:	2,574,332,100

Such figures, of course, indicate only the potential number of words,[4] but they should certainly still the voices that will claim that the Hawaiian sound system made a large vocabulary impossible. As a matter of fact, some writers from the middle of the nineteenth century complained that the vocabulary was too large, or, in their terms, "copious." For example, Hopkins (1862:347) wrote, quoting George Simpson:

> The indistinctness and confusion which arise from the scantiness of its elements, and its consequent repetition of the same sounds, are considerably aggravated by the copiousness of the vocabulary—a copiousness which is said to have been in a great measure caused by the pride and policy of the chiefs, who habitually invented new words for their own peculiar use, and

constantly replaced them, as soon as they became familiar to the people, with other novelties of the same kind. Under those circumstances, to say nothing of the intricacy and precision of the grammar, a foreigner can never hope entirely to master the tongue; and even the missionaries, in spite of all their industry and zeal, often find their ears at fault, more particularly when the natives, as is their custom in cracking their jokes at the expense of strangers, chant their barely articulate strings of vowels in a quick and monotonous strain.

Hopkins (ibid.) added his own comment on the copiousness of the language:

> The Hawaiians have, moreover, [a] different dialect for their poetry; or, at least, if the language be the same, its inflections and construction appear very different, and its metaphors and allusions, which give enjoyment to the native race, elude the comprehension of residents who are well acquainted with the Hawaiian language used in prose.

Donne (1866:87–88) complained about what seemed to him an unnecessarily large vocabulary:

> One thing that makes the Hawaiian language so difficult to foreigners is the great number of words it contains. It is said there are no less than 1400 beginning with the letter a.[5] Not that the Hawaiians ever needed so many words, but it seems, their chiefs had a foolish custom of trying to keep themselves separate from the common people by speaking in a different way from them, and so, it is said, they were always inventing new words for the same things; when one of their words began to be understood and used by the common people, they dropped it, and invented another, and so on, till at last their language became clogged with a vast number of useless expressions.

Working through this surfeit of words, however, some observers were not pleased that the Hawaiians divided their world into semantic categories that were different from their own. They expressed this displeasure by complaining about a lack of generalization in the organization of vocabulary. Typical of such comments are those by Lorrin Andrews (1854:19):

> In Hawaiian there is a great want of generic terms, as is the case with all uncultivated languages. No people have use for generic terms until they begin to reason; and the language shows that the Hawaiians have never been a reasoning people. They have been better warriors and poets, than philosophers and states-

men. Their language, however, richly abounds in specific names and epithets.

William D. Alexander echoed the sentiment in his introduction to Andrews's dictionary (1865):

> A few words should be added on the peculiar genius and structure of the Polynesian language in general and of the Hawaiian dialect in particular ... The vocabulary of the Hawaiian is probably richer than that of most other Polynesian tongues. Its child-like and primitive character is shown by the absence of abstract words and general terms.

Even years later, casual observers were making the same kind of comment. The following example is from Preston (1900a:51): "In this phrase we see again the lack of generalizing power of the Polynesians." Later in his paper (p. 57), he fitted this putative quality into a series of characterizations about the language:

> Here we have a distinguishing feature in Polynesian methods of thought. By its very simplicity, its lack of generic terms, and its flexibility, the Hawaiian tongue is capable of almost endless expression of the simplest ideas.

Throughout his discussion of the vocabulary, Preston seemed to be torn between the extremes of pointing out the "primitive" features of the Hawaiian, and then praising it for richness or detail in some aspect that European languages neglect.[6] The same kind of vacillating characterizes many comments about Hawaiian grammar, particularly with reference to the parts noticeably different from those of Latin and Greek. But in the early comments about Hawaiian, its features were seldom praised.

Grammar

One of the adjectives that crops up occasionally in early discussions of Hawaiian is "undeveloped." Although the term is seldom defined, it seems to refer to the fact that Hawaiian does not have the elaborate systems of declensions and conjugations that Latin has for its nouns and verbs.

Other characterizations are "simple, childlike." Probably these terms can be traced to a common Austronesian feature: *reduplication*, the repetition of part or all of a word to accomplish some grammatical or semantic purpose. For many writers, reduplication evoked the image of baby talk. For example, Sweet wrote (1900:47): "One of the most primitive and natural ways of strengthening, emphasizing, or otherwise modifying the meaning of a word is to repeat it ... "

Preston (1900a:50) echoed the theme: "As in all uncultivated tongues, intensity of expression is accomplished by repetition."

Chamisso as well used such adjectives (*kinderhaft* and *einfach* were his terms), but he gave what he thought was proof that the characterizations were appropriate. After his first visit, he commented at length on his general impressions of Hawaiian and some of its linguistic relatives. He wrote first that the people of the Polynesian triangle formed by New Zealand, Easter Island, and the Sandwich Islands (Hawai'i) spoke one language, with dialect differences only in pronunciation. Familiar with the rudiments of Tongan grammar from John Martin's grammar (1817), Chamisso gave this opinion of its nature (Kratz 1986:255):

> In this we recognize the Malayan language system in its greatest possible simplicity and, in our view, at the level of undeveloped childhood. It is a pleasant childish babble that can hardly be called a language.

Continuing with his pronouncements on the nature of Polynesian languages, he came to Hawaiian:

> The language of the Sandwich Islands really did seem much more childlike to us than the dialect of Tonga appears in its grammar. We have discovered only two pronouns in it, *wau* for the first person, *hoe* [*'oe*] for the second, and only two adverbs for determining the time of the action, *mamure* [*mamuli*] for the future, *mamoa* [*mamua*] for past time. The interrogative or doubting particle *paha*, which is a postpositive enclitic, is of frequent use. *Nue* [*nui*] and *nue nue* [*nui nui*] 'very' and 'large' form the comparative and superlative.[7] Some particles designate the relationships of nouns as prepositions.

In a note, Chamisso justified his assertion that Hawaiian contained only two pronouns by claiming that John Liddiard Nicholas's Māori vocabulary (1817) showed no "indication of greater extent."

As for the information gained from Nicholas's Māori word list, had Chamisso looked at some of the phrases more carefully, he would have found, in addition to forms for 'I' and 'thou', at least two more pronouns: *kodooa* (*kōrua*), second person dual (vol. 2, p. 345), *taooa* (*tā ua*), first person dual inclusive (p. 346).

Fortunately, Otto von Kotzebue, Chamisso's captain and compiler of the account of the expedition, corrected the statement about Hawaiian pronouns (1821, 3). Based on other works on Polynesian languages, such as Martin's Tongan grammar, and Kendall and Lee's Māori grammar, Kotzebue realized that, because of the similarity among the languages, Hawaiian would be certain to have more pronouns.[8]

Another grammatical anomaly frequently commented on, not only for Hawaiian, but also for a number of other Oceanic languages, was the absence of relative pronouns. For example, Preston (1900b:52) noted: "No relative pronoun has ever been found in Hawaiian." However, he went on to say that this did not indicate a "lack of logical clearness," for the meaning could still be conveyed without ambiguity.

Another feature of Hawaiian and many other Oceanic languages is the presence of many sentences apparently without a verb, and the absence of direct translations for the verbs *to be* and *to have*. Preston wrote (1900b:52):

> Some of the strongest and clearest affirmations are made in Hawaiian without any kind of a verb; there is no verb in the language to express the idea of existence. The structure of the idiom does not require it. Neither is there any verb to express having or possessing, nor to express duty or obligation, nor to affirm any quality as belonging to any substance ...

In contrast to some of his more judgmental statements, Preston did not condemn these features in Hawaiian, but explained how the notions were expressed indirectly. Still, even though he was writing in the last year of the nineteenth century, the idea of the Noble Savage and primitive language underlay much of his discussion. Sometimes it came to the surface, as in his treatment of syntax, particularly the Hawaiian pattern of moving important information to the beginning of the sentence and marking it as the topic. French, in contrast, he maintained, could not do this (p. 55):

> But the French language, proud mistress that she is, will not tolerate those liberties of construction that the Polynesian tongues not only permit but even court. The higher the civilization, the more acute are the forms of thought. The more exacting the rules of syntax become, the more limited appears the capacity for flexibility.

REASONS FOR THE JUDGMENTS

Even taking into account the adage *autres temps, autres mœurs*, it is sometimes difficult to imagine what prompted observers of the Hawaiian language to make the statements they did. For example, Chamisso had an established reputation as a naturalist when he was invited in 1815 to accompany Captain Kotzebue on his exploring expedition. Why did he make the outlandish statement that Hawaiian had only two pronouns? Chamisso unwittingly provided the answer himself in his description of his first contact with Hawaiian other than in the travel accounts he had read. It seems that he was introduced to the Hawaiian language by a fellow passenger on the *Rurik*—John Elliot de Castro, "of mixed English and Portuguese ancestry," who had lived in Hawai'i for two years, first as a pearl trader on O'ahu, and later as Kamehemeha's personal physician. Chamisso described his "benevolent teacher," as he called him (Kratz 1986:111–12):

> My discussions with our guest on the voyage across were incalculably instructive to me. To be sure, I had read what was written about the Sandwich Islands and had collected a good deal of data about their present condition, especially with regard to the commerce for which they have become a center. But there I had an O-Waihian (*Naja haore* [*nai'a haole*],[9] porpoise of the white men) before me who had lived with and among the people, who had belonged to a definite caste and from whom I could hear the language and learn about the customs. I used the opportunity industriously, and I was really well prepared, and even not completely ignorant of the childlike language, to visit the residence of this engaging people, at that time still not deprived of its natural character.

Thus, by the time Chamisso heard Hawaiian from native speakers, he had already formed his opinions about its nature, apparently accepting de Castro's version of it as authentic.

As for other observers, perhaps they were linguistically naive or lacked the intelligence to overcome the natural prejudices of their own culture and language. Chamisso certainly suffered from the first disadvantage, for accurate knowledge of these exotic languages made its way only slowly to Europe and America. And perhaps the idea of the Noble Savage and primitive languages acted as a screen through which data were observed. In other words, these early writers may have been preconditioned to find certain things and not to find others.

As for a lack of intelligence on the part of the observers, it might be fair to suggest this reason much later, when—in spite of evidence against the notion of primitive languages—observers continued their ethnocentric comments.

A third, and intrinsically more interesting, explanation is that the Hawaiians, realizing that visitors (whose languages were labeled as *namu* 'gibberish') constantly misunderstood them, simplified their language. This style, dubbed FOREIGNER TALK, was not uncommon in the

Pacific, especially in regions with more intergroup contact. For example, the earliest records of Fijian show that the speakers were accustomed to simplifying their language, especially the phonology, for the Tongans, who apparently couldn't handle the consonants [mb], [nd], [ŋg], [nr], [ß], and [ð]. William Beresford (Dixon 1789:268) made such an observation very soon after the first outside contact with Hawai'i:

> Their language is soft, smooth, and abounds with vowels. In their conversation with each other it appears very copious, and they speak with great volubility; but when conversing with us, they only make use of those words which are most expressive and significant, purposely omitting the many articles and conjunctions made use of when speaking to each other ...[10]

The outgrowth of Foreigner Talk, Pidgin Hawaiian, is discussed more thoroughly in chapter 3. Whatever the label, the phenomenon did not die out. The following warning appears in *Na Huaolelo* ... (Bishop 1854:3):

> There has long prevailed, between natives and foreigners, a corrupted tongue, which the former only use in speaking to the latter, but never among themselves. It is a method of speech which should be abandoned, as it gives a false impression, derogatory to all rule, and is without system or beauty ...[11]

More Recent Judgments

Often, misconceptions that should have been corrected after prolonged contact with the language lived far beyond their expected span. For example, Laura Fish Judd wrote in 1880 (p. 24):

> If the Italian is the language of the gods, the French of diplomacy, and the English of business men, we may add that the Polynesian is the dialect of little children. It is easier to say "hele mai," than "come here," and "i wai," than "give me water."

And in the preceding sections, the several quotations from Preston show that the Noble Savage was still alive and well in 1900. More recent appearances are less frequent, but by no means altogether absent. What is surprising is the sources of the reappearances.

Otto Jesperson, described on the back cover of one of his books as "perhaps the world's greatest authority on the English language," published *The Growth and Structure of the English Language* in 1905. It went through a number of editions; the ninth, the author wrote in 1938, was "carefully revised and brought up to date." But "up to date" is a relative term. Apparently Jesperson retained his nineteenth-century attitudes toward non-Indo-European languages, even though he lived well into the formative years of modern structural linguistics. Here are Jesperson's views of the overall qualities of specific languages, treating Hawaiian as a contrast to English (1939 [1956]:2–4):

> It is, of course, impossible to characterize a language in one formula; languages, like men, are too composite to have their whole essence summed up in one short expression. Nevertheless, there is one expression that continually comes to my mind whenever I think of the English language and compare it with others: it seems to be positively and expressly *masculine*, it is the language of a grown-up man and has very little childish or feminine about it ...
>
> To bring out clearly one of these points I select at random, by way of contrast, a passage from the language of Hawaii: 'I kona hiki ana aku ilaila ua hookipa ia mai la oia me ke aloha pumehana loa.' Thus it goes on, no single word ends in a consonant, and a group of two or more consonants is never found. Can any one be in doubt that even if such a language sound pleasantly [*sic*] and be full of music and harmony the total impression is childlike and effeminate? You do not expect much vigour or energy in a people speaking such a language; it seems adapted only to inhabitants of sunny regions where the soil requires scarcely any labour on the part of man to yield him everything he wants, and where life therefore does not bear the stamp of a hard struggle against nature and against fellow-creatures.[12] In a lesser degree we find the same phonetic structure in such languages as Italian and Spanish; but how different are our Northern tongues.

In the last half century or so, there have been local variants on such linguistic impressionism, but they have generally been at the other end of the pendulum swing, chauvinistically praising Hawaiian for some indefinable quality. The following quotation, by Henry P. Judd, is from a short pamphlet on the language, produced for a local commercial enterprise (1938:3–6):

> The Hawaiian dialect is a subtle and rhythmic language, soft and filled with musical cadences. Because of its rhythm, gesture is very important to the complete expression of the meaning, and as a result the gesture developed in tradition and became a distinct part of the oratorical, poetical and religious speech ...
>
> It might be said that each word resembles the face of a beautiful girl in that it is capable of many different shades and changes of expression ...
>
> Not only were words and sentences full of double meanings, but different words with entirely different meanings sound exactly the same to our unpracticed ears. Fortunately, the native Hawaiian

had a keen sense of hearing. These differences in sound are so small that a man who speaks English on hearing them would be positive he had heard only one sound. And yet a Hawaiian would have heard a number of different sounds.

In a longer work (1939a), discussed more fully in chapter 12, Judd could still not resist the capsule descriptive adjectives, based on a comparison with English. "Some expressions are cumbersome; for example in the Lord's Prayer the words, 'Forgive us our debts as we forgive our debtors' is but nine words in English and twenty-four in Hawaiian." Such naive statements as this ignore some of the fundamental differences between the languages, such as the different means they use to carry out grammatical functions. Obviously, if a language uses inflection and derivation to a great degree, many words consist of two or more morphemes—that is, pieces that contain meaning—and fewer words will be necessary to communicate an idea.

Nor has the Noble Savage been laid to rest in the years since Judd emoted over the language. In the first edition of their Hawaiian-English dictionary (1957:xiii), Mary Kawena Pukui and Samuel H. Elbert saw fit to quote the following flight of fancy, written by Lorenzo Lyons in 1878:

> It is an interminable language ... it is one of the oldest living languages of the earth, as some conjecture, and may well be classed among the best ... the thought to displace it, or to doom it to oblivion by substituting the English language, ought not for a moment to be indulged. Long live the grand old, sonorous, poetical Hawaiian language.[13]

Lyons's eulogy reflects his own affection for the language, and is perhaps appropriate as a lay opinion in the nineteenth century. But in a mid-twentieth-century professional treatment, no purpose is served by the uncritical quoting of such meaningless words (as applied to language) as *oldest* or *best*.

Still, such characterizations continue. The following quotations are from more recent, lightweight treatments of the language:

> The language of Hawaii is soft and has a musical sound (Hancock and Sadler 1969:15).

> The Hawaiian language is considered by linguists to be one of the most fluid and melodious languages in the world (*Say It As It Is* 1978:3).

-0-0-0-0-0-

First impressions are hard to shake off. Throughout much of what has been written about the Hawaiian language run several threads of ideas, such as *simple* and *primitive*. More than 120 years after Cook's first encounter with Hawaiian—a period of intense change within Hawai'i and of equal development in our understanding of language— one "scientist" (Preston 1900a: 59, 62) still viewed Hawaiian through a nearly opaque veil of romanticism, calling it "exceedingly primitive" and stating flatly that "the Hawaiian is a child of nature."

NOTES

---

[1] John Charlot (pers. comm., September 1993) pointed out the sibilant-like variant of /h/, discussed in somewhat more detail in chapter 4.

[2] Here, Andrews was referring to vowels separated by a glottal stop; see chapter 8.

[3] The Canadian explorer who traveled around the world in 1841–1842.

[4] These figures for potential words do not take into account the limitations on sequences discussed in various articles by Viktor Krupa (e.g., 1971), the absence of certain syllables (e.g., *wu*, except in borrowed words), and the low frequency of others (e.g., *wo*).

[5] Even though this figure includes both initial *a-* and *'a-* words, it still seems unrealistically high.

[6] A work such as Preston's would not normally warrant so much attention, since so much of its theme is the antithesis of how linguists today view language and culture. But it represents a particular point of view and contains, in just twenty-four pages, a wealth of examples of the attitudes that I am trying to illustrate. Besides, its straightforward title and prestigious publisher (*Bulletin of the Philosophical Society of Washington*) might cause the unsuspecting to take it seriously. In fact, one wonders why the publisher who has reprinted so many old works on Hawaiian language and culture has not made a tourist booklet out of this one.

[7] Some writers have suggested that such reduplication reflects a pidginized form of Hawaiian, but it is difficult to prove the assertion (John Charlot, pers. comm., September 1993). *Nuinui*, as an "intensive of *nui*," appears in older dictionaries, but not in the Pukui-Elbert dictionary.

[8] Judging from his comments on Chamisso's Hawaiian grammar (1969:iv), Elbert does not seem to have been aware that Chamisso's unfortunate statement was corrected in the same work.

[9] It seems more likely that the name was *nā i'a haole* 'foreign fish'.

[10] Because this narrative appears under Dixon's name, it is often assumed that it is his own work. Actually, it is that of William Beresford, who wrote the letters that now appear as chapters in the book. See chapter 3.

---

[11] Bishop's phrase book was reprinted many times. Editions from the turn of the twentieth century continue the condemnation of this form of Hawaiian; the latest printing I have seen is from 1991.

[12] This characterization is in sharp contrast with that of Hopkins, quoted earlier: "a people of bold and forcible character."

[13] Fortunately, this quotation does not appear in the latest edition of the dictionary.

CHAPTER THREE

The Early Collections

-0-0-0-0-0-

To help my memory, I formed all I learned into the English alphabet, and writ the words down with the translations ... It cost me much trouble to explain to him what I was doing; for the inhabitants have not the least idea of books or literature (Jonathan Swift's Gulliver's Travels, *A Voyage to the Country of the Houyhnhnms, chapter 3).*

B etween the time of Captain James Cook's and William Anderson's first observations on the Hawaiian language in 1778 and the first concentrated efforts by the Congregational missionaries to master the language, more than forty years passed, a time of increased European and American interest in Hawai'i. Are these intervening years completely devoid of Hawaiian language studies? If one looks at only published grammars or dictionaries, the period looks barren indeed. However, there is another source for information about the language: the journals, in both published and manuscript form, of the explorers and traders who visited Hawai'i during that time.

After Cook's contact with Hawai'i, no visits are recorded from the outside until 1786, when four ships called.[1] The reasons for the visits were occasionally scientific but more often commercial—at first connected with the fur trade that had opened up along the northwest coast of America, but soon broadening to include other commodities and places. As Ralph S. Kuykendall described it (1938:20):

> ... in a very short time Hawaii became well established as a port of call and wintering place, not alone for ships engaged in the fur trade, but also for those engaged in the more general trade which grew up between Asia and the west coast of North and South America.

At first, ship captains called at Hawai'i mainly to provision their vessels, but later to recruit sailors (both peaceably and by force) from among the Hawaiians. They also came for sandalwood, but not until nearly 1810 did that enterprise flourish.

As for trade in the other direction, the Hawaiians had already had an early opportunity to observe the power of firearms, and the internal fighting they carried on until 1796 produced a demand for weapons.

Thus, contact with the outside increased greatly, as one can see from such studies as Judd and Lind 1974, which is an index, year by year, of the ships that called at Hawai'i before 1860, and Sahlins 1989, which contains a list ("without claim to be exhaustive") of thirty-four explorers' or traders' accounts that describe some aspect of Hawaiian history or culture before 1820.

MOTIVES

For the most part, the rationale for the explorers' first attempts to write Hawaiian words and phrases was intellectual curiosity. Thus, if we try to place ourselves in the position of these early amateur linguists, we find ourselves, as John C. Beaglehole (1974:99) expressed it, "plunged suddenly into the middle of eighteenth-century science," for the intellectual curiosity of the explorers was to be directed mainly to astronomical matters: the observation of the Transit of Venus provided the main impetus for Cook's first voyage to the Pacific.

The social sciences, as we call them now, seem to have been much less important to the planners of the expedition. For example, the secret instructions given to Cook before the voyage did not instruct him specifically to gather any cultural information. Aside from the all-important astronomical observations that were to be made, they requested surveys, plans, and views of the islands' geographical features (Beaglehole 1955: cclxxx). Moreover, the instructions for learning about natural history are detailed, listing even the supplies needed (e.g., a library, nets, special equipment for catching and preserving insects, different gear for fishing, an underwater telescope).

Perhaps the planners of the expedition did not intend to give this impression, but it seems only a suggestion, not a requirement, that language and culture be observed: in a document from the Royal Society called "*Hints* offered to the consideration of Captain Cooke [*sic*], Mʳ Bankes [*sic*], Doctor Solander, and the other Gentlemen who go upon the Expedition on Board the *Endeavour*," the expedition is requested to pay some attention to the inhabitants of the new lands discovered, noting (Beaglehole 1955: 514–19):

> The natural Dispositions of the people; Their progress in Arts or Science, Especially their *Mechanics*, Tools, and manner of using them; — Their notions of Astronomy &ᶜ are principal objects of attention.
>
> Or if they have any method of communicating their thoughts at a distance, As the *Mexicans* are said to have done by painting, and the Peruvians by the Quipos.[2]

Next, the Character of their Persons, Features, Complection, Dress, Habitations, Food, Weapons

Then may be considered their tokens for Commerce,... Religion, Morals, Order, Government, Distinctions of Power, Police

Lastly, the Natural productions of the Country, in the Animal, Vegetable and Mineral Systems.

Finally, the local name for any animal was to be recorded. Other than this desire for animal names, the Royal Society seems to have been interested in language only to the extant that it could be "communicated at a distance"—that is, transformed into writing or some other method of symbolic representation.

SOURCES

Fortunately for historians of linguistics, some of the early observers, perhaps feeling that it was implicit in the "hints" above, also commented on the Hawaiian language. Naturally, the comments vary widely in their value, depending on such variables as the intellectual curiosity (and competence) of the writer, or the requirements of the sponsoring organization or the trading company.[3]

TABLE 3.1

HAWAIIAN WORD LISTS BEFORE 1820

Date Collected	Date Published	Collector	Nationality	Number of Words
1778	1784	Anderson	British	250
1779	1967	Samwell	British	143
1787	1789	Beresford	British	82
1789	1964	Martínez	Spanish	285
1791	—	Santelizes Pablo	Spanish	70
		Santelizes Pablo	Spanish	216
		Santelizes Pablo	Spanish	312
1791	1822	Quimper	Peruvian (?)	253
1804	1812, −14	Lisiansky	Russian	203
1809–10	1816	Campbell	British	400
1819	1823	Gaimard/Arago	French	200

(Adapted and expanded from Elbert 1954)

In a few of these reports, language takes center stage for a time, and we find sections that contain not only comments about Hawaiian but even sample word lists. Table 3.1 shows those that are known so far, discounting some probably spurious lists that have recently been published.[4]

These lists comprise one of the two major sources of information about the Hawaiian language from the time of Cook to the arrival of the American missionaries. The other is a largely neglected grammatical sketch by Samuel Ruggles, discussed in chapters 6 and 12. These sources are supplemented by the occasional linguistic observation made in passing that one can find in travel accounts, even though they may not contain a neatly organized word list. By themselves they may seem insignificant, but combined they often add to our knowledge of language use and attitudes.

Compilers of the Word Lists

This section (which is based first on the invaluable work by Judd and Lind [1974]) attempts to fill in the rough outline of table 3.1, adding (when available) such information as the compilers' ships, the time they spent in Hawai'i, the places where they collected the words, whom they used as consultants, their linguistic and educational background, and any other details that may help us better interpret what they wrote about the Hawaiian language.

Anderson 1778. The *Resolution*, with James Cook in command, arrived in Hawai'i 18 January 1778 and left 2 February. Acting as naturalist was William Anderson, a highly regarded but shadowy figure in the journals of Cook's second and third voyages. The particulars of Anderson's life are difficult to find. For example, the *Dictionary of National Biography* is cursory in its treatment, giving only the date and cause of his death, his official positions on Cook's second and third voyages, and a summary of his contribution as a naturalist. As another example, in the volume of Kuykendall's history (1938) covering this period, Anderson's name does not appear in the index.

We can add some detail to the rough sketches of the official biographies, mostly through Beaglehole's extensive research. Anderson was born in Scotland in 1750, and was educated at Edinburgh University. In December 1771, he joined Cook's crew for the second voyage, and the two ships—the *Resolution* and the *Adventure*—set sail from Plymouth on 13 July 1772. Anderson's position aboard the *Resolution* was that of surgeon's mate. For the third voyage, he was surgeon on the same vessel. Beaglehole (1974:500), summarizing Anderson's abilities and contributions to the expedition, wrote that he "was clearly one of the best minds of all the three voyages—professionally competent, but with an interest in all the departments of natural history as they were known at that time, acute as well as wide-ranging, and with a linguistic talent both eager and careful."

On 18 January 1778, as Cook and his crew were bound northwest from Christmas Island, they sighted land again—the Hawaiian Islands. They advanced toward the three northern islands and arrived at the eastern end of Kaua'i on the afternoon of the 19th. They then proceeded to the west, eventually anchoring in Waimea Bay, off the village and mouth of the river by the same name.

Just before the landing at Kaua'i, Anderson had been very ill.[5] But on 21 January 1778, he was sufficiently well to walk with Cook and Webber to a *heiau* about a mile up the river (Beaglehole 1974:574). There he collected his Hawaiian vocabulary.[6]

A little over six months later, Anderson died, a victim of tuberculosis (or the consumption, as it was called then). He was buried at sea off the northwest coast of the American continent.

Samwell 1779. After sailing to the northwest coast of America, the two ships of the Cook expedition returned to Hawai'i, lying at anchor (most of the time) from 17 January to 22 February 1779 at Kealakekua Bay. David Samwell was now surgeon on the *Discovery*, a position he assumed after William Anderson's death. According to Beaglehole (1974:500), he was interested in capturing the essence of Polynesian poetry, and his journal, more than any other, describes the lighthearted side of the voyage. In his diary entry for 4 February, near the end of a long description of customs and material culture, Samwell touched on the topic of language, mentioning the similarity of Hawaiian to Tahitian and promising: "A specimen of it will be hereafter given." However, Cook's death on 14 February provided a much more urgent matter for diarists to describe.

From Kealakekua, the ships headed northwest, hugging the shores of the islands and attempting unsuccessfully to find fresh water and other provisions. They ended at Waimea Bay on Kaua'i, where they had made the first contact with the Hawaiians a little over a year earlier. But yams were in short supply; nor did a stop at Ni'ihau prove successful at procuring them. But the promised specimen of the language appears after a description of people and events at Ni'ihau in the entry for 14 March 1779—the day before they left the island. It remained in manuscript form until Beaglehole published his edition of Cook's third voyage (1967:1231-34).

Beresford 1787. The *Queen Charlotte* (British registry, Capt. George Dixon) and the *King George* (Capt. Nathaniel Portlock) stopped at Hawai'i on their way from the west coast of America to China, initiating the fur trade on the northwest coast of America, described as "a new and inexhaustible mine of wealth."

Except for the introduction and navigational details in the appendix, Dixon's book was actually written by William Beresford. In the introduction, he was described simply as "a person on board the *Queen Charlotte*, who has been totally unused to literary pursuits, and equally so to a sea-faring life" (p. xxii). Each chapter is in the form of a letter, signed "W. B."

The crew of the *Queen Charlotte* sighted Hawai'i on 24 May 1786, and after spending some time at O'ahu, Kaua'i, and Ni'ihau as well, left on 13 June, heading toward the Pacific Northwest.

Beresford's word list appears as letter 41, dated September 1787, after the ships' return to the Hawaiian Islands. Because it was some six weeks too early to head northward, they spent the longest time at Kaua'i—specifically Waimea Bay. Here the crew seem to have had more personal contact with the Hawaiians, more leisure, and more time for observation. (The use of *t*, rather than *k*, adds strength to the argument that a speaker from Kaua'i [or Ni'ihau] was the informant for the list.) Interestingly, Beresford also went up the Waimea River, following the path that William Anderson had trod nearly a decade earlier.

-0-0-0-0-0-

The next five word lists in table 3.1, all collected by Spanish speakers, are intricately bound together by the Nootka Controversy—a struggle between Spain and England for control of the Pacific coast of North America. In spite of the waxing and waning, respectively, of England's and Spain's power, in 1789 Spain attempted to assert its authority over settlement and trade in the area by seizing two English vessels (the *Princess Royal* and the *Argonaut*). The first of the word collectors, Martínez, was directly involved in the fray after he had seized one of the ships. The next collector, Santeliz es Pablo, is somewhat of a mystery, for he seems to have compiled his three word lists from information available in Mexico City. However, the Nootka vocabulary included in his work places it in the same geographical and political area as the other lists. Finally, Quimper was also connected with the Nootka conflict, for in December 1789 he took command of the *Princess Royal*. Minson (1952:5) explained the significance of the aggression: "The seizure of these vessels threatened for a time to plunge Europe into war, an event which was averted by the diplomatic agreement between Great

Britain and Spain known as the Nootka Sound Convention [28 October 1790]."

Barring unrecorded visits before Cook's time (always a tantalizing possibility), these Spanish word collectors represent the extent of Spain's role in the linguistic history of Hawaiian.[7]

-o-o-o-o-o-

Martínez 1789. Esteban José Martínez, captain of the *Princesa Real* (the *Princess Royal* renamed), collected his vocabulary on the return voyage from Nootka Sound. Regarding its provenance, he wrote (Day 1991:24–25):

> This vocabulary comes from the Indian [Hawaiian] whom I have on board named José Mariano (alias) Matutaray. It is apparent in him that the natives of those islands use very few letters of the alphabet. His pronunciation is facile and they have many terms comparable to those of the language of the islands of Tahiti.

The Hawaiian "Matutaray" had been taken prisoner from the *Argonaut* (Day 1991:24) and, judging from the consistent use of *t* and *r* on the word list (rather than *k* and *l*), he probably came from Kaua'i or Ni'ihau.

Santeliz es Pablo 1791. We know little about the provenance of these lists except the signature, (Juan Eugenio Santeliz es Pablo), place (Mexico [City]), and date (16 March 1791) at the end of a three-page letter introducing the glossaries. Each list is arranged alphabetically according to the Spanish gloss, and two of them also include Nootka and "Mexican" words.

Quimper 1791. Manuel Quimper was master of the *Princesa Real*, one of the British ships captured by the Spaniards in 1789. The crew sighted Hawai'i on 20 March 1791, anchored on 23 March, and sailed for Manila 18 April, eventually bound for Macao, where the ship was to be returned to the British.

Known also for his discovery and exploration of the Strait of Juan de Fuca, Quimper described himself as an American-born Spaniard. From other evidence, William H. Minson (1952:ii) guessed that his birthplace was probably Peru (specifically Lima), and that the rough date of birth was the decade 1750–1760 (ibid., p. 4).

Although Quimper mentioned brief stops at Moanalua Bay (O'ahu), Waimea Bay (Kaua'i), and Paliuli Bay (Ni'ihau), it is likely that he collected the list on Hawai'i, where he spent more time. As for his linguistic prowess, "... he was not an educated man. He made many mistakes in grammar and spelling" (p. 13). Minson continued (p. 14):

It will be noted, particularly in the vocabulary of Castilian-Hawaiian words, that Quimper often caught by ear or understood only the last syllable or two of some Hawaiian words. The impossibility of making exact identification and translation of such words is thus readily recognized.

Lisiansky 1804. The *Neva*, of the Russian imperial service and commanded by Capt. Lieut. Urey Lisiansky (Jurij Lysjans'kyj) arrived in Hawai'i 8 June 1804 and left 20 June in the company of its senior vessel, the *Nadeshda*, commanded by Capt. Lieut. Adam John von Krusenstern. (See the next paragraph for details of the *Neva*'s visit in 1809.) Lisiansky was born in the Ukraine on 2 August 1773 and served in both the Russian and British navies. According to J. B. Rudnyckyj (n.d.), the English translation of the word list is an abbreviated version of the Russian original, reduced from 203 words (including a few phrases) to 172.

Campbell 1809. When the *Neva*, this time under the command of Capt. Hagemeister, called at Hawai'i again in late January 1809, Archibald Campbell was an "inbound passenger." The ship left after three months, but Campbell remained there for a total of thirteen months, eventually learning some of the language himself. For this reason, his sample of the Hawaiian language is significantly different from those of his predecessors, since it was not elicited from a native speaker, but was formed from his own recollection of the language.[8]

A Scot whose "rudiments" of formal education ceased at the age of ten, Campbell was apprenticed to a ship when he was thirteen and made three voyages to the West Indies. In Hawai'i a close association with Kamehameha and several prominent *haole* residents put him in the center of activities during his stay.

Campbell returned to Scotland in April 1812. Having earlier lost both his feet from having been frozen in the Arctic cold (hence the significance of his Hawaiian name *Moomooka te Wawyee* [*mumuku ka wāwae*] 'the feet are cut off'; see p. 255 in his narrative), for a time he crawled around the streets of Edinburgh and Leith, earning a "miserable pittance" as an organ grinder. James Smith, who eventually became his editor, found him playing violin for the passengers aboard a pleasure boat on the Clyde, an encounter that resulted in the publication of Campbell's remarkable story.

Gaimard/Arago 1819. The *Uranie*, a French ship commanded by Capt. Louis de Freycinet, was engaged in an exploring and scientific voyage. "The principal object of the expedition ... was the investigation of the figure of the earth, and of the elements of terrestrial magnetism ..." (p. i). It arrived in Hawai'i 8 August 1819 and left 30

August 1819. Jacques Arago held the position of draftsman on the voyage.

In his narrative (1823:270), Arago included a note of appreciation that justifies including not only a coauthor, but one who deserves first billing for the linguistic material:

> I cannot finish this article without informing the public, that I am indebted for nearly all the words here given, to the patience, zeal, and care of my friend, M. Gaimard. We made nearly the same excursions, and I can appreciate better than any other person, the trouble he took to obtain these fortunate results.

Joseph P. Gaimard was "second surgeon" aboard the *Uranie* (p. 139). About ten years later, he was a member of the Dumont d'Urville expedition, again collecting words from Pacific languages.

Both Captain and Mme. de Freycinet, who accompanied her husband, commented on the language in their journals; some of their remarks are noted below.

-o-o-o-o-o-

The following visitors collected no word lists, but their comments on the language, often scattered throughout their narratives, add a sociolinguistic dimension to the sometimes colorless lists of the other observers.[9]

Chamisso 1816. The *Rurik*, a Russian Imperial Navy brig, was commanded by Lieut. Otto von Kotzebue. The *Rurik* arrived in Hawai'i 21 November 1816, left 14 December 1816, returned 27 September 1817, and left 14 October 1817. Adelbert von Chamisso, mentioned in chapter 2, served as naturalist for the expedition. Born in 1781 in France, Chamisso and his family fled to Germany in 1792 to escape the fate of the nobility during those years of unrest (Kratz 1986:xiv). The editor and translator of a recent edition of Chamisso's narrative described his linguistic background (Kratz 1986:xxii):

> Although his native language was French, he did most of his writing in German, the language of his adopted country. His German apparently never became accent-free, and his German syntax, particularly in his earlier writings, occasionally shows French influence. He had taught himself some Spanish and was able to act as interpreter in the Spanish-speaking countries the *Rurik* visited. He knew some English but notes that Englishmen tended to laugh at his pronunciation whenever he opened his mouth. He once started to learn Russian but soon gave it up,

claiming at one point in his writings that it was an advantage for
him not to have to listen to the babble that went on around him.

At the time of the voyage, Chamisso's writings were already
widely known, particularly his *Peter Schlemihls wundersame Geschich-
te*. As for his views of the Polynesians and their languages, Kratz (p.
xviii) described Chamisso as "imbued with the idea of the 'noble
savage'," a stance that is easily recognized in his comments about
Hawaiian mentioned earlier.

Ingraham 1791. The *Hope*—American registry, brigantine, trader,
Joseph Ingraham, master—arrived in Hawai'i 6 October 1791, and left
12 October 1791. Ingraham's unpublished journal (1790-1792) is valuable for its unusual comments on the linguistic facility (or lack thereof)
of a Hawaiian crewman, quoted below.

MEANS OF COMMUNICATING

It is interesting to try to deduce, from the early explorers' accounts
of their first contact with the speakers of an unknown language, how
communication actually took place.

According to Hawkesworth's rendering of Cook's account of his
arrival in Tahiti in 1769, the first sign of communication seemed to be
"young plantains, and branches of a tree which ... as we afterwards
learnt, were brought as tokens of peace and amity ..." (1773ii:79). The
first attempt of the Englishmen to speak Tahitian was accompanied by a
gesture: "... we laid our hands upon our left breasts, and pronounced the
word *Taio*,[10] which we supposed to signify friend ..." (p. 85). Other
references to communicating often used such phrases as "gave us to
understand," "intimating by signs," "addressed myself by signs,"
"endeavoured to make them understand," or "by their gestures ..."
Although the first meeting was on 12 April 1769, not until 10 May did
the account make specific mention of any mutual language learning
taking place. In this case, it was the exchanging of names, with an
emphasis on the difficulties that the Tahitians had with English consonants, consonant clusters, and word-final consonants (p. 123).

But communication may have had a slight head start, for some of
Cook's crew had been on Wallis's voyage in 1767 and may have learned
a few words of Tahitian. At any rate, eventually it becomes clear from
the journals that something more than sign language was taking place:
because of extended contact between the Tahitians and the Englishmen,
each group learned something of the other's language.

Some accounts of similar situations for Hawai'i imply extensive
and rather elaborate communication without giving an idea of how it

was accomplished. For example, Bingham's secondhand account (1847:43) of Vancouver's second visit in 1793 used phrases such as the following:

> He [Vancouver] took laudable pains to convince the Hawaiian chiefs of the inexcusable mischief they occasioned by their war spirit and plans of conquest. Appearing to respect his judgment, they are said to have authorized him to propose to the leeward chiefs a general peace, allowing things to remain as they were.

But the question remains: how did the parties communicate with each other—especially to the extent suggested above? To answer the question, we must return to Cook's first voyage and his first contact with the Tahitians.

The Tahitian Connection

The longer Cook and his crew stayed in South Pacific waters, the more proficient they became in speaking Tahitian.[11] Thus, by the time of the second voyage, communication was much less of a problem than it had been on the first. On this voyage, William Anderson was the principal word gatherer, and his Tahitian word list was the only one printed in the official account of that voyage. David Samwell, first mate on the *Resolution*, reported that Anderson spoke and understood Tahitian better than anyone else on the expedition.

This ability to speak and understand Tahitian eased the way toward a rapid understanding between Cook's crew and the Hawaiians—at least at a superficial level. As a matter of fact, the similarity of Hawaiian and Tahitian was one of the first things that several writers mentioned, with a touch of surprise, because of the great distance from Tahiti. James King wrote (Beaglehole 1967:264n.):

> ... what more than all surprisd us, was, our catching the Sound of Otaheite words in their speech, & on asking them for hogs, breadfruit, yams, in that Dialect, we found we were understood ...

David Samwell was even stronger in his opinion, writing that the language was "the same as that of Otaheite."

Thus, since Anderson was already familiar with "the idiom," there was little need to use gestures or ad hoc sign language to gather information. For example, undoubtedly Tahitian (and perhaps Māori) helped him elicit the Hawaiian equivalents of three rather difficult grammatical concepts that begin his list: the Hawaiian forms for 'where (specifically)?', 'where (generally)?', and 'no'.

Because of this facility on the part of not only Anderson, but a number of the crew (including Cook), communicating with the Hawaiians did not require rudimentary signs and gestures. In fact, the explorers were struck very early by the unexpected level of uniformity among all the Polynesian languages, even though some of the island groups were separated by great geographical distances. For example, on the first voyage, Cook reported "perfect understanding" between the Tahitian interpreter and the Māori. In spite of doubts one might have about how "perfect" such communication was, obviously some was achieved.[12]

For Captain James Colnett of the *Prince of Wales* and the *Princess Royal*, the Tahitian connection saved both his ships and perhaps the lives of the crews. He reported the following incident (1786-1788:161):

> ... she went to the surgeon who had taken a good deal of pains to make himself acquainted with the Language, & understanding from her that it was plan'd by the natives to take both Ship and Smack[13] by surprise; they came into the Cabin & acquainted me with it, sent for the girl having some little knowledge of the Language, from its corresponding with the society Isles where I had been twice, learnt from the Girl ...

Tahitian did not always open the doors of understanding, however. George Mortimer (1791:50–51) found that sign language had to suffice, blaming the Hawaiians' "thick and guttural" pronunciation (mentioned in chapter 2) for the breakdown in communication, rather than his admittedly superficial knowledge of Tahitian. Fairly soon, especially when trade was concentrated among the Pacific Northwest, Hawai'i, and the Orient, knowledge of Tahitian became the exception rather than the rule, and other ways to communicate had to be found.

Mutual Language Learning

In the following decades, when information about Hawaiian was gathered, the methodology changed. Those successors to Cook who were not able to use Tahitian as a lingua franca must have used some other means of communication. Some lists show that gestures could have been used; for example, the collector could have pointed to such objects as mats or coconuts, or acted out such simple motions as throwing or walking. Yet to get beyond this point with gestures alone is not only difficult but also time-consuming. Here mutual language learning takes place.

For example, consider Beresford's list. A number of words refer to objects that could be pointed to, but others, such as kinship terms, imply a different methodology. Beresford wrote simply that he collected the meaning of the words during his stay. But six weeks would have been long enough for some mutual language learning, if there was interest enough. No specific mention of the means of communicating is made, although a good deal of trade was carried on so that they could reprovision their ships.

Nor was contact with the inhabitants confined to short business dealings: during Beresford's visit, two Hawaiians from O'ahu may have spent a good deal of time with the crew (Beresford 1789:107):

> Captain Portlock had Piapia, the King's nephew, on board, accompanied with the man who used to chew Ava for Teereteere. It seems Piapia was so exceedingly attached to Captain Portlock that he was determined to go with him to Pritane, as they call England; and the cup-bearer was inclined to follow the fortunes of his young master.

Thus, increasing contact between the two groups meant increasing familiarity on the part of each with the other's language.

Sometimes, keepers of journals, their goals thwarted by what they considered the insufficient linguistic talents of those about them, noted that the time away from Hawai'i had not made true bilinguals out of the adventurous Hawaiian seamen, but had produced instead speakers of some garbled mongrel tongue. Ingraham wrote of his difficulties with his crewman "Opye." He had explained earlier (p. 2, entry for 16 September 1790) that the young man from Kaua'i had sailed with him on his previous voyage; thus, Opye must have left Hawai'i on the *Columbia*, which was in Hawai'i in August 1789 (Judd and Lind 1974:68).

Ingraham's first linguistic surprise was finding that contrary to the notion of Polynesian "dialects" and "perfect understanding" among them, Opye could not understand the Marquesans very well (p. 50, April 1791):

> Their language bore a similarity to that of the Sandwich Islands many words were the same yet Opye understood them but very indifferently which seem'd to me a little extraordinary as the language of these people by Mr. Forsters who visited these Islands with Capt[n] Cook as before mentioned is very near the Otaheitian and it seems the Otaheitian and Sandwich Island language are so near alike that when Capt[n] Cook discovered the latter he understood them from his knowledge of the former.

Later, he expanded on this theme (pp. 58-59):

> I was much surprised to find Opye—could not understand the natives of Marquesas but I was still more so to find he could converse very indifferently with the people of his own country. Nay, I could apparently on our first arrival talk better with them

than Opye for he by blending the American language with his own form'd a kind of jargon unintelligible to every one but himself. This was on his first arrival but it soon wore off and his mother tongue became natural.

Some thirty years later, the newly arrived missionaries—with more stringent linguistic requirements—made a similar observation about the Hawaiian youths who had spent many years in New England: that they were unsatisfactory speakers of their native language (see chapter 5).

Resident Interpreters

Some of the comments above refer to the abilities of various Hawaiians to speak English, and thus bridge the inevitable communication gaps that appeared. But interpretation in the other direction was also necessary. With the number of long-term residents increasing, it was inevitable that some of them became proficient enough in Hawaiian to act as interpreters as needed. For example, Archibald Campbell reported this incident from 1809 (1816:130–31):

> I was then invited by the king to take my meals in his eating-house, and at the same time he desired a young American, of the name of William Moxely [Moxley; see note 2, chapter 7], who understood the language, to eat along with me, to act as my interpreter.

Kotzebue (1821) mentioned at least two European residents who acted as interpreters. The first was Elliot de Castro, mentioned in chapter 2 as the source of Chamisso's "primitive language" interpretation of Hawaiian pronouns:

> Elliot, who understood his language ... (p. 294).

> After the king had poured out some very good wine, and had himself drunk to our health, I made him acquainted with my intention of taking in fresh provisions, water, and wood. A young man of the name of Cook, the only white whom the king had about him, was quick, not without education, and spoke fluently the language of the country; he had formerly served as pilot on board a ship, but had been settled on the island for several years (p. 302).

> Cook was not always able to translate the words that the king used, which were peculiar to the Owhyee language, and so witty, that his ministers often laughed aloud (p. 305).

> They put to me several questions, which I answered to their satisfaction through Cook (p. 306).

He [the king] then said to me, through Cook, though he speaks tolerably good English himself ... (p. 311).

Other early writers also used longer-term residents as interpreters. For example, de Freycinet wrote (1978:23): "M. Rives,[14] who spoke the Sandwich Island language with ease, acted as interpreter." Don Francisco de Paula Marin was also used in that capacity, particularly after the missionaries arrived in 1820 (Bingham 1847:92): "Calling on the interpreter, Mr. Marin, a Spanish settler ... "

Apparently, not all the Europeans and Americans who claimed to be able to serve as interpreters were competent. For example, William Richards, writing from Honolulu in 1827, registered his dissatisfaction:

One of the foreign residents attempted to read the letter in the Hawaiian language, but his knowledge of the language was so incompetent that few, if any, of the chiefs were able to understand it at all. Kaahumanu said, "Write down a translation of it, that we may clearly understand it."

Thus, the abilities of the interpreters available varied widely.

ARTIFICIAL LANGUAGES

In addition to a simplified kind of language spoken to foreigners, referred to in chapter 2, there are also recorded two examples of made-up languages, both from the long-term and well-known early Spanish resident of Hawai'i—Don Marin.

The first concerns a priestly language, and was reported by Arago in 1819. He wrote (1823:143):

Marini the Spaniard, who has been settled here for a number of years, and speaks the language like a native, knows by heart all the prayers in use among them, and he assures me that none of them have any meaning whatever. They are, by his account, words taken at random, and placed after each other, which in a sitting position they pronounce in a disagreeable humming tone; and, what is very remarkable, the most offensive words form the chief portion of these prayers ... No one comprehends them; and does it not appear from the mysterious power which the priests attach to the unmeaning words they pronounce, that they merely wish to laugh at the credulity of the people, and to surround their power with a superstitious belief, that they alone possess the secret of understanding the supernatural language which they address to their gods?

Chamisso, as well, wrote that the common people were not able to understand what the priests were saying, speculating that it represented an "older, unchanged language of the people" (Kratz 1986:256). He also discussed the Tahitian phenomenon of word taboo (called *pi'i*) and noted that such changes had increased the distance between Hawaiian and Tahitian to the extent that the two groups could no longer understand each other.[15] Then he compared the Tahitian phenomenon to an unusual type of language change (Kratz 1986:257). Again, the source is Marin:

> Toward the year 1800, Tameiameia [Kamehameha], upon the occasion of the birth of a son, devised a completely new language and began to introduce it.[16] The newly devised words were not related to any of the roots of the current language, nor derived from any of them; even the particles that replace the forms of grammar were recreated in the same manner. It is said that mighty chiefs, whom this change displeased, sent the child who had given cause to it, on his way with poison. Upon his death that was given up which had been undertaken upon his birth. The old language was again accepted and the new forgotten. The innovation went from Hana-rura [Honolulu] out to O-Waihi [Hawai'i], where Tameiameia sojourned at the time. Mr. Marini was in O-Waihi when they barely began to penetrate. When we asked Mr. Marini how one or another word was said in the new language, he discussed the matter with natives of Hana-rura who were present, all of whom were well acquainted with the matter but had forgotten most of the words. Mr. Marini knew no other example of arbitrary linguistic change in these islands ...

In a note, Chamisso gave a few examples of this made-up language:

USUAL LANGUAGE	NEW LANGUAGE
Kanaka [kanaka]	*Anna*, man
Waheini [wahine]	*Kararu*, woman
Kokine [kūkine]	*Amio*, to walk
Irio ['īlio]	*Japapa*,[17] dog

Mr. Marini says *irio*, but otherwise one hears *lio*.[18]

As for gauging the validity of Marin's story, Chamisso's comment will serve well. He wrote:

> Thus we can adduce only inadequate examples of this entire linguistic process, which, although adequately attested for us, exceeds the measure of our imagination so much that we do not presume to demand credence.

On the other hand, note that at least two observers,[19] quoted in chapter 2, wrote that the chiefs invented new words to keep themselves separate from the commoners.

PIDGIN HAWAIIAN?

Although the data discussed in this chapter are mostly *word* lists, some of the early visitors went far enough beyond this level to write down a few phrases, many of them quite different from what we would expect to hear from a speaker of Hawaiian today. Julian M. Roberts (1993:8) cited an example from 1787 (Nicol 1822:92; 1936:99): *noue maccou*, the equivalent of *nui makau* 'the fishhook is big'; one would expect *nui ka makau* instead. However, it is not certain how accurately this example represents what Nicol actually heard, since thirty-five years passed before the event was recorded. Moreover, Nicol's command of the language is suspect. Although he wrote that he "was now picking up the language pretty fast, and could buy and sell in it, and knew a great number of words that were very useful," another citation is full of errors.[20]

Another early example is from 21 May 1791, when Ingraham (mentioned above) heard "Tiana" [Ka'iana][21] described as "Enoo, nooe nooe poo, makee Kanakka [*'ino, nuinui pū, make kanaka*] that he was bad and had many guns to kill men ..." Since Ingraham recorded this example at the time, not years later, there is a better chance that his transcription represented what he actually heard.

Individual words, too, can bear the mark of a pidgin. Also in 1791, Quimper collected a word, *kaukau* 'eat', that many people assume is authentic Hawaiian but is actually from the Chinese pidgin word *chowchow* (Carr 1972:4). A recent study by Bickerton and Wilson (1987:62) has used this evidence to support their statement, "The development of Pidgin Hawaiian began at a very early date ..." (p. 62).

In addition, Bickerton and Wilson described Campbell's phrases at the end of his word list "the earliest example of Pidgin Hawaiian" known to them, adding: "Campbell thought that the language was genuine Hawaiian, but it was not; indeed, it closely resembles Pidgin Hawaiian dialogues printed almost a century later ..."

To be sure, the examples from Campbell's phrases show some of the common features of a pidgin, but the authors did not describe the circumstances under which Campbell produced his Hawaiian examples. Nothing in the presentation prevents the reader from assuming that Campbell transcribed his Hawaiian directly from the lips of the speakers. On the contrary, it is significant that Campbell's word list was not collected on the spot from native speakers, but was recalled, some five or six years later, from the Hawaiian he knew. Nor could he refer to a written account; his editor wrote: "The author kept a Journal in the early part of the voyage; but it was lost in the events which succeeded, and he was afterwards placed in circumstances where it was not in his power to keep one" (p. 279). Later (p. 282), the editor wrote:

> The Vocabulary was written by the Author as he recollected the words, and transmitted to the Editor, who arranged them, and afterwards read them over to him, correcting the spelling from his pronunciation, according to the rules which are prefixed to it.[22]

Thus, these words and phrases passed through a number of filters before they reached the reader, and the background for the language sample is significantly different from what we are expected to believe. Campbell's Hawaiian was what he was able to learn in a thirteen-month stay, recalled after he had been away from the language for six years. And what finally appeared on the printed page was the result of a collaborative effort between Campbell and his editor.

As for the use of one word—*kaukau*—being accepted as the beginning of the development of Pidgin Hawaiian, how does that word differ from two other possible borrowings on Quimper's list: *tropi* (*ta ropi*?) for 'rope' and *tenu* (*tenū*?) for 'canoe'? Based on only these data, the argument steers closer to fiction than fact. The only thing this word list shows conclusively is that an informant used one word apparently from Chinese pidgin and two possibly from English.

Another study proposing a pidgin, this time called Hawaiian Maritime Pidgin (Day 1987), suggests that it may have begun as early as the late 1700s. However, the support for this proposal is also weak.[23] Still, the argument is less dogmatic than that of Bickerton and Wilson, admitting (p. 165) that the somewhat simplified Hawaiian that Beresford heard (Dixon 1789:268, see chapter 2) might have illustrated not a pidgin but simply Foreigner Talk.[24]

On the other hand, Roberts (1992a, b, 1993?) has offered more convincing lexical and grammatical evidence for the development of Hawaiian pidgin during the years from 1790 to 1820, basing his arguments on very extensive reading of the available sources, and concluding that "[a] pidginized variety of Hawaiian emerge[d] as the most widespread form of communication between Europeans of different language backgrounds and the Hawaiians ..." (1993:38).

In all this complexity there seem to be only a few pieces of solid evidence—each of these rather more general than specific:

1. Beresford observed that the Hawaiians simplified their language when talking to Europeans. But even this observation can be questioned: is this the kind of linguistic behavior that can be readily observed by a short-term visitor?
2. Many Hawaiian sailors, beginning in the late 1780s, spent enough time among English speakers to gain some control of their language.
3. The foreign population in Hawai'i grew rather rapidly after 1790.
4. A number of Hawaiians (other than sailors) were able to speak some English.
5. A number of foreign residents were able to speak some Hawaiian.
6. Through trade with the Far East, there must have been contact with speakers of genuine pidgins, *perhaps* providing the Hawaiians with an implicit model for communicating with outsiders.
7. Early transcriptions of Hawaiian show both words and constructions that differ from our conception of "standard Hawaiian," showing that either Hawaiians were simplifying their language for outsiders, or that outsiders were learning a simplified form of the language.

-0-0-0-0-0-

I have tried to show in this chapter and the preceding one that the earliest written records of Hawaiian cannot be treated as totally accurate reflections of the language spoken at that time, but have to be understood in the context in which the data were collected. For example, Chamisso first heard the language from a European who had lived in Hawai'i for only two years, but apparently he believed that what he heard *was* Hawaiian. Others collected their samples from or with the help of Hawaiians who had been away from their language long enough to cause problems in communicating. Finally, Campbell's Hawaiian, cited in one study as "the earliest example of Pidgin Hawaiian available," reflected not a native speaker's competence but instead Campbell's own facility in the language, recalled as long as six years later, and written down by his editor.

Yet, imperfect as these records are, they, and the pieces gleaned from other accounts, comprise the whole of our knowledge of the language for the first several decades after European contact. Moreover, they offer tantalyzing glimpses of the sociology of communication in

Hawai'i: the ways people with extremely disparate languages and cultures managed to talk with each other.

NOTES

Some of the material in this chapter is adapted from Schütz 1989b.

[1] The source for this historical sketch is Kuykendall 1938:20–28.

[2] A device made of cords, used by the ancient Peruvians for calculating and record-keeping (*Merriam-Webster III*).

[3] For example, the East India Marine Society in Salem MA decided in 1827 that its ship captains or clerks should request every member to keep a journal (Essex Institute M 656 1832B).

[4] Peter Lanyon-Orgill (1979) included four more Hawaiian word lists from the Cook voyages, but they are almost certainly not authentic. For example, the short list from Ni'ihau (p. 213) contains *k* to the exclusion of *t*—surely the reverse of what actually existed there in 1778. For a detailed review of the Lanyon-Orgill work, see Geraghty 1983.

[5] John Ledyard (Munford 1963:86) called Anderson's affliction "a lingering illness he had been subject to some years."

[6] It is not absolutely certain which of several *heiau* sites up the Waimea River the men visited, but from Samwell's journal (Beaglehole 1967:1083), we learn that it was about a mile upstream and "on the Banks of the River." Several sources specify that it was Ke'aali'i *heiau*; Bennett (1931:104) wrote that "so little remains that the rumor can not be substantiated."

[7] However, early in the nineteenth century, the Spaniard Don Francisco de Paula Marin served as an interpreter and provided some linguistic anecdotes, as described later in this chapter.

[8] In his narrative, Campbell commented indirectly on his ability to speak Hawaiian. On p. 175, he wrote: "I did not then understand the language ..." and on p. 177: "... and was not at that time sufficiently master of the language to understand the purport of the prayers." In the section on Pidgin Hawaiian, I question his control of the language.

[9] Almost every traveler's account contains some piece of information about the language, even if it is only the spelling of place and personal names.

[10] *Taio* 'friend' appears in John Davies's Tahitian dictionary (1851) but not in Yves Lemaitre's *Lexique du Tahitien contemporain* (1973).

[11] Some years later, William Bligh (who had served as master of the *Resolution* on Cook's third voyage) assured officials of the newly formed London Missionary Society that Tahitian was easy to learn.

[12] Judging from what some of Cook's crew wrote about Tupaia, the interpreter, he may have exaggerated his success with the Māori language for reasons of pride. As for the probability of perfect understanding, Peter Buck wrote (1938:198): "The person who says that he can immediately understand

all that is said in one Polynesian group because he knows the language of another group lays claim to extraordinary insight. Maori is my mother tongue but I freely admit that I could never understand all that I heard in the Polynesian islands which I visited for the first time."

[13] A type of sailing vessel.

[14] John Rives is discussed at greater length in chapter 13.

[15] It is interesting to compare this statement with the reports from various members of Cook's crew that the Hawaiians spoke "the same language" as the Tahitians. Is it possible that Tahitian *pi'i* could have separated the languages so much in forty years? Or was Chamisso's observation made on the basis of only casual questioning?

[16] Possibly Kamehameha Iwi or Kamehameha Kapuaiwa (not to be confused with Kamehameha III) (Emily Hawkins, pers. comm.).

[17] One assumes that *j* here has its German value of [y].

[18] Perhaps this can serve as a gauge of Marin's command of Hawaiian, as opposed to Chamisso's hearing of it, for the word is *'īlio*.

[19] Manley Hopkins (1862:347) and M. A. Donne (1866:87-88).

[20] Nichol stated (p. 99): "There is a great likeness in many of their words to the Latin:——

Sandwich Islands			*English*
Terra, -	-	-	Earth
Nuna, -	-	-	Moon
Sola, -	-	-	Sun
Oma, -	-	-	Man
Leo, -	-	-	Dog

[21] Ka'iana, "Prince of Kaua'i," the first Hawaiian chief to have traveled abroad (Miller 1988:1). Thanks to Robert J. Morris for the reference.

[22] Even the source of the examples in Bickerton and Wilson (they seem to have been taken from Clark 1977 rather than from the original) states clearly that his word list was not collected in Hawai'i (p. 28): "It must be admitted that Campbell's stay in Hawaii was relatively short, and that his Hawaiian was recalled from memory two years after he had left." But this explanation also misses the mark, for it was closer to six years. In the body of the narrative, Campbell wrote that he sailed from Honolulu on 4 March 1810, and arrived home on 21 April 1812. The editor did not sign the preface of their book until May 1816.

[23] Oddly, the date for the visits of Dixon and Portlock is given as 1784 and repeated at least three times; the correct date is 1786. The argument is also flawed by an apparent unawareness of the ability of various members of Cook's crew, particularly Anderson, to communicate with the Hawaiians through Tahitian, and a similar unawareness of the number of foreigners living in Hawai'i who could speak English, and the number of Hawaiians who learned English as members of ships' crews.

---

[24] Both articles might have benefitted from heeding Reinecke's suggestion (Bickerton and Wilson 1978:75) that some kind of "broken English" was used in the ports, especially Honolulu, and that many Hawaiian men (he said "thousands of," but this would refer to a later period) "picked up considerable English, mostly pidginized, on whaling and other ships and on the West Coast." Reinecke advised a thorough study of the written records available, which was not done until Roberts began his study.

CHAPTER FOUR

Reducing the Language to Writing: Explorers' and Traders' Alphabets

-0-0-0-0-0-

As all nations who are acquainted with the method of communicating their ideas by characters (which represent the sound that conveys the idea), have some particular method of managing or pronouncing the sounds represented by such characters, this forms a very essential article in the constitution of the language of any particular nation, and must therefore be understood before we can make any progress in learning, or be able to converse in it (William Anderson, Directions for the Pronunciation of the [Tahitian] Vocabulary, in James Cook's Voyage Towards the South Pole and Round the World, *1777, 2:319).*

The introduction to the Tahitian vocabulary published in the official account of Cook's second voyage, which contains the quotation above, was specifically requested by Cook, who wrote (Admiralty MS 55/108, pp. 243–44, quoted in Lanyon-Orgill 1979:47):

> This Vocabulary I had chiefly from M[r] Anderson Surgeons first Mate, who was indefatigable, in inriching it with all the Words he could collect ... In order to help the reader to a proper pronunciation of the different Words, I desired M[r] Anderson to draw up such Rules as he thought would answer this end, which he accordingly did ...

As was pointed out in chapter 3, neither the Admiralty's instructions given to Cook nor the list of hints from the Royal Society suggested that a facility in making alphabets for previously unwritten languages should be among the requirements for the crew, even the natural scientist. Actually, only the fact that a few people were interested in language and had a facility for it accounted for their collecting words along with specimens of flora and fauna.

We turn now to the way these words were written, trying to reconstruct something of how Hawaiian might have sounded over two centuries ago, and also trying to understand something of the complex relationships among the speakers, the observers, and their respective native languages. For example, are there clues in the transcriptions that show us that speakers of English, Spanish, and French perceived Hawaiian sounds in different ways? Two more ingredients in this verbal ollapodrida (a word that figures in chapter 13) are chronology and the ways available at the end of the eighteenth century for writing the sounds of an unfamiliar language.

It must be kept in mind, of course, that the creators of those temporary alphabets were very different from the missionary-linguists who arrived in 1820, for the latter had specific instructions to study the language and decide on the principles that would be used to represent it in writing. Moreover, explorers and traders did not approach the language in the same way as did the missionaries: the former seemed merely intellectually curious, while the latter were concerned with effecting literacy for the Hawaiians. Finally, whereas the earliest writers seldom had a chance to revise their work, their successors had ample opportunity to test their alphabets and improve them.

The complicated relationships among these variables means that in order to evaluate the works of the early makers of alphabets (mostly *pro tempore*), we have to know something of their backgrounds, their native languages, and their experience with other languages—much of which was treated in chapter 3. We now discuss another ingredient in the intricate mix: the tools that were available to them.

The earliest citation for the word *phonology* in the *Oxford English Dictionary* is from 1799, and at that time, it meant simply "the science of vocal sounds." But what was the nature of this "science"? What did a broadly educated scientist know about the sounds of language in the latter part of the eighteenth century? How much of this knowledge trickled down to the general educated public? In other words, what was the extent of professional and lay knowledge about the sounds of any language?

The answers to these questions require some idea of the general organization of language study at that time so that phonology can be fitted into its proper place. Here, Samuel Johnson enters the picture again, for his grammar can serve as a prototype for others written at that time.[1] In the preface to his dictionary (1755), he wrote:

> Grammar, which is *the art of using words properly*, comprises four parts: Orthography, Etymology, Syntax, and Prosody ... Orthography is *the art of combining letters into syllables, and syllables into words*. It therefore teaches previously the form and sound of letters.

In this four-part classification, orthography is the division that is closest to today's phonology. In treating it, Johnson began with the letters of the alphabet, illustrating their different values for English. For example, *a* was said to have three sounds: "the slender, open, and broad." Sample words showing these three different values of *a* are *face*, *father*, and *all*.

The rest of the letters were handled in the same way, with the result that one cannot avoid the conclusion that the accepted order of description was from symbol to sound, not the reverse. Even the terminology of the time supports this idea: note that the appropriate section of the grammar was called not *phon*ology, but ortho*graph*y; hence, not *sound* but *writing*. It is also significant that in the English tradition in the mid-eighteenth century, linguistics seemed to concentrate almost exclusively on the sounds of English, not on those of language in general.

Moreover, there was no established method for writing a previously unwritten language. The most common way to create an orthography for a new language was to use one's own, illustrating unfamiliar sounds with the closest familiar ones   Naturally this practice distanced readers from the foreign language, the extent dependent on the differences between it and the compiler's own. In addition, the compiler's intelligence and linguistic sophistication had a marked effect on the quality of the resultant alphabet.

In this chapter, we shall discuss not all of the eleven vocabularies listed in table 3.1, but a selection of five. Three English lists are presented: Anderson's and Samwell's, because of their position at the head of the chronological progression, and Campbell's, because it includes a pronunciation guide. The two remaining lists represent different languages: Spanish (Quimper's) and French (Gaimard's), with the hope that these different languages (and writing systems) may show some features of Hawaiian pronunciation from a different perspective.[2]

ANDERSON

The explorers and traders who figure in this chapter belong to two classes of alphabet innovators: the somewhat inconsistent write-it-as-I-hear-it type, and those who actually wrote Hawaiian according to some set of principles. William Anderson, the first of the group in terms of precedence, definitely fits into the second category, although at first glance his Hawaiian words look as though they were written according to no principles at all. Hence the paradox: why did the well-trained,

talented linguist (in the eighteenth-century sense of the word) write
Hawaiian so inconsistently?

Aside from Captain James Cook's own transcription of a few
Hawaiian words in an English context, most of the language sample
from the first visit of the expedition was collected by Anderson, the
surgeon aboard the *Resolution* and unofficial naturalist for the expedition. The list appears in the appendix to Cook's three-volume narrative:
it consists of 229 words and phrases, with another implicit 10—the
numerals "as at Otaheite."

Circumstances almost prevented Anderson from collecting this
list—indeed, from seeing Hawai'i at all.[3] When the expedition was
ready to sail north from Tahiti toward the American northwest coast,
Anderson and Charles Clerke (captain of the *Discovery*) had serious
reservations about leaving the tropics. Because they were both ill with
tuberculosis, they did not wish to "encounter the severities of a frozen
climate," but instead preferred to stay in the Society Islands. However,
as the ship progressed from one island to another, always they settled on
the next as the place to remain. Why the two men continued the journey
north is still unclear; John C. Beaglehole (1974:568-69) suggested that
Clerke's sense of duty lay behind his procrastination with the paperwork
that would have allowed him to resign his command. Perhaps we can
speculate further that Anderson might have dared the adventure with an
agreeable companion, but hesitated to risk it alone.

On 21 January 1778, three days after the expedition sighted Kaua'i,
Anderson accompanied Cook and John Webber to a *heiau* a short distance up the Waimea River. As Cook described the event (Beaglehole
1967: 269–70):

> I ... took a walk up the Vally, accompanied by Dr Anderson
> and Mr Webber; conducted by one of the Natives and attended by
> a tolerable train. Our guide proclamed our approach and every
> one whom we met fell on their faces and remained in that position
> till we had passed. This, as I afterwards understood, is done to
> their great chiefs. Our road lay in among the Plantations, which
> were chiefly of Tara, and sunk a little below the common level so
> as to contain the water necessary to nourish the roots. As we
> ranged down the coast from the East in the Ships, we observed at
> every Village one or more elevated objects, like Pyramids and we
> had seen one in this vally that we were desirous of going to see.
> Our guide understood us, but as this was on the other side of the
> river, he conducted us to one on the same side we were upon; it
> proved to be in a Morai[4] which in many respects was like those of
> Otaheite.

Unless Anderson had further contact with Hawaiians on board the *Resolution*, the time spent at the *heiau* was the extent of his work with native speakers. Although the ships stayed in the islands for a fortnight, Cook himself went ashore only on three days. Storms and heavy seas prevented repeated trips ashore, and on 2 February the expedition left the islands and headed north, leaving the balmy tropics for a much less hospitable climate.

As a physician, Anderson was able to diagnose his own illness but not cure it. He continued to write in his journal until 3 June (Beaglehole 1967:cxc), but died exactly two months later while the expedition was in the Bering Sea, off the northwest coast of America. He was twenty-eight years old.[5] King wrote: "If we except our Commander, he is the greatest publick loss the Voyage could have sustained" (Beaglehole 1974:614n). No memorial marks his resting place, for he was buried at sea. The next day, Cook named an island for him (in the Bering Sea), but unfortunately, "Anderson Island" was already St. Lawrence Island, sighted and named by Bering fifty years earlier.[6]

Anderson as Linguist

Cook himself has not always received high marks for his rendering of Hawaiian words. Perhaps the most negative assessment of his Polynesian spelling was that it was a "rough, inconsistent, quasi-phonetic spelling in Latin characters" (Wise and Hervey 1952:311). However, in Cook's defense, one wonders, of course, how it could have been otherwise. Besides, the examples that the authors cited show a greater degree of consistency than either they noticed or were willing to admit.

As for Anderson's spelling of Hawaiian, it has been—at best—superficially treated, or—at worst—ignored. Officially, he seems to be remembered mostly for his contributions to botany, not Hawaiian linguistics. For example, the *Dictionary of National Biography* (p. 393) gave Anderson credit for vocabularies from the second voyage, but not the third.[7]

From all accounts (and these are few in number), Anderson seems to have been one of those Renaissance men that eighteenth- and nineteenth-century Britain excelled in producing. And unlike some of the naturalists on previous voyages, he was not a difficult prima donna; fellow crew members seemed to like and respect him. As John Elliott summed it up, he was "a Steady clever Man" (Beaglehole 1967:872, 875).

The sketch of Anderson's background in chapter 3 showed that he was well trained, highly respected, and had a talent for language.

Drawing from several accounts, Beaglehole treated him in more detail in different places in his volumes on Cook:

> William Anderson ... was an extremely intelligent person, with a mind agreeably wide-ranging, interested in all the peculiarities of mankind, all the branches of natural history ... (1974:299).
>
> Anderson the patiently enthusiastic collector of vocabularies and island names ... (1967:cvci).
>
> He was clearly one of the best minds of all the three voyages—professionally competent, but with an interest in all the departments of natural history as they were known at that time, acute as well as wide-ranging, and with a linguistic talent both eager and careful. He took scientific equipment of his own. A pleasant and generous person, he thought independently and was capable of criticizing a course pursued by Cook; as a day-to-day chronicler he seemed to have an instinct, as he had the range of knowledge, for supplementing Cook; in scientific observation Cook could draw on his unhesitatingly. Everybody thought highly of him; Cook had an affection for him (1974:500).

But in spite of these accolades for his abilities, Anderson's linguistic work has, in the main, been ignored. When it has been noticed, it has generally been criticized. In a sense repeating Abel Tasman's and others' difficulties in using Iacob Le Maire's word list of 1616, some of the visitors to Hawai'i in the first two decades of the 1800s registered their frustration in trying to communicate with the Hawaiian vocabularies they had at hand. Rose de Freycinet told of her difficulties (Bassett 1962:152):

> The vocabularies of the Sandwich Islands language that we had with us were so inaccurate, and the spelling so little adjusted to our system of pronunciation, that it was almost impossible to make ourselves understood other than by signs. To give an example in writing, we will limit ourselves to citing the single word *Toaï-haï* or *Koaï-haï*, which means 'body of water' and which is the name of the principal bay on the west coast of Owhyhi. It is written *Toeaigh* by Vancouver, *Toe-yah-yah* by Cook, and *Towaïhae* by other British navigators.[8]

Earlier, another French explorer, Antoine Raymond Joseph de Bruni d'Entrecasteaux, made a similar complaint about Anderson's Tongan and Fijian word lists. He suggested that the difficulties existed (translated from Rossel 1808:300)

> either because of the difference that exists between the pronunciation of the Englishmen and ours, or because most of the words that Cook thought belonged to the language of the Friendly

Islands were most often words mispronounced by the English themselves and repeated by the islanders with a sign of approval, which could have made them believe that they could understand each other.

As for modern appraisals, the writers of a study of the development of the Hawaiian spelling system (Wise and Hervey 1952) discussed Cook's own spelling of the Hawaiian words that were scattered through his description, and that of several of his officers, but failed to mention either Anderson or his word list.[9] A later and mainly derivative article (Walch 1967) made the same omission. When his orthography was finally treated at length (Hervey 1968), it was almost totally misinterpreted. In short, Anderson's linguistic work has been neglected for the past two centuries. Why?

One might propose that the role of a historian can be compared to that of a director or a stage manager. Even if the plot and the cast of characters can seldom be altered, the focus can. Compared with the rest of Cook's officers and scientists, Anderson was rarely in the center of the narration, outshone by the brilliant if harsh light of such characters as the difficult Johann Reinhold Forster.[10] Perhaps it was because of the implicit competition from the natural sciences, for although they all collected samples for the European specimen case, zoology and botany were more conspicuous.

A more likely reason lies in the list itself—or, more specifically, the list as it was presented to the public.

To those of us familiar with modern written Hawaiian, one of the first things that strikes us about Anderson's list is that *t* and *r* are written regularly. (This practice is discussed in the next chapter.) There are a number of other differences as well, especially in the use of vowels. For example, the common word *hele* 'go' was written as *haire* (and *Pele* as *paire*); *he i'a* 'fish' as *haieea*; *he niu* 'coconut' as *eeneeoo*; *au* 'I' as *ou*; and *he ihu* 'nose' as *eeeheu*, with the unusual sequence of three *es*. *Oo* seems indiscriminately used for both /o/ and /u/, and there are many instances of *y* used as a vowel.

If one took the list at face value—that is, on its own and out of context—an analysis like the following might result. Wesley D. Hervey (1968:24) wrote that although Anderson gave no guide to the orthography he used, it was possible to reconstruct one. He went on to list such a system, one that bears little resemblance to Hawaiian. For example, his list of consonant phonemes includes /b/, /d/, and /f/, none of which is part of the system. As for the vowels, Hervey seemed to assume that all the vowel letters had their current values, except *oo*, which he correctly interpreted as /u/. Even fairly consistent relationships, such as Anderson's use of *ai* for /e/,[11] were explained as sound changes.[12]

Tables, included to show a variety of Anderson's spelling conventions, reflect little basic knowledge of Hawaiian grammar and linguistic history. For example, *heraee* 'forehead', clearly the modern form *he lae* 'it's a forehead', was annotated as follows: "Nothing resembling '*heraee*' was listed in Pukui & Elbert [1957]. '*He*' was most likely the demonstrative used at the beginning of the phrase." The explanation of *matta* 'eye' [*maka*] reveals that Hervey was ignorant of the extent of the [t] pronunciation on Ni'ihau and Kaua'i. He continued: "It is just possible that a shift from [t] to [k] did not constitute a phonemic change."[13] Another obvious form, *Heoo* 'nipple' [*he ū* 'it's a breast'], was interpreted as *hiu, hi'u, heo,* or *heu*—but not *he ū*.

The Tahitian Pronunciation Key

Even with an understanding of Hawaiian phonology and a rudimentary knowledge of Hawaiian grammar, one still finds problems with Anderson's transcription. However, most of this confusion vanishes when the Hawaiian list is examined not in isolation, but as a part of Anderson's total work, and with the knowledge that he was unable to advise the editor or printer about the conventions he used.

Even though Hervey was correct in saying that there is no guide to Anderson's orthographic conventions for the Hawaiian list specifically, there is certainly such a guide to his Tahitian list (Cook 1777, 2:319–22). The published version omitted Cook's introduction, which is quoted at the beginning of this chapter. In these rules, Anderson took the contemporary approach to orthography: he proceeded from spelling to sound.[14] And he concentrated on the vowels, considering them to be the "regulation of all sounds." Other writers seemed to assume this position as well; for example, in the only other pronunciation guide found so far, Archibald Campbell's, only the vowels are discussed. The consonants, it seems, were self-evident. (The problems that belie this assumption are discussed in chapter 5.)

Although it is impossible to be sure what Anderson's own pronunciation of English was like (the situation is complicated by the two variables of geographical dialect and time), table 4.1 is an attempt to convert his conventions into English phonetics, and from there, into Tahitian phonology. It allows us to see that Anderson used eleven separate vowels and combinations of vowels to represent eight sounds in Tahitian: five vowels and three diphthongs.

TABLE 4.1
A PHONETIC AND PHONEMIC INTERPRETATION OF ANDERSON'S
CONVENTIONS FOR VOWELS

Anderson's Transcription	English Phonetics	Current Tahitian Orthography
a	[ʌ], [a]	*a*
ai	[eʸ]	*e*
e	[e], [e]	*e*
i	[I]	*-i-* (?)
ee	[iʸ]	*i*
y / o[15]	[aʸ]	*ai*
o[15]	[oʷ]	*o*
oo	[uʷ]	*u*
eu	[yuʷ]	*iu*
u	[ʌ]	*a*
ou	[aʷ]	*au*

Anderson's diacritical conventions are as follows. The first, illustrated in the table: italics here reflect what was in the original manuscript: a ligature joining two vowels, indicating that they were to be pronounced as "one simple sound." Another convention is the use of dots over two vowels in succession to show that the sounds they represented were to be "expressed singly." In other words, they constituted two syllables. As an example, Anderson gave "roà" 'great, long, distant', probably to distinguish from the English spelling convention of *oa* representing a single sound, as in *boat*. Accent was marked before the syllable in question. Finally, a comma between parts of a word, especially reduplicated portions, represented a "rest or small space of time," but not a "full stop."

Table 4.2 shows Anderson's Tahitian examples (p. 322) respelled according to his conventions.

In the Tahitian list, the diacritics were preserved[16] through the printing. However, in the Hawaiian list, which is without any such modifications, one of two things must have happened: either the diacritics were discarded by Anderson himself, or they were used in his manuscript but lost in the printing process.

Having noticed other instances in which information was lost or confused in the transition from manuscript to printed page, I tend to favor the second explanation. The following examples may serve as possible evidence that this is indeed what happened.

Note "eeheu" (*ihu*) 'The nose'. Would Anderson have written "eee" as such? It is unlikely. In his directions for pronouncing Tahitian,

TABLE 4.2
TAHITIAN WORDS RESPELLED

Anderson's Spelling	Respelled Words	Current Spelling[17]	Gloss
roà	roa	roa	Great, long, distant
e'reema	e'rima	e rima	Five
ry'poeea	rai'poia	raipoia	Fog *or mist*
e'hoora	e'hura	e huri	*To* invert, *or turn upside down*
paroo, roo	paruru	paruru	A partition, *division or screen*

"e" represented /e/, whereas "ee" represented /i/. Thus, "eeeheu" would have been fairly close to *he ihu.*

Another example is "too" for 'sugar cane' (*kō*): did Anderson write "too" or "*too*"? The latter would have represented a mishearing of the vowel as [u], but in the Tahitian list, one of the transcriptions for 'sugar-cane' is "too," written without italics, hinting that Anderson might have heard the long vowel.

Still another example is underlined <u>ai</u>, which does not represent /ai/, but /e/, as (according to his example) in the second vowel of 'Arabia'. For instance, Anderson wrote "haire" 'to go'. As it is printed, it looks nearly like Māori *haere.*[18] However, "H<u>ai</u>re" would represent *here*, an accurate writing of what is now written as *hele.*[19]

Since the third part of Anderson's journal for the third voyage is lost (Beaglehole 1967:cxc), it is impossible to *prove* that for Hawaiian Anderson continued the conventions he described for Tahitian. But the earlier volumes, which cover the period up to 2 September 1777, add weight to the argument, for in them the conventions are followed regularly. For example, the manuscript word list from New Zealand, collected in February 1777,[20] contains the ligatures, dots, and accent marks that were by then a regular feature of Anderson's transcription methods.

Once we understand Anderson's conventions, many confused-looking forms become words that resemble those in the current spelling. This is not to say that his list is entirely accurate, but it is not a bad showing, considering the circumstances under which it was collected.

Table 4.3 shows the first twenty-five words in his list respelled according to the Tahitian conventions, so that they can be compared with the modern equivalents. *T* and *r* have been changed to *k* and *l*, respectively, and word division has been changed to match current conventions.

TABLE 4.3

SAMPLE FROM ANDERSON'S HAWAIIAN WORD LIST, RESPELLED

Hawaiian	Gloss	Respelling	Modern Spelling
tehaia	where	ke hea	i hea (specifically)
mahaia	where	ma hea	ma hea (generally)
aorre, or Aoe	no	aole	'a'ole, 'a'oe, 'a'ohe
he oho[21]	the hair	he oho	he oho
e poo	the head	e poo[22]	he po'o
pepaiee aoo	the ear	pepeiau	pepeiao
heraee	the forehead	he lae	he lae
matta	the eye	maka	maka
pappareenga	the cheek	papalinga	papālina
haieea	fish	he ia	he i'a
eeeheu	the nose	e ihyu	he ihu
oome oome	the beard	umiumi	umi'umi
haire	to go	hele	hele
erawha	tears of joy	elawa	? le'a
aee	the neck	ai	'ā'ī
poheeve	the arm	pohivi	po'ohiwi 'shoulder'
ooma ooma	the breast	umauma	umauma
heoo	the nipple	he u	he ū
peeto	the navel	piko	piko
hoohaa	the thigh	huha	'ūhā
he, wawy	the leg	he wawaihe	wāwae
eroui	wait a little	elaui	_____
myao	finger and toe nails	maiao	mai'ao
eeno	bad	ino	'ino

Rewriting Anderson's word list according to the conventions that were almost certainly lost in the editing and printing gives his work on Hawaiian a credibility that was missing before. Now perhaps the list can be reexamined for what it can tell us about the pronunciation of the Hawaiian spoken on Kaua'i in 1778.

One of the most unusual features of pronunciation is represented by five examples of *ng* spellings, apparently representing Anderson's hearing of [ŋ]: *pappareenga* (*pāpālina*) 'cheek', *Tangaroa* (*Kanaloa*) name of a god, *mango* (*manō*), 'shark'—and two examples showing alternation: *tanata ~ tangata* (*kanaka*) 'person' and *moena ~ moenga* (*moena*) 'mat'.

Treating Anderson's list as a serious document, Geraghty (1983: 557) interpreted these data as showing that Proto-Polynesian *ŋ was usually reflected as [n], but occasionally as [ŋ]. Such information would have added depth to other studies of Hawaiian phonology, particularly Newbrand 1951, Elbert 1979, and Elbert and Pukui 1979.

Hervey (1968:28) apparently dismissed the idea that Anderson's *ng* could be correct: he discussed only the example *papparee-nga* 'the cheek', commenting "The spelling symbols <ng> could indicate that Anderson thought he had heard [-inga] or possibly [-iŋga]." *Ng* does not appear on Hervey's list of "consonant graphemes" (p. 25).

Three unusual transcriptions—*eeeheu* 'the nose', *eahoi* for *he ahi* 'the fire', and *erahoi* for *he lahi* 'thin'—suggest that the Hawaiian pronunciation of /h/ at the time may have included a palatal constriction common in certain dialects of Māori spoken around the turn of the nineteenth century and still heard in the Marquesas.[23]

Ironically, Anderson's word lists from Cook's third voyage[24] seem to have suffered at every touch of an editor and a printer. First, Dr. John Douglas,[25] who edited the official publication of Cook's journals (1784) and used much from Anderson's journals as a supplement (Beaglehole 1967:vi), printed the Hawaiian word list with no diacritics whatsoever, thus changing a fairly accurate rendering to the "inaccurate" vocabulary referred to earlier.

Next, in his editing of the Cook journals, Beaglehole (1967:817) reproduced (from the original manuscript, one presumes) Anderson's Māori list of twenty-one words, including dots over vowels and accent marks, but excluding the all-important ligatures over *ai*, *ou*, *ee*, and *oo* to show that each was to be pronounced as a single sound. Beaglehole, although he partly understood Anderson's system,[26] dispensed with this convention because it would "often have meant a most unsightly page" (ibid.:ccxviii). In certain forms that would otherwise have been ambiguous (such as a succession of three *es*), he added the diacritics. But his altered system does not allow for a possible distinction between "oo" (for *ō* or *o'o*) and "oo" (for *u*).[27]

Finally, Lanyon-Orgill (1979:139-40) mentioned three versions of Anderson's short Māori list from the third voyage—the manuscript, the first printed version (1784), and Beaglehole's transcription of the manuscript—but seems to have chosen the last to reproduce, deleting one more diacritic in the process. Thus, we have a progression from (for example) "makka'reede" to "makka'reede" and finally to "makkareede."

Lamenting the loss of Anderson's final volume, Beaglehole wrote (1967, 1:cxci): "... and we should like our Anderson entire." So should we, especially with respect to the diacritics that change a "defective vocabulary" to a valuable document that gives us new insights into the nature of the Hawaiian language at the time of the first European contact.

SAMWELL

Although David Samwell, Anderson's friend and surgeon's mate, moved up in the hierarchy to become surgeon to the *Discovery*, he did not assume an official position as naturalist or philologist. For example, Clerke, captain of the *Resolution*, wrote of Anderson (Beaglehole 1967, 3:406, n. 1):

> ... and the loss of his superior Knowledge of, and wonted attention to the Science of Natural History, will leave a Void in the Voyage much to be regretted.

And James King, lieutenant aboard the *Resolution*, wrote (Beaglehole 1967, 3:406, n. 1):

> ... he has left no person in I believe either of the Ships, that can even on a less scale continue in making observations on the Objects of Natural History that may occur.

Thus, Samwell seems to have collected specimens of Hawaiian because of his own interest, not through any official capacity. Nor was he aware (apparently) of Anderson's conventions for writing Polynesian languages. Except for one macron (*coomakā* for *ku'emaka* 'eyebrows'), he used no diacritics.[28] And certain practices that coincide with Anderson's, such as *ee* for /i/ and *oo* for /u/, simply reflect common patterns of English spelling.

One of his own conventions is the use of *w* for the offglides of diphthongs, especially /au/. Examples are *raw-oho* (*lauoho*) 'hair', *apaw* (*ua pau*) 'finished', and *kawa* (*kauā*) 'slave'. *Pepeiaw* (*pepeiao* 'ear') shows a common problem: the inability to hear the difference between *au* and *ao*. Finally, in *oomawma* (*umauma* 'breast', which at least in slow speech is pronounced in two accent units: *uma.uma*), his transcription suggests that he heard a diphthong across accent unit boundaries.[29]

QUIMPER

The vocabulary collected by Manuel Quimper provides us with an example of Hawaiian heard by a speaker of a language other than English, and written with roman letters, but with the conventions of another European language.

The first major difference between this list and previous ones is its relative accuracy in representing Hawaiian vowels, the result of the fortuitous match between the Hawaiian and Spanish systems. In addition to the similarity in pronunciation of the five vowels in each system, they are now written in the same way—no accident, since the missionaries eventually chose to write the vowels according to the continental or European system, of which Spanish is a prime example. Thus, the gestalt of the words is familiar: no *oo*, *ee*, or other such combinations to make the written words look longer than what we are used to today.

Even so, the vowels are not quite perfectly transcribed. A common problem, as with other early attempts to write Hawaiian, is the confusion among unaccented vowels, which tend to move toward a more central position. For example:

metuatane	for	*makuakāne* 'father'
paparine	for	*papālina* 'cheek'

Much less frequent is an occasional mistake in an accented vowel:

toagine	for	*kuahine* 'sister'

The use of *j* and *g* (usually to represent Hawaiian /h/) is somewhat confusing, but it seems to reflect an overdifferentiation in Spanish orthography: *g* before the vowels *i* and *e* is pronounced [h] or [x] (as in German *ach*). But those sounds can be represented by *j* as well. Note that this pattern is reflected by the following items, which occur in succession:

agi	for	*ahi* 'fire' (glossed as 'hearth')
geaji	for	*he ahi* 'the fire'

Interestingly, there are two possible examples of the palatal pronunciation of /h/, discussed earlier in reference to Anderson's list, the first of these coinciding with his:

geijiu	for	*he ihu* 'nose' (Anderson wrote "eeeheu," probably "e*e*eheu")
enijiu	for	*he niho* 'tooth'

Many initial *h*s were missed altogether, but many observers from other language backgrounds had that problem as well. As for the convention of writing a [y]-like sound with double-*l*, as in *pepellau* for *pepeiao* 'ear', it simply reflects a pattern in Spanish spelling and tells us little about Hawaiian pronunciation.

Another pattern, however, does tell us something about the language. In contrast to many English transcriptions of Hawaiian, there are no instances of *b* for /p/. The importance of this practice is discussed in chapter 5.

The use of *b* between vowels to represent [β], rather than *u*, tells us that Quimper heard what is now written as *w* more like a fricative than a glide, for which he might have used *u*. Still, the lack of *w* in the Spanish alphabet may have caused some confusion in this area. For example, why did Quimper write *e ue* 'weep (imperative)' as *e gue*—which would represent a [gw]-like sound?

The single, rather than double, *r* shows that Quimper heard what is now written as /l/ as a flap, rather than a trill. And the use of *r* in the borrowed word *paura* 'powder' (one of the first borrowed words recorded and now written as either *pauka* or *pauda*) suggests that the Hawaiians associated an English /d/ between vowels with their [ř] sound, now written as *l*.

As a general comment about the language, Quimper noted that it was "analogous and very similar to that of the islands of Tahiti." He added:

> As to any difference there may be between my vocabulary and that of Captain Cook, I consider it to be the result of the pronunciation, since the language of the Indians is softer than Spanish; and the increase and arrangement[30] of the words acquired is a consequence of the aforementioned voyages made to these islands as well as to those of Tahiti.

CAMPBELL

Archibald Campbell's list, as noted in the previous chapter, is different from the others in that it was not transcribed directly from a native speaker, but recalled from his own acquaintance with the language, such as was gained during a little over a year in Hawai'i in 1809-1810. It is also different in that it includes a guide to pronunciation. However, we cannot be sure how many of the spelling conventions in the work are his own and how many are those of his editor, James Smith (p. 227):[31]

> In pronouncing the words as spelt in the vocabulary, *all the letters must be sounded*, with the exceptions after-mentioned.
>
> In sounding the vowels, A has always the sound of the initial and final letter in the word *Arabia*.
>
> E, as in the word *eloquence*, or the final Y in *plenty*.
>
> The double E as in *keep*.
>
> I, as in the word *indolence*.
>
> O, as in the word *form*.

The double O, as in *boot, good.*
U, as in the word *but.*
The dipthongs [*sic*] Ai, as the vowel sounds in *tye, fly,* or the I
in *diameter.*
Ei, as in the word *height.*
Oi, as in the word *oil.*
Ow, as in the word *cow.*
All other combinations of vowels are to be sounded separately,
thus *oe, you,* and *roa, distant,* are dissyllables.

Note that like the previous spellers of Hawaiian, Campbell stayed
very close to the conventions of his own language. The one exception in
the guide above is the use of *ai* and *ei* for the diphthong now written as
ai. Most other writers usually used *i* or *y.*

From a phonologist's point of view, Campbell's vowel system
itself has only three examples of overdifferentiation (writing one
phoneme two different ways), as table 4.4 shows. In terms of phonetics,
however, two of the examples are not overdifferentiated, but instead tell
us something about pronunciation. The use of *u* for allophones of /a/
(as in Campbell's transcription *mukapa* for *makapō* 'blind') shows the
raising of /a/ to [ʌ] in the sequence *a - a,* still a common feature of
pronunciation.[32] However, Campbell was by no means consistent in his
use of *u*: for example, he wrote *makana* 'give, gift' once as *mukunna* and
once as *makunna*; and in *mummee,* for *momi* 'pearl', *u* was used for *o.*

TABLE 4.4
CAMPBELL'S TRANSCRIPTION OF HAWAIIAN VOWELS

Simple vowels		Diphthongs	
Campbell's System	Modern Spelling	Campbell's System	Modern Spelling
a } u	a	ai } ei	ai
e	e	oi	oi
ee } i	i	ow	au
o	o		
oo	u		

The second example—*ee* as in *keep* and *i* as in *indolence*—reflects the difference between Hawaiian /i/ in accented and unaccented positions. Again, Campbell was inconsistent in his use of this convention. As a matter of fact, his identification of unaccented vowels, including those in diphthongs, is one of the most troublesome parts of his transcription—but he was by no means the only foreigner who had such problems.

GAIMARD

Although Joseph P. Gaimard's word list is not prefaced with a tabular guide to pronunciation, the following quotation (Arago 1823: 170) explains the compiler's system of writing Hawaiian words (and, incidentally, again faulting his English predecessors):

> The French orthography is preserved in these vocabularies. There are, however, some sounds in the languages of the savages, which our (the French) alphabet does not precisely give; and to signify them, I have used those letters which seem most nearly to give a correct idea of them. The vocabularies of the English navigators are so very imperfect, that even with their help, we often found it impossible to make ourselves understood. This probably arises from the different manner of pronunciation which exists in the two nations. Owhyhee, Woahoo, and Mowhee, for example, thus written by the English, are to be pronounced here as in England, *Ohahi, Houahou,* and *Mohoui.* Every difficulty of this kind is avoided in these vocabularies; and the only means of people making themselves understood, is to pronounce all the letters as here written.[33]

The word list collected by Gaimard shows a different set of problems in transcribing Hawaiian, for the French were no less prisoners of their alphabet than the English or Spanish. For example, Gaimard's list shows that he had a French speaker's expected problems with Hawaiian /h/. (Not that English speakers didn't also have problems with this consonant; elsewhere I noted that its occurrence in unaccented medial syllables was often missed.) On the other hand, astute observers from the French viewpoint (and Gaimard was certainly one) would notice certain phenomena, even if they didn't exist in their own language. Thus, he did not simply omit the *h* in his transcription, but instead used the letter for a number of sounds, including the glottal stop. Table 4.5 shows his different uses of *h* (with rough statistics).

TABLE 4.5
GAIMARD'S DIFFERENT USES OF *H*

h represents /h/	14	Ø represents /h/	38
h represents /'/	13	*b* represents /h/	1
h represents Ø	11	Ø ~ *h* represents /h/	2

Another French spelling convention that produced unexpected information is the practice of writing a dieresis over the second of two vowels to show that it represents a separate sound. In French spelling, *ai* and *ei* ordinarily represent [e], *oe* (or, more properly, *œ*) [œ], and *oi* [wa]. A dieresis over the second vowel of each of these pairs shows that Gaimard heard them as separate vowels, and, in a number of cases, there is actually a glottal stop between the vowels: an example is *kapouaï* for *kapua'i* 'sole, footprint'. But these observations are made after the fact; there is not enough consistency in these practices to allow us to propose that Gaimard was consciously writing a glottal stop, for he also used the convention to indicate a diphthong: *ivireï* for *iwilei* 'collarbone'.

One transcription—*poachou or poatu* (*pōhaku*) for 'stone hammer'—suggests palatalization of /t/ before /u/, a process common in many languages. Even recently, palatalization (usually before /i/) has occasionally been reported among *t*-dialect speakers of Hawaiian, but specific information is hard to find.

As with the Spanish list, the French transcription of Hawaiian shows a greater degree of consistency in its representation of vowels than do the English lists, simply because French orthography is more consistent in this aspect.[34] Unlike with Spanish, there is not a one-to-one match with the Hawaiian system. However, the five vowels corresponding to the Hawaiian set are without offglides (as opposed to English), and although some of the vowels can be written several ways ([o], for example), this overdifferentiation causes no difficulties in reading the transcription. As a theoretical example, Gaimard might have chosen to write the first syllable of *'ōpū* 'belly' as *o, ô, au,* or *eau* (he chose *o* fairly consistently for this sound).

Again according to French orthographic conventions, *é* is usually used for *-e*. However, like many other transcribers, Gaimard often confused final unaccented *-e* with *-i*, and *-o* with *-u*.

Gaimard ended his comments on the language with the following comment, which, if accurate, would indicate a feature of Hawaiian pronunciation not noted elsewhere (Arago 1823:143n.):

> I frequently put a final h to a number of words of the Sandwich Islanders, because the natives in pronouncing them, generally finish by a slight aspiration, or a kind of suppressed sigh.[35]

-0-0-0-0-0-

For the most part, this chapter has focused on vowels, not really as an echo of Anderson's opinion that vowels are the "regulation of all sounds," but more as a way to treat as a whole what the early explorers and traders found a very perplexing problem: the apparent instability of a number of Hawaiian consonants. In chapter 5 we shall discuss the matter as reflected in the earliest accounts of the language, and in chapter 7 we shall trace the development of the American missionaries' solution to not just one dilemma, but to a set of them.

NOTES

This chapter takes its title from the subtitle of Kenneth L. Pike's important textbook *Phonemics: A Technique for Reducing Languages to Writing*. Published in 1947, Pike's work was one of the first comprehensive statements of the methodology of phonemics and devising an alphabet for a previously unwritten language.

The earliest citation for *reduce (in)to writing* in the *Oxford English Dictionary* is 1659, stemming from a more general meaning of 'to bring into order.' This meaning of *reduce* is archaic now, and the phrase is somewhat fossilized into an idiom.

However, some people would assign a more common meaning to *reduce* in the phrase, maintaining that Hawaiian itself was reduced or simplified when the extraneous consonants were pared from the alphabet in 1826.

Some of this chapter is adapted from Schütz 1989b.

[1] "A Grammar of the English Tongue," part of the introduction to Johnson 1755.

[2] I had hoped that the Russian list would add some phonetic detail, especially with regard to possible palatalization of consonants (see the discussion of Anderson later in this chapter), but it provides no such evidence.

[3] This discussion is summarized from Beaglehole 1974:568–69.

[4] Cook, and other writers as well, regularly used the Tahitian term (which is actually *marae*); in a sense for them it had become an English word, its status later sanctified by being included in the *Oxford English Dictionary*.

[5] Clerke died on 22 August 1779. He was only thirty-eight—just ten years older than Anderson.

[6] The island is in the Bering Sea, 150 miles south of Bering Strait and 118 miles from the Alaskan mainland.

[7] The entry is as follows: "[He] accompanied Captain Cook as surgeon's mate in the Resolution in 1772-75, and as naturalist on board the same vessel on that commander's third voyage. He contributed the vocabularies of the

various languages printed in the official relation of the former voyage, and his observations during the early part of the latter are cited by Cook in his own words ... His health began to fail towards the end of 1777, and he died of consumption on 3 Aug. 1778; an island sighted the same day was named Anderson's Island in his memory ... His commander, in the narrative of the voyage, testified in strong terms to his sense of his abilities and devotion; and Robert Brown, in founding the genus *Andersonia* chiefly in honour of him, speaks in eulogy of his devotion to botany. In the Banksian Library in the British Museum there are manuscript lists of animals and plants noted by him during his two voyages."

[8] De Freycinet's criticism was unjustified; the last spelling is closest to the present one, *Kawaihae*. Her etymology also is incorrect, for the name means 'water of wrath' (Pukui, Elbert, and Mookini 1989).

[9] Perhaps the reason is revealed in the references, in which we find only secondary sources, with no mention of the official publication of Cook's journals.

[10] For example, a three-part television movie on Cook's voyages, which was shown in Honolulu in October and December 1989, eliminated Anderson's role entirely.

[11] Consistent in one direction at least. However, many instances of /e/ are written with *e* as well.

[12] This is Hervey's explanation of *ai* (1968:26): "In Kauai orthography, <ai> is pronounced [a-i], while in the manner of Pukui and Elbert, *mahea* is pronounced [mɑheɑ]. Pukui & Elbert indicate that there is a tendency for [a-i] to change to [e-i] in 'fast pronunciations.'"

[13] The phrase "just possible" is inexplicable, for the main part of Hervey's dissertation concerns the missionaries' decisions about such consonant alternations.

[14] With the advantage of hindsight, we now look on this approach as quite the opposite of the correct one. But so far as I know, it was not until Peter Duponceau's *English Phonology* (1817) that an attempt was made to reverse this direction and work from sound to symbol.

[15] Anderson's *o* doesn't seem to represent /o/ in today's Received Pronunciation [ɛʷ]. Perhaps it was closer to the vowel in Received Pronunciation *ought*, and hence closer to the Tahitian sound.

[16] Although the printer of the account of the second voyage did not do violence to Anderson's system (that is, no information was lost), the original is perhaps more elegant in appearance. Any two vowel letters used to represent one sound, such as "ai" for [e], were written with a ligature over them, or—in Anderson's own words—"joined together." This convention was translated by the printer into italics, and the text of the description altered accordingly. Another printer's convention was the substitution of a diaeresis over the first

member of a pair of vowels, rather than a dot over each, to indicate that they belonged to separate syllables.

[17] All the Tahitian words were found in Davies 1851.

[18] Although Lanyon-Orgill (1979:47–48) quoted verbatim Anderson's guide to the pronunciation of Tahitian, he apparently did not realize that the con-ventions applied to Hawaiian as well. Thus, he interpreted *haire* as *haele*, a dual or plural form for 'come'.

[19] Hervey (1968:26) explained elaborately, but wrongly, that another *ai* spelling represented Anderson's perception of a careful pronunciation of /e/ as [a-i].

[20] Lanyon-Orgill (1979:135), with the accuracy that characterizes all of his study, wrote: "Anderson's original manuscripts of the longer vocabularies have apparently not survived but the contemporary copies used as the basis for the account of the expedition would seem to have been accurate versions and were faithfully reproduced by the printers."

[21] Note that the majority of nouns occur with *he*. In a sense, each phrase is a discourse, and new information is introduced as such (Hawkins 1979a:10). Gregory Lee Carter (1991 [1994]) treated *he* as an existential verb. A more accurate translation of this phrase would be 'It's hair'.

[22] This is an instance in which we assume that Anderson made a distinction between "oo" and "*oo*."

[23] Kendall's Māori grammar (1815), reflecting the Bay of Islands dialect, contains many instances of /h/ written as *sh*. Elbert (1941:58) mentioned a similar sound still used in the Marquesas in the 1930s, and Michael Koch (pers. comm. 1987) observed it still in use there. Note that in the only examples from Anderson's list, /h/ is followed by a high vowel.

[24] Anderson's journals from the second voyage are lost as well; all the information we have from him comes secondhand, apparently copied by Cook into his own journal. Thus, except for the two volumes from the third voyage, Anderson's observations live only through Cook's and the editors' use of them.

Beaglehole described what remains (1967,1:cxc): "The journal is contained in two small quarto volumes ... ; a third is lost." As Beaglehole's introduction tells us, we have only volumes 1 and 2 of Anderson's three journals from the third voyage. Douglas edited the first published version (1784) and obviously used Anderson's third volume (which continues until 3 June 1778), which was then lost. The last entry in volume 2 is dated 11 July 1777, a little less than a week before the expedition left Tonga. Incidentally, in his transcription of Tongan words and place names (pp. 245, 251) Anderson still used his system of diacritics. For example, his transcriptions *Hēē'hēēfo* and *Fēē'nou* accurately represent *Hihifo* and *Finau*.

[25] "Canon of St Paul's since 1776 and fellow of the Royal Society since 1778" (Joppien and Smith 1987:162).

[26] He wrote that the stroke over two vowels represented *quantity*; actually, Anderson did not generally recognize quantity, but used this convention to indicate *quality*.

[27] I do not wish to criticize the historical content of Beaglehole's monumental work on Cook, but it cannot be left unsaid that his attitude toward, and treatment of, Pacific languages is decidedly cavalier. In the introduction to the third volume (1967:viii; the preface is dated July 1966), he presented his opinions on some aspects of language, immediately raising a linguist's hackles, as it were, by using the word *purist*:

> There are two matters that may infuriate the purist … [the first was the spelling of geographical names]. The second matter is Polynesian spelling and the use of the hamza or glottal stop ('). When I began to edit Cook I was specifically warned, as a non-philologist, against trying to use it in Tahitian, and the French have never adopted it officially. I therefore still present to the reader Raiatea, which should strictly be Ra'iatea; and I have written *arii* generally though not invariably, and not *ari'i*. But in Tongan the thing, ignored in earlier dictionaries, is now official; and in Hawaii pressure is strong for its general adoption. Hence Kalani'opu'u or Kalei'opu'u for the journal's Terreeoboo, and *ali'i* instead of my Tahitian *arii*. Here again I cannot claim total consistency, though I have done my best—whether the reason be weariness of the spirit, or what the eighteenth century, too often gratuitously blaming the printer, called 'faults of the press'.

One cannot help but wonder who gave Beaglehole this unfortunate advice. If a conscientious historian does not hesitate to consult other specialists to supplement his or her own knowledge, why not ask for linguistic advice as well? It is bad enough that the glottal stop is dismissed as "the thing," but even worse, vowel length is ignored altogether. As a result, the correct spelling and pronunciation of *every* Polynesian place name, personal name, and word is suspect. Granted, at the time Beaglehole began his research (approximately 1935 [Beaglehole 1974:xi]), except for Williams's work on Māori, few accurate Polynesian dictionaries were available. But work was well underway, and for each of the major languages, consultation with professional linguists, including native speakers, would have eliminated most of the errors. Besides, the field of Polynesian lexicography was by no means static, and by the end of the 1950s, full-scale dictionaries of Hawaiian and Tongan had appeared. (The mid-1960s saw Samoan as well on the list, but Sāmoa did not play an important role in Cook's exploration.) Perhaps a revision of the works will include a more professional treatment of Polynesian words, but with personal and place names especially, since the proper pronunciation of some of these is being lost with each succeeding generation.

[28] At least none appear in the published version (Beaglehole 1967, 3).

[29] However, such vowel sequences have a tendency to diphthongize in faster speech, thus shortening the form. Cf. *hána + úma -> hanáuma.*

[30] The original has *coordinacion*; the obvious English translation of 'coordination' does not make much sense in this context, unless it is a coordination between the Hawaiian words and their translations.

[31] It is difficult to know whether the apparent contradictions in the guide are simply inconsistencies, or reflect some feature of early nineteenth-century British pronunciation. For example, were the first vowel of *eloquence* and the last vowel of *plenty* really the same? Were the diphthongs in *fly* and *height* different (except for length)? It is possible that they were: some English dialects raise the diphthong in the second word (i.e., before a voiceless consonant).

[32] See Ruggles's use of *u* for the same purpose (chapter 6).

[33] This attitude caused some difficulties for the translator, who added a footnote here: "The Translator has retained these Vocabularies as the author has given them; the words must consequently be spoken conformably to the French pronunciation" (270n).

[34] Actually, the whole system is more consistent, at least in one direction: "French has a one-to-one system for conversion of graphemes to phonemes, but a set of one-to-many correspondences between phonemes and graphemes. That is, any given grapheme in French only receives one pronunciation, but a given sound of French—particularly the vowel sounds—can be written in many ways" (David Caplan 1987, *Neurolinguistics and Linguistic Aphasiology: An Introduction,* Cambridge: Cambridge University Press, p. 234).

[35] It is difficult to translate this observation into phonetic terms, but possibly some Hawaiian vowels were heard as partially devoiced at the end of an utterance (see Newbrand 1951:9).

CHAPTER FIVE

Consonant Confusion

-o-o-o-o-o-

In writing these words, I have spelt them as near the pronunciation as I possibly could; and yet it is probable many of them might strike the ear of another person very differently (William Beresford, Voyage Round the World, *September 1787 [Dixon 1789:270]).*

In this apologia, William Beresford attempted to explain why several observers might write the same Hawaiian word in just as many different ways. Such imprecision is not unexpected; after all, the visitors were recording their personal impressions of Hawaiian words, and because of their different native languages (or even dialects of the same language), varying linguistic expectations, and the inevitable slip between the speaker's lips and the writer's pen, it is surprising that there is any agreement at all in the way a particular word was spelled by different writers.

But the inconsistent spellings that we find are due to more than just those causes; they also stem from an unexpected degree of difference in the way outsiders heard certain Hawaiian consonants.[1] The recognition of this unusual flexibility came about piecemeal and gradually. For example, as noted in chapter 4, William Anderson was obviously aware of variation of a very limited kind when he wrote both *tanata* and *tangata* for 'man'. On the other hand, now we can see in his list many instances of variation that he was *not* aware of. For example, he apparently had no idea that what he wrote as *v, w,* and *wh* did not stand for three distinctive sounds, but only for one.

In the following discussion, we trace the development of the realization that certain classes of consonants in Hawaiian did not behave in the way that European observers expected. In particular, we shall examine the pairs *t - k, l - r, p - b,* and *v - w.*[2]

T OR *K*?

To those of us familiar with modern written Hawaiian, one of the first things that strikes us about Anderson's word list is that he wrote *t* regularly, to the exclusion of *k*. Had he been able to observe the speech of other communities in Hawai'i, he would have noticed that the *t*

76

pronunciation was by no means universal. David Samwell, who did visit other parts of Hawai'i, noted that different dialects used different sounds (Beaglehole 1967:1230–31): "These people [of Ni'ihau and Kaua'i] constantly make use of the T, where the others use the K, such as in the Name of the island Atowai which is called Akowai at Ou-waihee."[3]

If we examine Samwell's narrative description of Kealakekua and Ni'ihau, we find that for the former he wrote k[4] exclusively (except for *Etee* [*ki'i* 'image', perhaps a carryover from Tahitian]), and in the latter he wrote only t. Why, then, does his word list show a nearly even distribution of t and k? In chapter 3, we saw that Samwell could not fulfill his promise to provide a sample of the language, made while he was at Kealakekua, until he reached Ni'ihau. Thus, it is probable that his list represents a mixture of the two dialects.

Finally, Samwell's occasional wavering between c and k for /k/ tells us nothing about the language that he heard, but instead reflects an inconsistency in English spelling. In both lists, d for t reveals the mistake English-speaking transcribers of Hawaiian made in hearing the relatively unaspirated Hawaiian stops as voiced, a problem more conspicuous with p and b, and discussed later in this chapter.

Not all the early recorders were aware of the t - k variation. For example, Beresford wrote t exclusively, no doubt because, like Anderson, he collected his word list at Waimea on Kaua'i. Of the other collectors, Esteban Martínez and Juan Santeliz es Pablo are the only ones who used t exclusively, suggesting that their contact too was with Hawaiians from Kaua'i or Ni'ihau.

However, Urey Lisiansky, who used both t and k in his list, gave a choice for one form, 'cabbage': *tabetee*, or *kabekee* (a borrowing, of course).[5]

Archibald Campbell as well noted the variation and reported it to his editor, who, commenting on the spelling of "Tamaahmaah" (Kamehameha), wrote (1816:210n):

> The editor has not thought himself at liberty to alter the orthography of the king's name adopted by Vancouver and Broughton. Although, to his ear, it would be more correctly Tameamea. Every voyager has spelt it in a different manner. Captain King spells it Maiha Maiha; Mr Samwell, the surgeon of the Discovery, who published an account of Captain Cook's death, Cameamea; Portlocke, Comaamaa; Meares, Tomyhomyhaw; Vancouver and Broughton, Tamaahmaah; Lisiansky, Hameamea; Langsdorf, Tomooma; and Turnbull, Tamahama. As the hard sound of C and T is scarcely to be distinguished in the pronunciation of the

language, and the *h* is silent, the reader, from a comparison, will be able to ascertain the most correct way.

At the end of the guide to pronunciation (p. 227), Campbell's editor wrote that *k* and *t* were "frequently substituted for each other," giving as an example *kanaka, tanata* 'people'.

Within the list itself, Campbell took specific note of the alternation in several cases; in addition to the example above, he wrote the following:

to, ko	sugar-cane
poopoota, poopooka	contempt, a term of
te, he, ke	the

In successive entries on the list, Campbell wrote the same word two ways:

Russian	*Tanata Lookeene* (lit., *person-Russian*)
sailor	*kanaka hanna-hanna te motoo* (lit., *person-work-the-boat*)

And many short phrases as well have both *t* and *k*.

Unlike Samwell's list, Campbell's is less likely to be the direct result of collecting his data from two distinct areas, since he spent most of his stay on Oʻahu. However, it is possible that he was influenced by speakers from other islands who happened to be living in Honolulu while he was there.

Joseph P. Gaimard also noted the *t* - *k* alternation, writing *cacaou*—*tataou* 'tattoo'.

As for the shift from [t] to [k], Judd, Pukui, and Stokes (1945:13) noted that [t] was more common "between 1778 and 1809 according to the dozen vocabularies made in those years. By the time the present Hawaiian orthography was established in 1825,[6] the 'k' sound had become so general that the character 'k' was adopted."[7]

However, it is not clear just whose vocabularies these "dozen" were, for the authors did not list them. Moreover, they ignored the variable of geography. For example, if most of the earlier lists were collected on Niʻihau or Kauaʻi, and the later ones on Hawaiʻi, bare statistics will appear to support a *t* to *k* shift.

Although information on even the current distribution of [t] is surprisingly meager, it is clear from the missionary records of the 1820s that [t] was common, if not universal, on both Niʻihau and Kauaʻi, and some other parts of the Hawaiian group as well. However, this feature seems to have changed somewhat in the last two centuries:[8] more recent investigations (Newbrand 1951:106–8, Elbert and Pukui 1979:24-25) show that although speakers on Ni'ihau (and parts of Kaua'i?) definitely use *t*, they do not do so exclusively. For example, Helene L. Newbrand noted for a native speaker of the Ni'ihau dialect (who also spoke a *k*-dialect of Hawaiian) an interchange between the two sounds, with a dental [t] occurring consistently in some words, [k] in others, but varying in many.[9]

Newbrand collected data from two informants from the Hanalei side of Kaua'i, both using [k] exclusively. However, a man from Waimea, Kaua'i, who in 1950 or so was eighty-three years old, produced [t] not in his narrative, but under special circumstances: "The recollection of old days brought forth the exclamation 'maita'i! maita'i!' (good! good!)—showing the use of the [t] allophone of /k/" (p. 79).

As for the use of [t] elsewhere in Hawai'i, the early word lists and missionary reports show that in the late eighteenth and early nineteenth centuries, it was much more widespread than now. But it is difficult to know how to interpret the different patterns of distribution shown on table 5.1. Certainly, it is clear from Anderson's and Bereford's lists, both collected at Waimea, Kaua'i, that [t] was used exclusively there. It is the lists that show a mixture of [t] and [k] that present a problem (e.g., those of Quimper, Campbell, and Gaimard). Do their findings represent the result of a long-established variation between the sounds, a whole range of pronunciations, including "intermediate" sounds (discussed in chapter 7), or a mixture of dialects due to population movements? With the sketchy background information that most of the accounts provide, it is difficult to decide among these choices.

L OR *R*?

Judging from the evidence provided by the early word lists, the problem of *l* versus *r* (and sometimes *d* as well) is not one that arose immediately. For example, in his Kaua'i word list, Anderson wrote only *r*. As for other writers on Cook's third voyage, Judd, Pukui, and Stokes (1945:14) noted: "In the various lists and writings of 1778-79, the sound was 'r' (totals, 'r' 126 times, 'l' once and 'd,' four times)."

Although one might suggest that Anderson was conditioned by his experience with Tahitian to expect, and therefore to hear, [r] exclusively, his Tongan word list (Admiralty Records 51/4560/204, Beaglehole 1967, 3:956–57) belies this hypothesis. Collected only about six months before he wrote his first Hawaiian words, this list contains both *r* and *l*. Therefore, his transcription of *r* exclusively for Hawaiian words suggests that he perceived the /l/ phonemes in the two languages quite differently.[10]

No matter how the sound was produced, outsiders' perception of it changed over the next decades. Judd, Pukui, and Stokes continued their statistics (p. 14): "By 1792-94, from [the earlier] percentage of 0.7, the 'l' sound had increased to 8%, and by 1804, to 16%."

As with *t* and *k*, Campbell (or his editor) noted the variation between l and r, giving the following example: *ooroo, ooloo* 'bread-fruit'.

Because it is longer than the other lists, Campbell's provides some tantalizing suggestions of complementary distribution[11] for *l* and *r*.[12] For example, there is a tendency for *l* to occur most often before *a*: 19 of the 28 occurrences of *l* are in this position. There are instances of *r* before *a*, but not proportional to the total of 218, considering the high frequency of *a*. On the other hand, there are no instances of *li* syllables, but 2 of *ri*—admittedly not very convincing statistics, but at least suggestive.

Gaimard as well noted the *l - r* alternation in the forms *aloha - aroha* (Dumont d'Urville 1834).

P OR B?

In Hawaiian, this so-called pair, *p* and *b*, differs from the other groups of variable consonants in that the perception of the sound as [b] was probably a mistake from the very beginning. In English, /p/ and /b/ are kept apart not only by voicing, but in some positions also by aspiration—that is, the puff of air that accompanies the articulation of the sound.[13] Although it is possible that Hawaiian /p/, especially between vowels, might have occasionally been voiced,[14] it is more likely that speakers of English wrote it as a *b* because it is so much less aspirated than English /p/.

The confusion between what sounded like [p] versus [b] in Polynesian languages began with Daniel Solander's occasional transcription of Tahitian /p/ as *b* (as in *oboo* for 'stomach', now written as *'ōpū*). The mishearing was indelibly fixed in the English language when Cook borrowed Tongan /tapu/ as *taboo*.[15] And it was nearly as firmly fixed by geographers, who spelled the name of one of the major islands of Tonga as *Tongatabu* (or *Tongataboo*) long after *b* had been discarded from the spelling system.

The examples just given share one feature: in each instance the [b] was heard between vowels—a common occurrence in many languages in which [b] is only a variant of /p/. In some of the Hawaiian lists, there are tendencies toward such a distribution. For example, in Anderson's list, four of the five instances of *b* appear in that position. However, as counterevidence, there are many examples of *p* written between vowels as well.

Even though mishearing a lack of aspiration as voicing is more noticeable with *p*, it is not confined to that sound, but applies also to *t* and *k*. For example, Samwell, who wrote both *t* and *k* in the word list he collected, included three *g*s and five *d*s, all indicating the phoneme /k/.

Most of the early transcribers seemed to have no idea that *p* and *b* did not contrast. Campbell, however, mentioned the variation more directly: *boa, poa* 'a hog'.

The most convincing evidence that the *p* - *b* "variation" lay more in the minds of the English-speaking analysts than in the mouths of the Hawaiians comes from the word list collected in 1791 by Quimper, a speaker of Spanish. In his list, he wrote /p/ fifty-two times as *p*, but none at all as *b*.[16] Why this dramatic difference from, say, Beresford's orthography, in which the letters are nearly evenly divided? Did the Hawaiians stop saying *b* for Quimper and then resume it for later English-speaking visitors? No, it was a difference in perception, not production: like the Hawaiian /p/, the Spanish /p/ is also relatively unaspirated. Thus there was no interference from the native language to mislead the writer.

The evidence from the list collected by Gaimard, a speaker of French, is nearly as strong (French /p/ is also much less aspirated than English /p/): there are only six words transcribed with *b* (all between vowels, by the way), and one showing *p* - *b* alternation.

Finally, the statistics from Lisiansky, a speaker of Russian (another language with a /p/ less aspirated than English /p/), follow the same pattern, with forty-three instances of *p* and only four of *b* (and two of those from *Tabetee*, or *Kabekee*, representing the borrowings for 'cabbage').

V OR *W*?

As table 5.1 shows, there is no clear pattern in the early transcriptions of Hawaiian /w/. For example, Anderson and Samwell divided the sound nearly evenly between *v* and *w*. But unlike the other "pairs" of sounds, which were noticed as early as 1810 or so,[17] these seem to have been treated as though they were separate consonants. For this period, the first, and only, mention of the problem seen so far is that of Rose de Freycinet, the wife of Gaimard's captain, who included *v* and *w* in her list of "interchangeable" consonants that seemed to impede communication (Bassett 1962:153).

TABLE 5.1
CONSONANT VARIATION 1778-1819

	A	S	B	Q	L	C	G
K							
d	2	5	2	—	—	—	2
t	all*	23	38	65	24	209	22
k (c)	—	29	—	21	39	124	47
g	—	3	—	—	—	—	2
t ~ k	—	—	—	—	3	4	3
L							
l	—	—	1	6	22	28	16
r	69	57	19	64	46	218	70
n	—	—	1	—	—	—	—
d	—	—	2	2	—	2	—
l ~ r	—	—	—	—	—	1	—
P							
p	40	24	10	52	43	150	64
b	5	3	8	—	4	10	6**
f ~ p	—	—	—	1	—	—	—
p ~ b	—	—	—	—	—	1	1
W							
v	8	9	5	2	16	20	7
w	13	8	—	—	—	49	—
wh	4	2	3	—	—	1	—
b	—	—	—	10	—	—	1
u	—	—	—	3	—	—	—
p	—	—	—	1	—	—	—
o	—	—	—	—	1	—	—
ou	—	—	—	—	—	—	21

*Except for *d*   **All between vowels

A = Anderson   S = Samwell   B = Beresford
Q = Quimper   L= Lisiansky   C = Campbell   G = Gaimard

As for patterns in the distribution, there are not enough examples to examine *v* versus *w* before each of the five vowels; the only pattern that emerges is that before /a/ they are fairly evenly divided.[18] Comparing their distribution in accented and unaccented syllables also gives nearly even figures.

CONCLUSION

In the period from Cook's first contact with Hawai'i to 1820, when the first American missionaries arrived, one finds the following degrees of awareness of the consonant variation in Hawaiian that was later to prove such an obstacle to developing an efficient orthography:

1. Only one variant was transcribed. An example is Anderson's writing *t* and *r* consistently, to the exclusion of *k* and *l*.
2. It was noted that the dialect in question used one sound, whereas another dialect used a different one. Samwell's awareness of *t* and *k* dialects is an example.
3. More than one variant was transcribed, but not for the same word: i.e., the writer gave no overt sign that they were not separate sounds. An example of this level of awareness is Anderson's use of *v*, *w*, and *wh* to represent one phoneme, referred to at the beginning of the chapter.
4. It was stated overtly that sometimes one heard one sound, and at other times, a quite different one. Campbell seems to have been the first to make specific mention of variability, but several of his successors did so as well.

For the most part, observers accepted the variation simply as—from their point of view—an oddity. But de Freycinet's assessment of the "interchangeable" consonants as impediments to communication hints of the problems that later, longer-term residents had to deal with in a professional way.

NOTES

---

[1] Note that I have described this variation from the hearers' point of view, not from that of the speakers. This position is at odds with the usual way of describing the variation, which assumes that Hawaiian speakers were pronouncing the sounds differently. In chapter 7, I approach the problem from both points of view, and in more detail.

[2] These groups are set up as opposing pairs only in the sense of how the transcribers wrote them. The matter of whether these sounds were indeed alternates or various points on a continuum is discussed in chapter 7.

[3] However, his comments had a very limited distribution, for his journal remained unpublished until 1967.

[4] Realized as *k*, *g*, and *c*.

[5] The *ee* spelling was the invention of the English translator-transliterator.

---

[6] This is a mistake; the correct date is 1826.

[7] This observation seems at odds with the facts. As we shall see in chapter 7, *t* was still widely used in some parts of Hawai'i in 1826—and is today as well.

[8] Churchill (1912:13) labeled the *t*-to-*k* movement "kappation," a term not now generally used in phonetics.

[9] There is no indication that any sound "intermediate" between the dental and velar positions was used, and the discs from which the transcription was made are not available.

[10] Samwell, Beresford, and Quimper also wrote *r* exclusively, or nearly so (see table 5.1).

[11] This term implies that the distribution of the variants is patterned, and the environments are mutually exclusive. Thus, if *l* and *r* were in complementary distribution, *l* would never occur in an environment in which *r* is found, and vice versa.

[12] One must remember that here the transcription is several times removed from the pronunciation of a native speaker (see chapter 3).

[13] The usual test for noticing the different degrees of aspiration of English /p/ is to put one's hand close to the mouth and pronounce *pin* and *spin*. The /p/ in the second word is closer to that in Hawaiian and other Polynesian languages.

[14] In Beresford's list, the *p*s and *b*s are almost evenly divided (ten versus eight), but there is a marked tendency for *p* to appear at the beginning of words, and *b* between vowels. Newbrand (1951:107) noted "an occasional voicing of [k] and [t]" in the speech of one informant, but the only [b] I can find in her text transcriptions is in the borrowed word *Baibala* 'Bible' (p. 35).

[15] The earliest citation for this word in English is 1777. Until very recently, even the etymology in unabridged dictionaries perpetuated the misspelling, giving the Tongan source for the word as *tabu*. Now, the *Random House Dictionary of the English Language* (2d edition, 1987), for example, has corrected that mistake to *tapu* but added another—that Fijian *tabu* might be the source of the word. This etymology is impossible, for the Fijian form is pronounced [tambu]. The convention of writing [mb] as *b* was not established until about 1839.

[16] As table 5.1 shows, b was written for /w/ but not for /p/.

[17] I refer here to Campbell's observation in 1809 or 1810 that *t* and *k*, *l* and *r*, and *b* and *p* were "frequently substituted for each other."

[18] See Elbert and Pukui (1979:13) for a similar statement about the present-day distribution.

CHAPTER SIX

The Cornwall Connection: 3s, 8s, and Noah Webster

-0-0-0-0-0-

It may be useful to notify the public that it is the wish of many leading men in America that all the children in the different States should learn the language in the same book, that all may speak alike (Noah Webster to the publishers of the Grammatical Institute, *suggestions for advertisements, Warfel 1953:79-80).*

Our earliest example of a systematic[1] alphabet for Hawaiian is that used in a manuscript grammar written at Cornwall, Connecticut in 1819, and in the collection of the Hawaiian Historical Society since 1892.[2] The link between Cornwall and the history of Hawaiian linguistics was forged when 'Ōpūkaha'ia, born at Ka'ū on the island of Hawai'i in 1792, arrived at Yale University. One of his biographers gave a dramatic account of how and why he had spanned the vast physical and cultural distance from the Kona coast to the coast of New England (Bartlett 1869:3):[3]

> In the year 1809, a dark skinned boy was found weeping on the door-steps at Yale College. His name was Henry Obookiah ['Ōpū kaha'ia];[4] and he came from the Sandwich Islands. In a civil war, his father and mother had been slain before his eyes; and when he fled with his infant brother on his back, the child was killed with a spear, and he was taken prisoner. Lonely and wretched, the poor boy, at the age of fourteen, was glad to come, with Captain Britnell [Britnall], to New Haven. He thirsted for instruction; and he lingered round the College buildings, hoping in some way to gratify his burning desire. But when at length all hope died out, he sat down and wept. The Rev. Edwin W. Dwight, a resident graduate, found him there, and kindly took him as a pupil.

Had Captain Britnall[5] not been a New Haven resident, the history of Hawaiian language studies (and indeed, Hawaiian history in general) might have taken a different turn. Yale University, already more than a century old, had a rich tradition in studies both secular and sacred: the Yale Divinity School had long trained students for missions, first to Native Americans, and later to the inhabitants of places such as Ceylon,

Malta, and Turkey.[6] This, then, was the environment that helped shape
'Ōpūkaha'ia's future and that of Hawai'i as well.

Taken into a succession of homes and well looked after, 'Ōpūkaha-
'ia lived in this somewhat cloistered world until his death in 1818—
almost nine years, all told. Most of this time he was a student, not only
in New Haven, but also in other communities in Connecticut—Torrington, Litchfield, Goshen, and Cornwall—and in Andover, Massachusetts.
For his support, he relied partly on the kindness of friends but, like so
many students today, he often worked during the summers to help earn
his keep.

Quite naturally, one of his first challenges learning English. He
had received his first English lessons aboard the *Triumph* on the way to
New England: one of the crew, a young man from Yale, taught him the
"letters in [an] English spelling-book." The Reverend Mr. Dwight, who
eventually edited 'Ōpūkaha'ia's *Memoirs*, continued to teach him reading and writing, again using "the spelling book." He reported (p. 15):

> When he began to read in words of one or two syllables in the
> spelling-book, there were certain sounds which he found it very
> difficult to articulate. This was true especially of syllables that
> contained the letter *R*—a letter which occasioned him more
> trouble than all others. In pronouncing it, he uniformly gave it the
> sound of *L*. At every different reading an attempt was made to
> correct the pronunciation.

'Ōpūkaha'ia was also taught by others in his rounds of various
families, and in this way "he soon acquired a knowledge of the spelling-
book, and in a few months was able to read in the Testament. By this
time he had also made considerable proficiency in writing" (p. 19). In
one of the first letters he wrote (2 March 1810), he mentioned: "I spell
four syllables now."[7] Mr. Abbot, steward of the Theological Institution
at Andover, told of his desire to know both the sight and sound of a
word (p. 27):

> When he heard a word ... which he did not understand or could
> not speak, it was his constant habit to ask me, "How you *spell*?
> how you *spell*?" When I told him he never forgot.

In the fall of 1813, 'Ōpūkaha'ia attended a public grammar school
at Litchfield, and there he began to study English grammar, along with
geography and arithmetic.

'Ōpūkaha'ia's connection with the eventual mission to Hawai'i
came through his conversion to Christianity in 1815. By that time, he
had not only learned English and studied the usual curriculum of the
period, but had also experienced some of the fervor of the prevailing

general religious revival and the awakening of a mission spirit (called the Second Great Awakening of the New Light Theology) among the Protestant churches of New England.[8] ʻŌpūkahaʻia and others from the Sandwich Islands, as well as other Polynesians and Native Americans,[9] requested the training that would prepare them to return home and share the Gospel with their own people.

The presence of those islanders and Native Americans, especially ʻŌpūkahaʻia, along with their evangelistic zeal, inspired the founding of the Foreign Mission School in 1816, where ʻŌpūkahaʻia was one of the first students. Set up first in Morris, Connecticut, the school was administered by the American Board of Commissioners for Foreign Missions in Boston. In May 1817, the school was transferred to Cornwall, which became its home for its brief life of a decade. One historian summarized its history (Mitchell 1939:16):

> A movement had developed throughout the state out of sympathy with an Hawaiian, Obookiah, who came to the United States to get an education. The Board decided to establish a school in this country to train the natives of non-European races to become missionaries to their own peoples. It was set up in this town [Cornwall] because of the salubrious climate, the remoteness from city allurements, the excellent character of the townspeople, the persuasion of the pastor ... and the donations of Cornwall citizens ... In the ten years of its existence about one hundred students attended, including forty-three American Indians, thirteen Americans (white), and twenty Hawaiians; the rest mainly other natives of the Pacific, including two Chinese.

Support for the school was widespread, coming not only from the inhabitants of Cornwall, but from sympathetic donors elsewhere in Connecticut—and from Massachusetts and New York as well. Those who could not give cash gave clothing and provisions; in addition, the students worked at nearby farms to help support themselves.

The students also gave as well as received in the educational process, for learning took place in both directions. Not only did they take courses common in secondary schools at that time, but they also helped prepare the American missionaries by teaching them about the different languages and cultures they would encounter in their future missions to foreign parts.

But even before the official founding of the school, ʻŌpūkahaʻia was aware of the importance of the Hawaiian language in the work of the proposed mission. Dwight wrote (1818:81–82):

> After having acquired some slight knowledge of the English language in its grammatical construction, he entered upon the pro-

ject of reducing to system his own native tongue. As it was not a written language, but lay in its chaotic state, every thing was to be done. With some assistance he had made considerable progress towards completing a Grammar, a Dictionary, and a Spelling-book.

In 'Ōpūkaha'ia's own words (p. 36):

At this time [summer 1814], Mr. Mills[10] wished me to go and live with the Rev. Mr. Harvey, of Goshen. This was pleasing to me, and I went to live with him and studied geography and mathematics; and a part of the time was trying to translate a few verses of the Scriptures into my own language, and in making a kind of spelling-book, taking the English alphabet and giving different names and different sounds—(for this language was not written language.) I spent some time in making a kind of spelling-book, dictionary, grammar.

He mentioned the grammar again on 4 June 1815. In a letter from Goshen, Connecticut, to the Reverend Eleazar T. Fitch[11] at New Haven, he wrote:

I want to see you about our Grammar:[12] I want to get through with it. I have been translating a few chapters of the Bible into the Hawaiian language. I found I could do it very correctly.

Dwight continued:

He had also translated into his native tongue the whole of the Book of Genesis.

When Obookiah became a member of the Foreign Mission School, he had attended to all the common branches of English education. In reading, writing, and spelling, he was perhaps as perfect as most young men of our own country, of the same age and with common opportunities. He wrote a legible manly hand, and had acquired the habit of writing with considerable rapidity. He had at this time studied the English Grammar so far as to be able to parse most sentences with readiness ... He ... of his own accord, without a regular instructor, had acquired such knowledge of the Hebrew, that he had been able to read several chapters in the Hebrew Bible, and had translated a few passages into his native language. He had a peculiar relish for the Hebrew language, and from its resemblance to his own,[13] acquired it with great facility; and found it much less difficult to translate the Hebrew than the English into his native tongue.

The winter before he came to the school he commenced the study of Latin. This he pursued principally after he became a member of the Institution.[14]

So far as we know, none of 'Ōpūkaha'ia's works on the Hawaiian language survives, at least in its original state.[15] For the past century, it was thought that the manuscript grammar mentioned at the beginning of the chapter might be his, but now the research of James D. Rumford has shown that it is actually the work of Samuel Ruggles, one of the First Company of missionaries and a fellow student with Ōpūkaha'ia at Cornwall. Having become familiar with the handwriting in the manuscript while he was preparing a printed version (1993), Rumford was able to compare it with that in a letter from Ruggles (1819), in which the writer mentioned his own grammar, "much assisted by one which Obookiah attempted to form."

Even under the better-known name of 'Ōpūkaha'ia, until fairly recently this grammar remained curiously unanalyzed. For example, neither of two important early studies of the Hawaiian orthography (Spaulding 1930, Wise and Hervey 1952) mentions it or its unorthodox spelling system. However, in his dissertation on the Hawaiian orthography (1968), Wesley D. Hervey devoted a long chapter to 'Ōpūkaha-'ia, treating many aspects of the young man's life in rich detail, but curiously ignoring the alphabet (still, at that time, attributed to 'Ōpū-kaha'ia), even though its unique characteristics can be clearly seen in a reproduction of the first page included in Hervey's work.

Thus, even without examining the grammar, one is struck by the anomaly that although it has been accessible to scholars for nearly a century, and is purportedly the first grammar[16] of the Hawaiian language, it has never been critically evaluated.

Perhaps the reason is that beyond the title page, some forms are recognizable, but most look as though they were written in code. The first unusual thing that the reader sees—and which is all the more remarkable because it seems to have been accepted without comment or query—is that the alphabet is littered with numbers, specifically, the figures *3* and *8*, as shown in table 6.1.

This "code," as it were, is easy enough to break: one has simply to compare the spellings with the current ones, as in table 6.2. Besides illustrating the use of the numbers *3* and *8*, the examples also show unusual uses of the letters *a*, *e*, *i*, *u*, and the combination *ou*.

Table 6.3 shows the relationships between Ruggles's vowel system and the current system.

But what is the origin of the system? The answer lies in the history of American education and the backgrounds of the people who trained the Hawaiians in New England in the first decades of the nineteenth century, and especially in "the spelling book."

TABLE 6.1
RUGGLES'S SPELLING CONVENTIONS

Ha-h3-la	the house
Ha-k3-n3-k3	the man
Le-m3	hand
L8-n3	upward
M3-m8-3	forward
8-8-k8	little
3-o-la	no
Mi	from
O-ou	I
Wun-na	presently

TABLE 6.2
RUGGLES'S AND CURRENT SPELLING COMPARED

RUGGLES'S SPELLING	CURRENT SPELLING	GLOSS
Ha-h3-la	he hale	the house
Ha-k3-n3-k3	he kanaka	the man
Le-m3	lima	hand
L8-n3	luna	upward
M3-m8-3	ma mua	forward
8-8-k8	'u'uku	little
3-o-la	'a'ole	no
Mi	mai	from
O-ou	o au	I
Wun-na	auane'i[17]	presently

TABLE 6.3
SYSTEMATIC RELATIONSHIPS

e for /i/	*a* for /e/
o for /o/	*3* for /a/
8 for /u/	*u* for [ʌ]
i for /ai/	*ou* for /au/

In the biographical sketch above, the spelling book that was mentioned several times refers to a specific work: one volume of Noah Webster's *Grammatical Institute of the English Language*, later known as the *American Spelling Book*. Later accounts of the Hawaiian mission (particularly Loomis 1951) also mentioned that the basic reading primer used in Hawai'i after 1820 to teach English to the Hawaiians was Webster's speller. Thus, I was curious to see, first, what the speller was like, and next, how widespread was its use. The second question was easier to answer: first published in 1783, "more than 50 impressions of the book appeared before 1800, some of them 25,000-copy runs. Another 100 impressions were run off by 1829 when the number of copies sold throughout the United States reached at least 20 million" (Morgan 1975: 48–49). Since the population of the United States in 1830 was a little less than 13 million, this means that the Webster speller must have been familiar to nearly every American schoolchild at that time.[18]

As for its content, Webster's interest in the inconsistencies of English spelling eventually resulted in the *3*s and *8*s Ruggles wrote. Starting not from sound but from spelling (a principle discussed in the previous chapter), Webster tried to show that there were patterns in the use of the vowel letters.[19] Table 6.4 shows the part of his analysis that Ruggles adapted to Hawaiian. First we see that the basic values of four of the five vowel letters are their names. Thus, the letter *a* represents [e], *e* [i], *i* the diphthong [ai], and *o* [o]. As for the [a] sound, there was no vowel letter with that name, so he called it the third value of the letter *a*.[20] And since *u* represented [yu] and not [u], the letter *u* with an *8* over it was used for the vowel in such words as *room* and *move*. The only use of *u* in Ruggles's manuscript (other than for diphthongs) is in the form for future, *wun-na* (*auane'i*); here it seems to indicate Webster's "short *u*"— that is, [ʌ], as in *come* or *love*.

TABLE 6.4
LONG VOWELS IN ENGLISH (WEBSTER 1800:13)

1	2	3	4	5	6	7	8
a	a	a	e	i	o	o	u
late	ask	hall	here	fight	note	move	truth

At first, Ruggles's use of *ou* for [au] suggests simply a mistranscription, but Webster holds the key to this convention as well: for him, *ou* represented the diphthong in *house* or *loud*.[21] But was Webster the originator or borrower of such a system? Further reading, this time on the topic of English lexicography, shows him to be the latter. Sidney I. Landau (1984:57) cited William Kenrick (*A New Dictionary of the English Language*, 1773) as the innovator of the system of putting small superscripts over vowel letters to indicate the pronunciation. A few years later, Thomas Sheridan (*A General Dictionary of the English Language*) used a similar system. In the introduction to this work, Sheridan gave a pronunciation key (p. 13) showing three phonetic values of the letter *a*: $\overset{1}{a}$ = [a], $\overset{2}{a}$ = [e], and $\overset{3}{a}$ = [ɔ] (as in *call, talk, laud*). The entries in the body of the dictionary use this system as a guide to pronunciation.[22]

What all these scholars had in common was that they concentrated on the vowels,[23] further distinguishing among different "powers of the letters" to reduce the inconsistencies of English spelling and help overcome the disadvantage of having only five vowel letters to work with. Still, the system was designed expressly for English, for the purpose of promoting an "accepted" pronunciation over a "common" one.

In a sense, this convention was the beginning of the English lexicographic practice of respelling dictionary entries to indicate pronunciation. And until the missionaries in Hawai'i later abandoned the idea that the names of the vowel letters were their "basic" sounds, it was the only means available for showing the pronunciation of Hawaiian vowels.

Aside from the idiosyncratic use of numbers, how does the rest of Ruggles's orthography fare in the light of present knowledge? Some other spelling patterns in the manuscript are:[24]

1. Words are divided into syllables, usually ending with a vowel. Only rarely are double consonants used, and the syllables are divided between them. *Wunna*,[25] mentioned above, is one example. Perhaps the double-consonant spelling reflects the English convention of indicating a "short *u*" (that is, [ʌ]) rather than a "long *u*" ([yuʷ], as in *runner* versus *rune*.

2. Only *l* is used, not *r*.

3. With the exception of two words, one of them an exclamation, *k* is used, not *t*.

4. Only *w* and *wh* are used, not *v*. As opposed to some writing practices changed only recently, '*o au* 'I (as topic)' was not written with an excrescent *w* between the first two vowels, but as *o-au*. Such a *w* does appear in *o-w8 k3* (*o-wuka*, '*o uka*) 'inland',[26] but this time it follows a rounded vowel—the expected environment.

5. As opposed to the practice in many of the explorers' word lists, the use of *h* seems fairly consistent.[27]

Even discounting the use of numerals, it is still the vowel system that is most different from today's orthography, but in rather complex ways. For example, the use of *ou* (as in 'house') to represent /au/, perhaps combined with the influence of the English diphthongized pronunciation [oʷ] in words like 'go', led to a loss of distinction in the grammar between Hawaiian /o/ and /ou/. For example, Ruggles wrote *o-*

k3-ko (*o kako*) for *'o kākou* 'we (plural inclusive)', and *o-ko* for *'oukou* 'you (plural)'.

Another problem he had with vowels is one that was common in the explorers' lists as well: Ruggles did not always write final unaccented vowels consistently; for example, *m3-m8-la* (*mamule*) for *mamuli* 'backward' (p. 13), *oi* for *'oe* 'thou' (p. 5). However, he did write the final vowel in *'ae* 'yes' correctly (p. 13).

As expected, long vowels are not noted, except indirectly in an example from the small set of nouns, mainly kinship terms, that form a plural by lengthening the antepenultimate vowel. Ruggles's example is *kanaka* 'person', which becomes *kānaka* in the plural. The process is explained (and marked) as a change in accent.

Also consistent with the practice in this period is the fact that glottal stops are not indicated. However, there are at least two ways in which their presence was indirectly noted. First, as mentioned above, the sound /au/ was represented by the spelling *ou*. When the spelling *au* does occur, it represents /a'u/, as in *kau* (*ka'u*) 'my' (p. 5).

A second way of indicating glottal stops is the hyphen that marks syllable division. According to the Webster-based system that Ruggles used, the diphthong /ai/ is written *i*. However, the sequence /a'i/ is indicated by marking the syllable boundary: *m3-e-m3-e* (*ma'ima'i*) 'sick' (p. 13).

The almost complete absence of consonant variation in Ruggles's transcription of Hawaiian words left him and the other missionaries unprepared for what they found when they reached Hawai'i a few years later. One cannot help but ask why. Certainly, the possibility for dialectal variation was present, since George Kaumuali'i, another of the Hawaiians at the Foreign Mission School, came from Kaua'i and was very likely a speaker of the *t*-dialect.[28] And Ruggles must surely have known that the Hawaiian words in Cook's account were written with *t*. On the other hand, did the Hawaiians at Cornwall, thrown together after being away from their own dialects for years, develop some kind of standard pronunciation among themselves?

Another possibility is that Ruggles worked exclusively with 'Ōpūkaha'ia, who was most likely a *k*-speaker. If so, he may have influenced Ruggles in his choice of letters. For example, 'Ōpūkaha'ia's own difficulties with American English /r/ might have prompted him to suggest *l* for his alphabet.

Finally, we have no idea of the extent to which Ruggles used the material in 'Ōpūkaha'ia's grammar for his own. Nor do we know whose idea it was to use Webster's numbers in place of *a* and *u*.

But in spite of these uncertainties, this short manuscript is a remarkable document, being probably the first example of Hawaiian written on other than a hasty and impressionistic phonetic basis. In addition to its chronological and sociolinguistic importance, the grammar shows a good deal more orthographic consistency than many of the explorers' lists and such early Polynesian linguistic classics as William Mariner's and John Martin's work on Tongan (Martin 1817) and Kendall's on Māori (1815).

However, the unusual writing system was short-lived. Even before the missionaries set sail for Hawai'i, they found it cumbersome. After all, Webster's numbers were meant only to help explain part of a writing system, not to serve as part of the system itself. The following letter (Hiram Bingham to Samuel Worcester, Salem, MA, from Goshen, CT, 11 May 1819, Bingham family papers) shows that the convention of writing vowels with *3*s and *8*s, with the addition of the figure *4*, was used for only about two years:

> As to elementary books in the language of O[whyhee], something has been done & some passages of scripture have been translated. I do not think the character in which the language is to be written is yet satisfactorily settled. Our alphabet is used with the addition of 3 characters viz the figure 3 for the sound a in father, 4 for a in hall and 8 for oo in room. The fact that these are employed for a different purpose is an objection & another is that they are not used for this in Otaheite.

Thus, not only did the system mix the inviolate areas of language and arithmetic, it was also at odds with the Tahitian orthography, well established by this time.[29]

The Foreign Mission School at Cornwall was also short-lived, continuing only until 1826. Its demise was brought about by a social scandal—two interracial marriages that tested the residents' tolerance and found it wanting. In terms of its physical presence in Cornwall, all that remains of the building is a plaque where it stood; other material effects have been reduced to a key, a lantern, and some books from the school's library, all either in private hands or in the archives of the Cornwall Historical Society (Chamberlain 1968:22–23).

But both the school and its inspiration, 'Ōpūkaha'ia, had a profound effect on Hawai'i and the Hawaiian language: they were a catalyst for the Sandwich Island Mission and the first concentrated efforts to analyze the language.

NOTES

---

[1] This term must be qualified somewhat. Anderson's alphabet was also systematic, but in a different way: it was not designed especially for Hawaiian, but was his method for indicating the sounds of Polynesian languages in English letters. Ruggles went a step further in that his alphabet is nearly "phonemic": except for the expected omission of symbols for long vowels and the glottal stop, and some difficulties with diphthongs, each sound is generally written in the same way.

[2] A note attached to the ms. says that it was found among Queen Emma's private papers.

[3] Much of the following account appears in Schütz 1989a.

[4] The name means literally 'slit belly'; hence, 'cesarean'. ʻŌpūkahaʻia him-self might have been born by cesarean, or perhaps his birth coincided with that of a high chief born by cesarean. As another possibility, Charles W. Kenn stated that the name commemorated "an event in which a chief was disemboweled" (Dwight 1990 [1818]:[97]).

[5] Britnall provides an interesting connection between ʻŌpūkahaʻia and a popular modern aspect of Yale student life. Captain Caleb Britnall (1774-1850) married (as a second wife) Content Mix (1789-1865). The house in New Haven in which they lived was occupied by Britnall's widow after his death, and sometime later, after changing hands, became known as Mory's, immortalized in "The Wiffenpoof Song" (Nancy Martin, pers. comm., 29 May 1988).

[6] Yale Divinity School Library RC/Y12.

[7] See chapter 9 for more details about the syllabic method of teaching spelling.

[8] The First Great Awakening took place around the middle of the eighteenth century and produced a conflict, often intense, between conservative Protestants (Old Lights) and the revivalistic reformers (New Lights).

[9] "... eight Cherokees, three Stockbridges, two Choctaws, two Oneidas, two Caughnowagas, one Tahitian, one Marquesan, and one Malayan" (Bingham 1847:58).

[10] Samuel John Mills, Jr., 1783–1818.

[11] Eleazar Thompson Fitch (1791–1871), eventually D.D. He was at Yale from 1817 to 1852 as chaplain ("Pastor of the Church in Yale College"). He began his study of theology in 1812 at Andover and taught there for a time.

[12] The phrase "our grammar" immediately raises the question of the nature of this collaborative effort, but so far it is unanswered. ʻŌpūkahaʻia's *Memoirs* sheds no light on the problem, and the items under Fitch's name at the New Haven Colony Historical Library are mainly sermons and speeches, with no reference to his work with ʻŌpūkahaʻia on the grammar.

[13] It is not clear just what this resemblance is. Bingham (1847:27) wrote, rather vaguely, that "no trace of the Hebrew language is clearly discernible in

their tongue, though there is some resemblance in the structure and simplicity of the two."

[14] Note the chronology. This doesn't seem to have happened until 1817. Thus, 'Ōpūkaha'ia's work on Hawaiian would not have been much influenced by Latin, but instead by Webster's grammatical analysis of English.

[15] Of the three works mentioned in the *Memoirs*—the grammar, dictionary, and spelling book—apparently none has survived. A search that includes the Cornwall Free Library, 'Ōpūkaha'ia's church, and the Cornwall Historical Society, as well as the most likely libraries and archives elsewhere, has turned up none of his manuscripts—at least so far.

[16] Its grammatical content is discussed in chapter 12.

[17] I am grateful to James D. Rumford for this identification.

[18] Morgan (1975:49) wrote: "By then [1820] the speller had been read by almost every literate American."

[19] Because Webster started from spelling, rather than sound, his explanation of the English vowel system is rather confused. But he did realize that there were not just five or six vowels; his figure was nine.

[20] Not everyone's pronunciation of this sample word in English will match the Hawaiian sound, for English vowels in this phonetic area show significant dialect variation. In brief, the range of pronunciations is from [a] to [ɔ].

[21] Anderson used the same convention, as did Samuel Johnson.

[22] Perhaps we can take this system—or one very much like it—back another 150 years or so to the beginning of the seventeenth century. Then, as exemplified in such works as Giulio Caccini's *Nuove Musiche* (1602), the vocal line of a monodic piece was accompanied by a figured bass—so called because of the numbers over the notes that indicated the harmonic progression. It is easy to see how the idea of a number over a note, making finer distinctions, could be carried over to a number serving the same function for a vowel letter.

The history of the German convention of writing a diaeresis over certain vowel letters (popularly called an *umlaut*) is somewhat similar: the symbol was originally a small superscript *e*.

[23] This is not to say that there is a one-to-one fit for the consonants. But most of the consonants are fairly "stable" in comparison with vowels.

[24] In the following discussion, any word showing the idiosyncratic parts of the system is followed by two respellings: the first shows Ruggles's intention in modern spelling; the second shows the word as spelled today.

[25] Ruggles was inconsistent in the spelling of this word. Elsewhere, the letter *a* represents /e/.

[26] James D. Rumford (pers. comm., 20 October 1992) noted that this form was glossed 'southward' in the grammar. Consequently, one wonders where Ruggles was when he gave it such a meaning.

[27] The distribution of /h/ in English is complex; thus, it is difficult for speakers of English both to hear and reproduce an *h* in certain unaccented syllables in Hawaiian. For example, in an English context, *Kamehameha* is often pronounced *Kameamea*.

[28] However, as James D. Rumford has pointed out (pers. comm., 20 October 1992), George Kaumuali'i, who left Hawai'i at the age of six, was said to have forgotten his Hawaiian to the extent that 'Ōpūkaha'ia was teaching him his own language.

[29] Except, as with so many Polynesian writing systems throughout the rest of the century and beyond, for long vowels and glottal stops (if the latter existed in the language).

CHAPTER SEVEN

Fixing the Letters: Missionary Efforts 1820-1826

-o-o-o-o-o-

We have seen the name of Tamehemeha ... spelt in various publications twelve or fourteen different ways ... (William Ellis, Narrative of a Tour of Hawaii, *[1827 (1979):24-25]).*

The quotation above underscores some of the difficulties that the missionary-linguists faced when they arrived in Hawai'i in 1820. Up to this time, the only scholars who had tried to write Hawaiian in a systematic way were Samuel Ruggles and William Anderson,[1] and—as the preceding chapters show—each of their efforts was in effect a dead end. In the meantime, more than forty years had passed, and the language was still being written "as people heard it." Many common names, such as *Owhyhee*, were fixed by convention in a form that only suggested the actual pronunciation, persisting long after more appropriate spellings were devised. Others, less common, were spelled differently by each person who wrote them. As Hiram Bingham (1847: 153) described the problem:

> Those who had attempted to write the names of places and persons in the islands, had materially failed ... No foreigner or native, at the islands, could explain the peculiarities and intricacies of the language. Though we obtained a few words and phrases from Wm. Moxley[2] and others, we found the dialect in use by foreigners often materially misled us, so that none could be trusted as to accuracy; and it required time to detect and unlearn errors. In the oft recurring names of the principal island, the largest village, and of the king of the leeward islands, "Owhyhee," "Hanaroorah," and "Tamoree," scarcely the sound of a single syllable was correctly expressed, either in writing or speaking, by voyagers or foreign residents.

It is no wonder, then, that the first and most important step toward literacy for the Hawaiians was an efficient orthography. Other linguistic works, such as a grammar and a dictionary, although desirable and often discussed, were more of a convenience for the missionaries and other nonnative speakers than for the Hawaiians themselves. More than any other missionary innovation, it was the alphabet—but with fixed rules for its use—that would enable the Hawaiians to read religious materials written in their own language, thus preparing the way for their conversion to Christianity.

1820-1825: AN INTERIM ALPHABET

What philosopher ever formed an alphabet for the sounds of a language never before written? (Missionary Herald *19 [1823]:43*)

On the morning of 23 October 1819, a crowd gathered at Boston's Long Wharf to wish Godspeed to the *Thaddeus* and the First Company of Congregational Missionaries to the Sandwich Islands.[3]   From our language-centered point of view, the most important people there were four Hawaiians named Thomas Hopu, John Honoli'i, George Sandwich, and George P. Kaumuali'i (son of the "King" of Kaua'i); Hiram Bingham and his wife (of only six days), Sybil; and Elisha Loomis, who was to be printer for the mission.[4] Absent—miles away in his Cornwall grave—was the catalyst for the endeavor, 'Ōpūkaha'ia. His death, however, had enhanced rather than diminished his influence: for example, reading the *Memoirs of Henry Obookiah* convinced Loomis to leave his printing apprenticeship and join the mission.   Also, the *Memoirs* helped support the venture not only by producing revenue from sales, but also by convincing American church members to donate further money and goods to the mission.

Nor did the Prudential Committee of the American Board of Commissioners for Foreign Missions (ABCFM) forget 'Ōpūkaha'ia that morning in their lengthy address and prayers. But their only reference to the linguistic work that 'Ōpūkaha'ia, Samuel Ruggles, and Hiram Bingham had begun, and that the First Company now faced, made it sound formidable indeed:

> Some preparations may have been made toward conveying instruction, both by means of interpreters and in their own language; but the progress of divine truth among pagans, speaking a strange tongue, and not even having any language adapted to moral subjects, must be slow at first ... (*Instructions*, p. 40).

Just how to "convey instruction" was still somewhat of a mystery to the missionaries. Bingham, inspired by Thomas Hopkins Gallaudet,[5] a pioneer in teaching the deaf in America, even considered sign language as one approach (Hiram Bingham to Samuel Worcester, Salem, MA, from Goshen, CT, 11 May 1819. Bingham family papers, 1-1, p. 4):

> I have in my acquaintance with Mr. Gallaudet become so far acquainted with the language of signs as to [be] fully convinced that it must be of immense importance to the missionary to the un-lettered heathen. He thinks I ought to spend a little time at Hart-ford and this would certainly be desirable if there were time ...

Did Bingham think that gestures were universally understood and a way of achieving instant communication? Perhaps he had read Hawkes-worth's version of Cook's journal, which would have us believe that some fairly sophisticated messages passed between Cook's crew and the Tahitians solely through the medium of gesture (see chapter 3). What-ever his expectations, nothing more was mentioned about sign language as a means of communicating with the Hawaiians.

Bingham was also open to other ideas. A Russian visitor reported (Barratt 1988:265):

> ... as the English tongue is not equal to the expression of certain words in [Hawaiian], he [Bingham] is employing letters from other European languages too. In this connection, he even asked us about our Russian alphabet, learning the pronunciation of its letters and diphthongs.

For some time, none of these abandoned schemes was replaced by one uniform system: it seemed that each missionary had his or her own way of writing the language. For instance, table 7.1 illustrates how Loomis spelled some Hawaiian words in his journal on his arrival in Hawai'i (March 1820).

TABLE 7.1
LOOMIS'S AND MODERN SPELLING COMPARED

Loomis's Spelling	Modern Spelling
Krymokoo, one of the head chiefs,	Kālaimoku
Kirooah	Kailua
wihena	wahine
miti	maika'i
Woahoo	O'ahu
Witetee	Waikīkī
Hanaroora, Honorooru	Honolulu
Lahina	Lahaina[6]
hoo-dah hoodah	hula (-hula)
Tamahamaha	Kamehameha

Loomis wrote no numbers in his system, but, as did Webster, he used as the principal values of some of the vowel letters (*a*, *e*, and *i*) the names of those letters—that is, the way English speakers pronounce them when reciting the alphabet. And as the last example shows, he was not always consistent. There, in his transcription of *Kamehameha*, the letter *a* represents two distinct sounds: /a/ and /e/.

Thomas Hopu, as well, stayed close to the "English" method of indicating vowels. Table 7.2 shows how Hopu wrote the Hawaiian words in a letter mostly in English (Thomas Hopu to Jeremiah Evarts, 3 and 4 May 1821). Note the particularly "English" pattern of some of the vowels: *e* for /i/, *oo* for /u/, *i* for /ai/, and *u* for [ʌ].

TABLE 7.2
HOPU'S AND MODERN SPELLING COMPARED

Hopu's Spelling	Modern Spelling
O-ah-hoo	Oʻahu
Leholeho	Liholiho
nooe-nooe miti	nuinui maikaʻi
mah-moo-le	ma muli
Kummoree	Kamaliʻi

Perhaps if the missionaries had been forced to use Hawaiian for all their dealings in the community, their progress in analyzing the language would have been more rapid. As it was, however, the availability of speakers of English (at various levels) in the islands hindered, rather than helped, their progress by distancing them from the language. On the other hand, it was difficult to find qualified bilinguals to serve as interpreters. Bingham wrote (1847:103):

> We early used both English and Hawaiian together. For a time after our arrival, in our common intercourse, in our schools, and in our preaching, we were obliged to employ interpreters, though none except Hopu and Honolii were found to be very trustworthy ... Kaumualii, Kuakini, Keeaumoku and a few others could speak a little barbarous English, which they had acquired by intercourse with sea-faring men.

Although the presence of the Hawaiian students at Cornwall had given the missionaries an opportunity to hear and study Hawaiian, only after they reached the Islands did they hear the language in its natural environment. The differences between this style of Hawaiian and the one that they had become accustomed to suggested that the young displaced Hawaiians might not have been ideal speakers of the language (Missionary letters, p. 6. Joint letter from Bingham, Thurston, Ruggles, D. Chamberlain, E. Loomis to Samuel Worcester, 6 July 1821):

> You are aware of the very great difficulties which must meet us
> in the commencement of our work, difficulty in acquiring, &
> printing an unwritten & an almost unknown tongue, without com-
> petent instructors, & without any standard of pronunciation, as we
> have reason to believe that the youths who left this country at an
> early age, & have received the rudiments of an education in
> America, have but a very imperfect knowledge of their own
> language, & an equally imperfect acquaintance with ours ...

The Reverend Sheldon Dibble, who arrived in 1831 with the
Fourth Company, also faulted the returned Hawaiians for their linguistic
abilities (Dibble 1843:173):

> The native youth ... having failed in a great measure as
> interpreters, the necessity was the greater for the missionaries to
> acquire at once the language. And the same youth being of little
> service as helps in acquiring the language, the missionaries found
> nothing left but their own unassisted skill and application to
> accomplish the task.

In short, the missionaries found themselves inadequately prepared
for learning enough about Hawaiian to be able to develop a system for
writing it. The language, as spoken on its home territory, was somewhat
different from what they had come to expect, and none of the efforts so
far to write it had proved entirely satisfactory.

THE VOWELS

Even though the field of phonetics was in its infancy in the early
years of the nineteenth century, people who dealt with the English
language had long complained about the inconsistencies of its spelling
system. The focus for most of the complaints was the peculiar way
English handled vowels.[7] Tables 7.1 and 7.2 above show parts of the so-
called English system, mentioned as being used by Loomis: the names
we call the vowel letters when reciting the alphabet are considered their
principal values. Thus, *a* represented [e], *e* [i], *i* [ay], *o* [o], and *u* [yu].
Most early attempts at writing Hawaiian show other carryovers from
English as well, such as *oo* for [u], *u* for [ʌ], *ee* and *y* for [i], and *ou* for
[au].

The missionaries considered at least one imaginative way of
avoiding the problem of the vowels altogether: "A syllabic alphabet of
ninety-five characters[8] would have been tolerably convenient for all
native words ..." wrote Bingham (1847:154). Although we have no
idea how serious the proposal was, a syllabary would have been contrary

to the objectives the missionaries had in mind. In addition to wanting to represent the language faithfully and efficiently, the analysts listed three general goals for the new orthography, summarized as follows (Missionary letters, p. 6, joint letter from Bingham, Thurston, Ruggles, D. Chamberlain, E. Loomis to Samuel Worcester, Boston, 6 July 1821):

1. A system that would be understood by the scientific community in Europe.
2. One that would also help the Hawaiians learn English.
3. One that would give the readers equal access to books printed in Tahitian.

An underlying goal, occasionally stated explicitly, was that the alphabet be easy to learn and use correctly.

As with most of the earliest discussion of the proposed alphabet, these goals contain an implicit assumption that the consonants posed no problem and that once the vowel system was fixed, the alphabet would be complete. But it would have been impossible to achieve all these particular goals with the same alphabet. The "foreign sounds of the vowels" would satisfy both the European and Tahitian readers but would bear little resemblance to the English system, and vice versa. Still, the missionaries clung to these ideals, referring indirectly to at least two of them a few months later:

> The acquisition of the language is still & must be for a long time an object demanding much of our attention. We have not yet agreed upon an alphabet with which to write it — It is most probable that we shall adopt as the basis, "the foreign sounds of the vowels" & with the Roman character follow as nearly as is convenient the plan pursued in reducing to form the Language of Otaheite. We ask your deliberate advice on the Subject. — & if you can send us any books in the Otaheiten tongues,[9] or on the subject of *"Phonology"* you would contribute important aid in this difficult business   (Missionary letters, pp. 9–10, letter from Bingham, Whitney, Ruggles, "Atooi," 11 October 1821 [later corrected to 13 October]).

As was pointed out in chapter 4, in 1820 the term *phonology* did not mean quite what it does today. Studies of speech sounds were based on the assumption that somehow the correct pronunciation of a word should be derived from its spelling. In other words, one proceeded from symbol to sound.

A reversal of this principle, and thus a major advance in the study of speech, was proposed in Peter Duponceau's *English Phonology* (1817). The missionaries in Hawai'i may well have heard of Dupon-

ceau's work from their New England colleagues; at any rate, they would
have seen a reference to it in a work by Pickering, mentioned below. In
his essay, Duponceau explained his predecessors' failures (1817:231):

> Instead of applying the process of analysis to the sounds them-
> selves, independent of, and abstracted from, the signs which
> represent them, grammarians have looked to the signs in the first
> instance, and proceeded from them to the sounds which they are
> supposed to represent.

As a specific example, he criticized John Walker's *Pronouncing
Dictionary* for using two symbols (å and ȯ) to represent exactly the same
sound. "It will always be so when the alphabet of any language is taken
as the basis of a system of its sounds; for an analysis which proceeds
from the sign to the thing signified, can never produce a satisfactory
result ..." (p. 232).

As progressive as it was in theory, Duponceau's work was not so
advanced in its actual description of English sounds, particularly the
vowels. And because it described only English sounds, it did not present
a methodology for describing speech sounds in general. Although he
envisioned a phonetic alphabet (called a "phonology of language"),
Duponceau considered it a "Herculean Labour" and left it for someone
else to do.[10] Thus, even if the ABCFM did send *English Phonology* to
Hawai'i, it is unlikely to have been of much use to the missionary-
linguists in the field.

It is definitely recorded, however, that John Pickering's work, *An
Essay on a Uniform Orthography for the Indian Languages of North
America* (1820), did have some effect on the missionaries' decision to
use the European, or "continental," vowel system.[11] This essay, too,
was another step on the way to developing a phonetic alphabet, this one
dealing not with English, but with the "exotic" languages of North
America, thereby approaching in theory the goals of the missionaries in
Hawai'i.

Pickering could only have strengthened the missionaries' leanings
toward the Tahitian alphabet. After noting the most undesirable features
of the English orthography (e.g., four distinct phonetic values for the
letter *a*), he concluded (p. 11)

> that it would be best to adopt as the *basis* of our Indian ortho-
> graphy, what we call the *foreign* sounds of all the vowels; that is,
> the sounds which are usually given to them by those European
> nations ... who, like ourselves, use the *Roman* alphabet in their
> own languages.

As examples, he listed the following letters, each with the closest English pronunciation:

a as in *father*	*o* as in *note*
e as in *there*	*u* as in *rule*
i as in *machine* (or like *ee*)	*y* as in *you* (or like *ee*)

Pickering's advice, then, confirmed the decision to abandon the so-called English values of the vowel letters and use the continental system. This is not to say, however, that there was no opposition. But most of the criticism seems to have come from outside the mission family. Lorrin Andrews reported later (1836b:16) that their decision to use vowel values different from those of English was called a needless innovation and "an affectation of Italicising."

In spite of such criticism, the missionaries, after only a year and a half in Hawai'i, were fairly specific about the plans for printing and the kind of vowel system to be used (Missionary letters, O'ahu, 25 November 1821, Bingham, Thurston, Chamberlain, Loomis, pp. 13–14):

> Feeling more than ever, the need of the sympathies & the counsels of the Board, we again turn our eyes to you. In prosecuting the study of the language, which presents many obstacles difficult to be overcome, we are now encouraged to hope that as soon as January next we shall be able to put to press a Spelling book for the use of our schools containing about 1000 words of the Owhyhee Language, adopting as the basis of the alphabet what is termed the *foreign sounds of the vowels*, unless some new light on that point should induce us to commence printing with a different plan. Any books from you, in the language of Otaheite, New Zealand, or of the Indian tribes of America would be acceptable to us ...

Thus, we see that the missionary-linguists willingly sought guidance from a variety of sources to help them in the task for which they were so ill-prepared.

THE TAHITIAN CONNECTION AGAIN

Tahiti 1805: "In this first meeting an Alphabet had been drawn up consisting of the vowels a, e, i, o, and u ... to be pronounced as follows a as in lad, e as in met, i as in fin, o as in hop and u as in full or as oo in too, which seemed to be the real native sounds in quality, tho' the quantity is sometimes different. Mr D[avies] and several others thought simplicity and uniformity (neither of which is characteristic of the English Alphabet) ought to be aimed at, so that the natives might easily learn to spell their own words

*..." (C. W. Newbury's edition of John Davies' History of the
Tahitian Mission [1961:77n]).*

The wish that the Hawaiian alphabet match as closely as possible
that of Tahitian, mentioned in the preceding section, was not a new idea.
Bingham had expressed such a desire, at least implicitly, while he was
still in New England. It is not clear just when the mission received a
copy of the first Tahitian primer; since it was published in London in
1810, the members of the ABCFM may have had a copy long before the
First Company left for Hawai'i. At any rate, Daniel Chamberlain wrote
in his journal on 19 June 1820:

> Saw a man today a native of Otaheite, who can read well in his
> language—he had been acquainted with the missionaries there,
> and they had taught him to read. We have one Otaheite Spelling
> book.[12]

There were a number of reasons why the Tahitian alphabet was the
best model for the Hawaiian missionaries to use. First, ever since the
publication of Cook's journals, it was common knowledge that the two
languages were close enough to each other to enable a good deal of
communication to take place.[13] Next, the Tahitian alphabet had already
had twenty years to evolve. Finally, its official form had been settled by
the very capable Reverend John Davies.

Had it not been for Davies, possibly the best-trained and most
astute linguist in the Pacific in the first decades of the nineteenth century, the Tahitian alphabet would have been somewhat different from its
present form, and Hawaiian, having escaped an alphabet encumbered by
the numbers *3* and *8*, might have had one complicated by a Greek
epsilon instead. Davies had opted early for the continental values of the
vowels, but this system was outvoted, six to five, in March 1805. As he
expressed it (Newbury 1961:78), "The minority for peace sake gave up
the dispute and agreed against their judgement to adopt, to say the least
of it, the inconvenient way agreed upon by the majority."

This was the system that the majority accepted, and which served
as the official one for several years:

a	represented	/a/		o	represented	/o/
e	"	/i/		u	"	/u/
ε	"	/e/				

As the list shows, this system curiously retained one feature of the
English mode of spelling—that is, letting *e* represent the sound of its
name [i], rather than *i*, which would have been the foreign or continental

method. It would be easier to understand the motivation for this system if *i* had been used for /ai/, but instead, it was discarded altogether.

Although opposed in theory to this now-official orthography, Davies followed it in practice. As a matter of fact, he even used it to write Fijian words and place names during a brief stay in 1809–1810 (im Thurn and Wharton 1925).[14] Still, he was not happy with this mongrel system, and in 1807, when he sent the London Missionary Society his manuscript for a "Tahitian spelling book" (Davies 1810), he used the occasion to argue persuasively for the continental system. As a result, his work was printed using the five roman vowel letters according to the European system, thus influencing all the Polynesian alphabets from that time on.

INFLUENCE OF THE MAORI GRAMMAR AND DICTIONARY

As the letter quoted earlier shows, Bingham and his associates looked not only to Tahiti but also to New Zealand for orthographical guidance. Although the spelling system in Thomas Kendall's first Māori primer (1815) was fairly muddled, another five years' experience and the professional advice of Samuel Lee, a Cambridge professor specializing in Oriental languages, resulted in a version that was much improved (1820). The Hawaiian missionaries reported that they had received copies of the combined Māori grammar and dictionary on 1 January 1822, just a few days before the first sheets of the Hawaiian speller were run off the press in Hawai'i.

Even though the missionaries must have been impressed with the new work on Māori (the size alone was substantial: 230 pages), they were not really competent to judge its accuracy. In particular, they were unaware that beyond the vowel system, the improved Māori alphabet was still a provisional one, missing some important distinctions. For example, words now differentiated by *w* and *wh* were all written with *w*. This had no effect on the situation in Hawai'i, although had the missionaries made a comparative list of words, they might have found it strange that forms kept apart in Hawaiian by *w* and *h* were confused in Māori by the provisional alphabet. But the problem most closely related to Hawaiian was the question of *d* versus *r*. From the very first transcription of Māori, there had been some confusion over the use of these letters (and sometimes of *l* as well). Although eventually it was realized that they did not contrast (just like the Hawaiian *l* and *r*, discussed elsewhere), both letters were still written in 1820. But rather than varying randomly, they varied according to a pattern called *complementary distribution*: that is, for the most part, *d* was written before *i* and *u*, and *r* before the other vowels.

In spite of its faults, the Māori grammar and dictionary put the final seal of approval on the decision to use the five vowel letters in the "foreign" manner.[15] This is not to say that there were no more problems with that section of the alphabet; on the contrary, vowel length and its relationship to accent, some difficulty in distinguishing unaccented vowels, and a set of diphthongs quite different from those in English remained to puzzle the analysts for years to come. But this first move away from the English pattern of spelling was a major step toward an efficient alphabet.

THE FIRST PRINTING

> *When the king first examined the press, a sheet of white paper being laid on, he pulled the lever round, and was surprised to see the paper instantly covered with words in his own language (Bingham 1847:156).*

Soon after arriving in Hawai‘i, Elisha Loomis hoped to put his professional training to work immediately. He wrote on 5 August 1820: "Have been employed today in putting together the press and preparing to print a few alphabets for the use of our scholars ..." (Loomis and Loomis 1819–1827). But that work was postponed, not so much for practical or mechanical reasons as for the lack of a solid linguistic basis with which to operate. About five months later, he reported from Lahaina:

> 23 January 1821. Today the press was removed to this place. We have not yet made use of this powerful engine of knowledge but as we make the Owhyhee language a daily study we hope soon to be able to translate something. In acquiring this language we labor under many and great inconveniences. The want of an interpreter who understands the English language grammatically retards our progress.

Although many problems remained because of the missionaries' inadequate understanding of the structure of the language, it was essential to print something, even if the alphabet used in that material turned out later to be only provisional. This tentative, but epochal, step was taken early in 1822 (Missionary letters, p. 16, O‘ahu, 1 February 1822):

> We are happy to announce to you that on the first Monday of January [the 7th] we commenced printing, & with great satisfac-

tion have put the first eight pages of the Owhyhee spelling book into the hands of our pupils, copies of which we now transmit to you for the examination of the Committee, and as little articles of curiosity from these dark Isles. By the next conveyance we hope to send complete copies, with a preface. The edition will be small, about 500 copies, —We should be obliged, if the Committee should suggest alterations & amendments, from a perusal of the first 8 pages .

Plate 7.1 shows the alphabet that the missionaries decided to adopt. The "foreign" values for the vowels were used indeed; all remnants of the Webster system were discarded. However, fully a dozen consonants are used for Hawaiian words, and an extra four "used in spelling foreign words." The table of diphthongs (the word was misspelled, and the list omitted *oi* and *iu*) showed a problem that still plagues language teachers: the impossibility of giving English examples for *ai* versus *ae*, and *au* versus *ao*. Lesson 2, "Double vowels pronounced separately" (p. 3), shows that the missionaries certainly heard the glottal stop—but didn't quite know how to deal with it in terms of a writing system.

This sheet from the press contained the first eight pages (each 16 x 10.5 cm) of the book; the second eight pages did not appear until more than a month later.[16] On 26 February 1822, Loomis wrote:

> Engaged for several days past in printing ... The second sheet of our Spelling Book is now out. It contains several reading lessons, which have cost us much labor to prepare, and they are doubtless still very imperfect.

Five hundred copies of this sixteen-page booklet were printed. In September, Loomis began printing a second edition, this one of 2,000 copies.

The next year saw only two items emerge from the Mission's press, but one was of substantial size. The first, for which little documentation exists, seems to have been a four-page collection of vowel letters and punctuation marks (Judd, Bell, and Murdoch 1978:4). The major work was a sixty-page hymnal in an edition of 2,000 copies. In 1824, some 7,000 copies of a four-page Alphabet were printed, and in 1825, various editions of an eight-page Alphabet ran to 61,000 copies.

In summary, at least for those publications that are well documented, some 1,626,000 pages of Hawaiian were printed in a provisional system through 1826, the year that the Mission established its official orthography.

THE ALPHABET.

VOWELS.

Names.	SOUND. Ex. in Eng.	Ex. in Hawaii.
A a ...â	as in *father*;	la—sun.
E e ...a	— *tete*,	homo—cast of.
I i ...e	— *marine*,	marie—quiet.
O o ...o	— *over*,	ono—sweet.
U u ...oo	—*rule*,	nui—large.

CONSONANTS.

Names.		CONSONANTS.	Names.
B b	be	N n	nu
D d	de	P p	pi
H h	he	R r	ro
K k	ke	T t	ti
L l	la	V v	vi
M m	mu	W w	we

The following are used in spelling foreign words:

F f	fe	S s	se
G g	ge	Y y	yi

DIPTHONGS.

Ae	as in *eyes*, ...	ae—yes.
Ai	as in *aisle*, or *idol*, . .	ai—food.
Ao	as *a* in *far*, followed closely by *o*;	ao—bread.
Au	like *ow* in *now*, ...	pau—all.
Ei	as in *eight*, nearly, . .	lei—beads.
Eu	as *a* in *late*, followed by *oo*;	weuweu—grass.
Ou	as *o* followed closely by *oo*;	lakou—they.

TABLE 1.

LESSON 1.

Ba	be	bi	bo	bu
da	de	di	do	du
ha	he	hi	ho	hu
ka	ke	ki	ko	ku
la	le	li	lo	lu
ma	me	mi	mo	mu
na	ne	ni	no	nu

PLATE 7.1   A PAGE FROM THE HAWAIIAN SPELLING BOOK (*THE ALPHABET*), FIRST PRODUCT OF THE MISSION PRESS, 1822.

A SURFEIT OF CONSONANTS

"Is the dance called hulahula?*"*
"Ae. [Yes]"
"Is it hudahuda?*"*
"Ae."
"Or hurahura? *"*
"Ae." *(Albertine Loomis,* Grapes of Canaan,
p. 117)

Compared with some of their colleagues who prepared for missions among Native American tribes, Hiram Bingham and his associates were faced with a relatively simple consonant system: no glottalized or pharyngealized consonants—not even any consonant clusters.

Nor was there an extreme amount of dialect variation to plague those working with the language.[17] Unlike some other island groups in the Pacific (such as Fiji, whose individual languages are so diverse that on the largest island, roughly the size of Hawai'i, a number of mutually unintelligible languages are spoken), there were apparently only minor linguistic differences within the Hawaiian Group.

However, as described in chapter 5, among those outsiders who paid some attention to Hawaiian, the realization gradually developed that a different kind of problem faced those who would eventually create an alphabet for the language.

It is difficult to think of anything in the missionaries' training back home that could have anticipated a dialogue such as the one that introduces this section—one that symbolizes five years of questions, discussions, and disagreement. Their study of Latin or Greek had not prepared them for such an extent of consonant variation, and their English via Webster had led them to expect that once the vowels were settled, the rest of the alphabet would fall into place. Unfortunately, the early manuscript grammar of Samuel Ruggles gave no hint of what lay ahead, for it contained very little of the consonantal chaos that they found shortly after arriving in Hawai'i. Finally, they seem to have been unaware of the several comments on variation in the journals of explorers and beachcombers, mentioned in chapter 5.

Even their secondhand experience with Tahitian was no foreshadowing of the problems that awaited them: the Tahitian alphabet was overgenerous with its consonant letters, but mainly because it made provisions for writing foreign terms like *Jehovah, Jesus Christ,* and *Adam.*[18]

Moreover, the introductory quotation only suggests the variation that the missionaries found. In fact, a good deal more than just the word *hulahula* was affected. Before much time had passed, they discovered, as did the observers who immediately preceded them (such as de Freycinet and Gaimard), that words could be written with either *b* or *p*; *t* or *k*; *l*, *d*, *r*, or sometimes even *n*; and *v* or *w*—without changing the meaning.

The safest plan at first was to use all these letters, for, as with Tahitian, they could all prove useful for writing foreign terms. After all, as Bingham (1847:155) so fully expressed it, they could not,

> in good conscience, throw out every consonant in the names of Obed, Boaz, Ruth, David, Ezra, Russia, and Gaza, and nearly all out of such names as Sabbath, Christ, Moses, Joseph, Boston, and Genessaret, simply because such consonants could be dispensed with in writing the words familiar to the people.

Besides, a strong feeling persisted that words should be written "as they sounded"—that is, to an English ear. Thus, the first primer included all those troublesome consonants, along with the unambiguous remainder. However, although this larger alphabet could give the phonetic detail that the missionaries desired, the spelling and pronunciation of individual words became a matter impossible to resolve. For example, who was to decide which of the possible choices of consonant letters was appropriate for a particular word? How could the missionaries teach reading and writing quickly if the relationship between sound and spelling was not predictable? How could they write a dictionary if the spelling of so many words was not fixed?

The missionaries did not try to solve these problems only among themselves; time after time, they sought the advice of native speakers. But they found that the Hawaiians, for whom the differences were not significant, could not hear them.[19] In fact, one missionary thought it would be easier to teach the Hawaiians how to say a completely new sound like *s* than to teach them to distinguish among their troublesome variants (Richards to Anderson, 20 May 1828, HMCS letter 142).

The following account by Artemas Bishop (of the Second Company) gives a fair summary of how the missionaries perceived the problem (Bishop to Anderson, 30 September 1824, HMCS, v. 1–3, no. 96):

> ... I shall mention to you something, wh[ich] may perhaps appear strange & uninteresting, but to us is really a serious & difficult affair, and will require no little wisdom & address to adjust the dispute. It is concerning the true orthography of a great portion of the words in this language. There are two opinions on the subject, and we can gain no aid from the natives, for they can understand both methods with equal ease, and are in the habit of

using both as it may suit their inclinations. Perhaps I cannot give you a clear idea of the nature of this dispute, wh. may perhaps after all, arise wholly out of the indistinct method of pronunciation used by the natives. You must know then, that the use of an L, or an R, in any word when one of these letters is used, conveys precisely the same meaning, —thus to say, a*l*oha or a*r*oha, (love), either will be equally well understood. The same may be said with regard to the letters k & t. —and also v & w. "thus: *t*abu or *k*abu (forbidden) Ha*v*aii or Ha*w*aii, (proper name of this Island)—in the use of either method there is no difficulty in being understood. — The B. & the P. are likewise synonymous, thus we may say, *pure* or *pule, bure* or *bule* (prayer).

Bishop continued, saying that the situation had prompted all the missionaries to attempt a standard way of spelling. But there was not unanimity among the brethren. For example, the majority favored *l*, but Ellis and Bingham preferred *r*. (Bishop astutely observed that Ellis favored some letters over others because they were used in Tahiti and he was accustomed to them. Moreover, the British and American versions of *r* may have, by this time, become distinct enough to affect their respective perceptions of the sound they heard.) The conflict between *k* and *t*, on the other hand, was largely geographic: *k* for the windward islands, and *t* for the leeward.[20]

In the same letter, Bishop summarized the consonantal confusion:

... which then shall be the standard, is the question? Some are for retaining all the *various readings* as they now stand, in our Alphabet, others are for expunging the b, d, r, t, & v, as wholly unnecessary. Others still are for taking a middle course, and retaining them in the alphabet for the use of foreign words, and confine them here. I must confess myself of this latter class. "As far as my observation & hearing extends, I can find no native that comes so near the sound of R in his pronunciation as of L. —Tell a scholar to say R (ro), (and I have told more than 300 different ones) and he will invariable say, "lo," say v. (vi) ans[wer]; "wi." —and so of the rest.

This, then, was the crux of the matter: arbitrarily allowing some words to be spelled with *k* and others with *t* (and so on, through all the pairs or groups of potential letters) would severely reduce the desired "one sound, one symbol" nature of the alphabet and significantly increase the time necessary for Hawaiians to become literate. Hence the process of Christianization might be delayed for years.

From the very beginning, observers have described this problem as an *alternation* of consonants—that is, they called the sound either one

thing or another, but nothing in between.[21]   The missionaries had a
legitimate reason for so doing: they were concerned less about the nature
of Hawaiian phonology than about the problem of devising a practical
orthography. From this point of view, it is quite reasonable to ask: is it
more appropriate to write this sound (whatever it is) with a *v* or a *w*?
But now to call it an alternation is rather like saying, "*W* and *v* are
separate consonants in English; therefore, the sound in Hawaiian must be
one or the other."

Although in recent years writers have largely ignored the idea that
the sounds in question might have been something different from what
the English letters generally stand for, that is not an entirely new
approach. Note the following quotation (Hopkins 1862:347):

> The *k* and *t*, and the *l* and *r*, are so blended, that the distinction
> between the letters of each pair is not observed by the natives, or
> even by those who have been long resident in the islands. It is
> probable that the two interchangeable pairs were really two real
> letters [here he meant "sounds"], not found in European alphabets,
> and were analytically resolved into two elements by the mission-
> aries, in order to give them known phonetic expression.

Hopkins's explanation was only theoretical, but as the following
sections show, the observations of people closer at hand reveal that for
some of the "pairs," something other than simple alternation was taking
place. In the following discussion (which treats the so-called pairs introduced in chapter 5),[22] I shall try to reconstruct something of the phonetic
detail of these sounds from a composite of eighteenth- and nineteenth-
century accounts.

T or *K*?

To someone interested in phonetics, perhaps the most interesting
set of troublesome consonants in Hawaiian is *t* versus *k*. For the other
pairs—*p* and *b*, *r* and *l*, and *v* and *w*—it is easy enough for an English
speaker to admit that the sounds are similar. As a matter of fact, in his
discussion of the procedures for analyzing the sound system of a
language, Kenneth L. Pike (1947:70) included all those pairs on a chart
showing "phonetically similar segments." But *t* and *k*? Somehow we
expect them always to be distinct.

Nor would a familiarity with other Polynesian languages prepare
us for such a relationship. On a chart showing the consonant correspondences for forty-seven Polynesian languages and dialects (Biggs
1971:480–81), Hawaiian is the only instance of an earlier **t* (that is,
Proto-Polynesian) changing to *k* (thereby refuting R. L. Stevenson's

claim [1891:12] that the transition from *t* to *k* was a "disease of Polynesian languages").[23] In the majority of cases, *t* and *k* have remained separate phonemes (with *k* changing to a glottal stop in eight languages).

In the few reliable phonetic descriptions of modern Hawaiian that do exist, *t* and *k* are described as very similar to English *t* and *k*, with a minor difference of the point of articulation for *t* (made with the tongue touching the back of the upper teeth rather than the gum ridge) and a lesser degree of aspiration for both sounds.

In theory, however, the absolute placement of the tongue might have been anywhere along the roof of the mouth—so long as the sound was distinct from /p/ and /'/. Such a proposal was made obliquely by Hopkins, quoted above, and more directly by Claude M. Wise and Wesley D. Hervey (1952:319), who described Hawaiian as having one stop consonant articulated on the roof of the mouth

> for which the tongue contact might be anywhere between the teeth
> and the soft palate. Since the Hawaiian ear required only that his
> plosive distinguish itself from [p] and the glottal stop, it mattered
> not at all where the closure was made.[24]

From the evidence at hand, it is difficult either to prove—or disprove—that such an articulation existed. First the negative evidence: although for some of the so-called pairs (discussed later in this chapter) several missionaries wrote specifically of sounds "intermediate between the two," I have found only two writers to do so specifically for *t* and *k*. One was Hopkins, and he did not go into detail. Moreover, he was writing nearly forty years after the main debates on this matter. Lorrin Andrews, however, discussed the matter at greater length (1854:12):

> The letter *k* has some variety in its pronunciation. The people
> of the Island of Hawaii formerly had a sound now represented by
> the letter *k* which sound was a guttural, or rather perhaps, the
> sound was formed at the root of the tongue. The people of Kauai,
> on the other hand, had a sound of the same signification, but
> pronounced it near the tip of the tongue resembling the sound of *t*.
> Since the conquest by Kamehameha I., and the consequent mixing
> up of the people of the different islands; *this letter has all the
> intermediate sounds from a guttural to a dental* [emphasis added];
> that is, from the distinct *k* sound to that of the *t*. And the people
> appear to perceive no difference.

Thus, although it is unfortunate that more contemporary writers did not make the same observervation, Andrews's comments suggest a range of intermediate pronunciations of what is now written as *k*.

What do we know about the earlier geographical distribution of the sounds? First, it seems to have been general knowledge that [t] was more prevalent in some places than in others. For example, Artemas Bishop wrote on 30 September 1824 from Kailua, Hawai'i, that [k] was "used nearly altogether at the windward islands" and [t] "at the leeward" (A. Bishop to Rufus Anderson, Boston, HMCS 10, no. 96). In the more detailed discussion on settling the form of the alphabet, he wrote on 4 April 1826, again from Kailua, Hawai'i (Orthography, p. 2):

> ... or I might at Hawaii say T. should be omitted and our Tauai [Kaua'i] Brethren say it shall be K. ...

Joseph Goodrich wrote on 3 April 1826 from Hilo (Orthography, p. 6):

> Respecting k & t—I have no use for t in this place. I should say therefore exclude it.

The current distribution of [k] and [t] may match the earlier one in principle but not in detail: whatever the cause—standardization of the language, an independent sound shift from [t] to [k],[25] the diminishing number of speakers, or the increasing number of speakers who learn the language in formal classes—[t] speakers are concentrated primarily on Ni'ihau. However, [t] is not confined exclusively to that island; William H. Wilson has also observed [t] in speakers from Kaupō and Kīpahulu on Maui and Hālawa on Moloka'i (Elbert and Pukui 1979:24–25). In addition to its special geographical distribution, [t] is also sometimes used in chants (Roberts 1926:73).[26]

L or R?

As table 5.1 shows, the statistics for *l* versus *r* are rather different than those for *t* versus *k*: in only one list is the ratio of *l* to *r* as high as 1:3, and in three, *l* does not appear at all. Yet, it was eventually chosen to represent the sound. Is there any explanation for this apparent anomaly?

In the regrettable but inevitable absence of sound recordings from the 1820s, we must be careful to note the variables that might account for any discrepencies between what was heard and what was written. First there are the two dimensions of geography and time. There might well have been areas in which the sound was more like *l*, and others in which it was more like *r*. And through time, the *l* areas may have spread.

But it is just as important to realize that the symbol *r* meant different things to different people.[27] Perhaps Anderson (the Scot) and Cook (the Yorkshireman) might have spoken and heard English /r/ similarly, but how did their conception of the letter (or sound) compare with that of the American missionaries more than forty years later?

Whatever the exact value of the sound, the increasing confusion between *r* and *l* (and *d* as well) in the 1820s was just as troublesome to the missionaries as the *t* versus *k* problem. William Richards reported his own experiment with the set, rather like that in the quotation that heads this section. Based on the word now written as *lilo* 'be absorbed', he asked native speakers for confirmation of each of the following— *dido, dilo, diro, lido, lilo, liro, rido, rilo, riro*—and received a "yes" answer each time. He then described a variation on the experiment (Richards to Rufus Anderson, 20 May 1828, Missionary letters, p. 723):

> In another instance I asked a native to pronounce this word himself. Among the seven listeners there were four opinions as to the answer given. Three thought he pronounced the word *lilo*; two thought he said *lido*; one thought he said *liro* and one thought he said *rilo*.

His next sentence confirms that this problem was somewhat different from a simple alternation:

> All however were of [the] opinion that the sound was rather a medium one and not the full sound of the English letters.

Thus, it seemed that neither the letter *l* nor *r* exactly suited the sound. Unlike their discussion of *t* and *k*, in which the suitability of the letters was never questioned, several missionaries agreed in their assessment of the *r/l* sound: that it was something rather different from either English sound. For example, in the final debate over the consonants, Richards amplified on his earlier comment on the "medium" nature of the sound (Orthography, pp. 9–10) :

> I believe it is very generally agreed by all who have heard the Hawaiian language spoken that there is a peculiar sound which is something like a medium between the English *l* & *r*. I think too, it is generally agreed that the natives do differ some among themselves in the articulation of this medium sound; and that some approach nearer to the *l* or *r* than others. But if the natives do differ among themselves, or if the sound is neither *l* nor *r*, but a medium between the two or if the people are unable to distinguish between the sounds of the letters, then ... I can not see that the sounds of the language would be any more fully or definitely represented either to a native or a foreign ear by the two letters than by either one. Indeed the mere fact that the letters are acknowledged interchangeable, I think carries on the face of it the

evidence that some of the letters are redundant and ought therefore
to be dropped.

To add to Richards's opinion, we have that of Artemas Bishop
(Bishop to Rufus Anderson, ABCFM, from Kailua [Hawai'i], 30
September 1824):

> But after all, there appears to be a middle sound, neither l, or r,
> fully, it may be compared to the quick sound of the word, erlá,
> erló where there is at first an elevation of the tip of the tongue to
> the roof of the mouth, and from thence it rapidly descends to its
> former position.

Andrews (1854:12) provided a dissenting opinion:

> The letter *l* is a liquid, and is often interchangable with *r*; not
> the rolling French *r*, but the smooth *r* of the Americans.

With the exception of the last, all these pre-phonetic but sophisticated descriptions indicate that the Hawaiian sound was close to the
modern pronunciation of *r* in, for example, Tahitian or Māori—a tap
(made with the tip of the tongue on the gum ridge) that a phonetician
would transcribe as [ř]. The occasional transcription of the sound as *d*
(see table 5.1) supports such a conclusion: as mentioned earlier, Māori
/r/ was once (nearly) regularly written as *d* before /i/ and /u/, and the
Japanese /r/ before certain vowels is often perceived by English hearers
as [d]. As a negative example—that is, what it was *not*—Quimper's list,
with its absence of any words spelled with *rr*, shows that he heard the
Hawaiian sound as a tap [ř] and not as a trill [r̃].[28]

A corollary to the problem of *l* versus *r* is the addition of *n* to the
set. Judd, Pukui, and Stokes (1945:14) mentioned an alternation
between *l* and *n*, saying only that it applied to "some words." In the
introduction to the L section of the Hawaiian dictionary, Pukui and
Elbert (1986:188) noted: "In some localities *n* replaces more common *l*
...."[29] In the Hawaiian grammar (Elbert and Pukui 1979:25–26), the
authors loosely specified those areas, noting that it was more common
(perhaps) on Moloka'i and Lāna'i. Lists of examples show both
assimilatory and nonassimilatory changes, but the reader is still given no
idea of the extent of the replacement of *l* by *n*, or the effect that it has on
the phonological system of those particular dialects.

Whatever its extent, it does not seem to have been significant
enough to cause a problem in 1826. Besides, it is of a quite different
nature, for unlike the other groups of letters, both *l* and *n* are essential
for the alphabet. Thus, the replacement affects the spelling of only some

words, but with the reference materials that are now available, we have no idea of how many.

V or *W*?

As noted in chapter 5, although most earlier transcribers (with the expected exception of the French and Spanish visitors) wrote both *v* and *w*, so far as we know, this pair was not perceived as an alternation until 1819, when Rose de Freycinet described the two sounds as interchangeable consonants. An implicit missionary recording of the "alternation" appears in Sybil Bingham's manuscript primer (1823). Bingham's general practice was to write *v* in some words and *w* in others. However, above the word *raverave* (in the phrase now written as *kanaka lawelawe* 'servant'), she wrote an alternate: *lawelawe*—but without comment.

During the time of the most intense debate over consonant variation (1824–1826), few of the missionaries commented on *v* versus *w* to the extent to which they discussed the other problem consonants. One supporter of *w* over *v* was Asa Thurston, who prefaced his views by speculating a physical cause (Orthography, p. 13):

> Though the *v* may be used by some few natives whose upper
> lips are too short, & whose fore teeth are very prominent ...

It is tempting to ridicule the statement and allow it to color our opinion of the rest of Thurston's observation. To do so would be a mistake, for there follows some phonetic grain in the midst of this chaff:

> ... yet I question whether the proper sound of the *v* is found in the
> language. In my opinion there is no word in the language so far as
> I am acquainted with it, in which the *w* will not better fit the sound
> as spoken by the native than the *v* where either of them may be
> used, & where the *v* is now used in our printed tracts.

Note that Thurston did not say that *w* was the ideal representation of the Hawaiian sound, but that it would "better fit" it than *v*. His position suggests that he perceived the sound as neither *v* nor *w*, but something between the two. Such a point of view is supported by three other observers.

We begin with the comments of Horatio Hale, ethnologist and philologist for the United States Exploring Expedition.[30] Hale wrote: "In Hawaiian ... *w* is used for *v* (though the sound is properly intermediate between the two)" (1846:232).

Now, what exactly does "intermediate between the two" mean? First, it is important here to realize that Hale was more phonetically sophisticated than were many other recorders of Hawaiian sounds. For example, in his description of Fijian, he noted (p. 367) that the Fijian *v* is "like the Spanish *b* . . . pronounced by closing the lips together." This observation tells us that he was familiar with the articulation of [ß]—a sound that differs from [v] in that it is made with both lips, rather than the bottom lip and upper teeth. Moreover, it tells us indirectly that if he had considered the Hawaiian "intermediate" pronunciation to be a [ß], he would have said so.

William D. Alexander wrote a similar description (1864:5): "The sound of *w* is really between that of *v* and *w* in English, and in the middle of words it approaches more closely to that of *v*, as in *hewa*, *lawa*, &c." Here we are given, possibly for the first time, a statement (however oversimplified) of a distribution for [v]-like and [w]-like variants of /w/.

Lorrin Andrews corroborated the "intermediate" quality of /w/ (1854:13):

> The sound of the letter *v* is seldom as distinctly heard in Hawaiian as it is in the Tahitian dialect. The real sound represented by *w* from a Hawaiian's mouth is between that of *v* and *w*; but the double-you sound predominates; the letter *v* is therefore used only in words derived from foreign languages.

Andrews also noted that Hawaiians had difficulty pronouncing this "enforced" *v* in loan words: "*V* is not often clearly sounded by Hawaiians, they run it into the sound of *w*."

As evidence of a different kind, one might suggest that if Hawaiian had had a labiodental fricative [v], the phonetically similar /f/ sound in English would have been borrowed as /w/ and given this [v] pronunciation. However, English /f/ was usually borrowed as Hawaiian /p/—a bilabial sound.

Donald Billam-Walker (1979:40) recounted German bandmaster Henry Berger's difficulties with the Hawaiian sound. Berger, who lived in Hawai'i from 1872 until his death in 1929, was said to have spoken Hawaiian better than English. However,

> [d]ue to his Germanic background Berger always had great difficulty pronouncing the letter *w* both in English and Hawaiian. His *w* usually came out sounding like the letter *v*. This brought him criticism from many Hawaiians who were annoyed when he used the hard *v* instead of the soft liquid *w* or the semihard *vw* sound common to many Hawaiian words. When old-time Caucasians would hear some young Hawaiian mistakenly use a hard *v* they would laugh and say "there goes another native falling into the 'Berger trap.'"

Billam-Walker enlarged on the anecdote, adding that singer Ululani Robertson Jabulka considered that Berger had helped "to spoil our melodious Hawaiian language through singers imitating [his] mispronunciation of the Hawaiian 'w'".[31]

All this historical evidence points to one conclusion: that the *v*-like variant of /w/ was neither [v] nor [ß], but something different.

But what was its phonetic form? If we return to those earlier descriptions, we can reconstruct a tentative description of the *v*-like sound. Since the evidence seems to preclude any kind of slit fricative (either labiodental or bilabial), it is most likely that English hearers gained their [v] impression from a [w]-like sound in which the opening between the lips became constricted enough to produce some local friction—that is, a fricative quality. As supporting evidence, note that Newbrand (1951:8) described the *v* "alternate" as lax.

We are still confronted with a contrast between the situation that very likely held in the early and mid-nineteenth century, and the present one. The most plausible explanation is that although some variation existed before, an "alternation" between [w] and [v] was in the minds of the English-speaking analysts. By delaying an orthographical choice between *w* and *v* for so many years, they fixed in the minds of not only outsiders, but of many Hawaiians themselves (who were constantly being reminded of the prestige value of English) the idea that Hawaiian /w/ had to be pronounced as one of two extremes. Thus, what was originally a continuum was reformulated into a dichotomy—based on English models.

Alphabets for languages other than English and their resultant effect on printers' fonts also eventually played a role, albeit a minor one, in the *v-w* problem. Spaulding (1930:30) described the problem printers had in using Spanish fonts (with no *k* or *w*, at least for a conservative style of Spanish) to print English: *vv* had to serve for *w*. He continued, telling how the lack of those letters affected printing in Hawaiian:

> Something similar happened here when the French seized the Honolulu fort in 1849. Dr. N. B. Emerson, who was a boy at the time, remembered seeing "de Tromelin's proclamation, printed in the Hawaiian language, in which *vv* did duty for *w*, and *t* took the place of *k*, all of which peculiarities aroused the schoolboy's scorn and indignation."

In material printed by the Roman Catholic Mission later in the century, *k* appears, but a single *v* takes the place of *w*.[32]

An unexpected result of the forced (but necessary) choice of either *v* or *w* for a sound that seemed to fall between the two has been a century and a half's worth of arguments about the matter, often surfacing on the editorial pages of the local newspapers. For example, from 18 to 28 March 1936, nine letters on the topic of the pronunciation of Hawaiian *w* appeared in the *Honolulu Star-Bulletin*. (Incidentally, the last of these, written by the anthropologist, musicologist, and linguist Edwin G. Burrows, is the earliest account I have seen that approached the problem from a modern linguistic point of view: he referred to the so-called alternation as a "cluster of sounds," calling them a PHONEME. However, this major advance seems to have gone unnoticed by local Hawaiian language experts, and the concept was not used for Hawaiian, at least in print, until the late 1940s or early 1950s.)

ALPHABET BY ELECTION

The official movement toward a uniform orthography began early in 1824, when a committee was formed to frame a number of questions that the Protestant Mission should consider. The first of these questions was stated by William Richards and Charles S. Stewart on 6 March 1824 (Missionary letters, p. 917):

> Is a uniformity in the orthography of the Hawaiian language expedient? and what are the best means of securing it?
> Motioned that a Committee of three be appointed to correspond with the different members of the mission as to the expediency of establishing a uniformity in the orthography of the Hawaiian language, & to submit to this meeting for their consideration, propositions embracing the difficulties now felt in spelling the language.

The committee, appointed on 16 May 1825, consisted of Hiram Bingham, Stewart, and Levi Chamberlain. Their method was to poll all the members of the mission through a circular, which they summarized as follows:

> Very few, if any, of the natives seem to distinguish the difference between the sound of *k* & *t*, *l* & *r* or *v* & *w*. Many words at present in which *r* occurs, are by many uniformly pronounced as if written with *l*, and the same is true with respect to *k* & *t*, and *v* & *w*.
> Honolulu may be written four different ways and is constantly written two ways. Kaawaloa may be written eight and is written three.
> Every word in the language in which letters occur that are used interchangeably, may by permutation be written nearly as many different ways as the square of the whole number of interchangeable letters in the word.[33]

To the above I [Bingham?] may add, that the words are pronounced by different persons, in as many different ways as they are written and yet no native is aware of, or able to perceive the least variation.

Where we should use an *l* or an *r* or a *d*, the natives usually give a medium sound, which one foreigner thinks approaches nearest the *d*, another thinks it approaches nearest to the *r* and another still thinks it is the sound of *l*, so that the word which means *gone* is, pronounced by foreigners in all the following ways[:] *dido*, *lido*, *lilo*, *liro*, *riro*, *rilo*, and still the natives know no difference in all these different pronunciations.

The next sentence shows that the missionaries, quite naturally unaware of the far-reaching effects that their decisions would have, had no intentions of *changing* the language: "Now it is not for us to establish a uniform pronunciation of the language, for this would be impossible."[34]

The committee received most of the responses from April through July 1826.[35] The following summaries are based on a transcription of a number of missionary letters, referred to as "Orthography of the Hawaiian Language."

Artemas Bishop suggested that *b*, *d*, and *v* be dropped from the alphabet, explaining that "they are not sounded in the language, or at least not often. And even if they were expressed in the pronunciation of words, they can be fully expressed in the corresponding letters P, L, & W, without impairing in the least the regular pronunciation." He added that the Hawaiians could not distinguish between the members of the pairs, and did not use them consistently in writing. However, he recommended that the extraneous consonants be used for spelling foreign words. As for *l* versus *r*, and *k* versus *t*, he had no opinion and predicted disagreement among the brethren. Therefore, he recommended delaying the decision on these letters until the missionaries could meet and discuss the matter.

As light relief, Dr. Abraham Blatchely offered a medical parody, comparing the swollen alphabet with a disease and suggesting that *b*, *d*, *r*, *t*, and *v* were foreign substances to be removed.

Levi Chamberlain expressed his doubts about eliminating letters that represented sounds so clearly articulated by the Hawaiians. But he realized that continuing to write all the variants would only result in confusion. Thus, he could see no reason why one set of consonants should not be eliminated. Nor could he "see how the language will be more perfect for the use of characters which will perpetuate what we all regard as an imperfection in the language."

James Ely wrote a brief note recommending that *b, d, r, t,* and *v* be eliminated but suggesting that they be retained for foreign words.

As did his associates, Joseph Goodrich suggested that *b* and *t* be dropped, explaining that the latter was not suitable for the type of Hawaiian spoken at Hilo. However, he suggested that *r* was more appropriate than *l,* still referring to his particular need at Hilo. He had no opinion on *v* versus *w,* asking only for uniformity. The most insightful part of his letter is an implicit comment about the arbitrariness of letters:

> ... if I am at a place where the sound of t principally is heard; and yet t should be excluded, and k retained, I should not think it much of a trial, or effort to give the sound of the t to the k, while at such a place, and vice versa.

Loomis wrote a short letter in Hawaiian that illustrated how imprecise the current system was, with such spellings as *barapala, palabara,* and *barabala* for *palapala* 'writing'. He recommended that *b, d, r, t,* and *v* be eliminated.

William Richards wrote the longest reply, dwelling on the paradox that the consonant variation presented:

> I am aware that the orthography of a language is not perfect until all the sounds are correctly represented by appropriate characters. The object therefore in establishing an orthography, ought to be, fully and definitely to represent all the sounds of the language to be written.
>
> If the *characters* are sufficiently numerous, but yet are indefinitely or interchangeably used, then the language is no more fully represented than when the characters are too few.

He also made one of the few references to the early wish that the Hawaiian alphabet match those for other Polynesian languages:

> I agree with the committee in the opinion that it is desirable there should be a uniformity of spelling throughout all the group of isles in which the Polynesian language is spoken. But there certainly can not be such a uniformity while we differ so widely among ourselves. Neither do I think that a multiplication of characters to represent that which to all Polynesian ears is the same sound can possibly tend to uniformity.

As for his specific recommendations, he suggested that *b, t,* and *l* be eliminated, but he had no opinion about *d* (for /l/) or *v* versus *w.*

Asa Thurston recommended that *b, d, t, r,* and *v* be dropped.

The final letter in the collection "Orthography ..." summarizes the contributions of the remaining missionaries:

With respect to the orthography Mr Whitney in a letter to Mr Bingham remarks "You know my partiality for the R & W. but I shall contend for neither. I leave it to the judgement of the Committee. I pledge myself to abide by their decision."

Mr Ruggles has returned no answer.

Mr Bingham has not recently in a direct manner declared his opinion.[36]

Mr Ellis is regarded as in favor of all the letters.

Mr Stewart (as stated by Mr Bingham) as holding the opinion that none of the characters can be cast out without rendering the alphabet defective.

As the discussion above shows, those missionaries who responded were nearly unanimous in their choice of which consonants to eliminate and which to retain. The results of the voting (based on a letter from Bingham and Chamberlain to Rufus Anderson, 5 August 1826, ABCFM, Houghton Library), show that *l* was the only letter of the present alphabet that had to overcome any opposition:

B	9			P	0
D	8	R	6	L	2
T	8			K	0
V	9			W	0

In view of the prominence that several studies have given him,[37] it is interesting to note that William Ellis (as reported above) was in favor of retaining *all* the consonants. So strong was his opinion on this matter that an extract from the minutes of the General Meeting (Honolulu, May and June 1825, HMCS) reported that Ellis, whose opinion was regarded "as entitled to particular deference ... would probably print books independent of [the Mission], and therefore not conform to [their] method, should [they] fix upon one at variance with his own." Ellis's stance here —exactly the opposite of the missionaries' sensible decision—shows that his influence on the final form of the Hawaiian orthography has been totally misinterpreted.

Loomis and Loomis (18 August 1826, Journal) wrote a simple summary of the years of study, frustration, experimentation, and discussion:

We have rendered the orthography of the language much more simple by removing from the alphabet one of each of the interchangeable letters, and now hope to have uniformity of spelling.

AFTERMATH

Even after the orthography was settled, some of the missionaries found it necessary to justify the decision they had made. Answering a letter (23 October 1827) from Rufus Anderson in Boston, Richards addressed the problem again (20 May 1828, HMCS, letter 142):

> In my own mind, the question takes precisely this form. Shall we adopt an extremely intricate system of orthography[38] and one which is to natives inexplicable and in every respect arbitrary, with a hope and for the purpose of making the people apprehend distinctions in sound, which the most delicate ear among them is now unable to do?
>
> ... I say that with seventeen letters, the orthography is intricate. I mean, it would be very difficult indeed, if not quite impossible for common people to learn to write it uniformly, even though we should adopt a uniform system in all our books. More than half the words in the language contain one or more of the interchangeable letters and some words contain two, three or four, so that the interchangeables occur as often as once in every word.

Richards also discussed the interesting matter of the effect of the revised (and more limited) alphabet on pronunciation:

> Now I inquire to whose ear will the monotony of the language be increased, even allowing that the pronunciation is limited to 12 characters? Certainly not to native ears for the examples which I have given show that no native ears perceive any distinction in the sounds. There is no probability however that the pronunciation would ever be thus limited, although it might be less varied then it is now.[39]

He then suggested that John Pickering be consulted again, this time as a final authority: "The subject is one of immense importance, and I think we should have the advice of the best judges in relation to it."

Perhaps the best endorsement for the improved alphabet was its effectiveness. Richards stated it simply:

> But with our present alphabet a boy of fourteen, with common intelligence may in one month become a perfect master of the orthography of his language and be able to read and write the whole of it with correctness.

We shall see in chapter 9 that Richards's example was not an isolated one: the missionary correspondence contains repeated references to the excellence of the pared-down orthography and the speed with which the new scholars—young and old—learned to use it: the perfect testimonial for a writing system.

SUMMARY

The official Hawaiian alphabet has struck not only an intellectual but also an emotional chord for more than a century and a half since its adoption in 1826. People who are interested seem to fall into two groups. Those who understand the nature of an alphabet—that is, the arbitrary relationship between speech and writing—praise the missionaries' decision, hailing it as an insightful presage of the phonemic principle. Those without such an understanding condemn it, citing it as the cause of a number present ills. As an example of the latter opinion, consider the following excerpts from a letter that appeared in the University of Hawai'i student newspaper, *Ka Leo O Hawai'i,* 3 October 1990:

> ... In 1825 [*sic*], in Honolulu, a committee of seven self-appointed haole men decided through consultation by mail that the letters b, d, t, v, and r had no place in the alphabet they were constructing in order to make a written language of the indigenous speech of these islands, even though non-native informants had heard something like those sounds on the tongues of native speakers.
>
> King Liholiho, in fact, seeing his written name and having been instructed in the phonetics of the symbols, chose r rather then [*sic*] l as most approximate to its pronunciation. Nevertheless, the committee decided "for the sake of simplicity" to eliminate r and the other four sound values, and we live now with that diminished [ ].
>
> When I came to Hawaii sixteen years ago, I was told that the Hawaiian language had only seven consonants and five vowels, only twelve letters, the implication being that, compared to English with its twenty-six letter alphabet, Hawaiian is a simple language for simple-minded people.
>
> Surely we can connect the committee of 1825 and the subsequent banishment of a simplified, impoverished, trivialized Hawaiian language from the developing systems of instruction with the small number of students of Hawaiian ancestry on campus today.

This letter illustrates a complete naiveté about the most basic principle of a writing system: its arbitrariness. Moreover, it reflects a common lay assumption that a language should be written as it sounds to *us*. Thus, although one of the aims of the writer was to point out what she perceived as racial and sexual chauvinism on the part of the missionaries, the attempt backfired: what is revealed is the writer's *linguistic* chauvinism.   But more important, she simply ignored the implications of retaining the so-called alternate sounds—the resultant chaos.

But back to the accusations. Has Hawaiian actually been "simplified, impoverished, trivialized"?   If any of these processes have taken place, it is not because of the alphabet, but instead because of the importance that English has assumed over the years, the policies that discouraged the use of Hawaiian, the resultant moribund state of the language, and the generally poor quality of reference materials available. Had the use of Hawaiian continued normally, and had English not assumed such importance as a second, and then as the first, language, the choice of (for example) *l* to indicate a whole range of [l]-like and [ř]-like sounds would not have had so much effect in reducing the range of pronunciations.   As a matter of fact, in areas with minimal English contact (such as Ni'ihau), a tapped-*r* pronunciation is still heard. The survival of [t] as well on Ni'ihau shows that the choice of *k* for the official representation did not "diminish" the language in this respect either (note Goodrich's opinion, quoted above).   Finally, most speakers have retained a [v] pronunciation (albeit varying) in many words, in spite of the *w*-spelling.   Hence, it was not so much the alphabet itself that triggered any phonetic changes in the language as a variety of sociolinguistic factors.

The most important question to ask is this: did the missionaries have any choice other than to simplify the consonant confusion? The answer is obvious: no. Any other solution would have been unworkable— or, at the least, extremely inconvenient for readers and writers alike.

NOTES

"Fixing the letters" is a phrase often used in nineteenth-century accounts of the study of previously unwritten languages. The *Oxford English Dictionary* defines this sense of *fix* as "to settle or determine the form of, give a permanent form to (language or literature)."

[1] And perhaps 'Ōpūkaha'ia, although we have no way of knowing how consistent his orthography was.

[2] Campbell (1816:130–31) described Moxley as a "young American ... who understood the language" and acted as an interpreter (see chapter 3).

[3] The birth of the Mission to Hawai'i could be linked with any of various other events as well. As mentioned in chapter 1, Thomas Haweis, founder of the London Missionary Society, proposed a mission to the Sandwich Islands as early as 1795. *The Panoplist and Missionary Magazine United* (later *The*

Missionary Herald) for the year ending 1 June 1809 (p. 236) reported a "pleasing account" of the prosperity of the Sandwich Islands. The long residence of Isaac Davies [Davis] and John Young was mentioned, saying that they had "for some time the principal direction of [the king's] affairs." The king's army, vessels, and store of $12,000 were mentioned admiringly. "How happy should we be to add, they have also the privilege of hearing and knowing the joyful sound of the gospel!"

These mere suggestions were considerably strengthened by ʻŌpūkahaʻia's arrival at the doorsteps of Yale University, his conversion to Christianity, the founding of the Foreign Mission School in Cornwall, the ordination of the Reverend Messrs. Hiram Bingham and Asa Thurston on 29 September 1819 at the Goshen (CT) church, the formation of the Hawaiian Mission at the Park Street Church, Boston, on 15 October 1819, leading to the arrival of the *Thaddeus* at Hawaiʻi on 30 March 1820.

[4] The other Americans were: Asa and Lucy Goodale Thurston, Dr. Thomas Holman and Lucia Ruggles Holman, Samuel and Mercy Partridge Whitney, Samuel and Nancy Wells Ruggles, Daniel and Jerusha Burnap Chamberlain, and the Chamberlains' five children.

[5] Even after they were in Hawaiʻi, the missionaries continued their association with Gallaudet, translating three of his works into Hawaiian. See items 189, 200, and 238 in Judd, Bell, and Murdoch 1978.

[6] *Lāhainā* is an older version of this place name (Pukui and Elbert 1966:16).

[7] Reliance on the Roman alphabet was—and continues to be—at the root of the problem: English must use five vowel letters ("and sometimes *y*") to represent a much larger number of vowel contrasts.

[8] This figure breaks down to eighteen consonants and five vowels, the former including *b, d, r*, and others eventually pruned from the alphabet.

[9] As we shall see later, the mission already had a copy of the Tahitian speller. Perhaps they sought further examples of the Tahitian writing system.

[10] Duponceau was not the first to wish for such a system. Pickering (1820) quoted Sir William Jones, in *Dissertation on the Orthography of Asiatick Words*, 1788: "... every man, who has occasion to compose tracts on Asiatick literature, or to translate from the Asiatick languages, must always find it convenient and sometimes necessary, to express *Arabian, Indian*, and *Persian* words or sentences, in the characters generally used among *Europeans*; and almost every writer in those circumstances has a method of notation peculiar to himself: But none has yet appeared in the form of a complete system, so that each original sound may be rendered invariably by one appropriate symbol, conformably to the natural order of articulation, and with a due regard to the primitive power of the *Roman* alphabet, which modern Europe has in general adopted."

[11] Bingham (1847:155) wrote: "... the basis of [Pickering's] alphabet, in respect to vowel sounds, is followed." It is not clear whether the advice from Pickering was direct (which it could have been, since Pickering was from Boston), or whether it came about simply through his book. Since Bingham's reference also mentioned American Indian languages, it would appear that the latter was the source.

[12] Chamberlain may have been referring to the first imprint of the London Missionary Society in Tahiti: *Te Aebi no Tahiti*, a spelling book prepared by John Davies and printed in England. Other possibilities are a spelling book printed in Sydney in 1815: *Te Abi no Tahiti*, or one (with no title) printed in Tahiti in 1817. The copy in Hawai'i could have been any of these.

[13] For example, Ellis wrote to Jeremiah Evarts, 10 March 1823: "The analogy between the Hawaiian and Tahitian language was such as to enable me after a very short residence to preach I trust intelligably [*sic*] to the people whose attention was pleasing and encouraging."

[14] However, Davies's manuscript suffered a fate similar to that of William Anderson's: the editors, unfamiliar with the Tahitian system, neutralized the contrast between *e* and ε, thus producing what they called a "somewhat confused vocabulary" (Schütz 1980).

[15] Wise and Hervey (1952:313) enthusiastically credited the Māori grammar with helping the Hawaiian spelling "take a sudden and radical change for the better." However, they were apparently not aware of the Hawaiian mission's familiarity with the Tahitian system, which served as a foundation for all other Polynesian orthographies that followed.

[16] The bibliographic details for the following account come from Judd, Bell, and Murdoch 1978.

[17] At least this is our assumption. Writers of early accounts sometimes mentioned words associated with a particular island. Later in the present chapter, it can be seen that certain features of pronunciation were geographically distributed. But this variation does not seem extreme. Still, there is a dearth of information available on the topic, although Abraham Fornander (1878–1885) listed some variants (John Charlot, pers. comm., September 1993).

[18] The qualifying adverb is used in this statement because of the occasional *b* and *d* that reflect the way speakers of English heard (relatively) unaspirated /p/ and /t/.

[19] This sounds condescending, but it is a natural reaction. To change the linguistic roles, an analogy would be for a speaker of Arabic to ask whether a speaker of English had pronounced a fronted or backed *k* sound in a particular word—consonants that sound the same to the English speaker, but different to the Arabic speaker.

[20] A later writer looked on some pronunciations as old-fashioned, others as modern (Donne 1866:86):

Perhaps you wonder why we say Tauai or Kauai. The reason is this: the two letters t and k are allowed to be changed for one another in the Hawaiian language. The same word is sometimes spelt with a t, and sometimes with a k; for instance, there have been five kings of the Sandwich Islands called Kamehameha; the second always wrote his name Tamehameha, the present king writes Kamehameha. I believe that, as a general rule, t is considered an old-fashioned letter in the Sandwich Islands, and k is looked upon as the modern one that has taken its place, except that the t is still used in poetry. In the same way, but more strangely, the letters l and r are interchangeable in Hawaiian; r belonging to the old fashion, and l to the new; thus, the name of the capital of the Sandwich Islands used to be written Honoruru, but is now Honolulu.

[21] This terminology is still used. For example, see Elbert and Pukui 1979: 12: "The consonants *w* and *v* are variants (or alternates) of the same sound."

[22] As for the so-called alternation between *p* and *b*, the discussion in chapter 5 showed that this was more a matter of perception than of production.

[23] Stevenson was no doubt influenced by his long contact with Samoan, in which the choice between *t* and *k* is determined by the social context.

[24] It is difficult to know how to evaluate this proposal, since neither writer was a professional linguist, and we are given no data to support such a conclusion. Hockett (1958:97–98) described the Hawaiian stop system as follows (incidentally classifying the glottal stop as a "catch" and therefore putting it in a different category): "Hawaiian has bilabial /p/ and lingual /k/, the latter freely apical or dorsal." Note that this description still puts /k/ into two, and only two, slots. (So far as I know, this classification was based solely on written descriptions.)

[25] See the discussion of Beaglehole's treatment of the question in chapter 4.

[26] In discussing chanting, Helen H. Roberts (1926:72-73) noted that "a *t* or its softer substitute [apparently a [θ]- or [z]-like sound] is generally employed on Oahu and Hawaii as well [as Ni'ihau and Kaua'i]. If there is anything in the theory that songs and rituals tend to preserve archaic forms of language ... this use of a *t* sound in chanting ... would indicate that the sound was once common to the people of all the islands, possibly in an earlier home."

[27] Anderson's own production of English *r* was likely to have been an alveolar tap, quite unlike the more vowel-like, retroflex *r* from some other parts of Britain that seem to have developed into the present American English *r*. Whatever the exact phonetic nature of Hawaiian *r/l* at that time, it obviously sounded more like *r* than *l* to Anderson.

[28] Spanish has a contrast between these two types of *rs*—the former, as in *pero* 'but', written with a single *r*, and the latter, as in *perro* 'dog', written with double *r*.

[29] It is difficult to understand just what was meant by this statement, especially the phrase "more common *l*."

[30] Hale was not very explicit in telling how he obtained his Hawaiian data, other than mentioning Andrews's vocabulary (1836a) and his article "Peculiarities of the Hawaiian Language" (1838). As for his view of phonology, he approached it from a comparative point of view, so he was speaking of a proto *v*—that is, the "ancestral" sound that developed into the various reflexes that the present-day languages have.

[31] I can find no evidence that German [v] (which is written as *w*) is any more fortis ("strong") than English [v]. For example: "There is no significant difference in the production of [v] in English and German ..." (Hans-Heinrich-Wängler, *Instruction in German Pronunciation*, 3d, ed., St. Paul: EMC Corporation, p. 102). Thus, why were not English speakers' attempts similarly ridiculed? A possible answer is that Berger may have pronounced *all* instances of written *w* as [v], even the unnecessary *w* once written in such words as *'owau* 'I' or *auwē* 'alas' (now *'oau* and *auē*), never pronounced as [v] by native speakers.

[32] John Charlot (pers. comm., September 1993) pointed out that many Roman Catholic writers used *t* and *v* regularly.

[33] This formula is incorrect; the number is not exponential but linear—the product of the number of choices at each position. Thus, for *Kaawaloa* (*Ka'awaloa*), the formula is 2 x 2 x 3 = 12. (The writers apparently didn't take the *d* variant of /l/ into account.) Likewise, the explanation of the *lilo* example below is wrong; 3 x 3 = 9 variants are possible.

[34] Not to Samuel Marsden, guiding light of the Māori mission, who suggested that the Māori change their pronunciation and pronounce the vowels as speakers of English did.

[35] Some writers, working with secondary sources, have mistakenly given 1825 as the official date. John E. Reinecke's error (1969:28), can be traced to his misreading of a letter by Loomis, written on 27 July 1826 and quoted in Ballou and Carter (1908), in which Loomis referred to the resolution "about a year since" to vote on the selection of consonants. However, Loomis was not referring to the vote itself. Samuel H. Elbert, in his short history of Hawaiian dictionaries (1954:5), stated twice that the official orthography was established in 1829.

[36] Did Bingham abstain out of deference to his position as head of the Mission? In his discussion of the orthography in Bingham 1847, he did not mention the matter.

[37] For example, Reinecke 1969, Wist 1940, Wise and Hervey 1952, Elbert 1954, and Hervey 1968. Reinecke (p. 27) seemed to think that Ellis influenced

the final form of the Hawaiian orthography.   However, the evidence contradicts such an assumption. First, the main outlines of the orthography (illustrated in the first printing in January 1822) had already been set before Ellis arrived.   After that time, the only major change to the system was the elimination of the unnecessary consonant variants, a move that Ellis firmly opposed. Wist (p. 21) mentioned the progress made after the arrival of Ellis and his Tahitian helpers, making it appear as though the official alphabet of five vowels and seven consonants was the direct result of Ellis's presence. (He also wrote, incorrectly, that "this alphabet was the one already proposed by John Pickering in his essay on a *Uniform Orthography for the Indian Languages of North America*.")   Elbert seems to have based his opinions on Wise and Hervey's mistaken assessment of Ellis's contributions and overlooked, as they did, the revealing quotation about his insistence on keeping all the consonants in the alphabet. First he referred to Ellis as an intellectual giant, and then proposed that "he undoubtedly played a part in the ensuing controversy over the consonants." Next, he praised the missionaries' decision to eliminate the unnecessary consonants, little realizing that had Ellis had his way, Hawaiian would still be written with *b*, *d*, *r*, *t*, and *v*.

[38] John Charlot (pers. comm., September 1993) noted that one missionary letter suggested that there were over sixty distinct sounds in Hawaiian, but that to represent them all would result in an unusable system.

[39] An interesting position, this. One wonders if Richards's opinion would have been any different if he could have foretold the near demise of the Hawaiian language and the extent to which English took its place.

CHAPTER EIGHT

The Missing Elements: Problems with Glottal Stops and Long Vowels

-0-0-0-0-0-

Stranger still, that prevalent Polynesian sound, the so-called catch, written with an apostrophe, and often or always the gravestone of a perished consonant (R. L. Stevenson, In the South Seas *[1891:12]).*

Now that the vowels were written in the European fashion, and the list of consonants was trimmed of its excess fat, the Hawaiian alphabet moved closer to the principle of "one letter per sound (i.e., phoneme), one sound per letter" that characterizes an ideal writing system. But there still remained two subtle problems to be solved: the delayed recognition of long vowels and glottal stops, and the lack of proper symbols with which to represent them.

THE MISSING MACRON

Although the English grammatical tradition still speaks of "long" and "short" vowels, those labels are more appropriate for the English of a thousand years ago than for the variety spoken today. What the terms mean now is the difference between, say, the different sounds represented by the letter *a* in the words *fate* and *fat*—sounds that differ primarily in quality.

Vowel length in Hawaiian, on the other hand, is quite another matter, for the main difference between long and short vowels is quantity. The importance of this difference, however, was, if not totally ignored, at least misunderstood for well over a century. At first glance, this state of affairs presents a puzzle, for the framers of the orthography were familiar with another language tradition in which vowel length was equally important: Latin.

The Latin Precedent

One reason to suppose that the missionaries were familiar with the concept of a contrast between long and short vowels is that most of them had received, as part of their normal education, some training in Latin. The writers of modern textbooks for Latin, and teachers of the language as well, agree that vowel length was important, especially for verse. For example, when poetry was read aloud, all long syllables were accented. Theoretically, they were also to be pronounced twice as long as short syllables. As my own high-school Latin textbook explained it (Ullman and Henry 1941:383):

> Each of the Latin vowels may be pronounced long or short, the difference being one of *time*. This is called *quantity*. In addition, all the long vowels except *a* have a different *sound* from the short vowels. This is called *quality*.

This approach, however, masks the most significant aspect of vowel length in Latin—that it is CONTRASTIVE. The paragraph that follows makes implicit reference to this quality:

> It is very important to distinguish the *sounds* of the long and short vowels. For a person to say, *I heard the din in the hall*, when he meant the 'dean,' or *I forgot the debt*, when he meant the 'date,' is no worse than to confuse ĭ and ī, ĕ and ē in Latin.

An earlier text used a minimal pair (that is, two words differing in only one feature) to explain how important long vowels were in Latin (Magoffin and Henry 1928:17): "A Roman had to pronounce **māla**, **maala**, because if he said **mala**, he would have been talking about *evils*, not *apples*."

In Latin textbooks written around the turn of the twentieth century, long vowels were sometimes marked by a macron, sometimes by an acute accent, and sometimes by both (Miriam E. Sinclair and Robert J. Ball, pers. comm., March 1988). But earlier, it was more common to mark vowel length only when discussing meter.[1] This is the system used in the one Latin grammar I have at hand that might represent the knowledge and practices of the Hawaiian missionaries—Richard Lyne's *Latin Primer* (1817).

Thus, the earlier practice of marking vowel length in Latin only for prosodic purposes suggests that if the missionaries did indeed hear it, perhaps they followed the Latin precedent. The following quotation (Bingham 1847:153) strengthens the idea that in Hawaiian, vowel length was perceived, but not considered important enough to mark in the writing system.

> The slight variation in quantity, though not in quality, of sound in the vowels requires no mark of distinction, any more than in the variation of the sound of *a* in the English words *art* and *father*. Here the quantity may differ slightly though it is not necessary to put a distinctive mark, or make a different character[.]

However, this solution to the puzzle turns out to be an oversimplification for Hawaiian. Although vowel length was missed in most positions in the word, in a few places it was distinctly heard and commented on. These were positions in which it also produced a difference in *accent patterns*.

The Problem with Accent

At the time the missionaries were first studying Hawaiian, the goal of what was called phonology was to produce an efficient alphabet. Thus, most discussion was confined to consonants and vowels—that is, sounds that could be represented by letters of the alphabet. In this matter, those who studied languages were, in a sense, hindered by the writing systems as much as they were helped.

From the very beginning, long vowels were misunderstood because of their relationship to accent.[2] The problem is that this relationship is lopsided: although all long vowels are accented, not all accented vowels are long. Of the material I have examined so far, Ruggles's (1819) is the first that contains an explicit statement about a vowel-length contrast, but it is confused with accent. In Hawaiian, there are a few words, mostly kinship terms or other words referring to humans, that form plurals by lengthening the vowel in the third-to-last syllable. An example is *kanaka* 'person' (with an accent on the second-to-last vowel); *kā naka* 'persons' (with an additional accent on the long vowel). Ruggles was obviously aware of the difference, but he described it not as a difference in vowel length, but one of "a different accent or pronunciation," writing the words as *kanáka* and *kánaka*.[3]

Lorrin Andrews (1854:19–20) wrote that the "general law" for accent placement was that it should be on the second-to-last syllable, but he added that it was a law with many exceptions. To show these exceptions, he analyzed 117 words of more than one syllable, finding words accented not only on the second-to-last syllable, but also the last and the third to last. The *kanaka-kānaka* example above shows how he ignored vowel length in his reckoning of accent: he too wrote the words as *ka-nà-ka* versus *kà-na-ka*.[4]

Related to this asymmetrical relationship with accent is our different perception of vowel length, depending on its position in the word. If it occurs in a syllable that is not otherwise accented, it is more noticeable to the listener. For example, Andrews wrote *akā* 'but' as *a-kà*, for the accent on the long final vowel makes the word stand out from most other two-syllable words. On the other hand, if a long vowel occurs in a syllable that *is* normally accented (i.e., the second to last), the contrast seems more difficult to hear. For example, even as late as 1945 (Judd, Pukui, and Stokes), forms like *'aina* 'meal' and *'āina* 'land' were treated as homonyms.

Even the most obvious of the accentual "misfits" seem to have been ignored by the collectors of the earliest word lists. At first glance, Lisiansky's (1814) and Arago's (1823) lists look promising, for they abound in acute accent marks—at least on the vowel *e*. On closer examination, however, it turns out that in almost all the examples, the pattern follows normal French orthography—that is, using *-é* to represent a real sound (as opposed to *-e*, which has more subtle functions). A device that Campbell's editor used (1816) (but only twice) was to write a long final syllable as a separate word, as in *Muka pa* (*makapō*) 'blind'. Another method he used, but inconsistently, was to write a final /-ā/ as *aa*, as in *ahaa* (*'e hā*) 'four', contrasting with the following word *areema* (*'e lima*), which ends in a short vowel.

Only a few years later, Ellis (1826) also treated vowel length as accent, and with as limited a number of examples. At the end of a grammatical sketch in the appendix, we find the word for 'star' written as *hokú*. Actually, the form is *hōkū*, with two long vowels, but it is the second accented syllable that makes the word stand out from other disyllables, particularly a word like *Hóku* (so accented) 'night of the full moon'.[5] In 1848, a word with an identical prosodic pattern, *pā'ū* 'skirt', was similarly marked—but this time with a macron on the final syllable: *pa'ū*.[6] So far, this is the earliest example I have found of a macron used apparently to mark a long vowel. But note again that the writer missed the long vowel on the first syllable, and marked the second probably only because the word was so obviously different in accent from the similarly spelled *pau* 'finished' and *pa'u* 'smudge'.

Thus, it seems clear that during this period, vowel length was still treated as accent, if we can read between the lines of the following quotation (Andrews 1838:396):

> From the fewness of the letters and syllables in the language, it is plain that many words of the same letters must have different significations. This is remedied in the Hawaiian, as in some degree in other languages, by different tones, accents, etc., exhibited in pronunciation, and some of the tones and accents are exceedingly difficult for an adult foreigner ever to catch.[7]

To be more explicit, it appears that long vowels were noticed only when they distorted the "normal" accent pattern, and even then were considered as variations in "tones and accents"—difficult for the outsider, perhaps, but not to the native speakers and readers of Hawaiian, who could rely on context to determine which word was being used.

The Māori Model.

For a number of reasons, it seems strange that the publications of the Mission Press—especially those written to help people learn Hawaiian—did not include diacritical marks to delineate more finely those "tones and accents" they found so difficult. Perhaps the strongest reason they should have done so is precedent: English pronouncing dictionaries and Webster's speller used superscript numbers to aid in discriminating among different sounds represented by the same vowel letters. As for the material available for other Polynesian languages, all of William Anderson's word lists except that for Hawaiian made use of his system of diacritics, and Martin and Mariner's Tongan grammar and dictionary (1817) used acute accents and diaereses to add detail to its use of the vowel letters.

However, the Polynesian linguistic study that was most likely to have influenced the Hawaiian Mission was the Māori grammar and dictionary (Kendall and Lee 1820) mentioned in chapter 7. In this work, the authors used acute accents freely (if sporadically) to indicate vowel length. This work is especially important, for the presentation, clearly set out on the first page and reproduced here as table 8.1, refers not to accent, but to vowel length.

TABLE 8.1

MāORI VOWELS AS EXPLAINED BY KENDALL AND LEE

Vowels				Sound
Long	Short			
Á	á	A	a	as in *father*, and as in *pad*.[8]
É	é	E	e	as *a* in *bate*, and as *e* in *bet*.
Í	í	I	i	as *ee* in *feet*, and as *i* in *fit*.
Ó	ó	O	o	as *o* in *pole*, and the same sound shortened
Ú	ú	U	u	as *oo* in *boot*, and as *oo* in *good*.

Unfortunately, this concise and accurate analysis was better in theory than in practice, for Kendall and Lee also confused vowel length with accent. Immediately following the pronunciation exercises are words that would have been quite familiar to the Hawaiian missionaries, such as *mánu* 'bird', *máta* 'face', *díma* 'five', and *íka* 'fish' (1820:8, 9)—all written with the penultimate syllable accented (and hence, "long"). Not until page 12 does one find an actual long vowel so marked: *pá* (*pā*, form of address to male elder).

Even before the Māori grammar arrived in Hawai'i, at least some of the missionaries were using their own system of diacritics for the vowel sounds. For example, in his transcription of Hawaiian words, Hiram Bingham (1821) used macrons, breves, and acute accents.

From all these different sources, then, one can assume that Bingham, Loomis, and their associates were accustomed to using diacritics in their linguistic work to add some kind of phonetic finesse to the rough sketch of the orthography, even if they did not distinguish vowel length from accent. Why, then, did they not incorporate accented vowels into their system, at least for the material designed to explain Hawaiian to outsiders? The reason appears to be a very practical one: the missionaries' requests to the ABCFM in Boston for special type were never honored.

Shortage of Type

Even in the earliest correspondence from the Hawaiian Mission, one can find evidence that the missionaries were aware of a need for special type. For example, Loomis wrote to the mission headquarters on 1 February 1822, just after he had printed the first spelling book (Missionary letters): "We feel it necessary to ask for some additional type, a quantity of Small Pica *accented letters*." Later that same year, he requested special type again, adding (Bingham, Thurston, and Loomis, 12 October 1822. Missionary letters, p. 22): "Within 2 years we hope to print a grammar & vocabulary & shall need accented vowels."

To this end, Bingham and Loomis included a postscript to their letter to the ABCFM on 23 October 1823, a separate page showing different quantities of normal and special type needed. As table 8.2 shows, five kinds of diacritics for vowels were requested: macron, breve, circumflex, acute accent, and grave accent.

At least once the board complied with the request for special type—but sent the wrong size. On 31 December 1823, Loomis wrote (Ballou and Carter 1908:14):

> I am sorry to inform you that the type which you forwarded to us by the Octavia are of no service, they being of a size much larger than those which we had had here before. The font of types which we have here is what is called small pica, and it was for small pica accents (accented vowels) that we wrote. The accented

vowels were received by the Octavia but they are of the size called pica and of course much to large to be used with small pica ...

In consequence of this mistake we are under the necessity of printing our books without any characters to denote the different sounds of the vowels, a proper distinction of which is very desirable.

TABLE 8.2

TYPE REQUESTED BY BINGHAM AND LOOMIS

a	7,300	e	3,000	i	3,450	o	4,440	u	3,180
b	900	d	600	h	1,930	k	2,040	l	1,020
m	2,070	n	1,600	p	1,050	r	1,000	t	630
v	700	w	900	c	600	f	600	g	600
s	660	x	130	y	600	z	600	_	50

ROMAN LOWER CASE LETTERS

ā	210	ē	150	ī	150	ō	150	ū	150
ă	210	ĕ	150	ĭ	150	ŏ	150	ŭ	100
â	120	ê	60	î	60	ô	60	û	60
à	120	è	60	ì	60	ò	60	ù	60
á	120	é	60	í	60	ó	60	ú	60

ACCENTED LETTERS

Nor, it seems, was the problem of a type shortage ever solved—at least not in the nineteenth century. As late as 1845, with the publication of Emerson and Bishop's English-Hawaiian dictionary, there was still a lack of special type. In the preface to this work, Emerson wrote (p. iii): "But a still greater difficulty under which we have labored is the entire want of all points and marks for distinguishing the vowel sounds and the accents."

So, for want of the proper typeface, a convention was lost. It is difficult to say what might have happened had long vowels been correctly marked in the early grammars and dictionaries. The accent marks in Kendall and Lee's grammar certainly had no effect on Māori orthography, but then, grammars at that time were generally read and used by nonnative speakers.[9] The principal readers for the material produced by the missionaries in Hawai'i were the Hawaiians themselves, and at that time, they had no need to be shown where the long vowels (or glottal stops) were, except perhaps in new words introduced, especially biblical terms. This philosophy was summarized by Andrews (1854: 21):

As the Hawaiian books have been printed almost entirely for the use of Hawaiians, it has not been thought necessary to use any marks for accents, but if they should be used by those who wish to acquire the language, it would be very convenient for such to have certain classes of words accented.

Not until Parker's revision (1922) of Andrews's dictionary (1865) was any attempt made to use diacritical marks to indicate pronunciation, and that attempt failed (see chapter 11). As for the description of accent, in at least three editions of Pukui and Elbert's Hawaiian dictionary it was incorrectly stated that five-syllable words were accented on the first and fourth syllables, an assumption immediately disproved by the words (for example) *makùahíne* 'mother' and *Kalìkimáka* 'Christmas'.[10] Not until the 1986 edition was the statement corrected and a system introduced to show the accent(s) in each entry (Schütz 1986:xvii–xviii).

In summary, there were a number of reasons that vowel length was not incorporated into the writing system. The most important of these was that it was confused with accent, and thus (perhaps unconsciously) compared to English, in which accent is not marked. This confusion also obscured the parallels between Hawaiian and Latin long vowels. Besides, the convention of writing Latin at the time reserved diacritics for the discussion of poetic meter.[11] Next, it was felt that although those who wanted to learn the language would benefit from such aids to pronunciation, native speakers and readers of Hawaiian needed no such help. Finally, the wish to include pronunciation guides in grammars and dictionaries was thwarted by a lack of the proper type.

AND ONE CONSONANT TOO FEW

A glottal stop is a sound made in the same way a [p] or a [t] is, but instead of the lips or tongue serving as an articulator, the vocal cords do so. One can hear this sound between the vowels in the expression *Oh-oh*, or in the way many speakers of American English pronounce what is written as *tt* in *button*.[12] In some dialects of English, both American and British, it corresponds to *t* in many other positions as well. However, most speakers of English, unless trained in phonetics, do not think of this sound as a separate consonant, but simply use it as a kind of *t*, or as a transition from silence to a word that otherwise begins with a vowel. At any rate, the glottal stop does not function in English as a member of the sound system, except as a variant of another consonant. In Hawaiian, however, it has a quite different status, for here it is just as much a consonant phoneme as /p/ or /k/, serving to keep apart such words as *kau* 'your' and *ka'u* 'my', or *awa* 'passage' and *'awa* 'kava'.

Because of the way the glottal stop functions in English, it was quite natural that the early analysts did not recognize it as a consonant in Hawaiian. To them, the sound had all the stability of quicksilver. Even nearly a century later, this attitude had not changed. In addition to Stevenson's colorful metaphor that heads this chapter, a number of strange characterizations of the sound are scattered through the literature of Pacific linguistics. For example, William Churchill (1912:13) referred to the glottal stop as "an audible hole in the word." As late as 1929, the editors of *The Journal of the Polynesian Society* (38:83n) argued: "The glottal stop is not a recognized consonant. As observed, it is a catch or break in the voice."[13] Finally, in his *Rotuman Grammar and Dictionary* (1940:64), C. Maxwell Churchward referred to it as a "feeble consonantal sound."

Bingham and his associates were not the first to find it difficult to accept the glottal stop as a consonant. It is ironic that the very word *alphabet* is the result of the inability of the speakers of Greek to hear the glottal stop in another language. *'Elif* (or *'alif*), the first letter of the Arabic alphabet, generally refers to a glottal stop, but is also the sign of a long *ā*. The Greeks didn't hear the glottal stop and borrowed the word as the name of their first letter: *alpha* (Anatole Lyovin, pers. comm., October 1988). Moreover, paralleling somewhat the marking of the long vowels in Latin, writing the glottal stop in Arabic was a complicated matter. So even had the missionaries been familiar with Arabic, they might not have realized that the sound should be written. However, because of their training, they undoubtedly knew Hebrew, in which the first letter of the alphabet—*aleph*—is a glottal stop.[14] (Interestingly, the fact that this letter is not written in transliterations when the sound occurs at the beginning of a word may have affected the Hawaiian missionaries' inability to recognize the sound in Hawaiian words in that position.)

Because journalists, signpost designers, some scholarly publishers, and even some conservative speakers of Hawaiian have been reluctant to write the glottal stop in Hawaiian words or names until fairly recently, and because not only *malihini* but also many *kama'āina* seem unable to pronounce the sound properly, one might think that it was simply not noticed. Perhaps at first this actually was the case. There is nothing in Anderson's or Ruggles's transcription of Hawaiian words that hints at the presence of such a consonant.[15] Nor would John Pickering have been likely to help, either through correspondence or in his 1820 work on orthography: although he expanded the range of consonants to include such non-English sounds as [x] (as in German *ach*), he did not include in his repertoire of consonants a glottal stop or anything like one.

However, although I have not yet found a discussion of the question in the missionary correspondence, a very practical matter brought the problem at least close to the surface: certain words, written identically, could have very different meanings, resulting in serious misunderstandings. For example, if the Hawaiians read this line in the Lord's Prayer: *nou ke aupuni* 'thine is the kingdom', *nou* could be either /nou/ or /noʻu/, that is, 'thine' or 'mine'. Such ambiguity could have had an interesting effect on doctrinal understanding.

Because of this set of possessive pronouns, careful writers were using an apostrophe to mark the glottal stop in important pairs of words as early as 1823. For example, Sybil M. Bingham, teacher and missionary wife, wrote what is probably the first Hawaiian phrase book: *Select Hawaiian Phrases / Sentences Rehearsed at Table*. In this work, such words as *koʻu* 'my' versus *kou* 'your', which can appear in exactly the same context, were distinguished.[16]

This convention of marking obviously significant glottal stops was reflected in print only three years after Bingham's manuscript phrase book. In the description of Hawaiian that introduces his popular journal, William Ellis added to his summary of the orthography a passage suggesting that he was vaguely aware of the distinctive function of the glottal stop (1826:21):

> In the English language, two letters, called double vowels, are used to lengthen the same sound, as ee in thee, or to express one totally different, as oo in pool; but in Hawaiian there is often a repetition of the vowel sound, without any intervening consonant, or other vowel sound, as in a-a (*ʻaʻa*), a bag or pocket, e-e (*eʻe*), to embark, i-i (*ʻiʻi*), a name of a bird, o-o (*ʻōʻō*), an agricultural instrument; which must be sounded as two distinct syllables.[17]

Note that the troublesome phrase—the validity of which was still being debated a century later—was "without any intervening consonant."

This passage remained unchanged through various later editions. However, in the appendix of the same edition, Ellis was rather more specific, taking his description one step further than simply a "repetition of the vowel," suggesting that the vague awareness of the sound had actually gained form. Almost hidden in his analysis of pronouns are certain words (e.g., the possessives *naʻu, noʻu, kaʻu, koʻu, aʻu, oʻu*) that are written with an apostrophe to indicate the glottal stop. The convention is explained as follows:[18]

> A peculiar break in the first person singular possessive, which makes the pronouns resemble two syllables, while in the second person they are sounded as one long syllable, is the only distinction between them.

Ellis did not go so far as to reverse his previous opinion by suggesting that this "peculiar break" was a consonant. But the fact that this sound was the "only distinction" (foreshadowing the concept of minimal pair) between some very common forms is the reason that it was marked in such words.

By the time the Bible was translated, marking these few pairs was a regular practice. For example, we can still find such words as *kou* and *ko'u* so distinguished in the Hawaiian Bible: the copy I have at hand (printed by the American Bible Society in 1960) has *Ma ka hale o ko'u Makua* for 'In my father's house'.

Still, even though the glottal stop was written in some positions, there is evidence to show that it was considered merely a prosodic feature. For example, writers sometimes suggested implicitly that it was a way to show that two vowels were separate, and not joined together as diphthongs. Lorrin Andrews (1838:394) gave such pairs as *ai* (*'ai*) 'food' and *ai* (*'ā'ī*) 'neck', explaining that the difference between them was that the first was a diphthong, and the second was two "distinct syllables." Later (p. 396), while enlarging on this theme, Andrews gave at least a semiphonetic name to this syllable divider:

> As might be expected, where the letters are so few, and their combination into words so regular, the language, to foreigners, is very monotonous. The guttural[19] sounds are frequent, for many vowels come together which do not form diphthongs.

Thus, apparently the only function Andrews admitted for the "guttural sound" was that it kept two vowels from forming a diphthong. Bingham (1847:152) described the phenomenon in a somewhat different way, but still avoided the word "consonant": "There are, on the other hand, abrupt separations or short and sudden breaks between two vowels in the same word."

The convention of marking the glottal stop in only a few words was followed in some later grammars and dictionaries (e.g., Andrews 1838, 1854). William D. Alexander's grammar was a turning point (1864:5):

> Besides the sounds mentioned above, there is in many words a guttural break or catching of the breath, sometimes at the beginning, but more often in the middle of a word. This guttural is properly a consonant and forms an *essential* part of the words in which it is found. It almost invariably takes the place of the Polynesian *k*. Thus the Polynesian *ika*, fish, becomes *i'a* in Hawaiian. This guttural consonant is represented by an apostrophe, in a few

common words, to distinguish their meaning, as *ko'u*, my, *kou*, thy.

The source for this breakthrough was Pierre Gaussin's work on Tahitian, Marquesan, and Polynesian in general (1853),[20] acknowledged by Alexander in his preface. In his work (pp. 19, 21), Gaussin showed clearly how Polynesian *k* was "suppressed" in Hawaiian, "remplacé ... par l'explosive pharyngienne": Tongan *ika*, Hawaiian *iá* 'fish' (Gaussin, like other French writers, indicated the glottal stop by writing the following vowel as accented, thus making efficient use of French type fonts).[21] What is even more interesting about these observations is that, unlike many English-speaking analysts of Hawaiian, Gaussin accurately perceived glottal stops at the beginnings of words: he wrote (p. 30) *ópu* (*'ōpū*) 'belly' and *úla* ('ula) 'red'. Why this difference in perception? If a French word begins with a vowel, the onset is fairly smooth. In contrast, an English word beginning with a vowel has a strong glottal onset. Thus, for English speakers, a glottal onset is part of the package, so to speak, and hard to recognize as a separate entity. For example, it could only have been this English-based phonetic barrier that kept William D. Alexander's father, William P., from noticing the clearly laid out correspondences between Marquesan and Hawaiian in a substantial list of cognates between the two languages: all nineteen words beginning with *k-* in Marquesan actually begin with a glottal stop in Hawaiian. However, Alexander prefaced the list as follows (1838:19): "The Marquesan prefixes *k* to words which the Hawaiian begins with a vowel, or inserts *k* where the Hawaiian has a guttural break."

But interpretation, as well as perception, was a problem. Alexander's contribution was to expand the notion of a "suppressed" sound to that of a full-fledged consonant. But in spite of this advance, a cavalier attitude toward the sound continued well into the twentieth century (e.g., Judd 1939). Somewhat earlier, the guide to pronunciation in the Andrews-Parker dictionary (1922:xix) described the accepted orthographic convention:

> The glottal closure (') indicates an interruption of a sound that prevents two vowels from coalescing ... According to current usage the first person singular pronoun and its possessive (a'u, o'u, ka'u, ko'u, na'u, no'u, and io'u) always retain the glottal closure in writing and printing.

Note that the definition of the "glottal closure" does not suggest that it is a consonant. Nor is it listed among the letters of the alphabet. Consistent with this philosophy, all words except the pronouns in the quotation above are spelled without the glottal stop, the only indication of which is given in a respelled form in parentheses after the headword. Here, glottal stops are written, but not consistently.[22]

Perhaps the first recognition of the Hawaiian glottal stop as a real consonant (and not merely the echo or trace of one) is from the Judd, Pukui, and Stokes dictionary (1945). In it, the authors noted (pp. 8-9):

> The glottal closure, known to the early Hawaiians as **'u'ina**, we recognize as a consonant and include in the alphabet. It is represented by an inverted comma ... It represents the Polynesian (not the Hawaiian) "K," attenuated until almost complete elided. Not only by the Hawaiians was this Polynesian "K" so treated, but also by the Samoans and Tahitians, while it was retained in full volume by the other Polynesians in New Zealand, Tonga, Cook, Marquesas, Tuamotu and Easter Islands."

According to Charles McEwen Hyde (1888), another early Hawaiian term for the glottal stop was (in his spelling) *kaii*, possibly *kai'ī*, the closest form in either Andrews's or Pukui and Elbert's dictionary. Among several meanings, the sense of 'hard, rigid' is the only one remotely connected to 'glottal stop', and even here we must engage in semantic gymnastics to find a relationship. Another possibility is *ka'i 'ī* , meaning roughly 'leading into speech'.[23]

Even *'u'ina* has been replaced by a new term, *'okina*, lit., 'cutting'. Apparently Samuel H. Elbert (1991:100) considered *'u'ina,* which refers to a crackling noise, or that of thunder or guns, inappropriate and saw fit to introduce a replacement.

Moreover, the symbol itself has changed over the years. As noted above, a normal apostrophe was first used for the sporadic marking of the glottal stop. However, as the quotation from Judd, Pukui, and Stokes (1945) shows, the current symbol is a reversed apostrophe. Elbert and Pukui (1979:11) wrote that it made its first appearance in the 1945 work, but as noted above, Parker used it in his revision of the Andrews dictionary in 1922. However, there is an important difference in the way it was used: Parker included the symbol as a diacritical mark to indicate pronunciation; Judd, Pukui, and Stokes took the important step forward by calling it part of the alphabet.

SUMMARY

If linguists have been slow to recognize that long vowels and the glottal stop are essential features of Hawaiian's sound system, non-linguists have been even slower to accept the symbols as part of the alphabet. In a large measure, the works by Pukui and Elbert (both singly and in collaboration) have made dictionary users in particular more aware of the importance of using the symbols accurately, for they, especially Elbert, have served as missionaries, as it were, for the proper spelling of Hawaiian words.

Even in the academic community, which one might have expected to be open to accepting professional judgments, scholars in other disciplines have often resisted change, apparently considering themselves experts when it comes to language. As an example, note the attitude underlying the following comment from a review of a biography of a figure prominent in Hawaiian history, published not in 1887 but in 1987: "Purists may be offended that diacritical marks are not used throughout; others will be pleased that there is no affectation in this regard."[24]

As another example, the historian Oskar H. K. Spate, in the third and final volume of his history of the Pacific (1988:xxi), warned the reader that he would not indicate the glottal stop except in direct quotations from writers, quoting Katherine Luomala's disclaimer in 1949 (*Maui-of-a-Thousand-Tricks*, p. 15) that it was "almost impossible to be consistent in its use." We could quibble with Luomala's statement, arguing that it might be difficult to cite Polynesian words correctly, but it is not impossible. Moreover, better dictionaries were available in 1988 than forty years earlier.

In November 1988, *Honolulu* magazine began a trend-setting policy of spelling Hawaiian names properly, and some other publications have followed suit.

On 4 February 1991, the University of Hawai'i's student newspaper, *Ka Leo O Hawaii*, became *Ka Leo O Hawai'i*. However, the English translation remained *The Voice of Hawaii*, and policy for use of the name in text copy continued to follow that of the Associated Press, which writes the name without the glottal stop. The editor was said to be exploring ways to modify the typesetting equipment "to add glottal stops and macrons for Hawaiian words in the copy."

In July 1991, officials of the city of Honolulu and the state of Hawai'i issued directives providing that place names were to be written with glottal stops and macrons in official correspondence. However, the macron was questioned, apparently still considered some kind of punctuation mark.

Efforts by Hawaiian language teachers to convince Governor John Waihe'e of the importance of using the two symbols elicited a sympathetic response in September 1991, noting some of the difficulties with the proposal:[25]

> Although considerable progress has been made by people such
> as you and the dedicated group of Hawaiian language instructors

who are literally producing a written language, there are still
differences of opinion on whether, or when, or where, to include
diacritical marks in the written word . . .

While a positive response to your request is premature, I
sincerely appreciate your efforts. The discussion is pertinent,
necessary, and long overdue. I hope you will pursue the matter in
the community and, eventually, bring that discussion to the body
that can provide the legal and financial impetus, the Legislature.

In less than a year, the hope was fact. In June 1992, the governor
signed a bill permitting the use of glottal stops and macrons:

Macrons and glottal stops may be used in the spelling of words
or terms in the Hawaiian language in documents prepared by or
for state or country agencies or officials. Any rule, order, policy,
or other act, official or otherwise, that prohibits or discourages the
use of these symbols shall be void.[26]

In the following months, more and more publications of the University of Hawai'i changed their policy to use glottal stops and macrons
accurately. The 5 October 1992 issue of the *University Bulletin* (64[7])
used for the first time the spellings *University of Hawai'i* and *Mānoa.*
Within the body of the text, however, one finds, for example, both
Hawai'i and *Hawaii.* Also in October, the Department of Linguistics
was allowed to use macrons and glottal stops on its letterhead.

Even before these most recent changes, the city of Honolulu, in its
street-sign policy (the result of a 1979 ordinance), made perhaps the
most visible advance in Hawaiian spelling, but not without stumbling
blocks: in 1986 a naive transportation director provoked a loud outcry by
trying to override the ordinance. "I don't know how the law got on the
books in the first place," he complained. "Those markings make signs
very difficult to read—they're confusing both to tourists and to local
people. And they make signs much more expensive" (*Honolulu Star-
Bulletin*, 28 May 1986).

Nor did the newswriter help, for he referred to glottal stops as
"those backward apostrophes found in Hawaiian dictionaries." Although
macrons were not mentioned, the general term for the symbols was
"pronunciation markings." The caption on the picture accompanying the
article used an even less appropriate phrase: "punctuation and pronunciation markings."

All in all, the whole affair seemed made to elicit responses from
the uninformed. For example, a trustee of the Office of Hawaiian
Affairs was quoted as saying, "Nobody understands them (glottal stops)
except the linguists . . . Even the kupunas [elders] don't understand what
you're talking about" (ibid.).

Possibly he was right here. In some circles, there has been surprising resistance to changing the alphabet as it was fixed in 1826. Even
today, there is still a naive belief that the language is being tampered
with in some way. At the root of this belief is the notion that the
language of the Bible represents the "true" language. A recent
newspaper article (*Honolulu Star-Bulletin*, 16 August 1989, p. A-18)
illustrates this attitude, along with a total misunderstanding of what
marking glottal stops and long vowels really means. From an elderly
"educator, Hawaiiana expert":

> The Hawaiian version of the Bible—originally translated in the
> early 1800s—was the best example of the language ever put in
> writing ... To tamper with it meant that that example of the
> language as it was spoken at that time might be changed or lost
> forever.

It is ironic, first, that anyone could seriously consider the style of a
translation, however carefully done and however faithful to the original,
as the best written example of the language.[27] Next, the content —an
alien philosophy in a setting totally unknown to Hawaiians—does not
encourage a natural style. Moreover, the Bible was translated by
speakers of English with an imperfect control of Hawaiian, aided by
Hawaiians with the same deficiency in English.

However, the main fallacy of the argument is the idea that adding
glottal stops and macrons would be tampering with the language, when
actually it would reduce the guesswork that readers of the Bible must go
through, especially now that so many learners of Hawaiian must rely on
the printed, and not the spoken, word. To rephrase the last sentence of
the quotation from a linguist's point of view: unless glottal stops and
macrons are written, both the proper pronunciation and the meaning of a
significant part of the language will most certainly be changed or lost
forever.

NOTES

---

[1] Hanzeli (1969:37–38) discussed the seventeenth-century French tradition
of teaching the language in which there was "almost no indication of the
pronunciation of Latin, and no treatment of phonology whatsoever ... That
vowel length is functional in Latin is ignored in these grammars."

[2] Even as late as 1930, the two phenomena were confused. In a particularly
naive treatment (Atcherley 1930:9) we can read: "As a general rule in classifying vowels, long or short, it would appear that all accentuated vowels in a word

are long, and the unaccentuated, short. Prolonging the sound of a vowel soft-
ens the sound of a word, in the Hawaiian language."

[3] In many Oceanic languages, a vowel that is phonologically long can
shorten in faster speech, but the accent on the vowel still marks it as "long."

[4] It is not clear why Andrews used a grave, rather than an acute, accent;
perhaps, as on other occasions, the printer was limited in his choice of type.

[5] The only other word on the list that ends in a long vowel is a mono-
syllable, *la* (*lā*) 'sun'; the accent pattern on such words seems to have been
self-evident because of word division. All other long vowels on the list—in
other words, those that didn't distort the expected accent pattern—were
ignored.

[6] Letter from the mission, 2 June 1848, *Missionary Herald* xlv:21, quoted
in Anderson 1864:93. I am grateful to Robert J. Morris for the reference.

[7] A later writer (unidentified; see "On the Hawaiian Language, " n.d.)
commented on Andrews's difficulties with Hawaiian prosody and the glottal
stop:

> Judge Andrews, it is said, had not a musical ear, was not
> quick to detect difference in tones, and even insisted there
> was no such click or catch. His dictionary gives no clew to
> the right pronunciation of words and for want of any notice
> of the difference in words as they are pronounced with or
> without the guttural click, many mistakes are made in
> definition.

[8] This is not a particularly appropriate equivalent, but a British pronunciation (which of course is what is intended) is closer than an American one.

[9] Kendall included a scattering of accent marks in his 1815 primer. In the
following years, he developed an "elaborate accentuation system, which Professor Lee was to criticize" (Binney 1968:180). The system used in Kendall
and Lee 1820 was much more orthodox than Kendall's own creation.

[10] To explain the second "aberration," the compilers invented a long vowel
for the second syllable, since long vowels are always accented: *Kalīkimaka*.
The recommendations of the 1978 Hawaiian Spelling Project (see Wilson
1978) listed twenty-one additional misspellings of this type.

[11] Perhaps the main genre for European-styled verse in Hawaiian was
hymns, in which the notion of contrastive vowel length is usually meaningless,
since it is subordinate to the musical rhythm.

[12] Many varieties of Hawaiian English have [tʰ] in this position.

[13] The full quotation is as follows: "The glottal stop is not a recognized
consonant. As observed, it is a catch or break in the voice, as when some of
our Maori Atiawa folk slur the *h*. The peculiar sound is not represented by any
of our consonants, and it would be difficult, if not impossible, to isolate it.
The situation cannot be compared with that of *h* replacing *s*, or *k* replacing *t*,
etc." (I am grateful to John Mayer for finding this quotation.)

[14] John Charlot, pers. comm., September 1993.

[15] If Anderson had marked a glottal stop in some way, this notation, too, might have been lost in the printing process. However, there seems to be no indication in his Tahitian list (with its key to pronunciation) that he recognized the sound as a consonant.

[16] In Sybil Bingham's phrase book, the only word so marked that is not part of an opposing pair (like 'my', 'your') is *ia'u* 'to me'.

[17] The practice of using a hyphen to separate the "distinct syllables" continued sporadically for years.

[18] This note does not appear in the second edition (1826), but does in the third (also 1826). Elbert and Pukui claimed (1979:4) that Horatio Hale (1846) was "apparently the first to recognize the importance of the glottal stop." This is probably too strong an assertion, for such realizations are more often gradual than abrupt. Hale did not call the glottal stop a consonant, for it does not appear in his list of "elementary sounds proper to the Polynesian languages" (p. 231). He went on to note that in most Polynesian "dialects," "some of these letters are dropped entirely, and others changed." As an example of the former, he cited Samoan: "The *k* is dropped, its place being merely indicated by a hiatus or catching of the breath." In his comparative tables, he did, however, make a distinction between two types of "dropping" (p. 232):

> The hiatus caused by the omission of the *k* is represented by an inverted comma. An omission of a letter which does not cause a hiatus, or sensible break in the pronunciation, is denoted by a dash.

As further evidence that Hale considered the glottal stop only the manifestation of a missing consonant, see his comparative list on p. 235. Here, the only glottal stops on the list are those in Samoan, Tahitian, and Hawaiian, corresponding to *k* in related languages. He failed to recognize the sound in Tongan (in which it is inherited from Proto-Polynesian), writing *'eiki* 'chief' as *eiki*.

Thus, although Hale correctly identified the historical source of the glottal stop and provided valuable comparative data, he was probably not much closer to recognizing the sound as a consonant than was Ellis, whose publication preceded his by twenty years.

Finally, in spite of the high quality of Hale's work in general, it did not have the expected effect on Polynesian linguistics because the number of copies printed was very limited. In a letter written nearly fifty years later (1890, School of Oriental and African Studies Library, London), Hale complained that his early work had never had a wide enough distribution. The official publication of the Wilkes Expedition reports, which was plagued by congressional squabbles, was limited by law to 100 copies. The unofficial issue was an edition of only 150 copies.

[19] As the *Oxford English Dictionary* described the term, 'guttural' was

generally used to refer to sounds "produced in the throat." It was applied "by non-phoneticians [to] any mode of pronunciation which is harsh or grating in effect ...," such as—to English hearers—the sound represented by German *ch* before back vowels, represented phonetically by [x]. The first example of its substantive usage is particularly appropriate, as it applies to the misperception of the glottal stop, referred to earlier: "the first letter being such a guttural as could not well be pronounced by the Greeks."

[20] This work also provided much of the Polynesian data in Lepsius's work on orthography (1855, 1863), at least in the later edition.

[21] Perhaps this method of writing the glottal stop led to its being interpreted as a modification of the vowel, which one can still find in some current descriptions. Interestingly, in 1835, a Hawaiian teacher (who signed himself Nāpela) who had studied Greek at Lahainaluna suggested that vowels (or perhaps "units") should be divided into two types: light and prominent. Part of his argument was based on the Greek convention of marking "rough breathing" in otherwise vowel-initial position. The writer concluded such a practice would improve the writing system of Hawaiian, which, as written then, "was clearly understood when spoken but when we look at it in written form it is not clear." With such a system, he would no longer mispronounce the name *Ka'io* as *Kaio*. He concluded that the distinction between individual sounds should be maintained. Thanks to John Charlot for finding the letter (Hawaiian Mission Childrens Society, Lahainaluna folder, 10 April 1835), to Laiana Wong for translating it, and to Anatole Lyovin for explaining the relationship between Greek phonology and the writing system.

[22] In these semiphonetic transcriptions, the words are divided into syllables and four diacritics are added: a macron, a breve, a glottal stop, and an acute accent. Some serious problems of analysis and accuracy are discussed in chapter 11.

[23] Suggested by Laiana Wong.

[24] George Simson, review of *The Fantastic Life of Walter Murray Gibson, Hawaii's Minister of Everything*, by Jacob Adler and Robert M. Kamins, in *The Hawaiian Journal of History* 21:171–5, p. 175.

[25] Letter to Emily Hawkins, from Governor John Waihe'e, 5 September 1991.

[26] HB 2409, Act 169.

[27] Surely there is an element of circularity here, along with a difficulty in separating form from content: it is the language of the Bible, and therefore good.

CHAPTER NINE

The Printed Word

-0-0-0-0-0-

... The cry rings in our ears continually— "give us the palapala," "give us slates," — "give us pencils," "give us ink—" "make haste and give us the biber" (letter from Hiram Bingham to the American Board of Commissioners for Foreign Missions, 9 March 1824)

O ne of the most dramatic examples of the clash of cultures in the Pacific is the meeting between the Polynesians and the printed word. William Mariner's account (Martin 1817 [1981]:91–94) of the Tongan chief Finau's reaction to writing is a vivid description of the beginnings of what G. S. Parsonson (1967) called "the literate revolution." Having caught the castaway Mariner trying to smuggle a letter out of Tonga to warn other ship captains of the fate of the plundered *Port au Prince*, Finau

> sent for Mr Mariner, and desired him to write down something: the latter asked what he would choose to have written; he replied, put down me: he accordingly wrote "Feenow" (spelling it after the strict English orthography): the chief then commanded Mr Mariner to turn his back and look another way, he gave the man the paper, and desired him to tell what that was: he accordingly pronounced aloud the name of the king, upon which Finow snatched the paper from his hand, and, with astonishment, looked at it, turned it round and examined it in all directions; at length he exclaimed 'This is neither like myself, nor anybody else! where are my legs? how do you know it to be I?'

Finau thought that the whole process smacked of witchcraft, and it was no easy matter for Mariner to explain "the composition of elementary sounds, and of arbitrary signs expressive of them, to a people whose minds were already formed to other modes of thinking ..." When told that the histories of nations were recorded in this way, Finau

> acknowledged this to be a most noble invention, but added, that it would not at all do for the Tonga Islands; that there would be nothing but disturbances and conspiracies, and he should not be sure of his life, perhaps, another month. He said, however, jocularly, that he should like to know it himself, and for all the women

to know it, that he might make love with less risk of discovery, and not so much chance of incurring the vengeance of their husbands.

The reactions of the Hawaiians were much the same. As Sheldon Dibble (1909:156–57) reported:

> The people were amazed at the art of expressing thoughts on paper. They started back from it with dread, as though it were a sort of enchantment or sorcery. A certain captain said to Kamehameha, "I can put Kamehameha on a slate," and proceeded to write the word Kamehameha. The chief scornfully replied, "That is not me—not Kamehameha." The captain then said: "By marks on this slate I can tell my mate, who is at a distance, to send me his handkerchief," and proceeded to write the order. Kamehameha gave the slate to a servant, who carried it to the mate and brought the handkerchief. Kamehameha then took the two—the slate and the handkerchief. He looked at the writing and at the handkerchief—they did not look alike. He felt of the two—they did not feel alike. And what connection there could be between the one and the other he could not imagine. With this ignorance, it is not strange that the people formed very wild conceptions of the powers of letters. They even imagined that letters could speak. Every article of clothing that had a name upon it was for a time safe; no one would steal it—for there were letters there, and they did not know but they might tell the owner where it was.
>
> They also believed for a time, and the belief was a great stimulus to learn to write, that a wish for money, clothing or any property expressed on paper and handed or sent to the foreigner would be certainly and in all cases successful—that the paper would be regarded the same as money—that it possessed a kind of charm to procure whatever was expressed upon it. A few trials convinced them of their error, and many who had been industriously toiling from avaricious motives to learn to write were much chagrinned and disappointed.

KA PALAPALA

The earliest recording of the word *palapala* I have found so far is from Archibald Campbell's word list, recalled from the years 1810–1811. Here, *purra-purra* (in his editor's spelling) is defined as 'painting, printing, drawing, or writing'. Among the missionary material, an early citation is from Daniel Chamberlain's journal, in an entry dated 24 June 1820, only three months after the missionaries' arrival: "When I happen to fall into a circle of Indians and they begin to say pullah pullah [*palapala*] (learn to read) then I am anxious that some of my friends in America ... should come and teach them ... "

The current Hawaiian dictionary is strangely silent about the etymology of the word, which now refers to writing or printing of any kind. It does not seem to have been applied to carving petroglyphs, which is perhaps as close as pre-contact Hawaiians came to communicating through inscribed symbols. If we use only this dictionary, the most reasonable guess that we can make is that the word is the reduplicated form of *pala*,[1] defined as 'daub, smear, smudge, blot', fitting in with the occasional function of reduplication to refer to the frequent repetition of an action.

Lorrin Andrews's dictionaries (1836a, 1865), however, give much more satisfaction to the etymologically curious: *Palapala* (from *pala* 'to paint; to spot') is defined first as a verb:

> To stamp with marks, as in painting or printing tapa. (The figures ... were cut on pieces of wood or bamboo, dipped in the liquid coloring matter and then impressed with the hand on the tapa.) 2. In modern times, to write; to mark; to draw; to paint ...

and next as a noun:

> Characters made by impressing marks on kapa or paper like printing or by writing with a pen; hence, 2. A writing; a book either written or printed; a manuscript.

William Tufts Brigham, first director of the Bernice P. Bishop Museum, in his study of Hawaiian *kapa* (1911), also defined the term as 'to print on tapa'.

Thus, the modern use of *palapala* derives from the act of writing, not from its function, i.e., communication. Interestingly, Andrews also mentioned that "the whole system of instruction as first practiced on the Hawaiian islands was summarily called by the Hawaiians *palapala*." Thus, *palapala* (for at least a time) referred to European education as a whole.

And what of the relationship between the old and new *palapala*? According to Brigham (p. 2), the latter was largely responsible for the decline of the former. Explaining first that traditionally, tapa decoration was the "chosen work of the higher female chiefs," he continued:

> Almost from the coming of the American missionaries in 1820 these exalted dames had generally ceased to beat or rather decorate kapa for amusement, and betaken themselves to the more difficult task of learning to read and write with the new letters brought by these foreign teachers.

However, John Charlot (pers. comm., September 1993) noted that Brigham's statement was true only to a degree, since women (both royalty and commoners) continued to make and decorate tapa.

As for any communication[2] effected through the traditional *palapala*, it seems unlikely. Brigham wrote (p. 206):

> The kapa ornamentation is purely geometric ... and it is not symbolic; it is not intended to convey any esoteric meaning, it is simply to please the eye ... If any of my readers choose to see a cloud or a whale in any of the Hawaiian kapa designs they are of course at liberty to do so; some of the figures may be "very like" either. In naming the *bent knee* pattern it was not meant that the zigzag presents a human knee in such a position; it was never a symbol of a bent knee, or worship in the sense that the Egyptian hieroglyph for water (also a double zigzag) represented the motion of waves.

After their first exposure to writing, many Hawaiians seemed to believe that it had a *mana* of its own that would be transferred to them as soon as they learned its mysteries. Kamehameha, however, learned early of its practical, not mystical, power. Captain George Vancouver (1798, 2:141) reported in 1793 that the shipwrecked John Young had sent a letter to a ship captain via "Tianna" (Kaiana), who persuaded Kamehameha that because he had sailed to China in the company of Englishmen, he could read English. The contents, he declared (falsely), instructed the captain to seize Kamehameha, who in turn gave orders that anyone who carried a letter from Young or his companion Isaac Davis would be punished by death.

For most of the population, however, the first printing in January 1822 of 500 copies of the Hawaiian speller showed them firsthand the power of the printed word. In September of the same year another printing of 2,000 copies spread the effect even further. As Hiram Bingham described it (1847:160):

> The introduction of printing in the language of the country, not only awakened curiosity among the chiefs and people, but gave a new and decided impulse to our schools and the cause of education. From sixty to seventy pupils were at once furnished with copies of the first sheet, as they could not wait till the work was finished. They found the lessons easy. They not only soon mastered them, but were able to teach them to others. In a few months, there were not less than five hundred learners.

And who were these learners? Lorrin Andrews wrote (1834:156):

The first scholars consisted of a class of people immediately connected with the chiefs ... These schools had continued but a few months, when a desire was expressed by some of the high chiefs to attend to instruction, and schools were formed for their particular benefit. The missionaries of course were their teachers. The schools were generally made up of the chiefs and some of the principal people of both sexes in their trains. These schools for the chiefs were commenced at Oahu and Kauai about the same time. When the missionaries became the immediate instructors of the chiefs, their former schools were committed to the care of some of the natives; either to those who had resided some time in America, or those who had made the greatest progress in the schools here during the short time that the schools had existed.

One of the scholars was "Adams" (High Chief Kuakini), who more than a decade earlier had expressed a desire to learn to read and write English.[3] Shortly after the first speller was printed (Bingham 1847:157),

... Adams sent for the lessons we had printed in his language, and was quickly master of them. But a few days passed before I received a letter from him, which I immediately answered in the Hawaiian, under the date of Feb. 8th, 1822, one month from the first printing for the nation. Epistolary correspondence, thus commenced in that language, suddenly opened to the chiefs and people a new source of pleasure and advantage, of which hundreds soon availed themselves.

By the mid-1830s, letter writing had apparently become routine. Andrews wrote (1836b:15):

From the time the chiefs and people became acquainted with the art of writing, or marking characters representing articulate sounds, they have generally used this method of conveying ideas to each other. Many legal proceedings have been written, and news circulated over the islands by means of letters written by the common people.

Describing the Ladies Seminary at Wailuku, Maui, in 1841, Commodore Charles Wilkes, of the United States Exploring Expedition, which called at Hawai'i in 1840 and 1841, observed another stage in Hawaiian letter writing (1852 [1970], 4: 421):

One courtship has already taken place by letters; and I was informed that these were the first love-letters that had ever been written in this group. I was extremely desirous of obtaining the originals or copies, but was not successful. The correspondence appears to have been carried on under the eye of the missionaries, and the expressions they contained were very common-place.[4]

Kamāmalu, Liholiho's favorite wife, and a positive force for education in the earliest years of the mission, not only increased her own efforts to learn to read English and Hawaiian, but also ordered a schoolhouse built for her people. Liholiho (Kamehameha II) requested 100 copies of the speller for his "friends and attendants," but—according to Bingham—hesitated to let his subjects' schooling get in the way of the sandalwood cutting that would help pay his debts (Bingham 1847:163).

With the help of William Ellis, Bingham translated forty hymns into Hawaiian, and an edition of 2,000 copies was printed in 1823. But before that time, the powerful High Chiefess Ka'ahumanu as well joined the increasing number of scholars (ibid., pp. 164–65):

> ... Deeming it of great importance to induce her, if possible, to substitute the reading of divine truth for her heathenish or trifling engagements[5] at this period—more than two years after commencing our work—Mrs. B. and myself called at her habitation, in the centre of Honolulu ... We gave her ladyship one of the little books, and drew her attention to the alphabet, neatly printed, in large and small Roman characters.
>
> Having her eye directed to the first class of letters—the five vowels, she was induced to imitate my voice in their enunciation, a, e, i, o, u. As the vowels could be acquired with great facility, an experiment of ten minutes, well directed, would ensure a considerable advance. She followed me in enunciating the vowels, one by one, two or three times over, in their order, when her skill and accuracy were commended. Her countenance brightened. Looking off from her book upon her familiars, with a tone a little boasting or exulting, and perhaps with a spice of the feeling of the Grecian philosopher, who, in one of his amusements, thought he had discovered the solution of a difficult problem, leaped from the bath, exclaiming "*Eureka!* I have found," the queen exclaimed, "*Ua loaa iau [Ua loa'a ia'u]*! I have got it," or, it is obtained by me. She had passed the threshold, and now unexpectedly found herself entered as a pupil. Dismissing her cards [her "trifling engagement" at the time], she accepted the little book, and with her husband, asked for forty more for their attendants.

Later that year, she wrote to Kamamalu (p. 172):

> This is my communication to you: tell the *puu A-i o-e-o-e* [*pu'u 'ā 'ī oeoe* 'group of long necks'—a nickname applied to the missionary wives when they arrived] ... to send some more books down here. Many are the people—few are the books. I want *elua lau* (800) Hawaiian books to be sent hither. We are much pleased to learn the *palapala*. By and by, perhaps, we shall be *akamai*, skilled or wise.[6]

Occasionally, one finds a valuable linguistic observation nestled in a straightforward description of the educational process. Laura Fish Judd, who wrote about her experience in Hawai'i from 1828 to 1861, began by describing her school (1880:30):

> We have commenced a school for native women, which already numbers forty-five, including Kaahumanu, Kinau [Kīna'u], Namehana [Nāmāhana] [all high chiefesses], and several of their attendants. They are docile and very anxious to learn. I devote two hours a day teaching them to write on paper ...

But her next comment shows an important, but seldom mentioned, difficulty in transplanting the European idea of a written language to the Hawaiian culture: the foreign nature of the concept of "word":

> Mrs. B[ingham?] spends two hours more in giving them lessons on the slate, and teaching them how to divide words and sentences. Their preference is to join words together in continuous lines across the page, without stops or marks.

The problem of what constitutes a word in Hawaiian has plagued analysts from the very beginning of Hawaiian literacy, continuing to this day (see chapter 16).

A contemporary travel account enhances the usually matter-of-fact reports of such activities by allowing us a closer look at Sybil Bingham as a person (Barratt 1988:265):[7]

> Mrs. Bingam [*sic*], who seemed to be still a very young woman, was an energetic and zealous assistant for her husband. She questioned with particular gentleness those children, few in number, who were still learning the alphabet; and they, smiling, answered her without shyness.

METHODOLOGY

The missionaries' wish to teach the three Rs to the Hawaiians coincided with an important educational movement in Britain. Joseph Lancaster (1778–1838) was inspired at an early age to teach children who could not otherwise afford an education. Unable to hire assistants, he developed a system of training older pupils to teach the younger ones. The system was solidified into a military-like hierarchy, allowing the all-male student body to grow to as many as 1,000 pupils. In 1803, he described his methods in a pamphlet, *Improvements in Education*.

In addition to the feature of economy in matters of staff, his system employed a similar parsimony in regard to materials. There were no individual readers, notebooks, or slates; instead students referred to large sheets of paper affixed to boards at the front of each classroom and practiced writing on thin layers of sand on their desk tops.

Lancaster's reputation, and that of a contemporary with a similar scheme, Andrew Bell, reached a number of the Pacific missions. For example, Thomas Kendall, in his training for the Māori mission, was specifically advised to become familiar with the "new system" (Binney 1968:10). John Davies of Tahiti wrote in 1813 (Newbury 1961:161) that he had received pamphlets written by both educators and that he had attempted to use the ideas of mutual instruction and writing in sand:

> ... the miss[ionaries] with some assistance from the natives had a new place put up, and the boys and people were taught spelling by writing in sand.

However, the necessity for such Lancasterian methods diminished with the printing of the Tahitian spelling book: Davies wrote that the "considerable number" of copies sent (700, according to Lingenfelter 1967:2) were "found of great use."

Although the missionaries in Hawai'i knew of the Lancasterian system as early as their first year there (1820), slates and paper were used by the small number of students, and sand writing was not mentioned at all. Although it was never referred to directly, it is likely that the reason for the insistence on the printed page lay more in the attitudes of the Hawaiians than in the intent of the missionaries. Unlike Lancaster's English scholars, who, although illiterate, were familiar with the printed word and the books and newspapers that contained it, the Hawaiian scholars seem to have been intrigued not only by the process of writing, but by its physical manifestation as well. Bingham reported that Kamehameha II was presented with "an elegant copy of the Bible" (1847:87), as later were High Chiefs Kaumuali'i and Boki. Later he wrote (p. 257):

> An interesting youth begged of me a book. "My desire to learn, my ear to hear, my eye to see, my hands to handle; from the sole of my foot to the crown of my head I love the *palapala*."

Nearly a decade later (5 November 1834), Asa Thurston and Artemas Bishop reported from Kailua (*Missionary Herald* 31 (1835): 376):

> Books in a pamphlet form have lost their value in the eyes of the people, but bound books are in good demand, and are sought after even by those who have left the schools.

Is it any wonder then that the *mana* attached to books enabled them to win over the practical but ephemeral sand writing?

The part of the Lancasterian system that *was* used, however, was the hierarchy, or monitor, system, although it may not have been referred to as such. As noted earlier, Hawaiians who had learned to read very soon after the first printing in January 1822 served as teachers for others, but even this part of the system was considered by some to be a failure (Andrews 1832:165):[8]

> Several of us have frequently conversed on the subject of Lancasterian schools, as being suited well to the wants of this people; but I believe there is now more hesitancy in saying so, however we may feel. It is well known that, on the Lancasterian plan of conducting schools, much depends on the faithfulness of the Monitors. But at the Sandwich Islands there is no words [*sic*] for *faithfulness* in the language; of course the *thing* does not exist. And it is now my own opinion, after two years experience in teaching and introducing this system as far as I could, that if a school should be instituted entirely on this plan, it would fail. In the High School I employ some native assistants, but they act the part of professors, rather than monitors.

In spite of the inadequacies of the Lancasterian methodology for Hawai'i, the missionary schools flourished—for young and old alike. Occasionally the love of learning had to be given a helping hand. For example, Bingham reported (1847:474) that Hoapili, the "viceroy of Maui," exempted teachers from all other public labor; required all children older than four to go to school, and—with a shrewd understanding of human nature—forbade marriage to any couple unable to read.[9] The last clause, Bingham was quick to explain, was "intended, not as an obstacle to marriage, but as a spur to education, so far, at least, as to enable the people to read God's Word."

Samuel Kamakau, who had been a student at Lahainaluna, gave an insider's view of what the schools of that period were like (1866–1871 [1961]:270):

> The subjects taught were spelling in unison; reciting syllables of two letters; reciting a refusal to keep wooden gods; names of lands, names of months; a recitation relating the emotion of the people over the death of a king in a foreign land; portions of the books of Matthew, Psalms, Acts of the Apostles, and Luke; questions relating to God; the Ten Commandments; questions prepared for the exhibition; the desire of the rules proclaimed at Honuakaha; the first hymn about 'Opu-kaha-'ia; and the arithmetical processes of adding, multiplication tables, division, and fractions. Some schools taught how to get ready, to stand, to speak out, to take up a slate, how to place the pencil on the slate, thus: "Attention, get ready, wait, stand up, speak, give greeting."

These were some of the many things taught in old days which gave reading such prestige.

MATERIALS

Had the Webster-based orthography described in chapter 6 been closer to the mainstream of European writing systems, the missionaries might have arrived in Hawai'i with reading materials in hand, for 'Ōpū kaha'ia wrote that he had been working on a spelling book. However, because the system was rejected, the spelling book was never printed, and the manuscript seems to have vanished without a trace. The first Hawaiian language imprint, referred to earlier and called simply *The Alphabet*, served as the first vehicle for teaching the Hawaiians how to read.

The origin of the Hawaiian name for 'alphabet', *pīāpā*, is sometimes misunderstood. An early reference to it is as follows: Joseph Goodrich and Samuel Ruggles (Journal, 26 April 1824) described a particular school as being

> composed of adults & children, parents advancing in years & their rising offspring, sitting down together in long rows upon the ground, each with a B.A.B.A. in his hand, learning the first use of letters in their own language.

Here, the *B.A.B.A.* refers to *Ka Be-a-ba*, printed on 13 April 1824. It was another version of *The Alphabet*, which by this time had gone through 2,500 copies. Both versions were based directly on English primers used at that time, particularly that of Noah Webster.

Webster's work on English spelling and grammar has been mentioned several times in its role as a model for American missionary-linguists in the early years of the nineteenth century. His "speller" proved especially important for the teaching of reading. Its almost universal use in America guarantees that the missionaries in Hawai'i—in particular Sybil Bingham, the experienced teacher—would have been familiar with the book. In fact, Hiram Bingham (1847:104) mentioned using Webster's spelling book for instruction in English, and in Albertine Loomis's documentary novel, *The Grapes of Canaan*, based on the journals and letters of her ancestors, Elisha and Maria Loomis (1951 [1966]:58, 107), the speller also plays a small part.

However, Webster's speller affected more than just English instruction in Hawai'i, for it served as a model for the first Hawaiian primer. Moreover, it was the methodology used in this book that indirectly provided a name for the Hawaiian alphabet. Thus, if we know something of Webster's educational philosophy, we can better understand how the Hawaiians were taught to read.

Webster's Speller

The organization of Webster's speller, and in turn the contemporary methods of language teaching, are closely tied to the concept of the syllable. As E. Jennifer Monaghan described it (1983:14, 31), the main goal of the spelling book was to teach reading, for which spelling—in particular, spelling aloud—was a prerequisite. "As far back as one can trace the history of reading methodology, children were taught to spell words out, in syllables, in order to pronounce them." Webster himself wrote (1783 [1800]:28):

> Let a child be taught, first the Roman letters, both small and great—then the Italics—then the sounds of the vowels; not pronouncing the double letters *a* and *u*, &c separately, but only the sound that those letters united express—then the double letters. All this a child should know before he leaves the Alphabet and begins to spell.

In the edition just quoted, Lesson 1 (p. 29) begins with a table of syllables (called a "syllabarium") to be spelled aloud and then pronounced as units: *ba be bi bo bu by*.[10] Thus, students began to learn to read by reciting the names of the letters and then pronouncing the syllable the letters spelled: *bī, ā: bā*.[11] After this exercise, students could proceed to the lessons.

The Hawaiian version of this scene is as follows (Andrews 1832:159):

> The teacher takes a Pia-pa [i.e., speller], sits down in front of a row or several rows of scholars, from ten to a hundred perhaps in number, all sitting on the ground, furnished perhaps with Pia-pas, perhaps not. The teacher begins: says *A*. The scholars all repeat in concert after him, *A*. The teacher then says *E*. They repeat all together, as before *E*, and so on, repeating over and over, after the teacher, until all the alphabet is fixed in the memory, just in the order the letters stand in the book; and all this just as well without a book as with one. The abbs [?] and spelling lesson are taught in the same way.

This practice of spelling aloud, especially using the "syllabarium,"[12] gave the Hawaiian alphabet its name. Just as American schoolchildren taught with Webster's speller began their recitation by naming the letters that formed the first syllable, and then pronouncing the result: "B, A—BA," so did Hawaiian learners. However, they pronounced these sounds "*pī, ā—pā,*" which is now the word for 'alphabet'.[13]

As a speller, this first work in Hawaiian has one unexpected feature: it presents Hawaiian sounds (and then words) not from a Hawaiian point of view, but from that of English. Even the title is in English, and English "equivalents" for the sounds precede the Hawaiian ones. This practice is in direct contrast to the first printing in Tahitian more than a decade earlier (Davies 1810), in which the only English in the entire work (47 pp.) is in the colophon. But in spite of its English orientation, the speller was for some pupils the only book even partly in Hawaiian that they saw for years. Andrews (1832:159) reported that some schools continued for two or three years without advancing beyond the content of this sixteen-page booklet.

With this in mind, it is interesting to look at what the booklet offered in addition to the syllabic method of spelling. Unhappily, this little primer contains little to instill a love of reading in neophyte scholars. After the introduction of the letters, it is organized into a series of "tables" (in the manner of Webster)—thirteen in all. Of these, only five contain anything larger than isolated syllables or words to pronounce, and their content is decidedly sacred, not secular. Moreover, the sentences are mostly a series of rather disconnected affirmations of Christian doctrine (or occasional suggestions for modification of behavior), without the leavening effect that an Old Testament adventure or a New Testament parable might have provided.[14]

Later primers provided somewhat more interesting fare for the beginning reader. *O ke Kumumua na na Kamalii* [First lessons for children] (1835), sixteen pages of short but not altogether disconnected sentences, is graced by woodcuts on each page, equitably juxtaposing indigenous and introduced items. For example, a European sailing ship (*moku*) on p. 6 is balanced by a Hawaiian outrigger (*waʻa*) on p. 8. (Not all primers were so progressive: the woodcuts in *Ke Kumu Mua ano Hou* [A new primer], printed in Boston in the 1860s, show European children elegantly clothed in Victorian dress and engaged in wholly European activities.)

As for other books available in those early years, Judd, Bell, and Murdoch 1978 serves as an excellent guide, since it gives complete bibliographic information, including the number of copies printed. But for a contemporary summary of the first decade or so of printing, we must turn to the Mission records. In June and July 1834, the ABCFM sent the Hawaiian Mission a series of questions to be answered. In addition to asking for an account of how and when the language was reduced to writing, it asked: "Are books numerous? Some general account of their nature and origin?" The Mission responded as follows:

As yet, there is no grammar or vocabulary of the language published, and but few books, mostly of a religious character, or books containing the rudiments of science[:]

1822	first Book
1823	an edition of 40 hymns
1825	another Spelling Book ... containing 8 pages ... the reading part consisting principally in extracts from the New Testament, which has since gone through several successive editions to the amount of about 150,000 copies.
1825	Scripture Extracts
	Catechism
1826	the Decalogue, the Lord's Prayer &c
1827	the Sermon on the Mount
1828	the History of Joseph (32 pp.)
	an Arithmetic (8 pp.)
	an enlarged edition of the Hymns
	the Gospels
1829	the Acts of the Apostles
	historical parts of Genesis and Exodus, extracts from Leviticus
1830	Romans, 1st & 2nd Corinthians, remainder of the New Testament; History of Joseph enlarged and reprinted
1832	Geography of about 200 pp. 12 mo.
	tract from the Book of Joshua

After 1832:

Numbers and Deuteronomy
several small tracts
Judges , Ruth, 1st and 2nd Samuel
Two editions of Ninau Hoike (Catechism of Scripture History), 216 pp.
Two editions of Fowle's Arithmetic in the Hawaiian language
Enlarged edition of Hymns, with a gamut and tunes
Colburn's first lessons and Sequel (in press)
Translation of Holbrook's Geometry
"A few other works at the press of the High School"

The list continued, showing increased printing activity during the next four years. Years later, and writing of a somewhat later time (the 1840s?), Laura Fish Judd (1880:78–9) summarized the Mission's printing efforts, noting that the range of books available extended to "sixty volumes in all, and embracing a wider range of literature than constituted the library of many happy children in New England forty years ago."

But what kind of "literature" was this? Even in the late 1830s, Rev. Dibble considered that "everything connected with instruction was inseparably connected in the minds of the people with Christianity" (Westervelt 1912:20). Dibble himself organized and edited what seems to be the first publication in book form of Hawaiian literature, as opposed to works on Euro-American or Christian themes. Begun in 1835 or 1836 and published at Lahainaluna in 1838, *Ka Mooolelo Hawaii* (The history of Hawai'i) was the collective work of a number of students at the high school, including David Malo, A. Moku, Samuel M. Kamakau, and S. N. Hale'ole. It was based on the students' own memories and those of older experts who also contributed (Charlot, in progress, chapter 5, p. 156).

Twenty-five years passed before another such work was published: *Ka Kaao o Laieikawai: Ka Hiwahiwa o Paliuli* [The legend of Lā 'ieikawai, the beloved one of Paliuli], by Hale'ole. And nearly that many years separated this work from the next substantial book on Hawaiian themes: *Na Mele Aimoku, na Mele Kupuna, a me na Mele Ponoi o ka Moi Kalakaua I* (Chants for rulers, ancestral chants, and personal chants of the King Kalākaua I), published in 1886.[15] Thus, in a period of nearly fifty years, only three books on Hawaiian history and culture appeared, with a total number of pages under 650.

Supply and Demand

A theme emerging again and again in the missionary accounts and correspondence is that the printer was unable to produce enough books to keep up with the demand. In describing the state of the Mission in 1825, Bingham wrote (1847:256):

> Our pupils on the different islands now amounted to thousands, and the number of learners was rapidly increasing. The demand for books and stationery was far greater than could possibly be supplied by the mission. Many of both sexes, and of every age, required instruction and aid.

Loomis's letters at this time reflect the printer's viewpoint (Missionary letters, Loomis to Evarts, O'ahu, 26 December 1825):

> The demand for books has been so great that we have not been able at any time to furnish a supply, and indeed it is very possible we never shall be; but as I have before stated, the want of paper and types is the only objection to our keeping the press in constant

operation. A vast number of people have become able to read; and a vast number of others will be able to read by the time one of the gospels can be put into their hands.

As a postscript, Loomis added an interesting request, based on the different frequency of letters in the English and Hawaiian alphabets:

> In my letter of August last I mentioned 2000 additional a's and 2000 additional k's for the fount [font] of Long-primer; but 2000 k's and a's will not be enough for a fount of 300 lbs. I should have stated 4000 additional a's and 3000 additional k's.

Bingham continued his account of the demand for books and trained personnel (1847:257):

> Multitudes sought books and teachers whom we were obliged to deny. "Many are anxious to learn," said Mr. Whitney in respect to the people of Kauai, "but for want of books and teachers must for the present be denied that privilege." One school on Oahu was taught from a single copy of elementary lessons in spelling and reading.

The missionaries wrote to the headquarters in Boston (p. 258):

> Do, sir, send us *stationery* as well as *bread*: we cannot live without. Suppose that one-fifth of the population shall in a few years be furnished with books and slates, with ability to use them, what an engine our press becomes for carrying on the improvement of the nation. Had we slates and books sufficient, the number of native teachers increases so fast, that I should not be surprised if in three years from this time, there should be twenty thousand natives who shall have begun to read and write.

Inflation and Barter

In spite of repeated requests for supplies, however, they were slow in arriving: the ABCFM was in considerable debt, and the missionaries in Hawai'i feared that they might be "thrown upon [their] own resources for support."

And such a state did indeed come about, mainly through an unexpected increase in the cost of living, ironically caused by the "civilization" of Hawai'i so earnestly sought by armchair missionaries such as Haweis (see chapter 1). Bingham described what was for the missionaries an economic crisis (1847:161):

> The greatly increased demand for the productions of the country for the supply of foreign ships, and the growing desire of the people to possess themselves of money and articles of foreign

manufacture, combined to raise the prices of supplies, far above the trifling and wholly inadequate compensation, which had formerly been given them, when a bit of iron hoop was bartered for a hog, and a fish-hook for a fowl. Now the natives demanded a quarter of a dollar for a fowl, two or three dollars for a barrel of potatoes, and six or eight or ten for a hog, weighing two hundred pounds on the foot.

The problem was solved, at least in part, by taking advantage of a demand from the opposite direction: that for books. Agent Levi Chamberlain wrote from Honolulu on 2 January 1829 (Missionary letters, p. 556):

> Books are in demand in all the islands and may be turned for vegetables, fowls, eggs, wood &c:—with them we can get little jobs of work done about our premises, at some of the stations timber for native houses can be obtained and most of the labor of erecting them performed; but at this place where more families reside than at any other station we can get no houses built for books nor at the present time anything like a competent supply of vegetables & wood. What change may take place by & by in favor of the palapala I know not; but certainly we do not just distribute three quires a week.

But still, there had to be books enough to be sold. This barter system continued to be hamstrung by the lack of books. The following quotation (not identified, Missionary letters, p. 917) adds considerable detail to the account of the eagerness of the Hawaiians to obtain books:

> Wednesday 17th. We have recently received a new supply of spelling books & have now constant applications from the people for them. We have in three days taken the names of about two hundred new scholars, but can supply only one third of them with books. To one family of twelve persons we gave five books. Two of those who received none came to plead with us that they might not be denied. We examined them & found that they could not tell the printed letters of the alphabet, having never had a book. They made the strongest promises that if we would give them books they would not be lazy, but would learn them very quick, and that when they had learnt the word of God they would regard it. They said, moreover, "You have always told us we must learn your books, that we must learn the word of God. We desire to learn, we desire to know the word of God, for we believe it is a good word. We have now for two moons been seeking books, but cannot get them. We would buy, but you will not sell to us. You have now obtained books and give them to many lazy persons who will not learn them, but here we are intent on learning, but your own teachers will let us have no books. Think again, is this

proper?" We queried with them saying, perhaps you are not more industrious than others to whom we give books. They answered "yes we are, —you have seen none like us in Lahaina. We have had no books, you have not taught us at all, we have nothing to learn with except this stone board (holding up a slate) and still we can write." We said to them, "let us see." They each took the slate & wrote, "Ke noi aku nei au ia oe i wahi biaba." My entreaty of you is a spelling book.

By this very powerful argument we were convinced that we ought to give them books. Our feelings are frequently tried ...

Andrews summarized the result of the missionaries' inability to supply the Hawaiians with a suitable range of books and inadequate numbers (1834:156):

... In 1830, the *Pia-pa kamalii*, or child's spelling book, was published, since which time no visible change has taken place in the schools. Other books have been added, such as a historical catechism of the Bible, a part of the Epistles, Exodus, and Joshua. These are all the books of an Hawaiian student's library, when he has been so successful as to obtain them all. *But probably one half of all the schools on the islands have at this day nothing to read but the Pia-pa* [emphasis added].

MOTIVES, MEDIA, AND MESSAGES

In an age that occasionally recognizes the value of education for its own sake, we tend to forget to question the motives of educators nearly a century and three quarters ago. From a historical point of view, we are fortunate that such motives in the Hawaiian mission field were rather explicitly set out. In a report to the ABCFM in 1835, the missionaries explained their purpose in educating the Hawaiians (Bingham 1847: 471):

While it has been our business to teach a few hundreds personally, and superintend their efforts to teach others, our steady aim has been to extend a moral and religious influence over the whole community by means of the widely extended and, in some respects, loose school system.

They continued, saying that the main purpose of the schools had not been "merely or mainly literary," but [in my words] one of control. The general object [of the schools] was, they wrote,

to supply the want of family government and education; the want of a well regulated civil government; to restrain from vice and crime, and to supply amply, by a mild and salutary influence, the want of the power once derived from a horrid superstition.

The missionaries seemed delighted with the Hawaiians' newfound fascination for the printed word, since it diverted them from activities that they considered morally degrading (p. 471):

> It has afforded, to a great extent, by the pen, slate, pencil, and book, a substitute for the pleasure which the people once derived from games of chance, and of skill, and strength, connected with staking property; and in many cases instruction imparted by dictation and the exercise of joint recitation or cantillation of moral lessons by classes, has been a happy substitute for the heathen song and dance ...

Censorship?

As for the content of the reading material, it was strictly controlled (Bingham 1847:471):

> While then we have labored to afford the people the means of learning the arts of reading and writing, geography and arithmetic, for the discipline of mind and the purposes of life, and to facilitate their access to the sacred Scripture, it has been our steady aim to bring to bear constantly on the dark hearts of pagans and their children those moral and evangelical truths, without the presence and possession of which the design of their rational existence cannot be secured.

A glance at the list of Hawaiian imprints (mentioned in an earlier section) shows that two books on arithmetic, one on geometry, and one on geography[16] are the only works on secular subjects that existed until the first Hawaiian newspaper was printed (see below). Counter to the rich Hawaiian tradition of oral literature that already existed, reading fiction seemed anathema; even *A Pilgrim's Progress* was not translated into Hawaiian until 1842.

However, this approach was not very different from the contemporary norm. Thomas Dilworth (1740 [1787]:ix) advised the teachers who used his primer to

> banish from their Eyes such *Grub-street Papers*, *idle Pamphlets*, *lewd Plays*, *filthy Songs*, and *unseemly Jests*, which serve only to corrupt and debauch the Principles of those, who are so unhappy as to spend their Time therein.

Webster, as well—a source much more familiar to the American missionaries—used the content of his speller to instill Christian virtues.

As summarized in Monaghan 1983 (p. 45): "The value system displayed by Webster's spelling book was, as Dilworth's had been, thoroughly religious."

Newspapers[17]

The medium that allowed readers to range beyond the rather restricted diet of primers, catechisms, and textbooks was the Hawaiian language newspapers, the first of which, *Ka Lama Hawaii*, came from the new press at Lahainaluna in mid-February 1834.[18] To the ABCFM in Boston, Lorrin Andrews, the founder of the newspaper, explained the motives for the publication (ABCFM Report, 1835, p. 146, quoted in Mookini 1974:iv):

> Its object was First, to give the scholars of the High School the idea of a newspaper—to show them how information of various kinds was circulated through the medium of a periodical. Secondly, to communicate to them ideas on many objects directly and indirectly, such as we should not put into sermons, or into books written formally for the nation. Thirdly, it was designed as a channel through which the scholars might communicate their own opinions freely on any subject they chose ...

To its readers, the first issue of *Ka Lama Hawaii* explained something of the Western attitude toward knowledge (translated by Laiana Wong):

> In the enlightened countries, it is considered good to disseminate knowledge. Intelligent people feel that when they have discovered something new, something not previously known, and it is realized as being a valuable discovery, they have a desire to publish it, not conceal it, in order that all people might know of it.

Even if not specifically biblical in every article, the first issue was still significantly moralistic in content—as one would expect. A review of this issue[19] shows the following contents:

An introductory article (the first paragraph of which is shown above) on the advantages of knowledge over ignorance, and the righteousness of the word of God.
A discussion of sin as the source of ignorance.
An article on elephants.
Some facts about the college [Lahainaluna].
A letter reporting that some 396 students in Kaua'i could now read.

A letter expressing disappointment in the lack of progress in
    the Kingdom's common schools.
A song of lamentation for Ke'eaumoku.
An essay on the value of geography.
An interpretation of some parts of the Bible.
"Wealth from Christ."
An essay on anger and love.

    The next two issues contain similar stories, plus an additional two types of articles. First, there is an occasional world news story, obtained from arriving ships (e.g., the war in Portugal, ending with the advice that people and their rulers listen to God and love one another). Next, there are two stories on the "ancient ways," not actually containing moralistic judgments from the Christian viewpoint.

    The next Hawaiian-language newspaper to appear was *Ke Kumu Hawaii*, begun in 1834, and edited by the Reverend Reuben Tinker. In 1837, the *Missionary Herald* (33:72) described it as a "vehicle for conveying to the natives much important information on religious and other subjects ..." The *Herald* reported (p. 73) that 3,000 copies were circulated. "It is used to some extent in schools, and read more or less at their houses, as other books are read by such a people. Natives write more and more for it; and we hope it may prove more and more useful as their intelligence increases and also our skill in adapting it to their wants."

    However, there was some disagreement about what "their wants" were or should have been. In 1838 Tinker resigned over the policy of the Prudential Committee of the ABCFM to censor all materials written by the missionaries for publication. Wilkes, describing conditions in 1841, also criticized what he called the "restriction on the liberty of the press," blaming this directly on the board in Boston. (Later, this censorship must have diminished when the ABCFM relinquished direct control over the Hawaiian Mission.)

    Notwithstanding the battles over the control of the contents of the newspapers, the medium developed into a literary form that focused on Hawaiian history and traditions (Charlot in progress, ch. 5, pp. 135 ff.) Not surprisingly, such a topic was not universally accepted. Some Hawaiians encouraged the writing down of texts, since knowledgeable people were becoming fewer in number. Others objected to hithertofore oral knowledge becoming public, foreseeing the loss of prestige customarily due the traditional expert (p. 136). Then, too, the newly adopted Christianity complicated the matter. One view eschewed any attention to pre-Christian history on the grounds that it might glorify this "period of darkness." An opposing view suggested that such knowledge would show the old ways in disadvantageous contrast to the new enlightenment. Whatever the consensus, a great amount of historical and cultural material reached the reading public through the medium of these newspapers (p. 144).

Hawaiian-language journalism was offered to an even wider readership in 1856, when Henry Martyn Whitney printed the first issue of *The Pacific Commercial Advertiser*, which was planned to include "two or three columns ... in the Hawaiian language" (Chaplin 1993:B1). In the first issue, this section turned out to be a full page, with the name *Ka Hoku Loa o Hawaii*. The purpose was to give the Hawaiians better access to foreign news and other articles that would improve "the social habits of the natives." Thus, both the all-Hawaiian newspapers and the bilingual ones greatly expanded the material available for Hawaiians to read in their own language, serving as an important supplement to the rather plain Calvinistic fare offered by the missionaries.

SUCCESS?

It is easy to understand the attraction that writing had at first for at least some of the Hawaiians. Writing seemed to be a key to Western power—huge ships, riches, weapons, and other wonders. Today it is not clear just what doors this key actually opened. But aside from the possible material benefits from literacy, how successful was literacy as an end in itself? Different accounts from this period give different answers. However, most firsthand observers agreed that the excellence of the orthography, with a nearly one-to-one correspondence between phoneme and letter, greatly reduced the time required to learn to read. For example, Dibble reported (1839:80):

> The Hawaiian language contains but 12 articulate sounds, and of course the missionaries introduced but 12 letters ... They adopted also the simple method of avoiding all arbitrary spelling. Every word is spelt precisely as it is pronounced, so that to teach spelling is scarcely an object. Every one who can combine two letters in a syllable, and put two syllables together, can both read and spell with readiness. The art of reading, therefore, is very easily acquired. I think I am safe in saying, that the children of Hawaii learn to read their language in a much shorter time than our children do the English.

In the same vein, Artemas Bishop wrote (5 September 1828, Missionary letters, p. 651):

> About half of the scholars can read with facility in any of the tracts, and all who have passed through the elementary sheet can

spell any word in the language, so simple is the syllabic construction of words.

Laura Fish Judd wrote (1880:78):

> The construction of the Hawaiian language is so simple, when compared with the English, that it is no marvel that so many of the natives acquired the art of reading and writing it. The proportion is estimated as greater than in any other country in the world, except Scotland and New England.

One must remember, however, that these assessments were made after 1826, when the orthography was significantly altered. By this time, many Hawaiians had already been taught to read using the fuller (and inefficient) orthography, so they had to relearn the skills of reading and writing—or at least modify them. As for the material produced from 1822 to 1826, all of it had to be revised.

At any rate, according to some reports, the number of Hawaiians who had learned to read was impressive indeed. In answer to the questions on this topic asked by the ABCFM in 1834, referred to above, the missionaries wrote that more than 20,000 attended the schools, evenly divided between males and females, with a ratio of adults to children of three to one.

The general question also included the following more detailed ones: "Are the people disposed to learn? Are those who are able to read, fond of reading? Are they willing to receive & read Christian books?" To these, the mission gave much less sanguine answers:

> This cannot be called a reading people, nor can it be said, that they are "disposed to learn," as a characteristic trait of the nation. We doubt not their capacity, could sufficient motives be presented before their minds to induce application, and we have reason to believe that such as are actuated by religious principles are truly desirous to learn that they may read the word of unerring truth, and find therein the way of salvation. But of those who have not this motive, it cannot be said, that as a body, they are disposed to learn. This propensity to learn mechanically to read, without attending to the sense of the words, is a great hindrance in the way of becoming a reading people. Until this evil shall be remedied, there is little prospect that they as a community ... will become fond of books.

Dibble, writing only five years later, was much more optimistic in his appraisal (1839:114–15):

> Formerly they had not the least conception of writing, printing, and reading. The simple business of putting thoughts on paper, as

I have before described, was to them so great a mystery that they stood in amazement and wild conjecture. Now it is a common practice with them to write letters to each other. They have a newspaper in their language, published once in two weeks, and many of the communications are from their own pens. About one third of the whole population can read. Four printing presses and two binderies are in constant operation, except when stopped for want of funds, employing about 40 native young men in both departments, who execute their work well with very little superintendence. They have now in their language most of the Scriptures, several hymn books, —one printed with a gamut and notes, religious books and school books of various kinds—making in all quite a library.

Formerly they had no schools, except to teach their vile amusements and the art of breaking a man's bones for the purpose of robbery. They had something like schools for these purposes.[20] Now you can enter a High School, and see young men of intelligence demonstrating problems and theorems on a black board, or answering questions with readiness in geography, history, and religion. You can enter a Female Seminary too, and lower boarding-schools, look upon their sparkling eyes, their cleanly though humble dress; witness the ardor and propriety of their behavior, and listen to the readiness of their answers.

And wherever you go, throughout the whole group of islands, you will meet with schools of more or less interest. Every station has had at times from 50 to 150 district schools connected with it. Under my own care at Hilo at one time, there were 87 schools, and not far from 7,000 learners. When collected at the centre at a quarterly examination, they formed an immense crowd, no house could contain them. They might have been seen regularly arranged, with books in their hands, and covering a large enclosure. These schools were very imperfect, and soon accomplished most that they could accomplish. Schools are now less numerous—better organized and furnished with better teachers.

Later, Dibble wrote (p. 150):

Much has been effected, and much more can be effected, by the distribution of the Sacred Scriptures, and of religious books and tracts. Not far from 90,000,000 of pages have been printed at the islands and scattered among at least 30,000 readers.

Is the discrepancy among the reports a matter of different expectations, or did the passage of time solve the earlier problems? Writing nearly a century later, George F. Nellist (1925:19–20) also painted the scene in glowing colors:

King Liholiho [Kamehameha II], Kamehameha III and other chiefs were among the first to acquire a knowledge of the new arts of reading and writing. As soon as a few of the chiefs became proficient they assumed the roles of teachers, and within a comparatively short time were able to send out the best scholars among them to act as instructors in the several districts. It is said that before the end of 1824 more than two thousand natives had learned to read. For a few years following 1824 almost the entire adult population spent some time in school, a condition probably unique in history. In 1832 schools for native children were opened. These gradually took the place of the schools for adults. Each missionary station became a center for educational work.

Bingham, writing in 1847 about mission events in 1836, gave still another highly optimistic account, especially in terms of the content of the material (p. 472):

The simplest ideas of the true God and of the soul, and of our relation and duties to God and his creatures, are the most elevating, expanding, and purifying that can be first introduced into the minds of the heathen, whether aged or middle aged, in youth, or childhood. The Egyptians in the days of Moses, the Athenians in their glory, and the proud Romans, in the days of the Caesars, before the Gospel was preached among them, did not possess so much elevating and purifying knowledge as was taught in our 900 schools, among 50,000 learners, the first half generation after the missionaries set foot on these dark shores ...

On the other hand, Andrews,[21] writing in 1832, took the opposite side (p. 160):

... a great circulation of books does not prove *here*, that, the books are much understood. It is fully believed, that were the mission to print off an edition of logarithmic tables, there would be just as great a call for it, as for any book that has been printed ...

The truth is, a *palapala* is a *palapala*; it is all new to them, and all considered good. They have been told, that the perusal of these and similar books constitutes the difference between them and ourselves; that they are able to make people wise.

Here, Andrews brought up an important feature of literacy, one that proved both an attraction and a detraction: its novelty. From the Mission's Annual Report for 1833 (*Missionary Herald* 29:455), a little more than a decade after the introduction of printing to the Hawaiians, the Mission reported:

Nothing could be a greater novelty to a Sandwich islander, than a book, and the art of reading it. This novelty, and the curiosity which it awakened, are of course gradually passing away; and that, too, before the people have acquired so much knowledge as to realize its value, and to love and desire it for its own sake.

Andrews laid much of the blame on the teachers (1832: 157):

> The Pia-pa, therefore, in most cases, was all they could teach, for it was all they knew. And it is remarkable that the teachers have shown very little skill in teaching themselves; in other words, have added nothing of consequence to their stock of knowledge by their own exertions ...

Later, he noted that it was difficult to get teachers to sustain an interest in what they were doing (p. 160):

> When a teacher considers himself as having become expert, that is, when the novelty of his authority has gone by, and he has a little experience; when he arrives at the point just where *we* should say he might begin to be useful ... he stops and passes the job on to someone else.

A report two years later (*Missionary Herald* 30:284) echoed this sentiment: "Respecting our native schools, we have little to say that is encouraging," citing the poor quality of teaching for at least part of the difficulty. Andrews even reported (1832:159) one instance in which a teacher had to make one copy of the alphabet "suffice for both himself and the entire class, [and] the students learned all their letters upside down"!

Thus, he concluded that the best progress had been made not by people who had (necessarily) been in schools, but by those who had had direct contact with the missionaries. William D. Westervelt enlarged on this theme (1912:20):

> A distinction arose between schools. Those taught by the missionaries and their wives became known as 'station schools', sometimes called 'select schools' while those which were under the care of native speakers were ultimately recorded in the mission annals as 'common schools'.

Other missionaries as well reported difficulties. For example, Asa Thurston and Artemas Bishop, stationed at Kailua on the island of Hawai'i, wrote in May 1834 (*Missionary Herald* 31:338–9):

> Our schools have not been in vigorous operation for two or three months past. It is a time of great scarcity of provisions in this part of the island, and since the rains have commenced, the people have been engaged in planting. The schools which we teach ourselves have been continued, though with diminished

numbers. Those who have attended regularly and given their minds to their studies, have made commendable improvement, and exhibit evidence of being as able to make progress in reading, writing, arithmetic, and geography, as any other people. The great obstacles in our schools are the want of competent teachers, the indisposition both of children and adults to attend school, and the inactivity of their minds when they do attend.

Perhaps the strongest indictment of the teachers is the following statement (*Missionary Herald* 29:457): "The only sufficient remedy for the extremely inadequate system of schools now in operation, (if system it can be called,) must be found in the better education of the teachers." Lorenzo Lyons, stationed at Waimea, wrote in his journal two years later (*Missionary Herald* 31:113): "I do not wonder that there are so few good readers, or so few readers of any kind; but I rather wonder that there are so many, considering the qualifications of the teachers, and the other circumstances under which the schools have been taught."

But other groups as well shared in the criticism. In a rebuke that seems timeless and universal, the writers of the Hawaiian Mission's Annual Report for 1833 (*Missionary Herald* 29:456) stated that "the reins of parental government are held with so slack a hand, that when children arrive at the common age for attending school, they are usually unmanageable."

Wilkes provided a secular point of view. His description of the seminary at Lahainaluna is not optimistic: he did not criticize Andrews, but attacked instead the ambitious plans of the "Board" (the ABCFM), which took over the administration in 1836. In particular, he lamented the lack of the teaching of practical skills, noting (1852 [1970]:247): "In all the departments of this establishment I saw nothing but ill-directed means and a waste of funds ... The school has passed its meridian, and is now fast going to decay."

Wilkes also criticized the "loose and irregular" discipline of the scholars, as well as the plans for studying Greek (p. 249): "Fortunately for the students, however, they could not proceed for want of books." Still, in his opinion, the ABCFM, more than the missionaries, was at fault.

As is usual, the effect of these several weak spots in the eduction system was to hinder the students' progress, especially in reading and writing. In most of the enthusiastic reports on the speed with which Hawaiians learned to read and the impressive numbers of people who were able to read, the writers made no distinction between the mechanics of reading and the students' ability to understand what they read. On this topic, Andrews's views cast doubt on the appropriateness of

Bingham's adjectives used in a quotation earlier: *elevating, expanding,* and *purifying* (1847:166):

> The worst thing in their *reading* [wrote Andrews] is, that they get no ideas. I have taken great pains to ascertain this fact, and I am convinced that ninety out of a hundred that are called readers, hardly know that any meaning *ought* to be attached to the words. Indeed a great many think there is a kind of mystery, or perhaps magic, in reading. Their notion is, that they must say over a word or two, or a sentence and then from some quarter or another a thought will come to them ... I have spent hours at a time in the High School trying to make the scholars believe that a word written on paper or printed in a book, meant just the same thing as when spoken with the mouth. From several things it is manifest to me, that the common readers understand but very little of what they read. For *first*, they are not able after reading a sentence or paragraph, to tell any thing about it ...
> Oral instruction is better understood.

Nearly thirty years later, long after Andrews had resigned from the Mission and was serving in his new capacity as a judge in Honolulu, he looked back on Hawaiian literacy, softening somewhat his harsh earlier judgments (1860:94–07):

> One of the questions asked: "What are some of the things of specific value, which Hawaiians have gained through the medium of instruction in their own language?" ... In the summer of 1828, I commenced teaching, or rather hearing Hawaiians read, in their own language. That was about the time that the desire to learn to read became prevalent throughout the nation, and schools were established in almost every district on the Islands, and the great *mass* of the people, (adults,) began to *read* in their own language. It is true, they did not read very fluently, nor had they much in their language then to read. But a great many learned to read, and in some measure understood what they read. It will be remembered, that at that time, and for several years afterwards, no children were in the schools. The schools were composed entirely of adults, chiefs and people, men and women. Many who had passed the middle age of life, were proud to stand up in classes, and read their *palapalas*. The *masses* read, and continued to learn to read, as fast as the missionaries could get out books for them. The first book was a little Spelling-book; then followed "Thoughts on the Chiefs..." As before, it is not pretended that the adult Hawaiians, as a general thing, became good or fluent readers; but they did read, were anxious to get books, and got ideas from reading.

Again, simultaneously with reading, the people learned *to write*, just as far as they could get the apparatus; i.e., pen, or pencil and paper, (the ink they manufactured, or got from the cuttle fish,) or slates and pencils. My first efforts to understand the Hawaiian language, in 1828, consisted in reading and examining manuscripts written by Hawaiians. Letter-writing, even at that time, was considerably practiced, and would have been much more, but for want of materials.[22]

In addition to the constant want of writing materials, Bingham's reference to *oral instruction* above leads to another dimension in the picture of early literacy in Hawai'i: reading versus memorizing what has been heard.

Conflict between Oral and Written Traditions

It is a truism to say that, until the *palapala* arrived, Hawaiian culture was an oral one. An important question is: after the introduction of writing, how long did Hawaiian culture remain an oral one? In Bingham's report of the first year of the Mission (1820), he described the results of Sybil Bingham's school, then three months in operation (p. 114):

One of their exercises on this occasion, particularly engaging to pupils and spectators, was the cantillating, in concert, and with a degree of Hawaiian enthusiasm, one of their lessons *committed to memory* [emphasis added], and which they were accustomed to teach to their acquaintances, at their places of abode.

Andrews commented on the Hawaiian proficiency in memorizing and the effect it had on literacy (1832:157):

The reading consists in saying over the words in a book very slowly, with many stops, and repetitions, and blunders, until repeated so frequently as to [be] fixed in the memory

On the topic of committing to memory, he remarked:

At this the natives have ever shown themselves very skilful; but the ability to repeat and the fact they do repeat the Pia-pa and the Ui [lit., 'question'; hence, 'catechism'], and the Mataio [Matthew], and other books from beginning to end, *does not imply that they can read a word* [emphasis added].

Thus, at least early in the process, the practice of teaching reading by reciting aloud encouraged many Hawaiians to perform a skill at which they were adept: memorizing (what would appear to us) a large body of material and actually relying very little on reading.[23]

CONCLUSION: POWER AND PROMISES

Even for those pupils who did learn to read (without the intrusion of memorizing), understand, and synthesize, there remained a problem: the type of books in the Hawaiian language available to readers. Earlier, the point was made that the missionaries' control of the books printed in Hawaiian was not significantly different from that exercised by the writers of the major English primers of the period—Webster and Dilworth. Both those writers felt that the moral instruction of the young was the primary goal of the materials they presented.

In Hawai'i, however, this point of view seems to have been carried to an extreme. Judging from the definitive bibliography of Hawaiian imprints (Judd, Bell, and Murdoch 1978),[24] the missionaries did not seem to consider that people could read for a purpose other than instruction, whether sacred or secular. Even essentially secular subjects were often studied from a religious point of view: for example, of the nineteen works referring to geography, seven of them treat biblical geography. But the translators outdid themselves with their 1838 work on anatomy: as the compilers of the bibliography took wry pleasure in observing (p. 61), "Even the skeletons knelt in prayer."

Moreover, there is an important difference between the moral instruction at that time in Hawai'i and in America. In the latter, although Webster kept a firm grip on the type of material available for younger children to read, it was considerably loosened as they grew older and could range further afield in their reading. Even in the classroom, they came to have access to reading material that—although perhaps moralistic in intent—was distinctly secular in content. For example, in 1836, William Holmes McGuffey published the first two of his *Eclectic Readers* (Monaghan 1983:168–69), whose very title shows that the books contained a variety of reading matter. By the time pupils reached the sixth reader, they could read selections from Samuel Johnson, Shakespeare, and William Byrd (among many others), and—in later editions—an impressive range of such nineteenth-century authors as Scott, Irving, Longfellow, and Tennyson. The purpose of this sampling of cultural richness was to whet the appetite for the great quantity of material available beyond textbooks.

But for the Hawaiians, what did indeed lie beyond the textbooks? Very little, actually. For those Hawaiians born after the acceptance of Christianity and the rejection (to a degree) of the classical modes of Hawaiian education (see Charlot in progress, Introduction), the opportunity to learn of the cultural richness of their own past through reading was limited to just a few books and the numerous, but more ephemeral, articles in the Hawaiian-language newspapers.

This chapter began with a reference to Parsonson's treatment of literacy in the Pacific. It ends with his conclusion (1967:57):

> The literate revolution ... lacked any adequate economic or political base and could not therefore confer upon the local princes more than the limited jurisdiction which the Roman missionaries had long ago bestowed on the early Anglo-Saxon kings ... The great leap forward which the Polynesians had contemplated with such enthusiasm was thus finally frustrated and men turned away from the present to ponder the wreckage of their past.

But is Parsonson's judgment too harsh? Have the benefits of literacy for the Hawaiians been more subtle than economic and political power? At least one thing is certain: without literacy in the nineteenth century—particularly its role in recording the language and culture in a period when both were in decline—the current Hawaiian renaissance[25] would be doomed to failure.

NOTES

[1] See also *kāpala* 'to paint or print a design' (among other similar translations) and the discussion of the *palapala* in John Charlot's history of education in Hawai'i (in progress).

[2] Here we have a problem with terminology. Some would maintain that "communication" includes the kinds of moods or senses conveyed by music or abstract art; for this discussion, I apply the term only to human language and systems based on human language, such as writing, Morse code, shorthand, etc.

[3] See chapter 14.

[4] One wonders if the missionaries were innocent of *kaona*, the poetic device of hidden meanings!

[5] Bingham did not cover himself with glory at this point, speaking of "odoriferous necklaces" or "rude coronets," "vile songs," and "foolish stories" in describing the activities of the queen.

[6] Bingham described the letter as "characteristic," thus one assumes that it was customary for Ka'ahumanu to mix Hawaiian and English.

[7] The quotation is from the narrative of Aleksei P. Lazarev, March–April 1821.

[8] John Charlot (pers. comm., May 1993) suggested that another reason for the failure of the monitor system was the envy of other students.

[9] This was in 1835 (John Charlot, pers. comm., September 1993).

[10] This differs from Dilworth (1740 [1789]) in including *y* as a vowel. Of course, it was not necessary for Hawaiian.

[11] Monaghan (p. 14) noted that not until the appearance of McGuffey's *Readers* in 1836 did American children begin to learn to read from a "reader" rather than a "speller."

[12] See Monaghan 1983:33.

[13] Thus, the Pukui-Elbert dictionary (1986) is ambiguous in saying that Hawaiians began the alphabet by saying *pī-'ā-pā*; if they did so, they were simply giving their recitation a title: "The Alphabet."

Such a method of spelling out the syllables was widespread in the Pacific. Buzacott (1866:65) reported the following anecdote from Rarotonga. An unfamiliar noise in the night elicited this reaction:

> 'Oh, Tiaki,' exclaimed the wife, 'say the prayers you have learned.' Both immediately dropped on their knees, and Tiaki began most earnestly to cry, '*B a, ba; b e, be; b i, bi; b o bo*'.

Dibble, as well, mentioned indirectly the contemporary method of teaching reading syllable by syllable (1909 edition, p. 155): "Every one who can combine two letters in a syllable and put two syllables together can both read and spell with readiness."

[14] However, in defense of the compilers of the speller, one can note that contemporary works were much the same. But even in Dilworth's speller, the exceedingly moralistic sentences in the first sixteen pages are given in paragraphs that have some internal cohesion.

[15] Dibble's history is the only one of these three works published under the aegis of the Mission; there is some discussion in chapter 16 of how the missionaries opposed Kalākaua's revival of some pre-Christian customs. However, such feelings were not universal; Lorrin Andrews, although he left the Mission in 1842, retained his interest in Hawaiian literature and language, and was especially interested in the ancient *mele*.

[16] John Charlot (pers. comm., May 1993) has stated that the geography book (*He Hoikehonua* ... [JBM #75]) did have some literary value and enjoyed great popularity, so much so that Dibble complained that the Hawaiians liked it better than the religious publications. This book, by the way, was not entirely a translation, but contained some original material.

[17] For a comprehensive review of Hawaiian-language newspapers, an alphabetical index, and a useful list of references, see Mookini 1974.

[18] Esther T. Mookini has translated some of the secular articles and arranged them in a collection: *O Na Holoholona Wawae Eha O Ka Lama Hawaii*, or *The Four-Footed Animals of Ka Lama Hawaii* (1985). The work is described in Sachdeva 1985.

[19] By Laiana Wong.

[20] This statement seems incredibly naive when compared with Charlot's description of classical Hawaiian education (in progress).

[21] Andrews, in charge of the high school at Lahainaluna, begun in September 1831 (Bingham 1847:423), was extremely critical of the lack of progress made in literacy, as several quotations in this chapter show.

[22] John Charlot pointed out (pers. comm., May 1993) that because of the shortage of writing materials, many Hawaiians learned to read but not to write.

[23] This problem was not unique to Hawai'i. In 1826, John Williams wrote to the London Missionary Society headquarters:

> They have in all the Islands in these Seas got into a method of learning all by heart without being able to tell a letter hardly they will read of[f] Chapter after Chapter correctly I am about to turn about 5000 persons back again to A & commence over again with them on a new plan — It has occasioned a great stir amongst them they have their books in their hands night & day now.

[24] The following is a list of secular materials, other than the newspapers, available in Hawaiian from 1822 through 1838, selected from Judd, Bell, and Murdoch 1978. The English translations of the titles are given.

1828 Thoughts of the chiefs. 8 pp.
    Arithmetic: that is, the explanation of numbers
1829 First book for children, to educate them in their youth
1830 The fine decree of the King of Great Britain ... 4 pp.
1832 An arithmetic
    A geography
    First reading book, to teach Hawaiian pupils what is right,
        108 pp.
1833 An arithmetic
    An intellectual arithmetic
    Geometry
    Questions on geography
1834 Hawaiian almanac
    Tables for surveying and navigation
    History of quadrupeds
1835 Stories about animals for children
    Penmanship
1837 A publication showing the evils of intoxicating drinks.
    English grammar
    The history of Hawai'i
[25] See chapter 16.

CHAPTER TEN

Take My Word For It

-0-0-0-0-0-

> ... *the language of the Hawaiians was utterly destitute of all words for representing many ideas respecting the Christian religion, morals, social duties, terms of science, &c. It has been necessary, therefore, to introduce new words. All languages do this to some extent, even the German, though it is avoided there if possible. The English have no scruple on this head, but have received with open arms every new word or term that offered itself from any language (Lorrin Andrews, 'Remarks on the Hawaiian Dialect' [1836b:20]).*

Lorrin Andrews's lament for the lack of ready-made words in Hawaiian for totally alien concepts is a familiar one in Pacific mission history, tempered only by the knowledge that such a want is felt by all languages in contact. But even without such contact, every language has a need to form new words to keep up with cultural change. So before we discuss borrowing, a pertinent question needs to be asked: what other ways did (and does) Hawaiian have, other than borrowing, to increase its vocabulary?

HOW TO ADD WORDS

One way to add to the store of words in a language is to coin entirely new ones. As chapter 2 showed, complaints about the apparent poverty of the sound system and the resultant effect on the number of possible words in the language were unfounded, since some two and one half billion words from one through four syllables in length would be theoretically possible. Thus a "language planner" could take one of these unused shapes and assign an arbitrary meaning to it. And, according to Don Francisco Marin's account, reported by Adelbert von Chamisso (see chapter 3), Kamehameha I did just that, producing a new but short-lived vocabulary.

However, Hawaiian has other ways of word building as well. The first of these is through its system of derivation—adding prefixes or suffixes to broaden (or narrow, depending on one's point of view) the meaning of an existing root word. One of the most common affixes is *ho'o-*, used as a causative (among several different functions). For example, note the following pairs:

maka'u	afraid	*ho'o-maka'u*	to frighten
nani	pretty	*ho'o-nani*	beautify
nui	large	*ho'o-nui*	enlarge

Another very productive method is reduplication: simply repeating all or part of the root word. As do all other Polynesian languages, Hawaiian uses this process extensively and for a number of different purposes. One of the most common of these is to indicate frequent repetitions of the action of a verb:

ha'i	say	*ha'iha'i*	speak back and forth
ma'i	sick	*ma'ima'i*	chronically sick
hoe	paddle	*hoehoe*	paddle continuously

Next, a word can take on new meanings by modifying it, thus expanding or narrowing the usual meaning. As a means of dealing with new concepts, this device is discussed below.

makapa'a	blind in one eye (*maka* 'eye' and *pa'a* 'closed')
kinohou	beginning (*kino* 'body' and *hou* 'new')

In the first example, the meaning of the longer form is somewhat predictable from the meanings of the parts. However, the second example is much less obvious, and some forms, such as *i'a-lele-i-aka* 'Milky Way, lit., 'fish jumping in shadows', are true idioms, with the meaning of the constructed form totally unpredictable from the meanings of the parts.[1]

Finally, we assume that a word can take on new meanings with no changes in form at all. Unfortunately, we have no documentary evidence for such changes; the only clear examples of this process involve introduced concepts. However, we can make some guesses from various meanings grouped under one headword in the current Hawaiian dictionary. Here, metaphor plays an important role. For example, Pukui and Elbert (1957) explained the relationship between *limu* 'seaweed' and *limu* 'deceiving' as hinging on the octopus's ability to change color and imitate the motion of seaweed in water.

The need for words with which to refer to concepts not native to Hawai'i but introduced from the outside stems from Captain Cook's and the Hawaiians' reciprocal discovery, and the inevitable exchange of goods and ideas that grew out of this meeting.[2] After more than two centuries of contact, the exchange has been considerable. For borrowings from Hawaiian into English, the most authoritative study cites 205 loanwords (Tsuzaki and Elbert 1969:23). But by far, most of the borrowing has been in the opposite direction: from English to Hawaiian. This chapter presents a view of some of the borrowings as illustrations of the confrontation and accommodation between two very different languages and cultures. It also investigates a minor mystery: why should the Hawaiian borrowings show such very different phonological patterns from those in some related languages?

THE EARLIEST EVIDENCE

Perhaps even before we look at the earliest historical evidence for loanwords in Hawaiian, it is necessary to discuss the romanticized folk etymology that has grown out of stories of lost caravels and other hints of Spanish contact with Hawai'i before Cook. Of course, history and geography support the possibility of Spanish contact before 1778. But the idea of contact has been strengthened by the accidental resemblance between a few words in both languages. Although these putative relatives are probably due to the similarity between Spanish and Hawaiian vowels, they have given rise to the notion that Hawaiian has borrowed them from Spanish. The following example is typical of this kind of creative history (Preston 1900a:43):

> One of the most potent factors in the modification of language is commercial intercourse. Similarity has been noted between certain Hawaiian words and those of identical meaning in Spanish. They furnish evidence of early contact between the two nationalities. Here are a few examples:
> The words *mate* in Kanaka and *matar* in Spanish both mean to kill; *poko* in Kanaka means the same as *poco* in Spanish; *piko* means the same as *pico* in Spanish, as in *ka piko o ka mauna*.

Preston went on to explain a possible source for the "borrowings": by Hawaiian tradition, a Spanish shipwreck between 1525 and 1530. Had Preston looked beyond Hawaiian to other Polynesian languages, he might have revised his opinion: all three words can be traced back to Proto Polynesian. Thus the forms are inherited, not borrowed.

As for real borrowings, it would be illogical to expect them to crop up at the first meeting between Hawaiians and Europeans, but Cook's narrative does interest the philologist in at least two ways. First, from the Hawaiians' reaction to the various items of European material culture, Cook surmised that he was indeed witnessing their first encounter with Europeans (at least within the memories of those Hawaiians present): "I never saw Indians so much astonished at the entering a ship before, their eyes were continually flying from object to object, the wildness of thier [*sic*] looks and actions fully express'd their surprise and astonishment at the several new o[b]jects before them ..." (Beaglehole 1967:265). (Some of the new objects mentioned were looking glasses, beads, cloth, and china cups.)

Next, one item turned out to be less "new" than expected. As noted in chapter 1, the Hawaiians were already familiar with iron, most likely since it had been washed ashore attached to driftwood.[3] Thus, some of its superior qualities were already appreciated: "& of Iron, they only knew its use for boring & to make Tòès [*ko'i* 'hatchets']" (Beaglehole 1967:265n). As a matter of fact, it was in such demand that Cook was able to obtain a large hog for one or two 6d nails, and other provisions in exchange for chisels.

As more and more of Cook's successors reached Hawai'i, the impact of foreign products and the need to find names for them increased. If we reexamine the vocabularies discussed in chapter 3, it comes as no surprise to find that the later lists contain more borrowings than the earlier ones. Even so, those collected not long after the first effort in 1778 show some influence from the outside, although they contain no borrowings in the strict sense of the word. For example, William Beresford's list (collected in 1787) includes Hawaiian words that had taken on new meanings to cover European items:

1. *Booboo* [*pūpū*], a button. Evidently because of a button's shape and material, the Hawaiians gave it their general name for 'shell'. On the other hand, Tongan and Samoan chose the function, not the material, for their names: *fakama'u* and *fa'amau*, respectively; lit., 'to make fast'.

2. *Poreema* [*pūlima*], a number of buttons on a string. Here, the word for 'wrist' has taken on a new meaning, probably from the fashion, then as now, of a row of buttons at the wrist of a man's coat sleeve.

3. *Hou* [*hao*], nail. Now the word for 'iron', *hao* was originally the name for a hardwood tree.[4] Evidence for Beresford's intending *hao* rather than **hou* is found in his spelling of *kaula* 'rope' as *touro*.[5]

4. *Tabahou* [*ka pahu*], a pail or bucket. The Andrews-Parker dictionary explains the connection between this meaning and the basic meaning of *pahu*: 'drum': "A pahu was originally a hollow coconut or other tree with a shark skin drawn over one end and used for a drum: hence anything hollow and giving a sound when struck is a *pahu*."[6]

As these words show, borrowing a foreign concept does not necessarily produce a linguistic borrowing, for it is obvious that a foreign
word must be associated with the concept as well. For borrowings from
English, this did not take place until the influence of the language was
strong enough to cement the association between *Wörter und Sachen*:
words and the things they signified.

The first evidence we have for true borrowings comes as early as
1791. When Manuel Quimper collected his vocabulary, he included
some adapted English forms that were apparently well established by
that time. For example, 'rope' was translated as *tropi*, most likely from
ta ropi, with *ta* (now *ka* in most parts of Hawai'i) as the definite article.
'Canoe' was translated with the expected Hawaiian form: *gebago*
(Quimper's Castilian spelling of *he wa'a*), but also with a borrowed one:
tenu (probably *tenū*). It is significant that both of these words are
nautical, for at that time, the most likely interpreter for a word collector
was a Hawaiian who had spent some time at sea on a European vessel.

By the time Archibald Campbell stayed in Hawai'i in 1809–1810,
both European material culture and the English language had affected the
lives of the Hawaiians. From Campbell's collection of about 400 words
(1816:227-55), list 10.1 shows the forty-one that refer to recent additions
to the Hawaiian culture.[7] Because this sample was collected well after
the earliest European contact, but a decade before Bible translation
began to influence the language, we can use it to represent the different
ways in which Hawaiians referred to introduced concepts.

It was noted early that there were different ways to add to the
Hawaiian vocabulary. For example, Andrews wrote (1836b:20):

> With regard to new words in a language just reduced to writing
> and where improvements, or what is the same thing, where new
> ideas are brought in, there are two methods of proceeding. One is
> to introduce new words from other languages to express new
> ideas; the other is, to give new definitions to words already in use.
> Both of these methods have been pursued in the Hawaiian. New
> words have been introduced as noticed above. Caution however
> will be necessary lest words should be unnecessarily introduced, or
> such as are no more significant than some that are already in the
> language. The number of the words to which new ideas have been
> attached is not yet large, but will probably be greatly increased
> when moral, religious, and scientific studies shall be more
> extensively and systematically pursued. *Naau* the heart, *uhane* the
> soul, and *Akua* God, and several other words, have ideas attached
> to them now in the minds of the more intelligent natives that they
> had not a few years ago.

LIST 10.1

WORDS FOR INTRODUCED CONCEPTS IN CAMPBELL'S WORD LIST.

American	*Merikana*	iron	*how*
bee	*Narro*	knife	*okee-okee,*
horse	*edea nooee*		*kanee-kanee*
bees-wax	*tootai narro*	looking glass	*anee-anee*
biscuit	*bikete*	marshmallow	*etooa rere*
block,	*pockaka*	mustard	*totai kumaree*
bucket	*tabahoo*	nail	*how*
button	*opeehee,*	printing	*purra-purra*
	booboo	rum	*lummee*
buttons,		Russian	*tanata*
string of	*Poreema*		*Lookeene*
		saw	*pahe oroo*
cabbage	*tabete*	scissors	*oopa*
cannon	*poo nooee*	sheep	*peepe*
captain of		ship	*motoo*
ship	*eree te motooa*	stockings	*tookeine*
cat	*popokee*	tallow	*oila*
cockroach	*patte-patte*	white people	*tanata howree*
cow	*peepe-nooe*	James	*Keeme*
duck	*mora*	William	*Williama*
England	*Pritane,*	Isaac	*Itseeke*
	Kaheite	John	*Keone*
Englishman	*kanaka Pritane,*	handkerchief	*haneeka*
	kanaka Kaheite		
goat	*peepe kao*	gun, musket	*poo*

However, one can make further distinctions. The words in list 10.1 show that the Hawaiians had at least four ways of expanding their vocabulary to include the offerings from outside, in addition to making up an entirely new word.[8] (In the following discussion, note the similarities to the ways Hawaiians had of expanding their vocabulary internally, listed at the beginning of the chapter.)

Use of an Existing Word, with Expansion of Meaning

The Hawaiian word for 'bee' is *narro* [*nalo*], from the word for 'housefly' and other flies. For 'beeswax', Campbell elicited *tootai narro* [*kūkae nalo*], lit., 'bee excrement'. He did not ask for a translation for 'honey', but later, when the missionaries needed such a term for Bible translation, we can surmise that they ran into difficulties. Depend-ing upon their pronunciation of the first vowel of the English model, two forms were possible for adaptation into Hawaiian: **honi* and **hani*.

Both forms would be close enough to the English model to avoid "destroying its identity," as one early missionary warned against, but they violated his second restriction: that an adapted word should not be of such a shape as to cause confusion with an existing word. Either *honi* 'kiss' or *hani* 'act flirtatious' would have given an undesired risqué meaning to such phrases as 'land flowing with milk and honey' (especially with 'milk' translated by a phrase that means 'breast liquid') or 'lips of a strange woman drop honey'. The solution the translators adopted was to use *meli*, from Greek μελι.[9]

As for the Hawaiian use of *kūkae* as a generic term for items with a certain color and/or viscosity, another example from Campbell's list is *totai kumaree* [*kūkae kamali'i*], lit., 'infant excrement', for 'mustard'. Obviously not a missionary creation, the form was possibly modeled on existing phrases with *kūkae* as the head. (The Pukui-Elbert dictionary shows a number of such phrases, mostly idiomatic and often referring to substances with a brown or spotted appearance. An example is *kūkae-hao*, 'rust', lit., 'iron excrement'.) As for the form for 'mustard', it was apparently short-lived; the New Testament (Matt. 13:31) used a true borrowing, *makeke* [*mākeke*], and this is the form Andrews entered in his dictionary (1865).

The word for 'horse', *edea nooee* [*'īlio nui*] is another example of an existing Hawaiian word assuming an additional meaning. With their inventory of four-legged mammals restricted to rat (*'iole*), pig (*pua'a*), and dog (*'īlio*), the Hawaiians chose to refer to 'horse' as 'big dog'. The *d* in Campbell's transcription represents his hearing of Hawaiian [ř], which is now written as *l*. The *a* (probably representing [ə]) is apparently how he heard an unaccented *o*. Eventually, the first syllable dropped, as did the qualifier, *nui*, leaving *lio*.

On Campbell's list, the Hawaiian words for 'limpet' and 'shell' in general—*opeehii* and *booboo* [*'opihi, pūpū*]—have taken on an addition-al meaning: 'button'. Now, *pūpū* can refer to beads, and *'opihi* (as with *'īlio* for 'horse') has lost the first syllable, resulting in *pihi*.

True Borrowing: Total Adaptation

On Campbell's list, the first word, *Merikana* 'American', shows a loanword proper—that is, the wholesale transfer of a word from English to Hawaiian. Here, the confrontation between two sound systems as different as those of Hawaiian and English can reveal unexpected information about both languages. In the following sections, we look at some specific patterns in the transformation of an English word to a Hawaiian one.

Consonants and Vowels. The first step in explaining the form of a Hawaiian borrowing from English is to compare the consonants and vowels of the two languages. In general, we assume that an English sound will "become" the Hawaiian sound most similar to it. However, "most similar" is not something that can be measured exactly. Thus, the correspondences in table 10.1 were deduced from the borrowings themselves, not predicted just from the sound systems of the words concerned.

Table 10.1 also shows that since Hawaiian has an unusually small number of phonemes (eight consonants and five vowels, as compared with twenty-four consonants and approximately twelve vowels—discounting diphthongs—for English), the resultant correspondence chart turns out to be a lopsided one. However, these numbers are misleading, for the Hawaiian vowel system is much more complex than the writing system shows: five short vowels, five long vowels, nine short diphthongs, and six long diphthongs (see Schütz 1981).

TABLE 10.1
CORRESPONDENCES BETWEEN ENGLISH AND HAWAIIAN SOUNDS
IN BORROWINGS

English	Hawaiian	English	Hawaiian
p, b, f	p	y, i, ɪ	i
v, w	w	e, ɛ	e
hw	hu	æ, a, ɚ	
s, h, š	h	er, ə, ʌ	a
l, r	l	ɔ, o	o
m	m	u, ʊ	u
n, ŋ	n		
t, d, θ,ð, s, z, ž, č , ǰ, k, g	k		

Adapted from Carr 1951 and Pukui and Elbert 1957:xvii

Early borrowings also show an expanded range of consonants, at least in their spelling, for before the superfluous consonants were discarded in 1826, casual visitors wrote the sounds they thought they heard, including *b, d, r, t,* and *v.* For example, note from the sample in list 10.1 that Campbell wrote *b* and *p, t* and *k,* and *d, r* and *l.*[10]

Even after 1826, as we saw in chapter 7, the missionaries kept the otherwise discarded consonants simply as badges, as it were, to identify loanwords. The decision to set borrowed words apart from native ones was a conscious one, documented by the following report (Missionary letters, May 1825):

> Upon the first question—[on uniformity of the orthography] motioned—that it is expedient in transferring words & proper names from other languages to the Hawaiian to preserve their identity as far as the genius of the language will admit.

Andrews (1836b:20) justified this policy as follows, showing first how English had borrowed additional letters for its alphabet along with words:

> With these words, too, the English have borrowed several letters such as *x, z,* and hard *ch,* the French *ch,* and the Greek *ph.* Thus the number of sounds are increased in the language,[11] and thus the words are readily recognized by the eye as taken from a foreign language. So it has been necessary to do in the Hawaiian; for without it more confusion would be made than benefit gained. Thus the foreign word *mare,* to marry, in pure Hawaiian orthography would be *male,* to expectorate. *Rama,* rum, would be *lama* a torch. But the confusion would be more particularly manifest in proper names; thus *Ruta,* Ruth, in Hawaiian orthography would be *Luka,* Luke; *Sara,* would be *Kala,* name of a man, &c. Though these foreign letters are necessary, yet it is not necessary to introduce *every* letter, nor even every syllable of a word that may be brought into the language; only a sufficiency to show that the word is of foreign extraction is all that is requisite.

Because of this policy, some borrowed words looked, if not necessarily sounded, more like their sources than they do today. For example, note *bikete* 'biscuit'. Here, the freedom to use *b* and both *k* and *t* produced a word that looks more like its model than would **pikeke.*[12]

At any rate, such forms illustrate how the Hawaiians perceived an English word, and, in turn, how their pronunciation was interpreted by the English recorder, at least in terms of consonants and vowels.

Syllable Structure. Perhaps even more significant than the disparity between the vowel and consonant systems of the two languages is the difference between their syllable systems. The effect of the Hawaiian syllable structure on the final form of a borrowing was noted early (Ellis 1825:244):

> It may be proper to add, that both in the Hawaiian and Tahitian languages, every syllable, and every word, ends with a vowel. Accordingly, Mr. Ellis has observed, that the Tahitians never could pronounce his name, which ends with a consonant; and moreover, that as they cannot sound the consonant *s* at all, they used to pronounce his name in three syllables, *Eliki* .

There are two ways to interpret this practice. One, the traditional approach, distinguishes between vowels inserted between consonants (*epenthesis*) and those added at the ends of words (*paragoge*). Such was the approach taken by Denzel Carr (1951), who treated the two processes in Hawaiian (as compared with Japanese) in separate sections.

However, as applied to introduced words in Hawaiian, the terms *epenthesis* and *paragoge* are somewhat misleading, since traditionally they refer to two separate processes. It is more in keeping with the structure of the language to suggest that added vowels are used for only one purpose: to produce syllables that consist (at the most) of just a consonant and a vowel.

Looking at the phenomenon in a different way, one might propose that each English consonant, except those in homorganic clusters,[13] is heard as a sequence of consonant plus vowel—that is, as a syllable in Hawaiian. Thus, adding a vowel when necessary is perhaps a means of formalizing the way a Hawaiian hearer divides an English loanword into syllables.

TABLE 10.2

SOUND-TO-SYLLABLE CORRESPONDENCES FOR SAMPLE WORDS

E	k	rI	s	mə	s	Christmas[14]
H	ka	li	ki	ma	ka	
E	bI	l				Bill
H	pi	la				
E	ka	n	sə	l		consul
H	ka	ni	ke	la		

Table 10.2 represents this idea graphically. At first glance, the Hawaiian form for 'Christmas' seems unwieldy: a five-syllable word corresponding to a two-syllable English word. But perhaps the forms "match" in another way: in each of these examples, the number of English syllables corresponds to the number of Hawaiian accent units.[15] Note the following example, in which brackets enclose English syllables and Hawaiian accent units:

E	[krɪs]	[məs]
H	[kalíki]	[máka]

Thus, in the process of adapting an English word to the Hawaiian phonological system, more than just individual sound correspondences are involved: the syllable structure of Hawaiian has to be accommodated and, ideally, the accent patterns of the English model matched as closely as possible. This last detail is usually accomplished by vowel lengthening. For examples, we return to Campbell's list—at least to the modern renderings of two of the words he collected:

> *kāpiki* 'cabbage' *palaka* 'block'

In the example for 'cabbage', if the first vowel were not long, the word would be accented **kapíki*, which does not match the English model very well. And conversely, if the word for 'block' had the form **pālaka*, there would be an accent on the first vowel, which is an added vowel between the *p* and the *l*—again, not a good match with the English model.

This is not to say that the forms that have become accepted always match the model as well as they could have. Because long vowels were not consistently marked until fairly recently, some forms were fixed by eye rather than by ear (this distinction is from Carr 1951), and vowel length fell by the wayside. For example, note the following personal names (from Pukui, Elbert, and Mookini 1975):

Alika	Alex	*Alena*	Alan
Amoka	Amos	*Akoni*	Anthony
Hapaki	Herbert	*Pakile*	Basil

Since each of the English forms is accented on the first syllable, the Hawaiianized forms would better fit the models if, in each case, the first vowel were lengthened. On the other hand, once a word was well assimilated into Hawaiian, how well it matched the prosody of the English original was probably not very important.

Adaptation, with a Shift

For some borrowings, the meaning has shifted over the years, sometimes matching technological changes. For example, *oila* [now *'aila*] was first used for 'tallow', although the current dictionary gives 'any oil, grease, lard ...' The meaning of 'tallow' probably waned as the use of animal fats diminished in the manufacture of candles and soap.

The curious word *kao* for 'goat' is another example of an adapted form that has undergone a semantic shift, illustrating the early flexibility in the Hawaiian system of classifying new quadrupeds.

Loanblends

Peepe-nooe [*pipi nui*], lit., 'big beef', is translated as 'cow'. This form, and those for 'sheep' (*peepe* [*pipi*], now *hipa*), produce a set that is both confusing and tantalizing. From these examples, it appears that *pipi*—usually assumed to have come from 'beef'—was early used as a general term for domesticated meat-producing mammals. Sheep and beef cattle were known to the Hawaiians as early as the 1790s, when Captain George Vancouver brought them both from California. But it seems odd that the form for 'sheep' is the unqualified one, unless *pipi* is a portmanteau borrowing from both 'beef' and 'sheep'. Whatever the early situation, the shape of the current word for 'sheep'—*hipa*—shows an unmistakable missionary imprint, because of both its first consonant and its last vowel (see the discussion later in this chapter).

-o-o-o-o-o-

A list even as short as Campbell's raises many questions. For example, how does one explain *patte-patte* for 'cockroach'? Is it *pakī pakī* 'splatter'? Is *mackeroa* 'shoot' actually *make loa* 'die' or *maʻaalaioa* 'shoot with a sling'? Because of the early transcribers' unsuccessful battles with the glottal stop and unaccented vowels, it might be either.

LATER LISTS

Of Urey Lisiansky's 170 words (1814, but collected in 1804), 5 refer to European articles. Some earlier forms were reinforced: *opeehee* for 'button', and *tabetee* or *kabekee* for 'cabbage'. But 'goat' was translated as *rio kao* [ʻīlio kao], lit., 'cow-like dog'. 'Looking-glass' remained *aneeanee* [*aniani*], lit., 'transparent', as in Campbells' list, and 'nail' was glossed as *mayo*, unexplainable unless from *māio* 'furrowed, grooved, cut in ridges ...' or *māiʻuʻu* 'fingernail'.

In Joseph P. Gaimard's list (1823), only 4 words out of 235 refer to items of European origin. *Poumah* (most likely representing *puma*) for 'chalk' leads nowhere: one unrelated and obsolete meaning for *puma* is listed in the current dictionary, and now the word for 'chalk' is *poho*, which first referred to chalky, white earth. Curiously, *kenou* [kenū?] survived from at least Quimper's time, evidently competing with the indigenous form *waʻa*. The word for 'goat' was simplified to *tao* [*kao*], which is its current form, and *paka* 'tobacco' made its first insidious appearance.

In the early 1820s, the Reverend Artemas Bishop compiled a provisional Hawaiian vocabulary, part of which eventually appeared as appendix 5 in the 1825 edition of Ellis's *A Journal of a Tour Around Hawaii*. Of the 248 words printed, the following refer to items of foreign origin.

alani [*'alani*]	orange	*kaukama* [*ka'ukama*]	cucumber
aniani	glass	*kala* [*kālā*]	dollar
ao [*'ao*]	bread	*kapiki* [*kāpiki*]	cabbage
baka [*paka*]	tobacco	*kulina* [*kūlina*]	corn
boti [*poki*]	boat	*ohia* [*'ōhi'a*]	apple
buke [*puke*]	book	*Perikani* [*Pelekane*]	Britain
hao	iron	*uala* [*'uala*]	potato
hanika [*haina-*	handker-	*waina*	wine
kā]	chief	*kae* [*kao*]	goat

Of these, *aniani*, *'ao*, *hao*, *'ōhi'a*, and *'uala* are indigenous words that have taken on new meanings. *'Ao* originally referred to 'dried baked taro or sweet potato ... used on sea journeys'. *'Ōhi'a'ai (Eugenia malaccensis)* is 'mountain apple' and *'uala (Ipomoea batatas)* 'sweet potato'. The remainder are direct borrowings from English.

PERSONAL NAMES AS BORROWINGS

> ... *but after great pains taken we found it utterly impossible to teach the Indians to pronounce our names; we had, therefore, new names, consisting of such sounds as they produced in the attempt. They called me Toote; Mr. Hicks, Hete; Molineaux they renounced in absolute despair, and called the Master Boba, from his Christian name Robert; Mr. Gore was Toarro; Dr. Solander, Torano; and Mr. Banks, Tapane; Mr. Green, Eteree; Mr. Parkinson, Patini; Mr. Sporing, Polini: Petersgill, Petrodero; and in this man-ner they had now formed names for almost every man in the ship ... [this was on Wednesday, 10 May 1769]* (John Hawkesworth, An Account of the Voyages ... *(1773), vol. 2, p. 123*).

This quotation shows how the Tahitians renamed Cook's crew members in 1769, paring the English (or French) names of consonant clusters and adding vowels to make the syllables match their own.

As Campbell's list shows, names were very early borrowings in Hawaiian as well. But the records we have usually show simply English spellings, such as Henry 'Ōpūkaha'ia, Thomas Hopu, John Honoli'i, William Kanui, George Tamoree [Kaumuali'i] for the young men connected with the Foreign Mission School in Cornwall, Connecticut; we are not told how the Hawaiians themselves pronounced these names. But one important person had a name so assimilated into Hawaiian that the English origin was quite concealed. And perhaps just as well so. William Richards told how Boki, governor of O'ahu, got his name (Richards to Anderson, Missionary letters, no. 142, 20 May 1828):

> I would just remark respecting the name of Boki that even according to our present rules it may be spelt with the *B* for the name is of foreign origin. His original name was Ilio- ['Īlio] punahele, that is, favourite dog. When the king became acquaint- ed with a large American dog named Boss, he immediately changed the name of the young chief from *Ilio-punahele* to Boss, which in native language is Boki, pronounced by 99/100 of the people Poki.

Naturally, the missionaries' and other residents' names were Hawaiianized as well. Some examples are *Pinamu* 'Bingham', *Laumiki* 'Loomis', *Eliki* 'Ellis', *Bihopa* 'Bishop', *Temenena* 'Chamberlain', and *Marini* 'Marin'.

LOANWORDS FOR BIBLE TRANSLATION

With the Hawaiians' at least partial acceptance of Christianity in the 1820s came not only a dramatic increase in the number of new concepts for which words had to be found, but also a change in their nature and a different methodology for their introduction. If we refer back to the quotation that heads this chapter, we can see that by his unconscious choice of phrase—*to introduce* new words, rather than *borrow* them—Lorrin Andrews touched on the underlying theme of this chapter: the active versus passive role of the speakers of a language in adding new words to their vocabulary.

Andrews used the word *introduce* again on the last page of his *Vocabulary* (see table 10.3), where he listed words beginning with non-Hawaiian consonants, otherwise eliminated from the alphabet. He prefaced the list as follows (1836a):

> The following words, with many others, have been introduced into the Hawaiian language, and of course a sufficiency of foreign letters to show the derivation, and distinguish them from native words by their orthography.

No longer did the bulk of new expressions represent concrete (and practical) items, such as *horse, biscuit,* or *bread.* Instead, the Hawaiians were presented with ideas rather different from their own physical and cultural world—such concepts as *trinity, transubstantiation, angel,* and

TABLE 10.3
WORDS BEGINNING WITH FOREIGN CONSONANTS

baka (E)	tobacco	goula (E)	golden
bakeke (E)	bucket	rabi (S)	master
bale (E)	barley	rana (L)	frog
bama (E)	balm	rope (E)	rope
bapetiso (G)	baptize	rue (E)	rue (herb)
bato (H)	bath, measure	Sabati (H)	Sabbath
bea (E)	bear	satana (G)	satan
berena (E)	bread, food	sato (G)	a measure
berita (H)	covenant	sekona (E)	second (time)
bipi/bifi (E)	cattle	selu (H)	quail
bitumena (E)	bitumen	setadia (G)	furlong
buke (E)	book	sopa (E)	soap
daimonio (G)	demon	sukamino (G)	sycamore
dala/dola (E)	dollar	sukomorea (G)	sycamore
denari (L)	coin	talena (E)	talent
dia (E)	deer	tausani (E)	thousand
diabolo (G)	devil	vinega (E)	vinegar
diderama (G)	tribute	viola (E)	viol
falaoa (E)	flour	Ziona (H)	Zion
fiku (E)	fig	zizania (G)	tares
gola/gula (E)	gold		

E: English   G: Greek   H: Hebrew   L: Latin

baptism. Still, the new expressions can be classified in the same way as the more prosaic and substantial ones from the period of explorers and traders. For example, the translation of *trinity* uses existing words, this time in a new combination: *kāhikolu*, lit., 'one-three'—that is, a three-part unity. For *transubstantiation, ho'okū ā kino* is used, primarily a 'transformation, as from animal to human form'.

Illustrating the missionaries' point of view that Hawaiian lacked the terms necessary for talking about Christianity, Sheldon Dibble wrote (1839:137–38):

> In many instances they succeed, in a measure, but with circum-location; in others they use a sort of patch-work of native words. For instance: *manao* [*mana'o*] means thought, and *io* ['*i'o*] means true or real; —so the combination, *manaoio* [*mana'o'i'o*], is used for faith. Again, *manao* means thought, and *lana* means buoyant, —so the combination, *manaolana* [*mana'olana*], is made by us to express hope. *Ala* means to rise, *hou* means again, and *ana* is a participial termination;— so we make *alahouana* [*alahou'ana*] to

signify the rising again, or the resurrection. We are obliged to manufacture many of the most important words expressive of religious subjects. It is perplexing to the ignorant people, but it is unavoidable. Then again, in some cases we introduce words of English, Greek, and Hebrew origin.

The following list shows a few more examples of religious terms composed wholly of Hawaiian items:

nīnau hōʻike	catechism, lit., revealing question
ui	catechism, lit., question
nīnau pili hoʻomana	catechism, lit., question about religion[16]
puʻuwai hoʻāno	sacred heart
puʻuwai laʻahia	sacred heart
poʻe hemolele	saint, lit., perfect, virtuous person
lei aliʻi	diadem, lit., chiefly lei
palapala hemolele	scriptures, lit., perfect, virtuous writings
kahuna pule	pastor, lit., praying priest
hale kupapaʻu	sepulcher, lit., house for corpses

In contrast, the following terms are direct borrowings:

ʻānela	angel	*papakema*	baptism
kakekimo	catechism	*sana*	saint
Sabati	Sabbath	*kāna*	saint[17]
Kāpaki	Sabbath[18]	*kūpika*	cubit
saneta	saint	*lōkākio*	rosary
kaneka	saint	*ʻāmene*	amen

One of the alternates for "rosary" shows total adaptation of an English word, with a shift in meaning: *kolona* (or *kalaunu*), based on "crown."[19]

An example of a loanblend is *ui kula Sabati* 'Sunday School', with an indigenous word *ui* 'question' and two borrowings, adapted from *school* and *Sabbath*.

As for the methodology for such introductions, it differed in two significant ways. First, as the missionaries developed an orthography and the Hawaiians learned to read, the eye, and not the ear alone, played a part in making neologisms (e.g., *hīmeni* 'hymn', in which the *n* is based on spelling, not pronunciation). Next, many new forms show signs of having been created by the missionaries rather than by the native speakers, thus adding a new dimension to the concept of "borrowing." As the following section shows, these words are identified by the choice of vowels that are added, as discussed earlier, to break up consonant clusters and make sure that every syllable ends with a vowel.

Choice of Added Vowels

Previous studies of the shapes of loanwords in languages related to Hawaiian (Schütz 1970, 1978) have shown that the choice of added vowels is not arbitrary, but dependent primarily on the phonetic nature of the preceding consonant, and secondarily on the surrounding accented vowels. In both Tongan and Fijian, although *i* and *e* account for the majority of the added vowels, with a particular reinforcement of *i* after dentals, there is also a tendency for *u* to occur after *b*, *p*, *v*, and *m*, *a* after *k*, and *o* after *l*.[20] Such a patterning leads us to suggest that even when an English consonant is not followed by a vowel, speakers of Oceanic languages hear its release as vowel-like, varying according to the position of the consonant, and thus affecting the choice of added vowel.

Although Tongan and Fijian differ somewhat in the details of their rules for the choice of added vowels, they operate in the same general way. Therefore, while expecting even more variation in detail for Hawaiian (because of its smaller consonant system), one still expects it to share the same general patterns.

The Actual Patterning

With these patterns in mind, it comes as a surprise to find that the vowel-consonant combinations prominent in Fijian and Tongan are much less so in Hawaiian. For example, in his comparison of added vowels in Hawaiian and Japanese, Carr (1951:20) found that in spite of certain phonetically logical patterns—such as *u* following labials, *i* following "dentals and palatals in the original ... in Hawaiian the tendency in all eye-borrowed and many ear-borrowed words is to choose *a* [at the end of a word]. It is considered the most neutral vowel and is, incidentally the most frequent ... *A* has now become the standard fill-out vowel, but many of the older l o a n w o r d s exemplify a different state."

As an illustration of this "different state," note the following borrowings in Campbell's list:

bikete	biscuit	*lummee*	rum
tabete	cabbage	*Lookeene*	Russian
Pritane	Britain	*tookeine*	stockings
peepe	sheep	*Itseeke*	Isaac
teakete	jacket	*Keeme*	James

Although the editor's key to Campbell's pronunciation shows that *e* is pronounced like the accented vowel in *eloquence*, or *plenty*, and *ee* like that in *keep*, the modern spellings of some of the forms above—

kapiki 'cabbage', *pipi* 'beef', *Lukini* 'Russian', and *kakini* 'stocking'—
show that both *e* and *ee* at the end of a word probably represented *i*.

For these particular examples, the situation is also complicated by
the fact that some of the vowels at the end seem to "echo" the preceding
one. Still, the change from a final *-i* (or *-e*) in the older loanwords to *-a*
in later ones is puzzling. Why does this phenomenon in Hawaiian
pattern so differently than it does in related languages?

To find the answer, one must follow the lead ignored by Carr and
investigate the "different state" of the older loanwords. As an example,
note that the variations currently allowed for "Isaac" provide further evidence that something happened to change this earlier patterning. *Aikake*
is labeled as "not Biblical," *Ika'aka* and *Isaaka* as "Biblical." Such
variations lead one to wonder about the Bible translators' attitudes
toward the Hawaiianization of English words.

The compilers of the first Hawaiian dictionaries were well aware of
the effect of the Hawaiian syllable system on the shape of the
borrowings. In the introduction to his list of borrowings (1865:515–19),
Andrews noted:

> Owing to the peculiar structure of the Hawaiian (every syllable
> ending in a vowel sound), the forms of these words are somewhat
> modified, by dropping a letter or syllable of the original, but more
> frequently perhaps by inserting or adding a vowel in order to
> Hawaiianize them.

And why the eventual predominance of *-a* as a final added vowel
in contrast to an early favoring of *-i*? Hiram Bingham (1847:155) wrote
of two ways of dealing with English consonants that did not fit the
Hawaiian (consonant)-vowel syllable structure. First, one element of a
consonant cluster was chosen to represent the whole. His examples,
however, show a total reliance on spelling rather than sound, for they are
not consonant clusters, but digraphs—two letters representing one
sound: *ph* [f], *th* [θ] or [ð], and *ch* [č].[21] But in his explanation of the
second method—the addition of vowels—he revealed why the expected
patterns do not turn up in Hawaiian: "When two consonants joined in a
foreign word, need both to be preserved, we interpose the vowel *e*, and
after a final consonant add usually the vowel *a*—as *Bosetona* for
Boston."[22] Apparently unaware of the patterns that already existed, the
missionaries imposed their own.

Thus, foreign words used in Hawaiian fall into two distinct classes.
First, words that were actually borrowed by the speakers themselves
follow some of the general patterns found in the related languages
studied so far. But many words, especially those related to the
translation of the Bible and educational material, differ in two ways.

Not only did the motivation for their use come from outside, but their very form—the use of *-e-* to break up consonants in the middle of a word, and of *-a* to end the word—identifies them not as borrowings, but as impositions.

SUMMARY

If we examine Hawaiian words that refer to objects and concepts introduced from the outside, it is easy to see that like other languages, Hawaiian has increased its vocabulary in a number of ways. In the broadest terms, it has altered words already existing by expanding their meaning, made up new words, adapted words from another language, or combined these methods.

In spite of the influx of foreign material goods that affected the language, probably the most concentrated introduction of new words stemmed from translating religious and educational materials, especially in the 1820s, 1830s, and 1840s. Here, the coiners used all the methods mentioned above—with the possible exception of making up totally new words. From the records that are available, admittedly mostly from the foreign and especially religious point of view, there does not seem to have been chauvinistic avoidance of foreign elements. But then, did anyone record the Hawaiian point of view?

We will see in chapter 16 that in some ways, the language is again undergoing changes similar to those that took place over a century and a half ago: after a long period of relatively little coinage, new words are again entering the language, and in great numbers. But the social climate has changed significantly, and with it, the balance between adapting indigenous words and borrowing words from the outside, especially from English.

NOTES

Much of this chapter is adapted from Schütz 1976a.

[1] Although this topic has not been systematically investigated, Hawaiian does not seem to have compounds that can be defined phonologically—that is, noun-modifier combinations with idiomatic meanings of their own and separate accent patterns, such as English *greenhouse* versus *green house*.

[2] This notion excludes possible influence from other Polynesian languages before the time of European contact.

[3] As noted at the beginning of this work, the Hawaiians' comment about the iron they saw on Cook's ships is the first example of the language that we can read in Cook's narrative. To expand on this topic, we can add that Cook wrote

specifically about the value of iron to the Hawaiians: "... but valued nails, or iron above every other thing ..." (Beaglehole 1967:264). Although the notion of prior European contact is certainly possible, there is a simpler explanation (Fornander 1880, 2:168–69)): "Because the iron was known before that time from wood with iron (in or on it) that had formerly drifted ashore, but it was in small quantity, and here [on Cook's ship] was plenty."

[4] The Pukui-Elbert dictionary offers no help to the reader seeking the origin of this usage. The Andrews-Parker dictionary, however, makes the connection between the referents of the word: 'partaking of the nature of hao wood'. It also adds that the word was used for hard substances other than iron, such as "the horn or hoof of a beast."

[5] Writing *ou* for [aw] or [au] was the standard practice at the time. See, for example, Anderson's conventions for Tahitian (table 4.1).

[6] The Pukui-Elbert dictionary "defines" the term by simply listing English translations (e.g., box, drum, cask, chest, barrel, trunk, tank, case ...), providing no explanation of the connection among these meanings.

[7] Some forms are obviously misprints: e.g., the gloss 'clock' for *moa tannee* [*moa kāne*] should be 'cock'.

[8] Except for the items that cannot be positively identified (there are at least thirty-two on the list), there does not seem to be any possible concrete evidence that this happened.

[9] One cannot help but wonder if avoiding homophony was more of a missionary principle than a Hawaiian one. After all, the Hawaiian vocabulary is rife with homophones, a feature of the language that is common as a literary device, *kaona*. Thus, sets of words sounding exactly alike but with widely different meanings would not be unusual in Hawaiian.

[10] Elsewhere on the list (but not in any introduced words), Campbell also wrote both *v* and *w*.

[11] Here, Andrews did not distinguish between sounds and letters of the alphabet. For example, introducing loanwords with the spelling *ph* did not change the inventory of sounds, since this digraph has always been pronounced /f/. However, the huge influx of loanwords after the Norman conquest did result in a change, for certain sounds that were only variants before now had the status as phonemes (e.g., *v* and *z*). But Andrews's analogy is imperfect: in spite of the extra consonants added for the spelling of loanwords, the Hawaiian sound system has not really undergone any changes of this type, except perhaps an occasional concession to an [s] pronunciation in a few words.

[12] To make a closer match with the accent pattern of the English model, the first vowel might have been long: **pīkeke*. However, we have no way of telling, since the word seems to have been lost; the confusion between the British and American English meanings of *biscuit* may have hastened its departure.

[13] I added this qualification to account for the frequent reduction of such English clusters as *nd* and *nt* in their Hawaiianized form.

[14] Incidentally, Meiric K. Dutton (1972) found sixteen different spellings of the Hawaiian form for 'Christmas'.

[15] So far, I have not calculated the frequency of this "match."

[16] The third example is labeled "Protestant" in the definition; the other two are not labeled.

[17] These four versions for 'saint' fall into two main classes: those with *s*-reflecting the written word; those with *k*-, the spoken word. *Kana* is identified further in the dictionary as the version of 'Saint' that occurs in proper names.

[18] These and following alternate forms show some of the differences between borrowings that used only the indigenous consonants, and those that used the extra set discussed earlier.

[19] Perhaps a longer form, *lei kolona* 'crown-like lei', explains the rather dubious connection between the concepts *rosary* and *crown*.

[20] This last pattern perhaps reflects the velarized variant of English /l/ after a vowel.

[21] Perhaps *'ānela* 'angel' is a true example of Bingham's policy. Here, the cluster /nj/ is reduced to /n/.

[22] In spite of the examples from Campbell, perhaps a final -*a* was actually a natural pattern. Since the HAW "reflex" of the majority of ENG consonants is *k*, the missionaries might have (consciously or unconsciously) noted that -*a* ended words borrowed "naturally." As for fewer words with *i* as the added vowel (as opposed to the pattern in Fijian), Hawaiian has many fewer dental sounds. And of these (two), *l*, at least in Fijian and Tongan, is often followed by *o*.

CHAPTER ELEVEN

From Word List to Dictionary

-o-o-o-o-o-

We are unitedly studying the language daily, with a view to commence a translation of the Scriptures as soon as possible ... Our Vocabulary is considerably enlarged and we find with pleasure, the language much more copious and expressive than we formerly conceived it to be (letter from William Ellis, Oʻahu, 30 October 1823 to the Reverend G. Burder, London Missionary Society).

Many early comments about Hawaiian vocabulary were concerned mainly with its size (with judgments ranging from too small to too large) and its semantic mismatches with English (a perceived want of generic terms). Now, in order to understand these and other such statements, we take a brief look at the vocabulary from a semantic point of view, and then examine the content of some of the first collections of words in order to judge how representative a sample they were of the language and culture. Finally, we trace the progress of Hawaiian lexicography from the 1820s to the present.[1]

HAWAIIAN VOCABULARY AS A REFLECTION OF CULTURE

Leaving aside such matters as linguistic relativity—that is, the notion that a group's language determines its Weltanschauung—it is probably safe to say that a language's vocabulary reflects the interests of its speakers.[2] It has long been noted that Hawaiian is especially rich in words in particular domains deemed important by those who participate in the culture. For example, Samuel H. Elbert, drawing on his experience as co-compiler of the most recent Hawaiian dictionary, noted that the language provided its speakers with "33 terms about clouds, 179 pertaining to sweet potatoes, and 225 concerned with taro, the staff of life" (Schütz and Elbert 1968:196). Continuing in this vein, in the introduction to the first edition of the current dictionary, the compilers gave Fornander (1916–1920, 5:93–103) as a source for more than 100 wind names, and Nākuina 1902 for more than 200 names.

Words for rain comprise another semantic field that abounds with names: Harold W. Kent (1986:377–82) listed 53 different names for specific rains (usually associated with a particular place, or with a certain clouds or winds) and 87 kinds of rains and mists. Moreover, he found 89 terms connected with clouds. Other large categories well represented in the vocabulary are fish, birds, canoes, kapa, amusements and games, kin terms, tools, weapons, and deities connected with the indigenous religion—among many others.

General Terms versus Specific Terms

For a missionary intent on translating the Bible, some of this richness could be a double-edged sword. In chapter 2 are quoted two complaints about the lack of general or abstract terms in Hawaiian. The following quotation, from William De Witt Alexander's introduction to Lorrin Andrews's dictionary (1865:13), is an extended example of the intellectual climate of the time with respect to "primitive" vocabulary:

> The vocabulary of the Hawaiian is probably richer than that of most other Oceanic tongues. Its child-like and primitive charac-ter is shown by the absence of abstract words and general terms. As been well observed by M. Gaussin,[3] there are three classes of words, corresponding to as many different stages of language: 1st, those that express sensations, 2d, images, and 3d, abstract ideas. The Polynesian vocabulary was originally composed chiefly of words of the first two classes. As languages grow older, words acquire a figurative sense, and the original meaning is gradually forgotten. In English, for instance, how many are aware that *tri-bulation* originally meant threshing, *respect*, looking back, *reveal* to draw back a vail [*sic*], *affront* to strike in the face, and *insult* to leap upon the body of a prostrate foe?[4] Now there were compara-tively few Hawaiian words that had gone through this process.[5]
>
> Not only are names wanting for the more general abstractions, such as space, nature, fate, &c., but there are very few generic terms. For example there is no generic term for *animal*, express-ing the whole class of living creatures, or for insects or for colors. At the same time it abounds in specific names and in nice distinctions.
>
> The first step in the formation of language was no doubt the employment of particular names to denote individual objects. It was only afterwards by a process of abstraction that these individual objects were classified by those qualities which are common to a number of them. It is from the specific that we ascend to the general. The same principle applies to verbs or

names of actions as well as to nouns. The savage has in his mind a picture of the whole action, and does not always abstract or separate the principal circumstance from the accessory details. This is true of uncultivated languages in general, and is not peculiar to Hawaiian.

The following lament is more specific about such problems (Judd 1880:25) :

> There are great deficiencies also, especially in abstract terms. There is no word for "nature," or "virtue," or "enemy," or "gratitude," or "color." "Pono" means "goodness" in general, but nothing in particular. So also "aloha" signifies "love," "affection," "good-will," and may perhaps be twisted into "thank you," or "gratitude."

Artemas Bishop, who translated both sacred and secular material into Hawaiian, described some of the problems—and their solutions—in detail (1844a). Because his account sheds light on how the missionaries approached this challenge, it is quoted here at length. First he proposed that the limitation of words (as the missionaries perceived it) grew out of a paucity of ideas attained by an "untutored people." He continued:

> While our acquaintance with the Hawaiian language was limited, this [limitation] constituted a formidable difficulty, and one which for a long time retarded our first efforts at translation. But as our investigations into the structure of the language advanced, we discovered that by the combination of simple and familiar words descriptive of the thing intended to be expressed, whether a noun or a verb, we were able to form new words to an indefinite extent, in perfect accordance with the genius of the language, and intelligible to the native reader. The constant use of this power enabled us to meet and overcome nearly every difficulty arising from the paucity of Hawaiian words, besides enriching the language with many hundreds of new terms, which are now in common use throughout the archipelago.
>
> Another method of obtaining words, was to take those in vulgar [i.e., common] use, and appropriate them to a religious sense for a definite purpose. In these cases, their new meaning needed to be explained in some instances, and in others not. The word used for repentance is one instance out of many others.
>
> The names of things not originally known at these islands, have been taken as circumstances indicated. Such things as have been introduced here, are named in our translations according to the appellations given them by the natives; most of which, are

their foreign names, changed (or as some would say, corrupted) into the orthography adapted to the Hawaiian organs of pronunciation.

But apparently Bishop was not satisfied with the degree of subjectivity available for translating. The greatest defect, so he maintained, was (p. 75)

> the want of definite and well-settled terms in the Hawaiian language, to express the sense of the originals, and incapable of an equivocal meaning. As an instance, the word *aloha* is used by the natives, and in our translation, in a variety of senses, as there is no other term to express *salutation*, *love*, compassion, charity, mercy, etc.; and though the connection in which it stands will often modify its meaning, yet it does not in all instances.

Certainly these mismatches between languages were troublesome for the translators. However, more experience would have shown them that a perfect translation between any two languages is an impossibility. Lyons (1969:55) expressed this notion (albeit less emphatically) in linguistic terms: "To the degree that the meanings of one language can be brought into one-to-one correspondence with those of another we will say that the two languages are *semantically isomorphic* (have the same semantic structure) ... The degree of semantic isomorphism between any two languages will ... depend very largely upon the amount of overlap there is in the culture of the two societies using those languages. "

As the experience of the missionaries eventually proved, the overlap between the cultures in question was far from complete. Chapter 10 discussed the most obvious problem that this cultural distance produced with respect to vocabulary: particularly for Bible translation, a great many concepts were inexpressible in Hawaiian, and either new words had to be borrowed or old words adapted to fill the need. Later in this chapter we will see how ignoring the cultural distance has marred the latest Hawaiian dictionary.

Literal Meaning versus Figurative Meaning: *Kaona*

Another problem the translators faced was the difference between literal and figurative meanings of words. Certainly such differences are not unknown in European languages; indeed, what happens below the surface meanings of words is important for any understanding of language as an art form, particularly poetry. But Hawaiian used figurative meaning to an extent unknown in English. As Mary Kawena Pukui described it (1949):

> There were always two things to consider: the literal meaning and the *kaona*, or "inner meaning." The inner meaning was sometimes so veiled that only the people to whom the chant belonged understood it, and sometimes so obvious that anyone who knew the figurative speech of old Hawaii could see it very plainly [p. 247].
>
> The *kaona* told the straight, consecutive story, although dressed in a garb of colors that did not seem to match. Persons were sometimes referred to as rains, winds, ferns, trees, birds, ships, and so on. A person might be referred to in the same poem as rain in one place and as wind in another [p. 248].
>
> A poem with words of innocent sound may hide within it as good an example of untranslatable vulgarity as can be found anywhere, while perhaps a poem that sounds decidedly vulgar on the surface may yield a thought as pure as a hymn. The *kaona* is the important meaning [p. 249].

It is difficult to know to what extent *kaona* was a problem for the early translators, for they were concerned mostly with translating from English into Hawaiian. (One would, nevertheless, expect inadvertent double entendres.) However, for translating in the other direction, *kaona* is certainly a problem, particularly now that so much esoteric knowledge of the language has been lost. As Pukui wrote (p. 252):

> As we move farther off into modern times from ancient times it is increasingly difficult to understand the *kaona*. We have left the old atmosphere and associations, and it is no longer possible to re-create them.

The Early Word Lists: Imperfect Mirrors of Culture

By necessity, most of the words collected by short-term visitors to Hawai'i tell us little about the Hawaiians' world, for they refer to objects that could be pointed to (such as body parts, material culture, geographical features, and flora and fauna) or simple actions that could be demonstrated (such as sitting or standing). But William Anderson, the first word gatherer, was able to go beyond these limitations through his knowledge of Tahitian, which allowed him to include some grammatical words, as well as those connected with the *heiau* where he gathered his information. More specifically, Anderson's list shows the following semantic fields (examples are in English and in parentheses):

Grammatical words (*where, no*)	Adverbs, directionals
Pronouns	Body parts
Bodily activities (*retch, urinate*)	Ceremonial activities and objects
Numbers	Fauna
Flora	Food
Artifacts	Natural features (*sun, sky, wind*)
Simple activities that might be demonstrated (*go, pluck, pull, look*)	Verbs referring to mental activities (*understand*)
Qualities (*bad, sweet*)	Kin terms, other terms for humans (*woman*)
Personal names	Unidentified (*tears of joy, wait a little*)

Short phrases (*what is your name?*)

Out of the nearly 240 words on Anderson's list, there are still over two dozen not yet identified. One possible explanation is that these are forms that have since dropped out of general Hawaiian. Another stems from the scarcity of information about dialect differences two centuries ago.[6] A tantalizing suggestion comes from Wendell C. Bennett (1930: 59–61), who listed a number of artifacts (described but unfortunately without Hawaiian names) "distinctively or predominantly found on Kauai." Thus, some of the unidentified forms may be Kaua'i words not recorded elsewhere.

One botanical term poses an interesting problem. Anderson collected the word *Tearre* (representing either *kiale* or *kiele*), which he identified rather loosely as 'Gardenia, or Cape Jasmine'. Now, however, *kiele* has come to refer to the gardenia that was introduced later (*Gardenia augusta*). Note the pertinent part of the dictionary entry for *kiele* (Pukui and Elbert 1986, apparently based on Neal 1965):

> **1.** n. Gardenia (*Gardenia augusta*), introduced. (Neal 799–800.) (PPN *tiale.*) **2.** vi. To emit fragrance; to perfume with *kiele*, as garments.

The fact that a native gardenia, *kiele* (or *kiale*), existed at the time of European contact seems to have been missed by lexicographers and botanists alike. In Andrews's (1865) entry for *kiele*, we find further evidence that the plant was not recently introduced:

> The name of an odoriferous shrub or tree; he laau aala. Some say
> it was brought from a foreign country, but the word is found in
> two ancient meles [songs] at least. [The two *mele* are quoted.]

This information was included in the Parker revision (1922), but in no
later dictionaries.

It has been suggested (Derral Herbst, pers. comm.) that perhaps
kiele was an alternate term for *nānū*, a native species of gardenia, but
unrecorded since Anderson's time. Although this matter has been corrected in the latest printing (1991) of the 1986 edition, an examination
of Anderson's list would have kept this apparent contradiction—an
introduced plant whose name has a Proto-Polynesian pedigree—from
appearing at all. Similarly, study of the other lists may provide further
clues about geographical differences in the Hawaiian vocabulary of the
late eighteenth and early nineteenth centuries.

FOLK ETYMOLOGY

Once explorers and traders had collected Hawaiian words, it took
little time for them to begin citing fanciful etymologies for some of the
common words and names. One of the first, and most imaginative, I
have found is the explorer Otto von Kotzebue's explanation of *Liholiho*,
son of Kamehameha the Great and Keōpūolani (1821:308):

> The prince, as soon as he is admitted into the rights of his
> father, receives the name of Lio-Lio, that is, dog of all dogs; and
> such we really found him.

Pukui, Elbert, and Mookini provided a more authentic etymology
(1974:132): "Ka-lani-nui-kua-liholiho-i-ke-kapu (the great chief [with
the] burning-back taboo), referring to the taboo against approaching him
from the back." As for the connection with 'dog' (*'īlio*), it is convo-
luted but (in a sense) logical. First, the speakers of English from whom
Kotzebue must certainly have heard the story probably pronounced
Liholiho without [h] in the unaccented syllables—a common English
mispronunciation of Hawaiian words. Next, as shown by the evidence
we have from the early word lists, the word *'īlio* was often pronounced
by foreigners as *lio*. Hence the false association between two unrelated
forms.

But *lio* has provided another folk etymology, still believed today.
In chapter 10 we saw how the word for 'dog', shortened to *lio*, came to
serve as a general name for introduced quadrupeds, and then specifically
for 'horse'. Some years ago, one highly respected Hawaiian language

expert insisted that the word came from *līō*, 'wild-eyed', from the wild-eyed look of the horses as they were unloaded from ships.[7]

A similar pseudohistory exists for *aloha*, supposed from English *hello*. But one of the most-often repeated fables is the explanation of *haole* 'foreigner'. Here is a version of the standard explanation, from *Ka Leo O Hawai'i*, 3 October 1990, in a letter from a member of the University of Hawai'i English Department, who, incidentally, had at that time lived in Hawai'i for fourteen years (punctuation added):

> *Haole* literally means 'without breath': *Ha*, 'breath'; *ole*, 'lacking'. The word, its metaphor hunkering the marrow bone [?], originally designated one who could not speak the Hawaiian language. Ranging in meaning through the nineteenth century from "introduced" to "foreign," it now, according to Pukui and Elbert's *Hawaiian Dictionary*, means "white person, American, Englishman, Caucasian."

Actually, the writer might have chosen any of a number of colorful etymologies for *haole*. In an entertaining article, Charles Kenn (1944b) included these meanings: 'without covering or husk', 'boar's tusk', derived from *ahole* (*āhole*) 'silvery fish', 'thief, robber', or 'the breath that blows the bugle'. As for the source of the "without-breath" explanation, Kenn credited Fred Beckley,[8] who proposed: "The white people came to be known as *ha-ole* (without breath) because after they said their prayers, they did not breathe (*ha*) three times as was customary in ancient Hawaii."

Unfortunately, this type of misunderstanding indicates a casual dismissal of long vowels and glottal stops as essential elements of the Hawaiian alphabet, for the words cited are actually *hā* and *'ole*. We have no evidence in other words of similar (and regular) losses of vowel length and glottal stops, and in my reading of early records (and conversations with others more widely read) I have found no documentary evidence for such an etymology. Thus, so far as we know, the word *haole* cannot be separated into shorter words.[9]

VOCABULARIES AND DICTIONARIES AFTER MISSION CONTACT

When the missionaries arrived in 1820, word collecting became a more serious endeavor, for they felt that some kind of formalization, or "fixing," of the vocabulary was a prerequisite for language learning and translation. The first vocabulary referred to in the mission records is that of ʻŌpūkahaʻia, prepared at Cornwall, Connecticut, but it has disappeared. So far as we know, none of the First Company of missionaries even referred to the manuscript in their journals. But as an earlier chapter showed, ʻŌpūkahaʻia was certainly the inspiration for those who followed him, particularly Elisha Loomis, the first printer.

Loomis n.d.

From all accounts, it appears that the lineage of word lists and dictionaries that grew out of the Hawaiian Mission can be traced to an extensive vocabulary compiled by Elisha Loomis, whose work with the language began with his training at the Foreign Mission School at Cornwall. Loomis himself referred to the vocabulary, as the following entries from his journal show:

> Mr. Phelps[10] called to ask permission to take a copy of my Vocabulary of the language. He copied only a part for want of time [31 August 1821].
> I have devoted much of my time the past week to the rewriting and arranging of a vocabulary, which I find a work of no small magnitude [23 December 1826].

However, the manuscript remains a tantalizing gap in Hawaiʻi's lexicographic history, for it apparently does not exist itself, but only in the works of Loomis's successors. Ironically, in this form it did not reach publication until 1836, the year of Loomis's death. But a little more than a decade before this, a rather unusual vocabulary grew out of the extended mission family and was very widely distributed as part of a best-selling travel account by William Ellis.

Ellis 1825

William Ellis, whose deleterious effect on the orthography was discussed in chapter 7, published his *Journal of a Tour around Hawaii* shortly after leaving the islands in 1824. As one of several appendices, he included a list of 248 Hawaiian words with English glosses. His introduction tells something of the list's provenance (Ellis 1825:244):

> A larger vocabulary, from which the following was compiled, was prepared by Mr. Bishop,[11] the American Missionary at the Sandwich Islands ... A copy of the original manuscript was procured by Mr. Pickering,[12] early in the present year (1825,) and by him has been obligingly lent, for the purpose of making the selections which are here given, and which would have been more extended, had the prescribed limits of the volume permitted. The

words in *small capitals* are such as are contained in the list of radical words, made by the Empress Catherine of Russia, and forming the basis of her great *Vocabularium Comparativum*.[13]

Ellis's Hawaiian list was by no means the first published: it was preceded by several of the explorers' lists. But because his account was so well received by the reading public, information about Hawaiian would have reached a wider readership than did the collections published earlier.

The list itself contains 248 words and naturally is more semantically diverse than Anderson's, going beyond simple artifacts and actions to include Hawaiian forms for such concepts as *exalt*, *prepare*, *despise*, and *infanticide*.

In a letter written to the ABCFM, Boston, Artemas Bishop, who supplied the list, gave an account of its history that differs somewhat from Ellis's:

> I have received yours of Jany. last together with a vol. of the Journal of the Dep[utation] around Hawaii. I was not a little surprised to find extracts from a very imperfect & faulty vocabulary which I had given Mr. Ellis at his request, but which I should have been unwilling to have any part published without corrections (Kailua [Hawai'i], 20 November 1826).

Bishop then listed sixty-one forms to be corrected, ending his letter with the following grievance:

> I regret very much that the few words taken from my vocabulary should need so many corrections—It was my first collection of words, at a time when I had not the means of obtaining correct definitions, and from the rapidity with which this people pronounce was unable to catch the sounds of words so clearly as to write all of them in a correct manner.
>
> But the greatest source of the above errors was mistaking one letter for another. Had I had a moments [*sic*] warning of the thing, I should have set down and written out my vocabulary in a fair hand before sending it away—It is our purpose in the course of a few years to make out a large & complete grammar & Vocabulary of this language & send it to America or England to be printed. I have here corrected nearly all of the errors that I know of in the words inserted in the appendix to the "Journal." The correction of the interchangable [*sic*] letters I leave with you to make in case you shall see fit in a future edition —

But future editions of Ellis's book saw a much truncated version of the original published list. By the time of the fourth edition, 1828, it had shrunk to seventy-four words. Moreover, it was an entirely different selection, only occasionally coinciding with the Bishop list, and introduced as "some of the most common words" in the language. It is no surprise to find that Ellis did not adapt his spelling to the 1826 standard, but instead used the fuller alphabet, writing both *k* and *t*, *l* and *r*, and *v* and *w*. Since he was fully aware of the new official orthography, we can only conclude that he retained the cumbersome array of consonants out of stubbornness, refusing to move from his earlier position as the lone objector to the pared-down and economical alphabet.

Andrews 1836

In comparing the linguistic accomplishments of the various Pacific missions, one finds that the differences in timing and production are due mainly to two variables: requirements set out by a particular mission, and the abilities of its personnel. As for the former, there seems to be little in the official policies of the ABCFM that required its members to produce a dictionary with all deliberate speed, which is very different from the practices of the Wesleyan Methodist Missionary Society and the London Missionary Society, active in other parts of the Pacific. And although there were competent "linguists" in the first two companies of missionaries to Hawai'i (such as the Binghams, Loomis, and Bishop), before Lorrin Andrews arrived in 1828, the Mission did not really have a member who considered the language to be of *principal* interest.

There is, of course, one reason that no serious lexicographic work could have taken place before the official orthography was settled in 1826: the fact that certain words could be written in as many as a dozen different ways was enough to deter even the most dedicated worker. But even after that time, there were a number of reasons that the missionaries shied away from the time-consuming task of compiling a dictionary. As Andrews explained in the preface to his *Vocabulary* (1836a:ii):

> Perhaps the Sandwich Island's Mission owes an apology to the literary world for having reduced to writing a language of such variety and extent as Hawaiian, and published so many books in it, without having given any account either of the genius, structure or peculiarities of the language. Many reasons, how[ev]er, exist why so little has been done in this respect. The want of leisure in any member of the Mission for setting down to labors purely literary, is one reason. The want of proper materials here-

tofore, for authority, is another. But the reason that has had the greatest influence is, the fact that those who came first on the ground and acquired the language by the ear and by mixing with the natives, soon became independent of helps and *needed* neither a vocabulary or a grammar of the language: and those who came later, and most needed such helps, felt that they were not well *qualified* for the task of making them.

Andrews went on to explain that in June 1834 the Mission had, by vote, selected him to prepare the vocabulary and that he had used the following materials as a foundation for the work: first, what was believed to be Loomis's vocabulary, transcribed by Andrews on the voyage from the United States, and "put to use in 1828"; and next, another vocabulary of words by James Ely[14] and Artemas Bishop, received in 1829, with blank pages inserted for additional words.

He then listed the deficiencies of the vocabulary. Among them were: inexact alphabetical order; unfamiliar words, but taken on the authority of their compiler; errors in the orthography; and a confusion between the literal and figurative meanings of words. (Was this last problem a manifestation of *kaona*?)

The work itself contains approximately 5,700 entries.[15] Headwords are divided into Andrews's concept of syllables, a notion that is inextricably tied to glottal stops and diphthongs. For example, a hyphen between identical vowels is a fairly reliable sign that Andrews perceived a glottal stop in that position, as in *a-a-hu* (*'a'ahu*) 'clothing'. However, hyphens between unlike vowels could mean two things: that a glottal stop separated them, or that this particular vowel sequence was not perceived as a diphthong. Thus, judging from his use of hyphens, it appears that for Andrews, *ai* and *au* were diphthongs, but *ae* and *ao* were not. Still, in practice he was not entirely consistent, for he missed the separation (that is, the glottal stop) in some very common words, such as *'a'ole* (negative), spelled *ao-le*.[16]

The order of entries matches that of the Hawaiian alphabet: first the five vowels, then the consonants, and finally, words beginning with the "foreign" consonants *b, d, f, g, r, s, t, v,* and *z*.

In spite of its label as a "vocabulary," Andrews's work contains a good deal of material on phonetics/phonology and morphology, thus going beyond the scope of earlier word lists and approaching that of a full-scale dictionary. As an example of his treatment of sounds, note the following comment on the pronunciation of /a/, a prominent feature ignored in the most recent Hawaiian grammar and dictionary:

> A, the first letter of the Hawaiian alphabet. Its sound is gener-
> ally that of the English *a* in *father*, *ask*, &c. but it has sometimes,
> when standing before the consonants *k*, *l*, *m*, *n*, and *p*, a short
> sound somewhat resembling the short *u* in *mutter*; as in *paka*,
> *malimali*, *lama*, *mana*, *napenape*,[17] &c. pronounced nearly as we
> should pronounce pukka, mullymully, lumma, munna, nuppy-
> nuppy (p. 1).

Except for the comment about "quantity" in the description of /o/
(which actually refers more to quality, as with "long and short" *o* in
English), Andrews did not comment on vowel length. He did, however,
recognize the other *bête noire* of Hawaiian orthography: the glottal stop,
marking some instances more directly than separating syllables with
hyphens. For example, he made a distinction between *au* 'I' and *a'u*
'my' by writing an apostrophe in the second and explaining: "There is a
sensible [i.e., discernible] break in the pronunciation ... (p. 4)." But as
did Ellis ten years earlier, he indicated such a distinction only sporadically, generally with common words that would be confused even in
context, such as *kau* 'your' versus *ka'u* 'my'.

Andrews's observation that "nouns whose first letter is *a* take both
forms of the article *ka* and *ke*, but most frequently the former" is an
interesting example of the inability to discern glottal stops at the
beginnings of words resulting in an incorrect grammatical statement.
For example, because both *'awa* 'kava' and *awa* 'harbor' were heard as
the same word and spelled the same, Andrews found it puzzling that the
former was preceded by *ka* and the latter by *ke*. It was not until initial
glottal stops were recognized that such apparent exceptions were
accounted for.

The treatment of function forms shows the extent to which
Andrews's work (in certain areas, at least) approaches a full dictionary.
For example, note the following entry for *a*, which a "pure" vocabulary
would define simply as 'and':

> A, *conj.* and, and then, also; when it connects verbs it stands by
> itself; when it connects nouns it is usually accompanied by *me*: *a*
> *me*; and, and also, besides, together with. In narration it frequent-
> ly stands at the beginning of sentences or paragraphs, and merely
> refers to what has been said without any very close connection
> with it. In many cases it seems to be euphonic, or to answer no
> purpose but as a preparatory sound to something that may follow.

One feature of Hawaiian morphology that has long caused some
practical problems for lexicographers is the very common prefix *ho'o-*

(and some alternates), which has a causative function, among others. As an example, note the following set:

nui	large	*ho'onui*	enlarge
'ai	eat	*hō'ai*	feed

In this case, the main question for the dictionary maker is whether to list *ho'onani* separately, to enter it under *nani*, or to enter both forms. Each solution has advantages and drawbacks, usually connected with the conflicting goals of economy of description (and space), consistency, and convenience for the user.

Andrews took an intermediate course. His vocabulary contains about eight and one half pages of *ho'o* forms, duplicating, to some extent, the information in individual entries. In his entry for the prefix itself, however, after giving a fairly detailed description of the form and its variations, Andrews expressed this opinion: "Hereafter it will be proper to write them as distinct significations under the proper radicals which will be a much more convenient as well as philosophical arrangement."

As for an in-house assessment of this work, the mission publication *The Friend* (2 January 1854, p. 4), in an announcement of Andrews's soon-to-be-published grammar, referred to his earlier vocabulary as "very unsatisfactory." But Andrews himself was the first to admit this, as his own critical comments above show.

Chamisso ca. 1837

In chapter 11, we saw how Adelbert von Chamisso redeemed his linguistic reputation (which was on very shaky ground because of his naive comments about Hawaiian) by producing a respectable Hawaiian grammar in 1837, the first full-sized published description of the language. Had he been spared (as nineteenth-century missionaries phrased it), he might have made a similar contribution to Hawaiian lexicography. As it turned out, however, his dictionary never advanced beyond a collection of envelopes filled with slips, held with the rest of his papers by the Staatsbibliothek in Berlin.

In the introduction to his grammar, Chamisso mentioned that the missionaries had referred to a Hawaiian vocabulary in 1833, but it had not reached him.[18] Therefore, as was his grammar, Chamisso's dictionary was based almost entirely on the translations produced by the Hawaiian Mission.[19] However, this is not to say that Chamisso was happy with such a forced choice of materials: on the contrary, he expressed his displeasure that all the effort seemed to be in one direction—to introduce Western culture to the Hawaiians, while failing to preserve for them their own traditions (Chapin 1973:99):

> One should not applaud these pious missionaries: the thirst for knowledge, which separates man from the beasts, is also given by God, and it is not a sin for him to want to look back to his own history, in which God manifests himself in progress. But too late! before the new has fully taken shape, the old has already disappeared.

The information Chamisso wrote on the slips, the physical details of which are described in greater detail in the Bibliography, is organized in a somewhat unusual way, since the most prominent feature of each card is not a potential headword, but the identification of the biblical source, e.g., PS XXIII. (For some references, Chamisso used an English Bible as well as a German one.) On the other hand, keywords, possibly potential headwords, are underlined. As a result, it is difficult to imagine how these slips would eventually have been organized.

There is also a bound copy of the notes, including some sections consisting entirely of grammatical markers (which could have served as a foundation for the grammar), and a few pages of a Hawaiian-Tahitian-Māori-Tongan comparative vocabulary.

The catalog of Chamisso's entire works serves as a vivid reminder of the range of the man's interests: botanical notes and drawings, notes on zoological systems, anatomical drawings and notes, botanical bibliography, letters about the editing of his poetic works, a collection of French folk songs, and even an article about the language of deaf-mutes. Thus, his premature death at forty-seven (in 1838) was a loss to the worlds of both science and literature. Even though his work on the Hawaiian language seems slight in comparison with his output as naturalist, novelist, and poet, in a sense it served as a bridge between those two worlds. Had he lived, he would no doubt have produced a dictionary that, albeit limited by its distance from the spoken language, would have been fuller in its treatment of individual entries than Andrews's. In short, the two works would have complemented each other.

FULL-SCALE DICTIONARIES

Of course, there is no clear-cut distinction between a word list and a dictionary; the two are in a sense end points on a continuum. Earlier we saw how the detailed grammatical explanations in Andrews's *Vocabulary* moved it toward the dictionary end of the scale. His revision and expansion of this work completed the change, resulting in the first published Hawaiian dictionary.

Andrews 1865

In the true lexicographic spirit, Lorrin Andrews began revising and enlarging his *Vocabulary* as soon as it was published. He printed interleaved copies to encourage his colleagues[20] to contribute as well, but he maintained that with the exception of a few school texts and the Bible, which he termed a *classic* (italics his), the authoritative sources for definitions were native speakers, and more particularly, their printed and handwritten documents (1865:2). Moreover, he had his own ideas about a "standard" Hawaiian, preferring material "written by Chiefs to other Chiefs, and such as were written by one intelligent Hawaiian to another." He added that he "sought after the best and purist Hawaiian he could obtain," excluding "low, filthy, vulgar language of ignorant and sensual depravity."

Contemporary records give us an unusually clear picture of how Andrews's dictionary came into being as an actual book. In March 1864, *The Friend* announced that the printing had begun, and several months later whetted the reading public's appetite by printing a sample page. Toward the end of the year, the editor reported: "As we pass in and out of the printing office, we perceive that this great national work is approaching its completion."[21]

In April 1865, the appearance of the book was imminent, and the editor suggested that it

> be placed in every school-house, court-house and Government office of the Hawaiian kingdom, and be found also in every merchant's counting-room, on the counter of every shop-keeper, in the mechanic's work-shop, and in every family upon the islands.

A month later *The Friend* noted the "somewhat remarkable circumstance that Mr. Andrews should have gathered and defined about the same number of words as are to be found in the great folio edition of Johnson's English Dictionary." When Andrews's dictionary was finally ready for sale (June 1865), it turned out to be the most expensive work printed in Hawai'i, other than the Bible.

The nearly thirty years separating the *Vocabulary* from the *Dictionary* was a period of rapid growth in the educated public's knowledge of Polynesian and other Austronesian languages, and this growth is reflected by William De Witt Alexander's introduction to the

Dictionary (pp. 7–14).   In this state-of-the-art survey of Polynesian linguistics, he covered the field in general and Hawaiian in particular, noting, for example, Chamisso's grammar, "a work of rare ability, considering the meagre materials which the author had at his command."

The significance of the comparative work on Polynesian languages for Hawaiian lexicography lies in Alexander's explanation (adapted from Hale 1846) of consonant correspondences for eight Polynesian languages, showing clearly the relationship of Hawaiian glottal stop (indicated by ') to *k* in most of the other languages. However, the phonetics of English still prevented him from making the great leap to the realization that the glottal stop was a full-fledged consonant. The following statement (quoted in chapter 11) shows that, unlike the French grammarian/lexicographer Gaussin (1853), he could not distinguish the sound at all at the beginning of a word: "In Hawaiian ... *k* at the beginning of a word is dropped, but in the middle of a word is represented by a peculiar guttural catch or break."

In chapter 8, I explained why it is easier for a speaker of French to recognize a glottal stop at the beginning of a word than it is for a speaker of English. However, Horatio Hale was able to overcome this phonetic handicap of his native language: only three pages beyond his table of consonant correspondences (1846:235) is a similar table showing examples, including Hawaiian *'upena* 'net', clearly corresponding to such forms as *kupe(ng)a* in related languages. Did Alexander miss the significance of the form? Or did he doubt Hale's transcription? We can only guess.

At any rate, had either Alexander or Andrews paid closer attention to Gaussin and Hale (and of course, had they marked vowel length), dictionary users would have been spared sorting through, for example, fifteen entries spelled simply *A*, and twenty-four spelled *A-a*. Interestingly, we shall see later how the compilers of the most recent Hawaiian dictionary erred just as far in the other direction, not through a misanalysis of the sounds, but through a misguided idea of what should constitute an entry.

A final matter connected with the form of headwords is Andrews's use of hyphens. As he did in his *Vocabulary*, he separated syllables (that is, his concept of syllables) with hyphens. This practice shows us which vowel combinations he thought constituted diphthongs: again, *ai* and *au*, but now, apparently *ao* as well. But his treatment of *ae* is inconsistent.

According to Andrews's own estimate, this work contains about 15,500 entries. However, as Elbert (1954:15) pointed out, although technically accurate, this count is somewhat inflated because many words were entered twice: once as a noun, and once as a verb. Elbert suggested that perhaps 14,000 would be a more accurate count.

The order of the entries again follows the pattern begun in the *Vocabulary*: first vowels, then consonants, and finally foreign consonants. The words in this last section are of course borrowings—mostly from English, but also Hebrew, Chaldean, Syrian, Latin, and Greek. In this last section the entries were increased from the forty-one in his 1836 vocabulary (see chapter 10) to 175; however, the latter figure does not accurately reflect the number of loanwords adapted into the language, since it includes only those words beginning with the extraneous consonants. Other borrowings are scattered throughout the dictionary.[22]

An English-Hawaiian vocabulary was added, the choice of entries based on that in George Pratt's Samoan dictionary (1862). This section consists of about 4,200 words.

In this work, as opposed to his *Vocabulary*, Andrews could now refer to his grammar; one can find examples of this cross-referencing by looking up almost any grammatical marker. To continue the example begun in the discussion of his earlier work, consider the causative marker. As he explained in his *Vocabulary*, ideally *hoʻo-* forms should be listed under the root. However, Andrews found that this solution was not a practical one, since "a large class of words have been found beginning with the causative prefix *hoo,* whose roots are not known or have not come to light, or are out of use." Thus, the dictionary contains some seventy-three columns of *hoo-* entries, not including those listed under *ho-* or *ha-*. Here, his policy was squarely on the side of the user. But in practice, he included (as he had done in his *Vocabulary*) many *hoʻo* forms whose roots did exist, whose meanings were predictable, and which were redundantly listed under the root.

It would not be consistent with what we know of Andrews's character for him to have considered his work a finished or complete one. Indeed, in a sense he "pre-reviewed" his dictionary by listing what he saw as its faults. For example, he felt that the vocabulary in the legends, or in the philosophical views of the Hawaiians, was "but feebly represented." Moreover, he added this caveat:

> The Author would here state that four-fifths of the work were completed before he had any intimation that it would ever be printed. It was written solely for his own amusement and infor-

mation, and preparatory to a more full investigation of those departments of the language above mentioned. He has been desirous for many years of going more fully into the study of Hawaiian poetry, and as a preparation to it he was induced to collect specimens of the language of common life; hence the origin of this Dictionary. An appropriation of money for a Dictionary passed by the Legislature of 1860 without his knowledge, was the first intimation the Author had that such a work was desired by the Foreign community on the Island.

In *The Friend* (1 August 1878—almost exactly ten years after Andrews's death), an article announced that Andrews's dictionary was to be enlarged, and that the Reverend Lorenzo Lyons, "acknowledged the best Hawaiian scholar living," was to undertake this work. A month later, in the same periodical, Lyons declined, first praising Andrews for his diligence, patience, and perseverance. But there was no doubt in Lyons's mind that a revision was needed:

> On the examination of the book I was greatly disappointed. There was much that was good, and correct, and helpful and enlightening in it; but there were great defects—many blunders, wrong definitions, an unpardonable jumble of words spelt the same but differently pronounced, of different meanings according to the pronunciation and the article that should be used. There were no marks showing how words should be pronounced or what article should be used, except occasionally. There was a jumbling up of active and neuter verbs, used the one for the other. Many words were wrongly spelt, and hence not Hawaiian words. One great defect was in the guttural words, which are very numerous. There were some bad words that ought not to appear in a dictionary.
>
> Well, I said to myself, it is a good dictionary under the circumstances, but not good enough to be transmitted to posterity. I will go to work and revise it for my own use and for the use of others, perhaps, hereafter. So I obtained ... a Dictionary with blank leaves, and set about the revision, employing all my reliable Hawaiian help I could find ... I commenced in June, 1867, and ended September, 1870 ... [During the intervening years] some new words have been added. I might have added many more new words during those eight years, for they have been constantly occurring in the Hawaiian newspapers. I find some new words in every newspaper I read —i.e., new to me, and new, too, to some of the natives.[23] Had there been any prospect that a revised Dictionary would ever be printed, I should have recorded these new words and their definitions; but I was informed eight years

ago that the stock of the first edition then on hand was large enough to supply the present and the future community down to the end of the race, perhaps; that a printed revised edition would injure the sale of the old one. So it has rested till now.

I don't claim that my revision is perfect. Doubtless some of my corrections need correcting. Should the time ever come or the means be provided for the printing of a corrected edition of Andrews' Hawaiian Dictionary, my criticisms may be of some use. Should I be living, I would gladly aid in revising my revision.

This passage is quoted here in full because it gives us an unusually close, and firsthand, look at this period of Hawaiian lexicography. Note the lexicographic issues raised: incorrect definitions, the problems caused by not writing the glottal stop, a need to specify whether a word should be preceded by *ka* or *ke*, no indication of pronunciation—even prudery entered the argument. A larger issue is the suggestion that the supply of dictionaries might outlast the Hawaiian race, a statement that gives us a revealing look at mission attitudes in 1870.

From a linguistic point of view, the most unfortunate part of Lyons's account is that had he been encouraged by the prospect of a new edition of the dictionary, there would have been no eight-year hiatus in his word collecting, and the present lexicon would have been richer for it. But the economics of printing a revision with copies still in stock won out over scholarship, and the supply outlasted Lyons himself, who died in 1886. Ironically, only a few years later (1893), the earlier prediction was proven wrong, and it became necessary to print another edition—without the revisions that Lyons had felt so strongly about.

Andrews-Parker 1922

In the decades after 1865, Lyons was not the only scholar to try to improve on the existing dictionary. Marguerite K. Ashford (1987:7–12) discussed at length a number of missionary successors to Andrews who annotated their copies: Arthur Alexander, Anderson Oliver Forbes, Charles McEwen Hyde, and Elias Bond. She went on to sketch the beginnings of the next published revision of Andrews's dictionary (1987:12):

By the turn of the century Andrews' dictionary had been long out of print, and an increasing interest in other Polynesian languages, as well as the need for an authoritative source for the spelling, pronunciation, and definition of Hawaiian words, led to arrangements for the preparation of a new Hawaiian dictionary under the direction of the Board of Commissioners of Public Archives. A 1913 act of the Territorial Legislature provided for the compiling, binding, and publishing of the dictionary, and substantial grants in subsequent years by the legislature and by Bishop Museum provided the necessary funding.

The compiler chosen to revise the dictionary was the Reverend Henry Hodges Parker, a second-generation missionary already in his eighty-second year when the work began in 1915.

As Parker himself described it, Andrews's 1865 work served as a basis for his revision, to which he added "a mass of unclassified material," including Lyons's annotated copy,[24] manuscripts from the Catholic Mission, and contributions from W. P. Alexander, Hiram Bingham, and W. D. Westervelt (p. vi).   Ashford (p. 13) added more detail by noting that some 500 new words were added, and by describing the editorial contributions of the Bishop Museum staff, which helped to verify geographical and other scientific terms.[25]

Although Parker probably was not aware of the historical coincidence, he wrote in his introduction that he had received a copy of Herbert W. Williams's Māori dictionary (5th edition, 1917), which revealed "a remarkable similarity in the structure of many Hawaiian and Maori words." As we saw in chapter 7, almost exactly 100 years earlier the First Company of missionaries in Hawai'i received a copy of the first Māori grammar and dictionary, using it to confirm their decision to use the continental values of the vowels. And, as we will see below, just as a careful study of that first dictionary would have cleared up some problems with the interim orthography, so might a better understanding of Williams's orthography have saved Parker from wasting such a great amount of time and space rewriting each entry to give a nearly uniformly false notion of its pronunciation.

Although Parker had the advantage of speaking Hawaiian,[26] formal training seems to have been missing: unlike many other mission children, he received his entire education in Hawai'i. Unfortunately, the narrow confines of this education show only too clearly in his treatment of Hawaiian pronunciation.

Aside from the addition of new words and a change in the alphabetical order, Parker's most noticeable (and most unfortunate) addition to Andrews's dictionary stemmed from official sources. The legislative act referred to above included the following phrase: "In such a dictionary there shall be given the correct pronunciation of the ancient and modern Hawaiian words and phrases ... "

Parker followed these instructions to the letter, but according to his own peculiar understanding of Hawaiian pronunciation. It is no surprise to find that vowel length and the glottal stop were the source of his greatest misunderstandings. In terms of printing, at last the essential type was available, but there is no evidence that Parker understood the contrastive function of the sounds the symbols represented. For example, he wrote that a macron should be used "to mark long or normal vowels," and thus his entries abound with short vowels marked with a macron (as, for example, with the common words *hale* (hā'-le), *hula* (hū'-la), and *aloha* (ā-lō'-ha). "The glottal closure ('')," he wrote (p. xix), "indicates an interruption of a sound that prevents two vowels from coalescing ..." As for accent, Parker omitted a general statement, except to propose that there were two types of diphthongs, depending on whether the first or second element was accented. As a result, the pronunciation symbols that appear after each headword give *no* reliable information except, in some cases, to show a glottal stop in noninitial position.

There are two ways in which a careful examination of Williams's Māori dictionary could have improved the Hawaiian dictionary. First, although Williams apparently did not fully understand the phonemic nature of vowel length, he came close: even though he could perceive several degrees of length in speech, he marked vowels in headwords either short (with no mark) or long (with a macron).

Next, in the comparative table of consonants in Alexander's introduction to Polynesian languages, referred to above, the reader can see that a Hawaiian glottal stop corresponds to, for instance, a Māori *k*. Thus, had he been so inclined, Parker might have noticed that the Māori word *kai* 'eat' should correspond to Hawaiian *'ai* (as it does). As it was, however, Parker treated the difference between that word and *ai* (which he defined as 'coition') as a difference in vowel length.[27]

Pukui and Elbert (1957:ix) criticized Parker's concept of an entry, suggesting that it was "based on translation into English." This is not quite accurately stated. True, in the example given, *maika'i*, the division into three entries is based on English, but on English parts of speech: one each for a noun, a verb, and an adjective. But in another example (also cited by Pukui and Elbert), the words spelled *pua* are separated into five entries, each with a different pronunciation (that is, different according to Parker).

All in all, Parker's revision was a failure, as Williams concluded in his review (1926). But it did have the effect of making available a slightly enlarged version of the Andrews dictionary—at least until the extremely short run (400 copies; Ashford 1987:13) was exhausted.

Judd, Pukui, and Stokes 1945

With the publication of the oddly titled *Introduction to the Hawaiian Language*, Hawaiian lexicography retreated from the DICTIONARY end of the continuum toward the starting point of WORD LIST or VOCABULARY. As a matter of fact, the principal sections (E-H, H-E) are labeled "vocabularies." According to the authors' count, the English-Hawaiian section consists of 5,000 words, and (from my own sampling) the Hawaiian-English, about 3,060 words.[28] The choice of entries for the English-Hawaiian section (which is the principal part of the work— nearly twice as long as the Hawaiian-English section) was very professionally made: Thorndike's word-frequency counts were used, among other less-known works. In this section, the Hawaiian trans- lations were based on Harvey R. Hitchcock's *English-Hawaiian Dictionary* (1887) but also "modified" with material from English- Hawaiian vocabularies by John S. Emerson and Artemas Bishop (1845), Andrews (1865), and some minor twentieth-century contributors.

As for the mechanics of the production, there are some mistakes in alphabetical order (see, for example, pp. 301–302, on which some forms beginning with *pu-* are nestled in the middle of *pi-* entries). Also, the "pronunciation," to be treated below, was indicated for the Hawaiian forms only in the English-Hawaiian section.

On the positive side, the following quotation shows a significant and long overdue advance in the treatment of the alphabet (p. 9):

> The **ʻuʻina** is still part of Hawaiian speech, but has not previ- ously been indicated in writing except to distinguish between **aʻu** 'my' and **au** 'thy' and in a very few other words. It has been treated largely as a diacritical mark, although Alexander noted in his grammar: "This gutteral [*sic*] is properly a consonant, and forms an *essential* part of the words in which it is found." Its presence or absence in Hawaiian words marks distinct terms. For instance, three such words have been written **ai**, although pro- nounced differently. The correct forms would be **ʻaʻi**, meaning 'neck,' **ʻai**, 'food,' and **ai**, 'sexual intercourse."
>
> For clarity, we believe that the **ʻuʻina** should be indicated when writing .

Here we have, possibly for the first time, a paraphrase of the phonemic—that is, contrastive—nature of the sound, for although Alexander had called it an "essential sound," he did not emphasize its role in keeping otherwise identical words apart.

The authors fared less well with their treatment of vowel length. In this case, they regressed rather than advanced, giving (p. 9)

> three values to the Hawaiian vowels, instead of the two, "long" and "short" previously given. We added an "intermediate" after endeavoring in vain to reconcile some of the pronunciations in the latest dictionary with the spoken Hawaiian.

Thus, long vowels were marked with a macron, short ones with a breve, and so-called intermediate ones were unmarked. However, it is difficult to find any sort of pattern for what they perceived as vowels of intermediate length.[29] Here, as with Parker in his revision of Andrews's work, the authors would have done well to follow the practice of Williams in his Māori dictionary, discussed above.

But in one sense, the authors had less of an excuse for their sins of omission than did Parker. The more than two decades that had passed between the publications constituted a critical period for the treatment of such matters. In 1933, Leonard Bloomfield published his *Language*, in which were laid out very clearly the fundamental principles of phonemics, which emphasized the contrastive nature of certain sounds to prove their existence as separate entities in the sound system. Bloomfield even gave examples of vowel-length contrasts in German to show the phonemic nature of this feature. Journal articles as well treated the topic in detail, for American linguistics was at the time caught up in the excitement of this notion, which is fundamental for understanding how language works. Thus, for those willing to look for it, a professional methodology was available.

However, almost everything Judd, Pukui, and Stokes wrote about pronunciation bears the indelible stamp of the amateur. For example, although they admitted diphthongs for Hawaiian, they denied the existence of semivowels. English, we are told, has many silent vowels and consonants. As for an important difference between the two languages: "Hawaiian articulation is based very largely at the back of the tongue, while that of English is nearer the tip" (p. 10).[30]

As might be expected for a pocket-sized vocabulary, the focus is on translating, rather than explaining the language. For example, note the following entries, chosen to illustrate the distance between Hawaiian and European culture:

(ke) **aloha**, affection, sympathy, greeting.
kapu, ... forbidden; sacred.   **mana**, authority, power, might.

The first of these entries shows a useful feature incorporated into the Hawaiian-English section: words that take the *ke* (rather than *ka*) variant of the article are so marked.

The purpose of their vocabulary, the compilers wrote in the preface, was "to assist the English-speaking person so desiring to acquire readily a working knowledge of the Hawaiian language." It is unlikely that a serious student of the language would have much success if this work were the only dictionary available. Still, the compilers gave their readers the useful advice of seeking formal instruction in the language, or practicing the language with native speakers.

Pukui and Elbert 1957-1986

The extremely small printing of the Parker revision (400 copies) and the justifiable dissatisfaction with its content (Ashford 1987:16), combined with the inadequacy of the Judd, Pukui, and Stokes vocabulary, led to a need for a new Hawaiian dictionary. Of course, after a century of lexicographic tradition, no Hawaiian dictionary could be totally new: it would be foolish not to take advantage of the work already done, even if marred. Thus, the latest Hawaiian dictionary has a complicated heritage, tracing its beginnings from the lineage of Hawaiian dictionaries that preceded it, the many annotated copies of these works, and the card file begun in (perhaps) the 1930s by Mary Kawena Pukui at the Bishop Museum. In 1949, Pukui and Samuel H. Elbert were commissioned by the territorial legislature (Pukui and Elbert 1961:viii) either to revise the Andrews-Parker dictionary or to compile a new one. The latter course was chosen, for the changes were too dramatic to be considered a revision. For example, the entries were increased from about 14,000 (in Andrews-Parker) to 25,000. The compilers gave some idea of the types of vocabulary that were expanded in the 1957 edition (p. viii):

> As indicative of the increase: the old volume has some 6 types of *aha'aina* (feast) compared with 23 in this work, some 49 types of *hale* (house) compared with 133, and 2 types of *palapala* (document) compared with 63.   The number of illustrative phrases and sentences has been greatly increased and the system of cross references expanded.

By the time of the 1986 edition, the total number of entries had been increased to about 29,000. This impressive advance was due not only to the diligence of the compilers, but to the cooperation of a great number of specialists as well.

As for the philosophy of what should be included in a dictionary, the compilers can only be admired. (We must remember, of course that this was the first major dictionary to be produced wholly outside the aegis of the church!) Note this statement (p. ix):

> The implications of the descriptive approach pervade every aspect of the lexicographer's trade. He is permitted no personal predilections for words of native origin as opposed to words from foreign sources, for ancient words as opposed to newer ones, for words of one standard dialect as opposed to another, for pronunciations conforming to the spelling as opposed to pronunciations heard in the fast colloquial conversation of cultivated speakers. He must not frame condemnatory definitions of customs of which he may not privately approve, nor on the other hand may he glorify the past or purge from it what he may deplore. Nor may he blanch at risqué terms. In short, he is a reporter and in his role of lexicographer he never takes the part of teacher, missionary, innovator, or purist.

In addition to the expanded scope, an important contribution of this series of dictionaries has been a move toward a more accurate indication of glottal stops and long vowels. For the latter, at least, this has been a gradual process. One finds curious changes from edition to edition: for example, *māhalo* 'thank you' in the first two editions became *mahalo* in later ones. And the realization that no content words consist of just one short syllable came at the same time. Thus, for example, *ku* 'stand' became *kū*.[31] Finally, not until the 1986 edition were the incorrect statements about word accent corrected and a system for indicating accent adopted.[32]

One of the major changes from its predecessors is this dictionary's concept of an entry (p. ix). The close attention paid to glottal stops and macrons resulted in, for example, the separation of the "word" formerly spelled *pua* into three different entries: *pua, puʻa,* and *pūʻā*. This was definitely a step in the right direction.

However, the step was still not large enough, for one still finds widely disparate meanings under one entry. Ironically, the compilers criticized Parker, as mentioned above, for his concept of an entry. Specifically, they wrote (1957:ix):

> Some eleven meanings of *pua* that may be translated by English nouns form a single entry in the Andrews-Parker volume;

in this new book the words spelled *p-u-a* that have widely differing meanings constitute different entries.

One can only wonder, then, what constituted "widely differing meanings" for the compilers, for under *pua* in the current edition, one finds the following senses: flower, appear, progeny, arrow, shortened form of *olopua*, float, shortened form of *ʻo-pua*, and name of a goddess. For some entries, grammatical words and content words are thrown together—for example, *mā*, used after a noun to indicate that there are others involved, but also 'faded'. Thus, the basis for the head-word is the linguistic form (devoid of meaning), and different meanings are grouped together regardless of etymology. In following this practice, the compilers directly contradicted their stated principles.

This practice is also directly counter to that followed by major English monolingual dictionaries available at that time (such as the *Oxford English Dictionary* and *Merriam-Webster's Second New International Dictionary*) and major bilingual dictionaries (such as *Cassell's German-English, English-German* [ca. 1909]). Few modern Polynesian dictionaries were available at that time, but Williams's excellent work on Māori could have served as a model: although homonyms are entered under one headword, the different senses are numbered as separate paragraphs, making it much easier for readers to find the meaning they seek. One has only to look at similar entries (e.g., *mata* for Māori and *maka* for Hawaiian, with about the same number of subentries) to see how much easier it is to use the Māori dictionary.

As was mentioned above in the discussion of Andrews 1836 and 1865, it is useful to compare how different lexicographers have treated the prefix *hoʻo-*. Like its predecessors, the Pukui-Elbert dictionary is inconsistent. At the top of pages containing entries beginning with *ho-* are these instructions: "In causative/simulative forms beginning with *ho, hō-, hoʻ-, hō-*, delete the prefix and look for the stem." First, this implies an unrealistic degree of linguistic sophistication on the part of the ordinary user. Next, although the same directions appear on pages with *hoʻo-*entries, there still appear some four columns of entries, most of which are self-apparent. Note, for example:

hoʻo.haʻa.haʻa. See *haʻa.haʻa*, low, humble.

A more efficient solution would have been to include only idiomatic forms or those whose spelling obscures their morphological structure. As it is, the selection of the *hoʻo-* forms that have separate entries seems random or even whimsical.

Beyond the organization of entries, a much more serious fault of the *Hawaiian Dictionary* is an underlying assumption that definition equals translation. If we can return to John Lyons's comments about degrees of linguistic and cultural overlap (referred to earlier in this chapter), we can recognize the fallacy in assuming that in dealing with two such disparate cultures, one can find direct English translations for all Hawaiian words. Professional lexicographers have stated this warning more directly (Benson 1990):

> Linguists and lexicographers have recognized that, except for some scientific and technical vocabularies, many lexical items in any language are culture-specific or culture-bound, and that, consequently, one must be cautious about assuming the absolute equivalency of any two items in different languages ...

Yet, this assumption seems to be the foundation of the definitions in the *Hawaiian Dictionary*. For example, note the following entry:

> **auē, auwē.** Interj. and vi. Oh! Oh dear! Oh boy! Alas! Too bad! Goodness! (Much used to express wonder, fear, scorn, pity, affection ...)

Here, what I would consider the essence of the definition—an explanation of the circumstances that prompt such an exclamation—follows the awkward translations, appearing in parentheses. Further examples in combination are translated as 'Goodness! Alas! Oh!, Alas for us! Woe betide us! Woe is me!'

As a contrast, compare this with Andrews's economical and sophisticated definition (1836a), in which translation is subordinate to explanation:

> ... the cry of persons lamenting for the sick or dead ...
> ... alas! O! an exclamation of wonder, of surprise, of fear, of pity or affection.

Another revealing example is Pukui and Elbert's treatment of *kapu*:

> ... Taboo, prohibition; special privilege or exemption from ordinary taboo, sacredness; prohibited, forbidden; sacred, holy, consecrated; no trespassing, keep out. ...

With the exception of one explanatory phrase, the "definition" consists entirely of translations. Note also the compilers' tendency to use unnecessary synonyms. As James T. Collins has suggested (pers. comm., October 1992), a definition of this kind reads like an English thesaurus.

Still, those who use the dictionary mainly for translation find this a useful feature (John Charlot, pers. comm., September 1993).

In contrast, note Andrews's definition of *kapu*, in which he explained the culturally foreign concept first, and then added translations:

> ... a general name of the system of religion that existed formerly in the islands, and which was grounded upon numerous *kapus* or restrictions, keeping the common people in obedience to the chiefs and the priests. The word signifies prohibited, forbidden, sacred, devoted to certain purposes.

Similarly, note the difference between the treatments of the word *kūmākena*. First, Pukui and Elbert's translation method:

> ... To lament, bewail, mourn loudly for the dead, grieve ...

compared with Andrews's explanation:

> ... the general mourning that followed the death of the king or high chief, when the people wailed, knocked out their teeth, lacerated their bodies and at last fell into universal prostitution.[33]

Perhaps one of the clearest examples of their focus on translation, to the exclusion of explanation, is Pukui and Elbert's "definition" of the word *aloha*:

> Aloha, love, affection, compassion, mercy, sympathy, pity, kindness, sentiment, grace, charity; greeting, salutation, regards; sweetheart, lover, loved one; beloved, loving, kind, compassionate, charitable, lovable; to love, be fond of; to show kindness, mercy, pity, charity ...

As a contrast, consider the definition of *aroha* in Williams's Māori dictionary, in which the explanation is divided into five sections: (1) Love, yearning for an absent relative or friend; (2) Pity, compassion; (3) Affectionate regard; (4) Feel love or pity; (5) Show approval. Each of these different senses is followed by an illustrative sentence. Because of this sophisticated and lexicographically satisfying approach to explaining culture-bound concepts, the Māori dictionary serves its users well.

Beyond definition, another problem with the entries in the *Hawaiian Dictionary* is that although some example sentences and phrases are identified (referring to specific pages of works by, for example, Abraham Fornander and Samuel M. Kamakau), many are not. This omission makes it difficult for serious students to examine the context from which an example was taken.

Moreover, for the most part, the compilers' thesaurus approach presents the language as if it were static, not dynamic.[34] This is particularly true for concepts that have changed significantly since European contact. Take the word *pule*, for instance, usually translated as 'pray, prayer'. It is defined (i.e., translated) as

> Prayer, magic spell, incantation, blessing, grace, church service, church; to pray, worship, say grace, ask a blessing, cast a spell.

It is clear from some features of the translation, and especially from its Proto-Polynesian etymology, that this word was not introduced at the same time as Christianity. But we are not told how and when the meaning shifted. Moreover, is this meaning related to the second sub-entry, which is translated as 'week'? Is 'week' so named because of weekly church services? Again, we are not told. A similar example was presented in chapter 9: the connection between the meanings of 'tapa printing' and 'writing' for *palapala* was not only left unexplained, but was obscured by omitting the former meaning altogether. Here, as in many such examples, the reader is better served by Andrews's dictionary.

Perhaps what is needed for a future edition is a modest adaptation of the principles underlying the *Oxford English Dictionary*, in which dated citations document meaning change and verify the meanings as well.

Because of these serious limitations—translations that rely on definition rather than explanation, and a slighting of post-contact etymology (except for a simple identification of loan words and their sources)—one can only infer that notwithstanding its impressive coverage and its Proto-Polynesian etymologies, the current Pukui-Elbert dictionary is more a tool for translators[35] than a guide to understanding the language. However, as mentioned above, some users of the dictionary are interested mainly in translation. Moreover, with its some 29,000 entries, it is by far the most comprehensive of the Polynesian dictionaries available. Like Williams's Māori dictionary, it makes abundant use of quotations to enhance definitions. And, improving on the Māori work, it provides translations for the quotations, which are essential for users who do not know the language well. Finally, both compilers can only be admired for their years of dedicated work, during a time when Hawaiian studies were not so popular, that produced a reference now essential in the efforts to preserve the Hawaiian language and culture.

Kent 1986

The last dictionary in our review, coincidentally appearing in the same year as the latest edition of the Pukui-Elbert dictionary, is Harold Winfield Kent's *Treasury of Hawaiian Words in One Hundred and One Categories.* According to Kent's preface, the foundation of the book was a "bundle of listings of Hawaiian words arranged according to category or subject," part of the papers of Charles M. Hyde (1832–99). Among his other language-centered activities, Hyde translated hymns into Hawaiian and—according to the manuscript accompanying the dictionary slips—had prepared a draft of a Hawaiian grammar.

Since Andrews 1865 was the only full-scale dictionary available to Hyde, it was the basis of much of his work. But he also added his own contributions. Kent then supplemented Hyde's notes with entries from the current edition of Pukui and Elbert, which was also no doubt the source for the macrons and glottal stops missing in the earlier works.

Because it is organized according to semantic domains, rather than an alphabetical order, Kent's *Treasury* is in a class by itself. Readers curious about the meaning of a particular word will have a difficult time finding it unless they can guess the category it belongs to. On the other hand, those who want to learn something about the Hawaiian view of a particular subject can gain a wealth of information from this work.

One of the *Treasury*'s most attractive features is the short historical or cultural explanation that introduces each category. In this way, the work extends beyond the end point of the VOCABULARY-DICTIONARY continuum proposed earlier, reaching into the ENCYCLOPEDIA area. For example, the section on *kapu* consists of a half-page explanation[36] and eighty-five terms connected with the concept. Reading the complete section is rather like reading a detailed essay on the topic.

However, as useful as this encyclopedic feature is, it is limited to the 101 categories treated—in short, an encyclopedia with 101 extended entries. Still, the work is indeed a treasury and a celebration of Hawaiian language and culture.

CONCLUSION

The various lists of Hawaiian words, ranging in time over two centuries and in scope from a few hundred words to the most recent full-scale dictionary, represent three different types of motives for collecting and defining Hawaiian words.[37] The first was to satisfy intellectual curiosity, and those who gathered the words were generally short-term visitors. The second motive was to facilitate Bible translation and religious instruction. Here, both the makers and the users of the dictionary were most likely missionaries and teachers.[38] A third, and more recent, motive is to help preserve an endangered language—to keep it from extinction. Here, the users are different, including many Hawaiians who have nearly—or already—lost their own language.

In spite of these changing motives, however, the basic format of the dictionary has not been altered. There is still, of course, a need to translate documents and to record vocabulary as an aid to understanding a culture that largely no longer exists. As Pukui and Elbert wrote so eloquently in the introduction to the first edition of the *Hawaiian-English Dictionary* in 1957 (p. xi), "A complete lexicon is a picture of the whole of the life of today and of yesterday."

However, in view of the fairly recent renaissance in Hawaiian language and culture, and the efforts to educate young speakers in their own language, perhaps what is needed now is a monolingual dictionary: one that does not detour thought through translation, but gives a Hawaiian explanation of a Hawaiian word.

NOTES

[1] For some of the discussion in this chapter, especially for the backgrounds of the lexicographers and the provenance of their manuscripts and published works, I have drawn on the excellent article by Marguerite K. Ashford (1987), which traces the history of Hawaiian dictionaries (and word lists) from 1828 to about 1984. But although the scope of our treatments is similar, the foci are different: it was not Ashford's intent to concentrate on the linguistic content of the dictionaries, whereas that is the principal purpose in this chapter.

[2] Lest one be accused of participating in what Geofry K. Pullum (1991: 166) called the "'gee-whiz' mode of discourse," it should be made clear at the outset that there is nothing unusual about the fact that Hawaiian has an extensive vocabulary in any particular semantic area, something Pullum (p. 165) called an "obvious truth of specialization." But these matters have been considered noteworthy in the past, and this section is simply a review of such statements.

[3] Pierre Gaussin, discussed in chapter 8.

[4] With the exception of *insult* (the *prostrate foe* doesn't seem to be part of the etymology), Alexander's explanations coincide with those in the *Oxford English Dictionary*.

[5] One cannot help wondering how Alexander could be sure of this.

[6] Kotzebue (1821:305) mentioned some vocabulary differences between Oʻahu and Hawaiʻi that caused communication problems.

[7] No documentary evidence was ever offered for this etymology.

[8] This type of explanation is consistent with Beckley's other writings on Hawaiian. See chapter 16.

[9] John Charlot (pers. comm., May 1993) has pointed out that *haole* was used in chants to refer to Kamapuaʻa and to Kūaliʻi. See Charlot 1987:108 (note 61).

[10] Not identified.

[11] The Reverend Artemas Bishop (1795–1872) came to Hawaiʻi as a member of the Second Company and spent the rest of his life here, serving the Mission in various ways, but especially as a translator of sections of the Bible, other religious tracts, and educational books, including a Hawaiian-English phrase book. His most important published lexicographic works are an English-Hawaiian dictionary compiled with John S. Emerson (1845; see the Bibliography) and several vocabularies, principally a 368-page manuscript described by Ashford (1987:2–3).

[12] John Pickering, of Salem, Massachusetts, already well-known as the author of *Essay on a Uniform Orthography for the Indian Languages of North America* and as one of the advisers for the Hawaiian spelling system (see chapter 7).

[13] This ambitious project is discussed further in chapter 15.

[14] Ely (1798–1890) was from the Second Company, arriving in Hawaiʻi in 1823.

[15] Based on a count of twenty pages. Andrews himself (1865:2) gave a count of "a little over 6,000."

[16] Of course, this could simply be a misprint.

[17] All these words except the last show a noticeable raising of the /a/. Those followed by /i/ in the next syllable are examples of assimilation (to the high vowel); the raising of sequences of /a/s is not so easily explained on phonetic grounds, but also occurs in modern Hawaiian (Greg Lee Carter, pers. comm., 1987), as well as in Micronesian languages and languages of Vanuatū.

[18] This must refer to what was eventually Andrews's vocabulary, but as the preceding section shows, he was not officially chosen as the compiler until 1834.

[19] The grammar (1837:2–3) lists the sources, which consist of various portions of the Bible, hymnals, other religious tracts, and school texts.

[20] He acknowledged substantial help from missionaries Dwight Baldwin, William Richards, Artemas Bishop, Gerrit Parmele Judd, and from the historian Samuel M. Kamakau.

[21] We can also find from *The Friend* that Andrews received $1.00 per copy, and that the book would sell for $5.00. The editor suggested that the government give Andrews a grant for further work, but was not optimistic about that idea's success.

[22] Some earlier borrowings were removed, and for good reason: for example, *bitumena* 'bitumen, slime', *dederama* 'tribute'. But oddly, *buke* 'book' was removed without being replaced by *puke*.

[23] John Charlot (pers. comm., September 1993) that the newspapers reflected efforts by the Hawaiians as well to record vocabulary.

[24] Lyons's annotated copy of Andrews's dictionary, interleaved with copious notes, is in the Hawai'i State Archives (James. A. Tharp, pers. comm., 29 October 1990). Elbert wrote (1954:11–12): "Lyons spent eight years revising the dictionary, and some of his revisions are said to have been incorporated in Parker's revision." (The direct quotation from Parker (1922:vi) is: "An interleaved volume of Andrew's [*sic*] work with notes and criticisms by the late Rev. Lorenzo Lyons has been used to advantage.") Of course, as the long passage from Lyons shows, he spent not eight years, but a little over three years in revision; eight years was the period that had elapsed between the time he stopped serious work and the time he wrote the note in *The Friend.* But the oddest thing about this part of the history is that, insofar as we can tell from the introduction to their dictionary, Pukui and Elbert did not use Lyons's notes, but instead relied on Parker's interpretation of them.

[25] In spite of these changes, Pukui and Elbert wrote (1957:vii-viii): "Except for rearrangement according to the English alphabet and a surprising deletion of all Biblical references, the revised Andrews-Parker work of 1922 is nearly the same as the 1865 volume." It is difficult to understand the adjective *surprising* in the quotation, for Parker stated very clearly in his Introduction (p. vi): "Most scriptural references have been omitted in this review [i.e., revision] since alterations made in the text of later editions of the Hawaiian Bible make these references unserviceable."

[26] An examination of Parker's linguistic credentials shows that he "learned Hawaiian as a child and became so devoted to the language that he is said to have refused to preach in English."

[27] As further examples, the noun and the verb for 'coition' are said to be pronounced differently. In all, there are eight separate entries for the single spelling *ai.*

[28] Elbert (1954:13) gave the counts as 4,500 and 6,000.

[29] Incredibly, Elbert praised the work for its "rather careful indication of glottal stops and of vowel quantity" (1954:13). As the discussion shows, the authors' treatment of vowel quantity may have been "careful," but it was inaccurate, based, as it was, on a totally false premise.

[30] One wonders why these solecisms were not excised in the editing: in the preface, Denzel Carr, described as an accomplished linguist, was credited "for guidance in evaluating basic sounds." But how was the word *linguist* being used here? Carr was well-known for being able to speak a great many languages. But a reexamination of his article on loanwords in Hawaiian (1951) shows that he was apparently unaware that Hawaiian had a vowel-length contrast.

[31] This change was suggested by William H. Wilson. The matter could have been resolved much earlier by studying Williams's Māori dictionary.

[32] This system, which I devised originally for Fijian, indicates accent units on all words longer than three short syllables, for accent, contrary to earlier statements, is not predictable. Headwords in the 1986 edition of the Hawaiian dictionary separate accent units with periods. The system is meant only as a guide to pronunciation, and is not part of the spelling system.

[33] The *Oxford English Dictionary* suggests that perhaps in this use the word has been confused with *prostration*. But in this context it might be either.

[34] Of course, the dictionary was not meant to be a historical dictionary. But John Charlot suggested this as an area in which it could be improved.

[35] Note that the *Hawaiian Dictionary* has as part of its front matter a one-page essay "On Translating into Hawaiian." This is rather a futile effort: those seriously interested in translation realize that it is a special skill and not something that one can do with a one-page aid, while those translating only casually are not likely to read the front matter of any dictionary.

[36] Perhaps not quite balanced, since it gives the impression at once that the main function of the system was to subjugate women.

[37] Note that an early practical motive present for some other parts of the Pacific seems to be missing here. For example, the stated purpose of an 1811 list for Fijian was to facilitate communication for the sandalwood trade.

[38] It was often said about the Fijian-English bilingual dictionary that Fijians used it to learn English. Observation and questioning showed that such was not the case.

CHAPTER TWELVE

Hawaiian Grammars

-o-o-o-o-o-

The first and most important thing to be attended to in studying Hawaiian ... is the idiom, *or the manner of expression peculiar to that language. The definition of words is a matter of minor importance. Hence it is well in the outset to divest ourselves of the idea that the language we are about to study can be constructed or written or analyzed entirely on the principles of our vernacular tongue ... It should be remembered that different people have different modes of thinking and speaking, according as the objects with which they are daily conversant, and about which they think and speak, are different. Hence the idioms of no two languages can be expected to be alike. (Lorrin Andrews, Remarks on the Hawaiian dialect [1836b:13]).*

Whether it was stated explicitly or not, the earliest comments about Hawaiian grammar were comparative in nature. Those who made casual statements about the structure of Hawaiian nearly always compared it with that of Latin or their own language (usually English), which was often viewed through a Latin lens.[1]

This practice of explaining the unfamiliar by contrasting it with the familiar is an inevitable feature of human nature. But perhaps it can help us in the difficult task of evaluating a lineage of Hawaiian grammars beginning in about 1819 and continuing to the present. For such an evaluation, I propose two general criteria: first, how well the grammarians used the tools that were available at the time; and next, how successful they were at escaping the bonds of Latin or of their own languages.

For the first forty years after European contact, most of the observations about Hawaiian grammar are tiny nuggets to be mined from the accounts of explorers and traders. And for this topic, the pickings are much slimmer than they are for vocabulary and spelling. After all, as we have seen in previous chapters, any astute observer could use an ad hoc orthography to write down a collection of words. Observations about grammar, on the other hand, required analysis, which, in turn, needed motivation, time, and special skills.

One of the first (although indirect) comments about Hawaiian grammar was made by William Beresford and quoted in chapter 2. In noting that Hawaiians spoke differently among themselves than to outsiders, he mentioned the "articles and conjunctions" that were omitted for foreigners. Adelbert von Chamisso's bizarre report that Hawaiian had only two pronouns was also referred to in that chapter.

Two early writers mentioned a feature that we might interpret as reduplication—the repetition of part or all of a word to serve a number of different grammatical functions. The first, Archibald Campbell, wrote (1816:228): "It frequently happens, that the same word is repeated twice, in which case it is connected with a hyphen, thus *leepe-leepe* [*lipilipi*], an axe."[2]

The other observation is from Jacques Arago (or perhaps Joseph P. Gaimard), who wrote (1823:294): "It will be seen, that the language of the Sandwich islanders is principally formed of compound words." Judging from the word list itself, he could have been referring to either reduplicated forms (which are well represented in the list) or sequences of noun plus qualifier, such as *niho li'ili'i* 'incisors (lit., small tooth)'.

But what was the frame of reference for these early comparative statements and for the fuller grammars that followed? To answer this question, we need to know more about the linguistic backgrounds of the people who wrote about Hawaiian at this time.

THE CLASSICAL MODEL

In order to discover what an eighteenth- and nineteenth-century scholar expected to find in a grammar, we turn again to the ubiquitous schoolmaster and grammarian, Thomas Dilworth (1740 [1778]:85):

> Grammar is the Science of Letters, or the Art of Writing and Speaking properly and syntactically ... Grammar is divided into Four Parts; Orthography, Prosody, Analogy, and Syntax.

Note that the primary function of the study of grammar, at least as stated by Dilworth, was to enable us to write and speak "properly." Noah Webster's variation on this theme was: "Grammar is the art of communicating thoughts by words with propriety and dispatch." However, it is difficult to know how to apply this principle to the study of Hawaiian, since linguistic propriety could hardly be defined for such an unknown quantity, particularly by outsiders.

The next part of the contemporary concept of grammar is more pertinent. The first division, ORTHOGRAPHY, we have already discussed at length. The next term, PROSODY, referred at that time to the metrical study of versification, a topic that is outside the scope of this work. However, the last two parts—ANALOGY and SYNTAX—figure prominently in our review of Hawaiian grammars. Dilworth defined these two terms as follows (pp. 97, 121):

> Analogy teaches us how to know distinctly all the several Parts of Speech in the English Tongue.
> Syntax is the disposing of Words in their right Case, Gender, Number, Person, Mood, Tense and Place,[3] in a Sentence.

These concepts can provide a framework for studying the degree to which analysts tried to fit Hawaiian into a Latinate mold, or, on the other hand, successfully described the language on its own terms. In other words, the terms just listed give us an idea of what European observers at the end of the eighteenth century expected of a language.

First, words should be unambiguously categorized into (preferably) eight or nine classes, traditionally called PARTS OF SPEECH. Definitions according to the trinity of form, function, and meaning kept (for example) nouns, verbs, and adjectives strictly distinct.

Next, words should be marked for one or more GRAMMATICAL CATEGORIES: systems within a language that show certain relationships among the items in a sentence.

To understand better why Hawaiian grammar came as a surprise to many observers, we now sketch some ways in which the language differs from English or Latin.

Parts of Speech

In Latin, parts of speech are readily identified by their suffixes, and even if there is crossing over from one category to another (say, from verb to noun), the suffixes will still mark the function of the word in a sentence. For example, because of the forms of the words, we recognize *timēre* 'to fear' as a verb and *timor* 'fear' as a noun. In Hawaiian, many words can serve any of several functions without changing their form. In the following sentences, the word *aloha* functions (in the traditional sense) as a verb, a noun, an adjective, and an adverb (these examples are adapted from Andrews 1854:18–19):

*Ke **aloha** aku nei au i ku'u hoalauna.*	I **love** my friend.
*He **aloha** kona i kona hoalauna.*	He[4] had **love** for his friend.
*He ali'i **aloha** nō ia i kona hoalauna.*	He is indeed a **loving** chief to his friend.

Hana aloha a'ela kēlā ia ia. That person treated him in a **friendly** fashion.

In spite of the fact that the word itself does not change, the functions are still distinct, for they are indicated in other ways, such as by markers (that is, grammatical function words) or by position in the sentence.

The remaining terms in Dilworth's definition (plus a few others that figure in the comparison) can be grouped around four major parts of speech—NOUNS and PRONOUNS,[5] VERBS, and ADJECTIVES—and a more general category of SYNTAX.

Systems Connected with Nouns and Pronouns

Case. Latin uses different suffixes on nouns to show their function in a sentence. For example, the ending shows whether the noun is in one of these cases: NOMINATIVE (subject), GENITIVE (possessive), DATIVE (indirect object), ACCUSATIVE (direct object), ABLATIVE (object of certain prepositions), and sometimes VOCATIVE (direct address). Table 12.1 shows how the relationships shown in Latin with suffixes are indicated in Hawaiian with markers (adapted from Andrews 1854:43).

TABLE 12.1
COMPARISON OF "CASE" IN LATIN AND HAWAIIAN
(SINGULAR FORMS ONLY)

	Latin	Hawaiian	Gloss
Nom.	domus	ka hale	the house
Gen.	domūs	*o* ka hale, *a* ka hale *ko* ka hale, *ka* ka hale	*of* the house the *houses'*
Dat.	domuī	*no* ka hale, *na* ka hale	*for* the house
Acc.	domum	*i* ka hale *ma* ka hale	the house *at/ to* the house
Abl.	domū	*me* ka hale *e* ka hale	*with* the house *by* the house
Voc.		*e* ka hale	*O* the house

Gender. In Latin, gender is an arbitrary system of nomenclature that divides nouns into classes. The function of such a system is unclear, although one might suggest that because the suffix of an adjective must reflect the gender of the noun it modifies, some useful redundancy is added to the language.[6] Hawaiian has no such system. Unfortunately, the names for the traditional gender categories for Latin—masculine, feminine, and neuter—have resulted in a confusion between a grammatical system and physical sex distinctions. Starting with the very earliest grammatical sketch of Hawaiian, linguistic amateurs have cited names of male versus female animals to illustrate gender. Even a preliminary draft of a recent Hawaiian grammar contained a similar statement, until it was pointed out that the terms *moa kāne* 'rooster' and *moa wahine* 'hen' may be appropriate for poultry husbandry but have nothing to do with grammar. Such writers would have done well to read William Marsden's comments on the issue (1812:29):

> The absurdity of attributing difference of sex to things, or to the names of things not organised by nature to reproduce their kind, did not suggest itself to the framers or methodisers of the Malayan tongue ... Should it be maintained that ... a mare is effectively the feminine of ... a horse, that daughter is the feminine of son, and queen of king, we may answer, without denying the propositions, that such a distinction of terms does not belong to grammar, but like other names of things, they are best sought for in a dictionary.

The current use of the term *gender* in the context of the equality or inequality of the sexes is the latest example of the misunderstanding.

Number. In Latin (and English), when we deal with nouns that refer to entities that can be counted, we must use either a singular form or a plural. For example, in English, one must choose between *house* and *houses*. In contrast, number in Hawaiian seems optional, except for a small set of words that change their form by lengthening the third-to-last syllable (such as *wahine* 'woman'; *wāhine* 'women').[7] Samuel Ruggles (1819) wrote: "There is no distinction between the singular and plural of nouns," except for that small set of words just referred to.

As for other indicators of quantity, only *nā* seems unambiguously a grammatical marker, and it is difficult to know whether its use was obligatory or imposed through translation analysis.[8] Other so-called plural markers, such as *po'e* and *pu'u*, were early noted as referring to collections of things. Thus, in a phrase such as *ka po'e kaua* 'the warriors', the structure could possibly be NOUN + QUALIFIER, not PLURAL MARKER + NOUN.[9]

In its pronoun system, however, Hawaiian divides reality into finer categories than does English: it distinguishes among three numbers—singular, dual, and plural. The category of dual would not have surprised Biblical scholars: Hebrew and Greek use such a distinction in their number systems.

Person. This category, which seems to be a feature of all languages, refers to the distinction among the speaker, the person spoken to, and the remainder (neither speaker nor one spoken to, sometimes referred to as "spoken about"). In Hawaiian, this system extends beyond pronouns to words referring to location as well: *kēia* 'by me', *kēnā* 'by you', and *kēlā* 'by him/her/it'. Hawaiian also has an additional nuance: the INCLUSIVE-EXCLUSIVE category, which tells specifically whether the various words meaning 'we', 'us', or 'our' include or exclude the person spoken to.

Systems Connected with Verbs

Mood. Some languages use an affix on a verb to indicate the state of reality of the event or condition it refers to. This category marks verbs for an actual event differently from ones referring to commands, wishes, or possibilities. As with the previous categories, Hawaiian indicates such meanings with separate markers.

Tense/Aspect. Many languages use grammatical markers to indicate when an event took place. Like number, tense in English and Latin is obligatory, except for the infinitive and (in English) a few modals such as *must*. In Hawaiian, however, although the time of an event or state can be indicated by a time word or phrase, whether or not there are grammatical markers to specify tense is a disputed point.

Another category, ASPECT, seems more appropriate for describing Hawaiian. In this system, which is indicated by such markers as *ua, e ... ana*, and *ke ... nei*, time is not as important as whether or not an action or state has been begun, is continuing, or has been completed—or whether or not it contrasts with another state or action. For example, *Ua ola ka wahine* 'The woman is well', can imply that she is *now* well, or has *become* well, after being ill. Because so many treatments of Hawaiian grammar have been translation oriented, the aspect system has long been confused with tense, and still today it is neither well understood nor well described.

Although not part of a system, there is another feature of Hawaiian verbs that bothered early observers. In European languages, verbs for 'to be' and 'to have' seem *sine qua non*. However, Hawaiian (like many other Oceanic languages) has no words directly corresponding to those two meanings. Thus, the senses of 'be' and 'have' are indicated by other constructions.

Systems Connected with Adjectives

Much like nouns and verbs, adjectives in Latin show at least three different features by their suffixes. Although they do not inherently contain gender, number, or case, they are inflected for those categories, agreeing with the nouns that they modify. Moreover (and English shares this feature), they have a distinction of their own: different endings to show the comparative and superlative degrees. Hawaiian has no kind of agreement like the former system, and comparison is handled simply as modification: adding words to qualify the original meaning.

Possessives are another set of words that function like adjectives (that is, they modify nouns), but are distinguished for person, exclusiveness, and number. Within this set there is a distinction between otherwise identical forms that differ in the choice of accented vowel: *a* versus *o*. A prominent feature of (probably) all Polynesian languages, such a system does not exist in European languages. Forms with *a* are sometimes called ALIENABLE; those with *o*, INALIENABLE. Perhaps it is these names that have encouraged a misunderstanding that has continued to the present: it is not the "possessed" that is either alienable or inalienable, but instead, the *relationship* between the possessor and the possessed.[10] In general, relationships involving kin, body parts and other parts of a whole, and innate qualities fall into the *o* or inalienable category; others are *a*, or alienable. However, each Polynesian language has a slightly different interpretation of the system, and thus there are exceptions to these general patterns.

Syntax

If we return to Dilworth's definition of syntax, we see that this part of grammar was devoted chiefly to the fitting together of words according to their inflectional endings. However, because so much grammatical information is contained in the endings of Latin nouns, adjectives, and verbs, once they are presented (in series of tables, or PARADIGMS), a great many features of the language have already been described. Thus, word order—the essence of syntax in many languages —is not so important in a language in which the function of each word is apparent from its very form and not necessarily from its relationship to other words in a phrase or sentence. As a result, many nineteenth-century grammars devote no more than a few pages to syntax.

Since Hawaiian grammar was often presented in noun and verb paradigms (even though the writers realized that the language did not operate as Latin did), there was also a good deal of information presented: not necessarily how *words* are built, but *phrases*, the building blocks of Polynesian grammar. However, certain prominent features of both word and phrase order were commented on. The following brief statement (written fairly late, but reflecting a much earlier period) notes some easily recognized features of Hawaiian word order (Judd 1880:24):

> Nouns are placed before adjectives, as, "pua ala ['ala]," "flower fragrant." Verbs are also placed at the beginning of a sentence, as, "Plucked I the flower fragrant."

Finally, most descriptions of Hawaiian have assumed that all Hawaiian sentences can be divided into SUBJECT and PREDICATE, just like English, but with the order of these elements reversed.[11] Perhaps this is an example of translation analysis—unconsciously describing the structure of the English glosses rather than the Hawaiian sentences.

WHAT ADDITIONAL TOOLS WERE AVAILABLE?

By the time the missionaries in Hawai'i began to describe the structure of the language, they had in their armory not only the usual training in the grammars of English and classical languages, but also a number of published grammars from related languages: Malay (Marsden 1812), Tongan (Martin 1817), Māori (Kendall and Lee 1820), and Tahitian (Davies 1823). The correspondence and publications of the various linguists in Polynesia show that their studies were connected by a network of ideas that ran from scholar to scholar and from island to island. For example, John Martin, who served as John Mariner's amanuensis, referred to Marsden's work on Malay, as did William Ellis in his "Remarks on the Hawaiian Language." In his Tahitian grammar, John Davies acknowledged the help he had received from S. Greatheed's manuscript grammar of Marquesan and the published works on Tongan and Māori. And earlier in this work it was noted that the Hawaiian missionaries had received copies of both the Māori and Tahitian grammars. Thus, in no sense were the Hawaiian grammarians working in an intellectual vacuum. Rather, they had the advice and cooperation of their colleagues, both within and outside their extended missionary family.

In our discussion of this flow of ideas, we begin with Marsden's work on Malay, not only because it predates all the Polynesian grammars, but also because it was a very sophisticated, innovative description of a language related to Hawaiian.

Marsden 1812

Having spent the years between the ages of sixteen and twenty-four in West Sumatra, William Marsden[12] returned to England at the time books on Captain Cook's first voyage to the Pacific were being published.[13] Caught up in "the enthusiastic spirit of curiosity," Marsden met such contemporary naturalists as William Jones, Joseph Banks, Daniel Solander, and others.

In terms of his treatment of grammatical categories that were strikingly different from those of the classical languages, Marsden was far ahead of his time. For example, when he described nouns, he noted that gender, number, and case are missing. As the quotation above about gender shows, he was not at all apologetic or condescending about its absence, unlike Karl R. Lepsius, who considered languages without gender "in decline."[14]

Marsden carried this attitude through his treatment of the other parts of speech. In short, he made this kind of statement (but this is in my words, not his): from the languages we are accustomed to speaking and studying, we are familiar with certain mechanisms of grammatical function. These mechanisms lie within the morphologies of the languages. In other words, English, German, and Latin carry out a great many grammatical functions through inflection. However, Marsden noted that Malay used other means—generally "words and particles" before or after the main words—for similar functions.

Martin 1817

In the introduction to his account of William Mariner's extra-ordinary experiences in Tonga from 1806 to 1810, John Martin explained both the motives behind and the methods for arriving at his analysis of Tongan grammar (1817 [1981]:26–27). The passage is quoted in full, for nowhere else, either in works of the past century or the present one, have I found so straightforward a description of the methodology that underlies the presentation of a grammar on the printed page:

> One object which I had in view in constructing the grammar was to satisfy my curiosity, by ascertaining what sort of rules and idioms were preserved in a language spoken by a people, who have no notion of grammatical laws, and who have no other conception of the art of writing than as a species of witchcraft, but who take a pride, at least the higher classes, in speaking their language with a sort of aristocratic propriety. I conceived also, that such an investigation would be acceptable both to the philologist and the philosopher; — to the former as regards the peculiarities of human language — to the latter as respects the

phenomena of the human mind. The result did not disappoint me.
I discovered some interesting coincidences, and several peculiarities worthy of notice. Like Hebrew and Greek, the Tonga dialect
has a dual number. It has a peculiar pronoun belonging to the first
person plural, excluding the person spoken to; a peculiar plural for
intelligent beings; three words expressing the action of *giving*,
accordingly as it may regard respectively the first, second, or third
person to whom any thing is *given*;[15] and many other points highly
curious. The plan which I adopted to discover and assign the rules
of this heretofore unwritten language, was this: — After Mr
Mariner had carefully selected from an English dictionary all the
words to which he could find appropriate Tonga phrases, and after
having assiduously attended to the elementary sounds of the language, and their articulations from Mr Mariner's pronunciation,
and upon this basis determined upon a system of orthography, I
undertook the charge of arranging all the Tonga words alphabetically, according to the system of spelling previously adopted. In
the mean time, Mr Mariner recalling to his mind sundry dialogues,
popular tales, speeches, and songs, wrote them down in the Tonga
original, upon which I exercised myself, with his assistance and
that of the vocabulary, in making literal translations; thereby
learning the idiom and at the same time furnishing the vocabulary
with additional words. I also collected examples of the various
turns of phrase in English, and of all the parts of speech, for Mr
Mariner to translate into the true Tonga idiom.   Thus we
ascertained what could be readily translated, what not; where the
language was ample in expression, where poor; what was definite,
and what vague; where there were rules, and where anomalies. By
gradual but diligent procedure, the character and genius of the
language were unfolded, and we soon arrived at the theoretical
knowledge of its structure.

In the grammar itself, one of the first indications that Tongan
would not be forced into the Latin mold is this general statement about
parts of speech: "the noun, adjective, verb, and participle, being often
one and the same word, [are] distinguished only by the general sense of
the phrase."

Within these categories, the treatment is similarly innovative. For
example, the noun was said to have, "properly speaking, neither gender
nor number ... and the number is only distinguished sometimes by a
sign, or by some other word." He added that the sign of the plural was
not always used. And not only was the noun said to be devoid of cases,
even the functions of the phrases corresponding to the various Latin
cases were discussed under the heading of PREPOSITIONS. Thus, Martin
presented no array of nouns even resembling a declension.

The verbs are, however, presented in tables of conjugations.[16] Interestingly—in the light of recent discussions of the possibility of ergativity[17] in various Polynesian languages, including Tongan—he reported that there was no passive in the language.

Martin apologized for the lack of a minutely detailed syntax of Tongan, justifying the omission with a candor too seldom seen (p. 408):

> ... for we are not treating of a language the rules of which have been before systematically investigated and written down; we are at present only in the act of making an investigation, in which the reader is requested to accompany us.

Finally, the grammar closes with about seven pages of translated text and a short essay on the developing idea of a Malayo-Polynesian (Austronesian) language family (although not so named), based on a comparison of Tongan and Malay (courtesy of Marsden's "excellent work").

Kendall and Lee 1820

The first major Māori grammar (and dictionary) was the result of a forced collaboration between a missionary with a control of the language but no training in linguistic analysis (Thomas Kendall) and a Cambridge scholar with exactly the opposite problem (Samuel Lee).[18] The fortuitous arrival of this work shortly before the first Hawaiian imprint (1822) was ascribed a somewhat exaggerated importance in a work on the development of the Hawaiian orthography (Wise and Hervey 1952), but I have found no evidence that it influenced the description of Hawaiian grammar. This is odd: because the languages are very similar, and the grammar is a good deal more than a sketch, it might have had a significant influence. However, a flawed orthography (there still remained at least three major problems with the consonants) hindered the grammatical description somewhat. For example, because the analysts were unable to hear the difference between an initial *h* and a vowel with a smooth onset, they could not distinguish between such pairs of grammatical markers as *he* and *e*.

In the main part of their analysis, it is difficult to gauge Kendall and Lee's success in avoiding the trap of describing Māori as if it were Latin, for the text and the introduction seem curiously at odds with each other. On the one hand, declensions and conjugations fill up more than half of the pages (nouns: five; pronouns: five; verbs: twenty-three). On the other hand, Lee explained in the preface that these categories did not actually exist, referring the reader to Martin's work on Tongan and Marsden's on Malay. His justification for this apparent contradiction is instructive, for it sheds light on similar practices in Hawaiian grammar:[19]

> The other particular object of the work, is the instruction of the European Missionary in the Language of New Zealand ... and for this end it was that Examples in declension and conjugation have been given, after the manner of European Grammars; when, in fact, there exists no such thing in the language in question ...

As for the treatment of individual grammatical matters distinctively Polynesian, the grammar shows no significant breakthroughs. Here are some examples: The declensions on pp. 10 *ff.* show the *a/o* contrast by giving alternate forms for the genitive, but the difference is not explained.

Related to the traditional European part-of-speech classification, there is some difficulty in the analysis of stative verbs as adjectives. Although they may usually be translated as adjectives, they function in many ways as verbs. Such a dependence on meaning for defining parts of speech was a problem that persisted well into the twentieth century.

For pronouns, the three numbers were noted, as well as the inclusive/exclusive distinction, but the latter was not clearly explained. Similarly, some paradigms show possessive forms without *t-* (indicating plural) but with no explanation.

As for demonstratives, the three-way personal distinction (see *kē ia*, etc., above) is explained as "very near," "in sight," and "at a distance," which is a step in the right direction, but not quite far enough.

The treatment of verbs seems to be a direct overlay of a European tense system on what is essentially an aspect system, resulting in a rather confusing analysis. For example, *e ... ana* (progressive, incomplete) was labeled "indicative mood, present tense," and *koa* [*kua*] (perfect, inceptive) was labeled "past."

The treatment of syntax is interesting in that Lee explained that since there was no agreement or concord possible, "all that is given relates merely to the order of words."

Davies 1823

Even before 1820 there was close cooperation between the ABCFM and the London Missionary Society in Tahiti. As mentioned in chapter 7, the missionaries originally hoped that the materials developed for Tahitian would suffice for the Hawaiian "dialect" as well. Although they soon discovered that the two languages were too different for this to be practicable, there were still enough similarities to mean that any advances in the description of Tahitian grammar would be useful to the missionaries in Hawai'i. There was a good deal of correspondence between the two missions, and William Ellis, because of his prolonged stay in Hawai'i, served as a tangible bond between them. Thus, it is inevitable that the earlier work on Tahitian grammar, just as on the orthography, would influence the description of Hawaiian grammar.

However, Ellis's own role in the development of the Tahitian orthography and the study of grammar was minimal, for he arrived on the scene rather late (1817) and served mainly as mission printer and historian. Instead, John Davies was the principal grammarian for Tahitian (see chapter 7). From his grammar (p. 5), we learn that he produced a grammatical sketch of the language as early as 1807, which was sent to the mission headquarters in London. However, this manuscript seems to be lost. Not until 1823 did a purely grammatical work appear (Davies 1810 is a primer and reader).[20]

As with so many works of this period, the grammar begins by listing the parts of speech—nine, "as in English." However, Davies was careful to note how Tahitian differed, especially from Latin (p. 10): "there is nothing *commonly* in the noun itself to signify either number or gender." He did, however, discuss a marker of "limited plurality" (*na* [*nā*]) and cited the usual method of attaching *tane* [*tāne*] or *vahine* to the noun in case it was necessary to be specific about sex distinctions.

As for case, he warned: "If by case be understood the different endings of the noun, the Tahitian nouns have no cases." He compared Tahitian with English, which has only one variation of case—the possessive—and said that Tahitian performed this function with "little words."

Even though Davies used the declension format for illustrating such functions, he suggested in a note (p. 17) that to speak of such an arrangement as a "declension" would be misleading, since there are no differences in endings.

As was noted above, Kendall and Lee came close to describing accurately the Māori three-way distinction among demonstratives, but Davies was explicit and correct in his description of this set of markers in Tahitian. Although recognized today for Hawaiian as well (see the description above under PERSON), nineteenth-century grammars do not mention the second-person form, *kēnā*.[21]

Davies listed many conjugations for mood, etc., but of course he realized that the system was different from that of Latin. Noting such differences, and echoing Lee's comments about Māori, he wrote (p. 38):

> There is nothing inherent in the verb, (a few of the *reduplicates* only excepted) to signify persons, number or gender, and conse-

quently the rules about their concord or agreement with the verb have no place in the Tahitian.

Thus, his section on syntax—often, in that period, a proliferation of rules about concord and agreement—consists of only about a page and a half.

As with many other European-based descriptions, the work ends with two pages of praxis (John xiv:15).

Unfortunately, although John Davies's Tahitian grammar was published early enough to have had some effect on the study of Hawaiian grammar, it is a sketchy work (only forty-three pages) and was not soon enlarged.

-0-0-0-0-0-

It is quite clear that given the works that were available on Malay, Tongan, Māori, and Tahitian, the well-read and astute grammarian had ample warning that Hawaiian would differ from the Indo-European models in a number of ways. Andrews's quotation at the beginning of this chapter shows that at least some analysts were aware of such differences and did not find them as unexpected as we might think. In the words of a much later writer (Preston 1900a:49): "The fact is the Oceanic family of languages is a distinct and separate creation, and must be studied on entirely different lines from those followed in Western speech."[22]

HAWAIIAN GRAMMARS

As mentioned in chapter 11, missionary organizations in the Pacific differed both in their requirements for linguistic work and in the abilities of their personnel. For example, in the 1830s, the Wesleyan Methodist Missionary Society presented its fieldworkers with the following assignments (Cargill letters, 18 June 1839):

> To draw up a comprehensive statement respecting the character of the language, the difference between it and the other Polynesian dialects, the principles on which you have settled its grammatical form, and the rules by which you have been guided in translating into it the word of God.

So far as we know, the ABCFM in Boston issued no such brief to its representatives in Hawai'i. Perhaps because there were no definite instructions to write a grammar, the Mission took thirty-four years to produce anything more than a grammatical sketch.[23]

However, the intention was there. Less than two years after the arrival of the First Company, Elisha Loomis wrote (Missionary letters, Oʻahu, 1 February 1822, p. 16):

> We intend to print a catichism [*sic*] historical & doctrinal, a scripture tract, a grammar and vocabulary, as we make advances in the language. Our pupils will devour books in this language as fast as we can make them. "The translation of the Scriptures into any language is a great work, but especially if there are no learned men who write and speak that language fluently."

As for the differences between English and Hawaiian, William Richards considered that (letter to Jeremiah Evarts, ABCFM, Boston, 7 October 1828, Lahaina. HMCS XI, Letter 143):

> There is a greater difference between the idioms of these two languages [i.e., Hawaiian and English] than any other two with which I am acquainted.
>
> There are several sentences in this letter which lose much of their beauty in a translation, for want of that distinction that exists between the *kakou* and *makou/Kakou, we*, including both those who speak and those addressed — *Makou, we*, including only those who speak ...
>
> Permit me Sir here to inquire whether we ought to devote much attention to preparing a grammar of this language in English, or a vocabulary, or anything else of the kind? Whatever can be done for the gratification of the learned or the curious, we shall be ready to do, on a suggestion from you.

To justify the long delay between the intention and the deed, at least twice Lorrin Andrews explained why a grammar had not yet appeared. Sixteen years after the missionaries arrived in Hawaiʻi, he listed "formidable difficulties" that blocked a "thorough knowledge and investigation of the Hawaiian language" (Andrews 1836b):[24]

Not enough documents yet written by Hawaiians, essential for
    etymology and syntax
No agreed-upon standard for the language (great flexibility)
The reluctance of the Hawaiians to give critical judgments
The tendency of the Hawaiians to agree to any proposition sug-
    gested by a person of authority

In a work published in the same year (1836a:ii), Andrews gave a similar set of reasons, focusing more on practical matters. First, he mentioned that there was a want of leisure time in which to do the work. But more important, he felt, was the paradox mentioned in chapter 11: after the earliest missionaries had learned the language, they didn't need such a work; their successors, who did need it, didn't feel qualified to compile a grammar.

Thus, until Adelbert von Chamisso published his grammar in 1837, the only representations of the language's structure available to the outside world were short sketches, beginning with those compiled at the Foreign Mission School in Cornwall, Connecticut.

Prelude: ʻŌpūkahaʻia

As a background to his grammatical sketch (referred to in Dwight 1818), Henry ʻŌpūkahaʻia had only his native-speaker's knowledge of the language, his Webster-based view of English, and his study of Latin and Hebrew to rely on. Of the Polynesian and related grammars described earlier, only Marsden's Malay grammar had yet been completed, and there is no suggestion in the available material about or by ʻŌpūkahaʻia that he had access to it. However, one source of outside help was the Reverend Eleazar Fitch (later Chaplain at Yale), his friend and apparent collaborator (a letter to him mentions "our" grammar).

Unfortunately, no copy of ʻŌpūkahaʻia's grammar still exists; as chapter 6 showed, the manuscript long attributed to him is actually that of Samuel Ruggles. But because they were at the Foreign Mission School at Cornwall together, and because Ruggles acknowledged using ʻŌpūkahaʻia's work (letter to Lucia Ruggles Holman, March 1819), some of ʻŌpūkahaʻia's grammar is reflected in that of Ruggles.

Ruggles 1819

In Ruggles's sketch, the parts of speech (nine, "as in most other languages") form the framework for the whole piece. Within each category, the departures from the model—the idiosyncrasies, if we may call them that—are discussed. For example, Ruggles began his treatment of nouns as follows:[25]

> There is no distinction between the singular and plural of nouns, unless it is by giving the plural a different accent or pronunciation, as; *he kanáka*, man, *he kánaka*, men.[26]

> The genders appear to be distinguished by no other method than by prefixing[27] to the noun, *kanaka*, (man) for the masculine; and *wahíne* (woman) for the feminine.

> The cases are distinguished by prefixing the articles; as

N[ominative]	*he wai* = (water)
P[ossessive]	*o ko wai*
O[bjective]	*i ka wai*

In general, one of the problems with Ruggles's description of nouns and pronouns is that he treated each form in isolation. Thus, most forms are preceded by *o* ['*o*], which normally serves as a topic marker and is more appropriate for discourse than for sentence analysis.[28]

In his treatment of pronouns, Ruggles recognized three numbers, but mentioned neither the inclusive-exclusive distinction nor the *a/o* classes for possessives.

He proposed "at least" four tenses for verbs: present, imperfect, perfect, and future, but noted that the "variations of the verb" were made by helping verbs—that is, separate words, and not affixes. The following grammatical markers were treated:

e	present
ua	imperfect
ua … aku nei	perfect
e … auane'i	future

All in all, six verbs were conjugated through three persons, three numbers, four tenses, filling six pages of the original manuscript's total of fifteen. As for the accuracy of the analysis, earlier we mentioned that analysts usually tried to fit Hawaiian's aspect system into a European tense system, partly because they tended to analyze the glosses rather than the actual forms. Here, Ruggles was no exception.

The last three pages of the grammar contain lists of adverbs (twenty-two), prepositions (eighteen), conjunctions (nine), and interjections (six).[29]

It is unfortunate that Ruggles's grammar is so paradigmatic in nature that it contains no sample of the language larger than simple noun phrases or verb phrases, and an occasional short sentence. But then, the title does contain the qualifiers "short" and "elementary," and any revisions the author might have made on this work were halted by the realization that the writing system, with its *3*s and *8*s, was totally unacceptable. However, it is still an important work, for it must have been instrumental in introducing some members of the First Company of missionaries (such as Bingham and Loomis) to certain features of Hawaiian structure. Moreover, even though it was not published until 1993, it was, so far as we know, the first systematic description of Hawaiian grammar.

Bingham 1823

Among all the First Company of missionaries and their families, Sybil Moseley Bingham was perhaps the best-trained teacher. Born in Westfield, Massachusetts, in 1792, she became a teacher at nineteen to help support three younger sisters. Mrs. Titus Coan, her biographer (and daughter), wrote (1895:1–2): "Remarkable success attended her in this relation. Her pupils were ardently attached to her ... The experience was fitting her for future usefulness."

Sybil Moseley first met Hiram Bingham at his and Asa Thurston's ordination at Goshen, Connecticut, on 29 September 1819; they were married on 11 October; and they left for Hawai'i a little over a fortnight later.

As an American teacher, Sybil Moseley would have been familiar with Noah Webster's approach to English grammar, as well as that used in the textbooks for Greek and Latin. Because of the suddenness of her connection with the Hawaiian Mission, she had no chance to begin her study of Hawaiian as early as Hiram Bingham did, but as chapter 14 shows, she did begin aboard the *Thaddeus* on the way to the islands. The journals, correspondence, and books concerning the early years of the Mission contain many references to Mrs. Bingham's work in teaching reading and writing to the Hawaiians—both in English and in their own language. Her written work on the topic is much less well known, because it was never published (the title of her primer [1823]—"Select Hawaiian Phrases / Sentences Rehearsed at Table"—shows that the booklet was meant for family use). Although the work was obviously planned to be a primer (and therefore is discussed more fully in chapter 14), her nine-page treatment of pronouns is organized more as a grammar than a primer. The phrases illustrate a variety of constructions, including the *a/o* contrast in possessives (although not explained), the inclusive-exclusive distinction (explained by glosses), dual number, and three cases (nominative, possessive, and objective). Most of the phrases on the last three pages illustrate particular types of grammatical markers: locatives and question words. Still, the main purpose of her work was to teach the language, not *about* the language.

Ellis 1826[30]

In a complicated series of editions of his best-selling *Narrative of a Tour of Hawaii ...*, William Ellis's grammatical sketch of Hawaiian waxed and waned. At its height, it comprised five or six pages, organized under the major parts of speech: articles, nouns, pronouns, adjectives, and verbs. As for the other traditional parts of speech, he apologized for their omission as follows (1828:478): "The adverbs, prepositions, conjunctions, and interjections, are numerous; but a description of them, and their relative situation in the construction of their sentences,[31] would take up too much room."

Nouns, Ellis explained, undergo no inflections, various grammatical relations being shown by "distinct words or particles prefixed or added."

The discussion of pronouns, arranged in declensions, makes up the bulk of the sketch. Each person is declined through three cases: nominative, possessive, and objective, with each of these represented (in most cases) by at least a half dozen forms. The list for third person singular possessive is the longest of these, with fifteen forms. The cause of such a proliferation is Ellis's mixing together a number of different categories. For example, the lists of possessives contain both *a* and *o* forms, with no explanation of the difference. Also, the lists include *k-*, *n-*, and Ø forms (to use Elbert and Pukui's terminology [1979]), but again, the distinctions are not explained. Finally, some of the lists even include such demonstratives as *kēia* (near first person) and *kēlā* (near third person).

Because so many different constructions are included in Ellis's analysis of pronouns, his three pages of declensions (each with an illustrative sentence or phrase) are a rich source of examples of both noun phrases and verb phrases.

Although the section on verbs is only one paragraph long, the classification it contains is interesting. Ellis proposed three types: active, passive, and neuter; and then "conjugated" an active verb (*lohe* 'hear') not through various persons, numbers, and tenses, but into four types more related to VOICE, which we might label unmarked, causative, passive, and causative-passive.

Ellis was by no means lacking in the linguistic prejudices of his period, treating as serious faults Hawaiian's lack of an easy way to translate the comparative and superlative degrees of English adjectives or 'to be'. And for some reason, he seemed to dislike *e ... ana*, which indicates continuing, incomplete action. In spite of these "imperfections," however, he gave high marks to Hawaiian structure (1828:474):

> In every other respect their language appears to possess all the parts of speech, and some in greater variety and perfection than any language we are acquainted with.

In spite of its brevity, Ellis's essay is a significant document. Because there were so many editions of his work, most of which included some form of a grammatical sketch of Hawaiian, *Narrative of a Tour through Hawaii ...* would have been the principal means by which at least some part of Hawaiian grammar became known to the outside world, for it preceded the next works by more than a decade.

Chamisso 1837

Probably because his work was not only published but was also of a substantial size (79 pp.), Chamisso has sometimes been given credit for producing the first Hawaiian grammar. For example, Alexander wrote in the preface to Andrews's dictionary (1865:9):

> The earliest really scientific[32] analysis of the structure of a Polynesian language, with which we are acquainted, is the work on the Hawaiian language published at Berlin in 1837, by Adelbert von Chamisso, the poet, who had been the naturalist of the Russian Exploring Expedition, under Kotzebue, in the years 1815 to 1818. It is a work of rare ability, considering the meager materials which the author had at his command.

Some details of Chamisso's visits to Hawai'i in 1816 and 1817 were discussed in chapter 3. Nearly twenty years later, as Chamisso was rereading what he had written soon after his return to Germany, he became aware[33]

> how these pages have aged in the fast progress of natural history and science since that time. The future to which I looked has become the past; questions which I discussed have been settled by experience, and where I, groping about in the dark, had to guess, the scholar is now justified in demanding a clear insight.

Also, he noted, Hawaiian had become a literary language, for there were now sufficient text materials on which to base a grammar. However, Chamisso's notion of a literary language is somewhat different from current ones: one can see from a list of these texts that they were, almost without exception, biblical and teaching materials translated by the missionaries. Thus, although he was working outside the Mission organization, his work was totally dependent on it. (For a decidedly contrasting methodology, see the discussion of Andrews 1854). Chamisso himself realized the limitations of his materials: he strongly deplored the absence of any account "devoted to preservation of the memory of the history and culture of this race of men." To gain a perspective from other Polynesian languages, he used—as did his contemporaries—the published grammars of Tongan, Māori, and Tahitian.

Chamisso's efforts to describe Hawaiian sounds were doomed to failure, since they were based on written materials and his own distant memory of pronunciation. As with fellow analysts, he was especially hampered by his failure to recognize the glottal stop as a consonant. Even the missionary practice of marking the sound in certain possessives did not help: he mistook the convention for some sort of mark of a compound! Here, a closer comparison with possessives in Māori (he acknowledged using the grammar) might have evoked at least the notion of "dropped" consonants, which would have been closer to the facts than his own wild guess.

As for prosodic matters, his memory of Hawaiian sounds let him down badly: "Our ear perceived neither prosody nor accent in the spoken language of Hawaii," he wrote. For additional data, he used the mission hymnal, assuming (incorrectly, as it turned out) that European metric patterns applied to Hawaiian would reveal something about the prosody of the latter. This exercise allowed him to say that the word *aloha* could be accented either *alóha* or *álohá*.[34]

In the rest of the grammar, Chamisso performed much better. He noted clearly the lack of inflection, pointing out that the "life and the flexibility of the language" were manifested by position and particles. And although the nature of the written material consulted did not give Chamisso a glimpse of Hawaiian culture, at least its volume allowed him to be reasonably thorough in his listing of grammatical markers. Among these, he discussed the *a/o* distinction at length, using at one point the terms ABHÄNGIG (dependent) and UNABHÄNGIG (nondependent) to explain the difference. The exceptions to this general rule, however, led him to suggest that the system was similar to the German use of gender.[35]

The analysis of *ua*—one of the touchstones we shall be using to measure progress in understanding the grammar—suffers because of the material Chamisso had at hand. The examples he cited seem to use the marker as an obligatory marker of past tense. In particular, the following example, in addition to contradicting the notion of past tense:

Ua poepoe ka honua   'The earth is round'

seems to suggest that the earth *became* round, or that this state contrasted with some previous state.[36] Thus was Chamisso at the mercy of his materials: if the translators did not understand the functions of certain markers, neither could the readers of the translations.

In the syntactic part of the grammar, Chamisso attempted to "have a Hawaiian sentence result from the elements which we have been trying to explain up to now." However, his presentation is largely piecemeal; his numbered paragraphs obscure the higher-level organization. Within this section, however, he made an interesting comparison between Hawaiian and Tagalog:

> We must admire a language which, with all the rigidity of its elements, is able to lay the emphasis so vigorously on the deed, the doer, or the thing done, on action, subject, or object, and always to begin the utterance with the emphasized, more significant thing. Clearly the same spirit is at work here which it is the

principal task of the Tagalist to make clear to us in the genetically related, much more synthetic languages of the Philippines.

What Chamisso was noting in Hawaiian was the practice of highlighting important information by fronting the appropriate phrase and introducing it with 'o,[37] a function that Tagalog performs through adding affixes to the verb and the marker *ang* to the noun.

Apparently consistent with the European tradition, Chamisso ended his grammar with an annotated text—in this instance, necessarily biblical.

In summary, Chamisso's Hawaiian grammar is largely a listing of grammatical markers, with extended commentary on their meanings and distribution. It is indeed a much fuller description of Hawaiian than any of its predecessors, and—considering the limitations of the data Chamisso had at hand—a significant advance in Hawaiian grammatical studies.

Andrews 1838

A member of the Third Company of missionaries to Hawai'i, which arrived on 30 March 1828, Lorrin Andrews was well qualified for his eventual work with Hawaiian grammar and lexicography: he was educated at Jefferson College, Pennsylvania, and Princeton Theological Seminary, New Jersey. His entire service for the mission was based in Maui, where he and his wife established the Lahainaluna Seminary in 1831. Andrews remained there until 1842, when he resigned in protest against the ABCFM's policy of accepting financial support from slave states (*Missionary Album;* Benedetto 1982).[38]

The title of one of Andrews's first published works on Hawaiian grammar, "Peculiarities of the Hawaiian Language" (1838), reflects the theme introduced at the beginning of this chapter: that of comparison as a method of description. Andrews wrote specifically (p. 392) that his remarks were "intended to show *some* of the peculiarities of the language, by comparing it with English." He added that the reader would be expected to know something of English grammar.

After explaining the sound system, he began with the grammar proper by listing the parts of speech, "similar to what they are in English," but with "some peculiarities." He dealt first with the articles, noting not only a two-way contrast of definite and indefinite, but also a semidefinite: "definite as relating to some particular class, but indefinite as to the individuals of this class." The difference between *ka* and *ke* was described as similar to that between *a* and *an* in English. However, the distinction between the variants (which is determined by the first sound of the following word) was still hazy, for Andrews did not yet realize that the glottal stop functioned as a consonant.

In his discussion of prepositions, Andrews described their function as follows: "They serve ... to connect nouns or phrases with each other and show the relations of possession, duty, obligation, cause, manner, instrument and place." Note that these are relationships usually associated with case. In his treatment of this topic, Andrews was thus more concerned with the functions of case than the specific forms—that is, whether or not the nouns were inflected. His opening paragraph on DECLENSION OF NOUNS states his position clearly:

> Nouns are declined in Hawaiian, by prefixing the simple prepositions, and thus modifying the idea expressed by the simple noun. These modifications are numerous, and hence the cases are numerous. If case be admitted to exist at all in the language, there must be many cases.

Thus, it seems clear that Andrews was not trying to force Hawaiian into Latin paradigms, but was simply using the format as a way of describing the functions of various types of phrases.

Andrews noted the distinction between the *a* and *o* possessive forms, illustrating the difference with contrasting phrases, but not generalizing from the examples to provide an explanation. Instead, he said merely that to use the wrong form would be ungrammatical.

As was the common practice (except in Marsden's case), gender and the sex of the referents were confused: again, *kane* (*kāne*) and *wahine* were described as markers of masculine and feminine gender ... but with the stipulation that they were used only when necessary, thus (covertly) distinguishing between this system and true gender.

As Andrews himself commented in the introduction to his work, it was not a grammar but, instead, an essay on the language. In this sense, it was a skeleton, to be fleshed out sixteen years later with many more examples, but changing little in outline.

Hale 1846

The remarkable son of a remarkable woman (Sarah Buell Hale— editor, women's rights advocate, and author whose works range from learned volumes to the children's poem "Mary's Lamb"), Horatio Emmons Hale cannot be considered anything less than a linguistic prodigy. Having entered Harvard in the early 1830s, he published an Algonquin vocabulary at the age of seventeen, and before he finished his undergraduate studies, he had gained a reputation as an ethnological and linguistic specialist on American Indian languages. Thus, Hale differed from most of the others who treated Hawaiian, for he had already had contact with a language very different from the usual scholarly fare. As for his background in European languages, a significant portion of the Harvard curriculum for three of the four years was devoted to Greek, Latin, and modern languages.

As a result of this impressive performance, at the age of twenty he was chosen as the linguist and ethnologist for the United States Exploring Expedition, under the command of Lt. Charles Wilkes, which circled the globe during the years 1837–1842. The results of Hale's research were published in 1846 as volume 6 of the expedition papers: *Ethnography and Philology.*

Although Hale did not write specifically about Hawaiian, he compiled a comparative Polynesian grammar, discussing first for each topic some general principles, and then giving examples from individual languages. Thus, in a sense, his analysis of Hawaiian builds on data from Samoan, Tongan, Māori, Rarotongan, Mangarevan, and Tahitian as well.

As for the works consulted on Hawaiian, Hale wrote (p. 230) that he used only Andrews's vocabulary and "Peculiarities ..." However, to supplement the meager published works, he used the experience gained on the voyage: as he described it, he had spent three years in the Pacific islands, achieving a "familiarity with the general structure of the Polynesian speech, and with the minuter peculiarities of some of the dialects."

Because of his background, it comes as no surprise that at the outset Hale made note of the principal difference between Polynesian languages and those he had learned as a student (p. 235):

> The dialects of Polynesia have, properly speaking, no grammatical inflections. The only changes which words undergo are by affixed particles, or by the reduplication of one or more of their syllables.

The following points are a selection of Hale's grammatical interpretation of matters already referred to in this chapter. For example (p. 238), he wrote that since the plural was often unmarked, in those cases it must be inferred from context. Still discussing nouns (p. 241), he called ʻo a marker of the "nominative, or rather the agent, in a sentence." (He also called it emphatic.) And, like many other grammarians, he confused sex distinctions with gender.

Hale recognized the *a/o* distinction in the possessives but did not define it concisely. As did some other analysts, he came close to understanding part of the system by calling the *o* category 'belonging to': vague, but appropriate, when discussing parts of a whole.

Nor did Hale recognize the locative word *kēnā* as related to second person. However, his comments on inappropriateness of tense as a verbal category show a better insight into the language than most of his predecessors (p. 263):

> The most striking peculiarity of the Polynesian dialects, as respects the verb, is the fact that the distinctions of time, which in other languages are considered of so much importance, are in these but little regarded,—while the chief attention is paid to the accidents of place.[39] By far the greater number of the particles which accompany the verb are devoted to the latter purpose.

By "accidents of place," apparently Hale was referring to the set of function markers and nouns that are used for locatives and directionals. For example, for Polynesian in general (p. 279), Hale correctly identified a set of locative nouns[40] that "correspond in meaning with the English prepositions, above, below, before, behind, within, without, &c." This analysis is an improvement on an earlier treatment: Ruggles, for example, simply listed such forms as adverbs.

Although Hale did not deal with Hawaiian *ua* specifically, he noted (p. 264) that in the related languages, the form *kua* was used with all tenses, but not so often with future.

In speaking of Polynesian as a linguistic entity, he wrote (p. 265): "The indefinite article *se, he,* or *e,* is frequently used to supply the place of the substantive verb [i.e., like English *be*]." He gave no example from Hawaiian, but instead from Māori: *he pono* 'it is true.'

Foreshadowing future discussions of voice and ergativity in Polynesian languages, Hale observed (p. 270):

> The Polynesian dialects make a very frequent use of the passive form of the verb. In many cases it is employed where the English would have the active; and there are, in all the dialects, verbs which, though active in form, are only used in a passive acceptation.

and continued with a five-page treatment of the topic. He also linked passive forms with *ana,* usually treated as a nominalizer (p. 272):

> The verbal nouns being closely connected in this language with the passive forms, it will be most convenient to treat of them in this place. They are formed by joining to the verb certain suffixes which usually terminate in *ŋa.*

Although the Hawaiian material Hale had to work with was limited (as well as the time actually spent with native speakers, which is not well documented), his breadth of experience elsewhere in Polynesia gave him a perspective that few other observers had. Ideally, his "Polynesian Grammar" should have had a marked effect on Hawaiian language studies.   However, because of the small number of copies printed, *Ethnology and Philology* was somewhat of a rare volume, even at the time of publication (see chapter 8, note 10), and there is no indication that the Hawaiian Mission had access to a copy until much later.

Andrews 1854

Expanding the sketch he had produced earlier, Lorrin Andrews published a much fuller grammar in 1854. Compared with Chamisso, who found it necessary to use Bible translations for his data, Andrews was much closer to our modern idea of what a grammar should be based on:

> The materials for the following grammar have been taken almost entirely from native manuscripts or from documents print-ed from native manuscripts ... It is possible that some of the works written by the missionaries might be of equal authority; but as so much has been written by the natives themselves, it was thought best to appeal to them for authority in every case.

By looking at the large number of sample sentences and phrases in the grammar, we can see that Andrews was true to his principles: there are no examples obviously translated from Biblical sources. As a matter of fact, he even offered the following sample sentence, without moral judgment (respelled, p. 107):

> *Ua 'ona i ka rama, hele hīkākā.* 'He was drunk with rum;
> he went staggering.'

In the introduction to the grammar, Andrews stated his guidelines with respect to grammar:

> Every language has certain great fundamental principles upon which it is constructed. These principles differing from each other, constitute their peculiarity. Hence, every language in its etymology and syntax must be regulated by its own laws : though some general principles may run through the whole.

The general outline matches that of Dilworth's grammar (1740), but the explanations of some of the main parts seem somewhat more modern (p. 9):

> Grammatical Treatises are usually divided into several parts, viz. Orthography, Etymology, Syntax, and Prosody. Orthography treats of letters and their formation into words. Etymology treats

of words and their changes in relation to each other. Syntax teaches the rules whereby words are formed into sentences. Prosody
will hardly be included in this Grammar.

In other respects, the explanation is a step backward: note that there is no
mention of the sounds that underlie the letters of the alphabet.

In ETYMOLOGY, which comprises about two-thirds of the grammar,
Andrews organized the topic around his part-of-speech system, beginning with the articles and what he called the *o* [*ʻo*] emphatic (an
improvement over Chamisso's classification of the marker as a definite
article).[41] Here, the important addition to our knowledge is the word
emphatic, which hints at the discourse function of the marker. Unfortunately, it is impossible to draw any more substantial conclusions from
the data, which Andrews himself called "detached sentences"—that is,
sentences out of context.

Andrews's treatment of nouns may look superficially as though it
was based on the Latin model, but actually it is quite different. Although he wrote that "Hawaiian Nouns have *Person*,[42] *Number, Gender*
and *Case*" (p. 38), he was careful to explain that these categories are not
manifested in Hawaiian by suffixes, but by what he called "*signs* [that]
are therefore set before the nouns for this purpose."

Andrews described the category of gender with less insight than
did Marsden, but still, he stated explicitly that sex distinctions applied to
animals and humans (p. 42): "They have no word to express neuter
gender or to give the idea of gender to any nouns that are neither *male* or
female." In addition, he made a similar disclaimer for adjectives (p. 51):

> Adjectives, in Hawaiian, are words used in some way to qualify
> nouns. They have nothing however like gender, number or case
> connected with them.

In his section on syntax (pp. 140–41), Andrews went beyond this
traditional view of adjectives to suggest an analysis that developed very
slowly over the next century. After two example sentences—one with
nui 'big' and the other with *lehulehu* 'numerous'—he questioned
"whether such words ... with the words *ua* and *he* should be considered
as adjectives or verbs." After another set of examples he wrote:
"Participles, verbals and other words qualifying nouns are treated as
adjectives." Beginning perhaps in the 1950s or 1960s, it became
common in the field of Oceanic linguistics to class modifying words as
STATIVE VERBS, mainly because of their common use after verbal markers.

Andrews treated "compound prepositions" (that is, locative nouns)
as a separate class of words but noted that "they are declineable like
nouns."

In the introduction to his long treatment of verbs, Andrews noted an interesting feature of Hawaiian sentences (pp. 96–97): that many have no easily recognizable verb. "Some of the most common, clear and strong affirmations are fully expressed without any kind of a verb." Here, also, is the germ of a slowly developing idea: that the Indo-European notion of subject and predicate (or noun phrase and verb phrase) as complementary and obligatory parts of a sentence does not necessarily hold for Hawaiian.[43]

As for tense as a feature of verbs, Andrews was aware that there was something wrong with applying a rigid past-present-future template onto the Hawaiian Weltanschauung. "In practice," he wrote, "[the tenses] run into each other."

In highly inflected languages, a great deal of grammatical importance is often attached to CONCORD and GOVERNMENT—the agreement or matching of forms according to their gender, number, case, etc. Since these categories are either missing or handled very differently in Hawaiian, agreement in its usual sense does not exist. Position, or word and phrase order, has a much higher functional load.

Perhaps unconsciously reflecting this hierarchy, Andrews dealt first with position in his section of syntax, a set of fifty rather unrelated rules. As a matter of fact, few of the statements about agreement have anything to do with the traditional meaning of the term, except, perhaps, statements about *ke* versus *ka*. And here, the matter is phonological, not grammatical.

From today's point of view, Andrews's treatment of syntax shares a fault common to the grammars of that period: too much attention to the trees, to the neglect of the forest. As a consequence, it is difficult to turn to any one section and gain an impression of the most common sentence structures.

In his introduction to a reprinting of Chamisso's grammar, Samuel H. Elbert referred to this version of Andrews's grammar as a "padded" version of his earlier essay (1969c: ix). However, the "padding," which took the form of a great many illustrative sentences and phrases, is to our advantage, since it allows us to examine the data and test the analysis. Still, there are drawbacks: almost all the material is out of context, and the large body of written material from which Andrews drew his examples has not been preserved. Thus, any part of the analysis that has to do with discourse (such as the "*'o* emphatic," mentioned earlier) has to be taken at face value.

Elbert also called Andrews a "slave to Latin" (1969:xi).[44] However, as the discussion above shows, this is not a fair assessment, seemingly based on only a superficial understanding of the nineteenth-century descriptive model. As a matter of fact, Andrews repeatedly attached warning labels, as it were, to the sections in which traditional terms were used. For example (p. 42):

> Nouns are not declined in Hawaiian by any variations of their *terminations* as in European languages. They are declined by *prefixing* the simple prepositions ... and by thus modifying the idea expressed by the simple noun.—These modifications (called cases) are somewhat numerous.

In this simple statement, Andrews explained his untraditional use of a traditional term, using the word *decline* in the sense of to *indicate the various functions.* Similarly, he explained his opinion clearly with respect to verbs (p. 100):

> There is no variation of the verb itself to express number or person. These are shown by the form of the nouns or pronouns; hence, the nouns and especially the pronouns are much more generally expressed than in languages where number and person are expressed in the forms of the verbs.

On the next page, he rephrased this caveat: "The three numbers of Verbs are expressed not by any form of the verb itself, but by the noun or pronouns." As for the other distinctions, Andrews made it quite clear that they were indicated by various forms preceding or following the verb.

Thus, as the earlier quotations clearly show, Andrews was no "slave to Latin," but merely used the format grammarians were most familiar with at the time as a frame for the information he wanted to present. As for any mistakes his grammar might contain, he was modest enough to end his introduction thus (p. iii):

> After all, there will probably appear principles in the language which have been entirely overlooked, or mistaken in the developement [*sic*]. If so, future editions or future laborers must be looked to for corrections or for the supply of deficiencies.

The contemporary reviews of Andrews's grammar were glowing. Its impending publication was first announced in *The Friend* (2 January 1854). The staff of this periodical were privy to advanced information, since both the grammar and the journal were printed in the same office. A preliminary reading prompted this response, interesting in its opinion of the fate of the language:

> We could wish that the industrious author had had leisure to give a fuller exposition of the peculiar idioms, and colloquial phrases of the language, and also for an essay upon the language

of the old "Meles," for which work none is so competent, but we are glad that so much of a form of human speech apparently soon destined to extinction, is saved for the future [signed "J.W.M."].

In a later issue (1 March 1854), the editor suggested that the missionaries send copies of the grammar "to all colleges and Seminaries of learning in the U.S. and Europe. It is a work that professors and students engaged in philological pursuits will peruse with much interest." Incidentally, the London offices of the German publisher, Trübner, requested from Hawai'i "2–6 copies of each native Vocabulary, Grammar, Dictionary and Spelling Book" (ibid.) The editor compared the desire for such productions with that for artifacts:

> Polynesia has been ransacked for curiosities, until idols and warclubs are more rare here than in London or Boston, but still the demand often comes "send us curiosities" ... Professors and students ... would prize a copy of [Andrews's grammar] far more than a cargo of idols, warclubs, canoes, and whale's teeth.

Alexander 1864[45]

Although the publication dates of the grammars written by Lorrin Andrews and William De Witt Alexander make the writers seem like contemporaries, they were actually a generation apart in age. The latter, son of the Reverend William Patterson Alexander, was born in Hawai'i in 1833. After an attempt to establish a mission station in the Marquesas, the family returned to Hawai'i, where they served at Wai'oli on Kaua'i and at Lahainaluna on Maui. Thus, the younger Alexander had the opportunity to hear—and perhaps speak—Hawaiian from childhood.

Alexander graduated from Yale in 1855 and two years later assumed the position of professor of Greek at Punahou School in Honolulu, which he held for six years. He then served as president for seven years. *The Dictionary of American Biography* (1927 edition) referred to him as "probably the ablest scholar that Hawaii has yet produced."

The fact that only ten years separate the two grammars also obscures the fact that a number of advances in Polynesian studies had been made during that period. Alexander's preface to Andrews's dictionary (dated April 1865) reads like a *Who's Who* in nineteenth-century Polynesian linguistics: he referred to works by Forster, Anderson (in particular, the comparative table at the end of the account of Cook's third voyage), Müller, Humboldt, Marsden, Crawford, Dumont D'Urville, Chamisso, and Buschmann.

Thus, although Andrews could use as a foundation only the most rudimentary works in related languages, Alexander was able to draw on a number of works on Polynesian in general (as evidenced by the list above) and three grammatical studies (as acknowledged in the preface): Andrews's Hawaiian grammar, Robert Maunsell's Māori grammar (1842),[46] and—most important—Pierre Louis Jean Baptiste Gaussin's comparative grammar of Tahitian, Marquesan, and Polynesian languages in general (1853).

We have already seen in chapter 8 the significance of Gaussin's perception and analysis of the glottal stop, particularly in initial position (which eluded Hawaiian analysts for nearly another century). Thus, Gaussin was obviously the source of Alexander's enlightened views on the status of the glottal stop as a phoneme in its own right. However, had Alexander paid more attention to the examples in Gaussin's work, he might have noticed glottal stops at the beginnings of words: in the preface to Andrews's dictionary he wrote (1865:12) "... k at the beginning of a word is dropped, but in the middle of a word represented by a peculiar guttural catch or break ..."[47] Normally, such a small phonological problem would not have much effect on the grammar, but here it did, for, as noted earlier, it had an effect on the statement of distribution of the two variants of the definite article *ka/ke*.

Gaussin also perceived long vowels and marked some with a cir-cumflex. However, he described such vowels as rare and failed to mark them on most of the expected forms. Alexander as well noted long vowels, but he confused length and accent, as did most of his predecessors and many of his followers. Even his first example of vowel length contrast, *awa* 'harbor' versus *āwa* 'kava' (p. 7), is incorrect; the forms are instead *awa* and *'awa*. As for his list of "Similar words distinguished by the Accent" (p. 7), the pairs are distinguished mainly by vowel length.

Gaussin was also the source of Alexander's analysis of the *a/o* distinction, a definite improvement over previous treatments. Gaussin used the terms voluntary/active versus involuntary/passive; Alexander chose the active/passive description (pp. 9–10):

> "*O*" implies a *passive* or *intransitive* relation, "*a*" an *active* and *transitive* one. "*A*" can only be used before a word denoting a living person or agent, and implies that the thing possessed is his to make or act upon, or is subject to his will, while "*o*" implies that it is his merely to possess or use, to receive or be affected by.

Here, Alexander used the important word *relation*, and (implicitly) the idea of *control*, which are the keys to the distinction, but then assumed that the possessor had control over the possessed—a misconception that continued until fairly recently.

We turn again to the treatment of the aspect marker *ua* as a way to evaluate the various descriptions of Hawaiian. Gaussin made a significant advance when he noted that *ua* indicates that a particular state is a *result* of something (p. 177). Note his examples from Marquesan:[48]

úa mate	il est mort
úa po	la nuit s'est faite, il est nuit

This analysis apparently had an effect on Alexander, who wrote (p. 20): "It has been questioned whether [*ua*] is properly a tense sign. We think that it affirms the completion of an action or the resulting state."

Perhaps because Alexander's grammar does not present the many pages of declensions and conjugations that dominate Andrews's work, it seems rather more modern. Certainly there are some parts that are better organized: for example, the section on syntax begins (after some general statements) by defining simple sentences. The rest of the section as well is organized around major topics, whereas Andrews's treatment of syntax seems more like a list of rules that are only loosely connected. But because of Alexander's background, his training, and his extensive use of works on Polynesian in general and on individual Polynesian languages, it is only natural that his grammar reflects these advantages.

-0-0-0-0-0-

With the publication of Alexander's grammar, which went through several editions,[49] Hawaiian grammatical studies came to a near standstill. Even though the slim volume[50] did not pretend to be a "complete account of the structure and peculiarities" of the language (as explained by Alexander in his preface), it remained as the only scholarly treatment available for more than a century.

This hiatus prompts us to wonder why there was no professional interest in the language for so many years. One possible answer is that often, the mere existence of a published grammar leads people to believe that no more work on the language needs to be done. So perhaps it was felt that the combination of Andrews's and Alexander's grammars already covered the field. Elbert and Pukui (1979:8) suggested that the reason for the lack of interest was "because no professional linguists were interested in the language." However, the circularity of this argument neutralizes it. They continued: "The missionaries' interest had been pragmatic, and once the Scriptures were translated, they were no longer concerned." Unfortunately, chronology does not support this assertion: the translation of the entire Bible was completed before either Andrews or Alexander did his major grammatical study.

In keeping with the theme of the first several chapters of this work, one might suggest that the lack of interest in Hawaiian was because the language was considered "simple." This, however, is also a circular matter, for any simplicity involved was more in the minds of the analysts than in the language itself.

Whatever the reason, until fairly recently, almost nothing appeared after the 1860s except "phrase books" and—somewhat later— pedagogical works that also explained some structural features. Two grammar-primers that appeared in the 1930s fit into this latter category—those by Mary H. Atcherley and Henry P. Judd. These works, along with others that were primarily teaching texts, are discussed in chapter 14. Not until the 1950s did studies outside the area of language teaching began to appear. The first of these, a thesis on Hawaiian phonology, covers only a part of the grammar, but is included here because it was a milestone—the first modern linguistic study of any feature of the Hawaiian language.

Newbrand 1951

With the publication of Kenneth L. Pike's *Phonemics* in 1947, a methodology for determining the distinctive speech sounds of a language (PHONEMES) was made available not only to students of linguistics, but also to interested people in allied disciplines. One of these people was Helene Luise Newbrand, whose M.A. thesis, "A Phonemic Analysis of Hawaiian" (from the Speech Department, University of Hawai'i), was based directly on Pike's methodology.

Pike's approach to the topic emphasized first a careful phonetic description as a foundation for phonemics, and here Newbrand made her greatest contribution. In her work, she gave a detailed description of the phonetic range of each phoneme. As an example of her insightful treatment, here the common [ʌ] allophone of /a/ was described for the first time.

Some parts of her description are, however, open to question. For example, on p. 19 we can find what is apparently the origin of the incorrect belief that, in a five-syllable word, accent falls on the first and fourth syllables.[51] (The statement of accent distribution in six-syllable words is also incorrect.) Another problem is the impressionistic assignment of four degrees of phonetic length to vowels (pp. 22–24).

In spite of these minor flaws, however, her description is a valuable addition to our knowledge, in some ways unsurpassed by anything done since. Of special interest is a section of nearly 100 pages of text transcription, with notes and sociolinguistic data on the speakers, and, finally, a detailed study of the distribution of [v]-like and [w]-like allophones of /w/.

In summary, Newbrand's thesis fulfills almost perfectly the criteria mentioned at the beginning of the chapter, especially in her expert use of the tools available. Moreover, her perception of the work remaining to be done was remarkable for its foresight (see the quotation introducing the summary). It is ironic that more than forty years later, only the peripheral areas of "pidgin" studies and comparative Polynesian linguistics have been adequately approached. In the mainstream of descriptive studies of Hawaiian, the unsolved problems of prosodic features and dialect variation remain relatively untouched and—because of the precarious state of the language—perhaps even further from our grasp than in 1951.

Knappert 1954

Working only with dictionaries (Andrews 1865 and Judd et al. 1945) and texts (Fornander texts, vol. 4, 5, and 6, especially the Legend of 'Aukelenuiaiku, v. 4) but no grammars, Jan Knappert wrote an innovative sketch of Hawaiian, the first to use the methodology of structural linguistics beyond phonology.

With no speakers to provide data, Knappert had to rely on dictionary markings for his observations on accent. And here he was led astray. His examples of contrastive accent:

    kíki   to sting   *kikí*   rapid

come directly from Judd et al. (1945:258). The forms are actually *kiki* and *kikī*, with the long vowel on the second form accounting for the accent on that syllable. On that topic, Knappert wrote (p. 11): "In many words, but not in all, a long vowel attracts the accent." Again, he was at the mercy of the dictionaries he used, which are riddled with errors about vowel length (see chapter 11).[52]

Knappert treated morphology only briefly, apparently finding little productive morphology in the language. From some source he formed the idea that *hoʻo-* (causative, among other functions) derived transitive verbs, but he questioned this assertion.

From a structural linguistic point of view, Knappert's treatment of syntax is more sophisticated than those of all his predecessors and many of his successors. He organized his description around simple and complex sentences, relating ENDOCENTRIC and EXOCENTRIC properties of each.[53] Following the lines of this organization, Knappert may have been one of the first analysts to recognize an important syntactic difference between Hawaiian and (for example) English: that the subject-predicate relationship (which is exocentric) does not always hold for Hawaiian. Note his comment about simple sentences (p. 15):

> The predicate ... is the only position that is filled in the simple endocentric sentence, all other positions may be zero and are in this way opposed to the predicate. Hence this sentence type is called endocentric.

Thus, for Knappert (and I think this is a reasonable view), a sentence could consist of a predicate alone. His use of the endocentric-exocentric opposition also allowed him to avoid such English-biased terms as VERB-LESS SENTENCES to describe classifying or identifying constructions.

Unfortunately, Knappert had a tendency to proliferate examples and forgo explanations. Had he been a little *less* structural in his approach, perhaps the sketch would have made a greater impact on later grammatical studies of Hawaiian. Even so, some of the innovative ideas contained in this work might have improved later studies, had it been consulted.[54]

Pukui and Elbert 1957

Beginning with the first edition of the *Hawaiian-English Dictionary* and continuing through two more, Mary Kawena Pukui and Samuel H. Elbert prefaced the body of the dictionary with "Notes on Hawaiian Grammar," explaining (p. xv): "An analysis of the phonology and grammar of a language is a prerequisite to the compilation of a lexicon."

In just fifteen pages (but tightly packed in two columns of small print), the authors expanded on Elbert's view of Hawaiian grammar interspersed throughout his primer (1951b).

In some ways, it is difficult to guess the readership for this grammatical sketch. It is too disorganized to be of much use to the general user of the dictionary. Nor, on the other hand, does it satisfy the professional, for it contains many contradictions, half-formed notions, and generally unsupported statements.

The section on "sounds" is oddly weighted: there is no phonetic description at all, the reader being referred to a one-page pronunciation table that simply gives the closest English equivalent to the phonemes. Such matters as common allophonic variations are ignored altogether. Instead, almost two pages are devoted to casual discussions of variant spellings, assimilation in fast speech, loanword patterns, and frequency of sounds.[55]

In the section on stress, the questionable concept of CLITIC is introduced, explained as a word or particle "pronounced as though part of accompanying words." It is not clear what this means. One part of the explanation—that such particles are stressed only when followed by an unstressed vowel—is an interesting presage of the patterning better explained by the concept of the accent unit. However, the authors do not seem to have noticed that all "clitics" are simply grammatical markers consisting of one short syllable. But then, the fact that all other content monosyllables (such as *kū* 'stand') are long had also escaped them.

The major part of this sketch centers on morphology: the classification of words, the function of various grammatical markers, and word-building processes such as affixation, compounding, and reduplication. This treatment is a decided improvement on that in previous grammars, especially in its basic division between content forms and function forms.

Within this classification, there seems to be a difference proposed between MINOR WORDS and PARTICLES. Minor words are said to be such forms as pronouns, demonstratives, and possessives. By this classification, *ka/ke* (article) is in a different category than, say, *'o* (topic marker) or *me* 'with'. A third term, MARKER, was also introduced to this confusing array. (The authors defined the function of markers as indicating "whether or not the following modified words are members of one or the other of the syntactic subclasses called SUBSTANTIVES and VERBS.")

One overriding problem with the morphological treatment is that it seems to use spelling as a criterion for classification. For example, the distinction between particles and prefixes depends on whether the form is written with the base or as a separate word.

The short section on sentences (characterized with the qualifiers "brief and incomplete") begins with a definition based on phonology, rather than semantics, as with the traditional definition that mentions "a complete thought": "A SENTENCE is any utterance preceded and followed by fading or rising pause." However, there are several problems with such a definition. For example, can a pause have such qualities as fading or rising? How long is a pause? Are fading and rising logical opposites in a dichotomy? Is a grunt a sentence? Does every sentence have to be preceded or followed by something else so that there can be a pause?

For some years, this sketch was the only modern grammatical description of Hawaiian readily available. It was finally superseded by the authors' fuller treatment, which appeared a little more than twenty years later.

Elbert and Pukui 1979

In the introduction to Elbert and Pukui's *Hawaiian Grammar*, the authors state that the work is the culmination of, respectively, forty and eighty years' study. Thus, the reader has high expectations that this will be a work that will finally escape the slough of amateurism that Hawaiian grammatical studies slid into after Alexander published his *Short Synopsis*. At first glance, the new work is promising, for the overall organization is reasonable: a brief summary of previous works, a sketch of the phonology, and an innovative plan for the treatment of morphology-syntax, which is an attempt to begin with an overview of sentences and to proceed to smaller and smaller units. Thus, this section treats—in this order—sentences, phrases, words, particles, and affixes. However, it must be said that the opening statement in this section—"Sentences are sequences bordered by periods, question marks, or exclamation points"—does not leave the reader with high hopes for what follows.[56]

Within this plan, the treatment of morphology (the smaller units: words, markers, and affixes) comes closest to succeeding. For example, Bender (1982:617) praised the "encyclopaedic and eclectic" nature of the work:

> One gets the impression that no variant of any grammatical morpheme or syntactic structure that has existed in the language anywhere in the islands in this century has escaped the authors' notice or has been suppressed in the interests of accentuating main outlines.

As a casual statistical verification of Bender's assertion, one can find in the body of the text (in various tables and lists) at least 160 grammatical markers, not including pronouns and possessives—a far more comprehensive list than any previous grammar contains.

Beyond morphology, however, the grammar is much less satisfying. From the historical survey (which is interesting but only skims the surface) to the index, the whole work is rather more like an unfinished patchwork quilt than a carefully thought out, carefully executed whole. As an example, consider chapter 2: "The Sound System." Compared with Newbrand's professional treatment (see above), it is a collection of superficial and inaccurate phonetics.[57]

As for the rest of the work, if there is one overriding problem, it is that in the places in which Hawaiian and English grammar clash, a translation bias mars the analysis. The following quotations from just one section (pp. 57–58) suggest that the authors were preoccupied with translation:

Since *ua* does not mark tense,[58] tenses must be supplied in
English translations of sentences containing *ua* + verb.
Condition-marking verbs ... may often be translated by present
tenses.
Some legends are best translated entirely in the past tense.
Time words may make past tense of any verb.[59]

This focus on translation comes to a peak in the last chapter,
"Interjections," which, for the past century or so, has been considered a
topic more appropriate for a dictionary than for a grammar. And even in
a dictionary, interjections are better treated by describing the circumstances that give rise to such spontaneous utterances. In this work, an
English translation is given for each item, a methodology of doubtful use
to the reader. For example, do the translations 'Say! Listen!' tell us
much about the situation prompting the response *'Ea*? Even though a
caveat warns the reader that such utterances are difficult to translate,
either the context for the interjections should have been provided or the
section omitted altogether.

One of the main problems with Elbert and Pukui's syntactic
analysis is what seems to be a foregone conclusion that the syntactic
elements of English (or other Indo-European languages) apply directly to
Hawaiian. Thus, for example, although some rather different elements
are identified at various places as *subjects*, nowhere is that concept (or
predicate, for that matter) defined—either in the body of the text or in
the short glossary of grammatical terms.

One positive feature of the treatment of verbs is that the authors
adopted Wilson's four-way[60] classification (intransitive, transitive,
stative, and *loa'a* stative[61]) and noted formal confirmation of these
categories—in particular, the behavior of certain verbs when nomina-
lized and possessed with either *a*-forms or *o*-forms (one of the few
examples of parts of the grammar that fit together as a comprehensive
whole).

As Besnier pointed out (1980:63), the Elbert and Pukui grammar
falls short of being a theoretical statement about the structure of
Hawaiian. This raises an obvious question: at what level *does* it
succeed?

First, although its brevity might be an argument for considering it a
"softer" linguistic work (a term from Besnier 1980), it is certainly not
clearly enough written to qualify as a popular treatment.

Another possibility would be as a reference grammar. Here it fails
as well, for a number of reasons. Most important, it is very difficult for
a reader to get an idea of what the most common sentences in Hawaiian
are like. For example, simple sentences are defined (p. 39) as consisting

of a VERB PHRASE +/- NOUN PHRASE(s). It isn't until the next page that the minus part of that formula is mentioned, referring to the fact that the verb phrase in the examples given could occur without any following noun phrases. If this is the case, just what is the status of the subject phrase (as labeled)? Is it only third person noun phrases that can be deleted? Apparently not, for we are told that in the sentence

| *He* | *kumu* | *au* | I am a teacher |
| a? | teacher | I | |

au can be deleted. Would the sentence still have the same meaning? Would it occur in the same context? There is no way of knowing.

In this same discussion, on only the second page of the treatment of sentences, we learn that the order of the noun phrases can be changed to shift the focus. Thus, we are confronted with discourse phenomena before we have finished with the basic sentence types.

The unnecessarily complicated table on p. 41, purportedly showing the structure of phrases, could be improved in at least two ways. First, noun phrases and verb phrases should be separated. Next, the information would be much easier to absorb if it had been presented first as a bare-bones structure, with markers added gradually to show their formal and semantic effects.

Such problems recur often, with the result that it is difficult to read about any topic without being left with more questions than answers. A specific example is the discussion of *he* (pp. 154–57). Is it really an article? Why is "any word after *he* ... considered a noun" (p. 157)? The circularity of this kind of argument is obvious: *he* is considered an article because it precedes a noun; but a noun is defined as any word following *he*.

Some elementary statistics also indicate the failure of this work as a reference grammar. For example, the index (which includes only 207 entries in all, 52 of which are proper names) contains about 65 grammatical markers. Yet, as noted above, in the body of the text (in various tables and lists) there are at least 160, not including pronouns and possessives. One of the most productive of these, *ho'o* and its many variants, is not listed at all, but occurs only under the heading CAUSATIVE/SIMULATIVE.

In summary, one might make the point that perhaps lexicographers (and more particularly, those who produce bilingual dictionaries) have some prejudices to overcome when it comes to writing grammars. Whether it happens consciously or not, there is a tendency to let the translation take over. Thus, the reader must repeatedly ask: is it really the Hawaiian structure that is being analyzed, or is it that of the English translation?

Perhaps the most redeeming feature of the Elbert-Pukui grammar, in addition to its comprehensive treatment of grammatical markers, can be gleaned from Bender's review (1982:618). Here he made the point (albeit indirectly) that the information presented, together with the massive number of illustrative sentences and phrases from the dictionary and the references to their context, would provide invaluable data "for the work that needs to be done."

-0-0-0-0-0-

With the exception of Newbrand's excellent study of Hawaiian phonetics and phonemics, and Knappert's structural sketch, grammatical studies of Hawaiian did not leave hands of (more or less) gifted amateurs until the mid- or late 1970s. By that time, the requisite training—a combination of both Hawaiian language and linguistics—began to produce a generation of scholars with the proper tools with which to approach the language in a professional way.

However, the studies produced during this period have not been grammatical sketches or fuller descriptions, but instead, detailed examinations of particular problems.[62] For example, in her 1975 Ph.D. thesis (published in 1979), Emily A. Hawkins treated several aspects of Hawai-ian syntax in an adaptation of Charles Filmore's case grammar format, which attempts to explain the connection between syntactic functions and semantic relationships. In her *Pedagogical Grammar of Hawaiian* (1982), she explored a number of grammatical features that students had found puzzling or inconsistent, touching on the important notion of the effect of the early grammars on our conception of "Standard Hawaiian." In a more recent work (1989), she examined texts from different writers to determine their use of the troublesome (that is, from an outside point of view) aspect marker *ua*.

Another important set of studies, those by William H. Wilson (1976a, 1976b), focuses on the *a/o* contrast in Hawaiian possessives, mentioned several times earlier in this chapter. In these works, Wilson examined a number of possible explanations for the patterning of these forms. His solution was to dismiss gender and other explanations that were based on noun classes; instead he proposed that it is the relationship between the possessor and the possessed that determines the choice between *o* and *a*.

In their teaching materials (1977, 1979), Wilson and Kauanoe Kamanā have explored new paths for Hawaiian language study by proposing Hawaiian metaphors for grammatical terms and relationships. The principal metaphor is the *pepeke* 'squid',[63] representing a sentence and composed of three main parts: the *poʻo* 'head', the *piko* 'navel', and the *ʻawe* 'tentacles'. Of these three parts, the *poʻo* (roughly corresponding to a verb phrase) is the essential part, while the *piko* (the subject) and the *ʻawe* (phrases providing additional information, such as object, location, etc.) are optional. The hierarchy continues, with each of these categories divided into a number of different types.

For the most part, this metaphor does not present a new analysis of Hawaiian grammar, but merely casts the terminology into Hawaiian without wholesale borrowing from English (think of the awkwardness of "Hawaiianizing" a term such as *intransitive*). Andrews did much the same thing with his ten terms for case declensions, each a compound consisting first of the word *ʻaui* 'case (lit., turn aside)', based on the literal meaning of the Latin word for *decline* (Pukui and Elbert 1986:31). However, the idea that a sentence may consist of the *poʻo* alone is a significant move away from the English grammatical tradition, which maintains that every sentence must contain both a subject and a predicate.

THE STATE OF THE ART

There is much to be investigated in the area of Hawaiian. Certain features of the language, herein treated somewhat briefly, such as vowel length, or syllable stress, could well be further analyzed. Morphophonemics and morphology could be the basis for separate investigations. Dialect studies of the language, such as those being conducted on the mainland of the United States, could well be made: the problem of the selection of the v-w allophones might be solved definitively in this way. The contributions of Hawaiian to "pidgin" have never been evaluated. Studies are needed comparing Hawaiian to other Polynesian languages, and reconstructions of proto-Polynesian should be made. It is hoped that this research will interest others to continue study in this language (Helene Newbrand, "A Phonemic Analysis of Hawaiian" [1951:3]).

One feature that all the fuller grammars treated here have in common is that they are at least satisfactory in their treatments of morphology, especially Elbert and Pukui 1979, which excels in this area. Unfortunately, they share another feature: they are disorganized and cursory in their syntactic descriptions. From the earliest to the most recent, the so-called reference grammars treat syntax by giving a collection of details that often are not only difficult to follow but contradictory as well. As a consequence, there is no such thing as an adequate reference grammar of Hawaiian.

Some of the more serious problems with these works have already been discussed, such as a continuing tendency to view Hawaiian in terms of Indo-European grammatical categories. But other problems hinge on the misanalysis of phonological and grammatical details that may be small in size but very important in terms of frequency. For example, in the last century, the inability to recognize an initial glottal stop was one of these details, resulting in a confused description of the distribution of the common article *ka/ke*. A twentieth-century equivalent, but much more pervasive, has been the insistence on calling *he* an indefinite article, equivalent to English *a*, ignoring its common occurrence with (mostly stative) verbs. Another problem, with far-reaching effects on description, has been the relentless attempt to apply the notions SUBJECT and PREDICATE to each Hawaiian sentence.

The material on which one bases a grammar has also been a obstacle. Are there any speakers who are "uncontaminated" by English? On the other hand, is finding such speakers an impossible goal? After all, it is often said that an unchanging language is a dead language.

Notwithstanding these difficulties, what is needed is a reference grammar, entailing:

Adequate phonetic data based, in part, on acoustic analysis.

A reconstruction, if possible, of the dialect picture that existed before the standardization of the spelling system. Even for those pockets of speakers who still exist, the information we have about dialects is mostly anecdotal.

Some documentation of the grammatical changes that have taken place since the language was first written.

A description of phonetics, phonology and orthography, morphology, phrase structure, ways of combining phrases into sentences, and relationships among related sentences, as all of these apply to Hawaiian.

An analysis of Hawaiian discourse.

A complete and detailed index, which includes an exhaustive listing of grammatical markers, construction types, and technical terms.

A prerequisite for many of these topics within such a grammar is a large computer data base. At present, scholars cannot deal even with Hawaiian vocabulary using the many opportunities that computer analysis offers, since the Pukui-Elbert dictionary is not yet available in that form.

Some of the topics are already being investigated by individual scholars. As an example of one of them, beginning with a study by Patrick Hohepa (1969), which generated an interest in ergative languages, linguists have begun to take a fresh look at Hawaiian verb classification. Very early on it was noticed that certain verbs seemed inherently passive. For example, Andrews (1854:125) noted only *loaʻa* 'gotten, obtained'. Elbert and Pukui (1979:49–51) expanded the list to more than a dozen, noting that some speakers today, especially on Niʻihau, use some of these verbs as actives. Hawkins (1982:29) increased the list to thirty and added an insightful discussion of some common characteristics of the set. But still, the overall picture of verb classification seems elusive, offering a challenge to today's Hawaiian linguists.[64]

Other areas are being examined as well. For example, students are beginning to pay more attention to prosodic features of the language, studying such problems as the variable vowel length of certain markers and the raising of the vowel /a/ in unexpected positions. Thus, on the whole, the future of grammatical studies of Hawaiian is encouraging, for thoughtful scholars are finally beginning to question some of the errors that writers have accepted and passed along without examining them critically.

NOTES

[1] Some scholars, especially students of the Bible, made overt comparisons between Hawaiian and Hebrew. However, they were seldom specific about the nature of such resemblances. For example, Davies (1823:3), mentioning a similarity between Hebrew and Polynesian in general (and probably Tahitian in particular), cited the conjugation of the verbs and many "primitive" words. Ellis (1979 [1827]:336) also mentioned verb conjugation and added the construction of causative forms as points of similarity.

[2] The observation may have been made by James Smith, Campbell's editor.

[3] At first glance, *place* seems to be a special grammatical term. But the examples Dilworth gave (p. 121) show that by *place* he meant *word order*. For some writers, it seems to refer to location (as in locative case).

[4] The translations are quoted verbatim from Andrews. However, since Hawaiian does not distinguish gender in its third-person pronouns, *he/his/him* could also be *she/her/her*.

[5] Pronouns are somewhat different from the other parts of speech listed here, since they are a closed set.

[6] For instance, gender agreement might allow the hearer to make a better guess at a small part of the sentence that was somehow obscured in transmission.

[7] Elbert (1970:82) listed six forms, all referring to kin or humans in general: *kanaka* 'person', *wahine* 'woman', *kaikamahine* 'girl', *kahuna* 'priest', *kupuna* 'grandparent', *makua* 'parent'. In each word the antepenultimate syllable (the one that is lengthened) is also the first syllable of the morpheme.

[8] The word *mau* may also be purely grammatical, not lexical; however, Andrews (1854:40) noted that "the original idea of *mau* seems to be that of *repetition.*"

[9] Elbert and Pukui (1979:162) also classified *poʻe* principally as a noun.

[10] For an example of a common misunderstanding of the *a/o* contrast, see Elbert 1969c:xii, in which the author says that the system almost fits Hockett's (1958:231) definition of gender, suggesting that most Hawaiian nouns "belong" to one or the other class. On the contrary, it is always the RELATIONSHIP between two entities that dictates *a* or *o* (See Elbert and Pukui 1979:137–38).

[11] Greg Lee Carter (pers. comm., January 1993) noted that Andrews and Alexander did not make even this concession, analyzing some constructions as SUBJECT-PREDICATE, when the opposite order was more appropriate.

[12] Not to be confused with Samuel Marsden, an influential mission head in New Zealand and Australia, who obstructed, rather than facilitated, the growth of our knowledge about Polynesian languages. See chapter 7, note 30.

[13] Marsden described his own qualifications (p. xlix). While in Sumatra, he devoted more than the usual attention to learning Malay, and, helped by his brother, attained a speaking and writing ability. After his return to England in 1779, he studied Malay literature.

[14] Lepsius wrote (1855 [1863]:89):

> It is not accidental but very significant, that, as far as I know without any essential exception, only the most highly civilised races—the leading nations in the history of mankind—distinguish throughout the genders, and that the *Gender-languages* are the same as those, which scientifically by linguistic reasons may be proved as descending from one original Asiatic stock. The development of peculiar forms for the grammatical genders proves a comparatively higher consciousness of the two sexes; and the distinction not only of the masculine and feminine, as in the *Semitic* and *Hamitic* languages, but also of the feminine and neuter gender, exclusively expressed in the *Japhetic* branch, is only a further step in the same direction ...
>
> It seems however unquestionable, that the three great branches of gender languages were not only in the past the depositories and the organs of the historical progress of human civilisation, but that

to them, and particularly to the youngest branch of them, the Japhetic, belong also the future hopes of the world. All the other languages are in decline and seem to have henceforth but a local existence.

[15] The current forms are *'omai*, *'oatu*, and *'oange*, relating respectively to first-, second-, or third-person recipients.

[16] Martin's tense markers do not always correspond with those of current analyses. But for the purposes of this treatment, as a forerunner of Hawaiian grammars, we are more interested in the overall organization of the grammar than the accuracy of individual points.

[17] This term refers to a "formal parallel between the object of a transitive verb and the subject of an intransitive one [i.e., they display the same case]" (Crystal 1980:134).

[18] Kendall and Lee were aided by two native speakers as well.

[19] In particular, see the discussion of Andrews's grammar below, with respect to the accusation that he was a "slave to Latin grammar."

[20] As for assurance that the Hawaiian Mission had access to the grammar, in a letter from Burder's Point, Tahiti, to the Sandwich Island missionaries (28 January 1832), David Darling wrote that he had sent all the Tahitian mission books that are in print.

[21] On the other hand, present dialectal differences suggest that perhaps this particular form was not widespread at that time. John Charlot (pers. comm., September 1993) suggested another reason: that it had a pejorative sense (see the entry in the Pukui-Elbert dictionary).

[22] As noted in chapter 2, Preston wrote mostly impressionistic nonsense about Hawaiian. But occasionally he made a sensible comment—although one might question his use of the adverb *entirely*.

[23] To put this figure into perspective, we might note that under much more trying circumstances, the Wesleyan missionaries in Fiji produced a grammar and dictionary of high quality within fifteen years of their arrival.

[24] Note that some of these apply today, and to any language under investigation.

[25] In the examples here, I have changed Ruggles's vowel spelling to the conventional system but have not added macrons or glottal stops, or made any corrections to the forms. Italics have been added for ease of reading.

[26] Note that it was accent alone that was perceived, and not the combination of accent and vowel length. See chapter 8.

[27] This seems to be a slip for *suffixing*.

[28] Thus, this marker has discourse function and should be treated at that level, as well as at the level of the sentence.

[29] Some of these forms are interpreted differently today.

[30] The 1825 edition contains no grammatical sketch, but only a word list.

³¹ This is a tantalizing statement; such a description was a long time coming.

³² It is not clear just what this term means. Elbert and Pukui (1979:1) took Alexander's statement even further (perhaps too far): "The first scholar to characterize the structure of the Hawaiian language was ... Chamisso ..." I prefer to look at the succession of grammatical statements about Hawaiian as a growing body of knowledge, not a small number of huge leaps.

³³ Quotations in English are taken from Chapin 1973.

³⁴ It is my impression that those who have set Hawaiian words to European-style melodies have nearly ignored the prosodic patterns of the words, producing a plethora of what musicians call "barbarisms." See Schütz 1981:8.

³⁵ See note 9.

³⁶ Today, analysts disagree about the appropriateness of sentences such as this. A possible explanation is, of course, that the language has changed and that the function of *ua* has shifted.

³⁷ On the other hand, not all fronted phrases are introduced with *'o*.

³⁸ Terence Barrow, in his introduction to the 1974 reprint of Andrews 1865 (p. ix), wrote: "Lorrin Andrews was among the most humanitarian of New England missionaries ever to come to Hawaii."

³⁹ Preston (1900a:50) borrowed this idea and the actual phrase for his later sketch:

> The distinctions of time are never so definite as in other languages, the chief attention being centered on the accidents of place. The word *ana* denotes a continuance, and may be past, present, or future. Thus *e hana ana au* may mean, I *am* working, I *was* working, or I *will be* working, according to the connection.

⁴⁰ Chamisso as well (pp. 29–30) suggested that such words behaved more like substantives than prepositions.

⁴¹ Greg Lee Carter (pers. comm., January 1993) pointed out that Andrews confused four different markers of this shape.

⁴² The grammatical category of person applied to nouns is an odd concept, but the examples show that Andrews was referring to a kind of apposition or identification construction: for example, *Owau nei ke kahuna* ... 'I am the priest ...'.

⁴³ This aspect of Hawaiian grammar, like so many others, has not been well studied. But it is likely that a predicate is obligatory, with a subject optional. However, grammarians must be careful to define PREDICATE carefully if they are to avoid circularity.

⁴⁴ See also Elbert and Pukui 1979:6 and Elbert 1989a.

⁴⁵ Technically, Alexander's grammar is identified as 1864a in the Bibliography.

[46] At present, I do not have access to the 1842 edition of Maunsell's work, and so cannot judge what use Alexander might have made of his analysis.

[47] Elbert and Pukui (1979:5) suggested that Alexander "borrowed Hale's term 'guttural'", but if he had, he would have acknowledged Hale in his preface. There is no evidence that Alexander saw Hale's work until somewhat later: in the introduction to Andrews's dictionary (1865), he discussed Polynesian language relationships, acknowledging Hale. At any rate, as we saw in chapter 8, Andrews had already used the term in 1838.

[48] The accented vowel shows the French manner of indicating a preceding glottal stop.

[49] In addition to more recent reprintings, the Hawaiian Collection, Hamilton Library, University of Hawai'i at Mānoa holds editions from 1864, 1871, 1908, and 1924. The last is said to be a revised fifth edition.

[50] The book has only fifty-nine pages, and the printed area on each page measures only about 8.5 x 14 cm.

[51] Pukui and Elbert's creative solution to the problem of exceptions to this "rule" is mentioned in the notes to chapter 8.

[52] However, Knappert's transcription of long vowels in such one-syllable content forms as *kū* 'stand' reflect Judd et al.'s correct marking of most such forms, at least in the English-Hawaiian part of the dictionary.

[53] These two terms indicate the presence or absence of a center or nucleus in a construction. For example, a phrase that has the structure ADJECTIVE + NOUN is endocentric, since the noun serves as the center. However, the construction SUBJECT + PREDICATE is exocentric, since there is no center.

[54] For example, the work does not appear in Elbert and Pukui's (1979) references.

[55] For one of these topics, assimilation, the authors devoted nearly a half page to Ruby Kawena Kinney's detailed statistics for the pronunciations of individual words, rather than summarizing the results (see Kinney 1956 for a related study). For another topic, frequency of sounds (tabulated by a mathematician), we are not told the size of the sampling.

[56] A competent definition of *sentence* uses grammatical evidence, phonological evidence, or a combination of the two.

[57] Here are just a few examples. A glottal stop is described as a closing of the glottis, with no mention of the following buildup of air pressure and release. /n/ is described as dental-alveolar, which by normal phonetic conventions would mean that the teeth are placed on the gum ridge. We must assume that this means that some speakers use an apico-dental, others an apico-alveolar articulation. The Ni'ihau people are said to use an "*r*-like" sound, but we are not told whether the sound is a flap, trill, or retroflex, or at what position it is made. The relationship between what is written as *v* and *w* is made to seem like a dichotomy, whereas historical evidence shows that the sounds are at the extremes of a continuum (see chapter 7). The raising of /a/ is men-

tioned, but the environments for the raising are not. Short vowels are said to occur voiceless at the ends of utterances; examples show only /i/ and /u/, which is common in many languages. Do other vowels devoice as well? /iu/ is missing from a list of diphthongs. Long diphthongs are not mentioned at all.

[58] The authors' description of *ua* went beyond tense to include its inceptive use (that is, to mark a new or changed condition), but this observation was based directly on Dorothy M. Kahananui's observations (see Elbert and Pukui, p. 58).

[59] This statement illustrates a confusion between semantics and grammar.

[60] Five types are listed, but two of these (deliberate and spontaneous transitives) are subtypes of the category transitive.

[61] See note 65.

[62] Although a number of student papers have treated individual problems, for the most part they have not been collected and published. The Bibliography includes papers that I happen to have seen or that are referred to in other works.

[63] The Hawaiian term for 'squid' is *he'e*. *Pepeke*, like some other terms in this system, is based on an amalgamated Polynesian form (Tahitian has *pe'e*; Māori has *wheke*), but changed slightly, perhaps to give it an identity of its own. Emily A. Hawkins added (pers. comm., June 1993) that there is also a play on words involved, since Pepeke is the name of a character in a legend involving a squid.

[64] Based on the behavior of Fijian verbs, I suggest that the feature the so-called *loa'a* verbs have in common is that they are not only stative, but that two entities are involved. Hawkins (1982:31) came close to this idea by noting that sentences with statives could be expanded to show the cause for the state. But does this mean that the semantics of *any* stative includes the cause?

CHAPTER THIRTEEN

English for Speakers of Hawaiian

-o-o-o-o-o-

I understood him in many things, and let him know I was very well pleased with him; in a little time I began to speak to him, and teach him to speak to me; and first, I made him know his name should be Friday, which was the day I saved his life; I called him so for the memory of the time; I likewise taught him to say Master, and then let him know that was to be my name ... (Defoe's Robinson Crusoe, *p. 155 [Puffin edition]).*

In Daniel Defoe's fictional account of the confrontation between speakers of "island" and European languages, it seems to have been taken for granted that the former learn the language of the latter, rather than the other way around. In other words, the hero showed no interest in learning an exotic language, but took pains to teach English to Friday, starting naturally with the most important words.

In the first few decades after European contact in Hawai'i, linguistic reality imitated Defoe's art. Granted, longer-term foreign residents such as Archibald Campbell learned some Hawaiian, but most of the accounts show that language learning was pointed toward English.

The earliest opportunities for Hawaiians to learn English stemmed from the rising number of British and American vessels that visited the islands. There were two principal ways that this language learning came about. First, those who had been recruited for labor on these ships often spent several years among English speakers.[1] For example, Ingraham wrote in November 1792 (1790–1792:207):

> In the afternoon a young man came on board with a certificate from Cap Coolidge, he could speak tollerable [*sic*] good English and informed me his name was Charles that he had been to England with Cap^n Duncan and returned with Cap^n Geo Vancouver in the Discovery.[2]

Judging from the available records (Judd and Lind 1974), "Charles" would have had nearly four years to polish his English. Charles Duncan (was it he who bestowed his given name on the

Hawaiian?) was master of the *Princess Royal*, which left Hawai'i on 18 March 1788. The *Discovery* called at Hawai'i on 2 March 1792.

Another example is from Kotzebue, describing events in 1817 (1821 [1967]:296): "... one of them, who had been a sailor on board an American ship in Boston, spoke a little English, and was a clever fellow; he remained on board, at Elliot's request, to pilot our ship."

As for the second method, it soon became possible for Hawaiians to learn English without leaving home, for there was a community of English-speaking residents in Hawai'i at least by 1790. Ralph S. Kuykendall reported (1938:26–27):

> From about 1790, there grew up, very slowly at first, a foreign population in Hawaii ... In the early part of 1794, there were eleven foreigners with Kamehameha at Kealakekua ... Archibald Campbell, who resided on Oahu for more than a year in 1809–1810, states that at one time during his stay there were nearly sixty white people upon that island ...

estimating that about one-third of them were American and the rest nearly all English.

In the early years, there was some resistance on the part of the foreign residents to the Hawaiians learning English. Campbell wrote (1816:141) that Kuakini, who called himself John Adams, wanted Campbell to teach him to read, but "[Isaac] Davis would not permit me, observing, 'they will soon know more than ourselves.'"

Whether Kuakini learned to read then is uncertain, but later his control of spoken English impressed visitors. Ten years later (1819), Rose de Freycinet reported (Bassett 1962:153): "He speaks English very well and put a question to Louis [her husband] that reveals more education in geography than one would expect from a savage, even a prince." This is a view of the same event from the sword side (de Freycinet 1978:5):

> Kouakini surprised me by showing knowledge of which I would not have thought him capable. Having learned that I was on a voyage of discovery, he asked me in tolerably good English if I had come to the Sandwich Islands by Cape Horn or if I had first rounded the Cape of Good Hope.

Finally, Jacques Arago as well praised Kuakini (1823ii:62):

> The becoming manner, however, in which he introduced himself, his language, (he spoke English very well,) his choice of words; ... all these things soon convinced us that our visitor [Kuakini] was a person of distinction.

Note, however, that these were French speakers commenting on the quality of the English spoken. From the ear of at least one native speaker, Kuakini's English did not receive such high marks. Recalling his experiences in 1820, Hiram Bingham mentioned (1847:103) the "barbarous English" of Kaumuali'i, Kuakini, Ke'eaumoku, and others, learned from sailors. This means of the Hawaiians' acquisition of English presented a dilemma: a better control of English eased the problems the missionaries had in communicating with the Hawaiians, but "the thought of making young men and women better able to comprehend and use that language, while subjected to the influence of frequent intercourse with an ungodly class of profane abusers of our noble English, was appalling." (One wonders: was it the form or the content of the Hawaiian sailors' English that Bingham was criticizing?)

De Freycinet also mentioned other Hawaiians who were able to speak English (p. 4): "Poui knew a few words of English and, therefore, I had not so much difficulty in understanding him."

Otto von Kotzebue summarized the extent to which English was known before the arrival of the missionaries (1821 [1967]iii:252, 252n):

> Many Owhyeeans understand a little English, but none are provicients [*sic*] in it, not even those who have made voyages on board American ships, which a great many have done. None of them have probably learnt the letters.

and added this note:

> Tamaamaah understands English without speaking it. Lio-Lio learned to write two lines in English, in which he begged the captain of a ship to send him a bottle of rum.

Thus, the quality of the Hawaiians' English might have been adequate for simple commercial transactions, but for the detailed duties of Bible translation, most of these people with a smattering of the language were found inadequate for the task (Loomis journal, pp. 751a-53a. Lahaina, 23 January 1821):

> In acquiring this language we labor under many and great inconveniences. The want of an interpreter who understands the English language grammatically retards our progress.

ENGLISH SCHOOLS FOR HAWAIIANS

Perhaps reflecting the contemporary ranking of the written over the spoken word, writing seems to have been the focus of the first (reported) school for Hawaiians. William D. Westervelt noted (1912:16, from the

Kuokoa of 1869,[3] "Incidents of Hawaiian History") that in about 1810, John Rives,[4] a young Frenchman also known as Luahine,

> started a school in English for the Prince [Liholiho, and a few others] ... The young foreigner taught them all the letters ABC, writing on pieces of paper given to each of the pupils. It was very difficult to explain the letters and secure the right pronunciation of each one.

The school ended after three or four weeks, apparently the victim of a clash between the teacher-pupil relationship and the commoner-royal one, with the latter prevailing. Moreover, the dispute ended the *aikâne*[5] relationship between Liholiho and Rives: "The two also stopped living together."

How foreign was the concept of "school" to the Hawaiians at that time? In his description of pre-contact Hawai'i, Kuykendall (1926:41–42, quoted in Huebner 1987:181) noted that Polynesians had been

> trained in schools or under the directions of selected teachers. The young man who was to be a chief or leader studied astronomy, law, geography, and particularly history and language. Besides his regular studies, he must be trained as a warrior and a speaker and taught to read the meaning of the habits of the fish, the blossoming of trees, the flight of birds, and the movement and shape of clouds. In some Polynesian islands each young man learned some trade, such as house builder, wood carver, fisherman, sailor or farmer ...[6]

Samuel Kamakau (1866–1871 [1961]:270) compared the newly established mission schools with a pre-contact institution, saying that they were "conducted like schools of the hula in old days."

At any rate, no effort to teach reading was going to succeed without the support of the chiefs. Many performed successfully: Bingham reported (1847:113) that Kaumuali'i, the ruling chief of Kaua'i, was writing in English after only three months of instruction.

But not all royalty were similarly inclined. After a year's influence from the missionaries, Ka'ahumanu, the highest-ranking female of the chiefly lineage, had not "yet shown the least desire to learn to read or write."

In most of the accounts above, the impetus for learning English came from the Hawaiians themselves. After 1820, however, the pressure was external. Although the missionaries, who were the main framers of language policy in Hawai'i in the nineteenth century, would have preferred to begin their evangelization in Hawaiian, their ignorance of the language and the lack of any materials either *in* or *about* the language led them to consider English as at least a *pro tempore* way to present the gospel to the Hawaiians. As Bingham explained the dilemma (1847:101), the missionaries' object was "not to change the language of the nation but to bring to their minds generally, the knowledge of the Christian religion, and induce them to embrace and obey it." Thus, they "undertook with the English, with zeal, and with some success, in the case of a very limited number." Within four months of their arrival, they had established English schools in Kailua and Kawaihae on Hawaiʻi, Honolulu on Oʻahu, and (probably) Waimea on Kauaʻi (Westervelt 1912:17).

Westervelt described the progress of these early schools (ibid.):

> In three months the king [Liholiho] was reading a little in the New Testament and five others were reading easy lessons in Webster's spelling book. ... Mr. and Mrs. Bingham in May 1820 started a school for the children of foreigners who had native families in Honolulu.
>
> ... Thus the first schools were started in the Hawaiian Islands. The instruction was entirely in English and was limited to a small number of pupils. "The English New Testament" as Mr. Bingham says, "was almost our first school book."

He concluded (p. 18):

> It is worth while to note that foreigners had visited the Hawaiian Islands for thirty years, had settled among the people and had native families but had not done a thing toward educating them; while within four months after the arrival of the missionaries four English schools had been established in four important localities, each one able to influence the most influential people of the islands.

Materials and Methodology

From scattered references in a number of sources, it appears most likely that even though first-language and second-language learning are very different processes, formal instruction in English for the Hawaiians was conducted in the way the American missionaries had been taught themselves.

Moreover, it wasn't until the late 1830s that the Mission printed materials specially designed to teach English to Hawaiians. Thus, for the first two decades at least, works at hand had to suffice. One quotation above mentions using the English Bible and another book nearly as familiar: Webster's Speller, a work that served as a teacher's guide as well as a text. Some of the fundamental principles of the contemporary approach to teaching English (from Webster's *Grammati-*

cal Institute, 1783) were described in chapter 9. As we saw there, the method of oral spelling required the pupils to pronounce a syllable, such as *ba*, by letters: first the consonant *bi* (*pî*), then the vowel *a* (*'â*), and finally the combined sound of the syllable (*pâ*). With this fortituous overlap between Webster's methodology and Hawaiian syllable structure, it is no wonder that students excelled at the beginning of their English instruction.

As for more difficult pronunciations, Webster advised (p. 28n.):

> ... when the tender organs are brought to utter the easy sounds, let them be brought gradually to pronounce those that are more difficult. In this children may be much assisted by being told how to place the tongue and lips to make any sound; this is a point in which instructors are very deficient.

Much later in the course, actual reading material was introduced, the content of which was patently moralistic and designed more to instruct than to entertain, as this sample shows (p. 109):

> How do you like your master?
> Exceedingly well; he is an agreeable man.
> Is he pleasant and good natured?
> Always so: I never saw him angry.
> Is he strict in keeping orders in school?
> Very strict indeed. He will not permit us to whisper or play or be idle a single moment.
> Does he scold and fret and find fault at trifles?
> Not in the least. If one breaks a law, he is sure to be punished. But the master, though he is very severe, never appears to be in a passion.
> You esteem it a pleasure as well as an advantage to be under the care of such a man.
> Indeed I do and so do all in the school. I hardly know which we love most, the master or our books.

The following fable, from a somewhat later edition (1800:89–90), raises some obvious questions about the level of vocabulary for beginning (and especially nonnative readers):

> The Cat and the Rat A certain cat had made such unmerciful havockk [*sic*] among the vermin of her neighbourhood, that not a single Rat or Mouse dared venture to appear abroad. Puss was soon convinced, that if affairs remained in their present situation, she must be totally unsupplied with provision. After mature deliberation, therefore, she resolved to have recourse to stratagem ...

This cursory review of Webster's work shows that his beginning methodology was reinforced by the phonological structure of Hawaiian, providing students and teachers alike with a pleasing return on their efforts. But learning a language involves more than reciting simple open syllables. Could the Webster approach have anticipated the difficulties the Hawaiians had when they tried to pronounce closed syllables and consonant clusters? Or when they tried to assimilate the grammatical patterns of English, which would be well established in any native speaker old enough to learn to read? We now look at some contemporary reports on the degree of success in the first English schools.

A CLASH OF STRUCTURES

No matter how enthusiastic the students, and how novel the idea of learning to read a new language, it was not an easy thing to teach English to speakers of a language so different in sound and grammatical structure. Bingham (1847:102) summarized some of the difficulties, citing the problems the Hawaiians had in pronouncing English sounds, learning the meanings of the words when using English dictionaries was not practicable, and coping with the capricious English spelling system.

Lorrin Andrews elaborated on the first of these problems. To explain the difficulties in pronunciation, he suggested a physiological barrier (1864:102–3):

> The masses of Hawaiians have no such development of the organs of speech, as that they could articulate the sounds used in pronouncing the English language. Nor can the masses acquire the ability to do it after an adult age. Their own language has comparatively few sounds, and those mostly of the simple, infantile kind. Again, the construction of their language has but little affinity with the languages of Southern or Western Europe. With the Hawaiians, every syllable ends with a vowel sound—there are no double consonants—there are no sibilants; hence, a vast many words in English cannot be plainly articulated by them, after they have passed the age of childhood.

And what did the Hawaiians think about the sound of the English language, with its sibilants and long series of consonants? The following account is unusual, because it shows the other side of the coin (Howe 1988:72: observations from John Rae on Maui).[7]

> The Hawaiian being eminently a vowel language they speak one rotundo and having scarcely concealed contempt for our tongue with its sibilants and sounds forced out between the lips. I have often caught them ridiculing our talk by giving a sort of

caricature imitation of it. On the day to which I refer about half a dozen of them were in a room with me when one of them took up an English book and pretending to read gave utterance to sounds such as might be expressed thus psha psi chi cho sharo tum etc.

At any rate, Andrews despaired of the time and effort involved in teaching an accurate imitation of English sounds. "Where this has been effected in special cases," he wrote, "it has been done at the expense of long labor on the part of both the scholar and teacher. It never could be done for the masses ... "

He continued, citing a twenty-five-year history of failures in the attempts to teach English. The decline seemed to follow a pattern familiar to every teacher: an enthusiastic beginning, followed by diminishing interest until, as Andrews noted, "both teachers and scholars would become disgusted with themselves and each other, and give up." From his temporal vantage point, he cited these reasons (1864:104):

> 1. They could not *pronounce* English. The attempt to combine two, three, or more consonants in one syllable, so contrary to all the principles of their own language, would vex them; and at the end of a sentence or phrase, they could add, *ka-ha-ha! Aole hiki,* [Oh dear! I can't do it.]
> 2. Great irregularities in the pronunciation of the vowels, sometimes long, sometimes short, and sometimes broad; they never knew what to call a word from the letters in it.
> 3. Great irregularity of orthography; that is, the letters would appear to spell one thing, and be pronounced so as to mean another; then the great number of quiescent letters, both vowels and consonants.
> 4. They had no means of ascertaining the meaning of words, or phrases, except as the missionary told them.
> 5. A total want of books adapted to their circumstances, and no one to make them.

Eventually, the questionable success of the attempts to teach in English, combined with the missionaries' growing facility in Hawaiian, resulted in, if not an end to, at least an interruption of the use of English as a medium of instruction. Bingham (1847:104) described the end of that period of the history of education in Hawai'i:

> Though the heathen revelry of the king and others often disqualified them from making progress in study, or proved unwelcome hindrances, still, during the time which they did devote to instruction, though taught chiefly in a foreign tongue, they made such advances, that in three months the king was reading a little in the New Testament, and five of the others in the easy

reading lessons of Webster's spelling book. The young prince [Kauikeaouli], a promising pupil, though a mere child ... could spell English words of four syllables. But their studies in English were wearisome, and ere long chiefly suspended.

What Bingham did not expand on was the nature of the "reading." Did the pupils actually follow the thread of the discourse, or did they merely read aloud, without necessarily understanding the content of the words? If the latter, is this why the studies in English were "wearisome"?

Dibble (1843:173–74) also described some of the difficulties of trying to teach English to the Hawaiians:

During this period of acquiring the Hawaiian tongue some efforts were made to collect some few scholars at the different stations, and to give them instruction in the English language. Some success attended these efforts, but for various reasons they were not long continued. One reason was, that females of the schools when a little improved in manner and dress and taught a little English were beset by a certain class of foreigners with temptations and allurements, which in not a few instances proved successful and ruinous. But more especially was this class of schools discontinued on account of the necessity, which was continually becoming more and more urgent, to give the whole attention to the native tongue and to efforts of a general kind among the multitude.

As Bingham summarized it (1847:103):

This, then, is our answer to the oft-repeated and not unimportant question, "Why did you not teach the nation English, and open to them, at once, the rich stores of learning, science and religion, to be found in that language?" and here we show our warrant for applying ourselves to the acquisition of the Hawaiian language, reducing it to a written form, and preparing books of instruction in it, for the nation, and teaching all classes to use them as speedily as possible.

Here we are shown the main reason for the temporary demise of the English schools: the more pressing need to attend to Hawaiian. As the missionaries' facility in Hawaiian increased, and as the press began to print books in that language, it became less important for the Hawaiians to learn English. Thus, instruction in that language lay dormant, not to be renewed for nearly twenty years.

A REVIVAL OF ENGLISH SCHOOLS

One cannot help noticing from the account above that in most of their endeavors, the missionaries concentrated on Hawaiian royalty, hoping that they in turn would influence those subservient to them. For example, in Westervelt's account he used the word *influential*; who could be more influential than royalty? In 1839, through the initiative of a group of Hawaiian chiefs, Amos Starr Cooke and his wife Juliette founded the Chiefs' Children's School, later called the Royal School. Called "the most exclusive school in the kingdom" (Otaguro 1989:87), its plan was "to begin with the English language—to accustom the pupils from early years both to read and speak it" (*The Friend*, 1 January 1844).[8]

But notwithstanding the success of that particular school, at a later date at least one prominent missionary (actually an ex-missionary at that time) felt that the trickle-down theory was doomed to failure, at least where language learning was concerned.   Having asked, rhetorically, "Would it have been possible to have educated the *masses* of natives, even in the elementary branches, in any other language than their own?", Andrews answered his own question (1864:101–2):

> History does not show any instances, in any country, or in any
> age or tongue, where the masses have been educated in any
> language but their own. Why? Because it would have been a
> physical impossibility. We see this more or less among intelligent
> men, when they try to learn a foreign language after years of
> manhood. They never *speak* it (I refer to the pronunciation mere-
> ly) as a vernacular tongue. Witness a German, Frenchman, or
> Italian trying to speak English, or an Englishman attempting to
> speak those languages. They may understand the theory of the
> language, may write it correctly, and speak it intelligibly; but they
> never pronounce it like a native.

English Explained in Hawaiian

In a passage quoted earlier, Andrews also noted that in the missionaries' efforts to teach English to the Hawaiians, they were handicapped by the lack of appropriate materials. We have already questioned the suitability of Webster's Speller to teach reading to those not already native speakers of English. To remedy this problem, perhaps first at the newly formed Lahainaluna High School and later at the Royal School, the Mission began to produce more appropriate texts, now designed to explain English structure or vocabulary in Hawaiian.

Beginning in the late 1830s, the Mission published a number of such works—for example, an English grammar, written in Hawaiian (Andrews 1837a) and a primer, also in Hawaiian (Andrews 1837b): *Ke Kumu Kahiki: Oia ka Mea e Ao ai i na Hua a me ka Hookui, a me ka Heluhelu ana i ka Olelo Beretania* (The foreign teacher: this is the thing to teach the letters and spelling and reading in the English language). This was followed by two more works by Andrews: *He mau Haawina no ka Olelo Beretania* (A few lessons in English) (1841) and *O ke Kokua no ko Hawaii Poe Kamalii e Ao ana i ka Olelo Beritania* (The assistant for Hawaiian youths in learning the English language) (1843).

Only two years later (1845), Rev. John Smith Emerson and Rev. Artemas Bishop published an important reference work, an English-Hawaiian dictionary, translated from an abbreviated Webster's Abridgement. The preface of this work stated (p. iii):

> The design of this work is primarily to aid Hawaiian youth of intelligence in acquiring a knowledge of the English language; and it is intended, in connection with the grammar, to furnish them adequate help, under the direction of the living teacher, until they can use the English Dictionary with English definitions.
>
> The present work is mainly a translation of Webster's Abridgement still more abridged. Many words are thrown out, which are rarely used, and which will never be needed, till the student is able to learn their import from the English Dictionary ...
>
> It is also hoped that the English student of the Hawaiian language will find some help from the present work, while seeking to enlarge his stock of Hawaiian words. With this object in view, two or three or more native definitions have sometimes been introduced as conveying the meaning of an English word, when, for the benefit of the Hawaiian only, one would have been sufficient.

In 1854, Bishop published two versions of an English-Hawaiian phrase book—one with the title in English and the other in Hawaiian.

> The primary object of this MANUAL is to teach natives to converse in English. It is designed to help carry out the plan of the Government to extend English schools among the indigenous race of these Islands.

However, in spite of this stated purpose, the grammatical explanations (rather few in number) explain Hawaiian structure to speakers of English, not the reverse. For this reason, the content of this work is treated in the next chapter.

One of the last works in this nineteenth-century series is the Reverend William B. Oleson's *English Lessons for Hawaiians* (1884).

Oleson, principal of the Hilo Boarding School, was also editor of the Mission publication *The Friend*, and—as the next section suggests—was concerned about the standard of English spoken in Hawai'i. According to the preface of his work, it was offered to "furnish a basis for systematic and progressive instruction in the English language in Hawaiian schools." However, the book itself is simply an English-Hawaiian vocabulary, with words organized by part of speech and semantic category. It offered little for the teacher except suggestions on using the words (e.g., "Fix the meaning of each word by object lessons. Have the class write the words and learn them for a spelling lesson") and augmenting them with drills on tense, number, and comparison, and a final piece of advice: "Encourage the use of easy colloquial English."

What Kind of English?

With the mixture of languages that started as soon as foreigners began to settle in Hawai'i, the possibilities of a kind of foreigner or trade jargon developing as early as the 1790s, and the increasing admixture of nationalities (and hence, languages) through the nineteenth century, it was inevitable that there developed a form of English that was not reminiscent of Boston or New Haven. In an unsigned article in *The Friend* in 1886,[9] one writer speculated on the linguistic future of Hawai'i:

> It is an interesting inquiry as to what is likely to be the conquering language ultimately in these islands. The signs now are that it will be an emasculated English or English with variations. One cannot help thinking as he hears the street-talk of the rising generation that "they have been at a great feast of languages, and stolen the scraps." The native boy is a rarity who has not several phrases in Chinese and Portuguese and when it comes to single words the stock in trade of most native boys is not at all small. It is natural and inevitable that such should be the case. It is true of the Chinese, and Portuguese, and Japanese; for some of the latter, known to the writer, who have been in the country a very brief time, have picked up some Portuguese words and a few native expressions, and a stray English word of uncertain lineage, and count themselves rich in their acquisition. The worst of it is that they think this *ollapodrida* is "English undefiled."

The author went on to say that the Hawaiians could easily learn English if they were surrounded by the "constant stimulus" of the language. However, with the lack of proper English as a model, the Hawaiians suffered: "The Hawaiian loses his own language and gets what in return? The tide of foreign tongues leaves its debris all along his shores."

Moreover, the process was said to be already well under way:

> This work of crystalling a new language is now going on. The colloquial English of Hawaii nei is even now sufficiently *sui generis* to be noticeable to strangers. It is not a dialect, but a new language with English as its basic element, wrought upon by the subtle forces of other languages, not so much in the matter of a changed vocabulary as a changed idiom.

Therefore, those concerned with such matters had to be on their guard against improper English:

> It is a sober duty for every instructor of Hawaiian youth to check the use of pigeon-English [*sic*]. Very much can be done by watchfulness in this particular. And as we look forward into the years, and think of the possibilities, there is every incentive to make teachers chary in their use of doubtful English, and alert to correct the language of playground and street.

-0-0-0-0-0-

The quotation above expresses a concern about the quality of the English spoken in Hawai'i. We end the chapter with a different kind of concern, expressed by Andrews (1864:107):

> If English is taught to any advantage, many years must be spent,—much expense incurred,—qualified teachers must be employed,— the scholars must be kept learners, and there must be a watchful eye on the working of the whole system ... At all public institutions, English may be taught as a branch, and the expense may come out of the funds of that school; but for the Government to set up English schools, to the neglect of educating its own people in their own language, would, in my opinion, be a suicidal act.

Andrews was spared seeing what he warned against become reality, for he died in 1868. As we shall see in chapter 16, the next several decades after this period were a time of not only neglect of Hawaiian, but also a deliberate campaign to encourage English at the expense of the native language.

NOTES

---

[1] After Cook, there are no records of ships calling at Hawai'i until 1786. The half dozen or so foreigners who visited in that year signaled the beginning of fairly extensive contact.

[2] Captain Charles Duncan of the *Princess Royal* left Hawai'i on 18 March 1788; Vancouver arrived on 2 March 1792 (Judd and Lind 1974:3, 5). Incidentally, Ingraham added his own opinion about the advisability of the Hawaiians traveling in the outside world:

> Wether the several adventurers which have left the Sandwich Islands and return'd to them again will be of generall utility or diservice is not for me positively to say, yet I have a right to give my own opinion which is it would have been better to have let them remain'd in their own country.

[3] *Ka Nupepa Kuokoa* [*Nûpepa Kû'oko'a* 'independent newspaper'], a weekly which ran from October 1861 to December 1927 (Mookini 1974). The original is from an article by John Papa 'Î'Î, reprinted in *Fragments of Hawaiian History* (John Charlot, pers. comm., Sept. 1993).

[4] Rives was mentioned in chapter 3 as an interpreter for de Freycinet.

[5] *Aikâne*, lit., 'male intercourse', refers to a culturally acceptable homosexual relationship, often between a chief and a commoner.

[6] It was difficult to find a summary of a topic as complex as this one. For an extremely detailed treatment, see Charlot (in progress).

[7] Rae to [R. C. Wyllie?], [1854], Rae Papers (Hamilton Library, University of Hawai'i). Howe's account also gives a biographical sketch of Rae, including his philosophical background and especially his notions of an Aryan connection for Hawaiian.

[8] For a more detailed discussion of the school and its most notable students, see chapter 16.

[9] "The Resultant Language," *The Friend*, April 1886, p. 10, possibly by William. B. Oleson, Editor. He may have had his own ax (i.e., an English textbook for Hawaiians) to grind.

CHAPTER FOURTEEN

Hawaiian for Speakers of English

-o-o-o-o-o-

Our ignorance of the language of the people, and their ignorance of ours, was, of course, an impediment in the way of intercourse between the teacher and the pupil, at first very great; and the absolute destitution of suitable books for the work of teaching the nation, was an embarrassment rarely or never to be found among Asiatic tribes—an embarrassment similar to what the pioneer missionary, J. Williams, found in attempting among barbarians to build a missionary ship, on a heathen islet, with neither tools, materials, nor competent artisans (Hiram Bingham, A Residence of Twenty-one Years in the Sandwich Islands ... *[1847:101]).*

For the most part, the explorers and other early visitors to Hawai'i who gathered specimens of the language as curiosity pieces or contributions to science had scant interest in much beyond the few phrases that would allow them to engage in trade or to provision their ships. As for longer-term residents, what little we can discover about how they learned Hawaiian suggests that they did it informally. Not until the Hawaiian Mission was formed could anyone make a concentrated effort to learn how to speak the language. For the missionaries, it was essential to learn Hawaiian as well and as quickly as possible, for in their war of conversion, language was the first and most important weapon in their arsenal.

However, learning Hawaiian was no easy matter for those more accustomed to acquiring a new language through the eye than through the ear. Because of their experience with foreign-language education in the early nineteenth century, most Americans and Europeans expected to see the pieces of a language laid out as the orderly declensions and conjugations of Latin and Greek were. Formidable and page filling as such arrays were, at least they provided something to cling to, satisfying a reverence for the written word and illustrating the language "brought to system." But the complete absence of such tools for Hawaiian as a primer, a grammar, or a dictionary hindered the missionaries from the very beginning in their efforts to speak the language.

HOW THE MISSIONARIES LEARNED HAWAIIAN

Actually, the First Company of Congregational Missionaries began to study the language long before they set foot on Hawaiian soil. Even when the *Thaddeus* set sail from Boston, not all the missionaries were novices at the language: Hiram Bingham had been studying it for some time, Elisha Loomis had made notes on Hawaiian while still in Cornwall,[1] and as we saw in chapter 6, Samuel Ruggles advanced far enough in his study to write a grammatical sketch. Even so, the group as a whole needed to devote a great deal of time and effort to acquiring the language. Here, the voyage to Hawai'i—about 18,000 miles in distance and a little over five months in duration—provided an ideal opportunity for study, for the confined quarters shared by the missionaries offered few distractions.

We know little of how they went about this task; searching through their personal journals gives only a few hints.[2] For example, on 30 November 1819, Sybil Mosely Bingham wrote (Bingham Family Papers 2–31):

> This day commenced the study of the Owhyhee language. Shall I be permitted to speak in it, to those idolatrous natives, the wonderful works which Jehovah, the true GOD, has done ...

Later (25 January 1820), she described the daily routine aboard the ship, showing that language studies occupied only a small part of the regimen:

> A regular system has been strenuously recommended to all. It is variously regarded. I will give you some parts of mine. It commences with the hour 6 in the morning, closing with 10, evening. From 9 to 12 logic and theological reading—from 12 to 1 recitation of the class—1 to 2 dinner and exercise—2 to 6 miscellaneous reading, writing, and Owhyee language—from 6 to 8 tea, singing, social intercourse and exercise.

But Mrs. Bingham did more than participate in the lessons. As Daniel Chamberlain described in his journal:

> 1 December 1819. ... The females have schools on deck in good weather. Mrs Bingham is the principal instructress; her qualifications are excellent.

After reaching Honolulu, Bingham wrote of the difficulties of studying the language aboard the *Thaddeus*:

> 21 June 1820. I long to know more of their language, that I might be pouring into their tender minds more instruction than ab. [?] I think we make progress in that now. It was impossible to do much on the voyage, as, without books, all our knowledge of it must be acquired as it falls from the lips of the natives. There are a few females [here] who understand a little of English. With these we endeavour to gain influence, that so we may begin the sooner with our great object.

Although the exact method and materials the missionaries used remain a mystery, the fact that they did not refer to Ruggles's grammatical sketch or any other of his works suggests that they considered his unorthodox orthography too great an obstacle to overcome.

Thus, with no written materials at hand, one wonders why they did not look for help from the four Hawaiians who had attended the Foreign Mission School in Cornwall. However, as earlier chapters have pointed out, some Hawaiians who left home at a fairly early age seemed to have forgotten their language—or at least partly so. Sheldon Dibble (1843:173) reported that the four repatriated young men were less than satisfactory as teachers. He wrote:

> The native youth ... having failed in a great measure as interpreters, the necessity was the greater for the missionaries to acquire at once the language. And the same youth being of little service as helps in acquiring the language, the missionaries found nothing left but their own unassisted skill and application to accomplish the task.

Of course, Dibble's claim that the missionaries were unassisted ignores their total dependence on native speakers as the proper models for learning Hawaiian. Still, it was an anomaly in the nineteenth century (as it still is today) to learn a second language without the aid of written materials. As did Sybil Bingham, Dibble decried the lack of printed materials to assist in learning the language:

> The task was indeed a difficult one, for there was no vocabulary, no grammar and not a paragraph indeed printed or written in the language. Of course they were obliged to learn the language entirely by the ear—to collect the articulate sounds—to fix upon signs or letters to express those sounds and thus proceed from step to step to reduce a barbarous tongue to a written language. Those who have never been called to such a task can probably form

little conception of its difficulty. It is a toilsome work to be obliged to substitute any foreign language for one's mother tongue, and most of all an unwritten language and one wretchedly deficient in terms to express the ideas of an intelligent and religious mind. It was a toilsome work indeed—a work not of months only but of years.

SYBIL BINGHAM'S PRIMER

Somehow, amid the strenuous duties facing her as a missionary wife, Sybil Bingham continued to be simultaneously both a teacher and learner of Hawaiian. And as for the needed language primer, she solved the problem by making her own. So far as we know, the first mainly pedagogical work on Hawaiian is her manuscript booklet dated July 1823. As Chamberlain noted in the quotation above, she was well qualified as a teacher, and apparently the only one of the First Company with such experience. Perhaps divinity school training had given the males an edge in classical languages, but Sybil Mosely had been a schoolmistress with "remarkable success" for nine years years before her marriage to Hiram Bingham.[3]

The title of her booklet, "Select Hawaiian Phrases & Sentences Rehearsed at Table," shows clearly its pedagogical intent. The work itself is not only a collection of fifty-one (rather unconnected) phrases interspersed with biblical quotations, but also a few pages of connected discourse, "extracts from the Diary of Catharine Brown,"[4] sentences with English translations, tables of pronouns, and sentences illustrating the use of interrogatives and other grammatical function words. The last two pages consist of miscellaneous sentences and phrases, mostly question words, but other constructions as well, including those with such directional nouns as *waena* 'middle', *uka* 'inland', and *kai* 'sea-ward'. As for its orthography, we noted earlier that this work is our first example of the glottal stop written to keep common words separate. For example, in the set of pronoun paradigms (pp. 21–29), an apostrophe is used in such words as *na'u* and *ka'u* ('mine') to keep them separate from *nau* and *kau* (*nāu* and *kāu*, 'yours'). Another of Bingham's orthographic practices is that she discarded *r*'s after the first several pages and wrote only *l*'s. However, as useful as this embryonic primer might have been, it seems to have been a domestic affair, not meant for wider use.[5]

Quite naturally, during those first years after arrival, learning the language weighed heavily on the minds of the missionaries and their wives, as their diary entries show:

> Aided by the vocabularies and assistance of the Brethren, I have been enabled to commence preaching to this people in their own language, and on the last Sabbath I delivered my sixth sermon tho' it is with a stammering tongue that I speak. [This was after only eight months in the island.] (Artemas Bishop, Kaua'i, 7 January 1824).

> It is a grief to me, that my time is so much taken up with the secular concerns of the Mission, as to leave me very little for the study of the language (Levi Chamberlain, Honolulu, 12 January 1824).

That it was years before there were materials designed specifically to help foreigners learn Hawaiian is probably due to the same reason that the grammar and dictionary were delayed: those who, by some means or other, had already learned the language no longer needed such aids, and those who had just arrived did not yet have sufficient knowledge to produce them.

PRIMERS AS A REFLECTION OF ATTITUDES

More so than Bible translations, catechisms, or translated textbooks, primers sometimes allow us a glimpse into the social conditions of the time in which they were written. As has been mentioned before that the content of British and American primers was essentially moralistic, encouraging obedience to several higher powers, including a deity, the king (or president), and the schoolmaster. The Hawaiian primers add another dimension: the writers of phrase books often created dialogs between Europeans and Hawaiians that reflect the social levels of the period.

As noted in chapter 13, the Reverend Artemas Bishop published a Janus-like work in 1854: what seems to be the same bilingual book, but with two titles: one in English and the other in Hawaiian. One of its aims was to teach English—that is, "proper" English. The other was to apply the same standards to Hawaiian, making a special effort to avoid a type of Foreigner Talk that the Hawaiians had developed (1906:iii):

> There has long prevailed, between natives and foreigners, a corrupted tongue, which the former only use in speaking to the latter, but never among themselves. It is a method of speech which should be abandoned, as it gives a false impression, dero-

gatory to all rule, and is without system or beauty. To effect this end, colloquial words and sentences only have been chosen; and in order to make the one a literal interpretation of the other, the idiom has been frequently sacrificed while endeavoring to express the true meaning of the corresponding word.

The main part of the book begins with short noun phrases that show a strict correspondence between 'the' and *ke/ka*; 'a/an' and *he*.[6] (As is shown later in this chapter, that approach did not change much in the next hundred years.) For the most part, grammatical explanations are omitted, the reader being referred to the grammars of Andrews and Alexander. Phrases are grouped in semantic categories: e.g., "of trees," water, dwelling, kitchen utensils, edibles, body parts, clothes, animals, meals, relations, tools, colors, etc.

The phrases themselves, which begin on p. 34, make for more interesting reading. Not much imagination is needed to picture the social situation that would call for such phrases as the following, whether they are in English or Hawaiian:

> Get some wood. Get some coals. Make haste. Do not be so slow. Listen to me. Go to work. Come here. Go there. Carry this tea cup. Do not spill the tea ...
> John, make a fire. Warm me some water. Mix cold water with it. Bring a clean shirt. Look in the bureau. Take out the clothes. Have you found it? Now bring the shoes and stockings. Are the shoes brushed? Take and do them again.

One dialogue, entitled "A Conversation with a Native Woman," begins amiably enough, with (apparently) the speaker of English asking for household help. A few pages later (pp. 44-45), the interested student can learn how to handle an exchange like this:

> If I do wrong would you be angry [?]
> I should then be angry.
> At what wrong would you be angry?
> If you refuse to obey my orders. If you are saucy. And if you are lazy. If you forsake me and run off. If you take things without asking. If you give away my property. If you steal any of my plants. If you gossip and tell falsehoods. If you say yes and do not do it. And if you do not attend the family worship. If you persist in going to places of ill repute. And if you do not read the Bible constantly. If you leave the house without my permission. Then I should be angry.
> If I wish to go home, why may I not go?

> If you ask me when the work is done, then I will give my
> consent. It is proper that I should know of your going.

Perhaps one can understand, if not condone, this point of view for the period in which the book was written. What is more difficult to accept is that a publisher chose to reprint it in 1968, and that by 1991 it had gone through seventeen printings. The back cover of the recent edition proclaims: "'It teaches Hawaiian to English-speaking people.' That's exactly what this book does." Thus, in addition to the mistress-servant dialogue above, the serious student can also learn how to say "Take the wheels to the blacksmith and have the tires reset" (p. 88) and "My father is afflicted with leprosy" (p. 102). Let buyers indeed beware, for they must look inside the front cover, not at the copyright page, to find that the current whited sepulcher with a colorful cover was reprinted from the 1906 edition, and that, in turn, was a direct descendant of the first edition of 1854.

EARLY TWENTIETH-CENTURY PRIMERS

Other than reprintings and slightly revised editions of the phrase book just mentioned, very little pedagogical work on Hawaiian appeared for another three-quarters of a century. However, the 1930s saw two primers published, both lightweight in content and riddled with errors in their description of the language. Normally, such works would receive no more attention than a citation in a bibliography. But because there was nothing else available, they figured prominently in the efforts at that time to reintroduce the language to those who had lost it. And if we are to understand the complex picture of the long-drawn-out "renaissance" of the Hawaiian language (which is one of the themes of the final chapter of this book), we must look at the materials that were available to work with.

Atcherley 1930

If we examine Mary H. Atcherley's *First Book in Hawaiian* as either a grammar or a teaching text, we find that it is as flawed in one role as in the other. As a grammar, it duplicates and oversimplifies information that already exists in previous works. Pedagogically, it is nearly useless. The exercises begin with an array of all the two-letter combinations possible from a twelve-letter alphabet.[7] But are there glottal stops between the vowels? Will learning the thirty-five forms ending with a consonant help a student pronounce Hawaiian? And what of the forty-nine totally unpronounceable two-consonant combinations such as *hm, km, kp, kw*? Even in an amateur production such as this, common sense might have prevented such an embarrassment.

The author's presentation of vocabulary is reminiscent of the methodology of the eighteenth-century grammarians Thomas Dilworth and Noah Webster: first, words formed with one vowel, then words formed with two vowels, words formed with a consonant and a vowel, and so on. This section is followed by a list of nineteen Hawaiian names for punctuation marks, also of dubious use for beginning students. As for grading structures according to their difficulty, it seems overambitious to expect a student to cope with the Hawaiian translation of 'The woman has carried the water to the table' and 'The rice is being cooked in the iron pot' after reaching only lesson 2. To add to this burden, lesson 5 presents the student with dozens of pronouns and pronoun phrases to memorize.

In short, except for a superficial organization of the material into "lessons," Atcherley's treatment of Hawaiian is no more pedagogical than the much more scholarly grammars of Andrews and Alexander of the previous century. The fact that it was officially accepted by the territory of Hawai'i shows that government agencies have not changed much in their ability to deal with language education.

Judd 1939

The preface of Atcherley's work provides a transition to the next primer, for it reveals that Henry P. Judd was editor for the Hawaiian Board of Missions, which published her primer. Near the end of the 1930s, however, apparently Judd decided that a replacement was needed. He wrote in the preface to *The Hawaiian Language and Hawaiian-English Dictionary* (1939:3) that

> a new work in the Hawaiian language, based on modern systems
> of instruction such as are used in teaching French, Spanish,
> Italian or German should be prepared for use in class-rooms
> throughout the islands and also for individual study,

subtitling his work "a complete grammar."[8] Yet the section just quoted shows that it it was Judd's intent to write a primer, not a grammar.

After examining his book, one finds it difficult to reconstruct Judd's conception of "modern systems" of language teaching. For example, a Latin primer written at nearly the same time[9] begins with a brief history of the importance of the language, a discussion of the alphabet, and pronunciation exercises keyed to a detailed and fairly sophisticated guide in the Appendix. The lessons begin with short readings containing simple sentences based on a limited number of patterns. These patterns are then discussed from a grammatical point of view, and the material is presented piecemeal—only a few points at a time. For example, the first reading contains only the nominative singular and plural forms of feminine nouns, and the verb is confined to the third person singular and plural forms of *to be*.

In sharp contrast, Judd's first display of Hawaiian begins with thirteen forms of pronouns and twenty-two names of body parts. The next lesson conjugates a verb and lists twenty-eight more body parts; further lessons continue verb conjugations and noun and pronoun declensions, the latter containing six cases.[10] The only feature at all pedagogically satisfying is that each lesson contains a set of sentences that illustrate a particular grammatical category and use the pertinent vocabulary. After sixty-six such lessons, the format changes, presenting five lessons consisting of lists of unrelated sentences. Finally, twelve reading lessons round out the course, and the book ends with a Hawaiian-English vocabulary.

Consistent with a prominent theme in Hawaiian linguistics, Judd's *Hawaiian Language* seems to have survived[11] because it was the only such work available. It furthers the tradition—after the pioneering works of Andrews and Alexander—of descriptive and pedagogical work being carried on by enthusiastic amateurs, perhaps good speakers of the language, but lacking the experience and training necessary to produce adequate teaching materials.

WORLD WAR II AND A CHANGE IN METHODOLOGY

One of the less dramatic effects of World War II on Hawai'i (and the United States in general) was that it changed the way professionals approached language teaching. The reason was that suddenly there was a practical need to teach a number of different languages quickly and thoroughly, and the mantle of responsibility fell on the unlikely shoulders of the military, who then assigned the task to members of a fairly new field: linguistics. The result was not only a change in methods, but a series of texts incorporating the new methodology. In one of these, the German course, Jenni Karding Moulton and William G. Moulton sketched the beginnings of the movement:[12]

> Early in 1942, within a month of Pearl Harbor, the Joint Army
> and Navy Committee on Welfare and Recreation began consider-

ation of the means whereby large numbers of troops might be instructed in the colloquial forms of the numerous languages spoken in the areas in which they were likely to be employed. A survey of materials already available for such instruction confirmed their suspected inadequacy. Many of the pertinent languages had never been taught in the United States; few of them had ever been studied or described by competent linguists. Only the unusual textbook was designed to teach the spoken forms to linguistically untrained students ...

The authors explained how their course was organized (p. iii):

It contains all the essential grammatical materials for learning to speak [the everyday language], and its vocabulary, though small, is built around a number of the most common situations and current topics. It is based on the principle that you must *hear* a language if you are to understand it when spoken, and that you must practice speaking it in order to master its sounds and its forms.

In this series of texts, the emphasis was on speaking, especially imitating a native speaker. The editors believed that "ideally one learns a foreign language most efficiently when taught intensively by a bilingual trained technical linguist while resident in the country to which the language is native." Recognizing that this ideal situation seldom exists, the texts and accompanying phonograph records were planned to substitute—to varying degrees—for ingredients either missing or inadequate. Grammar was said not to be an end in itself, but an aid to showing students how words, phrases, and sentences are put together, to help them memorize what has been heard, and to demonstrate how what has been learned can be varied in conversations.

Elbert 1951

For Hawaiian, the first textbook writer to be in a position to take advantage of these techniques was Samuel H. Elbert, who had spent the war years preparing vocabularies for Samoan and various Micronesian languages. Elbert began teaching courses in Hawaiian at the University of Hawai'i in 1949, and in 1951 published the first in a series of primers: *Conversational Hawaiian* (1951b). In principle, the work is a giant step ahead of its predecessors, at least in terms of the promises made in the preface (p. iii):

The method used in this text is based to some extent on techniques of language teaching evolved by linguists during World

War II. Learning to speak is the primary objective. Speaking ability insures reading ability. The language learned is every-day colloquial speech, not a "purist" or Biblical speech. Grammatical explanations are tailored to Hawaiian, and not to Latin or English. Effort has been made to make these explanations so simple that a student working alone without a teacher can learn to read. Some 625 words are introduced, each used in at least five lessons unless otherwise noted. Textual material is drawn as much as possible from the rich treasury of Hawaiian song, legend, chant, and proverb. The lessons have been tested experimentally for two years in courses at the University of Hawaii meeting three hours weekly.[13]

In practice, however, the work does not live up to the theory. Note first the contrast here with the introduction to the German course, in which speaking the language, not reading it, is the main goal. Next, translation seems to be another aim. For example, lesson 2 (following an inadequate pronunciation guide) begins by explaining articles largely by translating them into English. In the same lesson, students are given two sets of sentences to translate: one into English and one into Hawaiian. Neither of these practices would have been tolerated by the "Army" method.

As for making the grammatical explanations simple, the usual technique in this text was to translate a Hawaiian form into an English one. This may have seemed simple to the author, but the result was unsatisfactory for two reasons. First (and this is a problem that pervades Hawaiian language pedagogy), many of the constructions were not adequately analyzed to begin with. Next, to suppose that the two grammatical systems match each other is not a simple approach, but a simplistic one.

However, other parts of the work are more satisfying: for example (p. 5), the introduction of the notion FRAME, with a suggestion of a substitution drill (see the next section for an explanation), and lesson 37, which asks students to look at a picture and answer questions about it. Here, at least, translation is avoided. But the precedent was set early in the lessons that translation is an essential part of learning a language, and this habit, once instilled, is difficult to break.

All in all, the work is disappointing, but it was certainly an improvement over the earlier attempts at primers by Atcherley and Judd. Moreover, through classroom use and contributions from students and colleagues, this first draft, as it were, was considerably improved by the time it reached the 1955, 1961 (for these two editions, Samuel A. Keala was coauthor),[14] and 1970 versions (the latter with a new title, *Spoken*

Hawaiian). However, the major flaws in explaining the pronunciation and grammar remained.

Still, teaching a language involves more than textbooks, and at least two descriptions of how instruction in Hawaiian evolved at the University of Hawai'i (Segrest 1977, Kimura 1978) show that Elbert's changes—setting high standards, emphasizing the importance of writing glottal stops and long vowels, and using tape-recorded drills—were as innovative in the 1940s and 1950s as the workshop that followed was in 1960.

ENGLISH AS A SECOND LANGUAGE
AND THE HAWAIIAN LANGUAGE-TEACHING WORKSHOP

If WWII planted the seeds of a more structured approach to language learning, the attention paid to teaching English as a second language in the postwar years nourished them. In the English grammars of this period we find structure presented as patterns to be filled with sets of words and phrases. For example, students might be presented with a sentence such as the following:

This is a **book**.

and asked to replace the boldface word with any of a long list of items to substitute in its place. (As with many approaches to language-teaching methodology, the novelty of pattern practice wore off, and it was considered passé by the late 1960s, when more innovative and creative approaches were recommended. But whether the method is in favor or out of favor, its basic premise is sound, and it could certainly be used as at least one activity [out of many] in the classroom.)

This method was first applied to Hawaiian in an experimental project in September 1960.[15] As a demonstration for language teachers, a native speaker of Hawaiian, Dorothy M. Kahananui, and a professional linguist, Floyd M. Cammack, conducted a workshop that presented the most important features of the method: imitation of a native speaker, pattern practice, and substitution drills. In this week-long workshop, the first five lessons of Elbert and Keala's *Conversational Hawaiian* (1955) were used as the basic material.

A number of years later, one of the participants, Pua Hopkins, looking back on the experience, noted that she had been intrigued by its apparent success as "instant teacher training" (Segrest 1977:14–15):

> Once it got embedded at the University it took. All the
> language teachers went to the workshop—it was instant brain-

washing. It worked so well in the first ten lessons. It was very efficient. Now I am finding it necessary to get away from this method because ... the material is never solidified. The basic concept never changed. Only in the last two or three years have I criticized it. Now we have a core of young teachers and advanced students who know enough to realize they do not know enough. Something is missing. They know a *code* but not a *language*.

Such sentiments marked the beginning of an attempt to introduce more Hawaiian culture into the lessons. But in the meantime, the influence of the workshop was strongly felt, and most textbooks concentrated on structure.

Brown 1963

Although recorded exercises carefully keyed to the exercises were an essential part of the "Army" method of language teaching, there is little overt mention of audio recordings before Ronald R. Brown published his text, *Learn Hawaiian*, in 1963. In this work, which seems to have been designed as a self-tutor, Brown advised students to listen to the recorded lesson first without looking at the book. As for the organization of the work, the author used pattern practice, but under another name—*keys*, which were patterns said to integrate learning. Thus, his material focused on common structures rather than situations.

Kahananui 1965

As a response to a request in 1961 (see chapter 16) to develop Hawaiian language teaching materials for the Kamehameha Schools, Dorothy M. Kahananui drew on her skill as a native speaker and her experience with the workshop the previous year to write her own teaching text: *E Pāpā-'ōlelo Kākou*. This work shows the extent to which she was influenced by methods courses and texts of the period. For example, she emphasized the importance of the MIM-MEM (mimicry-memorization) principle in fixing good pronunciation habits and learning structures and vocabulary. Equally important, and contrasting with Elbert's material, she avoided translation wherever possible. At the end of the notes to teachers (p. xiv), Kahananui warned:

NEVER TRANSLATE UTTERANCES WHILE TEACHING
KEEP THE USE OF THE FIRST LANGUAGE AT A MINIMUM

Moreover, she did not emphasize grammatical explanations, implying that patterns should be inferred from the repetition of related sentences. Accordingly, overt pattern-practice drills begin early in the work. To a large extent, the semantic content of these drills was based on the classroom, with the words for such items as pencils, books, chalk, flag, erasers, tables, and chairs used to fill in the blanks in simple sentences.

This principle extends through the whole work. According to Pua Hopkins (pers. comm., November 1992), the 1960 workshop instilled in Kahananui the idea that pedagogically, language and culture should be kept separate. Thus, one of the stories presented late in the text (pp. 161–68) is "Goldilocks and the Three Bears," and a glance at the vocabulary at the end of the text shows that one can find, in one semantic domain, words for *butter, milk, fruit juice, pudding, coffee,* and *roast beef*—but not for *poi* or *fish*, and, in another, for *car* and *pencil*—but not for *spear* or *fishhook*.

Still, choice of vocabulary is a personal matter. In terms of organization, execution, and methodology, Kahananui's work is far more sophisticated than any primer that preceded it, and even some that followed. She may have had some difficulty in describing pronunciation, but this seems to be a recurring problem in Hawaiian language pedagogy.

Kahananui and Anthony 1970

This work, *E Kama'ilio Hawai'i Kakou: Let's Speak Hawaiian* is an expansion of Kahananui's earlier text. Its methodology, in the form of instructions to the teacher, is set out explicitly in the introduction (p. vii):

1. Provide sufficient pattern practice to help develop proficiency in the use of the target language.
2. Extend the classroom work though use of the language laboratory. Produce tapes for laboratory use.
3. To encourage the use of the target language outside of class, use material related to daily activities.
4. Use rapid drill material to check on student progress and to develop fluency.
5. Avoid placing the English equivalent of basic utterances on the same page as the target language. In this work, the only place where English and the target language appear together is in section VII of each unit.

6. Use English in the classroom to elicit replies in the target language and to prevent confusion when making assignments.
7. Provide review material.

As in Kahananui's earlier work, the pronunciation guide is an unsuccessful attempt to describe the sounds of Hawaiian without a working knowledge of phonetics. For example, although macrons are used elsewhere in the work, they are omitted in the guide, and only the terms *stressed* and *unstressed* are used. Also, English examples are used to show the difference between the diphthongs *ae* and *ai*, *au* and *ao*, although English has no such contrasts. On p. xiii, minimal pairs that really concern vowel length are described as words spelled alike but pronounced differently. Nor is the glottal stop treated as a real consonant.

On the positive side, the authors made extensive use of dialogues, pattern practice, and substitution drills. The drills are set out in detail, requiring much less invention on the part of the teacher. In addition, the authors expanded the grammatical explanations somewhat, but did so in language easy to understand.

Finally, as for the imbalance of language and culture, some of the latter made its way into the work: e.g., an explanation of kin terms (p. 29). And, as for vocabulary, the menu, as it were, was now broadened to include *fish* and *poi*.

Kamanā and Wilson 1977

In *Nā Kai 'Ewalu*, the authors combined a knowledge of Hawaiian with a sensible approach to teaching a language. The lessons present first a vocabulary, then a short dialogue, and pattern-practice and trans-lation drills. Exercises, such as questions and clues for the answers, encourage students to begin using the language immediately. For the most part, the grammatical explanations are easy to understand, avoid-ing, as they do, unnecessary technical jargon. In general, the authors avoided the translation approach to grammar, except when they explained the article *ka/ke*. In the second-year text, the authors used Hawaiian terms, many of their own coining, for grammatical explanations.

Hopkins 1992

Ka Lei Ha'aheo: Beginning Hawaiian is probably the first Hawaiian textbook written by a specialist in language teaching.[16] Its proposed readership extends from high school to university students; accordingly, the grammatical explanations are written clearly and in a style free of technical terms. As examples, note how two of her explanations differ from previous treatments. First, Elbert and Keala (1961:99–100) treated the passive by simply attaching labels (verb, subject, agent) to the different pieces of the construction without explaining its function in discourse. Hopkins's approach is directly opposite (p. 156):

> Hawaiians are often more interested in the final outcome of an action, rather than who performs it. This is expressed through the use of passive voice sentences in which the subject receives the action.

Next, note the treatment of verbs that are inherently stative in nature, but which involve a cause of that state (p. 174):[17]

> *Maopopo* and *loaʻa* are stative verbs whose English translations make their use tricky for English speakers. *Maopopo* means 'clear, known, understandable.' In the Hawaiian sentence, whatever is known or understandable is the **subject**. The person who knows or understands (the perceiver) is treated the same way as causes with stative verbs.

Consistent with this analysis, the author glossed *maopopo* in the general vocabulary as 'understandable, known'. Compare this treatment with that of Elbert (1970:7, 228), who in the lessons glossed the word as 'understand to-me' and in the vocabulary as 'to understand'. In keeping with the difficulty of such words and the effect they have on the rest of the phrase,[18] Hopkins introduced *maopopo* about three-quarters of the way through the text, in contrast with Elbert, who used it in his second lesson. Of course, such constructions illustrate a common problem in presenting language patterns and vocabulary: difficulty versus frequency.

The organization of most of the lessons follows a common plan, as outlined in the teacher's guide (p. vii):

1. Basic sentences to illustrate grammatical patterns and vocabulary
2. Explanations of the constructions, special vocabulary, and cultural concepts
3. Dialogues based on both new and old material
4. Exercises on both new and old material
5. New vocabulary

As for language and culture, Hopkins's approach, more than that of any of her predecessors, was that the two should go hand in hand (p. xiii).

> Whenever possible I have explained distinctive features of the language in the context of Hawaiian culture, rather than as deviations from the English speaker's norms. For example, *kēia, kē nā*, and *kēlā* are explained in terms of a Hawaiian view of space and respect for others' territory and not as some peculiar quirk of the language. The text also contains notes about aspects of Hawaiian values and culture that are reflected in the dialogs.

Thus, the user of this text has a chance to see the language as an aspect of Hawaiian culture, not just a series of patterns to be memorized.

CONCLUSION

Language-teaching methodology is not easy to evaluate, for ideas and techniques come in and go out of style. Thus, one must judge a teaching text mainly by its consistency and the degree to which the author keeps any promises made in the general plan of the work. There are two more considerations that override the faddishness of methodologies: How well does the work serve the student? And how faithful is the presentation of the language to the language itself?

Although linguists try to make a distinction between teaching a language and teaching *about* a language (i.e., primer versus grammar), sometimes the two overlap. This is especially the case in the history of teaching the Hawaiian language. Under ideal conditions, a student learns the rudiments of a second language in the classroom and then polishes the rough edges or corrects misunderstandings by observing and participating in the society in which the language is spoken. Unfortunately, for Hawaiian language students, many years have passed since they have been able to do this. Thus, the materials and the grammatical analysis that supports them are much more important than for students learning, for example, English, Japanese, or German— languages that can be learned simply by talking with native speakers.

There is also another difference between the teaching of Hawaiian and that of the more commonly taught languages. In the absence of a professional tradition of Hawaiian grammar, in which ideas are constantly challenged, tested, and revised, there has been a tendency to accept provisional statements without question. As a small example, if the primers used in classrooms repeatedly classify *he* as an indefinite article that appears before nouns, and *ua* as a marker of completed action, and then make sure that sample sentences reflect this analysis, students—with few chances to participate in normal conversations—will use and perpetuate this narrow, perhaps partly incorrect, interpretation.

Unless the sociolinguistic prospects for Hawaiian improve markedly, students will always be at the mercy of pedagogical and reference materials. Improvement in the quality of these materials has been slow. But through the diligent and dedicated work of the present generation of scholar-teachers, serious students of the language are much better served now than they were before.

NOTES

----

[1] "Elisha listened carefully when the Islanders spoke in their own tongue, making notes to be used if he ever found himself in Hawaii" (Loomis 1966:12).

[2] The journals do, however, tell much about the characters of the people themselves. Although a popular fictionalized account of the first Mission to Hawai'i portrayed many of the company as a dour, joyless lot and the voyage as fifty pages of seasickness, constipation, priggishness, and conflict, the actual journals tell a different story. Naturally, there were storms, seasickness, and discomfort. But there was also a strong foundation of faith and conviction that supported the Mission family. The following passages are from Daniel Chamberlain's journal on board the brig *Thaddeus* (Houghton Library):

> 27 December 1819. Mrs C has spoke in particular to day, how much better she enjoyed herself than she expected to —says, if her friends could know her feelings, they would not be anxious about her. We have some porter yet which is good; —one bottle of it, with the addition of water & molasses, will make four bottles of good beer. For about a month the principal part of us have had water gruel for supper — I love it as well as I formerly did bread & milk at home, we feel well thus far as to food.
>
> 31 December 1819. When it is safe, almost all hands go in swimming, we experience no inconvenience in it only the women are afraid the sharks will catch their husbands. Mr Bingham is the best swimmer I ever saw.

[3] For more details about her background, see chapter 12.

4 I have not yet identified Catharine Brown. Note that in Bingham (1847: 172) we find that "half cast" children had been "encouraged to ... keep a journal." And Albertine Loomis (1966:132) mentioned a Captain Brown.

5 The fact that it was found in the Bingham papers and not in the collection of the ABCFM supports this suggestion.

6 As a matter of fact, each *he* phrase is actually a sentence: for example, *he piku* would be better translated as 'It's a fig' than 'a fig'.

7 This count does not include the glottal stop.

8 As I have noted elsewhere, perhaps publishers, not authors, should take the responsibility for such statements.

9 Ullman and Henry 1941.

10 Judd 1939 as a grammatical description is discussed in chapter 12.

11 My copy was reprinted in 1961; as of November 1992, newly printed copies were still in Honolulu bookshops.

12 This quotation and the following summary are from Jenni Karding Moulton and William G. Moulton. 1944. *Spoken German: Basic Course— Units 1-12* (1944). Reprinted for the Untied States Armed Forces Institute by the Linguistic Society of America and the Intensive Language Program, American Council of Learned Societies.

13 It is not made clear just what kind of experimental method was used or how the students' progress was measured.

14 In this edition, Elbert and Keala acknowledged Nelson Brooks's *Language and Language Learning, Theory and Practice* (1960) for providing a "new key" to language learning.

15 Aspinwall (1960:13) described the plan of the workshop: "Free classes in Hawaiian are to be given for University language teachers and for selected representatives of all local colleges and schools. A linguist from Cornell is going to offer four hours of work per day in the late afternoon and evening for a week. The Committee for the Preservation of Hawaiian Language and Culture is happy to finance the classes because we shall all be learning Hawaiian."

16 Hopkins received a master's degree in teaching English as a second language.

17 Following previous treatments by Elbert, most recent grammarians have referred to this verb class as *loaʻa*-type verbs.

18 Apparently, there is a tendency for young students in Nā Pūnana Leo classes to treat this word as an active verb (Laiana Wong, pers. comm., 1992). John Charlot added (pers. comm., September 1993) that this usage also appears in "some late texts."

CHAPTER FIFTEEN

Hawaiian and Polynesian

-0-0-0-0-0-

> *The origin of the language of the Polynesians, divided as it is into several different dialects, is buried in deep obscurity. The people themselves know not whence they are, as the fabulous accounts of their own origin sufficiently testify; and yet, on the slightest inspection and comparison of the different dialects, it cannot for a moment be doubted that they had one common origin. And a singular circumstance is, that the people at the extreme parts of Polynesia speak dialects of the general language the most resembling each other. It has been said that the dialects of the New Zealanders and the Hawaiians resemble each other more nearly than any of the other dialects ... But whence came the inhabitants of Polynesia? How did they come, or get possession of so many islands scattered over such a vast extent of ocean? When did they come? And why did they come? are questions that cannot now be answered without much conjecture. Yet, no doubt a careful and thorough examination of the several dialects, and a comparison of one with the other with a view to ascertain the groundwork of the general language, and a comparison with the languages of the neighboring continents, would not only be a subject of inquiry full of interest, but would go far to indicate the probable origin of this people (Andrews 1836b:12–13).*

Before Cook's voyages, the Western world's knowledge about Polynesian languages[1] was very limited indeed. However, the relationship between these languages and Malay, Javanese, Malagasy, and others had been known since 1706, when Hadrian Reland compared words from the better-known languages further west with the short Polynesian vocabularies published by the explorers Iacob Le Maire and Willem Cornelis Schouten (Ray 1926:19).[2]

These vocabularies, collected in 1616 at the Hoorn Islands (East Futuna) and Cocos Island (Niuatoputapu) are our earliest records of any Polynesian language. The explorers' narrative of their voyage contains just a few examples of words from those islands, but Le Maire wrote on 24 May that he had amused visitors aboard the ship (hostages, actually, taken in order to insure the safety of his own men visiting ashore) "with playing on the violins and other *musical instruments*, dancing, and in writing some words of their language" (Dalrymple 1771:41).

The lists themselves are short: only 32 words from East Futuna, and 114 from Niuatoputapu. But for years, they were the only Polynesian data available. Several later explorers, including Abel Tasman, reported that they had tried to use words on the list to communicate with people from other Pacific islands, but with no success. All in all, it was more than a century and a half before the outside world knew anything more about these languages, in spite of the fact that a number of European explorers had passed through the areas in which they were spoken. What finally opened the door to an increased awareness of the languages was of course Cook's three voyages.

EARLY COMPARISONS OF POLYNESIAN LANGUAGES

Fortunately, Cook and his naturalists were interested enough in language to treat it as a matter worth recording. On the first voyage, they began by collecting words from Tahitian, the language that served as a touchstone for all the others they encountered. Tupaia, the Tahitian who accompanied Cook to New Zealand, was the first to demonstrate that the languages of the eastern Pacific were not a group of unrelated isolates: observers claimed that he was understood perfectly when he spoke Tahitian to the Māori.

But Tahitian and Māori were the only Polynesian languages for which vocabularies were collected on Cook's first voyage.[3] On the second voyage, the range was extended to include Easter Island, Marquesan, and Tongan as well, and forty words from these five languages (along with two from Vanuatū and one from New Caledonia) appear in a comparative table at the end of Cook's account. The compilation was probably a joint effort on the parts of William Anderson[4] and Johann Reinhold Forster, who wrote (Cook 1777, 2, fronting p. 364):

> It may be easily perceived, that notwithstanding some words are entirely different, the first five Indian languages are radically the same; though the distance from Easter Island to New Zealand is upwards of fifteen hundred leagues. The principal difference consists in the mode of pronunciation, which in Easter Island, Amsterdam [Tongatapu], and New Zealand, is more harsh, or guttural, than at the Marquesas Isles, or Otaheite.

As this quotation shows, Cook's naturalists remarked on the amazing similarities among these five languages. Thus, perhaps the greatest linguistic surprise that Hawaiian presented to Cook and his crew was not so much that the language so closely resembled Tahitian (and several other languages already encountered), but that this resemblance existed in spite of the great distances among the island groups, especially

Hawai'i, New Zealand, and Easter Island. In fact, by plotting Hawai'i on the map, they provided the third vertex of what later became known as the Polynesian triangle, an area of over 2,000,000 square miles (Biggs 1971:466).

Languages as Curiosities

The discovery of a far-flung language family piqued the curiosity of naturalists eager to collect new specimens. For example, one of the objectives of the explorer Antoine D'Entrecasteaux was to make a comparative study of languages encountered on his voyage in the 1790s (Rossel 1808:300):

> The vocabularies of different people will be brought together in a public depository so that everyone will be able to determine the similarities and dissimilarities that exist between the same words understood by different individuals.

Even some heads of state took an interest in such matters. Catherine the Great's fascination with the vocabularies of "exotic" peoples is well known; she "directed her Secretary of State to write to the powers of Europe, Asia, and America; and application was accordingly made to President Washington for our *Indian* languages; several specimens of which were accordingly furnished" (Pickering 1820:4n–5n).[5]

To a great extent, these collectors gathered their samples simply to show something of the diversity of human languages, without attempting to analyze them. Moreover, the accuracy of the data in the published versions varied, since the lists were gathered by many different people, most of them amateurs with no special training in languages.

However, a different way of looking at language change and language relationships was soon to produce a more rigorous kind of language study. For the time being at least, amateurs were pushed to one side as there emerged a new kind of professional—someone who examined languages in a systematic fashion.

POLYNESIAN LANGUAGES AND THE BIRTH OF COMPARATIVE LINGUISTICS

The concept of RELATED LANGUAGES or of a LANGUAGE FAMILY implies that two or more languages have derived from a common ancestor. But this definition may suggest that languages reproduce and have offspring.[6] Perhaps it is more straightforward to state the relationship in terms of time and change: thus, to say that languages are related means that at some time in the past, they were actually the same language, spoken in the same community, but because of (mainly) geographical separation, have changed over the years to become less and less similar.

Because it figured in the formulation of this new science of languages, Sanskrit held the center of the stage in the development of rigorous procedures to explain such relationships, while Hawaiian was only in the background.[7] Europe's increased knowledge of both these languages can be traced to Britain's flourishing expansionist policy of the late eighteenth century. The connection between this policy and the opening of the Pacific is obvious. Less obvious is that the British presence in India awakened European scholars to the importance of Sanskrit.

Perhaps the most often quoted comments on the newly realized connection among Sanskrit, Greek, and Latin are those of William Jones, who in 1786 noted that the similarities among the three, both in words and grammatical forms, were so great that they must have "sprung from some common source."

Thus, the comparison of languages moved from eighteenth-century curiosity collecting to nineteenth-century scientific method, based on the principle that sound change is regular and that descriptions of language relationships should stem from patterns of sound and vocabulary correspondences, not from the similarities of just a few words (which may be due to chance). For Pacific languages, this methodological advance is reflected in the different terms historians have used to describe the genesis of the notion of a Malayo-Polynesian (or Austronesian) language family. Sydney H. Ray, referring to Reland's proposal mentioned at the beginning of this chapter, wrote (1926:19) that in 1706 Reland had *inferred* a relationship between the Malayan languages and the Polynesian languages. Pedersen (1931 [1962]:130) wrote that, in the 1830s, Wilhelm von Humboldt had *clearly proved* the kinship between the two groups.

However, intellectual curiosity has inspired some people to look further afield for Hawaiian's relatives, spreading the range in one direction as far as Indo-European languages, in the other, native American languages, and in the middle, vanished civilizations.

LOST TRIBES AND SUNKEN CONSONANTS[8]

Oddly enough, decades after such scholars as the Grimm brothers, Franz Bopp, Rasmus Rask, and others were improving the techniques for delving into the history of a language family, linguistic amateurs were still hanging complicated theories on slight threads of accidental similarities among words. As an extreme example, one of the most imaginative hypotheses about the origins of the Polynesians suggested that they were survivors from the inundated continent Mu.[9]

In comparison with such fantasies, some other theories sound, at first hearing, almost plausible. For example, note the following comments from Herbert H. Gowen, which also bring the concept of race into the picture (1899:91):

> One branch of the great Aryan family journeyed ever eastward ... [We can] welcome as fellow citizens the dusky children of Hawaii—recognized at last, not as aliens, but as long lost brethren of the same stock and blood.

He also suggested (p. 93) that the consonants that had somehow been lost on the eastward journey were in Hawaiian "even yet distinguishable in the best native pronunciation."

Gowen had taken Abraham Fornander (1878-1885) for his mentor, calling him the "best comparative philologist of them all" (see Samuel H. Elbert's assessment below). But Gowen's etymologies seem based more on imagination than on philological method (p. 95): "Umi ['*umi*], ten, appeared so great that umiumi ['*umi'umi*] became the word for beard, denoting a vast number of hairs."

As proof of the relationship between Hawaiian and the Indo-European languages, Gowen presented the following "cognates":

Hawaiian	Indo-European
ka, ke (article)	English *the, that*; German *das*
na [*nā*] (plural)	Sanskrit *nânâ* 'various'; Irish *na* 'they'
au 'I'	Latin *ego*, German ich, English *I*
wai 'water'	English *water*
maka 'eye, face'	English mouth

In the same vein, the Reverend D. Lobschied, after a "brief visit" to Hawai'i in 1871(?), did some freewheeling comparison of Hawaiian words with those from other languages, concluding (1872:4):

> The language of the Hawaiians retains some traces of a Japhetite origin, some of the forms pointing to an Indo-Germanic-elements [*sic*], whilst the absence of flexions indicates a Hamitic origin. Their course of migration was certainly not east to west.

He also questioned the origin of certain Hawaiian words, implicitly suggesting, by his use of the word "Hawaiianized," that they had been borrowed from European languages: *mauna* 'mountain', *alaula* 'aurora', *like* 'like', *mano-mano* 'many', *mana* 'divine, manes'. On the basis of such resemblances, he asked:

> Are the many Hawaiianized words reminiscences of accidental intercourse, of which all traces are lost, or is the similarity of sound pure accident? I think not; for the foreign words in other languages contradict the hypothesis of accident.

Probably the best-known proponent of the Aryan connection was Abraham Fornander, who published his findings in a three-volume work: *An Account of the Polynesian Race, its Origin and Migrations and the Ancient History to the Times of Kamehameha I.* Even though the study was published piecemeal from 1878 to 1885, the literary community in Hawai'i received advanced notices as early as 1877. Its impending publication was announced in *The Friend* in April of that year, with the following synopsis offered as its theme:

> The Polynesians were originally members of the Arian race, belonging to some outlaying [*sic*] branch of that race in the direction of Susiana and as far as Belouchistan and the head of the Persian Gulf.

For a time, Fornander's theories (along with those developed independently by Edward Tregear in New Zealand) received wide acceptance among scholars. Any flaws that appeared in his argument were certainly not due to a lack of language training: he was well versed not only in Hawaiian, but in classical languages and literature as well (Howe 1988:75). Nor was he unaware of the development of comparative linguistics in Europe. What Fornander failed to do was to keep abreast of refinements in the theory and methodology of the discipline, particularly in the 1870s, when a series of discoveries explained apparent exceptions to laws of sound change formulated earlier. As Elbert described it (1959:1-2):

> [Fornander] believed in an evolutional sequence of languages— an idea long since discarded—and considered the Polynesian languages as remnants of an ancient linguistic stratum from which developed later the inflected Indo-European languages, and by comparison of folk tales and word and spelling similarities he traced the Polynesians back to the highlands of Central Asia and even to Italy. He placed too much faith in genealogies and folk tales as valid historical documents; he did not suspect that superficial resemblances of Hebrew and Polynesian tales might have been due to coincidence, in view of the principle of limited possibilities, or that the Polynesian tales might have been altered so as to attain conformity to Biblical traditions. He was too

credulous. Nor did he realize that accidental word or spelling similarities can be found between almost any two languages on earth, that contemporary likenesses of tongues separated for millennia are usually without significance, as are spelling similarities, and that phonemic similarities of words are indicative of genetic relationship only after attestation of systematic sound shifts and reconstruction of hypothetical parent forms. It has long been known that the Polynesian languages are a simplified branch of the eastern Malayo-Polynesian languages rather than a progenitor, and that they bear no relationship to Dravidian, Indo-European, or Semitic.

In spite of the overwhelming evidence against such arguments as Fornander's, it seems hard to break the habit of building elaborate theories from a few chance resemblances. The most glamorous of these, and one that has commanded some public attention for more than forty years, is that of Thor Heyerdahl, who, by proving that ancient Peruvians *could* have reached the Polynesian islands by raft, proposed that they *did* so, thus influencing the languages and cultures. As for the linguistic similarities, they seem confined to a handful of examples, far outweighed by evidence that Polynesia's connections were to the west, not to the east. But still, the theory lives. And as Robert Wauchope has pointed out (1962:5), the topic sometimes resembles not so much a quiet, contemplative historical and theoretical problem as a battlefield, with divinely inspired books and balsa rafts serving more as ammunition than as evidence.

LANGUAGE VERSUS DIALECT

So far, this discussion has treated Polynesian as a family of languages and Hawaiian as one of those languages. But this view has not always been predominant: the earliest accounts (and many later ones as well) referred to the Polynesian language (in the singular) and to Hawaiian as a dialect of that language, or a dialect of Tahitian.[10] These different terms point to the obvious question: is Hawaiian a separate language or one of many dialects of the Polynesian language?

In the quotation from Anderson and Forster above, the authors begged the question of language versus dialect by referring to five languages, but then stating that they were "radically the same". With Hawaiian added to the collection in 1778, some lay opinion came down firmly on the side of "dialect." For example, as quoted in chapter 3, James King wrote of "catching the sound of Otaheite words in their speech," referring to Tahitian as a dialect. David Samwell wrote that the language of Hawai'i was "the same as that of Otaheite."

John Davies was certainly of this one-language opinion, as shown by the opening sentence of his Tahitian grammar (1823:3): "The inhabitants of most of the numerous Islands of the South Sea, called by modern Geographers by the general name of *Polynesia*, have one common Language, which for that reason may be called the *Polynesian* ... "

In spite of such statements, the question as to whether Hawaiian is a dialect of Polynesian or a separate language is unanswerable on linguistic grounds, for the differences between those terms involve more than language: political boundaries and writing systems often obscure the linguistic relationships. As an example, popular use has established the term "Chinese dialects," but in reality, some so-called "dialects," such as Cantonese and Hakka, are more different than, say, Norwegian and Swedish, which are usually called separate languages.

As another way of looking at the problem, within a language family, LANGUAGE and DIALECT are points on a continuum with SEPARATE LANGUAGES and SAME LANGUAGE at the end points. Thus, it is clear that German and English are separate languages. But are Dutch and Flemish?

Given the impossibility of establishing rigid linguistic criteria for determining whether a particular form of speech is a language or a dialect, we can still ask how observers have tried to measure the immeasurable. The first step seems to have been to examine the degree to which speakers understand each other.

Mutual Intelligibility

The incident mentioned earlier in this chapter—Tupaia's ability to communicate with the Māori—was no doubt the beginning of the notion of Polynesian dialects. Hawkesworth described the first contact (1773 [2]:286–87):

> Tupia [Tupaia] called to them in the language of Otaheite; but they answered only by flourishing their weapons, and making signs to us to depart ... Tupia was again directed to speak to them, and it was with great pleasure that we perceived he was perfectly understood, he and the natives speaking only different dialects of the same language.

However, sociolinguistic factors may have been at work on this occasion. Apparently relations between the crew and Tupaia were not good, since the latter's expectations of deference to his status as chief and priest were at odds with the former's ingrained prejudices about race. Thus, he would have been anxious to succeed in his duties as an interpreter and not to lose face.[11] As for how successful he was, even though we have only the Europeans' report that there was "perfect understanding" between the speaker of Tahitian and the Māori, obviously some communication took place, proven by the results of the crew's efforts to trade goods for fresh supplies.

When the topic of language versus dialect comes up today, scholars point out that in the passage of even 200 years (since first contact), the languages would have changed enough to make them less mutually intelligible than in the late 1700s, especially with Tahitian and its *pi'i,* or word-tabu system. As for an assessment from the present century, Peter Buck (1938:198) claimed that, even though Māori was his first language, he could not immediately understand all that was said to him in other Polynesian languages (see chapter 3, note 13).

For a linguist's view of the problem of language versus dialect, the comments of H. A. Gleason, Jr., serve well (1961:441):

> The very nature of language is such that the problem of classification into such categories as language and dialect is intrinsically difficult or impossible. Several criteria can be proposed, no one of which is satisfactory.

These criteria, Gleason said, were mutual intelligibility and common elements. In discussing the first of these as a test, he noted :

> Intelligibility is a relative matter. Anything from essentially one hundred percent to zero may be found if such a test is applied. How much do two people have to understand of each other's speech to indicate that they speak the same language? Moreover, the matter is much affected by various complicating factors. For example, intelligibility depends on the subject matter ... Intelligibility also depends on the intelligence and background of the informant.

Still, it is commonly agreed that no matter what the "complicating factors," the degree to which people understand each other is important for setting language/dialect limits. To date, the most comprehensive study of this aspect of Polynesian languages is Jack H. Ward's M.A. thesis (1962), which set out to shed light on the problem by measuring mutual intelligibility. His method was to test how well a speaker of one Polynesian language/dialect understood basic vocabulary and short utterances in another. For Hawaiian, some of the scores—that is, the degree to which speakers understood material in another language—were as follows (p. 62):[12]

Hawaiian	Marquesan	41.2%
Hawaiian	Tahitian	37.5%

Hawaiian	Samoan	25.5%
Hawaiian	Tongan	6.4%

Still, as Ward himself noted, no matter what kind of measurement is used, one still has to set an arbitrary figure for the division between language and dialect. And this is where the test becomes subjective.

But leaving aside the question of language versus dialect, Ward's study is a valuable one, because it was the first (and perhaps so far the only) attempt to measure the degree of understanding among pairs of Polynesian languages.[13]

Shared Vocabulary

Gleason's second potential criterion for deciding between language and dialect was to count common elements (usually vocabulary) shared by two forms of speech. This method, called LEXICOSTATISTICS, is often thought to have begun in the 1950s, but actually, it extends almost a century further back in time and—coincidentally—includes Hawaiian in its pedigree.

One of the pivotal figures in the relationship between Hawaiian and the origin of lexicostatistics is Joseph P. Gaimard, mentioned in chapter 3 as having collected the Hawaiian vocabulary published in the works of Jacques Arago, artist on the de Freycinet expedition. In the late 1820s he did the same for another explorer, J. S. C. Dumont d'Urville, who used similar data—not only from Hawaiian, but from five other languages as well (Malagasy, Malay, Māori, Tongan, and Tahitian) —to determine the degree of similarity among the languages.

Dumont d'Urville proposed a scale of six levels to measure the relationship between two forms with a common meaning (Hymes 1983: 83). The values assigned range from ∅ ("words wholly disparate") to 1 ("words perfectly or nearly identical"). Using this scheme, he arrived at a figure of, for example, 0.74[14] for the relationship between Hawaiian and Tahitian.

In a sense, this system anticipated the one developed by comparative linguists: the concept of COGNATE, which assumes that a pair of words in two related languages, similar in sound and meaning, evolved from one earlier form.[15] The method differs, however, in one crucial way: it assigns a higher degree of relationship to words that have not undergone any sound change. As an example, for the following words:

Hawaiian	Tahitian	Gloss
manu	*manu*	bird
lani	*ra'i*	sky

Dumont d'Urville's system would assign the first pair a value of 1, but the second, somewhat less—perhaps only .6 or .8. The comparative linguistic method, however, takes into account the fact that the two differences in the second set are not random but regular. Thus, the second pair is just as important as the first in terms of proving the degree of relationship between the languages.

Dumont d'Urville did not use these figures to determine whether, for example, Hawaiian and Tahitian were dialects of the same language or separate languages; he simply used the term POLYNESIAN DIALECTS without questioning the term. Others, however, have set arbitrary figures: for example, Isidore Dyen's (1965) 70% solution states that two forms of speech with more than 69.9% cognates from a list of (ca. 200) common words can be considered dialects of one language. Dyen admitted that the figure was arbitrary, but tried to justify it with arguments such as: "In general, lists with the same language name, but different local source, have common scores higher than 70.0%" (1965:18). The problem with this argument is that in some places, such as Fiji, a number of so-called dialects have scores lower than 70%. Moreover, although the concept of language name may be sociologically interesting, it has little bearing on wholly linguistic considerations.

SUBGROUPING

In recent years, classifying Hawaiian as a language or a dialect seems to have given way to another activity: determining smaller groups of a language family by examining, for the most part, shared innovations. Information of this kind, combined with findings from the fields of archeology, folklore, navigation, ethnobotany, and others, allow comparative linguists to make reasonable assumptions about the prehistory of a language, especially the relative times at which it split into groups, and these, in turn, into subgroups.

However, the current popularity of this area of study does not mean that it is a new one, for we can take it back at least as far as the 1820s, when John Davies, the Tahitian grammarian, estimated that among the languages he had observed, Hawaiian, Marquesan, and Māori were closest, with Tahitian coming next. Tahitian differed from those, he said, by "abridging the words, and dropping a great number of consonants, and in discarding entirely the nasal *ng*, the *g* and *k*."[16] And Tongan differed from them all; in addition to the different phonologies, he suggested that it may have borrowed many words from Fijian (1823:4–5). A comparative linguist might transform Davies's prose statement into the tree diagram shown in figure 15.1.

FIGURE 15.1
DAVIES'S CLASSIFICATION OF POLYNESIAN

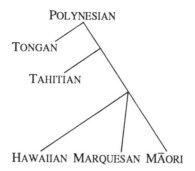

POLYNESIAN

TONGAN

TAHITIAN

HAWAIIAN MARQUESAN MĀORI

One must remember, of course, that Davies, in spite of his astuteness in recognizing regular consonant correspondences among the languages, was relying on his impressions for this scheme, as was Andrews (in the quotation that begins this chapter) in his assessment of the closeness of Hawaiian and Māori.

More than a century later, E. G. Burrows (1938), working from a common assumption that Polynesia was linguistically and culturally divided into east and west, argued for the homogeneity of a western group. This notion is perhaps still current as a lay opinion, but a study by Elbert (1953a),[17] impressive for both its breadth and depth, produced different conclusions. Firmly grounded in the comparative method, but supplemented by Morris Swadesh's "rediscovery" of lexicostatistics, Elbert covered a much wider range of languages (twenty) and used a much more systematic procedure. As a core, he compared approximately 200 "basic" words, but added phonological and morphological information as well. In terms of only the word comparison, his study arrived at the following cognate percentages (p. 159):

Hawaiian	Māori	71%
Hawaiian	Marquesan	69%
Hawaiian	Samoan	59%
Hawaiian	Tahitian	76%
Hawaiian	Tongan	49%

However, apparently on the basis of phonological correspondences (according to Pawley 1966:40n), he grouped the languages as shown in figure 15.2.

FIGURE 15.2
ELBERT'S CLASSIFICATION OF POLYNESIAN

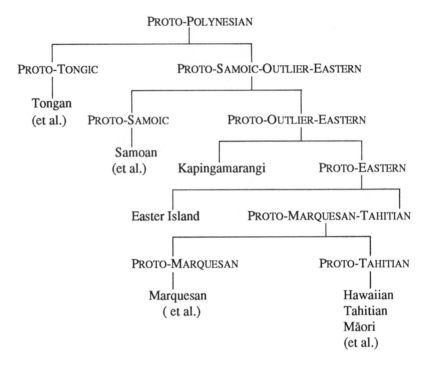

FIGURE 15.3
PAWLEY'S CLASSIFICATION OF POLYNESIAN

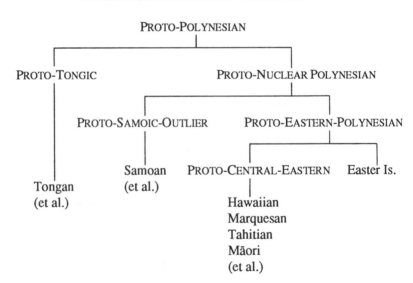

Elbert's study is significant because it refuted the notion of a western Polynesian group centered on Tongan and Samoan (and others), showing that Tongan and a few other languages formed a subgroup by themselves, with other subgroups splitting off. Most later researchers have agreed that the Tongan group belongs on a branch by itself, but have revised the right-hand branch. For example, based mainly on comparing grammatical function forms (such as pronouns, demonstratives, and articles), Pawley (1966) proposed the relationships shown in figure 15.3 (adapted by Clark [1979:258]).

To summarize the relationships shown in figure 15.3: Hawaiian belongs to an Eastern branch of the Polynesian family, which is divided into two groups: Easter Island forming one by itself, and Hawaiian, Tahitian, Marquesan, Māori, and five others forming the other. One of the other major[18] Polynesian languages, Samoan, is separated from Hawaiian by a longer time span, forming a group with a long list of Polynesian languages spoken by small pockets of speakers in Micronesia and Melanesia—outside the Polynesian Triangle—and some in western Polynesia. The last of the major Polynesian languages, Tongan, is separated from nearly all its Polynesian relatives by an even greater time span, making up (along with Niue) its own branch of the family tree.

Glottochronology: Time-Depth Studies

In the introduction to the section above, note the qualifier *relative* in connection with the word *time*. Within this constraint, we can deduce from figure 15.3 only that the division of Proto-Polynesian into Proto-Tongic and Proto-Nuclear Polynesian took place *before* the latter split into Proto-Samoic-Outlier and Proto-Eastern-Polynesian. In a sense, this methodology is the linguistic equivalent of stratification in archaeology: we can be fairly sure which of two events (or artifacts) precedes the other, but it is not clear how much time separates the two, and even less clear just when the events happened (or the artifacts were made).

However, archaeology has developed some ways to deal with absolute, not just relative, time. One of these is dendrochronology, which uses the number and relative width of tree rings to date a wooden object. Another is carbon-14 dating (and some more recent derivatives of this method), which can also give, within a margin of error, "absolute" dates for certain types of materials.

The linguistic parallel to these methods is a technique called glottochronology, an extension of lexicostatistics that assumes that after two languages split off from each other, they lose similarities in their basic vocabulary at a fixed rate, based on language pairs for which written records exist, such as Old English and Modern English, or Latin and Italian.[19]

Using this technique, Elbert (1953a:168) proposed a range of A.D. 930 to 1300 for the settlement of Hawai'i. However, taken on its own, glottochronology has too many variables for it to be considered seriously. Among them are the validity of the established retention rates, variation in the word lists used, cultural factors in word retention or replacement, unreliable sources for the data, and subjectivity in counting cognates. Still, Elbert compared the figures with the possible dates established by genealogies (A.D. 1050) or carbon-14 dating (A.D. 818–1190),[20] and found no serious contradictions. Thus, ideally, glottochronology provides some very tentative dates that need to be verified by other methods of dating, especially techniques used by archaeologists.

CONCLUSION

In his speculation on the origin of the Polynesians that introduces this chapter, Lorrin Andrews concluded by expressing the hope that "ere long ... ample data" would shed light on the problem. Unfortunately, such a revelation did not take place during Andrews's lifetime, for after Humboldt did his important work in the 1830s, most other professional comparative linguists ignored Hawaiian. As for the amateurs, most of them spent the remainder of the nineteenth century and part of the twentieth pursuing a Hawaiian-Aryan connection.

Nor were ample and accurate data forthcoming. It is ironic that for years, comparative linguists have been discussing the finer details of subgrouping while using as their sources of information dictionaries whose accuracy and comprehensiveness are questionable. For an extreme example of the lack of current and accurate data on specific Polynesian languages, we can note Bruce Biggs's comment (1971:467) that for Niuatoputapu, the short word list referred to earlier, collected in 1616, represents the extent of our knowledge about the language.

With Hawaiian, however, a diligent lexicographic tradition has given researchers a sizable data set to work with. Moreover, comparative linguists no longer study just sound correspondences and vocabulary alone, but include grammatical features as well. Thus, although in a chronological sense the origins of the Hawaiian language are slipping further and further away, through new techniques and cooperation among scholars in a wide range of disciplines, Hawai'i's past is becoming not less, but more, visible.

NOTES

---

[1] According to William Marsden (1812:i), "Polynesia" was once applied to the area around the Malayan peninsula—the islands of Sumatra, Java, Borneo, Celebes, and others. Referring to that area as Hither Polynesia, and the South Sea islands as Further Polynesia, he continued:

> The name POLYNESIA, as applied to this tract, was first used by M. DE BROSSES, and afterwards adopted by the late MR. A. DALRYMPLE ...
>
> To shew the general identity or radical connexion of its dialects, and at the same time their individual differences, I beg leave to refer the reader to the tables annexed to a paper on the subject which I presented so long ago as the year 1780 to the Society of Antiquaries, and is printed in vol. vi. of the Archaeologia; also to a table of comparative numerals in the appendix to vol. iii of Capt. Cook's last voyage; and likewise to the chart of ten numerals in two hundred languages, by the Rev. R. Patrick, recently published in VALPY'S Classical, Biblical, and Oriental Journal.

[2] The reference is from Grace 1959:3.

[3] In Lanyon-Orgill's collection of Cook vocabularies, he began with two word lists from the Tuamotus (1979:4-6), but they were almost certainly fabricated by the editor (see Geraghty 1983).

[4] The system of transcription, explained at the bottom of the table, is Anderson's, discussed at length in chapter 4.

[5] "As a result of her active interest, a great survey of more than two hundred languages of Europe and Asia appeared in 1786–1787, edited by the famous German traveller and natural scientist P. S. Pallas. A later edition included also African and American languages" (Pedersen 1931 [1962]:10).

[6] Some common terminology of this field of linguistics, such as *mother*, *daughter*, or *sister* languages, could reinforce such an interpretation.

[7] In one standard historical treatment (Pedersen 1931), Hawaiian does not appear in the index, and only about a page is devoted to Polynesian.

[8] This is based on the title of an entertaining account of such imaginative linguists and anthropologists, Robert Wauchope's *Lost Tribes and Sunken Continents* (University of Chicago Press, 1962).

[9] Mu is a shortened form of Lemuria, the Pacific counterpart of the centuries-old notion of the sunken continent Atlantis. The topic was popularized mainly by James Churchward, who was writing his imaginative works as late as the 1930s.

[10] The topic is not simple, for there are no absolute criteria to distinguish between a *language* and a *dialect*. The derogatory sense comes from popular usage, which somehow assigns a lower status to dialect. Writing comes into play as well: some years ago a national news magazine reported that certain

missionaries in New Guinea had made a written *language* out of a spoken *dialect*.

[11] Alan Moorehead (1966:39n) drew on the writings of John Marra, a crew member, who noted that Tupaia was "by no means beloved by the *Endeavour's* crew, being looked upon as proud and austere."

[12] For this and the following tables and figures, the number of languages has been reduced to show only the "major" ones: Hawaiian, Tahitian, Marquesan, Samoan, and Māori.

[13] But as Ward correctly pointed out (p. 57), this test measured the performance of individuals. To satisfy us statistically, it would have to be broadened to cover a much larger sample.

[14] Hymes found a minor error in the calculations and corrected the figure to 76%.

[15] George W. Grace (pers. comm., 1992) has noted that, technically, the words would no longer have to be similar in form and meaning if we had adequate historical records to show that once they were the same form. But for the lexicostatistical method, these criteria have to hold.

[16] For his evidence, Davies was using methods far ahead of his time. For example (p. 4), he discussed the consonant relationships among several Polynesian languages, as well as Fijian. That is, he didn't merely list related words, but noted that there were relationships between *t* and *k*, *h* and *f*, *n* and *ng*, and *l* and *r*.

[17] Written in collaboration with William H. Davenport, Jesse W. Dykes, and Eugene Ogan.

[18] That is, in terms of the number of speakers.

[19] Interestingly, the origin of the method goes back not only to Dumont d'Urville's Polynesian lists, but also to the work of Horatio Hale, discussed in chapter 12.

[20] Carbon-14 dates from more recent studies fall in this range as well. For example, Pawley and Green (1973:20), based on archaeological evidence presented by Patrick V. Kirch, deduced that Hawai'i was settled in the ninth century A.D. However, more recent studies have pushed that date back considerably. In 1985, Kirch wrote (p. 68):

> ... it is probable that the first settlement of Hawai'i occurred sometime *before* the fourth to fifth century. At present, it is difficult on strictly archaeological grounds to be more precise as to the date of initial colonialization of the Hawaiian Islands. In my own view, given that a number of permanent settlements were distributed throughout all the main islands by the sixth century, it is likely that the first colonalization occurred some two or three centuries earlier, perhaps by A.D. 300.

However, Kirch noted that not all his colleagues agreed with him.

CHAPTER SIXTEEN

Language and Power: The Past, Present, and Future of Hawaiian Language Policy

-0-0-0-0-0-

The rapid increase of a mixed race, as compared with the continued diminution of pure Hawaiians, seems to point to an early day, when the pure Hawaiian race will have given place to a mixed race compounded from several diverse stocks, but all speaking the English tongue (Sereno E. Bishop, The Friend, *November 1891).*

The language lives, with an astonishing resilience. It graces the conversations of older folk and not only those who dwell in Kona or Niʻihau; it is heard in the prayers uttered at weddings, funerals, family gatherings, meetings of clubs and societies, and dedications of buildings, offices, restaurants, and highways. It is spoken in fishing villages and cattle ranches. It quickens the songs and chants accompanying dances and rituals, whether solemn or profane. And it wells up daily in our speech and thoughts, almost in unconscious response to our island heritage ... (O. A. Bushnell, in the Foreword to Harold W. Kent's Treasury of Hawaiian Words *[1986:xi]).*

It must be said at the very outset that the first several companies of missionaries to Hawaiʻi did not intend to replace Hawaiian with English—at least, not in the beginning. On the contrary: they were instructed by their head organization in Boston "to give [the Hawaiians] the Bible in their own tongue, with the ability to read it for themselves ..." (Bingham 1847:60).[1] As Laura Fish Judd wrote (1880:78): "It was a maxim with the Mission that in order to preserve the nation, they must preserve its speech."

However well intentioned, this philosophy illustrates one of the many ironies of the period. In any society, language, culture, and the nation make up a three-legged stool, ready to topple if just one leg is removed—as it was in Hawaiʻi with the rapid destruction of many parts of the culture.

And even the second leg—language—was not so secure, for the protective attitude of some missionaries toward it was not shared by all. Nor was this stance necessarily a permanent one, as Bingham himself suggested (1847:103): "The progress of a generation or two may so alter the circumstances of the nation as to make the use of the English more feasible and useful."

These "altered circumstances," especially in the 1890s, figure prominently in the near demise of the Hawaiian language. But the seeds of change were sown a century earlier, for a language policy of sorts was put in motion as soon as the first English speaker set foot on Hawaiian soil.

LANGUAGE CHOICE

Looking back over the past two centuries of dynamic tension[2] between Hawaiian and English, we find that at different times and for different reasons, knowledge of the one language, and then of the other, was seen as a source of power. And, as in any language conflict, politics, religion, and economics were prominent in the fray.

The Early Period

Because of the increasing number of foreign visitors to Hawai'i after 1790, especially those who spoke English, it was only natural that Hawaiians should make a connection between the English language and the power and material wealth displayed by those who spoke it. The Hawaiians may have called English *namu haole* 'foreign gibberish', but they were quick to recognize the advantages of knowing how to use it. For example, we saw in chapter 13 that in 1809, Kuakini (a.k.a. John Adams) had wanted Archibald Campbell to teach him English, but another haole resident had objected, saying, "They will soon know more than ourselves." However, as the number of Hawaiians who had learned the language aboard trading ships grew, foreigners found it impossible to hoard English and dispense it at their discretion.

Kuakini was only one of a number of chiefs who expressed an interest in learning English. For example, ten years later, just two weeks after the arrival of the *Thaddeus* in 1820, the king (Liholiho) was "ready to try to acquire the act of spelling and reading our language, though unable to speak it ..." (Bingham 1847:92).[3] But here, rank complicated the educational process: the king was not willing to allow commoners to acquire the knowledge before he himself did (ibid., pp. 106–7):

> Liholiho, moreover, when he learned with what promptness we could teach reading and writing, objected to our teaching the common people these arts before he should himself first have acquired them. His self-respect thus manifested was on the one hand encouraging, for we wished him to take the lead, and on the other, embarrassing, for we wished to bring the multitude under instruction, without reference to the distinctions of birth or rank.

(Here we can observe one of the first ideological conflicts between the Hawaiians' hierarchical system and the New England missionaries' principles of selective democracy.)

From the missionaries' point of view, the only advantage to using English in the early 1820s was that it was a temporary way to communicate until they could speak Hawaiian well enough to handle the difficult topics of persuasion and conversion. Even the chiefly passion for English waned somewhat when the first printing in Hawaiian produced nearly two decades of frenzied interest in literacy in that language. From the mission press alone, from 1822 through the middle of 1845, there issued 149,911,383 pages, largely in Hawaiian (Bingham 1847:615). This basically religious and educational material was supplemented by newspapers, government documents, and—beyond the world of print—personal letters. In short, the spoken language was sustained and bolstered by the written language—a kind of literature perhaps different from the American and European concept of the term, but nonetheless, literature.

The Transitional Period

Still, it was inevitable that English would have some effect on language policy in Hawai'i. What is disputed is the extent of this effect in the nineteenth century. According to John E. Reinecke (1969:30),

> at the same time that the Hawaiian language was clothing itself with a literature in the Western style,[4] profound changes in the social and economic life of the natives and in the structure of the population were rapidly weakening the vitality of the native tongue.

Jumping ahead in his narrative several decades, Reinecke proposed that as part-Hawaiians grew in numbers (admittedly only "2.8 percent of the whole Hawaiian stock" in 1866), they "drove the wedge of bilingualism, of language dualism, deeper and deeper" (p. 31).

John Charlot (in progress, Appendix) has pointed out that even Reinecke himself, some fifty years after he wrote the M.A. thesis on which the published version is based, realized that he had underestimated the strength of Hawaiian, which continued until perhaps the second decade of the twentieth century. Charlot then, through a careful reading of Hawaiian-language sources, refuted many of the generally accepted statements of the rapid decline of the language in the nineteenth century.

Still, it is clear that English was on the rise, even in the early 1800s, and that the number of bilingual Hawaiians was also increasing. From the Hawaiian point of view, however, perhaps it is misleading to discuss bilingualism as if it were a conscious goal. It is much more likely that many Hawaiians took their own language for granted and wished to be able to speak and understand English as well, for although they were still fascinated with the written word in Hawaiian, this type of literacy was not an immediate stepping-stone to success and power in the rapidly changing world that intruded on their own. Perhaps it was as a reaction to such unfulfilled expectations that the Chiefs' Children's School was founded in 1839. As described in chapter 13, the king and chiefs requested Amos Starr Cooke and his wife, Juliette Montague Cooke, both teachers and members of the Eighth Company of Missionaries, to "educate the young chiefs of the Hawaiian nation." "For nearly a decade the Cookes were responsible for the important and delicate task of teaching the young chiefs those things which would be required of them to properly lead their people in the difficult transitional days to come" (*Missionary Album*, p. 74).

In its fifth year of operation, the Royal School, as it came to be called, was described in *The Friend* (1 January 1844), with the following comment on language policy: "The plan of instruction is, to begin with the English language—to accustom the pupils from early years both to read and speak it."[5] Such a policy was not always easy to carry out, as Mrs. Cooke noted (Richards 1970:48): "The scholars appear interested in their lessons, but it is very hard teaching in English." But later her husband reported (p.173):

> All their studies have been and are still in the English language. Hitherto they would have learned more if their studies had been pursued in native, but from this time forward they will learn a great faster for having the English language. They now use very little native even among themselves in common conversation.

Still, Hawaiian was not forbidden: one can find occasional quotations in Hawaiian from the students, particularly in Mrs. Cooke's portions of the diary. Moreover, her own English prose contains a liberal sprinkling of Hawaiian words.

The Royal School was immensely influential in Hawai'i's history for the next fifty years, for the class lists read like a Hawaiian *DeBrett*.

For example, *The Friend* (1 August 1844) included the following *ali'i* in its list of the Royal School's prominent pupils:[6] Alexander Liholiho (successor to Kamehameha III), Moses Kekūāiwa (hereditary Governor of Kaua'i), Lot Kamehameha (later Kamehameha V), William Chas. Lunalilo (first elected king), Jas. Kaliokalani (brother of Kalākaua and Lili'uokalani), David Kalākaua (last reigning king), Victoria Kamāmalu (last *Kuhina Nui*), Bernice Pauahi (granddaughter of Kamehameha and founder of the Kamehameha Schools), Emma Rooke (later queen consort), and Lydia [Lili'uokalani] Kamaka'eha (last sovereign of Hawai'i). The fact that these future leaders attended the Cooke school does not guarantee that any of them chose to speak English to the exclusion of Hawaiian outside the context of the school. But as the quotation above shows, the students became very proficient in English.

On the other hand, another prestigious school, serving the children not of chiefs but of missionaries, instituted a program to add Hawaiian to an otherwise classical curriculum (Alexander and Dodge 1941:276-77). In 1867, William D. Alexander, president of Punahou School,[7] drew up an outline for the study of Hawaiian, which the trustees adopted. From a modern perspective, it seems an innovative proposal, especially since Alexander considered the Hawaiian newspapers (in addition, of course, to the Bible) the most appropriate reading material. Examinations were to be based on:

1. A thorough knowledge of grammar (via Alexander's own grammar [1864])
2. A critical reading of at least one of the Gospels
3. Courses in writing Hawaiian and translating in both directions
4. A knowledge of common terms in Hawaiian schoolbooks.

Moreover, Alexander realized the limitations of learning from the written language alone (Alexander and Dodge 1941:290):

> We would add that the study of the language from books will be of little avail, without the frequent use of it in conversations with the natives themselves.

Still, in the next report (ca. 1870), the written, and not the spoken, word seemed to prevail (op. cit., p. 290):

> During the whole of the past year, classes have been exercised in writing Hawaiian, and I hope that some of our scholars will do good service in enriching the native literature by translations, and by aiding the native newspapers.

In 1873, apparently finding it difficult to provide a permanent teacher, the trustees voted that the president "communicate with the American Board in regard to teaching the Hawaiian language" at Punahou (p. 323), an action that seems to have ended the program.

LANGUAGE IMPOSITION

In spite of differing opinions on the suitability of teaching English to the Hawaiians, by the middle years of the century, that language had certainly made inroads into the educational system. However, the Cookes' school, just described, catered only to royalty. What of the commoners—those masses who Lorrin Andrews doubted could ever learn to control English at the level of native speakers? Here, the elements of power and control again come into play. When, in the early 1840s, it was asked if it would be "practicable and beneficial to introduce the English language entirely," the older missionaries were opposed to such a move (Wist 1940:70):

> There was obviously the fear that the introduction of English might tend to remove the natives from the close influence of the missionaries, who among the foreigners in the Islands were the most conversant with the Hawaiian language.

Also they feared that English would draw the Hawaiians from the land to the port areas, throwing them into contact with the "less desirable foreign element."

However, by at least the 1850s, the commoners too were slated for instruction in English. Reinecke reported (1969:44):

> No one seems to have questioned that some English should be taught in some of the schools. The practical question was in what proportions the foreign and the native language should divide the schools. The general opinion probably was that instruction should for the most part be given in the Hawaiian language, and that this was for the maintenance of a separate Hawaiian nation.

In this quotation, the important word is *proportions*. In many of the opinions cited, it is difficult to decide now whether the writer advocated that Hawaiian supplement English or replace it. Some contemporaries chose the latter interpretation, For example, on 10 April 1846, Rufus Anderson, corresponding secretary of the Mission board in Boston, wrote (ibid., p. 44n.):

> I trust you will not fall in with the notion, which I am told is favored by some one at least in the government, of introducing the English language, to take the place of the Hawaiian. I cannot

suppose there is a design to bring the Saxon race in to supplant the native, but nothing would be more sure to accomplish this result, and that speedily.

Richard Armstrong, who left the Mission and served as minister of public instruction from 1848 until his death in 1860, was a strong supporter of English in the schoolroom (ibid., p. 45n.):

> Were the means at our command, it would be an unspeakable blessing to have every native child placed in a good English school, and kept there until it had [acquired] a thorough knowledge of what is now, in fact, to a great extent, the business language of the Islands, and which would open to its mind new and exhaustless treasures of moral and intellectual wealth.[8]

Some outside observers, however, expressed strong opinions about the eventual winner in the struggle between the two languages. Berthold Seemann, naturalist aboard H.M.S. *Herald*, commented on the linguistic picture in the late 1840s (1853[2]:89):

> Although [English] is taught in the higher schools, yet few Hawaiians can speak it with any degree of fluency, and by far the greater number are ignorant of it. The peculiar construction of their own, disqualifies them in great measure for acquiring foreign languages. English however is rapidly gaining ground, and after the extinction of the aboriginal race it will become the vernacular tongue. In Honolulu nearly all the boatmen, and those connected with shipping understand it tolerably well, but speak it in a broken and disjointed manner. The chiefs have generally a good knowledge of English, and several converse in it fluently.

A novel theme here is that the structure of Hawaiian prevented its speakers from learning another language. However, Seemann contradicted his own assumption by observing that some chiefs already spoke English well and that soon, all Hawaiians would.

A more modern appraisal attacked Hawaiian from another angle. Educationist Benjamin O. Wist seemed to disapprove of the Hawaiian schools of that period because they were not progressive, whatever that means in terms of educational theory (1940:135):

> Very little had been attempted before 1870 toward curriculum reconstruction. Retarding influences lay in the use of the Hawaiian language with its lack of extensive literature, in the inadequate facilities for the training of teachers, and in the almost universal faith in the three R's.

Obviously, a "back-to-basics" movement lay far in the future.

From what one can glean from the various reports from the educational authorities, it was only lack of money, not desire, that kept them from conducting every school in English, even though Armstrong paid lip service to the linguistic integrity of the nation (Reinecke 1969:45n.): "The language of a nation is a part of its very being and never was and never will be changed except by a very gradual process." Armstrong's statement is, of course, self-contradictory: in one phrase he claimed that the language would not be changed, but then in the next said that the change would be gradual. Moreover, what did Armstrong mean by "gradual"? Did he envision a century-long process? Or one of a decade or only a few years?

Whatever the answer, the position of Hawaiian education was being weakened, the result of a number of events or conditions that, even taken singly, could have sapped the strength of the language:

1. Because Hawaiians had no immunity to certain imported diseases, their numbers were drastically reduced.
2. There were many obstacles to education in the vernacular: for example, the difficulty of producing materials in every subject, for every grade level, and in adequate numbers for the entire student body.
3. The increase in the number of immigrant laborers from a number of different language backgrounds made vernacular education an impossibility. As for their being educated in Hawaiian, it was the Portuguese who turned the tide toward English. Wist wrote (1940:73): "Particularly did the influx of Portuguese from the Azores Islands affect enrollment; for among early groups of new laborers, only the people from these Islands brought with them their families. Their choice of language for the instruction of their children was naturally English in preference to Hawaiian."
4. Teacher training in Hawaiian was also difficult. (See Reinecke 1969:49n., quotation from *Report of the President of the Board of Education to the Hawaiian Legislature*, 1884, p. 11: "Why worry over the quality of teachers in Hawaiian? We shan't need them much longer, anyway.")

The final push for the replacement of Hawaiian by English came from an unexpected development late in the century: a resurgence of "heathen" practices that Christianity had overlaid but had not completely stamped out.

THREATS TO POWER

As a contrast to the enthusiastic reports of the late 1830s that show the extent to which some Hawaiians had been pulled away from their own culture and religious beliefs, some decades later the voice of the Mission was much more pessimistic in tone. For example, in April 1889, the Reverend Sereno Edwards Bishop,[9] editor of the Mission publication *The Friend*, wrote (p. 27):

> If it be asked why sixty-eight years of Christian teaching has not availed to lift the Hawaiian people out of the mire of impure living, if it be thus efficacious, its teachers would point to the great increase of adverse influences for the last thirty years, and to the direct fostering of sorcery and *hulas* by authority during that time, and latterly to the promotion of hardly concealed worship of the gods.[10]

To explain the previous thirty years of pernicious backsliding, Bishop noted that for the majority of Hawaiians, the changes wrought by conversion were only superficial, and even for those who had been genuinely converted, "the more Christian minority gave place by death to another generation far less strongly impressed and less fervid in religious interest."

Bishop's comments were part of an article entitled "Why are the Hawaiians Dying Out." In the previous installment (March 1889, pp. 18–20), he listed these causes: unchastity, drunkenness, oppression by the chiefs, infectious and epidemic diseases, kahunas and sorcery, idolatry, and wifeless Chinese. His condemnation of the indigenous culture included this fulmination:

> One of the foul florescences of this great poison tree of Idolatry is the *Hula*. This is most intimately connected with the whole system, and forms an essential part of its services, just as Sacred Music does of Christian worship. The *hula* dances are habitually idolatrous in practice, having their special patron gods, whom the dancers invoke and worship. The chief posturings and movements of the *hulas* are pantomimes of unnameable lewdness, illustrated and varied with elaborate art, and accompanied with chants of unspeakable foulness of diction and description. This is the Sacred Music of Idolatry, its Opera and its Drama.

The late flowering of the hula, an art form that was suppressed during the height of the conversion frenzy, was matched by the resurgence of another segment of Hawaiian culture, even more reviled and feared by the missionaries—the *kāhuna* 'priests'. Both these symbols of pre-Christian Hawai'i were reinstated, or at least encouraged, during the Kalākaua reign, juxtaposed against the Victorian institutions of 'Iolani Palace, the court, and their retinue.

Diaries, records, photographs, and now the exquisitely restored palace show us the European trappings of royalty, with a Hawaiian overlay of *kāhili* and *koa*. Was the proportion of English to Hawaiian similar? It is unlikely; Reinecke (1969:36–37) wrote of the nativism of the Kalākaua court, a protest against the submersion of the upper (chiefly?) classes.

This revival of old traditions was displayed most conspicuously at the belated coronation ceremony for Kalākaua in 1883, celebrating also the completion of the palace in the previous year (Daws 1968:219–20). As part of the festivities (a combination of European and Hawaiian traditions), the king included hula performances. On this occasion, a language matter became a legal one, for the printed hula program was declared obscene, and William R. Castle[11] brought charges against one of Kalākaua's aides and the printer. Witnesses reported that it was traditional for poetry to honor body parts; others, no doubt referring to *kaona*, or hidden meanings, "testified that Hawaiian was a very ambiguous language" (ibid., p. 220). The lower court convicted the printer, but the Hawai' Supreme Court overturned the decision. Ironically, the judge did not dispute that the material was obscene, but ruled for acquittal only because the defendant, who allegedly did not know Hawaiian, was ignorant of the meaning of the words he had printed.[12]

Kalākaua dismissed such criticism as ignorance on the part of foreigners, and he (ibid., p. 220)

> continued to encourage his official genealogists in their reconstruction of the family lines of the old ruling chiefs; he collected and stored the stripped bones and feather cloaks of great men of the distant past; he supported legislation to permit the Hawaiian kahunas to practice their version of medicine legally;[13] he had the Hawaiian creation chant, the Kumulipo, recorded in writing for the first time; and he formed a secret society, Hale Naua [Nauā], whose object, according to its constitution was "the revival of Ancient Sciences of Hawaii in combination with the promotion and advancement of Modern Sciences, Art, Literature, and Philanthropy".[14]

Although the *kāhuna* did not head Bishop's list of reasons for the decline of the Hawaiian population, the topic became more and more prominent in the editorials of *The Friend* in the early 1890s, showing the reaction to another shift in the power structure in Hawai'i. As examples of the effect of this movement on one segment of the population, note the following warnings. In the September 1890 issue, the Reverend James Bicknell wrote (pp. 66-67): "Kahunas are centers of influence, and they do a vast amount of mischief in inciting the people to maintain their allegiance to the aumakuas (gods)."

A few months later (April 1891, p. 25), Bishop returned to his earlier theme of the forces at work to annihilate the Hawaiian people:

> Education, culture, religion, social and temperance reform are hard at work to save this noble and interesting people. But the Saloon has been set open to craze them. The Hula has corroded them with its leprosy. The majority succumb to drunkenness and social vice; and the Kahunas stand by to thrust them down into still earlier graves. And so the people are wasting away. Shall no Prince or prophet arise to lead the Hawaiians upward to purity and health? It may soon be too late.

In the June 1891 issue of *The Friend*, there was a complaint about the disruptive influence of the *kāhuna* and *'awa* in the marketplaces, mentioning a conflict between native priests and evangelists. In October, in an article entitled "Kahuna Work," the author complained of the "tenacity of Hawaiian superstition." In July 1892, the editor warned that the *kāhuna* were an obstacle to Westernizing the Hawaiians:

> Another and most poisonous effect [of the kāhuna] is in antagonizing the Hawaiians to civilized ideas and enlightened guidance. The Kahuna is the deadly enemy of Christian civilization. He and enlightenment are sworn foes, and he does his utmost to create aversion and jealousy toward the haole and particularly the "missionary." He organizes and consolidates the *heathen party*.

Other complaints were that the *kāhuna* interfered with the work of *haole* physicians, that they proposed that people with Hansen's disease no longer be segregated,[15] and that they wished to dismiss the Board of Health and create a Kahuna Board of Health. The writer continued: "We cannot be governed by Pulolos,[16] or by people of any of that turn of mind."

The following condemnation is from another church publication (*Twenty-Ninth Annual Report of the Hawaiian Evangelical Association, June 1892*, p. 13). It first raised the specter of a "colossal evil of a superstitious feeling that dallies with fetishism and spirit-worship," and continued:

> It must be frankly confessed that the power of this superstition rests as a pall on the spiritual life of the people. It has freely invaded the churches. It has been kept alive since the first by the

arts of the kahunas (medicine men). It has been very generally revived by the encouragement they have received in past years from persons high in authority. Licenses were granted to native Kahunas in 1864 [corrected in pen to 1868], and ever since these heathen doctors have been practicing their devilish arts on the people. From them the Hawaiians have received incalculable harm.

Apparently, from *The Friend*'s editorial point of view, there was no end to the corrupting influence of the *kāhuna*; at the time of the over-throw of the monarchy in 1893, Bishop wrote that they had encouraged the "half-maddened Queen."[17]

It was also Bishop who brought language into the discussion. In his paper on the topic of the diminishing number of Hawaiians (reprint-ed in the Blount Report, pp. 769–77), he concluded:

> Book knowledge, and even the much vaunted education in English, have sadly failed to arm Hawaiians against succumbing to superstition and its kindred impurity, either in the ranks of the lowly or lofty.

Thus, it was not enough to arm the Hawaiians with English. The next logical step was somehow to *dis*arm them.

A REMEDY FOR NATIVISM?

The 1890s were obviously a troublesome time for foreign interests in Hawai'i, both sacred and secular. Traces of Hawaiian culture, thought to have been subdued, kept resurfacing to threaten those in power. Even the most drastic political action—the overthrow of the monarchy—was not necessarily a permanent one: any coup can be subject to a counter-coup. It is obvious that one segment of foreign power—the second-generation missionaries (at least the most vocal ones)—had an almost pathological fear of the *kāhuna*'s ability to incite their audience to backsliding, sin, and even worse, insurrection. What was one possible solution? The *kāhuna*'s power could be reduced by taking away their audience. And this goal could be effected in just one generation by suppressing the Hawaiian language. If bilingualism had failed (the "much vaunted education in English" referred to above), then monolingualism (in English) might succeed. Such a move might also eliminate another thorn in the sides of the latter-day missionaries, for it would neuter the offensive and obscene (from the foreign point of view) language of the hula.

It is impossible to *prove* a direct relationship between discourag-ing the use of Hawaiian and crushing "nativism." However, if one refers to the latter by the euphemistic term "Americanization," it is easy enough to find clear statements of such a connection. For example, note this opinion from the Reverend Dr. Charles McEwen Hyde (*Blount Report*, p. 825):[18]

> The Americanization of the islands will necessitate the use of the English language only as the language of business, of politics, of education, of church service; and open the wide field of English literature to a people who have only poorly-edited newspapers and a meager number of very rudimentary manuals as their textbooks in science, as their highest attainments in culture.

Here, the intent is unambiguous: both the language and culture should be replaced, but only in certain areas.

The Forbidden Language

Even before the forced Americanization of the Hawaiians in the 1890s, educators attempted to foster the use of English by forbidding the use of Hawaiian. For example, Wist (1940:112), writing of the beginnings of The Kamehameha Schools in 1887, noted that William B. Oleson,[19] the first head, forbade the language to be used on the school grounds:

> Oleson, being a strict disciplinarian, did not propose to leave to chance the *esprit de corps* he desired ... Strict rules were set to prevent the use of other than the accepted tongue [English] on the campus.

In the early 1890s, a move was made by at least one arm of the church, the North Pacific Missionary Institute, to change the language of instruction from Hawaiian to English for students of a different type: those studying to be missionaries. The head of the organization, Hyde, whose views on the connection between the English language and the Americanization of Hawai'i are quoted above, gave the reason that the courses would be only "rudimentary in actual scope and reach" until English was the language of instruction. He continued (*Thirtieth Annual Report of the Hawaiian Evangelical Association, June 1893*, p. 26):

> The time seems close at hand, if it has not now actually come, when, in the new era of social development, with the accomplished change in the character of the national government, the attempt can hopefully be made to re-organize the work of the Institute, and make instruction through the medium of the English textbooks and reference books a prominent feature of the work of the Institute.

Thus, according to Hyde's logic, the change of government in January 1893 would somehow smooth the transition from Hawaiian to English.

The Moribund Language

In the last decades of the nineteenth century, those schools with instruction conducted in Hawaiian had a difficult time with both finances and personnel: more money was spent in schools in which English was taught,[20] with the result that the more qualified Hawaiian speakers who might have improved the quality of the schools chose better-paying occupations. The statistics in table 16.1, gleaned from Reinecke's fuller tables (1969:70–72), illustrate the dramatic drop in the number of Hawaiian-language schools and students.

TABLE 16.1
COMPARISON OF HAWAIIAN AND ENGLISH SCHOOLS

	Schools conducted in Hawaiian	Number of students	%	Schools in (or offering) Eng.	Number of students	%
1880	150	4,078	57.0	60	3,086	43.0
1886	77	2,018	22.4	95	6,998	77.6
1892	28	552	5.2	140	10,160	94.8[21]
1895	3	59	0.5	184	12,557	99.5
1897	1	26	0.2	191	14,496	99.8
1902	0	0	0.0	203[22]	18,382	100.0

The figures in table 16.1 are corroborated by statistics from a different source, an article on the history of education in Hawai'i (Alexander and Atkinson 1888): in 1878, the schools that taught in Hawaiian contained 61.8% of the total school population, but in 1888, only 15.7%. According to the authors, the reason for such a decline was

> the desire of the Hawaiians to have their children taught the English language. Petition after petition is constantly being received by the Board asking to have the Common Schools [i.e., those taught in Hawaiian] changed into English Schools. The result will be then in a very few years more the Common Schools will have ceased to exist.

The near-fatal blows to the Hawaiian-language schools were struck during the 1890s, when various educational policies not only ignored the language, but took deliberate steps to insure its demise—a stance

William E. H. Tagupa called "a concerted government policy of neglect and opposition" (1981:68). *The Biennial Report of the President of the Board of Education* (1890:22–23, quoted in Tagupa, op. cit.) considered the Hawaiian-language schools

> useful in places where it is absolutely impossible to obtain teachers who know anything of the English language ... In such places funds at the disposal of the Board hardly warrant the expenditure of even twenty dollars a month upon a teacher.

The most drastic step was described by Kalena Silva (1989:86–87):

> In 1896, three years after the overthrow of the Hawaiian monarchy by American expatriates, a law was passed which made the use of Hawaiian in schools illegal (Territory of Hawaii 1905:156). As English was then the sole legal language of instruction and the only language permitted on school grounds, children on all islands, with the exception of Niʻihau, were forced to abandon Hawaiian [in the schools].

The following quotation shows the understated reaction of one educationist, Wist (1940:219–20), to the way the linguistic balance between Hawaiian and English had shifted in just two decades:

> Perhaps the most interesting development in Hawaiian educational history was the change from the Hawaiian to the English language. Its use became almost universal before the end of monarchy. By legal enactment the English language was made the sole medium of instruction in the public schools during the period of the Republic.

Note also the use of the neutral word *change*, absolving the writer from the responsibility of discussing cause and effect. More recent opinions have been far less detached. For example, Larry Kimura asserted (Heckathorn 1987:50): "Hawaiians didn't lose their language. It was taken away from them deliberately."[23]

This political action did not, of course, spell an immediate end to the language, but it limited its use. It also meant that fewer foreigners learned Hawaiian, enabling those who did know it to use it as a kind of code if the situation demanded. An enduring example of this function of Hawaiian is the protest song of the period, "Kaulana nā Pua," with its ironic contrast between the sweetness of the melody and the bitterness of the text, which uses such phrases (translated) as "When the evil-hearted messenger comes/With his greedy document of extortion"; and "No one will fix a signature/To the paper of the enemy/ With its sin of annexation/And sale of native civil rights." As Martha H. Noyes described it (1993:22):

Only a handful of the new rulers understood the Hawaiian language. The song could be sung in the faces of the oligarchy, and they would only hear a pleasant Hawaiian melody, ignorant that in fact the very singing of the song was spit cast in their eyes.

But perhaps this is an overstatement, for at least one segment of the non-Hawaiian population still knew the language well. On 3 June 1895, Albert Francis Judd, son of Gerrit Parmele and Laura Fish Judd, delivered an address to the Hawaiian Evangelical Association, commemorating the arrival of the first American missionaries to Hawai'i seventy-five years earlier (*Thirty-Second Annual Report of the Hawaiian Evangelical Association, June 1895*, pp. 68–79). He spoke in Hawaiian.

THE RESULTANT LANGUAGE[24]

As laws were passed favoring English as the language of instruction and discouraging, even forbidding, the use of Hawaiian, one of the major threats to business, American nationalism, and Christianity was considerably reduced. The following quotation, from a report by the Reverend Dr. McArthur (*The Friend,* December 1895, p. 96) is particularly revealing of the motives that underlay such laws:

> The English language will be taught in all the public schools. For a time all former methods of mission work have been disarranged; but now there will be adjustments to new conditions ... The present generation will generally know English; the next generation will know little else. *Here is an element of vast power in many ways* [emphasis added]. With this knowledge of English will go into the young American republican and Christian ideas; and as this knowledge goes in, *kahunaism, fetishism and heathenism generally will largely go out* [emphasis added].

The most charitable interpretation of the writer's use of the word "power" is that it would be granted to the new generation of Hawaiians speaking English. However, the elimination of "kahunaism, fetishism, and heathenism" was definitely the goal of the outsiders, especially the missionaries.

In 1903, an anonymous writer[25] in *Paradise of the Pacific* predicted:

By the end of this century Hawaiian speech will have as little usage as Gaelic or Irish has now ... The native children in the public and private schools are getting a good knowledge of English, and, indeed, it would be doing them an injustice to deny them instruction in English speech.

The writer noted that those who spoke only Hawaiian found it difficult to find jobs, a reversal of the situation thirty years earlier, when foreigners needed to learn Hawaiian in order to do business.

The Changed Curriculum

Reflecting the statistics shown in table 16.1, the 1897 course of study for elementary schools began with a plan for the first year, conspicuous for its failure to mention the Hawaiian language at all (p. 3):

LANGUAGE—Teach children to express in English what they perceive and what they do in the schoolroom, on the playground, on the way to school, and at home.

Here, Hawaiian was not overtly, but covertly, discouraged: in a subtle way, the directive to describe home activities in English was a beginning at supplanting Hawaiian in even that domain.

In some of the courses of study (e.g., for 1897 and 1899), Hawaiian history played a small role in the curriculum, but again, the language was not mentioned at all.

The following mandate is an example of the official policy in 1905 (*Revised School Laws*, p. 8):

Sec. 211. ENGLISH LANGUAGE, BASIS INSTRUCTION. The English language shall be the medium and basis of instruction in all public and private schools; PROVIDED, that where it is desired that another language shall be taught in addition to the English language, such instruction may be authorized by the department, either by its rules, the curriculum of the school, or by direct order in any particular instance. Any school that shall not conform to the provisions of this section shall not be recognized by the department.

(Note that there is a distinction here between a language used as the medium of instruction and one that is taught as a subject.)

The law was essentially the same in the 1911 version. Thus, only a decade into the new century, instruction *in* or even *about* the Hawaiian language had become very much the exception, rather than the rule.

RESUSCITATION

In a surprisingly short time, such educational policies had the inevitable effect of cutting the language off at its roots. Many children may still have learned Hawaiian as their first language, but once Hawaiian instruction in the schools vanished, they found fewer and fewer opportunities to use the language outside the home. Thus, as the number of Hawaiian-language schools fell, the average age of native speakers rose. In 1919, J. McMillan Brown, described as the chancellor of the University of New Zealand[26] and writer on Polynesian topics, observed while traveling through Hawai'i that when his companion "spoke to the young people in Hawaiian, he received no answer" (1919:571). Brown, although an outside observer, was familiar with language policy matters in New Zealand, where, in contrast to Hawai'i, Māori was still taught in the schools. Obviously with this contrast in mind, he noted: "The worst of it is that when this generation of natives is gone, the language also will be dead." After describing the effects of English on a number of other subdued languages, he concluded (p. 573):

> It seems to me that it is the duty of a civilization that is wiping out an old culture and language, to provide for the conservation of what remains of them, and the study of their past ...
>
> Before it is too late, the legislature should see to it that there is a chair in the College of Hawaii devoted to the ethnology and language of the Hawaiians ...

Some observers from within the Hawaiian culture felt the same way. In 1917, a writer to the newspaper *Ka Puuhonua o na Hawaii* complained (26 January):[27] "There is no child under 15 years of age who can converse correctly in the mother tongue of this land." As we saw earlier, some writers, looking into the future, had warned that the Hawaiian nation (that is, race) could not survive without the Hawaiian language. For this writer, that particular future was just around the corner:

> A person is recognized as belonging to a particular nationality by his or her language. If the mother tongue of some particular nationality should vanish, then that nationality shall certainly vanish as well.
>
> Today, we no longer have our independence, and when we lose our language, that will be the end of the Hawaiians as a people.

However, the writer did more than forecast doom; he or she proposed a solution. First, the legislature should be persuaded that Hawaiian should again be taught in the schools. If that proved impossible, then the Hawaiian people should build schools for themselves. Finally, church services and Sunday schools should be conducted in Hawaiian. The writer ended with this eloquent plea:

> I hope that there will come a day when Hawaiian schools will once again stand on our land. But let us begin now to teach our children the Hawaiian language in the Sunday schools. All children should read the Hawaiian Bible, and we should not allow them to be instructed in English in our churches. If we begin by taking this stance, it won't take more than a few years and the Hawaiian language will flourish again. If it is difficult to obtain the support of the legislature, let us initiate things in the churches. O Hawai'i, send your children to the churches that conduct their Sunday school lessons in your mother tongue.

If there were any responses to this suggestion, the efforts were short-lived. However, in the next decade, some of the institutions that had, by forbidding the use of Hawaiian, contributed to the drastic fall in the number of speakers took steps to reverse the effects of their earlier policy.

Hawaiian Language Teaching in Primary and Secondary Schools

It is ironic (but perhaps predictable) that less than forty years after the founding of The Kamehameha Schools and the prohibition against using Hawaiian on the school grounds, it was felt necessary to teach the language as a subject (Wist 1940:115):

> The introduction of the study of the Hawaiian language in 1923 furnishes interesting evidence of a great change in the cultural and linguistic background of Hawaiian life occuring [sic] since the founding of the Schools in 1887. At that time Hawaiian was forbidden in order that English might be learned; by 1923 the former language had become so reduced in extent or effectiveness of use that its reintroduction seemed necessary, as a medium through which students of Hawaiian parentage might develop appreciation of the rich cultural background of their race.

Thus, whether intentionally or not, the language had been rendered harmless, since the subtleties, nuances, and emotional content that can be learned only through use had been, for the most part, lost. The kind of language learned from the inadequate grammars, dictionaries, and textbooks of the period could constitute a threat to no one.

However, notwithstanding Wist's assertion that instruction in Hawaiian was indeed introduced at the Kamehameha Schools, Harold Winfield Kent, the schools' president for sixteen years just after the end of World War II, provided a different view of the same event, bringing in another variable: the attitude of this generation of Hawaiians whose children might be affected by such a change in curriculum (1976:31–32):

> In the [Frank E.] Midkiff era [1923–1934] a sincere attempt was made to institute a formal and conversational course in the Hawaiian language. An excellent grammar was written by Mr. Midkiff. *There was however strong opposition from the parents and the project was abandoned* [emphasis added].

Here, then, we see how successful the campaign was, whether it was accidental or deliberate, to instill in Hawaiians a contempt for their own language. However, over the years, opinion changed. Kent continued:

> For many years to follow, Kamehameha touched lightly upon the teaching of the native tongue. It was made an elective in the Boys School and later an elective course in both upper schools. More recently it was introduced as a seventh and eighth grade required course. None of these efforts had the promise of permanent long range continuation of language study. What was needed was a sequence of perhaps three years in the high school. A course of this kind would have to be checked with the University of Hawaii for acceptance, a textbook written, tapes prepared and a teacher selected. Students, mindful of the limitations of possible future use of the language, would have to be located to assure a satisfactory class. All of these items were brought together in the summer of 1961. Mrs. Dorothy Kahananui was selected to do the work.[28] The University agreed to accept the three year program on the same basis as any modern language—Spanish, French, German. Mrs. Kahananui wrote a text for the first year's program and then proceeded to teach a class of twenty youngsters. The experiment worked exceedingly well. The first year course was revamped and a second year text prepared. The third year course would follow. It was hoped before it became too late that some of these students would have gone to the University to take further work in the Hawaiian language and qualify as teachers or users otherwise of this important course.

As for instruction in Hawaiian in the public schools, in the school laws for 1922, the section dealing with language was amended as follows (p. 26): "... provided however, that the Hawaiian language shall be taught in addition to the English at all normal and high schools of the Territory ..."[29] In the laws for 1928 (p. 24), the section remained mostly the same, but (p. 17) there was added (section 50) a notice that $2,000 was set aside for the "preparation, printing, binding and publication of school text books in the Hawaiian language."[30] Note that, as before, the phrase "in the Hawaiian language" is misleading as to whether Hawaiian was to be the topic or the medium of instruction. However, it is clear from the resulting work—Mary Atcherley's *First Book in Hawaiian* (and its subtitle, *A Text Book in the Hawaiian Language*)—that the former was meant.

Atcherley's small book has already been discussed as a primer (chapter 14). Now we look at the part it played in the territorial legislature's effort to reintroduce Hawaiian into the school curriculum. As with its previous role, it is difficult to find anything positive to say about *First Book in Hawaiian* except that it was the only work available. And as for the legislature's plans, they were—at best—farcical, and—at worst—insulting to the language and culture, for they proposed to teach the language with an embarrassingly inadequate text, no trained teachers, and no program with which to train them. However, in spite of these drawbacks, the program continued: in 1939, Henry P. Judd stated that five public schools in the territory taught Hawaiian at that time (1939b).

Jumping ahead a few decades, we find in the 1962 version of the *School Laws* (pp. 28–29) explicit instructions as to the time allotted to Hawaiian in particular schools, but no reference to trained teachers or adequate texts:

> ... and that daily instruction for at least ten minutes in conversation or, in [*sic*] the discretion of the department, in reading and writing, in the Hawaiian language shall be given in every public school conducted in any settlement of homesteaders under the Hawaiian homes commission ...

In the 1966 version, there are no entries in the index for *Hawaiian, language*, or *foreign language*, the attention to language apparently being devoted to raising the standard of English in all schools, now that the "English Standard Schools" had been abolished.[31]

Hawaiian Language Teaching at the University Level

At about the same time the public schools were considering adding Hawaiian courses to their curriculum, the University of Hawai'i was discussing the same matter. In 1921, the board of regents reported to the legislature (quoted in Kimura 1978):

> The matter of giving instruction in Hawaiian has received a good deal of serious consideration. Because of the very slight literature in the Hawaiian language it would seem desirable to combine instruction in Hawaiian with a wider study of the related Polynesian languages. The difficulty which has confronted us has

been that of finding anyone who was competent to give instruction of college grade in this field. It is not yet certain just how the
problem can be solved and it may be necessary to train someone
especially for the work.

Here, in contrast to the program proposed for the public schools,
we have evidence that planners had a realistic view of their task. Finding qualified teachers was indeed a problem,[32] and continues to be one.
The first teacher, Fred Beckley, who taught from 1921 to 1927, presents
something of a paradox. Although his wide experience with languages,
as well as his status as a "scholar of the Hawaiian language" (Kimura
1978:10), would seem to make him an ideal choice as a language teacher
at the university level, a competent speaker of a language is not necessarily qualified to teach or explain the language. Unfortunately, the only
evidence we have of Beckley's ability to explain the language is two
short articles (1926, 1932), and these show little understanding about
language in general and Hawaiian in particular. The following excerpt
quotes the first four sentences of the earlier article (1926:511):

> The Hawaiian language is a very simple language—all you
> have to do is to understand and appreciate one thing, that is the
> whole language in a nutshell. The Hawaiian language reduced to
> writing requires the use of five vowels and seven consonants, and
> you know some of the consonants are hardly pronounced for the
> simple reason that the Hawaiians have held themselves more aloof
> from the invasion from the Indian Ocean particularly, less in touch
> with the Javanese hordes, so that our language remains more like
> the primitive Polynesian than the rest from the South. If you
> follow the Southern dialects you will find more harsh consonants
> than used in Hawaii, and that is because the Hawaiian, to go back
> to time immemorial, had just his language and his religion.
> Expressing his ideas was as a child of nature speaking direct from
> the heart—everything goes out soft, sweet, musical.

Perhaps Beckley was trying to praise the language and its
speakers, but his naive comments turn the clock back to Noble Savage
times.

Still, the university did the best it could with what was available,
and a course in the Hawaiian language was first announced for the 1921–
1922 academic year: "Hawaiian language 1. A beginner's course in
reading, writing and speaking Hawaiian." More advanced courses were
offered in the following years (Kimura 1978:34–36).

Although enrollment figures for 1921–1938 are not available, those
for 1939 and 1940 show about 200 students per semester, a figure that
declined markedly with the beginning of World War II, rose somewhat

in the postwar years, and fell to a low of 27 in 1961–1962 (Kimura 1978:51–57).

For much of that period—at least until the end of the 1940s—Hawaiian was considered an easy course that attracted football players (Kimura 1978:16; Elbert 1989:132). When Samuel H. Elbert began teaching the language in 1949, his standards were higher, and gradually the reputation of Hawaiian language classes changed. In his own words, he "considered the Hawaiian language so precious that it should be taught as rigorously as French or German" (Elbert 1989:132).

RENAISSANCE

Like various periods of a rebirth of interest in literature, art, and culture in European history, the renewal of interest in the Hawaiian language and culture in the 1970s did not relight an extinguished flame, but fanned and fed the embers kept alive by dedicated scholars during the linguistically dark ages of the preceding years.[33]

Even in the late 1930s a renaissance was mentioned. In the preface to his Hawaiian grammar and glossary (1939a:3), Henry P. Judd wrote of an "increasing interest in the language of the Hawaiian people, amounting to a renascence in Hawaiiana." He expanded on this theme in a short article (1939b), explaining that an increase in tourism and more interest in Hawaiian music was responsible for the revival. However, a significant difference between this so-called renaissance and the one that followed several decades later is that for the former, the increased interest in Hawaiiana seems to have come mainly from outside the Hawaiian community itself. In contrast, the support that Hawaiiana now enjoys comes mainly from within the community.

George S. Kanahele, often credited with bringing the movement to the attention of the public, included language in the various cultural activities experiencing a surge of interest (1982:5):

> Another way to tell if a people are serious about reviving their culture is to see whether they are studying their language. Hawaiians, both young and old, are doing just that. Not only Hawaiians, but others as well. Not too many years ago you were lucky to get a handful of students registering for a Hawaiian language class at the University. Now there are hundreds of students each year ...
>
> Times have changed ... When I was attending Kamehameha, I had three choices in language study: German, French and Spanish, with Latin offered one year. Today students at Kamehameha and other private as well as public schools have Hawaiian classes.

How else can you explain this widespread interest in learning what some have called a "non-functional" language other than in terms of a cultural renaissance?

Whatever name one might attach to the movement, enrollment in Hawaiian language courses has climbed dramatically. For example, for just the University of Hawai'i at Mānoa, the comparative figures are as follows:[34]

1961–1962	27
1973–1974	623
1992–1993	1,277[35]

The increase in teaching staff and number of courses taught is also dramatic: in 1961-1962, one teacher handled four courses on the Mānoa campus. In the fall of 1993, nine full-time instructors, three native speaker consultants, and thirteen lecturers taught thirty-nine sections of the various courses, which can be as many as twenty-four in number (*Catalog for the University of Hawai'i at Mānoa*, 1993–1995).[36]

In addition to a very active Hawaiian language program at the University of Hawai'i at Hilo, the language is also taught at various community colleges, at the Mānoa campus through continuing education courses , at a number of high schools as evening courses , and even through private ventures, not only on O'ahu, but on the other islands as well.

However, in spite of the large increase in the number of students statewide, there is still no Hawaiian-language degree available higher than the baccalaureate and no training program for potential Hawaiian language teachers who want to teach at the university level.[37] Moreover, some departments at the University of Hawai'i offer doctorates in Hawaiian subjects without requiring some knowledge of the language (John Charlot, pers. comm., September 1993).

The Media

In chapter 9, we saw something of the early history of Hawaiian-language newspapers. Until the electronic media entered the picture, these newspapers were the principal means, other than the spoken language face-to-face and textbooks, by which communication in Hawaiian was carried on. However, newspapers, at least the secular ones, were commercial enterprises, and as the readership declined, so did the number of publications. Esther K. Mookini wrote (1974:xiv): "In 1948, when *Ka Hoku o Hawaii* ceased, there remained only ... a religious publication." The following statistics (ibid.) show the rapid drop in the number of such newspapers in the early years of the twentieth century:

1910	9 secular	3 religious
1920	5 secular	3 religious
1930	2 secular	1 religious

As the number of Hawaiian-language newspapers dwindled rapidly, there began in Hawai'i another medium, which had at least the potential of compensating for the meager supply of Hawaiian reading material. Radio broadcasting in Hawai'i, which began in May 1922, was an opportunity for the sound of the language itself—not just its trace in print—to reach a great number of potential learners. However, histories of the medium in Hawai'i show no evidence that in the 1920s, 1930s, and 1940s radio was recognized as a means of preserving and promoting Hawaiian. Or if it was, perhaps the project was impossible to finance. In 1953, the general manager of one station suggested Japanese language radio programs for Hawai'i (Hollinger 1953), but in his discussion of the multilingual population of the territory, he did not mention the possibility of Hawaiian broadcasts. However, at that time, people of Japanese ancestry made up 40.4% of the population, as opposed to 2.7% for Hawaiians.

From 10 April 1950 to 31 December 1951, the Reverend Edward Kahale produced a series of five-minute weekly sermons in Hawaiian (Kahale 1973). But the project neither lasted nor grew: a little over ten years later, in a study of foreign language broadcasting in Hawai'i (Klopf and Highlander 1965), there is no mention of Hawaiian, although programs in Japanese totaled 397 hours a week.

In the early 1970s, with the renewal of interest in the language and culture, this situation changed. Jonah Hau'oli Akaka described the origin of *Ka Leo Hawai'i*, which was then one of only two Hawaiian language radio programs in the world (1991:29):

> First organized by Kauanoe Lindsey Kimura and the Hui Aloha 'Āina Tuahine nearly 15 years ago,[38] Ka Leo Hawai'i features varied guests and topics weekly in a one-hour[39] Hawaiian language program co-hosted by Puakea Nogelmeier, Tuti Kanahele and Hau'oli Akaka. Ka Leo Hawai'i allows an opportunity for all—Hawaiian speakers and non-speakers—to bring the Hawaiian language into the home once more, via radio ...

Still, an hour a week is far below the figures for some other non-English language broadcasts. But it was not only a beginning but the inspiration for other Hawaiian broadcasts as well, such as a program on KTUH hosted by Iokepa De Santos: a Hawaiian music program conducted in Hawaiian. "With the number of Hawaiian speakers increasing rapidly, De Santos envisions the day when a commercial radio station

like KCCN will have their [*sic*] own music program *i ka 'ōlelo Hawai'i*"
(Nobori 1992).

In late January 1994, Hawai'i Public Radio began broadcasting a
five-minute Hawaiian-language news program Monday through Friday,
"Ke Aolama." A mixture of wire-services and print media news, items
of particular interest to the Hawaiian community, and proverbs from *'Ō
lelo No'eau* (Pukui 1983), the program is translated by university
language students (Yang 1994).

It is interesting to contrast Hawaiian radio policies with those of its
sister language, Māori. First of all, the overall systems are different.
Until recently, New Zealand radio, modeled on the British Broadcasting
Corporation system, was supported and administered by the government. In August 1986, it was announced that a Māori radio network
would be set up "as a priority." By May 1987, such a station had begun
broadcasting, mostly in Māori, on a trial basis. However, the 1989
Broadcasting Act, which established a government agency with the
objective "to promote Maori language and culture in broadcasting
through a network of Maori radio stations which reach Maori population areas of ten thousand or more," resulted in the birth of about twenty
iwi, or tribally based, stations.

Even though this picture is encouraging in theory, the reality is less
attractive. With less than 3% of the population as native speakers, the
remainder—after a thirty-year gap in which they had little contact with
the language—are not ready for a steady diet of language and culture.
Thus, much of the required seventy-two hours a week air time has to be
filled with deejay patter and "commercially successful" pop music.

In 1983, one of the two television channels began telecasting a
news program in Māori, *Te Karere* ('the messenger'), first two, then
five, and later ten minutes a day, five days a week. Within the general
television organization, a Māori department is responsible for news and
music broadcasts, as well as occasional documentaries. In 1987, a third,
all-Māori, channel was proposed, but as of mid-1993 had not come
about.

Both the differences between the funding structures of Hawaiian
and New Zealand television and the wide difference in the number of
speakers (i.e., potential viewers) mean that there is little likelihood (at
least in the near future) of a Hawaiian-language television channel. And
aside from some short series (*Pūnana Leo*, etc.), there have been no
regular television programs in Hawaiian, either on commercial or public
channels.[40]

IMMERSION PROGRAMS: HOPE FOR THE FUTURE?

Hawaiian is by no means the only Polynesian language in danger of becoming extinct; again, we look at Māori for comparison. After examining the falling numbers of native speakers of Māori, Bruce Biggs (1981:ix) concluded that in fifty years from the time of writing, children would learn only English, and that Māori would be

> used increasingly only in formalized, non-casual situations. Greetings and farewells will continue to be in Maori, but conversations will tend, more and more, to be in English. Formal speeches will begin and end in Maori but the *kaupapa* or body of the speech will often be in English. In church, prayers and hymns may continue to be Maori but the sermons will tend to be in English. More and more Maoris will use the language as an identity card, shown for a moment to establish one's Maoritanga [Maoridom], then returned to an inner pocket.

How the situation has changed can be seen below.

It is easy to point out parallels with Hawaiian. The rapid decline in the number of native speakers would relegate the language to an esoteric relic of the past, preserved in the *hula* by loyal keepers of the flame, or a static trace of a living language, recorded only on street signs and maps, and in a limited number of newspapers and texts held in archives.

Notwithstanding the sharp increase in the number of students in Hawaiian language classes over the past two decades, those concerned with the survival of a language on the brink of extinction have realized the futility of trying to preserve Hawaiian by teaching it to students for a few hours a week. Thus, the failure of such courses to affect the decreasing numbers of speakers of Hawaiian as a *first* language, in spite of some success in producing competent *second*-language speakers, has resulted in a reversal of conventional language-survival tactics.

Pūnana Leo

Earlier in this chapter, we saw that even by 1917, some Hawaiians were concerned that children under fifteen years of age were no longer competent speakers of their native language. If such a decrease in both the quality of the language spoken and the number of speakers had continued unchecked, there would be only a handful of able speakers alive today. But in the intervening years, some of the efforts to preserve the language have succeeded, and the figures are not as low as they might have been. Still, an estimate of 2,000[41] (Heckathorn 1987:48) is depressingly low, and the statistics become even bleaker when the age of the speakers is taken into account. Because most of them are elderly, "they will take the language with them when they die" (ibid., p. 48).

Certainly, these older speakers themselves have felt disheartened, not only for the future, but for the present as well: there are few people with whom they can speak Hawaiian. In 1977, Dorothy M. Kahananui, who was then teaching Hawaiian at Queen Emma's Summer Palace, reported that some retired teachers had made just this complaint. "Mrs. Kahananui suggested that they use [Hawaiian] in conversations with their grandchildren whom they often baby[sat], incorporating it into English sentences a little at a time until the children [were] familiar with each word or phrase and comfortable using it" (Segrest 1977:11). At the same time, Sarah Quick, Hawaiian language teacher at Kamehameha Schools, heard a similar complaint from the other end of the age range: her students. She suggested that they use their grandparents as a language resource. As another example of this cross-generational approach to language learning, Robert Snakenberg, who was then teaching at Kailua High School, began night classes for the parents of his language students (ibid., p. 12).

These seeds of an idea—using elders as resource people to teach the young—did not germinate for several years. Interestingly, it took a project developed by the Māori to inspire today's program for teaching Hawaiian to preschoolers in a monolingual environment.

In spite of Biggs's predictions for the future of Māori (quoted above), at first glance, its status seems very different from that of Hawaiian. Surveys in the 1970s showed that there were about 70,000 native speakers, a figure that would seem to place the language a comfortable distance from extinction. However, that number was from a total Māori population of some 300,000. And as with the Hawaiian figures, a look at the ages of these speakers was revealing: "Most native speakers are over forty years of age and in many tribal areas there are only a handful of native speakers who are under forty" (Douglas and Douglas 1983:1). Specifically, "less than one percent of Māori five-year-olds entering schools are native speakers."

In 1982, the Department of Māori Affairs established a program to teach the language to preschool Māori children. Named *Ngā Kōhanga Reo* 'language nests', this program was designed to expose infants to a Māori language environment daily for four to five years (ibid., p. 7).

Both the idea and the name have been borrowed into Hawaiian, resulting in *Nā Pūnana Leo*. In these "language nests," children between the ages of three and five hear and speak only Hawaiian for ten hours a day, five days a week. In short, it is a total immersion program. In the fall of 1992, there were 131 children enrolled in Pūnana Leo schools in the islands. Moreover, the parents have some responsibilities as well, ranging from participating in field trips to helping prepare "cut-and-paste" books to helping with janitorial duties (Laiana Wong, pers. comm., August 1993).

Immersion Programs in the Public School System

One of the main problems connected with the Hawaiian preschool immersion program has been to find a way to maintain and improve the language skills learned in the "language nests." The solution, instituted in 1987, has been to continue the program through primary education. At present (January 1993), six public elementary schools on Oʻahu, Kauaʻi, Maui, Molokaʻi, and Hawaiʻi use Hawaiian as the medium of instruction from kindergarten through the sixth grade,[42] serving about 500 children (*Ka Leo O Hawaiʻi*, 10 February 1992; Ramirez 1993: F6; figures updated by Noʻeau Warner). The program was slated to be extended through the eighth grade by 1994.

In February 1992, in response to pressure from those interested in preserving the language (including parents), the Board of Education approved a policy that would allow students in two high schools—one on Oʻahu and one on Hawaiʻi—to be taught in the Hawaiian language as well.

These hard-won advances, reversing the policies set by educational authorities nearly a century earlier, come with their own set of problems. In addition to resistance from the Department of Education, one of the main obstacles to the acceptance of the program is that some people have interpreted it not as *pro-bilingualism* but as *anti-English*. When the matter was still being debated in the legislature, A. A. Smyser warned, Cassandra-like, that such a move would be divisive (*Honolulu Star-Bulletin,* 26 February 1991). Later (24 March 1992), after the bill had passed, Smyser, drawing on his "instincts," predicted that the K–12 immersion program would "do both students and the community a long-term disservice." He then produced the opinions of an "educator" (but a specialist in politics and American studies, not in linguistics or languages), Lawrence Fuchs, who, in praising the virtues of *E Pluribus Unum* as a national characteristic, seemed to choose his own candidates for which features should be *pluribus* and which *unum*. Fuchs questioned whether schools should offer instruction "in a language that is spoken by a minuscule fraction of the world's population" and assumed that students in such a program would have no English at all:

> But how can we in good conscience take English away from
> these kids when it has become the international language of com-

merce, diplomacy and so many other parts of the world in which they are forced to live?

Such a point of view is ironic in light of earlier arguments in favor of teaching English to the Hawaiians: in the 1880s, some advisors maintained that the home environment, supplemented by an hour or two of reading and writing, was sufficient to preserve Hawaiian (Reinecke 1969:49). Might then the home environment, supplemented by several hours of TV and reading, suffice to preserve English?

It is no surprise that Smyser's "uninformed commentary" (as one critic called it) produced a flurry of letters, mostly critical. Possibly the most compelling argument against his point of view was a repeated theme that Hawaiians have a right to learn their own language.[43]

One exception to the critical majority was Billie Beamer (*Honolulu Star-Bulletin,* 14 March 1991), who also seemed to interpret the program as one that would produce monolinguals in Hawaiian, thus denying children the intellectual benefits of a putative 6,000,000-word English vocabulary for the sake of a 25,000-word Hawaiian vocabulary.[44]

What such arguments ignore is that the cultures and the educational systems of a number of countries, Switzerland one of the most conspicuous, produce bilinguals and even trilinguals. Just because the United States seems to have had a tradition of glorifying monolingualism does not mean that such a policy need continue.

This is not to say that the program is free from problems, the most obvious of which is the lack of teachers. However, the College of Education is now training teachers for the elementary level in the immersion program. At present, there are twenty-six teachers; six new teachers will be required each year, not allowing for attrition.[45] Still, most of these teachers are not native speakers, and the models of pronunciation they present to the students will vary widely. Thus, most students will not have the chance themselves to learn a native pronunciation (Gigi Glover, pers. comm., August 1993).

Another problem that has plagued Hawaiian language studies from the very beginning is the need for more and better reference and reading materials. The inadequacies of existing grammars and primers has already been pointed out (chapters 12 and 14). And it should be obvious that the Pukui-Elbert dictionary, although sufficient for adult learners, is not appropriate for children. As for reading material, in the last few years, quite a number of readers have been produced for the lower grades, but now, it is the older students who are at a disadvantage. A prominent example of the need at this level for better reading materials is the fact that for over thirty years, Fornander's *Hawaiian Antiquities and*

Folk-lore (Elbert 1959) has been used as an advanced reader, but except for the notes and list of illustrations, the entire text is lacking glottal stops and macrons. However, teachers are now beginning to tap the rich store of nineteenth- and early twentieth-century newspapers and books, annotating the material where necessary, and adding the essential glottal stops and macrons so that students are not forced to play guessing games as they read.[46] In addition, the Center for Hawaiian Language and Culture, University of Hawaiʻi at Hilo, has recently begun *Nā Maka o Kana*, a Hawaiian-language newspaper for students, offering readers a blend of traditional lore and current issues.

Thus, some of the problems connected with Hawaiian language teaching are being addressed. And in spite of those that remain, the immersion programs offer a glimmer of hope that the language will continue, an idea that seemed impossible as recently as twenty years ago.

CHANGING THE LANGUAGE

> *Since the time of Kamehameha the Great the Hawaiian tongue has been almost revolutionized, so many idioms have crept in and so many English expressions with Hawaiian spelling and pronunciation have been adopted. The old fashioned natives living in the country districts have an extensive vocabulary of words with which the younger generation in the city are wholly unfamiliar. A venerable native came over from Kauai a short time ago to visit his son, who is pure Hawaiian, and after they had conversed a few minutes the elder one exclaimed in Hawaiian: "You talk like a foreigner!" (The Hawaiian Language, 1903).*

This quotation touches on the most obvious kind of language change: an influx of new words, and the obsolescence of old words as a culture evolves. However, other parts of the language change as well. As a result of the long gap in the natural development of Hawaiian, some grammatical structures have been lost and others introduced. Such changes, observable in the differences between nineteenth-century text material and the language of today's classroom, suggest a concept almost certain to have been imposed from the outside: a standard language. For how do we know what Hawaiians considered "correct" or "incorrect" in their language? We can read in early reports the opinions of outsiders, such as those discussed in the early chapters about the (reportedly) poor language skills of the Hawaiians who had spent years abroad or on ships, or the inability of some residents to serve as translators. As for differences in pronunciation, we can find a wealth of commentary on the varying consonants in different parts of the islands. Finally, in a few cases, we can read about vocabulary differences from place to place. But was there one particular type of pronunciation, or the vocabulary of one region, that was considered "standard"? In spite of the lack of such a precedent, the nature of institutionalized education demands a degree of uniformity in the kind of Hawaiian now taught.

The Search for Standard Hawaiian

According to Reinecke (1969:29), the effects of English on Hawaiian (other than through borrowed words) could first be seen in the Hawaiian-language newspapers. But Reinecke gave no specific examples of such effects, basing his statement on an interview with the Hawaiian scholar John H. Wise in 1933. Another scholar of that period, John F. G. Stokes, reported that Samuel M. Kamakau (whose works are more widely known through an English version based on a series of articles for a Hawaiian-language newspaper) was "careless of his particles." But what does this mean? And according to whose standards? One problem may have been that the writing system at that time was still an imperfect way to represent the spoken language: for example, both *a* and *ā* are grammatical particles. But until fairly recently, no distinction was made in their written form. The same held for *e*, *ē*, and *'ē*; and *o*, *ō*, *'o*, and *'ō*. Moreover, some writers tended to ignore a single-vowel grammatical particle when it followed a word ending with the same vowel.[46] It is unlikely that these orthographical problems reflected any change in the speech of Hawaiians.

But did the notion of "Standard English" have an effect on Hawaiians' attitudes toward their own language? Possibly. We saw in chapter 8 that even in the 1980s, some Hawaiians believed that the Bible was the "best example of the language ever put in writing." As a reaction to such a statement, one wonders, first, about the size of the sample for comparison. Next, could translating from English to Hawaiian have fixed in the minds of many Hawaiian speakers (and eventually, teachers) a number of misconceptions about grammar and style—for example, that every sentence must have a subject and a predicate, that every noun must be marked for number, or every verb marked for tense? The earliest grammarians were careful not to make such assumptions: in Lorrin Andrews's treatment of tense (1854:103), he noted that the "grand divisions of past, present and future are somewhat distinctly marked; but in practice they run into each other." By the time Henry P. Judd produced his watered-down "complete grammar," verbs were neatly categorized into present, past, perfect, pluperfect, and future (1939a:8–11). Had a type of "learnéd" Hawaiian, based partially on the grammars, primers, and translations of the nineteenth century, become "Standard Hawaiian"?[47] Or was Judd merely an inept grammarian?

There was, however, aside from any ideas of correctness imposed on the language from mistranslations or inaccurate grammatical descriptions, a special type of Hawaiian—an "elevated," courtly style. However, we are told less of its nature than of its apparent demise (Reinecke 1969:37):

> The break-up of the royal court with its literary hangers-on was probably the critical blow to the prestige of elevated Hawaiian speech. Dispersed throughout the Islands, with no chiefly patron to look to, the composers of chants in the ancient manner and the masters of the meaning of the elevated poetic style no longer had a strong incentive to pass on their knowledge and attainments to their children. Literary Hawaiian began rapidly to disappear. John H. Wise told the author in 1933 that "probably I could count on the fingers of my two hands" the Hawaiians who could at that date understand the inner meaning [*kaona*] of the old poems.

Charlot (in progress, Appendix, pp. 16–17), however, disputed the idea that "literary Hawaiian" disappeared, quoting Ethel Moseley Damon, who wrote in 1935 (p. 465) that Hawaiian poetry was still a vital part of the culture—as it is today. Charlot's point here, and elsewhere in his work, is the idea, common today among language professionals but perhaps not so well known among the laity, that linguistic change is not only normal but inevitable. Perhaps Hawaiian poets of today cannot understand all the *kaona* in older works, but neither can today's English writers interpret the metaphors of yesterday without an annotated text.

Still, the sheer mechanics of formal language instruction seem to demand some kind of uniformity, even if it has to be imposed on the language. At the time the goal of Hawaiian instruction was changing from reading traditional texts[48] to learning a living language, Emily Hawkins wrote (1982:vii–viii):

> The Hawaiian language, as it is spoken and written today, represents many differing views on "correct" grammar. The *kū-puna* speak a language which they learned by reading the Bible and Hawaiian language newspapers while communicating orally with their *mākua* and *kūpuna*. Most of the new generation are learning Hawaiian by taking classes in the schools and university. These classes rely heavily on texts which have been written in "standard" Hawaiian. This standardized system is heavily based on the early grammars of Andrews and Alexander and native writings from 1840 to 1920, including works by Nakuina [Nā-kuina], Kamakau, Malo, Fornander, Ii ['Ī'ī] and Haleola [Hale'ole]. In using a standard which is based on the language as

it was spoken[49] nearly a hundred years ago, we teachers are opening ourselves for attack that the language we teach does not represent spoken Hawaiian of the 1980's.

In spite of the fact that some critics use the terms "University Hawaiian" or "UH dialect" for the type of language learned through tertiary instruction, it is impossible now to teach the kind of Hawaiian spoken two centuries ago. The language *has* changed and will continue to change, so long as it is still living. Some of those interested in the language, such as linguists, are concerned primarily with documenting those changes. However, others, sometimes termed language planners, are concerned more with influencing the direction and number of such changes.

The Académie

Like similar bodies set up for other languages (e.g., the Académie française), the 'Ahahui 'Ōlelo Hawai'i has been concerned with certain matters connected with the use of Hawaiian, especially spelling and the introduction of new words into the language.

Spelling. Even though adopting an official Hawaiian orthography in 1826 settled most of the spelling problems that had plagued the missionaries, there still remained a few smaller but troublesome matters. One of these, an unnecessary *w* added in some words (after the rounded vowels *o* and *u*), was noted by Lorrin Andrews as early as 1838 (p. 395):

> The letter *w* could, in many cases, be dispensed with, as *o au* would be the same as *owau*. Some Hawaiians write *o Akea*, the name of one of the ancient gods; others write *o Wakea*.

(Even though Andrews reported that Hawaiians themselves varied their spelling, it is possible that they were influenced by speakers of English, who have a *w*-glide after the vowels *o* and *u*.) The spelling recommendations of 1978 deleted this extra letter in certain words: *o wau* was indeed changed to *o au*. Other examples are *auwē* 'alas' and *kauwā* 'slave', which are now spelled *auē* and *kauā*.

Other corrections involved vowel length incorrectly marked in a number of words in the edition of the Pukui-Elbert dictionary then current, certain conventions of capitalization, the use of letters to indicate non-Hawaiian sounds in some words, the elimination of the apostrophe to indicate "dropped" letters, the use of hyphens, the writing of compounds,[50] and word division.[51]

One questionable recommendation concerns vowel length in one-syllable grammatical markers, some of which shorten in certain positions.[52] The most consistent way to deal with this variation is to write the markers long and describe the conditions under which they shorten. However, the vowel length in some of these forms seems to have been decided by vote rather than by investigation. Another problem in the spelling of such markers is that some that appear to be homophones are written differently to keep their meanings separate. These practices are counter to the phonological structure of the language and require that the language learner memorize the spellings.

New Words. In the period of Hawaiian's near dormancy following the 1890s until the renaissance of the 1970s, the language did not entirely encase itself in amber. For example, in the preface to the first edition of the Pukui-Elbert dictionary (1957), the compilers claimed to have included "recent vocabulary additions of World War II," and later editions contain translations of (for example) *atomic, computer,* and *escalator.*[53]

The point should be made that as lexicographers, Pukui and Elbert considered themselves recorders, not coiners, of words. Now, however, it has become necessary to create words. In an interesting repetition of history, language planners today find themselves facing the same problems that confronted the missionary-translators in the 1820s, 1830s, and 1840s: courses taught in Hawaiian, especially in the sciences, require a great number of new words. The demise of the last secular Hawaiian-language newspaper in 1948 meant that after that, for the most part, the only "literature" written in Hawaiian was an occasional language textbook. And until recently, the reference materials for teaching the language seemed to concentrate more on developing skills to translate old material than on those needed to discuss current affairs.[54] Thus, the flow of new words coming into the language had slowed down to a mere trickle.

As a result, advisory groups have found it necessary to coin words for such concepts as *charge account, aerobics, aerosol, air conditioner, smoke alarm, all-terrain vehicle, aluminum foil,* and *automated-teller machine.*[55]

As we saw in chapter 10, there are many different ways of enlarging a language's vocabulary. Realizing this, an advisory committee, now called Ke Alelo ka Hoe Uli, has produced lists of new words (*Papa Hua'ōlelo*), prefaced with a set of guidelines that ranks the legitimacy, as it were, of vocabulary, both old and new:[56]

1. A word that already appears in the Hawaiian-English dictionary.
2. A word not in the dictionary, but heard from native speakers.
3. A Hawaiian phrase that translates an English word.

4. A word made by broadening the meaning of an existing
   word.
5. A borrowing that has been "Hawaiianized."
6. A new compound or derived form.
7. A word made by shortening a word or several Hawaiian
   words.

Note that true borrowing (#5) is fairly low on the list,[57] not an
uncommon attitude among policymakers for other languages as well.
However, speakers themselves do not always share this disdain for
borrowed words. For example, in formal German, the word for 'tele-
phone' is *Fernsprecher*, a compound of native elements, literally 'distance speaker'. But in spite of the official sanction that this word has,
the borrowing *Telefon* is much more widely used.[58]

Ironically, English, traditionally much less opposed to borrowing
than German, was also sometimes caught in the tug-of-war between
foreign and native elements for increasing its word stock. As Richard
Foster Jones (1953:76) expressed it, "in some quarters, at least, borrowing was considered a reproach to the language."

However, one of the main ways in which borrowing in twentieth-
century Hawaiian differs from that in sixteenth-century English is that
for the former, the imported words and phrases would not be unfamiliar,
since the speakers already know English. Still, linguistic chauvinism
lives, and there seems to be a covert prejudice against loanwords,
especially those from the dominant language. On the other hand,
judging from the introduced grammatical terminology in a recent primer,
Nā Kai ʻEwalu, and some of the items in the lists of proposed forms,
borrowing from another Polynesian language is acceptable.

As for the general need to increase vocabulary, ironically, English
was in the same position in the sixteenth century (Jones 1953:68).
Writers found that the indigenous vocabulary could not "express all the
ideas found in the rapidly increasing knowledge of the Renaissance."
Yet, since one of their main goals was "the instruction and edification of
the unlearned," eloquent rhetorical devices from the classical languages
would not be easily understood. Moreover, this means of expanding the
vocabulary raised chauvinistic hackles, for "the nationalistic spirit, with
its pride in things native, resented the imputation of verbal deficiency
and the appearance of foreigners among good native citizens."

In addition to the form of new words, language planners also must
decide on the scope of new vocabulary.[59] Is it realistic to try to invent
Hawaiian vocabulary for *all* semantic fields? At first, one is tempted to
answer no. But on the other hand, as the immersion programs progress,

new words will be needed to cover the progress that the various sciences have made since schoolbooks were translated in the nineteenth century.

As these words are coined, it is important for our own enlightenment now, and for that of future historians, that language planners carefully record not only the outcome but also the reasons for their decisions. The early missionaries may have committed a number of linguistic and cultural transgressions, but at least they kept careful records so that we can look back and try to understand why they made certain decisions.[60] Their present-day counterparts are not so accommodating. Whatever the motives, it is shortsighted and anti-intellectual to conceal why certain words were chosen and others rejected. Moreover, it is condescending to language learners to presume that they will all be satisfied with that most frustrating of lexicographic labels, "Etymology unknown."

SUMMARY

The history of Hawaiian language policy is full of contradictions. For example, note the change in the tactics of the non-Hawaiians, who first wished to withhold English from the Hawaiians (to retain power), and then to replace Hawaiian with English (for the same reason). Another contradiction is that the early missionaries were convinced that the language was necessary to preserve the "nation" but that the culture could be replaced without harming either the language or the nation.

Ambiguities abound as well. For example, in the quotation that opens the chapter, did Bishop, in predicting that soon Hawaiians would be a mixed race "all speaking the English tongue," mean only English, or English as well as Hawaiian? This is only one of many policy statements in which it is not clear whether language planners intended that English supplement Hawaiian or supplant it. Finally, in reports from the Department of Education, it is often unclear whether the term "Hawaiian classes" meant that Hawaiian was the medium or the topic of instruction. And if the latter, it was seldom specified whether students were to learn the language or *about* the language.[61]

What does seem clear is that in the latter part of the nineteenth century there was a conscious effort to replace Hawaiian with English. But it is also clear that the motives for this policy were mixed. On the one hand, whether right or wrong, many people in authority believed that it was necessary for the sake of the Hawaiians themselves that they learn English, which would then open wide the door to American and European culture. On the other hand, the actions of those in power in the 1880s and 1890s seem much less philanthropic, for their position of control was being threatened. Still, they cloaked their actions with nationalism and religion, a combination that still appeals in some quarters.

In addition to its complicated past, Hawaiian also has a sketchily described present. For one thing, no one seems to know just how many native speakers there are, or how the language is being used. Moreover, it is generally agreed that the Hawaiian now being taught is, in a sense, a language that has been "reduced" in pronunciation, grammar, and vocabulary—although now language planners are trying to add new words. Both these conditions are at least partly the result of a long period of little scholarly interest in the language, as well as the decrease in the number of speakers.

Finally, it is obvious that Hawaiian has an uncertain future. Certainly it shows more signs of life now than it did twenty years ago, mostly due to the increased interest in immersion programs. But what is the prognosis for preservation? How long can Hawaiian be kept viable? And in what form and for how many speakers?

Perhaps the greatest uncertainty about the future of Hawaiian hinges on culture. To return to the metaphor of the three-legged stool, used early in the chapter: in order to survive, a language must have a cultural base—an environment in which to exist. Here, it might be useful to note the difference between the present-day Hawaiian and Māori cultures. In New Zealand, even though many Māori are urban-ized, many have maintained their tribal affiliations. And especially in the last two decades or so, many have been returning to the physical center of their tribe: the *marae* (an enclosed area that serves as a meeting place). Even if they do not live there permanently, they still participate in a number of cultural activities, ranging from such ritual greeting ceremonies as *te wero*, *te karanga*, *te pōwhiri* to communal cooking and sleeping to *mārena* (weddings) to *tangi* (funerals). Thus, the *marae* acts as a focal point of *Māoritanga*. And since the first language of the *marae* is Māori, the language is used there in a natural setting.

In contrast, nothing comparable exists in Hawai'i. The *heiau*, although referred to as a *marae* by Cook and his crew, was more limited in its function and, with the successful replacement of the indigenous religion by Christianity, is unlikely to survive except in the archeological sense. Still, Christianity, from its very introduction to Hawai'i, has been an institution that has fostered the Hawaiian language. The suggestion made in 1917, referred to earlier, that the church should take the initiative in restoring the language, is as valid today as it was then. Perhaps this introduced religion is not part of the traditional three-legged stool of language, culture, and nation, but it has become assimilated into the amalgam.

However, there is one traditional institution that could possibly become a focal point for Hawaiian language and culture, somewhat like the Māori *marae*. With the increased interest in traditional *hula* in recent years, much of the Hawaiian culture that still exists revolves around the *hālau*. Originally referring to the building in which *hula* instruction took place, the word is now more commonly applied to *hula* instruction or the combined body of *kumu* and students. Perhaps, expanding the earlier idea that Hawaiian might be kept alive mainly through song, the notion of the *hālau* will be further broadened, and *nā kumu hula* will become, even more so than now, *nā kumu ʻōlelo*. Thus, the *hālau* will be a place where people gather to speak Hawaiian, so that the language might change, grow, and continue as a living entity.

NOTES

Because of the complexity of the topic, Hawaiian language policy can only be sketched here.

[1] Berthold Seemann noted that some critics of the missionaries suggested that they chose to use Hawaiian because "they wanted to make it the medium of preserving their power, and exercising a censorship over the people." Seemann dismissed the explanation as an "absurd opinion" (1853:90). Still, it is easy to find comments about wishing to shield Hawaiians from what the missionaries perceived as the injurious influences of Honolulu, the dock area, etc.

[2] Apologies to Charles Atlas.

[3] We saw in chapter 13 that in about 1810, Liholiho had made another attempt to learn English. Perhaps Bingham was unaware of Liholiho's earlier brush with literacy.

[4] One might dispute this characterization.

[5] Although the Cookes themselves referred to the Royal School as an English-medium school, Bingham (1847:581) wrote: "They are taught both in English and Hawaiian."

[6] The identifications are from Otaguro 1989 and the *Missionary Album* pp. 74–75.

[7] Called Oʻahu College at that time.

[8] Years later, Armstrong's son, William Nevins, who accompanied Kalā kaua on his world trip in 1881, wrote, after observing English lessons in Malacca: "It is the knowledge of [English] which, more than any religious propaganda, acts like poison in the superstitions of the races" (1903:149).

[9] Bishop (1827–1909), a second-generation missionary (his father was Artemas Bishop), served as the editor of *The Friend* from 1887–1902 (*Missionary Album*, pp. 48–49).

[10] Here, Bishop was no doubt referring to Kalākaua's revival of such prohibited practices as *hula* dancing, discussed below.

[11] Son of the missionary Samuel Northrup Castle.

[12] The King *versus* Robert Grieve. *Hawaii Reports*, vol. 6. April 1883, pp. 740–46. Thanks to Robert J. Morris for the reference.

[13] John Charlot (pers. comm., September 1993) pointed out that such practice had already begun.

[14] William D. Alexander, another second-generation missionary and notable grammarian (see chapter 12), protested that the society was intended "partly as an agency for the revival of heathenism, partly to pander vice, and indirectly to serve as a political machine."

[15] A law passed in 1865 gave the Board of Health the authority to segregate people with Hansen's disease.

[16] Pulolo was a Hawaiian sorceress sentenced to life imprisonment on Lāna'i for allegedly committing three murders in February 1892. The case was reported in the San Francisco Examiner, 29 June 1892 (Rodman 1979:125–26.

[17] Charles T. Gulick responded, criticizing the missionary descendants, whom he dubbed "the saints" for their constant diatribes in their publications against the Hawaiians (Blount Report, Item # 23, Statement of Charles T. Gulick, pp. 745–69, p. 767):

> The bald fact stands out in plain view today [8 May 1893] ...
> that the sole prompting motive of the revolutionists was ... a lust
> for power coupled with a desire to possess themselves of the
> property of another without giving compensation therefor ...

[18] Hyde's opinions seem at odds with his long interest in the Hawaiian language and his grammatical and lexicographic work (see the discussion of Kent 1986 in chapter 11).

[19] See chapter 13 for Oleson's opinion of "street" English.

[20] From 31 March 1886 to 31 March 1888, $46,629.17 was spent on education in Hawaiian, $275,719.62 on education in English (Alexander and Atkinson 1888:11).

[21] At the time of the overthrow of the monarchy (1893), it was reported (*Missionary Herald* 89:92) that there were on the islands 94 government English schools, 36 government native schools, and 48 independent schools. This total of 178 does not quite match the total here (for 1892) of 168. Nor does the language breakdown match.

[22] One cannot help but wonder what happened to the teachers in the Hawaiian schools and where the Department of Education found competent teachers for instruction in English. Charlot (in progress, Appendix) found that the schools deteriorated as a result of the language shift.

[23] For an account of a Hawaiian being physically punished for not understanding English, see Nākoa 1979.

[24] This is the title of an 1886 article in *The Friend*, probably by William B. Oleson.

[25] Perhaps William M. Langton, Editor.

[26] At this time, all tertiary schools in New Zealand were colleges in a national system called the University of New Zealand. Brown was connected with what is now Canterbury University, in Christchurch (Linley E. Chapman, pers. comm., May 1993).

[27] Found and translated by Laiana Wong.

[28] See the discussion of Kahananui's participation in the language workshop in 1960 and her textbooks stemming from this experience (chapter 14).

[29] In the same work (p. 27), the notion of *foreign* is defined: "The term 'foreign language school,' as used in this Act shall be construed to mean any school which is conducted in any other than the English language or Hawaiian language, except Sabbath schools." Here we have a contradiction. The law specifies English as the language of instruction, whereas Hawaiian may be *taught*. However, in the definition of foreign language school, it is implied that some schools may be conducted *in* Hawaiian.

[30] Note that Judd's introduction to Atcherley's primer referred to the legislative session of 1923 as passing "an act to provide for the preparation and publication of a school text book in the Hawaiian language."

[31] For an account of the background of the English Standard Schools and the changing social and educational conditions that led to their dissolution, see Hughes 1993.

[32] Kimura (1978:11) disagreed with this point of view, pointing out that in 1920 or so, there were more "knowledgable [*sic*] sources in the language than there are now." He then set up an opposition between possession of higher degrees and knowledge of Hawaiian. I think that such an attitude, which can only be described as anti-intellectual, hinders efforts to preserve the language.

[33] Some obvious examples are Mary Kawena Pukui, Samuel H. Elbert, Ka'upena Wong, and 'Iolani Luahine, among many others.

[34] The figures for 1961–1962 and 1973–1974 are from Kimura 1978. Those for 1992–1993 are from Emily A. Hawkins, pers. comm., 14 April 1993. Note that these are figures for course enrollment, not individual students, some of whom may have been enrolled in more than one course. On the other hand, there are no statistics for the number of students who try to enroll but find sections closed. As for the dramatic increase of students since the early 1960s, one must also remember that the total enrollment at Mānoa has also increased.

[35] Since some of these students are taking the course to satisfy the university's two-year language requirement, the figures for more advanced classes are perhaps more significant: 3rd year, 70–80; 4th year, 35; and another

10 or so in other advanced courses. Thus, of the 636 students in the spring 1993 semester, approximately 120 were in upper division courses.

[36] Noenoe Moan, pers. comm., August 1993.

[37] Potential teachers in the immersion program for primary and secondary students, however, must take methodology courses.

[38] The tapes from the program held in the Language Laboratory at the University of Hawai'i at Mānoa begin with a broadcast on 22 February 1972 (Laiana Wong, pers. comm., August 1993).

[39] Earlier, there were many hour-and-one-half broadcasts.

[40] There are, however, several language-learning videos available.

[41] A much higher figure appeared in a summary of the 1990 census: in response to "the number of people aged 5 and older in Hawaii who speak a language other than English at home," 8,872 reported that they spoke Hawaiian. Moreover, the census reported 2,051 people in the same category for California. Of course, the figures do not necessarily refer to native speakers, but they still raise a number of questions. For example, is Hawaiian used exclusively by this many people? Do the figures represent fluent speakers? Does using a few common phrases in an essentially English context count? Do the figures include past and present students of Hawaiian learning their lessons? And finally, might they represent wish fulfillment: the response of people who identify themselves ethnically as Hawaiians and who would like to think that they speak the language as well?

At the other end of the scale, Carlos Andrade (1992:125) gave a figure of 400–500, but since he was referring to the integrated community of Ni'ihau, native speakers outside that community would not be included.

[42] As of mid-1993, only two schools included the sixth grade.

[43] See, for example, a letter from Helen B. Slaughter, *Honolulu Star-Bulletin*, 3 April 1992; and from Keith Haugen, *Honolulu Star-Bulletin*, 18 April 1992.

[44] According to Landau (1984:64), the largest lexicon compiled for English is *Webster's New International Dictionary* (second edition, 1934), which contains 600,000 entries.

[45] Emily Hawkins, pers. comm., April 1993.

[46] For example, in 1991 Gregory Lee Carter recast a 130-page Hawaiian book into the modern orthography, making it much more accessible to students at Windward Community College. Other scholars are engaged in similar projects as well.

[47] Suggested by Noenoe Moan, pers. comm., July 1993. Puakea Nogel-meier, who has been editing some of Kamakau's writings to use as an advanced reader, notes that, taking these orthographical practices into account, Kamakau was definitely not "careless of his particles." Charlot (in progress, Appendix, p. 17) added that "the variable use of particles is ... a characteristic of classical style."

[48] John Charlot (pers. comm., September 1993) noted that Hawaiian writers such as Nākuina (1902) or those who wrote for the newspapers did not use such a style.

[49] See, for example, the preface to Elbert 1970: "The objects of the book are to present the principal conversational and grammatical patterns and the most common idioms, and to prepare the student for a final reward: the capacity to read and enjoy the rich heritage of Hawaiian traditional legends and poetry."

[50] Actually, the standard is based on the language as *written* (Laiana Wong, pers. comm., August 1993).

[51] Here, the committee used semantic criteria—that is, the concept of an idiom—rather than phonological ones for their decisions. As for phonological criteria, it is debatable whether in Hawaiian there is an accent difference (as there is in English and German, for instance) to distinguish a compound from a combination of noun and modifier.

[52] Briefly, the committee recommended whether to write certain combinations of two grammatical markers as one word or two: e.g., *me he* versus *mehe*, *a me* versus *ame*, etc.

[53] Elbert and Pukui (1979:20) show the markers *a* 'of', *o* 'of', *ma* 'at', *na* 'by, for', and *no* 'for' long before a long vowel or diphthong, and short before a short vowel. This distribution exactly matches that of one-syllable Fijian markers. However, the Hawaiian phenomenon has never been systematically studied.

[54] However, the sources for these new words are not given, so we are uncertain whether they were actually heard or read, or simply made up by the compilers.

[55] For example, in the English-Hawaiian vocabulary in Elbert's *Spoken Hawaiian* (1970), the only words I can find referring to European technology more recent than the first missionary contact are those for 'moving picture' and 'car'. But this was a deliberate policy on the part of the author, who explained ([vii]):

> The words have been chosen on the basis of frequency of use in classroom situations, in general conversation, and in legends and songs ... No attempt is made to provide Hawaiian names for everything in a supermarket, as few, if any, students today will make their purchases in Hawaiian.

[56] From the first page of the draft of the English-Hawaiian section, *Papa Huaʻōlelo* (1992).

[57] This list is adapted from Laiana Wong's translation of the guidelines.

[58] For a similar attitude from language planners for Māori, see Harlow 1993.

59 This topic was suggested by John Charlot.

60 For example, see chapter 10 for Sheldon Dibble's explanation of certain terms that the missionaries introduced.

61 For example, see the quotation above, which shows that in 1921, the board of regents for the university suggested that because of the perceived lack of literature in Hawaiian, courses be filled out with the study of other Polynesian languages as well.

ANNOTATED BIBLIOGRAPHY

-0-0-0-0-0-

Few bibliographies are wholly original, and this one is no exception. Its foundation is the Hawaiian Collection at Hamilton Library, University of Hawai'i at Mānoa, supplemented by the holdings of the Hawaiian Mission Children's Society Library, the Hawaiian Historical Society Library, and the Bernice Pauahi Bishop Museum Library. A fuller list of collections consulted appears in the Acknowledgments.

For one type of material in particular, the items cited only hint at the richness that awaits more thorough research. In the voluminous correspondence among the missionaries themselves, and between the Hawaiian Mission and its parent organization in Boston (much of which is contained in the Hawaiian Mission Children's Society Library and the papers of the American Board of Commissioners for Foreign Missions, Houghton Library at Harvard University), the missionaries carried on lively discussions of the problems they encountered in trying to write the language efficiently, learn it well enough to carry on the work of the Mission, teach it to others, explore its vocabulary, and analyze its structure. Here, I have concentrated mainly on the early years of the Mission, especially the mid-1820s, when the orthography was developed.

In general, this bibliography excludes Hawaiian language text material unless it contains linguistic analysis as well. I have included articles on the etymology and semantics of individual words only when they reflect the linguistic attitudes of their period.

Within the entries, these conventions are used:

    { }   translation
    [ ]   annotation
    < >   holdings (for rare books and manuscripts)
    *   a work that does not contain material about the structure or use of the Hawaiian language but contains material useful for the historical or general linguistic background

Abbreviations

In the following list, Austronesian language names are abbreviated in the conventional way. Such abbreviations are used in the annotations, but not in titles of works, or in direct quotations (except for HAW).

ABCFM American Board of Commissioners for Foreign Missions, Boston
Adm Admiralty Records, London
ATL Alexander Turnbull Library, National Library of New Zealand, Wellington
BPBM Bernice Pauahi Bishop Museum Library, Honolulu
DJK David J. Kittelson, *The Hawaiians: An Annotated Bibliography* (1985). [The compiler gave me permission to quote his annotations.]
EAS Easter Island (language)
ed. edition
ENG English (language)
FR French (language)
HAW Hawaiian (language)
HHS Hawaiian Historical Society Library, Honolulu
HMCS Hawaiian Mission Children's Society Library, Honolulu
HRK H. R. Klieneberger, *Bibliography of Oceanic Linguistics* (1957).
HTL Houghton Library, Harvard University, Cambridge, MA
JBM Bernice Judd, Janet E. Bell, and Clare G. Murdoch (1978), *Hawaiian Language Imprints, 1822–1899.*
JHW Jack Hale Ward, *Hawaiian Language History* (1992)
MAO Māori (language)
MKA Marguerite K. Ashford, "The Evolution of the Hawaiian Dictionary ..." (1987)
ML Mitchell Library, State Library of New South Wales, Sydney
MQA Marquesan (language)
ms. manuscript
mss. manuscripts
NJM Nancy J. Morris et al., "Preliminary Bibliography of Hawaiian Language Materials at the University of Hawaii, Manoa Campus" (1974). [The principal compiler gave me permission to quote the annotations.]
PN Polynesian (languages)
RT John E. Reinecke, Stanley M. Tsuzaki, David DeCamp, Ian F. Hancock, and Rochard E. Wood, *A Bibliography of Pidgin and Creole Languages* (1975).
SAM Samoan (language)
TAH Tahitian (language)

TON   Tongan (language)
UHM   University of Hawai'i at Mānoa, Hamilton Library,
        Honolulu

Some Notes on Periodicals

One long-lived periodical, commonly known as *Thrum's Annual*, or *All About Hawaii*, has gone through a number of name changes:

1875–1924: *Hawaiian Almanac and Annual*
1925–1940: *The Hawaiian Annual*
1940/41–1946/47: *Thrum's Hawaiian Annual and Standard Guide*
1948–1968, 1974: *All about Hawaii* (suspended 1969–73)

The missionary periodical *The Friend*, originally titled *The Temperance Advocate, and Seamen's Friend*, appeared with an old series of volume numbers, a new series, and a short run with no volume numbers. Here, I give only the month and year of publication.

Alphabetization and Spelling of Hawaiian Words and Names

Hawaiian titles are alphabetized according to the first letter of the first content word after the markers *he, ka, ke, nā,* and *o*. Macrons and glottal stops are generally added to Hawaiian words and names, except in quotations or titles, where the proper spelling may be added in brackets. Proper names present a special problem: for example, Mary Kawena Pukui [Pūku'i] wrote her name as "Pukui" (Elbert 1989:132), and I have used this spelling.

Holdings for Hawaiian Imprints

For Hawaiian imprints of the nineteenth century, see Judd, Bell, and Murdoch 1978, which lists holdings in major Hawaiian collections.

-0-0-0-0-0-

Abbott, Isabella Aiona, and Eleanor Horswill Williamson. 1974. *Limu;
An Ethnobotanical Study of Some Edible Hawaiian Seaweeds.* Lā
wa'i, HI: Pacific Tropical Botanical Garden. 20 pp.

Abe, Isamu. 1965. Hawaiian Pronunciation. *Bulletin of the Tokyo
Institute of Technology* 63:25-30. [A list of phonemes, interesting
observations about diphthongs and the original pronunciation of /l/,
consonant alternation, word accent (incorrect), isochronous rhythm,
and intonation.]

———. 1966. Phonetic Transcription in an Old Hawaiian Phrase Book
(in Japanese). *Bulletin of the Phonetic Society of Japan* 121:20–22.

———. 1965. On Hawaiian Intonation. *Le Maître Phonétique* 30:5–6.

———. 1970. Hawaiian Accent and Intonation. *Bulletin of the Tokyo
Institute of Technology* 100:107–18. [The description of accent is
limited by a reliance on incorrect published descriptions. Study of
intonation based on the recordings accompanying Brown 1963.
Sentences transcribed on a four-level scale, with falling and rising
terminals (based on perception), and analyzed instrumentally as well.
The author proposed that Hawaiian follows certain universal features
of intonation.]

Achiu, Jerry, et al. 1980. Hawaiian Translations. IN *Cross-cultural
Caring: A Handbook for Health Care Professions in Hawaii,* ed. by
Neal Palafox and Anne Warren, 66–72. Honolulu: University of
Hawai'i John A. Burns School of Medicine. [DJK: Brief introduc-
tion to the pronunciation of the HAW language, followed by a list of
HAW translations of medically related ENG terms referring to body
parts, specific health conditions, and physical complaints.]

Addleman, W. C. 1938. See JONES AND ADDLEMAN 1938.

Adelung, Johann C[hristoph]. 1806–1817. *Mithridates, oder Allgemeine Sprachenkunde, mit dem Vater Unser als Sprachprobe in bey
nahe fünf hundert Sprachen und Mundarten.* 4 vols. Berlin:
Vossische Buchhandlung. [Two-paragraph description of HAW,
including sources for word lists (Anderson, Dixon), vol. 1, p. 640.
11 HAW words (from the Lord's Prayer) compared with TON,
TAH, MQA, MAO, EAS, and "Cocos" (Niuatoputapu), p. 621.]

'Aha Kūkākūkā 'Ōlelo Hawai'i {Hawaiian language confer-
ence}. [1972]. Program for First Hawaiian Language Conference,
The Kamehameha Schools, 20 May 1972. 16 pp., [2], 4 *ll.* <UHM
Hawn PL6441 .H39 1972> [Includes proverbs, riddles, a folktale in

HAW, facsimiles of early printing in HAW, hints on pronunciation, partial list of dictionaries and language texts, phrase books, and grammars. The last 4 *ll.* contain an annotated list of HAW language books in print.]

Akaka, Jonah Hauʻoli. 1991. Ua Ola ka ʻŌlelo Hawaiʻi!! The Hawaiian Language Survives. [Honolulu]: *The KCCN Hui,* 25th anniversary issue, pp. 28–29.

Akana-Gooch, Collette L. 1980. See HANDBOOK OF EXPRESSIONS IN ENGLISH AND HAWAIIAN.

Alakai Mua No na Kamalii {First guide for children}. 1854. Honolulu: Mea Pai-palapala a na Mikionari. 16 pp. Illustrated. JBM #321.

Alexander, Mary Charlotte, and Charlotte Peabody Dodge. 1941. *Punahou 1841–1941.* Berkeley and Los Angeles: University of California Press. xiii, 577 pp. [Contains a description of a HAW language program in the 1860s and 1870s.]

Alexander, William De Witt. 1864a. *A Short Synopsis of the Most Essential Points in Hawaiian Grammar: For the Use of the Pupils of Oahu College.* Honolulu: Whitney. 2 parts: 19, 34 pp. 1871, 2d ed., 52 pp. (Honolulu: Whitney). 1891, 3d ed., 59 pp. (Honolulu: Press Publishing). 1908, 4th ed., 61 pp. (Honolulu: Thrum). 1924, 5th ed., revised, 61 pp. (Honolulu: Hawaiian News & Thrum). 1968 reprint, 59 pp. (Rutland, VT: Tuttle). See JBM #409, 410 for title variations. [Later editions expanded somewhat by adding (un-numbered) paragraphs of examples. In the 5th edition, although the glottal stop is said to form "an *essential* part of the words," it is not written consistently. Long vowels are also said to be important, but are inconsistently marked. Fuller critique in Elbert 1969c:viii–xiv. See chapter 12.]

——. 1864b. *Exercises for Translation from English into Hawaiian.* Cover title: *Progressive Exercises in Hawaiian Composition.* Honolulu? 12 pp. [Date on title page corrected in pencil to "1869?" Twenty-seven sets of exercises keyed to Alexander's grammar (1864a).]

——. 1864c. Essay on the Best Mode of Teaching Hawaiian. *Maile Wreath* 4(1):12–18. <HMCS > ["Written for the Hawaiian Evangelical Association, but not read before them in English." Although Alexander suggested that the scientific study of HAW might be considered unusual ("The idea of its being taught in an institution of learning on the same footing as Latin, Greek or French is a novelty

& an experiment"), he noted that it had "a structure as regular & philosophical as that of any other language, ancient or modern." To learn the language, he advocated a combination of conversation and a theoretical knowledge of HAW grammar.]

——. 1865. Introductory remarks in Andrews 1865: 7–14. [Discussion of the early history of the study of PN languages, comparative consonant and vocabulary charts, impressionistic discussion of HAW vocabulary.]

——. 1901. Vigesimal System of Enumeration. *Journal of the Polynesian Society* 10(4):203. [Note on changes in HAW numbering system wrought by the missionaries, including introduction of words for 'hundred' and 'thousand'.]

——. 1903. *Hawaiian Geographic Names*. Treasury Department: U. S. Coast and Geodetic Survey. Appendix no. 7: Report for 1902, pp. 365–424. Washington: Government Printing Office. [Brief description of the language, including a distribution for the [v]-like allophone of /w/ ("approximates to that of *V* between two vowels"), and the following description of /'/: "... a slight guttural break between two vowels, where the Polynesian *K* has been dropped, as in *i'a* for *ika*, a fish," p. 373. Glossary of 296 words often forming parts of place names. In this section, however, the glottal stop only sporadically marked; e.g., *po'o* 'head', but *puu* 'hill'. Long vowels still treated as accent: "The accent of about five-sixths of the words in the language is on the penult." A few of the proper names are accented on the final syllable, as Puakó, Maná, etc." These are so marked in the list; e.g., *hokú* (*hōkū*) 'star', *manó* (*manō*) 'shark', pp. 396–99.]

——. 1909. The Origin of the Polynesian Race. *Hawaiian Hist. Soc. Annual Report* 17:14–24. Also in *Paradise of the Pacific* 23 (May 1910):12–14; 23 (June 1910):13–16. [DJK: Discusses similarities between Hawaiians and other Polynesians and reviews theories of Polynesian origins. Concludes that the Hawaiians' prehistoric origins lie in northern India.]

——. 1911 [1927]. Dr. Alexander on Hawaiian Pronunciation. *The Friend*, May, pp. 105–106. [A letter written in 1911 to Mrs. Harriet Castle Coleman, complaining of the deterioration of Hawaiian pronunciation, particularly the intrusion of [v]: "It is like the low class Australian pronunciation of lydy for lady, piper for paper, etc." Quoted by William D. Westervelt.]

———, and Alatau T. Atkinson. 1888. *An Historical Sketch of Education in the Hawaiian Islands.* Honolulu: Board of Missions. 12 pp.

Alexander, William Patterson. 1838. Marquesan and Hawaiian Dialects Compared. *The Hawaiian Spectator* 1(1):17–22 (Nr. 381) (January 1838. ["Der Verfasser war einer der von August 1833–April 1834 in Taiohae weilenden Haw. Missionare." Used by Horatio Hale in his comparative PN grammar (1846:230n).]

The Alphabet. 1822. 16 pp. Oʻahu: Mission Press. JBM #1, 2. [First eight pages printed in January, second in February. 2d ed. September of that year. See chapter 7.]

Ancient Hawaiian Civilization. A Series of Lectures Delivered at the Kamehameha Schools by Handy, Emory, Bryan, Buck, Wise and Others. 1933. Honolulu: The Kamehameha Schools. 323 pp. Rev. ed. 1965. Rutland, VT: Tuttle. 333 pp.

Anderson, Rufus. 1864. *The Hawaiian Islands: Their Progress and Condition under Missionary Labors.* Boston: Gould and Lincoln. xxii, 23–450 pp. [Discussion of the development of the orthography and printing in HAW, pp. 258–59.]

*Anderson, William. 1776–1777. Directions for the Pronunciation of the Vocabulary. IN Cook 1777, pp. 319–22. <Adm 55/108 (Public Record Office); UHM microfilm 4057, reel 36> [Cook wrote: "This vocabulary I had chiefly from Mr Anderson ..."]

*———. 1777. Journal, vol. 1 and 2 (vol. 3 is missing). Great Britain Admiralty Log Books. Captains' logs. 1763–1821. *Resolution* 1776–1780. <Adm 51/4560/203-4; UHM microfilm 4057, reel 23>

———. 1784. Vocabulary of the Language of Atooi, One of the Sandwich Islands. IN COOK 1784, vol. 3, Appendix 5, pp. 549–53. [Collected in 1778.]

Andrade, Carlos. 1992. Extinction Alert: Who Will Take the Challenge? *The Kamehameha Journal of Education* 3(2):125-27.

Andrews, Lorrin. n.d. Vocabulary ["of words in the Hawaiian language, not dated, but, judging from the penmanship, written a few years after the lexicon." From Gay Slavsky's (expert on Hawaiian books) annotation.] The lexicon referred to is the first part of the bound ms.: A Pocket Hebrew Lexicon, Translated and Enlarged from the Manual Lexicon of J. Simonis. <Punahou: Cooke Library Pun R-HC/499/An2o> [Pages are divided into two columns; there are 177 columns. Alphabetical according to the HAW. Diacritics used:

acute accent, breve, and hyphen. Judging from their use with *a, a-a*, and *a-a-a* words (col. 3 & 4), there is not much consistency. Col. 5. One orthographical distinction made is *ai* vs. *a-i* (neck). It doesn't capture all the distinctions, but is a beginning. The order of the words is vowels first. Col. 109: *kii*. Shows that /i'i/ at least was not perceived as a long vowel. The selection of consonants shows that the list was compiled after the resolution of the orthographical problems, for there is no *r, t*, or *v*. Col. 176, 177: loanwords, some of which contain consonants not in the regular alphabet, such as *buke*, 'book', *berena*, 'bread', *fiku*, 'fig'.]

——. [183-]. A Vocabulary of Hawaiian Words with English Definitions Illustrated by Short Sentences in the English Language. Ms. (unidentified hand); [O'ahu? 183-]. 181 *ff*. (345 pp.). <HTL ms., microfilm 72–2825. UHM microfilm S10110>. [Alphabetical order: begins with vowels. Definitely after 1826: no *r, t*, or *v*. On the first few pages, some marks (accents *after* the vowels seem to indicate glottal stops, such as in the words for 'neck' and 'lava'. Later, contrasting with *hui* are *húi* and *húihúi*, 'cool, cold, chilly'. Some penciled-in additions. There are several hundred *hoo* [*ho'o*] entries. Following is a partial count of entries, including alternate forms such as *kolu, ekolu*: A: 427; *E*: 69; *I*: 139; *O*: 257; *U*: 131; *H*: 818. These comprise 143 pp. The total number of pages with writing is 336.]

——. 1832 [1834]. Essay on the Best Practicable Method of Conducting Native Schools at the Sandwich Islands. Read at the General Meeting of the Mission, June 13, 1832, by Lorrin Andrews, Principal of the High School at Lahaina. Appendix 3 of the *Annual Report of the ABCFM read at the 25th Annual Meeting* (1834), pp. 156–68.

——. 1836a. *A Vocabulary of Words in the Hawaiian Language.* Lahainaluna: Press of the High School. iv, 132 pp. JBM #142.

——. 1836b. Remarks on the Hawaiian Dialect of the Polynesian Language. *Chinese Repository* 5 (May 1836 to April 1837), Article II: 12–21. [Dated February 1836. Some philosophical remarks about language, estimate of minimum dialect differences in Hawai'i, justification of the orthography, discussion of HAW poetry and the differences between it and conversational speech, the necessity for loanwords and non-HAW letters in the alphabet, and the role of language in the "improvement" of the people. Extracts of this article appeared in the *Sandwich Island Gazette*, 24 December, 1836, p. 1, and 31 December 1836, p. 1.]

——. [1837a]. *He Piliolelo no ka Olelo Beritania* {A grammar of the English language}. Lahainaluna: Press of the High School. 40 pp. JBM #161. [Andrews was the translator.]

——. 1837b. *Ke Kumu Kahiki: Oia ka Mea e Ao ai i na Hua a me ka Hookui, a me ka Heluhelu ana i ka Olelo Beretania* {The foreign teacher: a way to teach the letters and spelling, and reading in the English language}. 1837. Lahainaluna: Press of the High School. 36 pp. JBM #147.

——. 1838. Pecularities of the Hawaiian Language. *The Hawaiian Spectator* 1(4):392–420. [Pp. 394–96, discussion of diphthongs, distribution of /w/, and the effect of a small number of vowels and consonants. The glottal stop not yet recognized as a phoneme. Paradigm of a HAW verb, in its conjugations, moods, tenses, numbers, and persons, (folded) facing page 416.]

——. 1841. *He mau Haawina no ka Olelo Beretania* {A few lessons in English}. Lahainaluna: Press of the High School. 40 pp. JBM #222. 2d ed. 1844. *He mau Haawina no ka Olelo Beritania. Ka Lua o ka Pai ana.* Honolulu: Mea Pai Palapala a na Misionari. 36 pp. JBM #273.

——. 1843. *O ke Kokua no ko Hawaii Poe Kamalii e Ao ana i ka Olelo Beritania* {The assistant for Hawaiian youths in learning the English language}. Lahainaluna: Press of the High School. 104 pp. JBM #263.

——. 1854. *Grammar of the Hawaiian Language.* Honolulu: Mission Press. iv, 156 pp. JBM #324. 2d ed. 1885. Honolulu: Thrum. 156 pp. JBM #324. [See chapter 12.]

——. 1860. Degrees of Relationship in the Language of the Hawaiian Nation. Typescript copy of ms. Dated Honolulu, August 1860. 12 *ll.* <BPBM Hms/La8/storage case 5> [209 phrases. E.g., "my elder brother (said by a male)." Accented vowels and diphthongs marked, but accent marks and glottal stops (for such pairs as *kou* versus *ko'u*) confused.]

——. 1864. Value of the Hawaiian and English Languages in the Instruction of Hawaiians. IN *Hawaiian Evangelical Association's Proceedings ... 3* June to 1 July 1863, pp. 94–107. Boston: Marvin.

———. 1865. *A Dictionary of the Hawaiian Language, to which is Appended an English-Hawaiian Vocabulary and a Chronological Table of Remarkable Events.* Honolulu: Whitney. xvi, 17–559 pp. JBM #213. Facsimile ed., with introduction by Terence Barrow, 1974; Rutland, VT: Tuttle. x, 559 pp. [Original introduction by W. D. Alexander (1865). Introduction in 1974 edition contains a short discussion of orthography and lexicography. See chapter 11. For a discussion of annotated copies held by the Bishop Museum, see MKA.]

———. 1870. Notes on the Hawaiian Degrees of Relationship.   IN *Systems of Consanguinity and Affinity of the Human Family*, ed. by Lewis Morgan, 451–57. Washington, D.C.: Smithsonian. [DJK: Extensive listing of the HAW terms of relationship.   Includes definitions.]

———. 1875. Remarks on Hawaiian Poetry. *The Islander* 1:26, 27, 30, 31, 35.

———. 1922. *A Dictionary of the Hawaiian Language.*   Revised by Henry H. Parker. Bernice P. Bishop Mus. Spec. Publ. no. 8. Honolulu: Board of Commissioners of Public Archives of the Territory of Hawaii. xx, 21–674 pp. [(Referred to in this work, mainly in chapter 11, as Andrews-Parker.) As listed in the preface, Parker's additions were incorporating Lorenzo Lyons's revised definitions (see LYONS 1878), revising many definitions himself, using word lists from several sources, and supplying diacritical marks to indicate pronunciation (although often incorrectly).   For a discussion of annotated copies, see MKA. For a detailed and critical review, see WILLIAMS 1926.]

Andrews' Hawaiian Dictionary. 1865a. *The Friend,* May, p. 37. [Short notice of the impending publication of the work, praising its coverage.]

Andrews' Hawaiian Dictionary. 1865b. *The Friend,* June, p. 44. [Short announcement of the appearance of the dictionary; second only to the Bible in cost of printing.]

Annual Report of the Hawaiian Evangelical Association, 1878–1962. Honolulu.

Ka Ano o na Huaolelo. Mahele Alua {The nature of words. Division two}. 1860–1869. 20 pp. <IN Hawaiian Glossary in the Archives of the Sacred Hearts in Honolulu. UHM microfilm S11041> [The focus is HAW grammar, beginning with an explanation of *ana* and its morphophonemic changes. Names, and their various cases. ENG translations (and FR-spelled pronunciations of the ENG) given. Names of numbers (HAW, ENG, FR-pron. of ENG). Fractions, multiples, etc. adjectives. Pronouns (personal, interrogative, possessive, indefinite).]

Anthony, Alberta. For other works by this author, see both PUNG and HOPKINS.

——. 1970. See KAHANANUI AND ANTHONY 1970.

——. 1965. The Changing Position of the Hawaiian Language. Unpublished research paper. [Not seen; ref.: SEGREST 1977.]

——. 1979. Hawaiian Nonverbal Communication: Two Classroom Applications. Unpublished ms. 7 *ll.* [DJK: Describes aspects of nonverbal communication ... Notes the differences in interpretation of these signals between Hawaiians and Westerners.]

——. n.d. English Phonemic Correspondences to Hawaiian Consonant Phonemes in the Adaptation of English Loanwords. 6 pp. [JHW: With fifteen pages of words, 965 loan words. IN Ward 1992:157–85]

Anthropology Club of Kaua'i Community College. 1977–1978. The Bicentennial of the Discovery of the Hawaiian Islands by Captain James Cook 1778–1978. *Archaeology on Kaua'i* 6(2):1–15; 7(1):1–9. [Provides identification of some names of artifacts in Cook and Anderson's word list.]

Ao Hoku {*A'o hōkū* 'astronomy'?}. n.d. [but written between 1826 and 1836]. Hawaiian-English vocabulary. Ms. 63 pp. Compiler(s) unknown, but probably Ely, Andrews, or Loomis. <HMCS MS/H/499 /M68>

Ke Ao Spela ... See JOHNSON 1844.

Apoliona, S. Haunani. 1973. Hawaiian *Neia*. Unpublished ms. [A study of the use of *neia*, a "rare demonstrative." Not seen; ref.: ELBERT AND PUKUI 1979.]

Arago, Jacques. 1823. *Narrative of a Voyage Round the World in the Uranie and Physicienne Corvettes, commanded by Captain Freycinet, during the years 1817, 1818, 1819, and 1820 ...* London: Treuttel and Wurtz. Reprinted in 1971 as Bibliotheca Australiana no. 45, New York: Da Capo. xxx, 285, 297, [2]. [Translation from the French original. Vocabulary of 236 words and some brief notes on consonant alternation, pp. 291–94.]

———. 1839–1840. *Souvenirs d'un aveugle. Voyage autour du monde par m. J. Arago, ouvrage enrichi de soixante dessins et de notes scientifiques*. 5 vols. Paris: Hortet et Ozanne. [Duplicates the list found in the the 1823 publication, v. 4, pp. 402–10.]

Arai, Saku. 1891 [1892]. *Hawaiian, Japanese and English Phrasebook*. Tokyo: Shusai Byoin. [3], 123 pp., 1 *l*. JBM #574.

Armand, Abraham. 1834. See BACHELOT AND ARMAND.

Armitage, George Thomas. ca. 1939. *How's your Hawaiian?* Honolulu: Advertiser Publishing Co. New York: Stechert. 103 pp. <HMCS 817/Ar5> [Mostly stories, many apocryphal, centering around language. Glossary, pp. 99–102; place names, pp. 102–3. No glottal stops or macrons marked, but accent marked in a crude effort to indicate pronunciation after each entry.]

Armstrong, Louise B. 1933. *Facts and Figures of Hawaii including a Glossary of Hawaiian Names and Words*. New York: Snyder. [14,] 3–159 pp. [Brief vocabulary of HAW words and their meaning, pp. 141–59.]

Armstrong, Richard. 1838. Have All the Polynesian Tribes a Common Origin? *Hawaiian Spectator* 1(3):286–96. [Terms in TAH, HAW, and MQA.]

*Armstrong, William Nevins. 1903. *Around the World with a King*. New York: Stokes. xiv, 290 pp. Reprinted 1977, Rutland, VT, and Tokyo: Tuttle. xxvi, 290 pp. [A narrative, by a member of his cabinet, of King Kalākaua's world trip in 1881.]

Ashford, Marguerite K. 1987. The Evolution of the Hawaiian Dictionary and Notes on the Early Compilers, with Particular Attention to Manuscript Resources of the Bishop Museum Library. *Bishop Museum Occasional Papers* 27.1–24. [A valuable discussion of "some of the sources now in the Bishop Museum Library manuscript collection that were used by ... (various compilers of HAW dictionaries). A linguistic analysis of each source has not been attempted; instead, an indication of the type of source, its extent, and a glimpse of the material contained is presented," p. 2.]

Aspinwall, Dorothy B. 1960. Languages in Hawaii. *Modern Language Association of America Publications* 75(2):7–13. [A short history and description of language use in Hawai'i, including HAW language instruction.]

[Atcherley, Mary W.] 1930. *First Book in Hawaiian: a Textbook in the Hawaiian Language.* Honolulu: (Published for the Territory of Hawai'i by the Hawaiian Board of Missions; printed by the Honolulu Star-Bulletin). 94 pp. [Surprisingly amateurish, considering the period in which it was written and its support by the territorial government. Confused accent and vowel length. In order to determine the proper accent, it was suggested that the learner put the word "into a Hawaiian Poetical Phrase or Song." Long vowels incorrectly marked; e.g., *lēi, līo, alōha.* Some parts of the grammatical explanation were taken directly from earlier works. See chapters 12 and 14.]

Ayer, Edward E. See BUTLER 1942.

Bachelot, Alexis, and Abraham Armand. 1834. *Notes grammaticales sur la langue sandwichoise, suivies d'une collection de mots de la même langue.* Paris: Imprimerie de Decourchant. 76, [1], pp. [The pagination is uncertain: ML has [39]–77, and Yzendoorn (1912) noted that only the first thirty-seven pages were printed. The vocabulary contains some 2,000 words.] <ML, ATL>

Ballou, Howard M., and George R. Carter. 1908. The History of the Hawaiian Mission Press, with a Bibliography of the Earlier Publications. *Papers of the Hawaiian Hist. Soc.* 14:9–44.

Barreiro-Meiro, Roberto, ed. 1964. Colección de Diarios y Relaciones para la Historia de los Viajes y Descubrimientos, 6: Esteban José Martínez (1742–1787). Madrid: Instituto Histórico de Marina. [Contains a HAW word list of 285 items, collected in 1789. See A. G. DAY 1991.]

*Barratt, Glynn. 1988. *The Russian View of Honolulu.* Ottawa: Carleton University Press. xiv, 424 pp.

Barrow, Terence. 1974. Introduction to 1974 ed. of Lorrin Andrews's *Dictionary of the Hawaiian Language* (1865), pp. vii–x. Tokyo: Tuttle. [A brief sketch of HAW word lists and dictionaries, early spelling differences, and some biographical details about Andrews.]

Bartlett, Samuel Colcord. 1869. *Historical Sketch of the Hawaiian Mission and the Missions to Micronesia and the Marquesas Islands.* Boston: ABCFM. 322 pp. plus map. 1893 ed.: C. M. Hyde, co-author. 43 pp.

Bassett, Marnie. 1962. *Realms and Islands. The World Voyage of Rose de Freycinet 1817–1820*. London: Oxford University Press. xii, 275 pp.

Ka Be-a-ba {The alphabet}. 1824. Two editions in 1824. O'ahu: Mission Press. 4 pp. JBM #5, 6.

Ka Be-a-ba {The alphabet}. 1825. O'ahu: Mission Press. 8 pp. JBM #7.

Beaglehole, John Cawte, ed. 1955. *The Journals of Captain James Cook on his Voyage of Discovery*. Vol. 1. *The Voyage of the* Endeavour *1768–1771*. Hakluyt Society Extra Series no. 34. Cambridge: Hakluyt Society. cclxxxiv, 684, 12 pp. [See also HAWKESWORTH 1773.]

———. 1961. *The Journals of Captain James Cook on his Voyage of Discovery*. Vol. 2. *The Voyage of the* Resolution *and* Adventure *1772–1775*. Hakluyt Society Extra Series no. 35. Cambridge: Hakluyt Society. clxx, 1021 pp. [See also COOK 1777.]

———. 1967. *The Journals of Captain James Cook on his Voyage of Discovery*. Vol. 3. *The Voyage of the* Resolution *and* Discovery *1776–1780*. Hakluyt Society Extra Series no. 36. Cambridge: Hakluyt Society. Part 1: ccxxiv, 718 pp.; Part 2: viii, 723–1647 pp. [See also COOK 1784.]

———. 1974. *The Life of Captain James Cook*. Stanford: Stanford University Press. xi, 760 pp.

Beamer, Billie. 1991. Program Could Produce Students Unprepared for Complex World. *Honolulu Star-Bulletin*, 14 March, A-21. [Criticism of Hawaiian language immersion program.]

Beckley, Fred. 1926. The Hawaiian Language. *Mid-Pacific Magazine* 32(12):511–14. ["The Hawaiian language is a very simple language ... some of the consonants are hardly pronounced ... the *l* is soft, the *k* is soft ..." Well meaning perhaps, but linguistically naive and inaccurate.]

———. 1932. Voice Culture in Ancient Hawaiian [*sic*]. *Paradise of the Pacific* 45(12):25–28. [Describes (with no supporting evidence) a relationship between an early Hawaiian's "modulated and controlled use of his voice" and his environment. Some sample phrases: "laws of vibration and consequent color reaction." "His language was that of the angels ..." "Consonants, whenever used, were pronounced as semi-vowels." "He is taught to utter only the most pleasant of thoughts ..." As a conclusion, Beckley suggested that the introduction of jazz disrupted the Hawaiians' unity with their surroundings.]

Bell, Janet E. 1978. See JUDD, BELL, AND MURDOCH 1978.

Bender, Byron W. 1982. Review of Samuel H. Elbert and Mary Kawena Pukui, *Hawaiian Grammar* (1979). *Journal of the Polynesian Society* 91(4):614–19.

Benedetto, Robert. 1982. *The Hawaii Journals of the New England Missionaries 1813–1894.* Honolulu: Hawaiian Mission Children's Society. ix, 85 pp.

Bennett, Fe. 1985. Directionals in Hawaiian Language. Course paper for Hawaiian 452, University of Hawai'i. [Not seen; ref.: HAWKINS 1989.]

*Bennett, Wendell C. 1930. Kauai Archaeology. *Papers of the Hawaiian Hist. Soc.* 17:53–62. [Contains a discussion of customs and artifacts "distinctively or predominantly found on Kauai." Such differences may explain some of the unidentified items on Anderson's word list.]

*———. 1931. *Archaeology of Kauai. Bull. Bernice P. Bishop Mus.* no. 80. iii, 156 pp., [8] *ll* of plates. [Contains an index to and map of *heiau* sites, including a possible identification of the site at which Anderson collected his Kaua'i word list.]

*Benson, Morton. 1990. Culture-Specific Items in Bilingual Dictionaries of English. *Dictionaries* 12:43–54.

[Beresford, William]. 1789. *A Voyage Round the World, but More Particularly to the North-west Coast of America: Performed in 1785, 1786, 1787, and 1788, in the King George and Queen Charlotte, Captains Portlock and Dixon* ... By Captain George Dixon. London: Goulding. xxix, [2], 360 pp. [Although Dixon is listed as the author, he was actually an editor; the forty-nine chapters appear as letters signed W. B. HAW word list, pp. 268–70.]

Besnier, Niko. 1980. Review of Samuel H. Elbert and Mary Kawena Pukui, *Hawaiian Grammar* (1979). *Pacific Studies* 3(2):63–67.

———, and Albert J. Schütz. In progress. *Annotated Bibliography of Polynesian, Fijian, and Rotuman Linguistics.*

Bickerton, Derek. 1991. The Origins of Hawaiian Pidgin and Hawaiian Creole. Lecture to East-West Center Institute for Culture and Communication seminar, Honolulu, 13 November 1991.

——, and William H. Wilson. 1987. Pidgin Hawaiian. IN *Pidgin and Creole Languages: Essays in Memory of John E. Reinecke*, ed. by Glenn G. Gilbert, 61–76. Honolulu: University of Hawai‘i Press. [Discussion, examples, and analysis of forms of (possible) pidgin HAW as early as 1809.]

Bicknell, James. 1890. Hawaiian Kahunas and Their Practices. *The Friend*, September, pp. 66–67.

Biggs, Bruce. 1959. Review of Mary Kawena Pukui and Samuel H. Elbert, *Hawaiian-English Dictionary* (1957). *Journal of the Polynesian Society* 68(1):52–53. [Praises choice of entries, criticizes the looseness of word classification and the imprecise notion of compounds. Praises the marking of long vowels and glottal stops (missing the fact that long monosyllabic words were not marked as such).]

——. 1967. The Past Twenty Years in Polynesian Linguistics. IN *Polynesian Culture History. Essays in Honor of Kenneth P. Emory*, ed. by Genevieve A. Highland, Roland W. Force, Alan Howard, Marion Kelly, and Yoshiko H. Sinoto, 303–21. Honolulu: Bishop Museum Press.

*——. 1971. The Languages of Polynesia. *Current Trends in Linguistics 8. Linguistics in Oceania*, ed. by Thomas A. Sebeok, 466–505. The Hague: Mouton.

*——. 1981. *The Complete English-Maori Dictionary*. Auckland: Auckland University Press / Oxford University Press. x, 227 pp.

Billam-Walker, Donald. 1979. Article on Henry Berger, IN KANAHELE 1979, pp. 34–44.

Bille, S. A. 1849–51. *Beretning om Corvetten* Galathea’*s Reise omkring Jorden 1845*, 46, og 47. Deel 1–3. C. A. Reitzel, Kjobenhavn. Typescript translation of Hawai‘i sections in Carter Coll., BPBM [MKA].

Bingham Family Papers. Jimerson, Randall C., and Rena R. Weiss. <Yale University, Sterling Memorial Library Manuscripts and Archives. Ms. group no. 81> [Hiram Bingham I papers are in Series I (two boxes). Correspondence is microfilmed. Section called *Writings of Hiram Bingham I*: diaries, journals, notebooks, and other mss. 1811–1826. *Writings of Sybil (Moseley) Bingham*: Journal 1811–1847. Ms. ‘Select Hawaiian phrases’ (see entry). Some selections follow. 1–1: Hiram Bingham to Samuel Worcester,

Salem, MA, from Goshen, CT, 11 May 1819. (Contains a short discussion of the drawbacks to an orthography that uses numbers. Mentions discussion with Thomas Hopkins Gallaudet about the possibility of using sign language with the "unlettered heathen.") 1–5: Hiram Bingham to Jeremiah Evarts, from Oʻahu, 12 November 1824. (Discussion of the problems of the Mission publications in the United States using the old spellings; it would be better to use the mission orthography developed thus far in the publications.) 1–7: Letter written from Oʻahu, 15 November 1830 [?] to "Pinamu wahine." (In HAW. Also uses the apostrophe for glottal stop in certain possessives: *koʻu, naʻu*. But not in *aole, hoo-*, etc.) 2–27: Writings of Hiram Bingham I. "Original hymns, or first attempts at metrical composition in the HAW language. Feb. 1823." Unnumbered, but well over 100 pp.]

Bingham, Hiram. 1821. Journal of a Tour to Kauai. <HTL> [Vol. 1:180–93: transcription of place names includes macrons and breves.]

———. 1847. *A Residence of Twenty-one Years in the Sandwich Islands; or the Civil, Religious, and Political History of Those Islands; comprising a particular view of the missionary operations connected with the introduction and progress of Christianity and civilization among the Hawaiian people.* Hartford, CT: Huntington; New York: Converse. xvi, 17–616 pp. Later editions in 1848, 1849, 1969, and 1981. [Discussion of linguistic matters, especially literacy, throughout. Discussion of the problems of adopting an orthography, including the possibility of a syllabary, and the use of some of Pickering's orthographical principles (1820). pp. 154–55. Discussion of borrowed words, p. 531. For an index to the work, see CASEY 1988.]

———. 1991. *The Hawaiian Language; a Short Sketch.* Honolulu: Printing Office [Mission Houses Museum]. v, 18, [1] pp. [Written between 1826 and 1841. Printed by James D. Rumford from a ms. in the HMCS Library.]

———, and Elisha Loomis. 1823. Letter to Jeremiah Evarts. <HTL ABC 19.1, vol. 1 (141–56)> [Letter describing orthographic problems and requesting special type, including diacritics, vol. 1:141–56.]

Bingham, Sybil Moseley. 1819–1823. Typewritten copy of journal, 8 November 1819–19 Mar. 1823. IN BINGHAM FAMILY PAPERS 2–31. 30 November 1819 (on board the *Thaddeus*).

——. 1823. Select Hawaiian Phrases / Sentences Rehearsed at Table./ July 1823. (Title on cover: Selections for the Table.). IN BINGHAM FAMILY PAPERS, Series I, 2–34. [Possibly first HAW primer. Also first (so far as we know) example of glottal stops marked. In addition to sentences to be learned, there are also grammatical sections. Discussed in chapters 12 and 14]

*Binney, Judith Mary Caroline (Musgrove). 1968. *The Legacy of Guilt /A Life of Thomas Kendall.* [Auckland]: published for the University of Auckland by the Oxford University Press. xv, 220 pp. [Contains a thorough discussion of Kendall's pioneering work on the MAO language, especially the orthography, and his collaboration with Samuel Lee on the *Grammar and Vocabulary of the Language of New Zealand.* An excellent bibliographic treatment as well.]

Birgham, F. 1882. Farbensinn und Farbenblindheit bei den Hawaiiern. *Das Ausland. Wochenschrift für Länder- und Völkerkunde* 55:337. [Contains comment about and a few examples of reduplicated words for color terms.]

Bishop, Artemas. 1825. Hawaiian vocabulary IN ELLIS 1825. [The 1825 edition says that the vocabulary was obtained "this year." William Ellis described the list (249 words, sixteen sentences) as part of a larger one procured from Bishop by John Pickering.]

——. 1828. Vocabulary of the Hawaiian Language. Holographic ms., original in Copenhagen Ethnografisk Samling National Muset. Microfilm. Canberra: Pacific Manuscripts Burean. <Photographic copy in BPBM, Ms. Grp. 43; UHM microfilm S50060 no. 198> [Preface signed "A. B. May 12th, 1844." "This vocabulary is ... the first rough copy before it was corrected."]

——. 1844a. A Brief History of the Translation of the Holy Scriptures into the Hawaiian Language. *The Friend*, 1 August, pp. 74–75. [DJK: Summation of the linguistic difficulties involved in using HAW words to express the sense of the ENG text. Calls the Bible translation "far from perfect."]

——. 1844b. Hawaiian Vocabulary, with Notes on the Structure of the Language. Introductory page dated 12 May 12 1844. [Unpaged frames] 35mm. microfilm, positive of original ms. Original in Copenhagen Ethnografisk Samling National Muset. <HMCS> [Schuhmacher (1989) explained the provenance: the result of the Danish naval vessel *Galathea* calling at Hawai'i. The vocabulary is dated 12 May 1844 and signed "A. B." in the foreword.]

———. 1845. See EMERSON AND BISHOP 1845.

———. 1854a. *English and Hawaiian Words and Phrases, for the Use of Learners in Both Languages* ... Honolulu: Whitney (Polynesian Press). 112 pp. JBM #322.

———. 1854b. *Na Huaolelo a me na Olelo Kikeke ma ka Beritania, a me ka Olelo Hawaii, no na Haumana e Ao ana i Kela a me Keia, na A. Bihopa* {Words and conversation in the English, and Hawaiian languages, for students who will be learning one or the other, by A. Bishop}. Honolulu: Whitney. 112 pp. 2d ed., revised, 1871, title preceded by *Hawaiian Phrase Book* (Honolulu: Whitney. iv, 5–120 pp.) 5th ed., revised, 1884. Honolulu: Oat. Reprint, 1967, 1968 (Rutland, VT: Tuttle, 112 pp., with note "First published in 1906"). JBM #327: "Title variations: 1854, *Na Huaolelo a me na Olelo Kikeke ma ka Beritania, a me ka Olelo Hawaii*; 1871, 1878, 1881, 1884, 1893, *Hawaiian Phrase Book.*" [No glottal stops or long vowels marked. Words and phrases organized by topics. The 1968 edition was based on the 1906 edition. In spite of its uselessness as a guide to speaking HAW today, it was in its seventeenth printing in 1991.]

[Bishop, Sereno E.]. 1887. Anglo-Saxonizing Machines. Editorial in *The Friend*, August, p. 63. [A prediction that the "coming people of Hawaii are to be a thoroughly Anglicized people."]

———. 1889. Why are the Hawaiians Dying Out? Elements of Disability for Survival Among the Hawaiian People. *The Friend*, March, pp. 18–20; April, pp. 26–27. Reprinted in the BLOUNT REPORT, pp. 769–77.

———. 1891a. Decrease of Native Hawaiians. *The Friend*, April, p. 25.

———. 1891b. The Hawaiian Census Report for 1890. *The Friend*, November, p. 83.

———. 1893. A Wonderful Week. *The Friend*, February, p. 9.

Bleek, H. I. 1858. See GREY AND BLEEK.

Blount Report. See *FOREIGN RELATIONS OF THE UNITED STATES*.

Bloxam, Andrew. See DIARY OF ANDREW BLOXAM ...

Boelen, Jacobus. 1836. *Reize naar de Oost-en Westkust van Zuid-Amerika en, van daar, naar de Sandwichs-en Philippijnsche Eilanden, China enz, Gedaan, in de Jaren 1826, 1827, 1828, en 1829.* Amsterdam: Ten Brink and De Vries. [HAW section, vol.

3:20–178. Vocabulary and notes on orthography and pronunciation (e.g., "A ... als bij ons in het woord *vader* ..."). Problems with *l* ~ *r*, *k* ~ *t*, *v* ~ *w*, *b* ~ *p* noted, with examples, pp. 169–78. 246 words. Additional 253 words introduced by: "Lijst van woorden en spreck wijzen, door mij zelven uit den mond der inboorlingen, en volgens de ons voor domende uitspraak, van tijd tot tijd opgeteekend." Verzamelde Spreekwijzen: 30 phrases.]

Bond, Elias. n.d. Annotations to Andrews's dictionary. <BPBM> [Extensive corrections and additions. See MKA.]

Boom, Robert, and J. S. Christensen. 1971. *Important Hawaiian Place Names.* Honolulu: Robert Boom Co. 34 pp. 1978 edition: co-edited by Fred Kalanianoeo Meinecke. Hilo: Boom. 47 pp. [For a review, see *'AHA KŪKĀKŪKĀ 'ŌLELO HAWAI'I* (1972).]

*Bopp, Franz. 1841. *Über die Verwandtschaft der malayisch-polynesischen Sprache mit den indisch-europäischen.* Berlin: Dummler. 164 pp.

Botta, Paolo Emilio. 1841. Word list in Auguste Bernard du Hautcilly (A. Duhaut-Cilly)'s *Viaggio Intorno al Globo, principalmente alla California ed alle Isole Sandwich, negli anni 1826, 1827, 1828, e 1829 ...* 2 vols. in 1. Torino: Fontana. [HAW word list, pp. 360–65.]

Bowman, Sally-Jo. 1990. Pūnana Leo: The Quest to Save the Hawaiian Language. *Aloha* 33(1):38–41. [A history and description of Pūnana Leo, HAW language immersion preschool program. Includes interviews with Larry Kimura and others, a description of activities in one school, and Hawai'i Department of Education plans for helping to preserve the HAW language.]

Brigham, William Tufts. 1908. *The Ancient Hawaiian House.* Honolulu, Mem. Bishop Mus. 2:185–378. [House-building terms, pp. 301–4.]

——. 1911. *Ka Hana Tapa: the Making of Bark-cloth in Hawaii.* Honolulu, Mem. Bishop Mus. 3. iv, 273 pp. [Tapa-making vocabulary, pp. 215–29.]

Broca, Paul. 1862. La Linguistique et l'Anthropologie. *Bulletin de la Société d'Anthropologie de Paris.* Lecture, séance du 5 Juin 1862, pp. 264–319. [Not seen.]

Brown, J[ohn]. McMillan. 1919. A Plea for the Vanishing Culture of the Hawaiian. *Mid-Pacific Magazine* 17 (June 1919):571–73.

[DJK: Advocates college-level teaching of Hawaiian ethnology and language in order to keep traditions from being obliterated. See chapter 16.]

Brown, Ronald R. 1963. *Learn Hawaiian.* [No publication data except copyright 1963 by the author.] 145 pp. [Most recto pages are blank or contain illustrations. Sophisticated discussion of vowel length and glottal stop, ō versus *ou*, etc. Set of phonodisc recordings to accompany text. See chapter 14.]

Bryan, Edwin H., Jr. 1951. A Check List of Hawaiian Artifacts. Compiled for the Mokihana Club ... with the assistance of Kenneth P. Emory. 6 pp. Mimeographed. <BPBM GN Ethn. Pam. 3663>

Buck, Elizabeth Bentzel. 1986. The Politics of Culture: A History of the Social and Cultural Transformation of Hawaii. University of Hawai'i Ph.D. dissertation. vi, 264 *ll.* [Published as BUCK 1993.]

————. 1993. *Paradise Remade: The Politics of Culture and History in Hawai'i.* Philadelphia: Temple University Press. vii, 242 pp. [Published version of BUCK 1986. See chapter 6: Transformations in Language and Power, pp. 121–61.]

Buck, Peter Henry [Te Rangi Hiroa]. 1932. Recording of Polynesian Texts and Proper Names. *Journal of the Polynesian Society* 41 (4):253–61. [Discussion of the inadequacies of the orthographies of many PN languages. Recommends using diacritics (for the glottal stop; long vowels are not mentioned) and hyphens for compound names.]

*————. 1938. *Vikings of the Sunrise.* New York: Stokes. xiii, 335 pp.

*————. 1964. A*rts and Crafts of Hawaii.* 1st ed. 1957. Bernice P. Bishop Mus. Spec. Publ. no. 45. viii, 606 pp.

Budnick, Rich, and Duke Kalani Wise. 1989. *Hawaiian Street Names. The Complete Guide to O'ahu Street Name Translations.* Honolulu: Aloha Publishing. [4], 170 pp. 2d ed.: 1993. Honolulu: Aloha Press. 170 pp. [Preface by the Reverend Abraham Akaka, foreward by Samuel H. Elbert. The title page credits Budnick for the compilation, Wise for the translations. The collection includes 4,000 HAW street names and nearly 100 HAW place names, with their translations.]

Budnick, Rich, and Hokulani Holt-Padilla. 1991. *Maui Street Names: The Hawaiian Dictionary and History of Maui Street Names;* Honolulu: Aloha Press. 142 pp. [Translations are by Holt-Padilla.]

Burningham, Robin Yoko. See SNAKENBERG 1982.

*Burrows, Edwin. G. 1938. Western Polynesia. A Study in Cultural Differentiation. *Etnologiska Studier* 7:1–192.

Buschmann, J. E. Eduard. See HUMBOLDT 1836, 1838, 1839. [Ref.: ELBERT AND PUKUI 1979.]

*Bushnell, O[swald] A. 1986. Foreword to *Treasury of Hawaiian Words* (KENT 1986), pp. xi-xiii.

——. 1991. Aftermath: Britons' Responses to News of the Death of Captain James Cook. *The Hawaiian Journal of History* 25:1–20.

Butler, Ruth Lapham. 1942. *The Newberry Library. Edward E. Ayer Collection. Hawaiian Language.* Chicago: 1941. 33 pp. [DJK: Checklist of HAW linguistic material held by the Newberry Library. Most of the 301 items are translations of biblical material into HAW, but there are references to a number of grammars and dictionaries, as well as to glossaries of HAW words appearing in late eighteenth- and early nineteenth-century explorers' journals.]

*Buzacott, Aaron. 1866. *Mission Life in the Islands of the Pacific*, ed. by J. P. Sunderland and A. Buzacott. London: Snow. xxii, 288 pp.

Campbell, Archibald. 1816. *A Voyage Round the World, from 1806 to 1812; in which Japan, Kamschatka, the Aleutian Islands, and the Sandwich Islands, were visited. Including a narrative of the author's shipwreck on the island of Sannack, and his subsequent wreck in the ship's long boat. With an account of the present state of the Sandwich Islands and a vocabulary of their language.* Edinburgh: Constable; London: Longman; Glasgow: Smith. 2 *ll*, 288 pp. 1967 ed., Honolulu: University of Hawai'i Press for Friends of the Library of Hawai'i. 220 pp. 1969 ed.: Amsterdam: Da Capo. [Guide to pronunciation and HAW word list, pp. 227–55.]

*Cargill, David. Letters to the Secretaries of the Wesleyan Methodist Mission Society, 1832–1840. <ML ms. A2809>

Carr, Denzel. 1951. Comparative Treatment of Epenthetic and Paragogic Vowels in English Loan Words in Japanese and Hawaiian. IN *Semitic and Oriental studies ... [for] William Popper*, ed. by W. J.

Fischel. *University of California Publications in Semitic Philology* 11:13–25. [See chapter 10.]

Carr, Elizabeth Ball. 1972. *Da Kine Talk: From Pidgin to Standard English in Hawaii.* Honolulu: University Press of Hawai'i. xvii, 191 pp. [Literacy and rise of ENG, p. 4; HAW and ENG phonology compared, p. 5; dictionaries, p. 82; courses in HAW, p. 82; influence of HAW on HAW ENG, pp. 83, 86; words from HAW in ENG, pp. 82, 85; HAW and ENG structures compared, pp. 162–63.]

Carter, George R. 1908. See BALLOU AND CARTER.

Carter, Gregory Lee. 1991 [1994]. Hawaiian Prepositions and the Word *He. Working Papers in Linguistics* 23:1–44. University of Hawai'i, Department of Linguistics. [The 1991 volume appeared in 1994.]

Casey, Dawn. 1988. Subject and Name Index, a Residence of Twenty-one Years in the Sandwich Islands by Hiram Bingham. 29 pp. ["Chapters i–xii indexed by Dawn Casey, September 2, 1987; chapters xiii–xxvi indexed by Judy Roquet, June 9, 1988." Paper prepared for School of Library and Information Studies, University of Hawai'i. See BINGHAM 1847.]

Cassella, Nancy, and Nancy Martin. 1978. The Hawaiian Connection. *Journal of the New Haven Colony Hist. Soc.* 26(1):15–19.

Chamberlain, Daniel. 1819–1820. Journal on Board the Brig *Thaddeus.* <HTL>

Chamberlain, Maria Patton. ca. 1828. A Hawaiian-English Vocabulary. Ms., 15 pp. <HHS> [292 words with definitions, but not beyond the letter A (Forbes 1992). Words divided into syllables; no long vowels or glottal stops marked.]

Chamberlain, Paul H. Jr. 1968. *The Foreign Mission School.* Cornwall, CT: Cornwall Historical Society. 23 pp.

Chamisso, Adelbert von. 1821. *Bemerkungen und Ansichten.* Vol. 3 of KOTZEBUE 1821. [Contains the author's early comments about HAW.]

———. 1835. *Reise um die Welt mit der Romanzoffischen Entdeckungs-Expedition in den Jahren 1815–1818.* See KRATZ 1986.

———. 1837. *Ueber die Hawaiische Sprache.* Vorgelegt der Königlichen Akademie der Wissenschaften zu Berlin am 12. Januar 1837. Leipzig: Weidmannischen. 79, xxii pp. 1969 ed. has the subtitle *Facsimile Edition with a Critical Introduction and an Annotated*

Bibliography of Literature Relating to the Hawaiian Language by Samuel H. Elbert ... Amsterdam: Halcyon Antiquariaat. [Elbert's portion appears on pp. i–xxii. For a review, see Chapin 1971.]

———. n.d. Nachlass Chamisso. Werke. <Staatsbibliothek zu Berlin / Preußischer Kulturbesitz> [A collection of six envelopes of dictionary slips (cut from larger sheets and uneven in size), apparently ready to be ordered into a rough draft of the dictionary. One envelope marked "Grammatisches." The other envelopes are marked by letters. Box 12: H, E, BD &c, Aa, grammatisches. Box 15: U, W, P. The ms. that these slips were cut from seems to be a duplicate of an intact version of notes in two sections (some on both sides): 211, 97 *ll.*, Unterlagen zu "Hawaiisches Wörterbuch," also n.d. One large box with three folders. Large sheets, ca. legal size. Some pages nearly blank. Long vowels and glottal stops not indicated. Citations often biblical, with book, chapter, and verse numbers given. For example, abbreviations for books of the Bible and mission books and pamphlets fill an entire page. There is also a separate numbered list of 124 grammatical particles and grammatical terms (e.g., *adverbia*). Interspersed in the pages: botanical drawings, garden plans. In some sections, the majority of the "entries" are grammatical markers. Thus, this work would have served as a foundation for the grammar. There are a few pages of HAW-TAH-MAO-TON comparative vocabulary. The contents of Part II are similar.]

———. 1973. On the Hawaiian Language ... Translated from the German by Paul G. Chapin. *Working Papers in Linguistics* 5(3):89–167. University of Hawai'i, Department of Linguistics.

Chapin, Paul G. 1971. Review of Adelbert von Chamisso, *Ueber die Hawaiische Sprache*, 1969 edition. *Oceanic Linguistics* 10(2):152–57.

———. 1973. See CHAMISSO 1973.

Chaplin, George. 1993. The Honolulu Advertiser: Men Who Made the Paper. *Sunday Star-Bulletin & Advertiser*, 31 January 1993, pp. B1, B3.

Charlot, John. 1987. *The Kamapua'a Literature: The Classical Traditions of the Hawaiian Pig God as a Body of Literature*, Monograph Series no. 6. Lā'ie, HI: The Institute for Polynesian Studies, Brigham Young University—Hawai'i Campus. x, 165 pp.

——. 1992. Aspects of Onomatopoeia in Hawaiian Literature and Thought. *Rongorongo Studies: A Forum for Polynesian Philology* 2(1):14–21.

——. In progress. *Classical Hawaiian Education.*

Christensen, Jack Shields. 1967. *Instant Hawaiian.* Coedited by Fred Kalanianoeo Meinecke. Honolulu: [Star-Bulletin Printing Co., for the author]. 51 pp. 1978 ed. by Chris Christensen, coedited by Kalani Meinecke and Robert Boom. 47 pp. [A useful guide for visitors lurks behind the somewhat trivializing title, but mainly for pronunciation. Accent rules are incorrect. Word and phrase lists are divided into semantic categories; no grammatical information is given. For an overly praising review, see *'AHA KŪKĀKŪKĀ 'ŌLELO HAWAI'I* (1972).]

Churchill, William. 1907. *Weather Words in Polynesia.* Lancaster. *Memoirs of the American Anthropological Association* 2(1):1–98. [Organized by topics: clouds, precipitation, wind movement, temperature, optical meteorology, electrical meteorology, climate in general. Sources not given. No long vowels marked, although the author recognized TON double vowels as such; glottal stop written as *k* in SAM, but not at all for HAW.]

*——. 1912. *Easter Island: The Rapanui Speech and the Peopling of South-East Polynesia.* Washington, D.C.: The Carnegie Institution Publications, vol. 174. 340 pp.

*Churchward, Clerk Maxwell. *Rotuman Grammar and Dictionary.* [Sydney]: Methodist Church of Australasia, Department of Overseas Missions. 363 pp.

Clark, Ross. 1977. In Search of Beach-la-Mar: Historical Relations among Pacific Pidgins and Creoles. *Working Papers in Anthropology, Archaeology, Linguistics and Maori Studies*, no. 48. University of Auckland, Dept. of Anthropology.

——. 1979. Language. IN JENNINGS 1979, pp. 250–70.

Coan, Mrs. Titus (Lydia Bingham). 1895. *A Brief Sketch of the Missionary Life of Mrs. Sybil Mosely Bingham.* Honolulu (?): Woman's Board of Missions for the Pacific Islands ("Published by Request"). 73 pp.

Colnett, James. [1786–1788]. The Journal of Captain James Colnett aboard *The Prince of Wales & Princess Royal* from 16 Oct. 1786 to 7 Nov. 1788. Carbon of typescript copy. 250 *ll.* <Admiralty 55 Series II 146, Public Record Office in London; UHM Hawn G/460/C65 > [The Hawai'i portion is from pp. 133–83.]

Cook, James. 1777. *A Voyage Towards the South Pole and Round the World. Performed in His Majesty's ships the Resolution and Adventure, in the years 1772, 1773, 1774, and 1775.* Vol. 2. London: Strahan and Cadell. [See also BEAGLEHOLE 1961. Note also that there are many editions of the Cook journals.]

———. 1784. *A voyage to the Pacific Ocean, undertaken by the command of His Majesty, for making discoveries in the Northern Hemisphere.* London: Straham, for Nicol, & Cadell. [See also BEAGLEHOLE 1967.]

———. n.d. Log Book and Journal (second voyage). <British Museum, Adm. MS 27886, Journal, Add. MS 27888>

Cook, Kenneth William. 1994. The Temporal Use of Hawaiian Directional Particles. Paper presented at the Symposium on Language and Space, University of Duisburg, Germany, March; and the Seventh International Conference on Austronesian Linguistics, Leiden, the Netherlands, August. Typescript, 8 *ll.*

Costa, Robert Oliver. 1951. Beginning Studies in Linguistic Geography in Hawaii. Typescript, [2]. 850 *ll.* University of Hawai'i M.A. thesis. [Includes a short phonetic description of HAW. Compares ENG pronunciation of Chinese, Japanese, and HAW speakers.]

Coulter, John Wesley, ed. 1935. *A Gazetteer of the Territory of Hawaii.* Honolulu: University of Hawai'i. 241 pp. [References on Hawaiian place names, pp. 238–39.]

*Crystal, David. 1980. *A First Dictionary of Linguistics and Phonetics.* Boulder, CO: Westview. 390 pp.

Cust, R. N. 1886. ...Ueber unsere gegenwärtige Kenntniss der Sprachen oceaniens. London: Trübner. 22 pp. VII Internationaler Orientalisten-Congress, Wien. Malaisch-Polynesische Abtheilung. Mittheilung. <HMCS 499/ C95/S–P> [Hawaiiana, pp. 4–5.]

*Dalrymple, Alexander. 1771. *An Historical Collection of the Several Voyages and Discoveries in the South Pacific Ocean.* Vol. 2, containing the Dutch voyages. London: for the author. xxxii, 204, [3] pp.; 224, 20, [60] pp. 1967 reprint: Amsterdam: Da Capo. 2

vols. in 1. [The comparative PN vocabulary (see chapter 15) is in vol. 2, following the twenty numbered pages.]

Damon, Ethel Moseley. 1935. *Na Himeni Hawaii, A Record of Hymns in the Hawaiian Language.* The Friend, March, pp. 470–72; April, pp. 488–91; May, pp. 506–509. Facsimile ed., 1935. Honolulu: The Friend. 34 pp.

Das, Upendra K. 1930. Terms Used on Hawaiian Plantations. Mimeographed. Honolulu: Agricultural Department, Experiment Station, Hawaiian Sugar Planters Association. [ii], 17 *ll.* See HANCE 1954.

Dates Relating to Language History of the Hawaiian Islands. 1987. Photocopy of typescript. 4 *ll.* <UHM Hawn PL6441 .D37 1987>

Davenport, William H. ca. 1952. See ELBERT, DAVENPORT, DYKES, AND OGAN.

*Davies, John. 1810. *Te Aebi no Taheiti, e te Parou Mata Mua i Parou Hapi Iaitea te Perini e te Ridini te Parou no Taheiti.* London: London Missionary Society. 47 pp.

*——. 1823. *A Grammar of the Tahitian Dialect of the Polynesian Language.* Burder's Point, Tahiti: Mission Press. 43 pp.

——. 1839. The Polynesian Nation. *Hawaiian Spectator* 2 (January): 49–51. [DJK: Argument for Hawaii's linguistic affinity with other Polynesian islands. Provides tables of selected words, numbers, and the 'Lord's Prayer' in HAW, MQA, MAO, Rarotongan, SAM, TAH, and TON.]

*——. 1851. *A Tahitian and English Dictionary, with Introductory Remarks on the Polynesian Language and a Short Grammar of the Tahitian Dialect: with an appendix containing a list of foreign words used in the Tahitian Bible, in commerce, etc., with the sources from whence they have been derived.* Tahiti: London Missionary Society Press. vi, 40, 314, 7 pp. 1991 ed.: Tahiti: Haere Po No Tahiti. 470 pp.

*Daws, Gavan. 1968. *The Shoal of Time. A History of the Hawaiian Islands.* New York: Macmillan. xiii, [xv], 494 pp. 1974: University of Hawai'i Press. xiii, 494 pp.

Day, Arthur Grove. 1949. *Ka Palapala Hemolele, Comments on the First Hawaiian Bibles.* Reprinted from *Kokua*, November 1949. Honolulu: University of Hawai'i Press. 4 pp. [Some discussion of the problems caused by the high frequency of *k* and *a* in HAW.]

——. 1951. How to Talk in Hawaii. *American Speech* 26:18–26. Reprinted in *The Hawaii Book: Story of Our Island Paradise* (1961). St. Paul, MN: Ferguson, pp. 128–32. [Sophisticated treatment of sounds, including glottal stop (but long vowels not mentioned). Mostly a discussion of vocabulary ("20,000 words"—a figure that appears elsewhere as well). Ends with a discussion of local ENG.]

——. 1991. An Early Hawaiian Vocabulary. *The Hawaiian Journal of History* 25:21–30. [Historical background for, and reproduction of, Martínez's 1789 HAW word list. Some items identified (with ENG glosses) and respelled, pp. 28–29.]

——, and Albertine Loomis. 1973. *Ka Pa'i Palapala, Early Printing in Hawaii*. Honolulu: Printing Industries of Hawaii. 36 pp., illus.

Day, Richard R. 1985. The Ultimate Inequality: Linguistic Genocide. IN *Language of Inequality*, ed. by Nessa Wolfson and Joan Manes, 163–81. New York: Mouton. [Discussion of the "death of HAW," pp. 165–71.]

——. 1987. Early Pidginization in Hawaii. *Pidgin and Creole Languages*. IN *Essays in Memory of John E. Reinecke*, ed. by Glenn G. Gilbert, 61–76. Honolulu: University of Hawai'i Press. [Argues for the development of a HAW Maritime Pidgin after European contact, a possible contributor to HAW plantation pidgin.]

Dean, Love. See MORRIS AND DEAN 1992.

DeCamp, David. 1975. See REINECKE et al. 1975.

de Freycinet, Louis Claude de Saulces. 1823. *Voyage autour du monde entrepris par ordre du roi ... Exécute sur les corvettes de S. M. l'Uranie et la Physicienne, pendant des anées 1817, 1818, 1819, et 1820 ...* Paris: Pillet Anie. [Opposite the preface to vol. 1 (*Histoire du Voyage ...*) is a list of volumes resulting from the voyage, including the second, *Recherches sur les langues*, 1 vol. in -4°. However, although the name appears in some Pacific bibliographies, it was never published (Renée Heyum (Emeritus Pacific Curator, UHM), pers. comm., Honolulu, November 1993.]

——. 1978. *Hawai'i in 1819: A Narrative Account by Louis Claude de Saulces de Freycinet*. Translated by Ella L. Wiswell, notes and comments by Marion Kelly. *Pacific Anthropological Records* no. 26, xii, 136 pp. Honolulu, Bernice Pauahi Bishop Museum. [Occasional references to difficulties with HAW consonant alternation and pre-1820 spelling. Appendix A (pp. 121–26): Glossary of HAW words and names, with de Freycinet's spelling, present spelling, and definitions.] Delalande, A. Raymond. n.d. The Hawaiian People Has Been Connect-ed with the Semitic Race; Proved 1st by Similarity of Manners and Practices, 2ly, by the Comparison of Both Languages. Ms. [42] pp. <Cambridge University, Widner ms. Am/588f>

Del Rocco, David. 1989. Index and Vocabulary List for *Nā Kai 'Ewalu*. Paper for LIS 687 (Hawaiian Resource Materials), University of Hawai'i, Summer Session 1989. [36] *ll.* <UHM Hawn. PL 6443 .K35 1977a. Supp. [See KAMANÂ AND WILSON 1977, 1979.]

Diary of Andrew Bloxam / Naturalist of the "Blonde" / On Her Trip From England to the Hawaiian Islands 1824–25. 1925. Bernice P. Bishop Mus. Spec. Publ. no. 10. 96 pp. [Sixty-six place names, personal names and words in Bloxam's spelling and "modern" [1925] spelling, pp. 94–95.]

Dibble, Sheldon. 1835. *O ka Ikemua, he Palapala ia e Ao Aku ai i na Kamalii, i ka Heluhelu ana a me ke Ano no Hoi o na Olelo a Lakou e Heluhelu ai* {A primer, a book instructing children, in reading and in the meaning of the words they read}. Lahainaluna. 48 pp. JBM #130. [Other editions in 1835, 1837, 1840.]

——. 1838. *Ka Mooolelo Hawaii. I Kakauia e Kekahi mau Haumana o ke Kulanui, a i Hooponoponoia e Kekahi Kumu o ia Kula* {The history of Hawai'i. Written by some scholars of the high school and corrected by one of the teachers of this school}. Lahainaluna: Mea Pai Palapala no ke Kulanui. 2 p.l., 116 pp.

——. 1839. *History and General View of the Sandwich Islands' Mission.* New York: Taylor & Dodd. xii, 13–268 pp.

——. 1843. *History of the Sandwich Islands.* Lahainaluna: Press of the Mission Seminary. viii, 464 pp. [Language, pp. 5–11.] 1909 ed.: Honolulu: Thrum. v, [3], 428 pp. Based on the 1843 edition, with some changes. [Difficulties of the missionaries in acquiring the HAW language and reducing it to writing; Hawaiians' reactions to writing, pp. 148–57. Lord's Prayer in HAW, compared with TAH, Rarotongan, MAO, MQA, SAM, and TON, p. 409. HAW numerals, compared with those in twenty-nine other Austronesian languages, pp. 411–12. List of works in the HAW language, pp. 416–18.]

Dickison, Roland. 1985. Geolinguistics in Hawaii. IN *Geolinguistic Perspectives, Proceedings of the International Conference Celebrating the Twentieth Anniversary of the American Society of*

Geolinguistics, pp. 157–63. [A sketch of changes in the pronunciation of place names, especially patterns of mispronunciations, such as omission of glottal stops and long vowels, misinterpretation of such sequences as *oo,* and misplaced accent.]

*Diderot, Denis. 1955. *Supplément au Voyage de Bougainville, publie par Herbert Dieckmann.* Geneve: Droz. clv, 86 pp.

*Dilworth, Thomas. 1740 [1788]. *A New Guide to the English Tongue.* 52 d ed. Gainsbrough: Mozley. 154 pp.

Dinswood, Elsie. 1939. The Hawaiian Language. *Paradise of the Pacific* 51(11):18, 29. [An overpraising review of Judd's grammar (1939a), referring to the author's work as "intellectual, intelligent and energetic," none of which adjectives seems appropriate.]

Dixon, George. 1789. See BERESFORD 1789.

Doane, E[dward] T[oppin]. 1896. A Comparison of the Languages of Ponape and Hawaiian ... With additional notes and illustrations by Sidney H. Ray. Read before the Royal Society of N.S. Wales, September 5, 1894. *Journal of the Royal Society of New South Wales* 29:420–53. [Divided into the following sections: 1. Introduction; 2. Sounds; 3. Syllables; 4. Accent; 5. *O* emphatic; 6. *La* directive; 7. Prepositions; 8. Nouns; 9. Adjectives; 10. Numerals; 11. Pronouns; 12. Verbs; 13. Participles; 14. Verbal directives; 15. Syntax; 16. Comparative vocabulary. The article adds little to our knowledge of HAW, since the pieces of the descriptive sketch were taken from "the Grammar."]

Dodge, Charlotte Peabody. 1941. See ALEXANDER AND DODGE 1941.

Donne, M. A. [1866]. *The Sandwich Islands and Their People.* London: Society for Promoting Christian Knowledge. iv, 5–188 pp. [Discussion of HAW language, possibly based on those in various editions of Ellis's *Journal* ..., pp. 84–87.]

Donnelly, Milly Lou. 1943. "G.I." Hawaiian. *Paradise of the Pacific* 55(4):10–11. [Primitive guide to pronunciation. An ENG-HAW word list of 185 items, arranged in semantic categories. HAW words divided into syllables. No glottal stops or macrons.]

Dorton, Lilikalā. 1984. E Hoʻomau ana ka ʻŌlelo Hawaiʻi? or Will the Hawaiian Language Survive? An Update on the Status of the Native Language in Hawaiʻi. Conference on Pacific Languages: Directions for the Future. Port Vila, Vanuatu. 30 August 1984. Mimeographed. 16 *ll.* <UHM Hawn PL6441 .D67 1984> [Mostly political in content, with some statistics on number of speakers and programs for language survival.]

*Douglas, Edward M. K., and Rahera Barrett Douglas. 1983. Nga Kohanga Reo: A Salvage Programme for the Maori Language. Paper read at the Symposium on The Survival of Indigenous Languages, Multilingualism, and the Emergence of Pidgins and Creoles. 53 d ANZAAS Congress, Perth, W. A., Australia.

Drechsel, Emanuel J., and T. Haunani Makuakane. ca. 1979. Hawaiian Loanwords in Chinook Jargon and Eskimo Jargon. Photocopy of typescript. 12 *ll.* <UHM Spec Creole PMB1 .H3 D74 1979>

Dumont d'Urville, J .S. C. 1834. *Voyage de Découvertes de l'Astrolabe, éxecuté par ordre du Roi, pendant les années 1826—1827— 1828—1829, sous le commandement de M. J. Dumont d'Urville.* Paris: Ministère de la Marine. [Word list: pp. 196–306. See also HYMES 1983]

Duncan, Janice K. 1972. *Minority without a Champion: Kanakas on the Pacific Coast, 1788–1850.* Portland: Oregon Historical Society. 24 pp.

*Duponceau, Peter Stephen. 1817. *English Phonology.* Paper read 24 May 1817. No. 17 of [ ], pp. 228–64. Philadelphia: Small. [The offprint does not give the title of the volume.]

Dupont, John. 1973. Linking *Ai.* Unpublished ms. [Not seen; ref.: ELBERT AND PUKUI 1979]

Dutton, Meiric K. 1972. Mele Kalikimaka. Editorial in *The Sunday Advertiser*, 24 December 1972. [Includes different spellings for the words.]

Dwight, Edwin Welles. 1818. *Memoirs of Henry Obookiah, a Native of Owhyhee, and a Member of the Foreign Mission School; who died at Cornwall, Connecticut, February 17, 1818, Aged 26 years.* 1968: Honolulu: Woman's Board of Missions for the Pacific Islands, the Hawai'i Conference, the United Church of Christ. 112 pp. 1990: Women's Board of Missions for the Pacific Islands. 112 pp.

Dwight, Theodore. 1850. Sketch of the Polynesian Language, drawn up from Hale's Ethnology and Philology. *Transactions of the American Ethnological Society* 2. [Not seen; ref.: MARTIN 1867.]

Dyen, Isidore. 1965. *A Lexicostatistical Classification of the Austronesian Languages.* Indiana University Publications in Anthropology and Linguistics. Memoir 19 of the *International Journal of American Linguistics*. 64 pp.

Dykes, Jesse W. ca. 1952. See ELBERT, DAVENPORT, DYKES, AND OGAN.

*Edwards, B. B. 1832. *The Missionary Gazetteer; Comprising a Geographical and Statistical Account of the Various Stations of the American and Foreign Protestant Missionary Societies of all Denominations, with their Progress in Evangelization and Civilization.* Boston: Hyde. xi, 13–431 pp.

*Elbert, Samuel H. 1941. Chants and Love Songs of the Marquesas Islands, French Oceania. *Journal of the Polynesian Society* 50(2): 53–91.

——. 1951a. Hawaiian Literary Style and Culture. *American Anthropologist* 53:345–54. [DJK: Suggests that Hawaiian literary style owes its distinctiveness to special features of its culture. This results in literary emphasis on the chief, personal and place names, natural features, and figurative rather than literary expressions. Based on an analysis of 900 pages of tales printed in Hawaiian newspapers between 1870 and 1890.]

——. 1951b. *Conversational Hawaiian.*   Honolulu: University of Hawai‘i Extension Division. Mimeographed. vi, 98 pp. 2d ed.: 1955. Later editions: see ELBERT & KEALA 1961. <UHM Hawn PL6445 .E4> [See chapters 12 and 14.]

——. 1952. Hawaiian Language—"Handle with Care." *Paradise of the Pacific* 64(2):34–35. [Popular discussion of similar-sounding words and *kaona*, glottal stops, and long vowels, and a preliminary report on the Pukui-Elbert dictionary in progress (1957).]

——. 1953a. Internal Relationships of Polynesian Languages and Dialects. *Southwestern Journal of Anthropology* 9 (summer):147–73. [Written in collaboration with William H. Davenport, Jesse W. Dykes, and Eugene Ogan. See chapter 15.]

——. [1953b]. The Hawaiian Language and its Relatives. "Address delivered by ..." Mimeographed. 4 *ll.* <UHM Hawn PL6441. E43> [Brief sketch of phonology, structure, and vocabulary, with a page of statistics on number of speakers of various Austronesian languages.]

——. 1953c. A Literature in Polynesia. *Journal of Oriental Literature* 6:52–55. [DJK: Discusses ways by which Hawaiian oral folklore ceases to be merely ritualistic or genealogical in nature and deserves to rank as literature. Points out, and gives examples of, facets of Hawaiian literature that have literary value, such as: sublime themes, detailed attention to nature, sophisticated poetic style, and predilection for finding the abstract in the concrete.]

———. 1954. The Hawaiian Dictionaries, Past and Future. *Sixty-second Report of the Hawaiian Hist. Soc. for the Year 1953*, pp. 5–18. [Discussion of premissionary word lists and lexicographic methodology for PUKUI AND ELBERT 1957.]

———. 1956. Art and Language in Hawaii. *Paradise of the Pacific* 68(1):34–35, 100. [General comments about the structure of HAW and both grammatical and cultural features illustrated by Jean Charlot's drawings from *Conversational Hawaiian.*]

———. 1957a. Possessives in Polynesia. *The Bible Translator* 8(1):23–27.

———. 1957b. See PUKUI AND ELBERT 1957.

———. 1959. See FORNANDER 1916–20.

———. 1960. The Structure of Hawaiian as a Factor in Symbolic Proliferation. Extrait des *Actes du VIᵉ Congres International des Sciences Anthropologiques et Ethnologiques* Tome 2, 1ᵉ vol., pp. 67–70.

———. 1962. Symbolism in Hawaiian Poetry. *Etc.: A Review of General Semantics* 18:389–400. [DJK: Examination of HAW poetry shows interrelationship between symbolism and elements of the culture. Observes that HAW symbols are not the same as American or European symbols.]

———. 1964a. Hawaiian Reflexes of Proto-Malayo-Polynesian and Proto-Polynesian Reconstructed Forms. *Journal of the Polynesian Society* 73(4):399–410. [DJK: Comparison of 155 HAW forms, on the basis of meaning similarity and perfect conformity, with known sound correspondences.]

———. 1964b. See PUKUI AND ELBERT 1964.

———. 1966. See PUKUI AND ELBERT 1966.

———. 1968. See SCHÜTZ AND ELBERT 1968.

———. 1969a. Hawaiian. *Collier's Encyclopedia.* New York: Crowell-Collier Educational Corp. Vol. 11:717–18.

———. 1969b. Reviews: *Hawaiian Phrase Book; A Short Synopsis of the Most Essential Points in Hawaiian Grammar,* by W. D. Alexander; and *An English-Hawaiian Dictionary with Various Useful Tables,* by H. R. Hitchcock. *Modern Language Journal* 53:20–21. [Short review of these works as recent reprints by Tuttle.]

———. 1969c. Introduction and Bibliography for Adelbert von Chamisso, *Ueber die Hawaiische Sprache, Facsimile Edition, with a Critical Introduction and an Annotated Bibliography of Literature relating to the Hawaiian Language by Samuel H. Elbert.* Amsterdam: Halcyon Antiquariaat. xxii pp.

———. 1969d. See TSUZAKI AND ELBERT 1969.

———. 1970. *Spoken Hawaiian.* Honolulu: University of Hawai'i Press. [xiv], 252 pp. [See chapters 12 and 14.]

———. 1971a. Hawaiian Place Names. *Working Papers in Linguistics* 3(7):1–88. University of Hawai'i, Department of Linguistics.

———. 1971b. See PUKUI AND ELBERT 1971.

———. 1974. See PUKUI, ELBERT, AND MOOKINI 1974.

———. 1975a. The Domain of Place Names in Hawaii. IN *Linguistics and Anthropology: Essays in Honor of C. F. Voegelin,* ed. by M. Dale Kincade, Kenneth L. Hale, and Oswald Werner, 137–85. Lisse: de Ridder.

———. 1975b. See PUKUI, ELBERT, AND MOOKINI 1975.

———. 1976. Connotative Values of Hawaiian Place Names. IN *Directions in Pacific Traditional Literature: Essays in Honor of Katharine Luomala,* ed. by Adrienne L. Kaeppler and H. Arlo Nimmo, 117–33. Bernice P. Bishop Mus. Spec. Publ. no. 62.

———. 1982. Lexical Diffusion in Polynesia and the Marquesan-Hawaiian Relationship. *Journal of the Polynesian Society* 91(4): 499–517.

———. 1989a. A Note on the Hawaiian Language. IN *Hawaiian World, Hawaiian Heart,* by Robert A. LaBrucherie, 222–23. Pine Valley, CA: Imágenes Press. [Language sketch for the layman. Somewhat misleading, perhaps because of its brevity. The missionaries are mildly chastised for not knowing in the 1820s what we know today.]

———. 1989b. See PUKUI, ELBERT, AND MOOKINI 1989.

———. 1990. See PUKUI, ELBERT, AND MOOKINI 1990.

——. 1991. Shifting Attitudes in Hawai'i 1920s to 1990. *Currents in Pacific Linguistics: Papers on Austronesian Languages and Ethnolinguistics in Honour of George W. Grace*, ed. by Robert Blust, 99–102. *Pacific Linguistics*, C-117.

——. 1992. See PUKUI AND ELBERT 1992.

——, William H. Davenport, Jesse W. Dykes, and Eugene Ogan. ca. 1952. Internal Relationships of Polynesian Languages and Dialects. Mimeographed. <?> [Published version: ELBERT 1953.]

——, and Samuel A. Keala. 1955. *Conversational Hawaiian*. 2d ed. Honolulu: University of Hawai'i Press. 131 pp. 3d ed.: 1961, ix, 224 pp. [Described as 3 d edition of Elbert 1951]. 4th ed.: 1963, ix, 226 pp. 5th ed.: 1964, 226 pp. [Pronunciation, pp. 5–6; sixty-eight lessons of dialoguess, drills, and grammatical explanations. HAW-ENG vocabulary, pp. 201–9; ENG-HAW vocabulary, pp. 210–20. See chapters 12 and 14.]

——, and Edgar C. Knowlton, Jr. 1957. Ukulele. *American Speech* 32 (December):307–10. [DJK: Account of the adaptation of the word *ukulele* for the Portuguese stringed instrument that was introduced to the islands in the late nineteenth century.]

——, and Noelani Mahoe. 1970. *Nā Mele o Hawai'i Nei: 101 Hawaiian Songs*. Honolulu: University of Hawai'i Press. 110 pp. ["Structure of the Hawaiian Language and the Poetic Style," pp. 10–17. Includes an inventory of sounds, a discussion of poetic repetition, reduplications, rhyme, terseness, and vagueness, ambiguity, and veiled meanings. "Symbolism, Indirection, and Kaona," pp. 17–19. Other topics of linguistic intererest are "The Power of the Word," "Translations," and "Poetic Vocabulary."]

——, and Mary Kawena Pukui. 1971. *Hawaiian Grammar*. Draft. Honolulu: University of Hawai'i Press. Photocopy of corrected typescript. xiii, 232 *ll*. <UHM Hawn PL6443 .E37>

——, and Mary Kawena Pukui. 1979. *Hawaiian Grammar*. Honolulu: University Press of Hawai'i . xvii, 193 pp. [Reviews: BESNIER 1980, BENDER 1982, KRUPA 1981, MEIER 1985. See chapter 12.]

——, and David B. Walch. 1968. Correspondence: The Development of the Hawaiian Alphabet. *Journal of the Polynesian Society* 77(2): 191–92.

Ellis, William. 1823. Letter to Jeremiah Evarts, 10 March. <HTL> [Discussion of similarity between HAW and TAH.]

——. 1825. *A Journal of a Tour around Hawaii, the Largest of the Sandwich Islands by a Deputation from the Mission on Those Islands*. Boston: Crocker and Brewster. xii, [13]–264 pp. ["The following Journal was drawn up by Mr. Ellis, from minutes kept by himself, and by his associates on the tour (Asa Thurston, Charles S. Stewart, Artemas Bishop, Joseph Goodrich), who subsequently gave it their approbation" (p. vii). In this edition, the comments on the language (pp. 243–52) are confined to a short discussion of the alphabet, including "interchangeable letters." The word list is the fuller one (248 items, based on vocabulary collected by Artemas Bishop and used without his permission), with italicized forms matching those in Catherine the Great's "radical words," and a very large number of mistakes and misprints. "General remarks on the Polynesian language. Copied from the Introduction to a Grammar of the Tahitian Dialect of the Polynesian Language printed by the English Missionaries at the Society Islands, in 1823," pp. 252–54. "Vocabulary of the Fejeean language," from John Pickering's copy of William P. Richardson's word list, collected in 1811, pp. 254–58. In the 1826 edition (London), the Appendix was expanded considerably to include a discussion of the language family, the alphabet, "defects" and "excellencies" of the language, and a grammatical sketch. The word list was corrected and shortened to seventy-four words, including *hokú* 'star', with the final long vowel marked with an acute accent. The 1979 edition, based on the 1827 edition, includes on the title page: *With an introduction by Thurston Twigg-Smith and an introduction to the new edition by Terence Barrow, Ph.D.* Rutland, VT, & Tokyo: Charles E. Tuttle Company. xxiv, 363 pp. [In the appendix, "Remarks on the Hawaiian language" (pp. 334–42), approximately three pages of pronoun paradigms have been omitted.]

——. 1831. *Polynesian Researches*. 4 vols. 1st ed., 1829: London: Fisher, Son and Jackson. 2 vols. Hawaiʻi section reprinted in 1969 as *Polynesian Researches: Hawaii*. Rutland, Vt.: Tuttle. xiv, 471 pp. Foreword by Edouard R. L Doty, pp. xi–xiv. [Vol. 4 (vii, 471 pp.) treats Hawaiʻi. Sketch of HAW and explanation of orthography, pp. 49–54. *T, k*, and *r, l* still used. Appendix (pp. 459–70): Remarks on the Hawaiian Language. Repeats sections on HAW from various editions of his *Journal of a Tour ...*]

*E. Loomis—Printer. 1967. *The Friend*, January, p. [5]. [A brief biography of Elisha Loomis, concentrating on his work as printer, with a reproduction of the first two pages of the 1822 *Alphabet*.]

[Emerson, John Smith, and Artemas Bishop]. 1845. *He Hoakakaolelo no na Huaolelo Beritania, i Mea Kokua i na Kanaka Hawaii e Ao ana ia Olelo* {An explanation of English words, as an aid to Hawaiians learning this language}. Lahainaluna: Mea Pai Palapala o ke Kulanui. x, 184 pp. [An ENG-HAW dictionary, a translation of an abridged Webster's dictionary. Preface in ENG, signed by J. S. Emerson: "from letter *O* to end was furnished by Rev. A. Bishop."]

Emerson, Joseph Swift. 1921. Polynesian Alphabets. *Report of the President, Annual Report of the Hawaiian Hist. Soc.* 29:10–15. [HAW treated as a dialect of PN, which is described as a "simple, primeval language." Consonant correspondences among PN languages discussed. Excellent explanation of the function of the glottal stop (p. 12): "It is no curious affectation on the part of the Hawaiian thus to respect the memory of a lost *k*; it is an absolute necessity in order to distinguish words of a totally different etymology and meaning which are unfortunately spelled in the same way and are only distinguished from each other by the pronunciation ... "]

Emerson, Nathaniel Bright. 1839–1915. Word Meanings; Proverbs and Sayings. In his Collections, Folder #2. <HMCS MS B Em 35>

————. 1909. *Unwritten Literature of Hawaii; the Sacred Songs of the Hula Collected and Tr. with Notes and an Account of the Hula ...* Washington, D.C.: Government Printing Office. 288 pp. Later editions in 1965, 1972, 1977. ["Elocution and rhythmic accent in HAW song," pp. 158–75. The glossary begins with notes on HAW pronunciation. Each vowel is said to have two sounds, but many of the examples are incorrect. The glottal "closure" is mentioned, but its use in the glossary is not accurate. The list of diphthongs is incorrect, including such vowel combinations as *ia* and *ua*. There is an attempt to describe the distribution of allophones of /w/: [w] at the beginning of a word, [v] in the middle. The accent rule (penult and alternate preceding syllables) is incorrect, pp. 265–70.]

*————. n.d. Notes credited to N. B. Emerson in the collection of H. P. Kekahuna [Not seen; ref.: HOLMES 1981].

Emory, Kenneth Pike. 1924. *The Island of Lanai. A Survey of Native Culture. Bull. Bernice P. Bishop Mus.* no. 12:1–129. [Gazetteer; 323 place names, following the Andrews-Parker orthography. Glottal stops marked, but not long vowels. However, accent other than the penultimate syllable marked; e.g., *hōkū* is written *hokú*. Dialect variation: "*K* is always sounded *t* in Ohikupala; *w* is sounded *v* in Luahiwa, Iwiole, and Makaiwa. The older natives favor the *t* and *v* sound in place of *k* and *w* in many words," pp. 28–37.]

———. 1963. East Polynesian Relationships; Settlement Pattern and Time Involved as Indicated by Vocabulary Agreements. *Journal of the Polynesian Society* 72(2):78–100. [DJK: Application of glotto-chronological techniques to the problem of the settlement of Hawaii suggests that the HAW vocabulary is not purely derived from either the TAH or MQA languages.]

English-Hawaiian Translator; ke Kumu Mahele Olelo. 1969. Addison, TX: International Travel Mate. 1 card. [NJM: Plastic card with ENG/HAW terms.]

The English Language as a Qualification for Office. 1862. *The Polynesian* 19(10):2. [A reaction to a legislative proposal that office-holders should know HAW, and a counter proposal that they should know ENG.]

*Fairchild, Hoxie Neale. 1928. *The Noble Savage: A Study in Romantic Naturalism.* New York: Columbia University Press. Republished in 1961: New York: Russell & Russell.

Faye, Lindsay Tony. 1960. See HANCE, FAYE, AND HANSON 1960.

Fell, Barry. ca. 1974. An Introduction to Polynesian Epigraphy with a Special Report on the Moanalua Stele known as Pohaku ka Luahine. Arlington, MA: Polynesian Epigraphic Soc. 10 *ll.*

Fernandez, Zelie Duvauchelle. ca. 1955. *Beginner's Hawaiian.* Parts 1 and 2. Mimeographed. Honolulu: Privately printed. Part 1: v, 47 pp; part 2: iv, 60 pp. [See Sherwood 1981. Naive guide to pronunciation. The statements on grammar are essentially ENG-based: for example, modifications to verbs are considered tenses. "*He* is the Hawaiian indefinite article corresponding to the English words 'a' and 'an'"—an example of the translation bias that underlies this treatment.]

*Findlay, Katherine. 1993. Maori Radio: Where is it Going? *Mana (Maori News Magazine)* January/February, pp. 9–10.

First Book in Hawaiian. 1930. See ATCHERLEY 1930.

The First Book in Hawaiian. 1930. *The Friend,* March, p. 67. [An announcement of the publication of ATCHERLEY 1930.]

Flink, Stanley E. 1988. The Hawaiian Connection. *Yale Alumni Magazine* 51(4):46–50.

*Forbes, David W. 1992. *Treasures of Hawaiian History from the Collection of the Hawaiian Historical Society*. Honolulu: Hawaiian Historical Society. 126 pp. [Catalog of the exhibition at the University of Hawai'i Art Gallery, 22 November to 18 December 1992. 175 items, with annotations.]

Foreign Relations of the United States. 1894. Affairs in Hawaii. The Executive Documents of the House of Representatives for the Third Session of the Fifty-Third Congress 1894–95. Washington: Government Printing Office. 2 vol. 1,437 pp. [Commonly known as the Blount Report.]

Fornander, Abraham. 1878–1885. *An Account of the Polynesian Race, its Origin and Migrations and the Ancient History to the Times of Kamehameha I*. 3 vols. London: Trübner. 1969 ed., Rutland, VT: Tuttle, 3 vols. in 1. x, 247; v, 399; x, 292. Index to "The Polynesian race," compiled by John F. G. Stokes, with a brief memoir of Judge Fornander, prepared by W. D. Alexander. xiv–86 pp. [Vol. 3: comparative vocabulary study. Language: I: pp. 31, 37, 139–41, II: pp. 3, 59, III: pp. vi, i, 15, 63, 86, 229. Other topics connected with language: "PN one of the oldest," "fundamentally Aryan," "Aryan affinities," "in which may be found the solution to many etymologi-cal riddles in the Aryan," and Indo-European morphology, "not an offshoot of the Malay," dialectal variations. All of volume III is devoted to : "Comparative vocabulary of the PN and Indo-European languages."]

——. 1885. Hawaiian Names of Relationship, etc. *Hawaiian Almanac and Annual* 11:46–53. [NJM: HAW names and kinship terms.]

——. 1916–1920. *The Fornander Collection of Hawaiian Antiquities and Folk-lore*. Bernice P. Bishop Museum Memoir, vol. 4–6. Items from vol. 4 and 5 appear as *Selections from Fornander's Hawaiian Antiquities and Folk-Lore*, ed. by Samuel H. Elbert (1959). Honolulu: University of Hawai'i Press. 297 pp. [Glottal stops and macrons appear only in four pages of notes at the end, and in the captions for the drawings.]

French-Hawaiian Dictionary. E to ZZ. <HMSC   MS/499   Anonymous>

[French-Hawaiian Dictionary]. 1860–1869. Irregularly paginated. ([14], 90, [92] pp.) <IN Hawaiian Glossary in the Archives of the Sacred Hearts in Honolulu. UHM microfilm S11041> [Begins with names of trees, plants, seaweed, fish, birds, etc.   The remainder is an incomplete glossary from FR to HAW, very finely written in two columns (over a hundred words to a page), with rather few of the HAW words filled in.]

Fukuoka, Nobujirō, and Tetsutaro Taki. 1890. *Sankoku Kaiwa* {Three languages dictionary}. Tokyo: Airindo. 2 p. l., 114, [1] pp. JBM #561. 2d ed.: 1898. Hiroshima: Yasukichi Toda. 2 p. l., 113, [1] pp. JBM #598. [ENG, HAW, and Japanese phrase book, but somewhat misnamed: the first fifty-seven pages are single words arranged in semantic and grammatical categories (in three columns for the three languages), with ENG and HAW written in *kana*, Japanese written in both *kana* and *kanji*.]

Fuller, Josiah [J. Pula]. 1862. *Ke Kumu Mua Ano Hou, i Hoonaniia i na Kii Maikai* {New first teacher, decorated with nice pictures}. Honolulu: Na ka Papa Hoonaauao/ Boston: Maka [Na ka?] Hale Paipalapala o Oliver Ellsworth. Photocopy. 48 pp. <HHS H/428.6/F95> [Not in JBM. Alphabet, short sentences, first words (one-syllable), numbers. Short stories, increasing in difficulty. Instructions on how to write correctly, punctuate. Sermon on the Mount. Lord's Prayer.]

Gaimard, Joseph P. 1823. See ARAGO 1823.

Gaudichaud, Charles. 1826–1830. *Voyage autour du monde entrepris par ordre du Roi ... sur les corvettes l'*Uranie *et la* Physicienne *1817–1820. Botanique.* Paris: Pilet Ainé. 522 pp.; atlas 22 pp., 120 pl. [Not seen; ref.: St. John 1989.]

Gaussin, Pierre Louis Jean Baptiste. 1853. *Du dialecte de Tahiti, de celui des îles Marquises, et en général, de la langue polynésienne.* Paris: Firmin et Didot Frères. 284 pp.

Geraghty, Paul. 1983. Review of Peter A. Lanyon-Orgill, *Captain Cook's South Sea Island Vocabularies. Journal of the Polynesian Society* 92(4):554–59.

———. 1984. Meeting of Tongues; Question—Will the Hawaiian Language Survive? Answer—What We Really Need is Some Sort of Miracle. *Islands Business* 10(10):54–55.

Gerard, W. R. 1899. Language of the Hawaiians. *Paradise of the Pacific* 12(1):1–2, 9. [DJK: The HAW language is characterized by soft and indistinct sounds, a large vocabulary, and difficulty in expressing abstract ideas.]

Girvin, James. 1913. The Language of Hawaii. *Mid-Pacific Magazine* 6 (August):133–39. [DJK: Overview of notable characteristics of the HAW language, including its capacity for double entendre, sensitivity to vowel sounds, and its adaptivity to poetry.]

*Gleason, Henry Allen, Jr. 1961. *An Introduction to Descriptive Linguistics.* 2d ed. (1st ed., 1955). New York: Holt, Rinehart and Winston. viii, 503 pp.

Gleason, William B. 1884. *English Lessons for Hawaiians.* Hawaiian revised by A. O. Forbes. Honolulu. 32 pp. [Not seen.]

Gowen, Herbert Henry. 1899. The Hawaiian Language and Indo-European Affinities. *The American Antiquarian and Oriental Journal* 21:91–97. ["Let us first consider the Grammar, then the Vocabulary—remembering at the same time that in tongues so primitive the grammar is but slight, the endings are unknown, and but little distinction is made between noun and verb (p. 94)." The comparison treats a few grammatical markers, finding similarities between HAW and, variously, Sanskrit, Greek, Latin, German, etc. E.g., HAW *ka/ke* and German *das.* Numerals and twenty-three words also compared.]

Grace, George William. 1959. *The Position of the Polynesian Languages within the Austronesian (Malayo-Polynesian) Language Family.* Memoir 16 of the *International Journal of American Linguistics.* Bloomington: Indiana University Publications in Anthropology and Linguistics. v, 77 pp.

Gramare Havaii-Pelikani. 1877. 31 *ll.* Ms. <IN Hawaiian Glossary in the Archives of the Sacred Hearts in Honolulu. UHM microfilm S11041> [Description of ENG alphabet in HAW, including the pronunciation of the names of the letters, first in a HAW spelling and then in FR spelling. The remainder is a glossary of ENG words, with meanings in HAW, and pronunciation in FR spelling.]

Gramare Havaii-Peritani. 1860–1869. 30 pp. <IN Hawaiian glossary in the Archives of the Sacred Hearts in Honolulu. UHM microfilm S11041> [A primer, beginning with letters of the alphabet. On the third page begins a word list, with ENG, HAW meaning, FR-based pronunciation of the ENG, which continues to the end.]

[Gregory, Herbert E.] 1922. Annual Report of the Director for 1922. *Bull. Bernice P. Bishop Mus.* 4:5–38. [Pp. 25–26: A description of the Parker revision of the Andrews dictionary, noting that "the manuscript was incomplete in several essential features, demanding an unexpected amount of work on the part of the museum staff (and others) ... The revised Dictionary is obviously incomplete and the way is open for the preparation of a volume that will draw material from all available sources."]

Grey, George, and H. I. Bleek. 1858. The Library of His Excellency Sir George Grey, K.C.B. *Philology.* Vol. 2, part 4. *New Zealand, The Chatham Islands and Auckland Islands.* London: Trübner. 154 pp. [Section VII. The HAW language, pp. 138–49. The divisions are: [introduction], grammars, vocabularies, phrase book, elementary books, catechism, New Testament, Old Testament, tract, geography, arithmetic, proclamation, parliamentary papers (in ENG), and periodicals.]

Grey, George, and another. n.d. Sandwich Islands. Notes on Sandwich Islands language. Photocopy of ms. <Auckland Public Library G MSS/93/GMSS/D8> [Source unidentified. A discussion of HAW syllable structure and a statistical analysis of the possible number of one-, two-, three-, and four-syllable words.]

Groos, J. H. 1873–1874. Hawaiian and Malay Dialects. *China Rev.* 2:185–86.

Gulatz, Scotty. 195-. *Speak Hawaiian: Will Help You Have More Fun on Your Hawaiian Holiday.* Honolulu: South Sea Sales. 31 pp. [See 'AHA KŪKĀKŪKĀ 'ŌLELO HAWAI'I (1972) for review: "Filled with gross inaccuracies of pronunciation, and numerous deliberate tongue-in-cheek definitions, this item is better considered an unfortunate source of humor rather than an attempt to provide accurate and helpful information on speaking HAW. It is an example of commercialism and exploitation of the HAW language, treating the subject matter as a joke."]

Gurczynski, Ethel A. 1980. See HANDBOOK OF EXPRESSIONS IN ENGLISH AND HAWAIIAN.

Haawina Hawaii: Being a Lesson in the Hawaiian Language in Verse and Pictures and 1000 Words Defined. 1942. Honolulu: Honolulu Star-Bulletin. 16 pp.

He mau Haawina no ka Olelo Beritania {A few lessons in English}. 1841. Lahainaluna: Press of the High School. 40 pp. JBM #222. 2d ed., 1844. Honolulu: Mea Pai Palapala a na Misionari. 36 pp. JBM #273. [By L. Andrews.]

Hale, Horatio. 1846. *Ethnography and Philology.* Vol. 6 in *United States Exploring Expedition 1838–42.* Philadelphia: Lea and Blanchard. 666 pp. Unofficial issue; reprinted 1968. Ridgewood, NJ: Gregg. [Includes "A Comparative Grammar of the Polynesian Dialects," pp. 229–89; a PN-ENG vocabulary, pp. 294–339; and an ENG-PN vocabulary, pp. 341–56.]

*———. 1890. Letter to [   ], Ontario, Canada (11 July). <School of Oriental and African Studies Library, University of London>

Hance, John C. 1954. Plantation Terminology; 101 Words Commonly Used on Hawaiian Sugar Companies. Mimeographed. Honolulu. [i], 7 *ll.* <UHM Hawn P381.H3 H34> ["Revised from Das' list." See DAS 1930.]

———, Lindsay Tony Faye, and Noel S. Hanson. ca. 1960. Plantation Terminology; Words Commonly used on Hawaiian Sugar Plantations. 9 pp. <UHM Hawn P381.H3 H35> ["Revised from Das' list."]

Hancock, Ian F. 1975. See REINECKE et al.

Hancock, Sibyl, and Doris Sadler. 1969. *Let's Learn Hawaiian; a Word Picture Book.* Rutland, VT: Tuttle. 76 pp. [NJM: Includes common HAW words. Intended for juvenile readers.]

Handbook of Expressions in English and Hawaiian. 1980. Translated by Ethel A. Gurczynski, edited by Collette L. Akana-Gooch. Honolulu: Department of Education. Photocopy of typescript. 23 pp. Rev. ed., May 1991. Honolulu: Office of Instructional Services /General Education. [Glottal stops and long vowels marked, but long vowels misleadingly described: "Vowels are stressed when marked with macrons ..." Phrases organized by semantic category. In the revised edition, the wrong explanation of the macron not corrected; guide to pronunciation naive and misleading. Glottal stop inadequately explained.]

Handy, Edward Smith Craighill. 1940. *The Hawaiian Planter.* Vol. 1: His Plants, Methods, and Areas of Cultivation. *Bull. Bernice P. Bishop Mus.* 161:1–227. [The work is rich in HAW terms for plants, seasons, phrases of the moon, place names, etc. The appendices (pp. 219–27) contain lists of terms. No glottal stops or macrons marked. See HANDY AND HANDY 1972.]

——, and Elizabeth Green Handy. 1972. *Native Planters in Old Hawaii: Their Life, Lore, and Environment.* With the collaboration of Mary Kawena Pukui. *Bull. Bernice P. Bishop Mus.* 233. xviii, 641 pp. [An expanded version of HANDY 1940. 1992 ed. includes an index to subjects and chants.]

——, and Elizabeth Green Handy. 1972. *Native Planters in Old Hawaii: Their Life, Lore, and Environment.* With the collaboration of Mary Kawena Pukui. *Bull. Bernice P. Bishop Mus.* 233. xviii, 641 pp. [An expanded version of HANDY 1940. 1992 ed. includes an index to subjects and chants.]

——, Mary Kawena Pukui, and Katherine Livermore. 1934. *Outline of Hawaiian Physical Therapeutics. Bull. Bernice P. Bishop Mus.* 126:1–51. [NJM: Medical terms; names of medicinal plants.]

Hansen, Jim. 1992. Hawaiian Language as the Key to Understanding Hawaiian Heritage. IN *The Second Annual Conference on Issues of Culture and Communication in the Asia/Pacific Region.* Honolulu: East-West Center, 101–15. [Contains a sketch of the decline in the number of speakers, and the results of a survey (1989) on the language attitudes of students in HAW language classes.]

Hanson, Noel S. See HANCE, FAYE, AND HANSON 1960.

*Hanzeli, Victor Egon. 1969. *Missionary Linguistics in New France. A Study of Seventeenth- and Eighteenth-century Descriptions of American Indian Languages.* Janua Linguarum, Series Maior 29. The Hague: Mouton. 141 pp.

Harby, Bill. 1993. Living the Language. *Island Scene* 2(4):14, 16–17. [A description of Pūnana Leo preschools.]

*Harding, George L., and Bjarne Kroepelien. 1950. *The Tahitian Imprints of the London Missionary Society 1810–1834.* Oslo: La Coquille Qui Chante. 95, [1] pp. [Contains details on the printing of early readers and grammars, and the dispute over the orthography.]

*Harlow, Ray. 1993. Lexical Expansion in Maori. *Journal of the Polynesian Society* 102(1):99–107. [A discussion of the policies of a MAO language committee with respect to coining new words—in particular, the committee's reluctance to borrow from ENG.]

Harmsworth, Robert Leicester. 19--. *A Check List of the Books Printed in the Hawaiian and Other Pacific Island Dialects in the Library of Sir R. L. Harmsworth.* London: Printed for private circulation only. 28 pp. Butler #174.

Hawaii Library Association. 1958. See *NAMES AND INSIGNIA OF HAWAII* 1958.

Hawaii Visitors Bureau. 196-. *Primer of Hawaiian Language.* Honolulu. Mimeographed. 8 *ll.* [No glottal stops or long vowels marked. Point of view illustrated by: "However, the unhurried relaxed approach to pronunciation of these words backed by some simple technical rules makes it easy." The word list consists of "most frequently used words" (actually, most are HAW words used in ENG), names, place names, and greetings.]

[Hawaiian annotations to a printed Hawaiian-French dictionary]. 1860–1869. 112 pp. Ends with "Fin de la premiè[?re] partie.") <IN Hawaiian Glossary in the Archives of the Sacred Hearts in Honolulu. UHM microfilm S11041> [No glottal stops (except for words like *a'u*) or long vowels; *v* rather than *w* used.]

Hawaiian Dictionary. 1860. Unpaginated ms. <IN Hawaiian Glossary in the Archives of the Sacred Hearts in Honolulu, M38. UHM microfilm S11041> [The organization is unusual. It begins with an alphabetical listing of particles, one to a page (later, more than one), with grammatical explanation and examples. The second section is entitled *Idiotisme* (idioms). Next, separate pages contain grammatical categories or terms. E.g., *Article, Comparatif, Imperatif,* etc. The convention of marking the glottal stop only in words like *o'u* (versus *ou*) is followed. The most significant feature is that HAW words are not defined in FR, but given either HAW explanations/ definitions or quotations. One section is entitled *Comparisons*; another, *Aina* ['*āina*] (place names and locations). As in some other French publications, *v,* and not *w,* is used.]

Hawaiian Glossary in the Archives of the Sacred Hearts in Honolulu, Hawaii, M38–M49. 1860–1869. <UHM microfilm S11041> [Various works, descriptive and pedagogical, on HAW. The general title refers only to M38. The ten items, not all of which are lexicographical, are listed herein under their various titles, with 'IN Hawaiian Glossary ... '.]

Hawaiian in the English Classroom. 1978. 18, [11] *ll.* [A handbook by the 'Ahahui 'Ōlelo Hawai'i on how to handle the correct pronunciation of HAW. Discusses common mistakes; has exercises (with tapes) on trouble spots (unaccented *-e* versus *-i*, glottal stops, long vowels, *w*).]

Hawaiian, Japanese, and English Phrase-book. See ARAI 1891.

The Hawaiian Language. 1903. *Paradise of the Pacific* 16(11):7–8. [A prediction that by the end of the twentieth century, "HAW speech will have as little usage as Gaelic or Irish has now ..." Discusses changes to the language, particularly from borrowed words.]

The Hawaiian Language. 1942. *Thrum's Hawaiian Annual and Standard Guide* 68:159–86. [Unsigned. Two pages of fanciful comments on the language: "Vowels seemingly fall all over each other ... most melodious and liquid ... Polynesian dialects." Discounts diphthongs. Long vowels not marked, glottal stop mentioned but not used in word list. HAW-ENG, ENG-HAW, pp. 161–86. Unchanged through a number of editions of *Thrum's Annual.*]

Hawaiian Language and Dictionary. 1940/41. *Thrum's Hawaiian Annual and Standard Guide* 67:215–33. [Unsigned. Short phonological and grammatical sketch, more sophisticated and accurate than some later versions. ENG-HAW word list compiled by the Kamehameha Schools "for textbook purposes," appearing in the *Hawaiian Tourfax Annual,* August 1937, pp. 217–32.]

Hawaiian Language, Easy It Isn't. 1984. *Hawaiian Realtor* 11(4) (November):82–84.

Hawaiian Language League. 1936. See PROFESSOR OF COLUMBIA UNIV. [Possibly the ENG-HAW vocabulary referred to in Judd, Pukui, and Stokes 1945:6.]

Hawaiian Language Program Guide. 1979. Honolulu: Office of Instructional Services/General Education Branch. Hawai'i Department of Education. v, [i], 100 pp. [Contains notes on phonology and grammar. 'Recommendation of the 'Ahahui 'Ōlelo Hawai'i / 1978 Hawaiian Spelling Project' appended.]

Hawaiian Language Workbook: Puke Ho'opa'a Ha'awina he mau Ha'awina Pāku'i no nā Haumana 'Ōlelo Hawai'i {Workbook with lessons appended for Hawaiian language students}. 1980.

Honolulu: Hawai'i Department of Education. 151 pp. [DJK: A group of secondary HAW language teachers planned and produced this book of HAW language exercises that were designed to help students overcome some of the difficulties in learning vocabulary and structures. Includes cultural commentary and pictures to reinforce the importance of culture in language instruction.]

Hawaiian Made Simple. 1975. Honolulu: World Wide Distributors. 48 pp.

Hawaiian Manuscript. 192-. An anonymous Hawaiian manuscript. [Judd, Pukui, and Stokes 1945:6: "an anonymous manuscript used in Hawaiian classes at the University of Hawaii by F. W. Beckley in 1925 and by J. F. Woolley in 1928, and subsequently published for the Hawaiian Language League (1936), the Hawaii Tourist Bureau (1937), and O. Shaw (1938)." Judging from two of those works (1936, 1939), the ms. seems to have been a vocabulary rather than a grammar.]

Hawaiian Miscellany. 1868. [Various publications bound in one by Samuel C. Damon.] <HMCS919.69/H31>

Hawaiian Personal Names. 1899. *Hawaiian Almanac and Annual* 25: 113–20. [Naming practices, meanings of some common names.]

Hawaiian Personal Names. n.d. Typescript 5 *ll.* <HMCS MS /929.4>

Hawaiian Phrase Book. Na Huaolelo a me na Olelo Kikeke ma ka Olelo Beritania, a me ka Olelo Hawaii. 1854. See BISHOP 1854.

Hawaiian Place Names: The Significance of Hawaiian Sites, their Locations, and Interpretation of their Names. 1986. Irregular Series. [Honolulu]: The Kamehemeha Schools.

[Hawaiian primer]. 1862. Boston: Bazin & Ellsworth. 48 pp. <Widener Mss 817.2> [Not in JBM.]

Hawaiian Sentence Book. 1988. See SNAKENBERG 1988.

Hawaiian Slang: Words, Phrases and Medical Terms in Current Use. 193-. 27 pp. [No publication data. In English and Hawaiian. Cover title: *Speak Hawaiian.* However, contents identify the work as MALERWEINY 1935.]

Hawaiian Sugar Planters' Assn. 1930. See DAS 1930.

Hawaiian Tourfax Annual. 1937. Vol. 1. Honolulu: Hawai'i Tourist Bureau. 50 pp. [Comments on HAW language, practical phrases, p. 5. HAW-ENG word list, p. 50. ENG-HAW, pp. 52–62.]

[Hawaiian tract primer]. [18--]. Hawaiian language. Chrestomathics and readers. New York: American Tract Society. 80 pp., illus. <Widener Mss 817> [Not in JBM.]

Hawaiian Word Book. 1982. See SNAKENBERG 1982.

Hawaiian Words and Phrases; a Quickie Primer for Fun with the Hawaiian Language. ca. 1957. Honolulu: Tongg. [36] pp. illus. <HMCS 499.9/ H31>

*Haweis, Thomas. 1733–1796. Autobiography, vol. 1. <ML B1176–B1177, CY 950 >

*——. 1795–1802. Collection of papers *re* early South Seas missions. <ML Haweis Papers, MSS. 4190x. CY 933>

Hawkesworth, John. 1773. *An Account of the Voyages Undertaken by the Order of His Present Majesty for Making Discoveries in the Southern Hemisphere and Successfully Performed by Commodore Byron, Captain Wallis, Captain Carteret, and Captain Cook, in the* Dolphin, *the* Swallow, *and the* Endeavour: *Drawn up from the Journals which were Kept by the Several Commanders, and from the Papers of Joseph Banks, Esq.* 2d ed. London: Strahan and Cadell. 3 vols.

Hawkins, Emily A. 1975. Hawaiian Sentence Structure. University of Hawai'i Ph.D. dissertation. vi, 163 *ll.* [Published as HAWKINS 1979a.]

——. 1979a. *Hawaiian Sentence Structure.* Pacific Linguistics Series B—no. 61. Canberra: Australian National University, School of Pacific Studies. 111 pp. [The author listed the following as principal features treated: *A/o* possession; reanalyzed in terms of case relationships; relationship among pronouns, common nouns, and proper nouns as subjects; other possessive constructions (*k-* versus *k*-less); relationship between phrase order in verbless sentences and specificity; topicalization; the preposition *'o* in certain constructions shows that it is case-neutral; *iā* + pronoun/name analyzed for the first time.]

———. 1979b. A New Look at the Determiner System in Hawaiian. University of Hawai'i 5th Annual Linguistic Society of Hawai'i Oceanic Festival, 3 May. [An innovative analysis of the marker *he* not as an indefinite article, but as a predicate marker of new information.]

———. 1982. *Pedagogical Grammar of Hawaiian: Recurrent Problems.* Honolulu: Hawaiian Studies Program, University of Hawai'i—Mānoa. xi, 194 pp. [This work provides students with an explanation of some of the most puzzling (or seemingly inconsistent) features of HAW grammar, stemming from a lack of agreement about what is "correct" HAW grammar, and the minimal amount of competent, professional attention paid to HAW grammar, particularly in the twentieth century.]

———. 1984. Review of *The Polynesian Languages*, by Viktor Krupa (1982). *Modern Language Journal* 68:87–88.

———. 1989. Hawaiian Verb Phrase Stylistics. IN *VICAL 1. Oceanic Languages. Papers from the Fifth International Conference on Austronesian Linguistics. Auckland: Linguistic Society of New Zealand*, 237–45. [A detailed study, with data spanning over a century, of the use of the aspect marker *ua* and some postposed markers.]

———. 1990. See SHOJI AND HAWKINS.

———. 1991. Hawaiian Immersion Education: Where Will it Take the Language? Sixth International Conference on Austronesian Languages. Honolulu, 20-24 May. 9 *ll.*

Hayes, Casey. 1929. *Hawaiian Place Names.* Honolulu: Headquarters Hawaiian Dept., Fort Shafter. 15 pp. [P. 1: "The authorities are also divided as to the marking and pronunciation of a number of these names." The author relied on John H. Wise for a system to indicate pronunciation. After each headword, macrons, breves, glottal stops, and accents are marked—but incorrectly. For example: *hā-le* 'house', *o-lē-lo* 'language', *pu-'ū* 'hill', *lō-a* 'long'. Some of these errors are from Parker's edition of Andrews's dictionary (1922); others are introduced.]

Heckathorn, John. 1987. Can Hawaiian Survive? *Honolulu* 21(10) (April):48–51, 82, 84–86. [Description of efforts of "language activists" to keep HAW alive. Topics treated: number of native speakers, history of language attitudes in Hawai'i, the rise of pidgin, the Pūnana Leo schools, HAW as a medium of education, HAW on Ni'ihau.]

Heeren-Palm, Clementine Henriette Marie. 1955. Polynesische Migra- ties. Ph.D. dissertation, Faculteit der Geneeskunde, Universiteit op Dinsdag. J. A. Boom en Zoon - Uitgevers - Meppel. 189 pp. [Discusson of linguistic relationships, pp. 82–89, Table of pho- neme correspondences for HAW and nine other PN languages, p. 86. But with errors: e.g., *ng* for HAW, no *wh* for Māori, and no glottal stops marked for any language.]

Helbig, Ray. 1970. *Let's Learn a Little Hawaiian.* Honolulu: Hawai- ian Service, Inc. [4], 5–94, [1] pp. [HAW called a dialect of PN. In spite of its date, no mention of the glottal stop or long vowels for pronunciation. Word list consists of ENG names translated into HAW and about 2,000 ENG-HAW entries. For a review, see *'AHA KŪKĀKŪKĀ 'ŌLELO HAWAI'I* (1972).]

Hervas, D. Lorenzo. 1800–1805. Catalogo de las Lenguas de las Naciones conocidas, y Numeracion, Division, y Classes de estas segun la Diversidad de sus Idiomas y Dialectos. 6 vols. in -4°. Madrid. [HAW: vol. 2, chapter 1. Not seen; ref.: Martin 1867.]

Hervey, Wesley David. 1952. See WISE AND HERVEY 1952.

——. 1968. A History of the Adaptations of an Orthography for the Hawaiian Language. University of Oregon Ph.D. dissertation. 324 *ll.* [This work is useful almost solely for its extensive bibliography (especially manuscript materials) and for a straightforward, if superficial, account of the missionary solution to the problem of consonant variation. Insurmountable difficulties are the author's ignorance of basic phonemic principles, an inadequate treatment of William Anderson's word list and the grammar attributed to 'Ōpū kaha'ia, an exaggerated opinion of William Ellis's effect on the HAW orthography, and an attempt to inflate the study with sociological jargon that has little to do with the topic.]

——. 1969. An Alphabet for the Hawaiians. *Pacific Speech* 3(3):39– 47, 3(4):15–29. [(Part 3 was promised, but the journal ceased publication.) A condensed version of the misinterpretations men- tioned in the entry above. E.g.: William Anderson's *evy* for 'water', almost certainly *he wai* 'it's water', is interpreted as *e wai (*actually *ē wai)*, a vocative form! Words are cited from the Pukui-Elbert dictionary with macrons deleted. As an example of imaginative phonetics: some Hawaiian sounds are said to have an "implosive-explosive phase." To explain double letters in early ENG transcriptions of HAW words, the author suggested consonant length for the latter.]

Hirata, Fumio. 1976. Hawaiian—The Language of a Minority (in Japanese). *Area Studies* No. 12, Institute of World Affairs, Takushoku University, Tokyo, pp. 1–11. [Not seen.]

Hitchcock, Harvey Rexford. 1887. *An English-Hawaiian Dictionary; with Various Useful Tables: Prepared for the Use of Hawaiian-English Schools.* San Francisco: Bancroft. 256 pp. Reprinted 1968: Rutland, VT: Tuttle. [9], 10–256 pp. [HAW pronunciation, p. (3); ENG pronunciation and morphology, pp. 4–7; ENG-HAW, pp. 9–231. Back matter: abbreviations, HAW version of ENG names, events in HAW history, and Greek, Latin, etc. phrases translated into HAW.]

He Hoakakaolelo no na Huaolelo Beritania ... 1845. See EMERSON AND BISHOP 1845.

*Hocken, T. M. 1900. Some Account of the Beginnings of Literature in New Zealand: Part I., the Maori section. *Transactions and Proceedings of the New Zealand Institute* 33:472–90.

Hockett, Charles F. 1955. *A Manual of Phonology.* Memoir 11 of the *International Journal of American Linguistics.* v, 246 pp. [Discussion of various aspects of HAW phonology, pp. 98, 108, 120, 121, 126.]

———. 1958. *A Course in Modern Linguistics.* New York: Macmillan. xi, 621 pp. [Discussion of HAW phonemic system, p. 93.]

Hohepa, Patrick W. 1969. The Accusative-to-Ergative Drift in Polynesian Languages. *Journal of the Polynesian Society* 78(3):295–329. [Earlier version in *Working Papers in Linguistics* 1(6):1–70, University of Hawai'i, Department of Linguistics, 1969.]

*Hollinger, Fin. 1953. Should We Have Japanese Language Radio Programs in Hawaii? *Paradise of the Pacific* 65(5):28–29, 33.

Hollyman, K[enneth]. 1962. The Lizard and the Axe; A Study of the Effects of European Contact on the Indigenous Languages of Polynesia and Island Melanesia. *Journal of the Polynesian Society* 71(3):310–27. [DJK: Numerous HAW examples support discussion on bilingualism and lexical and phoneme borrowing.]

Holmes, Tommy. 1981. *The Hawaiian Canoe.* Hanalei, Kaua'i: Editions Limited. viii, 191 pp. 2d ed., 1993. Honolulu: Editions Limited. vii, 220 pp.

Holt-Padilla, Hokulani. 1991. See BUDNICK 1991.

Honolulu Star-Bulletin. 1936. Nine letters to the editor on the apparent *v-w* alternation in Hawaiian, from 18 to 28 March.

He Hope no ka Pi-a-pa {Supplement to the speller}. 1828. O'ahu: Mission Press. 8 pp. JBM #34. 2d ed.: 1829. 8 pp. JBM #43. 3d ed.: 1830. 8 pp. JBM #51.

Hopkins, Alberta Pualani. For other works by this author, see PUNG and ANTHONY.

———. 1985. Hawaiian Insults: A Preliminary List. Material from Hawaiian 321, Spring 1984, University of Hawai'i. Ms. [11] pp. [151 items collected from the Pukui-Elbert dictionary as a class project.]

———. 1989. *Ka Lei Ha'aheo. A Hawaiian Language Textbook. Beginning Level.* Photocopy of typescript. vi, 235 pp. [Published as Hopkins 1992a.]

———. 1992a. *Ka Lei Ha'aheo: Beginning Hawaiian.* Honolulu: University of Hawai'i Press. xiv, 278 pp. [See chapters 12 and 14.]

———. 1992b. *Ka Lei Ha'aheo: Teacher's Guide and Answer Key.* Honolulu: University of Hawai'i Press. xiii, 105 pp. [ENG translations and answers to the textbook's exercises.]

Hopkins, Manley. 1862. *Hawaii: The Past, Present, and Future of its Island-Kingdom.* London: Longman. xxiv, 423 pp. [European-biased, impressionistic sketch of the language, mostly of the sound system, paucity of letters in the alphabet, an especially slanted view by Sir George Simpson (but with sociolinguistic manifestations), and an interesting anecdote about *kaona*, pp. 346–49.]

Hopu, Thomas. 1821. Letters to J. Evarts (3 and 4 May). <HTL> [Contains samples of Hopu's own system of spelling HAW.]

Horie, Ruth H. 1979. A Sample Bibliography of Materials Relating to Land Tenure and Real Property Terminology in the Hawaiian Language. Paper for UHM LS 601 (Miles M. Jackson). Photocopy of typescript. 25 *ll.* <UHM Hawn Z7164.L3 H67>

Horne, Perley. 1911. Conservation of the Hawaiians. *The Friend,* December, pp. 38–42. [DJK: Argues for increased use of the HAW language and establishment of HAW language schools in order to encourage Hawaiians to express their sentiments more adequately.]

Houston, Victor Steuart Kaleoaloha. n.d. Collection of notes on Hawaiian vocabulary and language, with a summary by Houston. <BPPM Ms, Case 5, La29> [Annotated copies of vocabularies from Arago, Freycinet, and other explorers. Correspondence and notes: Langdon, Houston, Houston to Kenn, Kenn to Houston; misc. clippings, missionary comments; Kenn to Houston, Kenn, Anderson, *Missionary Herald,* James Cook, Goodrich, Hitchcock, ABCFM, Chamberlain, Richards, *Chinese Repository*, Pickering, Houston, and some misc. notes. Ms. papers on development of orthography. Two ms. articles, which constitute the following entries.]

——. n.d. The Pi-a-pa and the Palapala. Typescript. 31 *ll.* <BPBM Ms, Case 5, La29> [A detailed and well-researched history of the early years of the development of the HAW orthography, including an analysis of the system attributed to 'Ōpūkaha'ia (actually, Ruggles), but incorrectly guessing the rationale for the symbols *3* and *8*. Reviews a number of writers' comments on the language. The long discussion of the paring of extra consonants from the alphabet is from a historical, not a linguistic, point of view.]

——. [1936]. Further documents on the Hawaiian alphabet. Typescript. 8 *ll.* <BPBM Ms, Case 5, La29> [Basis of a letter to the *Honolulu Star-Bulletin* 27 March. The writer did not understand the phonemic principle, for he emphasized "euphony" as a key to understanding HAW sounds. He concluded (*l.* 7) "This [euphony] may have been the apparent enigma, which stumped the early missionaries in their inability to grasp the reason for the interchangeables, and in their ardor to advance common learning they may well have destroyed the genius of the language."]

Howe, K. R. 1988. Some Origins and Migrations of Ideas Leading to the Aryan Polynesian Theories of Abraham Fornander and Edward Tregear. *Pacific Studies* 11(2):67–81. [A historical account of the development of the idea of an Aryan connection for HAW and other PN languages.]

Huebner, Thom. 1985. Language Education Policy in Hawaii: Two Case Studies and Some Current Issues. *International Journal of the Sociology of Language.* 56:29–49. [Traces HAW literacy not only through the years of first contact with the written language, but also through the period of the rise of ENG and decline of HAW.]

———. 1987. A Socio-Historical Approach to Literacy Development: A Comparative Case Study from the Pacific. IN *Language, Literacy, and Culture: Issues of Society and Schooling,* ed. by Judith A. Langer, 178–96. Norwood, NJ: Ablex.

*Hughes, Judith R. 1993. The Demise of the English Standard School System in Hawai‘i. *Hawaiian Journal of History* 27:65–89.

Humboldt, Wilhelm von. 1836, 1838, and 1839. *Ueber die Kawi-Sprache auf der Insel Java, nebst einer Einleitung über die Verschiedenheit des menschlichen Sprachbaues und ihren Einfluß auf die geistige Entwickelung des Menschen-geschlechts.* Ed. by J. E. Eduard Buschmann. 3 vols. Berlin: Abhandlungen der königlichen Akademie der Wissenschaften zu Berlin.

Hunnewell, James Frothingham. 1869. *Bibliography of the Hawaiian Islands.* Boston: For the author. 75 pp. Kraus Reprint, 1962. [Introduction includes an account of printing. The main body includes publications of the Mission Press and detailed accounts of Bible translation, voyages, and European and American descriptive accounts.]

Hyde, Charles McEwen. 1884a. Some Random Notes on the Hawaiian Language. *Hawaiian Monthly* 1(9):209–11; 1(10): 236–38. [Classifies HAW as an "agglutinating or terminational" language. Includes amateur phonetics ("... the Hawaiian uses chiefly the upper part of the throat ..."). Cites opinion of Hawaiians themselves who claim that the phonetic structure of HAW is due to a diet of soft foods like poi. Some discussion of the phonological adaptation of ENG loanwords.]

——. 1884b. Hawaiian Names of Relationships of Consanguinity and Affinity. *Hawaiian Almanac and Annual* 10:42–44. [Corrections to Louis H. Morgan's (1871) treatment of HAW kinship terms.]

——. 1886. Some Hawaiian Conundrum. *Hawaiian Almanac and Annual* 12:68–69. [Sixteen HAW riddles, some involving puns.]

——. 1887. Hawaiian Poetical Names for Places. *Hawaiian Almanac and Annual* 13:79–82. [Discusses relationship of place names to personal names and climatic features such as rains and winds.]

——. 1888. Hawaiian Words for Sounds. *Hawaiian Almanac and Annual* 14:55–59. [Mentions a HAW term for the glottal stop: *kaiʻi*. DJK: Discussion of some onomatopoeic peculiarities in the HAW language. Includes lists of words for musical, animal, irregular, and oratorical sounds.]

——. 1893. See BARTLETT 1869.

——. 1896. *He Wahi Olelo Ao no ka Piliolelo Hawaii i Hakuia e Rev. C. M. Hyde, D.D.* E kuaiia ma ke keena o ka papa Hawaii {A bit of instruction on Hawaiian grammar composed by Rev. C. M. Hyde, D.D. Sold at the Hawaiian Board rooms}. Honolulu: Hawaiian Gazette. 41 pp. JBM #592. [Includes discussion of sounds, consonant alternation, and changes in ENG words borrowed into HAW, and a grammatical section organized around parts of speech.]

——. n.d. Draft of a Hawaiian grammar. Ms. <BPBM> [Not seen; ref.: Kent 1986.]

——. n.d. Annotated copy of Andrews's dictionary. <BPBM> [See MKA.]

Hymes, Dell H. 1983. Lexicostatistics and Glottochronology in the Nineteenth Century (with Notes toward a General History). IN *Essays in the History of Linguistic Anthropology*, 59–113. Amsterdam/Philadelphia: John Benjamins. [Describes Dumont d'Urville's lexicostatistical treatment of PN vocabulary.]

ʻĪʻĪ, John Papa. 1959. *Fragments of Hawaiian History, as Recorded by John Papa Ii*. Translated by Mary Kawena Pukui; edited by Dorothy B. Barrere. Honolulu: Bishop Museum Press. xii, 183 pp.

1963 ed., Honolulu: Bishop Museum Press. 202 pp. Rev. ed., 1983. Preface by Zadoc W. Brown, pp. vii–viii; foreword by Kenneth P. Emory, pp. ix–x. Bernice P. Bishop Museum Spec. Publ. 70. Honolulu: Bishop Museum Press. x, 202 pp.

*Im Thurn, Everard, and Leonard C. Wharton (eds). 1925. *The Journal of William Lockerby Sandalwood Trader in the Fijian Islands During the Years 1808–1809: with an Introduction and Other Papers Connected with the Earliest European Visitors to the Islands.* London: Hakluyt Society, series 2, no. 52. 251 pp. Reprinted by Kraus, 1967. 1982 ed., Suva, Fiji: Fiji Times & Herald. iii, 120 pp.

Ingraham, Joseph. 1790–1792. Journal of the Voyage of the Brigantine *Hope* from Boston to the North-west Coast of America. Photocopy of original in Mss. Division, Library of Congress. 208 *ff.* <ATL qMS 1790–92 P> [An account of contact in May 1791. Some pidgin-like HAW recorded, along with comments on various kinds of difficulties in communicating—especially those of "Opye," who had spent some time in America and spoke "a kind of jargon unintelligible to every one but himself."]

Na Inoa o na Kanaka Hawaii {Hawaiian personal names}. 1958. *Ka Hae Hawaii* 3(3):10.

Instructions of the Prudential Committee of the American Board of Commissioners for Foreign Missions to the Sandwich Islands Mission. Lahainaluna: Press of the Mission Seminary. 1838. 122 pp.

I Wanna Learn to Speak Hawaiian. 1949. *Paradise of the Pacific* (Travel Supplement) 61(8):8. [Lightweight, accurate with respect to HAW words often used in ENG. But the attempt to describe the pronunciation fails.]

Jennings, Jesse D., ed. 1979. *The Prehistory of Polynesia.* Cambridge, MA; London: Harvard University Press. 399 pp.

Jesperson, Otto. 1905. *Growth and Structure of the English Language.* 9th ed., 1956. Garden City, NY: Doubleday Anchor Books. 274 pp. [Characterization of HAW as childlike and effeminate, pp. 3–4.]

Jimerson, Randall C., and Rena R. Weiss. 1919. See BINGHAM FAMILY PAPERS.

Johnson, Edward. 1844. *Ke Ao Spela; he Palapala ia e Ao aku ai i na Kamalii i ka Mahele Pono ana o na Huaolelo, a me ka Hai Pololei ana o na Hua* {The speller; a book to teach children in the division of words, and in the correct pronunciation of words}. Honolulu: Mission Press. 46 pp. JBM #269. [Reader and spelling book.]

Johnson, Rubellite Kawena. For other works by this author, see KINNEY.

——, ed. 1976. *Kūkini 'Āha'ilono [Carry On The News]. Over a Century Of Native Hawaiian Life and Throughts From Hawaiian Language Newspapers of 1834 to 1948, Published In Honor Of The Bicentennial.* Honolulu: Topgallant. xiv, 436 pp. [Articles and notes on language and education scattered throughout this interesting and valuable work.]

——, and John Kaipo Mahelona. 1975. *Nā Inoa Hōkū: A Catalogue of Hawaiian and Pacific Star Names.* Honolulu: Topgallant. xiv, 170, A–E pp.

——. 1986. Hawaiian Language and the Geometry of Arts and Crafts ... for the Hawaiian Culture Lecture Series, fall 1986 and spring 1987, a Program of the Continuing Education Program, Extension Education Division, The Kamehameha Schools/Bishop Estate. [Honolulu]: The Division. [30] pp.

——. 1987. From Orality to Literacy in Hawaii. IN *Literacy and Orality: The Transformation of Thought,* ed. by Donald Topping and Victor N. Kobayashi, 9–13. Honolulu: The Hawai'i Committee for the Humanities.

*Johnson, Samuel. 1755. *A Dictionary of the English Language.* London: Strahan. No pagination. [The introduction allows us a glimpse of eighteenth-century knowledge about phonetics and orthography.]

Jones, Davis, and W. C. Addleman. 1938. *Dictionary of Hawaiian Place Names, Including the Islands of Oahu, Hawaii, Kahoolawe, Kauai, Lanai, Maui, Molokai & Niihau; also Beacon Lights and Channels.* Revised by Addleman. Honolulu: U.S. Army, Hawaiian Div. 45 pp. 2d printing 1942. [Naive pronunciation guide: long vowels and glottal stops ignored. Etymology for most place names, map coordinates given for all.]

*Jones, Richard Foster. 1953. *The Triumph of the English Language: A Survey of Opinions Concerning the Vernacular from the Introduction of Printing to the Restoration.* Stanford: Stanford University Press. xiii, 340 pp.

*Jones, William. 1788. On the Orthography of Asiatic Words in Roman Letters. *Asiatic Researches* 1:1–56. Republished in an edition of Jones's works, London, 1799.

*Joppien, Rudiger, and Bernard Smith. 1987. *The Art of Captain Cook's Voyages: With a Descriptive Catalogue of all the Known Original Drawings of Peoples, Places, Artefacts and Events and the Original Engravings Associated with them.* Melbourne/New York: Oxford University Press. 3 vols. in 4.

Judd, Bernice. 1929. *Voyages to Hawaii before 1860. A Record, Based on Historical Narratives in the Libraries of the Hawaiian Mission Children's Society and the Hawaiian Historical Society.* Honolulu: Hawaiian Mission Children's Society. 108 pp., 1 *l.*

——, and Helen Yonge Lind. 1974. *Voyages to Hawaii before 1860. A Record, Based on Historical Narratives in the Libraries of the Hawaiian Mission Children's Society and the Hawaiian Historical Society, Extended to March 1860.* Earlier edition by Bernice Judd (1929) enlarged and edited by Helen Yonge Lind. Honolulu: University Press of Hawai'i for Hawaiian Mission Children's Society. xviii, 129 pp.

Judd, Bernice, Janet E. Bell, and Clare G. Murdoch. 1978. *Hawaiian Language Imprints 1822–1899. A Bibliography.* Honolulu: Hawaiian Mission Children's Society and University Press of Hawai'i. xxix, 247 pp.

Judd, Charles Sheldon. 1936. Hawaiian Place Names. ["Compiled largely from the HAW dictionary by C. S. Judd."] Honolulu. Typewritten copy, 8 *ll.* <HMCS 499.9/J88ha; UHM Hawn/ DU622/ J83> [184 names, no macrons or glottal stops marked.]

Judd, Henry Pratt. 1923-? Hawaiian Proverbs and Words for his Dictionary. <BPBM Ms. Case 5 La32> [MKA.]

——. 1930. *Hawaiian Proverbs and Riddles. Bull. Bernice P. Bishop Mus.* 77. 91 pp. [828 proverbs (with explanation) and 282 riddles. Each genre is divided into semantic categories.]

——, ed. 1930. See ATCHERLEY 1930.

——. 1938. *Hawaiian Language.* Honolulu: Castle and Cooke. [2], 3–10 pp. ["'Hawaiian Language' is Number One of a series of booklets prepared under the direction of Castle & Cooke, Limited ...." An impressionistic and lightweight essay on the language.]

——. 1939a. *The Hawaiian Language and Hawaiian-English Dictionary: a Complete Grammar.* Honolulu: Star-Bulletin Ltd. 116 pp., . 5th printing: 1944. 10th printing: 1961. Honolulu: Hawaiian Service. 117 pp. [Nouns are declined, verbs conjugated, the glottal stop or long vowels only very rarely marked in the vocabulary, *a* versus *o* possessives not explained. The grammar shows little improvement over those written eighty years earlier.]

——. 1939b. Renascence of the Hawaiian Language. *Paradise of the Pacific* 51 (Dec.):89. [A short discussion of some reasons for increased attention to HAW, such as more tourists, and a growing interest in Hawaiian music. Some comments on language policy, such as the opposition to the Congregational Church's proposal of "a union of the various races in their assemblies," which the Hawaiians feared would "result in the rapid decay of their native tongue."]

——. 1944. Pronouncing Hawaii's Place Names. *Paradise of the Pacific* 56 (12):26. [A naive, amateurish treatment that ignores glottal stops and long vowels.]

——, Mary Kawena Pukui, and John F. G. Stokes. 1945. *Introduction to the Hawaiian Language (An English-Hawaiian Vocabulary. Comprising Five Thousand of the Commonest and Most Useful English Words and their Equivalents, in Modern Hawaiian Speech, Correctly Pronounced, with a Complementary Hawaiian-English Vocabulary.* Honolulu: Tongg. 314 pp. [Grammatical notes, pp. 10–29. Interesting statistics on the variation among (written) *r*, *l*, and *d*, based on early writings. The description of [v] versus [w], although not modern in terminology, is probably more accurate than recent attempts, p. 15. Interlinear text with annotations, pp. 26–29. In the ENG-HAW section, pronunciation, including glottal stops and vowel length (long, short, and unmarked) marked on pronunciation following entries—but not accurately. For the HAW-ENG section, long vowels not marked, because of type restrictions. See chapter 11.]

Judd, Laura Fish. 1880. *Honolulu: Sketches of Life Social, Political, and Religious in the Hawaiian Islands*. New York: Randolph & Co. xiv, 258 pp. [Brief sketch of the alphabet, grammatical system, and vocabulary, pp. 24–25.]

Kaʻanoʻi, Patrick, and Robert Lokomaikaʻiokalani Snakenberg. 1988. *Hawaiian Name Book*. Honolulu: Bess Press. 64 pp. ["Hawaiian translations of English first names based on the true meanings of the names, also given in the text."]

Nā Kaʻao Kahiko. Illustrated Bilingual Hawaiian Tales. n.d. Honolulu (?). ix, 258 pp. [No date, no publisher noted; however, ca. 1980s. Designed for "upper elementary Hawaiian Studies classes and the secondary Hawaiian language classes." Written by Evaline "Tuti" Kanahele Sanborn, based on Laura Green and Mary Kawena Pukui's Hawaiian folk tales.]

Kahale, Edward. 195-. The Hawaiian Language–1st–2d year. Mimeographed. 2 vols. [ii], 71 *ll*; vol. 2 unpaginated, but 66 *ll*. <UHM Hawn PL6443 .K28> [No macrons or glottal stops (except, as was the practice, the latter marked in essential pronouns and possessives). Gram-matical notes in traditional mode. Referred to in Newbrand 1951. UHM copy identified as 2d ed.]

———. 1973. *Nu Maikai* {Good news}. [Honolulu]: Hawaiʻi Conference of the United Church of Christ. [xi], 90 pp. [A series of five-minute sermons in HAW, broadcast weekly on KGMB from 10 April 1950 to 31 December 1951.]

Kahananui, Dorothy Mitchell. 1965. *E Pāpā-ʻŌlelo Kākou* ... Hawaiian level one. Honolulu: The Kamehameha Schools. 175 pp. 2d ed.: 1969, xiv, 175 pp. [Audiotapes accompany the book. Organized primarily around the principle of pattern practice. Pedagogically satisfying, but phonetically and grammatically less so. The author was careful in her explanation of long vowels but did not use the macron consistently (see, for example, the personal names on pp. 4 and 5. For a review, see *'AHA KŪKĀKŪKĀ 'ŌLELO HAWAI'I* 1972.]

———, and Alberta P. Anthony. 1970. *E Kama'ilio Hawai'i Kakou: Let's Speak Hawaiian.* Honolulu: University Press of Hawai'i. xx, 427 pp. Revised 1974. xxi, 431 pp. [For an index to the work, see DEL ROCCO 1989.]

Kahapea, Kehau. 1974. See MORRIS ET AL. 1974.

Kailiehu, L. S. 1865. Na Inoa o na Makani o Hana {Names of the Winds of Hāna}. *Ke Au Okoa* 1(8):3.

Kamakamailio ma ka Olelo Beritania, Hawaii a me Farani. I Hooponoponoia na na Haumana o ke Kula o Ahuimanu {Conversation, words in English, Hawaiian and French. Edited for the students of the Ahuimanu school}. 1873. Honolulu: Paipalapala Katolika. 38 pp. JBM #470.

Kamakau, Samuel Mānaiakalani. 1866–1871 (1961). *The Ruling Chiefs of Hawaii.* Translation of *Ka Moolelo o Kamehameha I* and *Ka Moolelo o na Kamehameha,* by Thomas G. Thrum, Lahilahi Webb, Emma Davidson Taylor, John Wise, and Mary Kawena Pukui (translation reviewed by MKP). Honolulu: The Kamehameha Schools Press. xiv, 440 pp. Rev. ed., 1991. Honolulu: The Kamehameha Schools Press. x, 513 pp. Introduction by L[ilikalā] K. Kame'eleihiwa, pp. iii–v. [Sources: *Ka Nupepa Kuokoa* 1866–1869, *Ke Auokoa* 1869–1871. The new edition includes an index.]

———. 1991. *Nā Mo'olelo a ka Po'e Kahiko.* Translated from the newspapers *Ka Nupepa Kuokoa* and *Ke Au Okoa* by Mary Kawena Pukui. Edited by Dorothy B. Barrère. Honolulu: Bishop Museum Press. [x], 184 pp.

———. 1869–1870 (1976). *The Works of the People of Old / Na Hana a ka Po'e Kahiko.* Translated from the newspaper *Ke Au 'Oko'a* by Mary Kawena Pukui. Arranged and edited by Dorothy B. Barrère. Bernice P. Bishop Mus. Spec. Publ. no. 61. viii, 170 pp.

———. 184- Lorrin Andrews: Quotations from his Dictionary. <Ms. in BPBM. [MKA].

Kamanā, Kauanoe. 1979. See SILVA AND KAMANā.

——, and William H. Wilson. 1977. *Nā Kai ʻEwalu. Beginning Hawaiian Lessons.* Photocopy of typescript, 331 pp. Rev. ed., 1990: 223, [19] pp. [No place of publication or publisher.] [Careful marking of glottal stops and long vowels; some other important features of pronunciation (such as vowel raising) not treated. Discussion of *ua* moves away from tense slightly, but not far enough. Innovative treatment of verbs.]

——. 1979. *Nā Kai ʻEwalu / Papa Makahiki ʻElua* {Second year}. No publication data. Revised 1991. Photocopy. 49, [1], pp. [ENG used only for glosses. Grammatical terms in HAW, such as *kikino* 'noun', *ʻaʻano* 'stative verb', *hehele* 'intransitive verb', and *hamani* 'transitive verb'.]

——. 1991. Immersion Program May Save Hawaiian Tongue from Extinction. *Honolulu Star-Bulletin*, 14 March, A-21.

Kanahele, George S., ed. 1979. *Hawaiian Music and Musicians: An Illustrated History.* Honolulu: University Press of Hawaiʻi. xxx, 543 pp.

——. 1982. *Hawaiian Renaissance.* Honolulu [?]: WAIAHA. vi, 39 pp. ["Three lectures delivered between 1977 and 1982. They trace the beginnings and progress of a rekindled interest in several different cultural areas, including language and literature."]

Kawaiʻaeʻa, Keiki K. C. 1980. Hawaiian Pathological Terms. *Ka ʻUnuhi, The Translator* 2:1–70. [The first part, Pathology (pp. 4–42), consists of 898 terms with their translation/explanation; the second part, Physical Ailments and Remedies as Used by the Hawaiians, is a four-column list (276 items) of HAW names of ailments, ENG translation, Hawaiian plants used for treatment, and the scientific name of the plant.]

Kawaiahaʻo Church Burial Records, 1894–1906. [Includes Hawaiian phrases and sentences. 1 bd. vol. in pocket file. Evidently this book was used in the study of the HAW language before it was used to record the burials.] <HMCS mss. Church Records>

Kawaikaumaiikamakaokaopua, Z. P. W. 1922. Kekahi mau Olelo Noeau Pookela, ame ke Kaona o ka Olelo {Some notable proverbs and their hidden meaning}. *Ka Nupepa Kuokoa* 61(49):7.

Kay, E. Alison. 1968. The Sandwich Islands. From Richard Brinsley Hinds' *Journal of the Voyage of the* Sulphur *(1836–1842)*. *Hawaiian Journal of History* 2:102–35.

Keala, Samuel A. 1955. See ELBERT AND KEALA 1955.

Kellerman, Elizabeth. 1955. History of Linguistic Problems in Hawaii. Paper given at International Conference of Pan-Pacific Women's Association, Manila, 1955. 4 pp., mimeographed. <HMCS MS/ 499/ K28>

Kelly, Marion. 1978. See FREYCINET 1978.

———. 1982. Some Thoughts on Education in Traditional Hawaiian Society. IN *To Teach the Children: Historical Aspects of Education in Hawai'i. Commemorating the 50th anniversary of the College of Education and the 75th Anniversary of the University of Hawai'i.* An exhibition at the Bishop Museum, 25 September 1981–31 December 1982. 68 pp.

Kelsey, Theodore (main compiler). 1922–193- Notes Saved to be Used in Compiling a New Hawaiian Dictionary. 6 folders. <BPBM> [MKA.]

*Kendall, Thomas. 1815. *A Korao no New Zealand; or, the New Zealander's First Book; being An Attempt to compose some Lessons for the Instruction of the Natives.* Sydney: Howe. 54 pp.

*———, and Samuel Lee. 1820. *A Grammar and Vocabulary of the Language of New Zealand.* London: Church Missionary Society. [v], 230 pp.

Kenn, Charles. 1939. Some Hawaiian Relationship Terms Reexamined. *Social Process in Hawaii* 5:46–50. [Discussion of the terms *'ohana, hānai, ho'okama, 'ōhua,* and *punalua.*]

———. 1943. The V and W in Hawaiian. *Honolulu Star-Bulletin*, 13 August. [Historically interesting, but linguistically uninformed and opinionated, ending with "... HAW is a euphonic language."]

———. 1944a. How Do You Say Hawaii. *Paradise of the Pacific* 56 (12):62, 64. [DJK: Commentary on the 1826 missionary decision to establish the format of the HAW written language. Argues for pronouncing the *W* as a soft *V*.]

——. 1944b. What is a Haole? *Paradise of the Pacific* 56 (8):16, 31. [An amusing listing of various accounts of the etymology of *haole* (with one unexplained comment that "the word was in use as early as 1736"!). See chapter 11 for some of these etymologies.]

——. 1947. The Meaning of Aloha. *Hawaiian Digest* 2 (Oct.):2–4. [DJK: Comparison of the meanings and concepts of the words *anoai* and *aloha*.]

——. 1948. In Support of 'Ha-vai-i'. *Honolulu Advertiser*, 30 August.

Kent, Harold Winfield. 1976. *The Kamehameha Schools 1946–1962.* Honolulu: Masonic Public Library. 132 pp.

——. 1986. *Treasury of Hawaiian Words in One Hundred and One Categories.* Honolulu: Masonic Public Library. xxviii, 475 pp. [Based on ms. notes of Charles M. Hyde (in BPBM). Sample categories are Age, Amusements and Games, Bananas, Birds of Hawai'i ... See chapter 11.]

*Kern, Rudolph A. 1948. The Vocabularies of Iacob Le Maire. *Acta Orientalia* 20:216–37.

Kihara, Ryukichi. 195-. Japanese-English-Hawaiian Vocabulary. Honolulu. Typescript, 53 *ll.* <UHM Hawn PL678 .K54> [No glottal stops or long vowels marked.]

Kimura, Larry L. 1978? A Review of the Hawaiian Language Program 1921–1972, University of Hawai'i, Mānoa. Photocopy of typescript, 66 *ll.* <UHM Hawn PL6441 .K48 1978a> [Bibliographic and "state of the art" information about how the grammar was viewed. Also short biographies of the people who taught HAW and prepared language materials, and class enrollment figures.]

——. 1980. The Hawaiian Language. IN *Hawaii*, ed. by Leonard Lueras, 361–62. Hong Kong: Apa. [DJK: Describes HAW as a language of emotions, poetry, and nature-related sounds and nuances. Traces the language's antecedents, establishment of its alphabet and written format by the missionaries in 1823, and its twentieth-century decline in use.]

——. 1983. Language Section IN *Native Hawaiians Study Commission Report*, vol. 1, pp. 173–203, 216–23 (notes), 623–27.

——. 1989. The Revitalization of the Hawaiian Language. *Hawaii Review*, Issue 27:74–46.

King, Robert D. 1935. Hawaiian Words Used in Naming Lands and Features. IN COULTER 1935:206–207.

Kinney, Rubellite Kawena. For other works by this author, see JOHNSON.

——. 1953. Hawaiian Poetry: Some Problems in Translation. *Journal of Oriental Literature* 6:55–58.

——. 1956. A Non-purist View of Morphophonemic Variations in Hawaiian Speech. *Journal of the Polynesian Society* 65 (3):282–86. [An argument for recognizing features of HAW pronunciation not considered "standard," and against prescriptivism.]

——. 1957. Changes in the Social Setting of the Hawaiian Oral Tradition. *Social Process in Hawaii* 21:25–33. [An autobiographical account of Hawaiian tradition in the author's family, along with two stories, with background and context.]

Kirch, Patrick Vinton. 1985. *Feathered Gods and Fishhooks: An Intro-duction to Hawaiian Archaeology and Prehistory*. Honolulu: University of Hawai'i Press. x, 349 pp.

*——. 1990. Regional Variation and Local Style: A Neglected Dimension in Hawaiian Prehistory. *Pacific Studies* 13(2):41–54. [A discussion of regional variation in (among others) material culture, agricultural systems. Mentions "the fallacy of assuming cultural uniformity throughout the archipelago."]

Kittelson, David J. 1973. Hawaiianized English Given Names. Honolulu: Hawai'i Library Association. 5 pp. [DJK: List of 660 modern ENG names with their HAW equivalents. Includes a formula for shifting words from other languages into HAW.]

*——. 1985. *The Hawaiians: An Annotated Bibliography*. Honolulu: Social Science Research Institute, Hawai'i Series no. 7. xi, 384 pp.

Klieneberger, Hans Rudolph. 1957. *Bibliography of Oceanic Linguistics*. London Oriental Bibliographies, vol. 1. London: Oxford University Press. xiii, 143 pp.

*Klopf, Donald, and John Highlander. 1965. Foreign Language Broadcasting in the Western States. *Western Speech* 29:219–27.

Knappert, Jan. 1954. Concise Structural Sketch of the Hawaiian Language. Leiden: Koninklijk Instituut voor Taal-, Land- en Volkenkunde, no. yy 10 N+ / V. Mimeographed, 57 *ll.* <UHM Hawn Pl6441.K52> [Possibly M.A. thesis (*doctoraalscriptie*). Introductory short chapters on ethnic origin, history, present state of native population, and comparative PN languages. The grammar per se begins on p. 10 with phonology. Following sections are morphology, syntax, a text, vocabulary, and bibliography. See chapter 12.]

Knowlton, Edgar C., Jr. 1957. See ELBERT AND KNOWLTON 1957.

Kotzebue, Otto von. 1821. *Entdeckungs-Reise in die Süd-See und nach der Berings-Strasse zur Erforschung einer nordöstlichen Durchfahrt. Unternommen in den Jahren 1815, 1816, 1817 und 1818, auf Kosten Sr. Erlaucht des Herrn Reichs-Kanzlers Grafen Rumanzoff auf dem Schiffe* Rurick. 3 vols. Weimar: Hoffman. English translation (1821): *A Voyage of Discovery, into the South Seas and Beering's Straits, for the Purpose of Exploring a North-east Passage, Undertaken in the Years 1815–1818 ...* 3 vols. Translated by H. E. Lloyd. London: Longman. Da Capo Press, 1967.

Kratz, Henry, ed. 1986. *A Voyage Around the World with the Romanzov Exploring Expedition in the Years 1815–1818 in the Brig Rurik, Captain Otto von Kotzebue, by Adelbert von Chamisso.* Translated and edited by Henry Kratz. Honolulu: University of Hawai'i Press. xxiv, 375 pp.

Kreisel, Werner. 1980. Assimilation in Hawaii am Beispiel des Vordringens der englischen Sprache. *Sociologus* 30(1):29–52.

Kroeber, Alfred Louis. 1921. Observations on the Anthropology of Hawaii. *American Anthropologist* N.S. 23:129–37.

Kroepelien, Bjarne. 1950. See HARDING AND KROEPELIEN 1950.

Krupa, Viktor. 1966. The Phonemic Structure of Bi-vocalic Morphemic Forms in Oceanic Languages. *Journal of the Polynesian Society* 75(4):458–97. [Table showing percentages of vowel combinations in bi-vocalic forms in HAW, p. 462. Statistical data on frequency and types of HAW morphemes consisting of two vowels (with optional consonants). "Three significant associative tendencies (*e* –

e, i – i, u – u) and three dissociative tendencies (*e – i, i – e, u – o*) have been found," pp. 463–64.]

———. 1971. The Phonotactic Structure of the Morph in Polynesian Languages. *Language* 47(3):668–84.

———. 1979. *Ghavaiskii Iazyk* {The Hawaiian language}. Moskva: Glav. red. vostochnoi lit-ry. 74, [2] pp., map. [Polansky 1974: "Bibliography: p. 73–(75)—69 items ... Covers phonetics, phonology, lexicology, words and phrases, sentence structure. Supplement includes two texts in HAW with a Russian translation and dictionaries."]

———. 1981. Review of Samuel H. Elbert and Mary Kawena Pukui, *Hawaiian Grammar. Asian and African Studies* 17:218–19.

———. 1982. *The Polynesian Languages: A Guide.* Languages of Asia and Africa, vol. 4. London: Routledge & Kegan Paul. vii, 193 pp. [Review: HAWKINS 1984.]

Krusenstern, A[dam] J[ohann] von. 1813. *Wörtersammlungen aus den Sprachen einiger Völker des östlichen Asiens und der Nordwest Küste von Amerika.* Bekannt gemacht von A. J. Krusenstern. St. Petersburg. [Not seen; ref.: Martin 1867.]

Kulamanu 1962. See WILLIAMS, EDITH, 1962.

O ke Kumumua na na Kamalii; he Alapala e Ao aku ai i na Kamalii Ike Ole i ka Heluhelu Palapala {First lessons for children; a book to teach the children, who do not know how to read books}. 1835. Oahu: I mea Pai Palapalana na Misionari. 16 pp. JBM #133. 2d and 3d ed.: 1837, 32 pp. 4th ed.: 1840, 32 pp. 5th ed.: 1844, 32 pp. [Handwritten in: "by Hiram Bingham, per R. Anderson." But JBM (p. 48) gives J. Emerson as author. Syllables are usually separated by hyphens, often illustrating an awareness of the glottal stop. For example, *wa-a, ka-a, mo-a, o-o, po-o, pu-u* versus *nui, oi.* But dissylables without a glottal stop are also written with a hyphen: e.g., *mo-a.* And there are some inconsistencies, such as *kii.*]

O ke Kumumua Hou {New first primer}. 1863? New York: American Tract Society. 80 pp. JBM #402. Editions in 1863, 1866. 1950: reprinted by The Kamehameha Schools Press, [2], 80 pp. [Translated by Elias Bond.]

Ke Kumu Mua Ano Hou i Hoonaniia i na Kii Maikai, na J. Pula i Kakau {A new primer ... with nice pictures ...}. 1862. Illus. Boston: Hall & Whiting. 48 pp. <HHS H/428.6/ M88.> [Not in JBM.]

Kumulua {Second primer}. 1843. Honolulu: Mission Press. 32 pp. JBM #259. [Editions: 1843, 1848.]

Kuykendall, Ralph Simson. 1926. *A History of Hawaii.* New York: Macmillan. x pp., 1 *l.*, 375 pp.

———. 1938. *The Hawaiian Kingdom.* 3 vols. Vol.1: *1778–1854: Foundation and Transformation.* Honolulu: University of Hawai'i. Reprinted 1947, 1957, 1968, University of Hawai'i Press. vii, 453 pp.

*Landau, Sidney I. 1984. *Dictionaries: The Art and Craft of Lexicography.* New York: Scribners. xiii, 370 pp.

[Language study (English/Hawaiian)]. Untitled. 1860–1869. 27 pp. [ENG word list in semantic categories, with HAW meanings and FR pronunciation. Adjectives, with comparative and superlative. Pronouns.] <IN Hawaiian Glossary in the Archives of the Sacred Hearts in Honolulu. UHM microfilm S11041>

Lanyon-Orgill, Peter A. 1979. *Captain Cook's South Sea Island Vocabularies.* London: by the author. xv, 287 pp. [Review: GERAGHTY 1983.]

Lau Kukui. Level II Hawaiian Language Reader. 1981. Honolulu: Office of Instructional Services. xiii, 134 pp. [*Level I* never published. Project coordinated by Larry Kauanoa Kimura. Pp. 1–51: teachers' guide, with grammatical notes.]

Ledyard, John. 1783. See MUNFORD 1963.

Lee, Alice Keakealani. 1937. *A Study of the Hawaiian Vocabulary of Certain Groups of Preschool Children in Hawaii.* University of Hawai'i M.Ed. thesis. v, 94 *ll.* [RT: Lists 148 words, some used only by Hawaiians. Simple recorded conversations, pp. 77–81.]

Lee, Kehau. 1973. Distinctions between the *Ko*-Noun Locative and the *O*-Noun Locative. Unpublished ms. [Not seen; ref.: Elbert and Pukui 1979.]

Lee, Makanani. 1973. The Particle *La.* Unpublished ms. [Not seen; ref.: Elbert and Pukui 1979.]

Samuel Lee. 1820. See KENDALL AND LEE 1820.

Ka Leo o nā Kūpuna {The voice of the elders}. 1986. Cassette and booklet. Honolulu: Ka Leo o nā Kūpuna, Inc. 22 pp. [Language-learning exercises for kindergarten through the second grade.]

Lepsius, Karl Richard. 1855. *Das allgemeine linguistische Alphabet. Grundsätze der Übertragung fremder Schriftsysteme und bisher noch ungeschriebener Sprachen in europäischen Buchstaben.* Berlin. [No publication data available for German edition. See next entry.]

———. 1863. *Standard Alphabet for Reducing Unwritten Languages and Foreign Graphic Systems to a Uniform Orthography in European Letters.* 2d ed. London: Williams & Norgate; Berlin: Hertz. xvii, 324 pp. [Discussion and charts of the alphabets of MAO, RAR, Gambier, TAH, MQA, HAW. Sample of TAH in recommended orthography, pp. 264–65. Glottal stops and long vowels recognized; no separate *wh* for MAO. PN data from Gaussin 1853.]

Liliʻuokalani. n.d. Notes on Hawaiian Words and Definitions. <BPBM Mms.La7, storage case 5> [In a writing tablet with ruled paper. Partly organized into semantic categories: e.g., names of sugarcane, trees, birds, etc. The largest section is a numbered list of 1,779 items, more like a HAW-ENG glossary than a dictionary. However, some of the semantic sets (e.g., trees) contain long explanations. An accompanying note says: "Reviewed by M. K. Pukui in 1938; words found filed in her dictionary."]

Lind, Helen Yonge. 1974. See JUDD AND LIND 1974.

Lingenfelter, Richard E. 1967. *Presses of the Pacific Islands 1817–1867. A History of the First Half Century of Printing in the Pacific Islands.* Los Angeles: Plantin. ix, [xi, xii, xv], 129 pp.

Lisiansky, Urey (Lisianskii, Iurii Fedorovich). 1812. *Puteshestvie Vokrug Svieta v 1803, 4, 5 i 1806 godakh po poveleniyu ego Imperatorskago Velichestva Aleksandra Pervago na Korable* Neve. St. Petersburg: Tip F. Drekhslera. [See next entry.]

———. 1814. *A Voyage Round the World, in the Years 1803, 4, 5, & 6; Performed, by Order of his Imperial Majesty, Alexander the First, Emperor of Russia, in the Ship* Neva. English translation by the author. London: Booth. xxi, [2], 388 pp. [Some 170 HAW words collected ca. 1804, pp. 326–28.]

Livermore, Katherine. 1934. See HANDY, PUKUI, AND LIVERMORE 1934.

Lobschied, D. 1872. Ethnological and Philological Notes Respecting Hawaiians. *The Friend*, January, p. 4. [Based on chance resemblance of words, an impressionistic linking of HAW with the Japhetic and Indo-European language families.]

*London Missionary Society. 1803. *Transactions of the Missionary Society*, vol. 1 (1795–1802). London: Published for the Benefit of the Society. [Compiled from missionary journals and correspondence. Vol. 1 includes TAH journals, TON journal.]

*London Missionary Society Correspondence. London, School of Oriental and African Studies Library.

Loomis, Albertine. 1951 (1966). *The Grapes of Canaan: Hawaii 1820*. New York: Dodd, Mead & Company. x, 334 pp. 1966 ed.: Honolulu: Hawaiian Mission Children's Society. [vii], 334 pp. [Contains an account of early work on the language, the first printing, difficulties with the alphabet. Glossary of HAW words, pp. 332–34.]

——— 1973. See DAY AND LOOMIS 1973.

Loomis, Elisha. n.d. Vocabulary. [No copy is known to exist, but according to Gay Slavsky (annotation for Lorrin Andrews n.d.) and based on the introductory notes in Andrews 1836, the vocabulary identified as Andrews n.d. was based on "a vocabulary of words collected mostly, it is believed, by Mr. Loomis, formerly a member of this Mission. This was transcribed by the Compiler on his voyage from the United States, and put to use in 1828 ..." Slavsky wrote: ""Based on Mr. Andrews' statement, the dates in the Hebrew lexicon MS, and the close resemblance of the penmanship in the two works, the appraiser believes that, in all probability, the vocabulary MS is the transcript from the original attributed to 'Mr. Loomis and others,' made by Mr. Andrews while on his voyage to join the Mission, aboard the ship Parthian, between November 3, 1827, and March 30, 1828, later added to and revised for the 1836 work."]

——, and Maria Loomis. 1819–1827. Journal. <Albertine Loomis's copy, HMCS>

Lothian, Christina R. N. 1985. An Index of the Articles on Hawaii in the New England Newspaper Collection 1806–1900 in the Lyman House Memorial Museum, Hilo, Hawaii. Photocopy. 62, [3] *ll.* <UHM Hawn DU625 .L83 1985>

Luomala, Katharine. 1947. Missionary Contributions to Polynesian Anthropology. *Specialized Studies in Polynesian Anthropology. Bull. Bernice P. Bishop Mus.* 193:5–31. [Review of linguistic work, principally in Hawai'i and Tahiti, pp. 11–15.]

——. 1985. Bibliographic Survey of Collections of Hawaiian Sayings: Proverbs—Hawaiian Language—Hawaii. *Proverbium* 2:279–306.

Lydgate, John Mortimer. 1914. The Hawaiian Contribution to English. *Hawaiian Almanac and Annual* 40:131–35. [DJK: Speculates on the nature of HAW words adapted into the ENG language, viewing these contributions as primarily of an ephemeral nature. Foresees no HAW word in common ENG use in a hundred years.]

——. 1917a. Early Missionaries and Primitive Education. *The Friend,* April, pp. 84–85. [An accurate sketch of the linguistic activities of the early missionaries, especially establishing the orthography and translating the Bible.]

——. 1917b. Hawaiian Personal Names. *Hawaiian Almanac and Annual* 43:80–86.

*Lyne, Richard. 1817. *The Latin Primer: In Three Parts.* 6th ed. London: Law and Whittaker. xii, 256 pp.

Lyons, Curtis Jere. 1868. *First Lessons in Hawaiian.* [Not seen.]

——. 1901. The Meaning of Some Hawaian Place Names. *Hawaiian Almanac and Annual* 27:181–82. [Etymology of thirteen common place names.]

*Lyons, John. 1969. *Introduction to Theoretical Linguistics.* Cambridge: Cambridge University Press. x, 519 pp.

Lyons, Lorenzo. 1878. [Letter from Waimea, Hawaii, 9 August 1878, on the Hawaiian language and Andrews's dictionary]. *The Friend*, 2 September, p. 73.

McAllister, J. Gilbert. 1933. Archaeology of Kahoolawe. *Bull. Bernice P. Bishop Mus.* 115:1–61. [Place names, pp. 56–68.]

McArthur, [   ]. 1895. Note on growth of English language in Hawai‘i. *The Friend*, December, p. 96.

McClellan, Edwin. 1929. The Much-mooted Pronunciation of 'V' and 'W' in Hawaiian. *Paradise of the Pacific* 42(5):11–14. [DJK: Review of the literature dealing with the pronunciation of the HAW *w*, ranging from the early missionary reports to modern scholarly analyses.]

MacDonald, Alexander. 1935. I Want to Learn to Speak Hawaiian. *Honolulu Sunday Advertiser*, 8 September. [Discussion of the dying language ("... some give the HAW language but another generation to live") and the development of the orthography. Ends noting the appointment of H. P. Judd to the University of Hawai‘i faculty and quotes Judd's statements about his dedication to preserving the HAW language.]

McDonald, S. 1938. How do you Pronounce 'Hawaii'? *Paradise of the Pacific* 50(10):19–21.

McGregor-Alegado, Davianna. 1980a. A Comparison of the Terms Malo Used for 'steal', 'theft', 'rob', and 'covet', with the Terms Used to Translate These Concepts in *Baibala Hemolele* and the First Penal Codes. *Ka Unuhi, the Translator* 1(May):23 pp. [DJK: Study reveals that while the Hawaiian Bible ... utilized twelve different HAW words to translate forms of 'steal', 'theft', 'rob', and 'covet', Hawaiian historian David Malo's *Moolelo Hawaii* contains twenty-one terms to identify these concepts. There are only six corresponding terms in the two sources.]

———. 1980b. A Translation and Analysis of No ka Moe Kolohe, a Law of King Kauikeaouli Enacted on September 21, 1829. *Ka Unuhi, the Translator* 1 (May):16 pp. [DJK: Consists of linguistic research into the background of this law of Kamehameha III, which prohibits adultery. Includes two differing ENG translations of the law.]

*Mackert, Michael. 1994. Horatio Hale and the Great U.S. Exploring Expedition. *Anthropological Linguistics* 36(1);1-26.

Mackintosh, S. D. n.d. Vocabulary of the Hawaiian Language. <BPBM Hms.La1, storage case 5> [Begins with pronunciation key. Alphabet post-1826. No glottal stops or long vowels marked, but occasionally vowels are marked with an acute accent. Part-of-speech classes given. 114 pp.; roughly 3,400 entries. 9 pp. of *hoo-* (*hoʻo*) entries.]

*Magoffin, Ralph Van Deman, and Margaret Young Henry. 1928. *Latin—First Year*. New York: Silver Burdett. xiii, 433, 32 pp.

Mahelona, John. 1979. Tradition, Archaeology, and Linguistics: On the Migrations between Hawaii, Tahiti, and New Zealand. Paper for Directed Reading 699 (Peter Pirie), University of Hawaiʻi. 36, 11 *ll*. <UHM GN671 He M3 1979a> [Summary of lexicostatistical and other kinds of evidence for approximate dates of PN migrations, pp. 13–16.]

Mahoe, Noelani. 1971. See ELBERT AND MAHOE 1971.

Maigret, Louis. 1860. *Langue havaienne*. Honolulu: Catholic Mission Press. 8 pp. <HMCS>

Makanani, Russell Kawika. 1973. Some Observations Concerning the Hawaiian *Haʻa*-type Prefix and Related Items. Paper for Hawaiian 452, University of Hawaiʻi, fall semester (Emily Hawkins). 30 *ll*.

Mālamalama has 'Dash'. 1993. *Mālamalama* 17(3):24. [A letter asking about the significance of the macron and opening single quote used in recent issues of the publication, and an accurate, concise explanation of these symbols and their use in HAW spelling.]

Malerweiny, Adam S. 1935. *Hawaiian Slang. Words, Phrases and Medical Terms in Current Use*. U.S.A.: [by the author]. 32 pp. <Peabody Museum, Salem, MA> [Preface dated Wailuku, 1935. No glottal stops or long vowels marked. Accented syllables marked in boldface. As an example of its tone: "People are forever arguing over whether or not 'W' in some particular words should be pronounced 'V'. Whatever you do is wrong. Remember that when the language was reduced to writing, many of the old boys were in need of false teeth; also, on different islands the people had their own colloquial pronunciation," p. 3. Or, "KOHE—that which all young girls hold dear and sacred," p. 12; "MIMI—to make room for more beer; to see a man about a horse; to inspect the plumbing," p. 16; "ULE—an instrument used for emptying the opu-mimi; also useful on other occasions," p. 20.]

*Mariner, William. See MARTIN, JOHN.

*Marsden, William. 1812. *A Grammar of the Malayan Language with an Introduction and Praxis.* Vol. 2 of *A Dictionary and Grammar of the Malayan Language.* London: Cox and Baylis. Reprinted 1984, Singapore: Oxford University Press. lii, 225 pp.

*Martin, John. 1817 (1981). *An Account of the Natives of the Tonga Islands, in the South Pacific Ocean. With an Original Grammar and Vocabulary of Their Language. Compiled and Arranged From the Extensive Communications of Mr William Mariner, Several Years Resident in Those Islands.* 2 vols. London: John Murray. 4th ed.: Tonga: Vavaʻu Press. 461 pp.

Martin, Nancy. 1978. See CASSELLA AND MARTIN 1978.

Martin, William. 1867. *Catalogue d'ouvrages relatifs aux iles Hawaii. Essai de bibliographie hawaiienne.* Paris: Commissionnaire pour la Marine, les Colonies et L'Orient. vi, 92 pp.

Martínez, Esteban José. 1789. Diario de la navegación que yo, el alferez de navío de la Rl Armada Dn Estevan Josef Martínez, boy a executar al puerto de Sn Lorenzo de Nuca mandando de frag[a]ta Princesa, y paquebot Sn Carlos de or[de]n del Exmo Sor Dn Manuel Antonio Florez Virrey, Govern[ad]or y Capitan Gral de N.E. en el presente año de 1789. 318 pp. <Original in the Public Archives of Canada, ms. group 23, J12. UHM microfilm S10111> [For published version, see BARREIRO-MEIRO 1964, and for an analysis, see DAY 1991.]

*Maunsell, Robert. 1842. *A Grammar of the New Zealand Language.* Auckland: J. Moore. xvi, 186 pp.

Meier, Georg F. 1985. Review of Samuel H. Elbert and Mary Kawena Pukui, *Hawaiian Grammar.* Zeitschrift für Sprachwissenschaft und Kommunikationsforschung 38(6):756–58. Berlin-Ost: Akademie-Verlag.

Meinecke, Kalani. 1976. *Language Books About Hawaii.* Honolulu: Hawaii Bicentennial Commission. 7 pp. [DJK: Annotated bibliography of twenty-two dictionaries, language texts, and phrase books.]

Menton, Linda Kristeen. 1982. "Everything that is Lovely and of Good Report": The Hawaiian Chiefs' Children's School, 1839–1850. University of Hawai'i Ph.D. dissertation. vii, 376 *ll.*

Midkiff, Frank Elbert, and John H. Wise. ca. 1931. *A First Course in the Hawaiian Language.* Mimeographed, some leaves printed. Honolulu: The Kamehameha Schools. 132 *ll.* 1937 rev. ed.: 70 pp. [The date is uncertain: Judd, Pukui, and Stokes say "about 1929;" the card in HMCS gives 1931.] Intended for pupils of senior high schools or university. Macron and glottal stops well described under "diacritical marks," but the marks themselves were not inserted in this copy. Includes vocabulary.]

Miller, David G. 1988. Ka'iana, the Once Famous "Prince of Kaua'i." *Hawaiian Journal of History* 22:1–19.

Milne, [Dr.]. 1839. Comparative Vocabulary of Malay and Polynesian. *The Hawaiian Spectator* 2:51–54.

Minson, William Harvey. 1952. The Hawaiian Journal of Manuel Quimper. University of Hawai'i M. A. thesis. iii, 114 *ll.*

Missionary Album. Portraits and Biographical Sketches of the American Protestant Missionaries to the Hawaiian Islands. 1969. Enlarged from the edition of 1937. Sesquicentennial Edition. Honolulu: Hawaiian Mission Children's Society. [ii], 222 pp.

Missionary Letters (typed copies) from the Sandwich Islands Mission to the American Board of Commissioners for Foreign Missions 1819–1837. 8 vols. [The volume count is apparently for the original; the typed copies are contained in 3 vols. "Supplementary to the letters published in the Missionary Herald for the same dates."] <HMCS 266.858/M69.>

Mitchell, Donald Dean. 196-. Communication, with Special Reference to the Hawaiian Language. Honolulu. 15 *ll.*

*Mitchell, Sydney K. 1939. *Phases of the History of Cornwall. An Essay First Delivered in 1939 and Republished in 1981.* Torrington, CT: Cornwall Historical Society. 39 pp.

Moan, Noenoe. 1991. A Brief Historical Survey of Attitudes toward Hawaiian Language. Paper for Linguistics 325 (Albert J. Schütz), University of Hawai‘i. 22, [2] pp.

Möller, Wendelin. 1897. Linguistisches aus Hawaï. *Die katholischen Missionen* 25:192. <Deutsche Bibliothek, Marburg> [Not seen; ref.: HRK.]

*Monaghan, E. Jennifer. 1983. *A Common Heritage. Noah Webster's Blue-Back Speller.* Hamden, CT: Archon. 304 pp.

Mookini, Esther K. 1974. *The Hawaiian Newspapers.* Honolulu: Topgallant. xiv, 55 pp.

——. 1966, 1974, 1975, 1989. See under PUKUI.

——. 1985. *O Na Holoholona Wawae Eha O Ka Lama Hawaii, or The Four-Footed Animals of Ka Lama Hawaii.* Introduction by Samuel H. Elbert. Honolulu: Bamboo Ridge Press. xvi, 129 pp.

Moore, Anneliese. 1977. Henry Maitey: from Polynesia to Prussia. *Hawaiian Journal of History* 11:125–61.

*Moorehead, Alan. 1966. *The Fatal Impact. An Account of the Invasion of the South Pacific 1767–1840.* New York: Harper & Row. xiv, 230 pp.

*Morgan, John S. 1975. *Noah Webster.* New York: Mason/Charter. vi, 216 pp.

*Morris, Nancy J., and Love Dean. 1992. *Hawai‘i.* World Bibliographical Series, vol. 146. Oxford/Santa Barbara/Denver: Clio Press. xxxv, 324 pp., map.

Morris, Nancy J., Verna Young, Kehau Kahapea, and Velda Yamanaka. 1974. Preliminary Bibliography of Hawaiian Language Materials at the University of Hawaii, Manoa Campus. *Miscellaneous Work Papers* 1. Honolulu: University of Hawai‘i Pacific Islands Program. 60 pp. [DJK: Comprehensive classified listing includes call number, brief annotation, and an author and title index.]

Morris, Robert J. 1990. *Aikāne*: Accounts of Hawaiian Same-Sex Relationships in the Journals of Captain Cook's Third Voyage (1776–1780). *Journal of Homosexuality* 19(4):21–54.

Morse, Peter. n.d. *Lorrin Andrews: Pioneer of Many Talents.* [10] pp. [No publication data, but perhaps Honolulu Academy of Arts.]

Mortimer, George. 1791. *Observations and Remarks Made during a Voyage to the Islands of Teneriffe, Amsterdam, Maria's Islands near Van Diemen's Land; Otaheite, Sandwich Islands; Owhyhee, the Fox Islands on the Northwest coast of America, Tinian, and from Thence to Canton, in the Brig* Mercury, *Commanded by John Henry Cox, Esq.* London: For the author. viii, [8], 71, [1] pp. [Comment on "thick and guttural" nature of HAW, and the crew's inability to communicate by using rudimentary TAH, pp. 50–51.]

Mosblech, Boniface. 1843. *Vocabulaire océanien-français et français-océanien des dialectes parlés aux iles Marquises, Sandwich, Gambier, etc., d'après les documens recueillis sur les lieux par les missionnares catholiques et les ministres protestans.* Paris: Jules Renouard et Cie. xiv, 318 pp. [A multilingual (-dialectal) dictionary, mostly MQA and HAW, based on documents from several missionaries, especially R. P. Mathias Gracia, who supplied material on MQA. Declensions and conjugations from MQA and HAW, pp. xi–xiv. Entries have alternate forms showing cognates: e.g., "FA (ha), quatre." No long vowels or glottal stops marked. YZENDOORN 1912: the author made use of a ms. HAW dictionary and other publications of both Catholic and Protestant missionaries.]

Mühlhäusler, Peter. 1990. 'Reducing' Pacific Languages to Writings. In *Ideologies of Language*, ed. by John E. Joseph and Talbot J. Taylor, 189–205. London, New York: Routledge. [A brief account of literacy in the Pacific, including Hawai'i. However, the comments on HAW are oversimplified and inaccurate. For example (p. 195): "In 1853 the first English-language schools for Hawaiians were set up and by 1892 English had replaced Hawaiian as the language of instruction and literacy . . . "]

*Mulrony, M. A. 1929. Radio in Hawaii. *The Hawaiian Annual* 55: 66–69.

Munford, James Kenneth, ed. 1963. *John Ledyard's Journal of Captain Cook's Last Voyage.* Corvallis, OR: Oregon State University Press. i, 264 pp.

Murdoch, Clare G. See JUDD, BELL, AND MURDOCH 1978.

Myers, Muriel. 1981. Phonological Innovations of Bilingual Samoans in San Francisco. *Anthropological Linguistics* 23(3):113–34. [Comparison of HAW and SAM patterns for paragoge and epenthesis, along with innovations (consonant clusters) among SAM speakers in San Francisco.]

Nakamura, Cathleen. 1980. Legal Terms Regarding Marriage, Divorce, and Lewdness in 1841. *Ka 'Unihi, the Translator* 1(May): 49 pp. [DJK: Contains a 125-word HAW-ENG glossary and a ninety-word ENG-HAW glossary.]

Nākoa, Sarah K. 1979. *Ka Lei Momi o 'Ewa.* Honolulu: Ka 'Ahahui 'Ōlelo Hawai'i. 32 pp. [In HAW. Includes an instance of a Hawaiian being "slapped on the cheek for not recognizing her English name" (Cited in WONG 1992:2n).]

Nākuina, Moses K. 1902. *Moolelo Hawaii o Pakaa a me Ku-a-Pakaa, Na Kahu Iwikuamoo o Keawenuiaumi ke Alii o Hawaii, a o na Moopuna hoi a Laamaomao! Ke Kamaeu nana i Hoolakalaka na Makani a pau o na Mokupuni o Hawaii nei, a uhao iloko o kana Ipu Kaulana i Kapaia o ka Ipumakani a Laamaomao* {The Hawaiian legend of Pāka'a and Kūapāka'a, the trusted personal attendants of Keawenuia'umi, King of Hawai'i, the descendants of La'amaomao. The mischievous child who tamed all the winds of the islands of Hawai'i, and put them inside his famous gourd named the wind gourd of La'amaomao}. Honolulu: Published by the author. 3 vols. in 1, 128 pp. Facsimile reprint in 1991: Honolulu: Kalamakū Press.@Q

Names and Insignia of Hawaii. 1958. Hawai'i State Public Library System, Hawaiiana section. 5 pp. 1993 ed., Hawai'i State Public Library System. RS 93–4309 (Rev. of RS 88–5030). [8] pp. [A few common place names explained, along with such information as the state motto, state bird, etc. Glottal stops and long vowels marked, but not consistently.]

Native Hawaiians Study Commission (U.S.) 1983. *Report on the Culture, Needs and Concerns of Native Hawaiian Pursuant to Public Law 96–565, Title III / Native Hawaiians Study Commission*. Washington, D.C.: The Commission. 2 vols. [Vol. 2 has a special title: *Claims of Conscience: A Dissenting Study of the Culture, Needs and Concerns of Native Hawaiians.* See KIMURA 1983.]

Neal, Marie. 1948. *In Gardens of Hawaii*. Bernice P. Bishop Museum Special Publication 40. Honolulu: Bishop Museum Press. 805 pp. New and rev. ed., 1965. Bernice P. Bishop Museum Special Publication 50. Honolulu: Bishop Museum Press. xix, 924 pp.

Nellist, George F., ed. 1925. *The Story of Hawaii and Its Builders, With which is Incorporated Volume III Men of Hawaii. An historical outline of Hawaii with biographical sketches of its men of note and substantial achievement, past and present, who have contributed to the progress of the Territory.* Honolulu Star Bulletin.

Nemoy, Leon. 1949. Henry Obbokiah: the First Hawaiian Student of Hebrew. *Publ. Amer. Jew. Hist. Soc.* 39.190–92. [Not seen; ref.: HRK.]

Neves, Paki. 1976. Some Problems with Orthography Encountered by the Reader of Old Hawaiian Texts. *Oceanic Linguistics* 15:51–74. [DJK: Contends that the HAW language's partially deficient writing system ... leads to ambiguity as to the form, and consequently the meaning, of individual words.]

The New Hawaiian Dictionary [by Lorrin Andrews]. 1864. *The Friend*, December, p. 89.

Newbrand, Helene L. 1951. A Phonemic Analysis of Hawaiian. University of Hawai'i M. A. thesis. iii, 133 pp. [See chapter 12.]

Newbury, Colin W., ed. 1961. *The History of the Tahitian Mission 1799–1830, written by John Davies, Missionary to the South Sea Islands, with Supplementary Papers from the Correspondence of the Missionaries.* Hakluyt Society, series 2, no. 116. Cambridge: University Press. liv, 392 pp.

Nichi-Ei-Ha Kaiwasho: Furoku Nichi-Ei Shokanbun Hachi-jippen. 1919. Honolulu: Hawaii Benrisha Shuppanbu. [39], 512,

166 pp. [A trilingual (Japanese-ENG-HAW) work based on SOPER ca. 1906. The second part contains letters (ENG, Japanese), vocabulary (HAW-Japanese), formal phrases for letters (ENG, Japanese), and abbreviations (ENG, Japanese).]

*Nicholas, John Liddiard. 1817. *Narrative of a Voyage to New Zealand, Performed in the Years 1814 and 1815 ...* London: James Black. [MAO and TON word list, vol. 2, pp. 327–52.]

Nicol, John. 1822. *The Life and Adventures of John Nichol, Mariner.* Edinburgh: Blackwood. viii pp., 2 *ll.*, 215 pp. 1936 ed., with foreword and afterword by Alexander Liang. New York / Toronto: Farrar & Rinehart. vii, 214 pp.

Niedzielski, Henry Z. 1992. The Hawaiian Model for the Revitalization of Native Minority Cultures and Languages. IN *Maintenance and Loss of Minority Languages,* ed. by Willem Fase, Koen Jaspaert, Sjaak Kroon. Studies in Bilingualism, vol. 1, 369–84. Amsterdam/Philadelphia: John Benjamins. [Useful for its treatment of current language programs, but the historical sections contain too many misinterpretations and errors of fact to be taken seriously.]

Nishizawa, Yū. 1990. See PUKUI, ELBERT, AND MOOKINI 1990.

Nobori, Raplee K. 1992. KTUH DJ Keeps 'Ka 'Olelo Hawai'i' Alive. *Ka Leo O Hawai'i,* 16 April 1992, pp. 12–13.

Nogelmeier, Puakea. 1985. *Puowaina.* [Honolulu]: Research and Development, Hawaiian Studies Institute, The Kamehameha Schools. 89, [5] *ll.* <UHM Du629.P78 N64 1985>

Note on "Alphabet of the Language." 1823. *Missionary Herald* 19:42–43.

Notes grammaticales sur la langue sandwichoise. 1834. <ATL Hawaiian Islands Collection 499.Haw.Is./1834>

*Noyes, Martha H. 1993. We Will Eat Stones. *Honolulu* 27(7):20, 22–23. [An account of the protest song, "Kaulana nā Pua."]

O'Brien, Eileen (McCann). 1957. *Hawaiian Words and Phrases.* 12th printing, revised 1959. Honolulu: Tongg. 1964 ed., Honolulu: Aloha Airlines. [32] pp. [Long vowels and glottal stops marked, but not consistently. From *'AHA KŪKĀKŪKĀ 'ŌLELO HAWAI'I*

[1972]: "From the initial unclear attempt at describing Hawaiian pronunciation to the poor job of interpreting Hawaiian place names, this work perpetuates more misinformation than it succeeds in clearing up."]

——. 1964? *Aloha Airlines Guide to Hawaiian Words and Phrases; a Quickie Primer for Fun with the Hawaiian Language.* Honolulu: Aloha Airlines. 32 pp. <UH: Hawn.PLd6445.02.>

Obookiah. See ʻŌPūKAHAʻIA.

Often Used Hawaiian Words in One Easy Lesson. 1947. *Paradise of the Pacific* (Travel Supplement) 59(5):24. [Oversimplified and misleading. Words respelled in an attempt to show the pronunciation. A number of accents incorrectly marked.]

Ogan, Eugene. ca. 1952. See ELBERT, DAVENPORT, DYKES, AND OGAN.

Ke Ola {The Verb}. 1860–1869. Ms. <IN Hawaiian Glossary in the Archives of the Sacred Hearts in Honolulu. UHM microfilm S11041> [36 pp. Contents: verb paradigms in ENG & HAW, through various tenses, moods, and voices; a list of verbs, with pronunciation written in FR spelling, and meanings in HAW; adverbs (*Ka liki-ola*); prepositions (*Ka hoolauna*), simple and phrasal; interjections.]

He Olelo Kike no ka Olelo a Hawaii Nei. n.d. [32] pp. JBM #645. <HMCS> [Not seen. "A dialogue concerning the language of Hawaii."]

Na Olelo Ao Liilii. Helu I {Words teaching little by little. No. 1}. 1865. Hoopukaia e ka Papa Hawaii {Published by the Hawaiian Board}. Honolulu: Paiia e H. M. Wini. 32 pp., illus. JBM #414.

Na Olelo Noeau {Proverbs}. 1922. *Ka Nupepa Kuokoa* 61(38):2.

Oleson, William B. 1884. *English Lessons for Hawaiians.* Hawaiian revised by Rev. A[nderson] O. Forbes. Honolulu: Thrum. [2], 31, [1] pp. [See chapter 13.]

——. 1886. See THE RESULTANT LANGUAGE 1886.

On the Hawaiian Language. n.d. Unsigned. 12 *ll.* <BPBM Ms/Case 5/La30> [A paper read at a monthly meeting of an unidentified society, probably after 1880 (Fornander' *Account of the Polynesian Race ...* is mentioned). Contains a brief survey of language types (e.g., agglutinating); classifies HAW as "Turanian." Discusses some mistakes in Andrews's dictionary. Discussion of the glottal stop: "The difference in pronunciation between *ai* [*'ai*] to eat and *a'i* [*'ā'ī*], the neck is the guttural sound or click rather, a peculiarity of the Hawaiian language which it is not easy for foreigners to catch," p. 11. Connections with Hebrew, Latin, Greek, etc., p. 13.]

'Ōpūkaha'ia, Henry. ca. 1817. Hawaiian Grammar, Vocabulary, Speller. [So far as we know, none of these works, referred to in Dwight 1818, 1819, still survives. The ms. 'A Short Elementary Grammar of the Owhihe Language to Which is Added a Large Vocabulary in English and Owhihe' <HHS Library>, long attributed to 'Ōpū kaha'ia, was actually written by Samuel Ruggles. See RUGGLES 1993 (1819) and RUMFORD 1993.]

Orthography of the Hawaiian Language. 1826. Typescript copies of original letters at HMCS, made by Bert N. Nishimura, 1936. 13 pp. <Photocopy in UHM Hawn. PL6445. 078> [A selection of correspondence from 1826 concerning the paring of extra letters from the HAW alphabet, including Messrs. Bishop, Chamberlain, Bingham, Blatchely, Ely, Goodrich, Loomis, Richards, and Thurston. This selection includes only the replies to the joint letter sent by the committee appointed to correspond with all the members of the Mission. HMCS contains a much fuller set of correspondence on the question of consonant variation and the difficulties it presented in establishing an official orthography.]

Ostrom, Frank Edison. 1945. *Ostrom's Languages of the Pacific. Words and Phrases in Pidgin English (New Guinea, Solomon Islands, and the Bismarck Archipelago), Polynesian (Hawaii and vicinity), Japanese (Japan), Spanish (Philippines), Moro (Sulu Archipelago, Philippine Group).* Los Angeles: Global Publications. 60 pp. [HAW: pp. 14–27. Guide to pronunciation. Word list organized by part of speech and semantic category. A note after the first instance of an apostrophe hints at the glottal stop.]

Otaguro, Janice. 1989. The Class of 1850: Most Likely to Succeed. *Honolulu* 24(5):86–89, 145, 147–49. [A history of Amos Starr and

Juliette Cooke's Royal School, with biographies of its pupils of chiefly rank.]

He Palapala Mua na na Kamalii e Naauao ai i ko Lakou Wa Opiopio {First book for children, to educate them in their youth}. 1829. Oʻahu: Mission Press. 36 pp. JBM #48. [Translated by H. Bingham. Editions 1830 (2), 1831, 1833, 1835.]

Pallas, Peter Simon. 1789 (1978). *Linguarum Totius Orbis Vocabularia Comparativa*. 2 vols. Hamburg: Helmut Buske. xxvi, 411; xiv, 491 pp. [The main publication of the comparative linguistic work of Catherine II, czarina of Russia. HAW is one of 200 languages compared through 273 words, and the numbers from 1 to 10, 100, and 1,000. However, there are only 44 entries for HAW.]

The Panoplist and Missionary Magazine United (later *The Missionary Herald*) for the year ending 1 June 1809. <UHM Hawn BV2350 .M5>

Papa Huaʻōlelo. He mau Huaʻōlelo i Hōʻiliʻili ʻia no ke Kōkua ʻana i ke Kumu Kula e Aʻo ana i ka ʻŌlelo Hawaiʻi {A list of terms. Words collected to help schoolteachers teaching the Hawaiian language}. 1992. Honolulu: ʻAha Pūnana Leo, Inc. Photocopy of typescript, [ii], 37, 32 pp.

Papa Huaʻōlelo / Hōʻiliʻili ʻia, Haku ʻia a ʻĀpono ʻia e ke Kōmike Huaʻōlelo Hoʻokuleana ʻia {Word list collected, composed, and approved by the Lexicon Committee}. 1993. Hilo: Hoʻomalele ʻia e ka Hale Kuamoʻo, Kikowaena ʻŌlelo Hawaiʻi, Kulanui o Hawaiʻi ma Hilo {Distributed by Hale Kuamoʻo Hawaiian Language Center, University of Hawaiʻi at Hilo}. 104 pp. <UHM Hawn PL6446 .K66 1993>

Papa o na Ola me na Hoolauna e Piliana me Lakou (Hopena). Verb Study (English-Hawaiian). 1860–1869. 41 *ll.* (14 x 22 cm). <IN Hawaiian Glossary in the Archives of the Sacred Hearts in Honolulu. UHM microfilm S11041> [List of ENG verbs in infinitive form, HAW translation, and use as phrasal verbs. E.g., *break, break in upon, break through, break up, break down.* Sample sentences with HAW translation.

Parsonson, G. S. 1967. The Literate Revolution in Polynesia. *The Journal of Pacific History* 2:39–57. [Discussion of the birth and growth of literacy in Hawai'i, based mainly on published sources, pp. 51–54.]

Pawley, Andrew K. 1966. Polynesian Languages: A Subgrouping Based on Shared Innovations in Morphology. *Journal of the Polynesian Society* 75(1):39–64.

*Pawley, Andrew K., and Roger Green. 1973. Dating the Dispersal of the Oceanic Languages. *Papers of the First International Conference on Comparative Austronesian Linguistics, 1974—Oceanic. Oceanic Linguistics* 12(1, 2):1–68.

*Pedersen, Holger. 1931 [1964]. *The Discovery of Language: Linguistic Science in the Nineteenth Century.* Bloomington, IN: Indiana University Press. [viii], 360 pp.

Perkins, Leialoha Apo. 1978. The Aesthetics of Stress in 'Ōlelo and Oli: Notes Toward a Theory of Hawaiian Oral Arts. University of Pennsylvania Ph.D. dissertation. lxvii, 379 ll. <UHM ML3560 .H3 P46>

Perkins, Roland F. 1980. *Greek and Hawaiian Terms of Authority and Emotion in Ka Baibala Hemolele.* Kamalu'uluolele. Monograph Series no. 1. Studies in Language, Culture, Literature, and Folklore. 51 pp.

Pi-a-pa {Alphabet}. 1835? Honolulu: Mission Press. 12 pp. JBM #135. [Spelling book.]

*Pickering, John. 1820. *Essay on a Uniform Orthography for the Indian Languages of North America.* Cambridge, MA: University Press—Hilliard and Metcalf. 42 pp.

Piianaia, Abraham. 1952. *An Introduction to Conversational Hawaiian. A Compilation of Lessons Used in a Ten-Weeks Course in Conversational Hawaiian.* Reproduction of typescript. 41 ll. <UHM Hawn PL6443 .P55> [Prepared for the faculty at the Kamehameha Schools. "... time alloted [*sic*] to grammar was reduced to the minimum and whatever time remained was divided between building a workable vocabulary and learning common phrases and sentences for use in conversation." Glottal stop discussed, but written only to show minimal pairs. Long vowels neither mentioned nor marked. Only penultimate "word" accent mentioned, and then tempered with the phrase "in general." *Ua* treated as past perfect tense.]

*Pike, Kenneth L. 1947. *Phonemics: A Technique for Reducing Languages to Writing.* Ann Arbor: The University of Michigan Press. xx, 254 pp.

He Piliolelo no ka Olelo Beritania {A grammar of the English language}. 1837. Lahainaluna: Press of the High School. 40 pp. JBM #161. [Translated by Lorrin Andrews.]

Plews, Edith Rice. 1933. Poetry. IN *Ancient Hawaiian Civilization* (1933), 169–93.

Poepoe, J. M. n.d. Dictionary Notebook, with Anecdotes and Short Chants to Illustrate Meanings of Words. 100 pp. <BPBM Ms. Case 4.L10> [In HAW only. Long explanations and illustrations. Range: *A* to *ahiehie.*]

Pohakumauna, Eneki. ca. 1942. *Ka Haawina Hawaii; Being a Lesson in the Hawaiian Language in Verse and Pictures and 1000 Words Defined.* Honolulu: Printed for Laszlo's Honolulu-laughs by Honolulu Star-Bulletin. 16 pp, illus. <HMCS 499.9/P75>

Pohl, Jacques. 1974. Les observations linguistiques de Jacques Arago. *La Linguistique* 10(1):123–42.

*Polansky, Patricia. 1974. Russian Writings on the South Pacific Area. A Preliminary Edition. Honolulu: Pacific Islands Program, University of Hawai'i. i, 156 *ll.*

Pratt, George. 1886. A Comparison of the Dialects of East and West Polynesian, Malay, Malagasy, and Australian. Read before the Royal Society of N.S.W., 2 June 1886. 22 pp. <HMCS 499/P88/S-P>

Preston, Erasmus Darwin. 1900a. The Language of Hawaii ... Read before the Philosophical Society of Washington, 9 December 1899. *Bulletin of the Philosophical Society of Washington* 14:37–64. <UHM Hawn PL6441 .P728> [Relates HAW words (*mate, poko, piko*) to Spanish. Treatment of glottal stop more accurate: "This break is an essential part of the word, and a disregard of it completely changes the meaning." But the statements about the general nature of the language revert to the Noble Savage philosophy.]

——. 1900b. The Language of Hawaii. *Science* 11: 283–84. [A condensed version of Preston 1900a.]

"Professor of Columbia University." 1936. *Vocabulary of Common and Every-day Words Compiled by a Professor of Columbia University*. Translated into the Hawaiian Language by the Hawaiian Language League. Honolulu: Royal Printing Press. 39, [1] pp. <HMCS 423/P94/P> [Possibly the ENG-HAW vocabulary referred to in JUDD, PUKUI, AND STOKES 1945:6. Guide to pronunciation adapted from Andrews's grammar. Ca. 2,400 words, ENG-to-HAW. No diacritics.]

A Protest. 1913. *The Friend*, April, p. 84. [Expression of dismay at Americans' constant mispronunciation of the name *Honolulu*.]

Pukui [Pūku'i], Mary Kawena. 1930s–1950s. Hawaiian dictionary card file. <Ms. in BPBM> [MKA]

——. 1934. See HANDY, PUKUI, AND LIVERMORE.

——. 1945. See JUDD, PUKUI, AND STOKES.

——. 1949. Songs (*Meles*) of Old Ka'u, Hawaii. *Journal of American Folklore* 62 (July–September):247–58. [Originally presented at a meeting of the Anthropological Society of Hawai'i in May 1940, this article contains a discussion of *kaona* 'inner meaning'.]

——. 1967. Poi Making. *Polynesian Culture History: Essays in Honor of Kenneth P. Emory*, ed. by Genevieve A. Highland, Roland W. Force, Alan Howard, Marion Kelly, and Yoshihiko Sinoto. Bernice P. Bishop Mus. Spec. Publ. no. 56, pp. 425–36. [Contains a number of terms related to poi and poi making, explained in context.]

——. 1971, 1979. See ELBERT AND PUKUI.

——. 1983. *'Ōlelo No'eau: Hawaiian Proverbs & Poetical Sayings*. Bernice P. Bishop Mus. Spec. Publ. no. 71. xix, 362 pp. [2,942 proverbs, with literal translations and explanations.]

——, and Samuel H. Elbert. 1957. *Hawaiian-English Dictionary*. Honolulu: University of Hawai'i Press. xxx, 351 pp. 2d ed.: 1961,

Honolulu: University of Hawai'i Press. xxx, 362 pp. 3d ed.: 1965, Honolulu: University of Hawai'i Press. 369 pp. [For a review of the 1st ed., see BIGGS 1959. See also chapters 11, 12.]

——, and Samuel H. Elbert. 1964. *English-Hawaiian Dictionary.* Honolulu: University of Hawai'i Press. xii, 188 pp.

——, and Samuel H. Elbert. 1966. *Place Names of Hawaii.* Honolulu: University of Hawai'i Press. x, 53 pp. [1,125 place names, with correct spelling, and etymologies for about 88%. Includes HAW reflexes of Proto-PN and Proto-Malayo-PN. For revised editions, see PUKUI, ELBERT, AND MOOKINI 1974, 1989.]

——, and Samuel H. Elbert. 1971. *Hawaiian Dictionary. Hawaiian-English, English-Hawaiian.* Honolulu: University of Hawai'i Press. xxxix, 402 pp., x, 188 pp. Revised and enlarged edition (1986), xxviii, 572 pp. Reprinted in 1991 with corrections. [See chapter 11.]

——, and Samuel H. Elbert. 1992. *New Pocket Hawaiian Dictionary, with a Concise Grammar and Given Names in Hawaiian.* With Esther T. Mookini and Yū Mapuana Nishizawa. Honolulu: University of Hawai'i Press. xii, 256 pp. [An apparently hasty revision. The incorrect explanation of accent and listing of diphthongs, corrected in the last edition of *Hawaiian Dictionary*, remains unchanged, as do similar mistakes in the grammatical sketch. The sketch itself, which is indeed concise, is also fragmentary and disorganized, containing several topics for discussion not chosen with the user in mind.]

——, Samuel H. Elbert, and Esther T. Mookini. 1974. *Place Names of Hawaii.* Rev. and enl. ed. Honolulu: University Press of Hawai'i. xvi, [xvii–xxii], 289 pp., 6 maps. [The appendix (pp. 235–90) includes an analysis of place names, both structural and semantic. See PUKUI, ELBERT, AND MOOKINI 1966 for 1st ed.]

——, Samuel H. Elbert, and Esther T. Mookini. 1975. *The Pocket Hawaiian Dictionary with a Concise Hawaiian Grammar.* The University Press of Hawai'i. x, 276 pp. [See PUKUI, ELBERT, AND MOOKINI 1990 for Japanese translation.]

——, Samuel H. Elbert, and Esther T. Mookini. 1989. *Pocket Place Names of Hawai'i.* Honolulu: University of Hawai'i Press. xvi, 79 pp. [See PUKUI, ELBERT, AND MOOKINI 1966, 1974 for previous eds.]

——, Samuel H. Elbert, and Esther T. Mookini. 1990. *Hawaiian-Japanese Dictionary*. Tokyo: Chikura Shobo. xiv, 225, xi pp. [Translation of PUKUI, ELBERT, AND MOOKINI 1975 by Yū Nishizawa.]

——, E. E. Heartig, and Katherine Lee. 1972–1979. *Nana i ke Kumu (Look to the Source)*. Honolulu: Hui Hanai, Queen Liliʻuokalani Children's Center. Vol. 1 (1972): xvii, 221 pp; vol. 2 (1979): xi, 333 pp.

Pula, J. 1862. *Ke Kumu Mua Ano Hou, i Hoonaniia i na Kii mai Kai* {New first primer, decorated with pictures from the sea}. Bosetona. 28 pp. Illus. <Widener 2234.75.10> [Not in JBM.]

*Pullum, Geofrey K. 1991. *The Great Eskimo Vocabulary Hoax and Other Irreverent Essays on the Study of Language*. Chicago and London: University of Chicago Press. x, 236 pp.

Pung, Alberta. For other works by this author, see ANTHONY and HOPKINS.

——. 1960. Language Notes of a Part-Hawaiian. *Social Process in Hawaii* 24:100–101. [DJK: Account of the author's revitalization of interest in Hawaiiana and the role of her parents and grandparents.]

Purvis, W. Herbert. 1930. *Vernacular Plant Names in Polynesia*. London. Offprint from *Man* 30(2). 39 pp. <UHM Hawn GN670 P87>

Quick Guide to Speaking Hawaiian. 1968. Honolulu: Orchids of Hawaii International, Inc. 23 pp. [Glottal stop mentioned, but not marked. Long vowels not marked. "It's easy to speak like a native" illustrates the level.]

Quick, Sarah. 1977. *Ka Lama Hawaii*: Hawaii's First Newspaper. A paper submitted for the Pacific Islands Program, University of Hawaiʻi at Mānoa M.A. 20, [4] *ll*. <UHM Hawn PN 4899.L34 L346> [Detailed listing of contents of each issue (1–25), pp. 12–20.]

Quimper, Manuel (Manuel Quimper Benítez del Pino). 1822. *Islas de Sandwich. Descripcion sucinta de este Archipiélago, Nombre que les Dió su Célebre Descubridor el Captain Cook, reconocidas por el teniente de fragata de la armada nacional.* Madrid: E. Aguado. [7], 8–32 pp. [Word list, pp. 28–31. See MINSON 1952 for an analysis of this work.]

Rae, John. 1862. Polynesian Languages. *The Polynesian* 19(22):1–2; 19(23):1–2; 19(24):1–2. [See RAE 1930 for annotation.]

———. 1892. *An Essay on the Great Antiquity of the Hawaiian People and their Language.* Honolulu. [Not seen; ref.: HRK. Listed in HUNNEWELL 1869]

———. 1930. Polynesian Language. IN *Human Speech*, by Richard A. S. Paget. New York: Harcourt, Brace & Co.; London: Kegan, Paul, Trench, Trübner & Co., 318–53. [Written in 1862, this article appears as Appendix 8. Also published in various issues of *The Polynesian* (See RAE 1862). Rae was identified as a resident of Hā na, Maui, and the author of *Political Principles*. An attempt to answer two general questions: where did the Polynesians come from (and when); what is the nature of their language, its connections with other languages, and relationship to the formation of language itself. The article itself is nonsensical fantasy, with an attempt to give a meaning to every syllable of the language and relate a number of words to those in Indo-European languages.]

Ramirez, Tino. 1993. Speaking the Language. *Honolulu Advertiser*, 5 September, pp. F1, F2. [An account of current HAW language immersion programs, serving more than 400 students at six public schools.]

Te Rangi Hiroa. See PETER BUCK.

*Ray, Sidney H. 1926. *A Comparative Study of the Melanesian Island Languages.* Cambridge: Cambridge University Press. xvi, 598 pp.

Rehg, Kenneth, and Richard Schmidt. 1990. Predicting Transfer: English Loanwords in Hawaiian. [Paper presented to the University of Hawai'i Austronesian Circle, Honolulu, 5 April.]

Reinecke, John Ernest. 1935. Language and Dialect in Hawaii. University of Hawai'i M.A. thesis. xi, 371 *ll.*

———. 1936. The Competition of Languages in Hawaii. *Social Process in Hawaii* 2:7–10. [Includes an estimate that from 500–1000 loanwords "have passed from HAW into all grades of English," reflecting the prestige that HAW had (and has) "as the language of native administration and culture."]

———. 1938. Pidgin English in Hawaii: a Local Study in the Sociology of Language. *Amer. J. Sociol.* 43(5):778–89. [Includes a brief mention of a late eighteenth-century trade language, "chiefly English adapted to Hawaiian syntax and pronunciation and containing a large number of native words though it never took a definite form. Whether the English or the Hawaiian tongue was the language of command on the plantations which about 1850 began to dominate Island economy is uncertain."]

———. 1938. A List of Loanwords from the Hawaiian Language in Use in the English Speech of the Hawaiian Islands. Honolulu: University of Hawaii. Mimeographed. 32 *ll.* <UHM Hawn./P381/ H3R4> ["… all loanwords from the HAW tongue (flora and fauna excepted) in general use …" (p. 1). Collected by the author, students, and friends from 1932–1935, while at Honokaʻa, Hāmākua District, Hawaiʻi. Discussion of common errors in pronunciation, pp. 5–6. Ca. 394 words and short phrases. See also REINECKE AND TSUZAKI 1967.]

———. 1969. *Language and Dialect in Hawaii.* Ed. by Stanley M. Tsuzaki. Honolulu: University of Hawaiʻi Press. [xvii], 254 pp. [A source of information about the decline in the use of HAW and its replacement by ENG in most areas of communication. However, the study is faulted by the author's unfamiliarity with the extent to which HAW was still used as late as the 1890s.]

———, and Stanley M. Tsuzaki. 1967. Hawaiian Loanwords in Hawaiian English of the 1930's. *Oceanic Linguistics* 6(2):80–115. [Based on Reinecke 1938. 420 entries, with HAW pronunciation and English glosses. Original introduction supplemented with information about currency of the forms in 1967.]

———, Stanley M. Tsuzaki, David DeCamp, Ian F. Hancock, and Richard E. Wood. 1975. *A Bibliography of Pidgin and Creole Languages.* Oceanic Linguistics Spec. Publ. no. 14. Honolulu: University Press of Hawaiʻi. lxxii, 804 pp.

Rémy, Jules. n.d. Vocabulaire français-hawaiien. Recueilli dans l'archipel de Havaii pendant les années 1852–1855. Ms. 250 pp. Vol. 2: Vocabulaire havaiien-français. 167 pp. <Newberry Library, Edward E. Ayer Collection 1768–1769. UHM microfilm S00631>

*Rensch, Karl Heinz. 1991. The Language of the Noble Savage: Early European Perceptions of Tahitian. *Currents in Pacific Linguistics: Papers on Austronesian Languages and Ethnolinguistics in Honour of George W. Grace,* ed. by Robert Blust, 403–14. *Pacific Linguistics,* C-117. [Quotes many early impressionistic statements about TAH, and comments on the earliest renderings of English names into TAH.]

The Resultant Language. 1886. *The Friend,* April, p. 10. [Probably by the editor, William B. Oleson. In general, a condemnation of colloquial ENG in Hawai'i, which he called "a new language with ENG as its basic element, wrought upon by the subtle forces of other languages, not so much in the matter of a changed vocabulary as a changed idiom." See chapter 13.]

*Reuman, Otto G. 1968? *The Influence of One Man—Henry Oboo-kiah.* Cornwall, CT: First Church of Christ in Cornwall. [1] *l.,* [16] pp., [2] *ll.*

Revised School Laws and Revised Rules and Regulations of the Department of Public Instruction of the Territory of Hawaii. 1905. Honolulu: Hawaiian Star Print. 50 pp.

Rice, William Hyde. 1923. *Hawaiian Legends. Bull. Bishop Mus.* 3:1–137. [HRK: Glossary (of native terms), pp. 133–37.]

Richards, Mary A. 1937. *The Chiefs' Children's School, a Record Compiled from the Diary and Letters of Amos Starr Cooke and Juliette Montague Cooke, by their Granddaughter Mary Atherton Richards.* Honolulu: Star-Bulletin. xx, 372 pp. 1970 rev. ed., Rutland, VT, and Tokyo: Tuttle. xx, 372 pp. [Includes some discussion of the difficulties students had with ENG.]

Roberts, Helen H. 1926. *Ancient Hawaiian Music. Bull. Bishop Mus.* 29. 401 pp. Reprint: New York: Dover Publications, 1967. [Discussion of poetry, pp. 57–69. "The cleverness of the composers was aided materially by the structure of the language, for with its paucity of sounds the same phonetic combinations perforce carry many meanings not necessarily allied in sense," p. 58. Stylistic consonant substitutions, p. 72. Use of *t* outside Kauaʻi and Niʻihau (see notes to chapter 7), p. 73. Vowel changes and the importance of writing the glottal stop, pp. 73–74.]

Roberts, Julian M. 1991. Language in Hawaii in the Nineteenth Century and its Relation to Hawaiian Pidgin English. 89 *ll.* <UHM Hawn./PM7891.79/H376>

——. 1992a. Origins of Pidgin in Hawaiʻi. University of Hawaiʻi Department of Linguistics Tuesday Seminar, 28 April. Handout. 10 pp.

——. 1992b. Pidgin Hawaiian: The Dominant Contact Language in Nineteenth-Century Hawaii? [Honolulu: The Author]. 50 *ll.* <UHM Hawn./PL6449/R63>

——. 1993? Pidgin Hawaiian: A Sociohistorical Study. Photocopy of typescript. 55 pp. Revised version, June 1994, 56 pp. [A very thorough study of early voyage accounts and HAW-language newspapers supporting the theory that a pidginized variety of Hawaiian was the original plantation language, only later (1880s and 1890s) to be replaced by an ENG-based pidgin. Bibliography, pp. 48-55.]

Rodman, Julius Scammon. 1979. *The Kahuna Sorcerers of Hawaii, Past and Present.* Hicksville, NY: Exposition Press. xvi, 399 pp.

Roll of Yale Men on the Foreign Mission Field 1701–1913. <Yale Divinity School Library ms. RC Y12>

Root, Eileen M. c a. 1987. Hawaiian Names—English Names. Kailua: Press Pacifica. 163 pp.

Roquet, Judy. 1988. See CASEY 1988.

Rose, Katie. 1980a. Glossary of Legal Terms, Hawaiian-English. *Ka Unuhi, the Translator* 1 (May):1–7. [DJK: List of 300 HAW words and ENG translation, which was compiled for a university class studying the history of legal terminology in the HAW language.]

——. 1980b. Ka Makani: Mai ka Puke Wehewehe ʻŌlelo ʻo Hawaiian Dictionary e Samuel Elbert a me Mary Kawena Pukui. Photocopy of typescript. 26 *ll.* <UHM Hawn PL6449 .M34> [Selection of wind names from the Pukui-Elbert dictionary, 1971 ed.]

——. 1980c. Ka Ua: Mai ka Puke Wehewehe 'Ōlelo 'o Hawaiian Dictionary e Samuel Elbert a me Mary Kawena Pukui. Photocopy of typescript. 33 *ll.* <UHM Hawn PL6449 .U3> [Selection of rain names from the Pukui-Elbert dictionary, 1971 ed.]

*Rossel, Elisabeth P. E. de, ed. 1808. *Voyage D'Entrecasteaux envoyé à la recherche de La Pérouse.* Paris: Imprimerie impériale. 2 vols.

Rousseau, Jean Jacques. 1749. *Discours dur les sciences et les arts.*

Rowell, George A. n.d. List of words (ms.) found in a book belonging to George A. Rowell. <BPBM PL Phi. Pam 615>

Rudnyckyj, J. B. 1989[?]. Jurij Lysjans'kyj's Toponymic Output. *Onomata* 12:472–79. [A discussion of Lisiansky's practices in his naming of geographical features, including Hawaiian place names.]

——, ed. n.d. Lisiansky's Hawaiian Dictionary of 1804. Ms., 7 *ll.* <AJS> [This copy is a handwritten draft of the introduction. The author makes the point that the English translation of Lisiansky's word list is an abbreviated version. "Unfortunately, Pukui-Elbert's dictionary quotes (and excerpts) only the abbreviated English version ..."]

[Ruggles, Samuel]. 1993 [1819]. *A Short, Elementary Grammar of the Owhihe Language.* Introduction by James D. Rumford. Honolulu: Manoa Press. [18] pp. [Just after the book was printed, Rumford discovered, from records at HMCS and BPBM, that the ms. long attributed to 'Ōpūkaha'ia was actually that of Samuel Ruggles. See RUMFORD 1993.]

——. 1819. Letter to Lucia Ruggles Holman, March 1819. <Original in BPBM; copy in HMCS> [Written from Cornwall, CT, this letter confirms that Ruggles had written a HAW grammar, based to some extent on that of 'Ōpūkaha'ia.]

Rumford, James D., ed. 1993. [Introduction to Ruggles's grammar (1819), attributed to 'Ōpūkaha'ia.]

——. 1993. Authorship of the Henry 'Ōpūkaha'ia Hawaiian Grammar. *Hawaiian Journal of History* 27:245–47.

*Sachdeva, Meena. 1985. Teacher Creates a Learning Tool in Hawaiian History and Language. *Mālamalama* 9[4]:4.

Sadler, Doris. 1969. See HANCOCK AND SADLER 1969.

*Sahlins, Marshall. 1989. Captain Cook at Hawaii. *Journal of the Polynesian Society* 98(4):371–423. [A list of "pertinent pre-1820 chroniclers, together with the dates of their visits and references to their accounts," p. 375.]

St. John, Harold. 1989. Gaudichaud's Record of Hawaiian Vernacular Names for Plants: Hawaiian Plant Studies 125. *Pacific Studies* 13(1):121–25. [Charles Gaudichaud collected plants in 1819 at Kealakekua, Lahaina, and Honolulu. The author's analysis of Gaudichaud's FR spelling of HAW plant names is not entirely accurate: CG used both *r* and *l* (not just *l*) for /l/, both *y* and *i* for /i/, and *ou*, *u*, and *v* (not just *v*) for /w/.]

Salmon, Jo-An. 1991. A Selected Annotated Bibliography of the Teaching Materials for the Hawaiian Language. Paper for LIS 693, University of Hawai'i at Mānoa, summer session. Photocopy of typescript. Honolulu: Pacific Islands Studies. [ii], 20 *ll.* <UHM Hawn PL6441 .S35 1991>

Samwell, David. 1789? [HAW word list in Beaglehole 1967:1231–34.]

Sanborn, Evaline "Tuti" Kanahele. n.d. See *Nā Ka'au Kahiko.*

Sandwich Islands Mission. 1833. Answers ... to the Circular of March 15, 1833, pp. 50–54. <HMCS 266.858/Sa5a> [Statement concerning HAW, both spoken and written, in 1834.]

Sankoku Kaiwa. See FUKUOKA AND TAKI 1890.

Santeliz es Pablo, Juan Eugenio. 1791. [Vocabulario Castellano Nutkeño, Sandwich, y Mexicano]. Ms. <British Library ADD 17631> [A collection of three word lists: (1) Castellano—Nutkeño—Sandwich—Mexicano, 70 words; (2) Castellano—Sandwich—Mexicano, 216 words; (3) Castellano (this time also called Español)—Nutkeño—Sandwich—Mexicano, 312 words. Each is arranged alphabetically, according to the Spanish gloss. Peter A. Lanyon-Orgill (1979:182) referred to the Nootka list as a "defective copy" (apparently of Cook's list) and Santeliz es Pablo as a compiler (rather than collector).]

Say It As It Is! Learn to Speak Hawaiian. Plus! Island Pidgin and Hanai Words. Authentic Easy Pronunciations. 1978. "Written by MeneHune, illustrations by Masaru Yamauchi, pronunciations by

Velda Yamanaka, edited by Valjeanne Budar." Honolulu: Hawaiian Isles Publishing Co., Ltd. 112 pp. [Anachronistic amateur phonetics ("considered by linguists to be one of the most fluid and melodious languages of the world." "Some linguists consider the glottal stop as a true consonant. It is actually a minute pause or break in the air stream."). Diphthongs misunderstood. Long vowels and accent confused in pronunciations. No grammatical notes; actually a word list organized into semantic categories.]

[Schools of Missionaries]. [1829]. Letter re work of missionaries in teaching Hawaiians to read. 3 pp. <HMCS> MS/266.58/ H31s> [Handwritten by unknown author.]

Schott, Wilhelm. 1838. Review of Adelbert von Chamisso, *Ueber die Hawaiische Sprache* (1837). *Jahrbücher für wissenschaftliche Kritik* 103:838–40, 104:842–48. [The reviewer praised Chamisso for allowing the reading public to see, for the first time, the *spirit* of the Malayo-PN.]

Schuhmacher, W. Wilfried. 1989. A Hawaiian Vocabulary in Denmark. *The Hawaiian Journal of History* 23:233–34. [Explains the provenance of Bishop's 1844 vocabulary in the Ethnographic Museum in Copenhagen—the result of the Danish naval vessel *Galathea* calling at Hawai'i.]

*Schütz, Albert J. 1970. Phonological Patterning of English Loan Words in Tongan. *Pacific Linguistic Studies in Honour of Arthur Capell*, ed. by S. A. Wurm and D. C. Laycock, 409–28. *Pacific Linguistics* Series C, no. 13. [An examination not only of consonant and vowel correspondences between the two languages, but also of the patterning of the added vowels, which depends partly on the surrounding consonants.]

——. 1976a. Take *My* Word for it: Missionary Influence on English Borrowings in Hawaiian. *Oceanic Linguistics* 14(1):75–92. [A history of early English loanwords in Hawaiian, with an explanation of the missionary imposition of specific added vowels. Parts of this article appear in chapter 10]

*——. 1976b. Fijian Prosody I: Syllables and Groups. *Working Papers in Linguistics* 8(2):75–100 University of Hawai'i, Department of Linguistics.. [The foundation paper for the development of the accent unit, or measure, as a phonological

building block. The concept's influence on HAW linguistics can be seen in its use to indicate accent in Pukui and Elbert's *Hawaiian Dictionary* (1986).]

———. 1978. Accent in Two Oceanic Languages. *Anthropological Linguistics* 20(4):141–49. [An exploration of the prosodic systems of HAW and Fijian, positing for each the *measure* as a phonological unit, and showing that accent in words longer than four syllables is unpredictable, notwithstanding repeated statements to the contrary.]

*———. 1980. John Davies's *Hibernia* Journal: Missing Epsilons and the Tongan Presence. *The Journal of Pacific History* 15(2):108–9. [An account of how the printer eliminated the contrast in Davies's transcription between *e* and *ɛ*.]

———. 1981. A Reanalysis of the Hawaiian Vowel System. *Oceanic Linguistics* 20(1):1–43. [A description of the HAW vowel system from a prosodic point of view, concluding that the language has twenty-five vowel nuclei, including short and long simple vowels and short and long diphthongs. The underlying theme is that all too often the writing system, not the phonology, has been analyzed, giving the false impression of a simple sound system.]

———. 1986. Section on accent in Pukui and Elbert 1986:xvii–xviii. [An explanation of the phonological background of the concept of using accent groups (measures) to indicate the prosodic behavior of Hawaiian words four or more syllables in length. Revised for the 1991 reprinting.]

———. 1989a. 'Op8k3h3'e3's Grammar of H3wie. *Honolulu* 25(5): 126–27, 169–70, 173. [A historical treatment of the 1819 grammatical sketch of Hawaiian attributed to 'Ōpūkaha'ia (but actually the work of Samuel Ruggles), with the numbers 3 and 8 representing *a* and *u*.]

———. 1989b. Early Studies of Hawaiian. *VICAL 1. Oceanic Languages. Papers from the Fifth International Conference on Austronesian Linguistics*, ed. by Ray Harlow and Robin Hooper, 497–525. Auckland: Linguistic Society of New Zealand. [An examination of the period between Cook's first contact with the HAW language and the first published grammars and dictionaries, showing the importance of early word lists, the ms. grammar attributed to ʻŌpūkahaʻiaʼs (but now identified as Rugglesʼs), and Ellisʼs published grammatical sketch.]

———. 1990a. Hawaiian in the 1820s: a Decade of Language Reform. IN *Language Reform: History and Future*, vol. 5, ed. by István Fodor and Claude Hagège, 329–50. Hamburg: Buske. [A treatment of how the orthography affected allophonic variation, the imposition of patterns on epenthetic and paragogic vowels in borrowings, and how the grammatical tradition has simplified the language—at least as it is learned in classrooms.]

———. 1990b. William Anderson: Hawaiʻiʼs Forgotten Philologist. Ms. <Albert J. Schütz collection> [A treatment of Andersonʼs life, work, and death, focusing on his pioneering recording of Hawaiian vocabulary.]

———. 1991. William Andersonʼs Hawaiian Word List. *Currents in Pacific Linguistics: Papers on Austronesian Languages and Ethno-linguistics in Honour of George W. Grace*, ed. by Robert Blust, 453–64. *Pacific Linguistics*, C-117. [A description of Andersonʼs generally neglected 1789 word list from Waimea, Kauaʻi, pointing out previously ignored lexicographic data, and examining the thesis that Andersonʼs diacritical marks were lost in the editing and publishing.]

———, and Samuel H. Elbert. 1968. The Hawaiian Language. *Thrumʼs Hawaiian Almanac: All about Hawaii*, ed. by Charles E. Frankel. 90:193–97. Honolulu: Star-Bulletin. [A short grammatical sketch, followed by a list of names (pp. 204–10), and a glossary (pp. 211–24) word list from previous volumes. The authorship of the last two parts is unknown.]

*Schweizer, Niklaus R. 1973. *A Poet among Explorers: Chamisso in the South Seas*. Bern and Frankfurt: Lang. 55 pp.

Seemann, Berthold. 1853. *Narrative of the Voyage of H.M.S. Herald during the years 1845–51 ...* London: Reeve. 2 vols.: xvi, 322 pp.; vi, 302 pp. [Impressionistic comments on HAW; some observations (from 1849) about the extent to which Hawaiians spoke ENG, and predictions about ENG supplanting HAW, vol. 2: 88–90.]

Segrest, Dana. 1977. The Hawaiian Language: Perspectives, Reflections, and Attitudes. Paper for Anthropology 486, University of Hawai'i at Mānoa (S. Boggs), spring semester. 30 *ll.* <Albert J. Schütz collection> [An important paper with much information not found elsewhere, based largely on interviews with such central figures for HAW language teaching as Samuel H. Elbert, Dorothy Kahananui, Pua Hopkins, Larry Kimura, and Sarah Quick.]

Shaw, O. 1938. *English-Hawaiian Words. Translations Which Will Enable You to Speak and More Thoroughly Understand the Hawaiian Language.* Honolulu: Driscoll. 96 pp. [No glottal stops or long vowels marked. ENG-HAW glossary, pp. 7–73; ENG-HAW in semantic categories (names, body parts, occupations, kinship, food, animals, fish, religious terms, etc., pp. 74–96.]

Sherwood, Zelie Duvauchelle. 1981. *Beginner's Hawaiian.* Honolulu: Topgallant Publishing Co., Ltd. [xvi], 152 pp. [An unfortunate anachronism. Glottal stops discussed, but not marked consistently. Long vowels not marked at all. The inclusive-exclusive distinction called an "irregularity." "The definite article is used as in ENG," p. 17. Latin case system used. 'Hen', 'rooster' given as examples of gender. *Ua* called tense. No reference to any other work on the language.]

Shōji, Kakuko, and Emily A. Hawkins. 1990. *Hawaigo Nyūmon* {Introduction to Hawaiian}. Tokyo: Tairyusha. 141 pp.

Silva, Kalena. 1989. Hawaiian Chant: Dynamic Cultural Link or Atrophied Relic? *Journal of the Polynesian Society* 98(1):85–90. [Includes short discussion of the language policy instituted near the end of the nineteenth century that resulted in a greatly reduced number of speakers of HAW.]

——, and Kauanoe Kamanā. 1979. *The Hawaiian Language: its Spelling and Pronunciation.* With audio cassette. Honolulu: Sturgis. 55 pp. [DJK: Offers an introduction to modern HAW orthographic symbols and proper pronunciation, including the use of the glottal stop.]

Simpson, George. 1847. *Narrative of a Journey Round the World, during the Years 1841 and 1842.* 2 vols. London: Colburn. [Discussion of HAW language, vol.2: pp. 2–9, 23–30.]

*Smith, Bernard William. 1960. *European Vision and the South Pacific*. Oxford: Clarendon Press. xviii, [xix], 287 pp plus 171 plates on 60 pp.

———. 1987. See JOPPIEN AND SMITH 1987.

Smith, William C. 1933. Pidgin English in Hawaii. *American Speech* 8:15–19. [Includes a brief account of literacy, instruction in Hawaiian, and the rise of English.]

Smyser, Adam A. 1991. 'Hawaiian Immersion' Idea May Divide Us. *Honolulu Star-Bulletin*, 26 February, A-14

———. 1992. Immersion May Fail a Careful Examination. *Honolulu Star-Bulletin*, 24 March, A-10.

Snakenberg, Robert Lokomaika'iokalani. 1979. *Hawaiian Language Program Guide.* Honolulu: Office of Instructional Services, Department of Education, State of Hawaii. 100 pp. [Mixed in with the pedagogical guides are pieces of structure. Much material on perception and writing of long vowels and glottal stops. 1978 spelling recommendations appended.]

———. 1982. *Hawaiian Word Book*. Illustrated by Robin Burningham, foreword by Lokomaka'iokalani Snakenberg. Audio cassette available. Honolulu: Bess Press. [5], 95 pp. ["... designed to teach over 200 basic HAW words and to introduce the HAW language and culture to everyone." Words and pictures organized by semantic and grammatical categories. Glossary, pronunciation guide accurate and easy to understand.]

———. 1988a. *Hawaiian Sentence Book*. Illustrated by Robin Burningham. Audio cassette available. Honolulu: Bess Press. 112 pp. ["For every picture in this book, ... two or more sentences using different structural patterns in HAW." Although meant to serve as a "supplementary resource work for students and teachers" (p. vii) and not as a grammar of the language, it does offer a well organized and readable sketch of five sentence types: equational sentences, descriptive sentences using stative verbs/predicate adjectives, *Aia* locational sentences, active verb sentences (both transitive and intransitive), and passive verb sentences. This short treatment of HAW sentences gives the reader a clear introductory look into HAW grammar.]

———. 1988b. See KAʻANOʻI AND SNAKENBERG 1988.

Snelling, George Howard. c. 1936. *Hawaiian Interpretations. A Glossary of Words and Terms in Common Use.* San Pedro, CA: Hansen. xii, 32 pp. [A guide for tourists. Surprising etymologies, such as "*Luau* means 'chicken'." *Kaukau* thought to be a HAW word. In the entries, accents are marked, but sometimes incorrectly (e.g., *Wáikíki*). HAW-ENG entries, including place names.]

Some Points on the Language of the People. 1893. *Paradise of the Pacific* 6(8):114. [DJK: Focuses on the changes English words undergo in their adaptation into the Hawaiian language.]

Soper, John Harris. ca. 1906. *Hawaiian Phrase Book: Na Huaolelo a me na Olelo Kikeke ma ka Olelo Beretania a me ka Olelo Hawaii* [Words and phrases in English and Hawaiian}. Honolulu: Hawaiian News Co. 126 pp.

*Spate, O[skar] H. K. 1988. *Paradise Found and Lost: The Pacific since Magellan*, vol 3. Minneapolis: University of Minnesota Press. xxii, 410 pp.

Spaulding, Thomas Marshall. 1930. The Adoption of the Hawaiian Alphabet. Honolulu, *Papers of the Hawaiian Hist. Soc.* 17:28–33. [A short, but readable and accurate, account of how the missionaries reduced the number of consonants for the official alphabet of 1826, based on the materials in HHS and HMCS. Written for historians rather than linguists, it ignores problems such as vowel length and glottal stops.]

———. 1956. The First Printing in Hawaii. *Papers of the Bibliographical Society of America* 50.313–27. <HMCS 659.1/Sp2f>

*Stam, James H. 1976. *Inquiries into the Origin of Language.* New York: Harper & Row. xii, 307 pp.

Standardized Hawaiian Orthography. 1976. Photocopy of typescript. 51 *ll*, but paginated by section. <UHM Hawn PL6443 .S73 1967a> [1: Glottals and macrons in grammatical words. 2: Word division suggestions. 3: Punctuation marks. 4: The spoken versus the written language. A valuable work that should be incorporated into a reference grammar. See WILSON 1977b.]

*Stevenson, Robert Louis. 1891. *In the South Seas, Being an Account of Experiences and Observations in the Marquesas, Paumotus and Gilbert Islands in the Course of Two Cruises on the Yacht "Casco" (1888) and the Schooner "Equator" (1889)*. New York: Scribner. iii, 370 pp.

Stewart, Charles Samuel. 1828. *Journal of a Residence in the Sandwich Islands, during the Years 1823, 1824, and 1825: Including Remarks on the Manners and Customs of the Inhabitants ... with an Introduction and Occasional Notes by William Ellis*. London: H. Fisher, Son & P. Jackson. xxiv, 25–407 pp. Facsimile reproduction of the 3d ed. (1830), with index added, Honolulu: University of Hawai'i Press (1970), 430 pp. [The 5th ed. includes a defense of the written language adopted by the missionaries, pp. 330–31.]

Stillman, Amy. 1978. Young Composers Have Trouble with the Hawaiian Language. *Ha'ilono Mele* 4 (July):6–7. [DJK: Examines current trends in the use of the HAW language in HAW music and concludes that songwriters and performers have difficulties in writing and pronouncing lyrics.]

Stokes, John Francis Gray. n.d. Hawaiian Language: Comparisons on Different Islands; Comparisons with Spanish. In his Papers. <HMCS MS B St6>

————. 1945. See JUDD, PUKUI, AND STOKES 1945.

Suzuki, Keikun. 1892. *Nan'yō Tanken Jikki* {Authentic record of South Seas exploration}. Tokyo: Hakubunkan. ix, 286 pp.

Sweet, Henry. 1900. *The History of Language*. London: Dent. xi, 148 pp.

Syntax. Mahele Alua. 1860–1869. 38 *ll* <IN Hawaiian Glossary in the Archives of the Sacred Hearts in Honolulu. UHM microfilm S11041> [Explanation of English syntax in Hawaiian, concentrating on adjectives. List of adjectives with pronunciation given in FR spelling, and HAW translations. Next, transitive sentences with direct and indirect objects. List of phrasal verbs.]

Tagupa, William E. H. 1981. Education, Change, and Assimilation in Nineteenth Century Hawai'i. *Pacific Studies* 5(1):57–70. [Includes an account of the attempt to replace HAW with ENG.]

Tate, Merze. 1962. The Sandwich Island Missionaries Create a Literature. *Church History*, pp. 182–202. <HMCS/ 996.9/T18> [Useful bibliography: A Catalogue of Publications by the Sandwich Island Missionaries, pp. 197–202. Based on a list by the Reverend Luther H. Gulick and published in ANDERSON 1870.]

*Taylor, Clyde Romer Hughes. *1951. A Pacific Bibliography: Printed Matter Relating to the Native Peoples of Polynesia, Melanesia and Micronesia.* Wellington: Polynesian Society. xxix, 492 pp. 1965 ed., Oxford: The Clarendon Press. xxx, 692 pp.

Thrum, T[homas] G. 1899. An Hawaiian Salutation. *Hawaiian Almanac and Annual* 25:132–34. [DJK: Observations on the popularity of the word *aloha* as a greeting in contrast to its earlier meaning. Notes that *anoai* was the ancient term for a warm greeting.]

———. 1905. On Hawaiian Duplicated Place Names. *Hawaiian Almanac and Annual*, pp. 150–54. [Rather than the expected topic of reduplication, the article deals with the repetition of place names in different parts of the islands. Unsigned.]

———. 1922. Wrestling with Place Names. *Hawaiian Almanac and Annual* 48:82–87. [Includes a history of the study of place names, including a series in the 1880s in the *Saturday Press*, based on the book of land claims. Discusses some colorful names, lists a few common components (such as *wai* and *pu'u*), and discusses some well-known disputed etymologies.]

Thurston, Asa. 1826. Letter from Kailua to L. Chamberlain, Honolulu, 5 April. IN ORTHOGRAPHY OF THE HAWAIIAN LANGUAGE.

Tinker, Spencer Wilkie. ca. 1978. *Fishes of Hawaii: A Handbook of the Marine Fishes of Hawaii and the Central Pacific Ocean.* Honolulu: Hawaiian Service. xxxx, 532, xxvi pp. [Glottal stops indicated but not long vowels, even though the Pukui-Elbert dictionary had long been available. Hyphens separate HAW words into "syllables" (taking no account of diphthongs).]

Titcomb, Margaret. 1952. *Native Use of Fish in Hawaii.* With the collaboration of Mary Kawena Pukui. Wellington: The Polynesian

Society. 162 pp., 1 plate. Supplement to the *Journal of the Polynesian Society*, Memoir no. 29. Published in 1972, Honolulu: University Press of Hawai'i, 192 pp. [HRK: Anatomical terms, p. 52; list of fishes by scientific family names, pp. 53–54; descriptive lists of Hawaiian fishes, pp. 54–139.]

———, et al. 1978. Native Use of Marine Invertebrates in Old Hawaii. *Pacific Science* 32:325–86. [DJK: A listing of 467 of these animals includes its Hawaiian name and meaning, scientific name, and general description.]

Tomlinson, Lucia R. 1931. *Journal of Lucia Ruggles Holman.* Bernice P. Bishop Mus. Spec. Publ. no. 17. Honolulu. 40 pp.

Tregear, Edward. 1891. *The Maori-Polynesian Comparative Dictionary.* Wellington: Lyon and Blair. xxiv, 676 pp. ["In 1897 Whitcombe and Tombs took over the remaining stock, and issued them with a new title page ..." City of publication: Christchurch, N.Z.]

———. 1892. Polynesian Causatives. *Journal of the Polynesian Society* 1(1):53–56. [A sketch of the form and function of the causative prefix in HAW and seven other PN languages.]

Tsuzaki, Stanley. 1967. See REINECKE 1967.

———. 1968. Common Hawaiian Words and Phrases used in English. *Journal of English Linguistics* 2:78–85. [A list of fifty-seven most commonly used HAW words and phrases in everyday ENG.]

———. 1969. See REINECKE 1969.

———. 1971. Common Hawaiian Loanwords in English. *Working Papers in Communication* 2(1):32–71, Pacific Speech Association and Department of Speech Communication, University of Hawai'i. [278 words. Introductory discussion of phonological adaptations of HAW words borrowed into ENG.]

———. 1975. See REINECKE 1975.

———, and Samuel H. Elbert. 1969. Hawaiian Loanwords in English. *General Linguistics* 9:22–40. [A list of 205 commonly used HAW words and their meanings. Based on written sources.]

Turner, George. 1861. *Nineteen Years in Polynesia.* London: Snow. xii, 548 pp. [A comparative view of the PN dialects (Butler 1942:539).]

*Ullman, B. L., and Norman E. Henry. 1941. *Latin for Americans.* New York: Macmillan. xvi, 422, xxxi pp. (Based on *Elementary Latin*, Macmillan, 1936).

U.S. Board on Geographic Names. 1954. *Decisions on Names in Hawaii. Cumulative Decision List no. 5403.* Washington, D.C.: Dept. of the Interior. 50 pp. [No long vowels or glottal stops marked. Some former spellings disapproved of: e.g., *Kau*, not *Kaoo*.]

U.S. Hydrographic Office. 1943. *Gazetteer (no. 4). Hawaiian Islands.* Nov. 1943. Washington, D.C.: Govt. Print. Off. iv, 51 pp. [Includes a list of "words frequently occurring in Hawaiian geographic names." For each entry, designates site as hill, peak, ridge, stream, land division, etc.]

Vancouver, George. 1798. *A Voyage of Discovery to the North Pacific Ocean ... performed in the years 1790, 1791, 1792, 1793, 1794, and 1795, in the Discovery ... and ... Chatham ...* London: Robinson and Edwards. 3 vol. and atlas.

Vincent, Joseph Eugene. 1961. The Hula; the Hawaiian Sign Language. *Science of Man* 1(3):81–83.

Vocabulary of Terms Used in Kapa Making. 1896. *Hawaiian Almanac and Annual* 22:84–86. [Also appended to BRIGHAM 1911. 110 terms, with ENG explanation. No macrons or glottal stops.]

Voegelin, Carl F., and Florence M. Voegelin. 1964. Hawaiian Pidgin and Mother Tongue. Section 2.3 of *Languages of the World: Indo-Pacific Fascicle Two. Anthropological Linguistics* 6(7):20–56. [In addition to a short historical account of language use in Hawai'i, the article contains a phonological sketch (which proposes a six-vowel system and six additional consonants in "expanded Hawaiian") and a grammatical sketch illustrated by 100 sentences with interlinear glosses. Both these sections are largely derivative, adapted from Pukui and Elbert 1957.]

Waiau, Hawea Desha Brown. 1990. An Assessment of the Needs of the Hawaiian Language Teachers of the Public Secondary Schools of Hawaii. University of Michigan Ed.D. dissertation. ix, 225 pp. [See Hawaiian Language Publications and Materials, pp. 80-97.]

Walch, David. 1967. The Historical Development of the Hawaiian Alphabet. *Journal of the Polynesian Society* 76(3):353–66. [Leans heavily on Wise and Hervey 1952, including some unacknowledged phrases. Once away from more reliable sources, the author ventured some novel opinions, such as: "Those few Hawaiians who today speak the native language pronounce it as it was originally transcribed during the early missionary days of 140 years ago" (p. 361). This misconception and others are discussed in ELBERT AND WALCH 1968.]

Wallin, Doug. 1975. *Hawaiian Made Simple.* Honolulu: World Wide Distributors Ltd. 48 pp. [Organization by semantic categories. Sophisticated pronunciation guide.]

Ward, Jack Haven. 1962. Mutual Intelligibility between Certain Polynesian Speech Communities. University of Hawai‘i M.A. thesis. iv, 561 *ll.* [See chapter 15.]

———. 1974. Review of Lorrin Andrews, A Dictionary of the Hawaiian Language. *The Modern Language Journal* 58(7):352.

———. 1976. The Publications of Samuel H. Elbert. *Oceanic Linguistics* 15(1, 2):8–13.

———. 1992. *Classroom Materials and Resources in Hawaiian Language History.* Text for UHM Hawaiian 454, packet 129. Honolulu: Dittos. 399 pp.

Warfel, Harry R., ed. 1953. *Letters of Noah Webster.* New York: Literary Publishers. xlvi, 562 pp.

Warner, Sam L. 1988. The Influence of Hawaiian on Syntactic Structures of Hawai‘i Creole English. Paper presented at Hawai‘i Educational Research Association (January), Honolulu. [Not seen.]

———. 1989. The Hawaiian Language Immersion Program: The Social, Political and Linguistic Background of the Inception of Hawaiian Language Medium Education. Paper presented at the 79th Annual Convention of the National Council of the Teachers of English (November), Baltimore. [Not seen.]

——. 1990. The Delay of the Introduction of English in the Hawaiian Language Immersion Program Until Grade Five. Paper submitted to Office of Instructional Service and Hawaiian Education Affairs Committee, Board of Education, State of Hawai'i Department of Eduction. [Not seen.]

——. In progress. The Acquisition of Hawaiian by Children in an Immersion Setting. University of Hawai'i Ph.D. dissertation.

*Wauchope, Robert. 1962. *Lost Tribes & Sunken Continents: Myth and Method in the Study of American Indians.* Chicago & London: University of Chicago Press. x, 155 pp.

*Webster, Noah. 1783 (1800). *A Grammatical Institute of the English Language.* Boston: Thomas & Andrews. Evans Index 18297–98, 1800 ed., Evans Index 39040.

Weiss, Rena R. 1919. See BINGHAM FAMILY PAPERS.

Westervelt, W[illiam] D. 1912. The First Twenty Years of Education in the Hawaiian Islands. *Nineteenth Annual Report (Twentieth Year) of the Hawaiian Hist. Soc. for the Year 1911.* Pp. 16–26.

——. 1913. Obituary—W. D. Alexander. *Journal of the Polynesian Society* 23(1):iii.

——. 1927. See ALEXANDER 1911.

White, Raoph Gardner. 1959. A Descriptive Comparison of Maori, Tahitian & Hawaiian (circa 1850 A.D.). 8, [6] *ll.* <UHM Pacc PL6465 .W48 1959> [Comparative phonology.]

Whitney, Mercy Partridge. 1993 [1823]. *The Hawaiian Language, As Copied by Mercy Whitney.* Ed., with introduction and notes, by James Rumford. Honolulu: Manoa Press.[iv], 25, [1] pp. [Based on material compiled by several members of the Mission. The editor has noted, in detail, those portions that seem to stem from Sybil Bingham 1823 and notes that eventually appeared in Ellis 1825 (1826 edition).]

Wight, Kahikāhealani. ca. 1992. *Learn Hawaiian at Home.* 147 pp., with two audio cassettes. Honolulu: Bess Press.

*Wilkes, Charles. 1852. *Narrative of the United States Exploring Expedition* ... Vol. 4. Philadelphia: Lea & Blanchard. 1970 (facsimile reprint), Upper Saddle River, NJ: Gregg Press. xvi, 539 pp.

Williams, Edith Beatrice. 1962. *Ka 'Olelo Hawaii no na Keiki* {The Hawaiian language for children}. Honolulu: South Sea Sales. 40 pp. [Glottal stops written, but macrons seem to be used only in the appendix (an attempt at a grammar), and then very inaccurately. Pronunciation guide naive and misleading. For a review, see *'AHA KŪKĀKŪKĀ 'Ō LELO HAWAI'I* [1972].]

*Williams, Herbert William. 1917. *A Dictionary of the Maori Language,* 5th ed., edited under the auspices of the Polynesian Society and based upon the dictionaries of W. Williams and W. L. Williams. Wellington: Marks. xxi, 590 pp. [Significant for PN language studies for its accurate interpretation and marking of vowel length; considered by Bruce Biggs (1967:304) to be "the best dictionary of any PN language."]

*——. 1924. *A Bibliography of Printed Maori to 1900.* Wellington: Government Printer. xvi, 198, [4], 5–24 pp.

——. 1926. Review of Andrews-Parker 1922. *Journal of the Polynesian Society* 35(3):248–54. [A careful, insightful review. "The new edition adds little to the vocabulary of Andrews and nothing to the elucidation of the genius of the HAW language."]

——. 1928. Some Observations on Polynesian Verbs. *Journal of the Polynesian Society* 37(3):306–17. [Some comments on HAW grammar scattered throughout; see p. 313 for reference to the relative infrequency of the passive in HAW.]

——. 1929. Some Elements of Polynesian Grammar. *Journal of the Polynesian Society* 38(1):60–80. [Concentrates on MAO, but draws from a few HAW examples. See p. 69 for a comparative table of noun markers in ten PN languages.]

——. 1938. Some Problems of Polynesian Grammar. *Journal of the Polynesian Society* 47(1):1–15. [Focuses on MAO, but includes a few comments on HAW.]

*Williams, John. 1826. Letter to the Reverend Mr. Burder, London Missionary Society. Raiatea, 6 March. <University of London,

School of Oriental and African Studies Library, LMS correspondence, Box 5>

Williams, Paul Koki. 1982. Niʻihau Dialect. *Archaeology of Kauaʻi* 9(3):1–2. [A brief description of some differences in pronunciation and vocabulary, with a suggestion for further research.]

———. 1985. Niʻihau Vocabulary. Photocopy of typescript. 4 *ll.* <BPBM Ms.Doc.118> ["List of vocabulary of Niʻihau children compiled by Williams while teaching them on Kauaʻi. Presented at fall 1985 meeting of the ʻAhahui ʻŌlelo Hawaiʻi Committee on Orthography. Annotations by Emily Hawkins." 140 words and phrases.]

Williamson, Eleanor. 1976. Hawaiian Chants and Songs Used in Political Campaigns. IN *Directions in Pacific Traditional Literature: Essays in Honor of Katharine Luomala,* ed. by Adrienne L. Kaeppler and H. Arlo Nimmo. Bernice P. Bishop Mus. Spec. Publ. no. 62, pp. 135–56. [Some discussion of the rhythmic and phonetic characteristics of HAW chants and songs.]

Wilson, William H. 1972. Possession in Hawaiian: -A- versus -O-. Typescript. Honolulu. [ii], 27 *ll.* <UHM Hawn PL6449 .W54>

———. 1976a. The *O* and *A* Possessive Markers in Hawaiian. University of Hawaiʻi M.A. thesis. xii, 188 *ll.* [Traces the development of three explanatory theories: 1. the arbitrary noun class theory, which relates the category to gender; 2. the feature-based noun class theory, which would classify nouns according to semantic features; and 3. the relation-based theory, which proposes that it is the relationship between the possessor and the possessed that is marked. Choosing the third theory as "potentially more nearly adequate than the [other] two," Wilson suggested certain refinements, especially those concerned with location, to help explain the apparent exceptions. This study represents the most comprehensive treatment of the topic to date.]

———. 1976b. The o/a Distinction in Hawaiian Possessives. *Oceanic Linguistics* 15:39–50. [An elaboration of one portion of Wilson 1976a: "the *o/a* choice in the possession of tangibles (concrete objects, or those believed to be concrete)."]

———. 1977a Hawaiian in the English Classroom. Photocopy of typescript. For 'Ahahui 'Ōlelo Hawai'i. [ii], 18 *ll*, [4], *11* (two to a page). [Discussion of pronunciation, especially long vowels, glottal stops, and accent. Also PN sound correspondences and language policy. Spelling, listening, and pronunciation exercises, apparently for accompanying tapes.]

———. 1977b. Hawaiian Orthography. Photocopy of typescript. [66] *ll*. [A report on the results of a project, approved by the University of Hawai'i Committee for the Preservation and Study of the Hawaiian Language, Culture, and Art, to "standardize the glottal/ macron orthography used by Hawaiian language teachers." Expanded version of 'Standardized Hawaiian orthography'.]

———. 1978. Recommendations of the 'Ahahui 'Ōlelo Hawai'i 1978 Hawaiian Spelling Project. Photocopy of typescript. [i], 7, [2] *ll*. [A summary of the longer recommendations for Hawaiian orthography, with a list of grammatical words, many with a problematic vowel-length variation. Also treated: word division, capitalization, hyphenization, /w/ vs. [w]-glide.]

———. 1980. Proto-Polynesian Possessive Marking. University of Hawai'i Ph.D. dissertation. xv, 199 *ll*. [Published as WILSON 1982.]

———. 1981. Developing a Standard Hawaiian Orthography. *Pacific Studies* 4(2):164–82. [A discussion of past problems, such as failure of missionary orthography to indicate glottal stops and long vowels, and present problems, such as wavering spellings in reference works, word division, excrescent *w*, and colloquial versus formal style. A recommendation for some prescriptive standards.]

———. 1982. *Proto-Polynesian Possessive Marking*. Pacific Linguistics Series B—no. 85. Canberra: The Australian National University. xv, 137 pp. [Published version of WILSON 1980.]

———. 1983. Hawaiian Language and Education for Ni'ihau People. Ms. [Not seen; ref.: HUEBNER 1985]. .

———. 1985. A Look at Hawaiian Orthography. Paper presented at fall 1985 meeting of the 'Ahahui 'Ōlelo Hawai'i Committee on Orthography. Photocopy of typescript. 2 *ll*. <BPBM Ms.Doc. 117> [Discusses some difficulties with the recommendations of the committee, such as the problem of deciding on compounds based on "evident meaning," and some of the grammatical markers that vary in length. Notes that the varying pronunciation of some markers represents dialectal differences. Notes discrepancies between the current dictionary marking of glottal stops and vowel length and what the writer has heard spoken.]

——. 1987. See BICKERTON AND WILSON 1987.

——. 1991. Hawaiian Language Making a Comeback. *Ka Wai Ola o OHA* 8(2):15, 18.

Windley, L[arry]? 1966. Lahainaluna Printing. *Hawaii Historical Review* 2:275–87. [MKA]

Wise, Claude Merton. 1951. Chiefess—a Hawaiian Word. *American Speech* 26 (May):116–121. [DJK: Discussion of missionary use of the word to convey the idea of female *ali'i.*]

——, and Wesley Hervey. 1952. The Evolution of the Hawaiian Orthography. *Quarterly Journal of Speech* 38(3):311–25. [A fairly detailed discussion of the events that led to an official HAW alphabet, especially the problems caused by consonant alternation. Oddly, it omits Anderson's work, concentrating mainly on Cook's transcription of HAW words in his narrative and that of several of his officers. The authors exaggerated both the role of Kendall and Lee's MAO grammar (1820) and the influence (and competence) of William Ellis in helping the missionaries in Hawai'i come to a decision. They also misinterpreted some minor details about the glottal stop, and the supposed *p—b* alternation. The material suffers from the authors' reliance on published sources and the HMCS typed selection from a much larger body of ms. material, but otherwise it is a careful and well-balanced sketch.]

Wise, Duke Kalani. 1989. See BUDNICK AND WISE 1989.

Wise, John H. ca. 1927. See MIDKIFF AND WISE ca. 1927.

——, and Henry P. Judd. 1933. The Hawaiian Language. IN *Ancient Hawaiian Civilization* (1933), 155–60. [Lightweight, impressionistic essay with a few comments about grammar and vocabulary.]

Wist, Benjamin O. 1940. *A Century of Public Education in Hawaii.* Honolulu: Hawaii Educational Review. xi, 221, viii pp. [A section titled "The Problem of Language," in addition to a number of references to the replacement of HAW by ENG in the school system, pp. 68–73.]

Wiswell, Ella L., and Marion Kelly. 1978. See FREYCINET 1978.

Wong, Kerry Laiana. 1992. Covert Prescriptivism and Language Survival. Paper for Linguistics 615 (George W. Grace), fall semester, University of Hawai'i. 15 pp. <Albert J. Schütz collection>

Wood, Richard E. 1975. See REINECKE ET AL. 1975.

Words Frequently Used in Hawaii. 1947. *Nisei* 1(summer):8.

Yamanaka, Velda. 1974. See MORRIS ET AL. 1974.

Yang, Joyce. 1994. Native Tongue Hits the Airwaves. History-making Show in Hawaiian Language. *Ka Leo*, 4 February, p. 7.

Young, Verna. 1974. See MORRIS ET AL. 1974.

Yzendoorn, Reginald. 1912. Bibliography of the Catholic Mission in the Hawaiian Islands. Typescript. [21] *ll.* <UHM Z4708 C3Y9> [118 items, including several on grammar and lexicography.]

Zimmermann, Heinrich. 1781. *Heinrich Zimmermanns von Wisloch in der Pfalz, Reise um die Welt mit Capitain Cook.* Mannheim: Schwan. 110 pp. [Observation that the language of Hawai'i is the same as that of Tahiti, p. 74.]

-o-o-o-o-o-

INDEX

This index includes not only topics and people, but also works from the bibliography that are cited in the text. Thus, it shows, for example, the number and location of references to Bingham 1847. If the author is also discussed, the reference precedes that to the work: *Bingham, Hiram* will precede *Bingham 1847*.

Counter to the usual practice, a Hawaiian phrase (for example, the name of a newspaper) is alphabetized according to the first word, even if it is an article such as *ka* or *ke*.

A

/a/
raising, 283
a/o possessives, 247, 252, 258, 261, 263, 264, 271–72, 280, 284
as gender, 261
Académie, 372–75
accent
incorrect description, 273
to show plural, 256
accents
difficulty for foreigners, 17
Adams, see Kuakini, 157
Age of Enlightenment, 3
'Ahahui 'Ōlelo Hawai'i, 372
Akaka, Hau'oli, 363
Akaka 1991, 363
Alelo ka Hoe Uli, Ke, 373–74
Alexander and Atkinson 1888, 352, 378
Alexander and Dodge 1941, 343
Alexander, Arthur, 225
Alexander, William De Witt, 378
biography, 270
proposes Hawaiian for Punahou School, 343
perceives *v/w* as intermediate sound, 120
Alexander 1864a, 120, 270–72, 343
Alexander 1865, 22, 207, 260

Alexander, William Patterson, 226, 270
alienable
defined, 247
American Board of Commissioners for Foreign Missions (ABCFM), 11
administers Foreign Mission School, 87
instructions from, 99
lack of linguistic guidelines, 254
criticized by Wilkes, 178
Anderson, William, 1
ability to speak Tahitian, 41
at Waimea heiau, 1
biography, 34–35, 72
comparative Polynesian word list, 323
death, 35, 57
Hawaiian word list, 1, 2, 3, 35, 210–12
limitations of, 10
semantic categories, 211
illness, 35
journal, 3
Māori word list, 62, 64
missing journals, 73
spelling conventions, 60–62
Tahitian word list, 10
use of *v* and *w*, 81